Christian Leaders' Comments on the Unabridged Edition "Beyond Calvinism and Arminianism"

Dr. Earl D. Radmacher, President Emeritus of Western C. B. Seminary: "I have been teaching systematic theology in seminary for 45 years and published numerous books and articles, but I have never found anything on the biblical doctrine of salvation as helpful and thorough, especially on the controversial areas.... Olson exercises great care in the word studies and is faithful to the biblical context. Furthermore, his attitude and style of writing is gracious rather than pugnacious. I wish I had it in my earlier days of teaching but, praise God, *I am still learning*."

Dr. Robert L. Sumner, Editor, The Biblical Evangelist: "...one of the finest on the subject... Olson annihilates the ideas of irresistible grace, limited atonement, and unconditional election.... we highly recommend this volume."

Dr. Don Fanning, Director of Missions at Liberty University, was the first to use it as a textbook in a theology course: "I have thoroughly enjoyed devouring its contents. Naturally one is especially delighted to read something that helps define one's own beliefs." He told me that Dr. Jerry Fallwell has read it and agrees with the viewpoint.

Dr. John F. Walvoord, longtime President of Dallas Seminary, before his homegoing told me that he thought that he agreed with me and wrote a proviso: "At my present age of 92 I find it difficult to read through very detailed arguments in theology that would have been taken in stride years ago." He then affirmed, "In [God's] plan some people will be saved and some would be lost but on the basis of their own choices. God did not condemn them Himself." In 1991 he wrote, "I do not believe either the words 'unconditional' or 'conditional' are properly added to the doctrine of election."

Pastor Leith Anderson at Wooddale Church, Eden Prairie, MN, (former Interim President of the NAE): "What I have so far read has been interesting and challenging. Thanks for all your hard work and all your research/scholarship. May God use your writing to bless, benefit and shake-up students of soteriology.... I hope you will receive broad readership as you have sought to bring new scholarship to old issues."

Dr. James Bjornstad, Professor of Philosophy at Cedarville University: "... your exegesis and thinking are fascinating--very refreshing.... Included are frequently neglected exegetical considerations, inferences from history, and other important insights. A tremendous contribution...."

Tim Johnson, Exec. Director, Minnesota Church Ministries Assoc.: "... a welcome perspective which ...a great number of evangelicals embrace and would be encouraged to see laid out in a systematic way.... a blessing and underscored so much of what I have believed and taught for years."

Dr. Thomas Edgar, Professor of New Testament at Capital Bible Seminary: "...a thorough and biblically based discussion of soteriology.... All who believe the clear and most probable meaning of the numerous biblical passages on this subject will appreciate this work."

Dr. Glenn Carnagey, late President of Austin Seminary of Biblical Languages, wrote: "A breath of fresh air has just wafted over the realm of theology. Olson's book takes a mediate position, avoiding the pitfalls of both extremes.... Many issues are explored--all fascinating and different. He covers all the issues one might want to study in connection with the theology of salvation.

Dr. Edward P. Meadors, Taylor University: "...a word of appreciation for your fine book on salvation theology.... The Scriptures are taking me in a very similar direction.... Thank you for your comprehensive, detailed work."

GETTING THE
GOSPEL
RIGHT

A BALANCED VIEW OF
SALVATION TRUTH

AN ABRIDGED AND REVISED EDITION OF

BEYOND CALVINISM AND ARMINIANISM:
AN INDUCTIVE, MEDIATE THEOLOGY OF SALVATION

C. GORDON OLSON

GLOBAL GOSPEL PUBLISHERS

GETTING THE GOSPEL RIGHT
A BALANCED VIEW OF SALVATION TRUTH

GLOBAL GOSPEL MINISTRIES, INC
adba GLOBAL GOSPEL PUBLISHERS
74 Mountain Avenue
Cedar Knolls, New Jersey 07927
Telephone: 973-267-2511
e-mail: gordolson@att.net

All Scripture quotations, unless otherwise noted, are taken from the New American Standard Bible © 1960, 1962, 1963, 1971, 1972, 1973, 1975, 1977, 1995 by the Lockman Foundation and used by permission.

The diagram by Dr. George W. Peters on page 10 is from p. 56 of his book, *A Biblical Theology of Missions*, copyrighted 1972 and is used by permission of Moody Publishers, Chicago, IL.

Cover layout: Bob Heimall, Inc., Sussex, NJ
Book manufacturer: Berryville Graphics, Inc., Berryville, VA

First edition: November, 2005

1   2   3   4   5   6   2011 2010 2009 2008 2007 2006 2005

TABLE OF CONTENTS

Chapter

DEDICATED TO:

Brother Hidayat Masih, Elder and Evangelist
of Bethany Assembly in Lahore,
Pakistan for half a century,
a faithful servant of Yisu Masih (Jesus the Messiah),
a man of one book, the Bible.
He is representative of myriads of indigenous
pastors, elders, evangelists, and missionaries
in the two-thirds world,
who because of limited education
probably have never heard of Calvinism and Arminianism,
but whose effective ministries have
suffered not the least thereby.
I suspect that I, as a seminary graduate and missionary,
learned far more of eternal significance
from him than he did from me.

What in the World Is God Doing?
The Essentials of Global Missions

"It is simply superb: . . . mastery of the entire global situation; . . . fine biblical exposition; command of history, world religions; and very practical approach."
-- Dr. Keith J. Hardman, Author, Professor Emeritus, Ursinus College

" concise, **highly readable** . . a strong biblical and historical framework to view the world from God's perspective solidly conservative and biblical." -- Mike Stachura, in *Evangelical Missions Quarterly*

"an introductory text that respects missiology's interdisciplinary nature, and treats the areas of concern for modern missionary ministry."-- Dr. Keith E. Eitel, Southeastern Baptist Seminary

"Gordon Olson has saved me a lot of time and effort. He has already published the book I planned to write! It will be a pleasure to use it in my classes." -- Dr. Justice C. Anderson, Professor Emeritus, Southwestern Baptist Theological Seminary

"Succinct yet comprehensive, solid but **readable**, creative yet biblical. . . a boon to mission teachers, students, and practitioners alike."   – Dr. David J. Hesselgrave, Emeritus Professor, TEDS

"I like your book's **readability**.... the best introductory guide I have seen."-- Grover G DeVault, OCSC

"The best introductory text available--excellent." -- Dr. Paul Lund, Vennard College

"not only valuable for teachers in schools, but also for Missions pastors and committees who wish to build missionary vision in their churches."   -- Charles Hall, Temple Baptist Seminary

---

Published by: **GLOBAL GOSPEL PUBLISHERS** --
Paperback: 384 pages, ISBN 0-9624850-5-5, 5th ed., July 2003,   List Price: US $ 13.00
Available from: Scripture Truth Book Co. (540-992-1273); Wm. Carey Library (1-800-MISSION); Amazon.com; Barnes & Noble.com; John Ritchie, Ltd., Scotland

FOREWORD
by Dr. Tim LaHaye

Three years ago I was introduced to the delightful writing style of Gordon Olson when I read his classic book, *Beyond Calvinism and Arminianism.* He articulated in scholarly yet easy to understand prose what has been my long-standing belief of what the Bible really teaches on these controversial subjects. He is a master at inductive Bible study and uses it to solve the age's long controversy that exists when writers use the proof-text method to prove their previously held position. It has been enthusiastically received by many ministers, missionaries, seminarians, Bible professors, and Christian laypeople. What I find interesting is that in spite of its incredible distribution, no scholar to date has attempted to refute it or anything in it. As another who was impressed with the book said, "The reason no one has attempted to refute it is that they cannot." I would agree.

Now he has produced a more popular version of that scholarly book, which will be accessible to many more knowledgeable Christians. His well defined position is unadulterated Biblical truth. The polarized positions he examines are based on the writings and thought of two men (and others); Olson's position is based on the Bible. It should be called "the faith of the early church" for at least four hundred years, or "the evangelical position about salvation," which it is. In fact, I think that most evangelical Christians believe it, even if their pastor holds a different view.

This book should be distributed everywhere. Gordon Olson is to be commended for having the courage and stamina to produce such a well researched, yet easy-to-understand book on a subject that has confused Christians for centuries. Every serious Bible student, preacher, and Bible teacher should read this book. It can truly be a life changing experience.

RESOURCES

BIBLE TRANSLATIONS USED:

Unless otherwise identified, all Scripture quotations are from the New American Standard Bible

TAB   *The Amplified Bible* GR. Zondervan, ©1965
FFB   Bruce, F F. *The Letters of Paul: An Expanded Paraphrase* Eerdmans: ©1965.
ESV   *The English Standard Version* Wheaton: Crossway, ©2001.
HCSB *The Holman Christian Standard Bible*, Nashville: Holman Bible Publishers, ©2004.
KNX   Knox, Msgr. R. A , *The New Testament: A New Translation*. NY: Sheed & Ward, ©1953.
NAB   *The New American Bible*. NY: Catholic Book Publishing, ©1970.
NEB   *The New English Bible: New Testament*. Oxford: Oxford Univ. Press, ©1961.
NIV   *The New International Version*, International Bible Society, ©1984.
NKJV *The New King James Version*, Nashville: Thomas Nelson, ©1982.
NLT   *The New Living Translation*. Wheaton: Tyndale House, ©1996.
TNIV *Today's New International Version*, International Bible Society, ©2001
JBP   Phillips, J. B. *The New Testament in Modern English*. NY: Macmillan, ©1962.
RSV   *The Revised Standard Version*. NY: Thomas Nelson, ©1957.
JBR   Rotherham, Joseph Bryant, *The Emphasized Bible*. Cincinnati: Standard Publishing, 1897.
LXX   *The Septuagint Version of the Old Testament,* with trans. By Brenton. London: Bagster, n.d.
NBV   Verkuyl, Gerritt, ed., *The Modern Language Bible: The New Berkeley Version* (rev. ©1969).
WAY   Way, Arthur. *The Letters of St. Paul*, London: Macmillan, ©1926.
WEY   Weymouth, Richard Francis, *The New Testament in Modern Speech*. Boston: Pilgrim, 1943
WILL Williams, Charles B *The New Testament*. Chicago, Moody Press, ©1958.

SYMBOLS USED:
All words defined in the Glossary are identified by an asterisk. *

BCAA - The original unabridged edition of this work, *Beyond Calvinism and Arminianism: An Inductive Mediate Theology of Salvation*, Global Gospel Publishers, 2002.

The various editions of the Bauer, Arndt, Gingrich, Danker lexicon are designated:
BAG - First edtion, A translation and adaptation of Walter Bauer's work by W F Arndt and F. W. Gingrich, 1957, mostly used in this work.
BAGD - Second edition, 1979, further edited by F. W. Danker.
BDAG - Third edition, 2000, more radical editing by Danker, some of which is questionable.

TGNT - Gerhard Kittel, ed. *Theological Dictionary of the New Testament*, trans. Geoffrey W. Bromiley, 10 vols. (Grand Rapids: Eerdmans, 1964-76).

PREFACE

As the gospel of the Lord Jesus Christ penetrates into thousands of people groups around the world and His church is planted among them, the global church is increasingly becoming non-Western. One of the most astounding phenomena of the last thirty years has been the explosion of tens of thousands of non-Western missionaries of the cross, who have joined their Western colleagues in fulfilling the Greatest Decree of the Sovereign of the universe. The decline of the churches in Europe, the battleground of the Reformation, raises real questions about the soundness of the form of Christianity which developed from the Reformation. It was the radical Reformation which sought to break free from the overhanging legacy of medieval scholasticism and thus took the lead in world evangelization.

Paul, the greatest theologian of the church, was also its greatest missionary. Western churches desperately need an inductive biblical theology, which will break free from the deadening influence of deductive scholasticism and polarized traditions, a crippling legacy of Western church history. We must move on to a missions-centered theology, conducive to world evangelization, since Christ died for a whole world of lost sinners.

My unabridged, inductive theology of salvation, *Beyond Calvinism and Arminianism*, has been received with enthusiasm. It is my earnest prayer that this abridged and revised edition will advance that goal. In setting out positively the actual Bible teaching about God's wonderful plan of salvation, the legacy of the past requires dealing with the widespread serious misconceptions and distortions of God's truth. There is such a strong tradition of misinterpretation and even of mistranslation of the Scriptures that we desperately need a paradigm shift in our whole approach to God's truth.

Many of my readers may need to undergo a radical paradigm shift. I have been on a more gradual theological pilgrimage for over thirty years. Many are thoroughly dissatisfied with the polarized traditions of Western theology, but many in those traditions will be upset with this book. I get encouragement from the fact that the Christ spent His ministry countering the religious traditions of a nation which desperately needed to repent. He spared no words in rebuffing adherence to human traditions.

We must constantly keep in mind that Calvinists, Arminians, and those in between are brothers and sisters in Christ, not sub-Christian or enemies. Yet much of the literature of the last five centuries reflects the intolerance of the post-Reformation period, when Christians persecuted other Christians! We have an overwhelming responsibility to manifest love to our fellow believers, even in the way we dialog doctrinally. If I have failed to do this in this book, I ask your forgiveness. However, if the truth makes you angry, I cannot apologize for that!

I have radically restructured the sequence from the unabridged volume. The first section deals with foundational truths and should not be a problem to read and understand for those not theologically trained. The second section deals with more controversial issues and is more challenging. The third section deals with the heavy doctrinal issues relating to Calvinism, which require constant reference to the original languages and are, therefore, quite challenging to those who are not theologically trained.

Although this is an abridged edition I have added three new chapters: 4, 6, and 9. I also rewrote the chapters on God and man, since a 'Biblical Theology' approach is more inductive. A survey of Old Testament anticipations of the gospel springs from teaching a diachronic Old Testament theology for a quarter century. Assurance is the bottom line of it all and requires more extensive discussion.

Providentially, I stumbled across new material on the doctrinal roots of the modern missions movement, some of which was published previously and some of which is brand new to this edition. It is of great significance in understanding the spiritual lineage connecting key personalities. I have "connected the dots," in telling "the rest of the story," as Paul Harvey says. This research into the primary sources of this lineage reveals the connection between theology, evangelism, the two Great Awakenings, and missions.

Readers will notice some stylistic peculiarities. After years in the Muslim world, I find it unthinkable to refer to "Jesus" without giving Him His proper titles, since Muslims never refer to *Hazrat Isa* without using terms of respect. Do we Evangelicals show less respect for God incarnate than Muslims do, even though they do not believe in His deity? I am convinced that this is a key reason for the weakness of evangelical communication of the gospel. Additionally, the proper translation of the two Greek titles of Christ's herald is John the Baptizer. Are translators in such a rut that they can't correct the misnomer?

One reviewer has picked up minuscule format inconsistencies in the unabridged edition. Please consider that these chapters were originally written over a dozen years on a number of different software platforms. It has been a major task to try to bring them into consistency, but some details remain unresolved. I have tried to keep the cost of my books to a minimum so that students can afford them.

I have had no support staff to get this work to press but am grateful to the many, too numerous to mention, who have helped and encouraged me. I am especially appreciative of the editorial help of Dr. Keith J. Hardman and Vicki Burnor. Naturally, I am grateful for the support and encouragement of my family, and especially to my dear wife, Miriam.

C. Gordon Olson, October 12, 2005

There is a great danger, when once we have adhered to one particular school of thought or adopted one particular system of theology, of reading the Bible in the light of that school or system and finding its distinctive features in what we read. . . . The remedy for this is to bear resolutely in mind that our systems of doctrine must be based on biblical exegesis, not imposed upon it.

-F. F. Bruce

INTRODUCTION

What Is the Gospel?

The goal of this book is to "get the gospel right." The word 'gospel' means 'good news,' so it is crucial to make sure that the message really is 'good news' for those who respond to it. It is the good news that the Lord Jesus and His Apostles proclaimed to a lost world of sinners–Jew and Gentile. The essence of the gospel is the person and work of the Lord Jesus and how the benefits of His life, death, and resurrection are realized in the lives of individuals. Most evangelical Christians agree about the person and work of Christ: that He was God incarnate in human flesh to provide eternal life to a spiritually dead humanity through His death and resurrection. However, many who accept this statement might not agree with each other as to how a sinner can be saved. Indeed, there has been a serious polarization among Evangelicals in regard to salvation truth.

It is the thesis of this book that the gospel is that any sinner can be saved by grace only through explicit repentant faith in the finished work of Christ alone. This means that the gospel is a valid offer for every last human being, available by God's unmerited favor, apart from human performance either before or after conversion. Christ is the only way of salvation, that is, no one can be saved apart from explicit trust in the merits of His saving death and resurrection. Although the new birth and right standing with God are given instantaneously upon the exercise of saving faith, there is a process by which unbelievers come to trust in Christ for salvation. Also, it is the privilege of every true believer to have assurance of ultimate salvation.

It is clear that many mainline Protestants would no longer agree with Evangelicals about even the deity and passion of Christ. This book will only briefly deal with those issues. Traditional Catholics and Eastern Orthodox

1

might agree with Evangelicals about His deity and passion, but they would not accept our teaching about how people can be saved. This was the crucial issue of the Protestant Reformation. However, within a century after the Reformation a sharp division developed among Protestants. Martin Luther and John Calvin had followed Augustine in a deterministic approach to salvation, with doctrines of unconditional election (absolute predestination) and irresistible grace. It is widely recognized that Calvin's successor in Geneva, Theodor Beza, developed a more extreme form of Calvin's doctrine by adding the notion of limited atonement–that Christ died only for the elect.

A century after the Reformation a reaction against this extreme Genevan Calvinism developed around Amsterdam pastor and theologian, Jacob Arminius (1560-1609). After Arminius' untimely death, some of his followers, called Remonstrants, pressed his denial of Calvinism in five points. At the Synod of Dort (1618-19) the Arminians were banished from the Netherlands Reformed churches by the extreme Calvinists, who set out their doctrine in five opposing points, the famous acronym, TULIP. Most Protestants, except Lutherans and the Anabaptist-Mennonite*heritage, can trace their lineage back to either the Calvinism or Arminianism.

It is the burden of this book to show that both Calvinists and Arminians have got it half right and half wrong, with the truth being in the middle. Diligent inductive study of the whole Bible, without traditional or philosophical preconceptions, confirms the above definition of the gospel message. A middle or mediate view is also confirmed by the views of the early church fathers* and a score of evangelical movements which reacted to the determinism of the Reformers. It is also harmonious with the Great Commission of the Lord Jesus to His church. British scholar, I. Howard Marshall expressed this goal so aptly: "The full Arminian position is as much open to error as is extreme Calvinism. My aim is to reach beyond the Calvinist-Arminian controversy to a position which is biblical, and which therefore accepts whatever is true in both Calvinism and Arminianism."[1]

What Are the Various Views?

Moderate Calvinism. The essence of Calvin's theology, which he got from Augustine a millennium earlier, is in the doctrines of unconditional election and irresistible grace. According to this view, God predestined some individuals to be elected to salvation based upon His own hidden reasons. God then sovereignly gives the new birth and faith only to those elect individuals. Christ died for all mankind, without exception or discrimination, but only the elect will respond to the gospel and be saved. This view is commonly referred to as four-point Calvinism.

Extreme or HyperCalvinism. Calvin's successors extended the implications of Calvin's views to become the five-points of the Synod of Dort and the Westminster Confession. The acronym **TULIP** stands for these points. **T** is for **T**otal Depravity, which means that mankind is so depraved that sinners can do nothing to please God, including repentance or faith. Spiritual death means total inability to respond to God, so God must give faith to the sinner. **U** is for **U**nconditional Election or predestination. **L** is for Limited Atonement, that Christ died only for the elect and not for the "non-elect." (Some prefer the term, "particular redemption.") **I** is for **I**rresistible Grace, which means that the elect are sovereignly given regeneration to enable them to believe. **P** is for **P**erseverance of the saints, which means that the truly elect prove their election by perseverance in faith and obedience to the end. Section III deals with issues raised by extreme Calvinism.

Classic Arminianism. Some Christians would go back to the moderate views of Arminius himself. They reject eternal security, although Arminius only had doubts about this doctrine. They reject the other points of Calvinism. Four chapters of this book deal with eternal security.

Remonstrant Arminianism. The Remonstrant successors to Arminius not only rejected all five points of Calvinism, but many also denied that Christ's death was as a substitute for sinners. This denial was an attempt to explain how Christ could die for all sinners without all mankind being saved.

Wesleyan Arminianism. Over a century after Arminius, John Wesley (1703-91) restored an "Evangelical Arminianism." He rejected the extreme views of the Remonstrants by holding to a stronger view of human depravity and God's sovereignty, which was important to his very fruitful evangelism. However, he began to teach that believers can attain sinless perfection, which became the basis for the subsequent 'holiness movement.'

Mediate theology. The Synod of Orange (AD 529) affirmed Augustine's emphasis upon grace, but rejected his doctrines of unconditional election and irresistible grace, which could be called a semi-Augustinian view. Over a dozen movements after the Reformation rejected the determinism of the Reformers and sought to find a middle position. Hundreds of theologians, Bible commentators, and church leaders in recent centuries have held to election being conditioned on repentant faith alone, while also affirming the eternal security of the true believer. *Research for this book has confirmed this mediate position as the biblical one.*

Biblical Doctrine Is Foundational

Since God uses true Christians in all of the above movements, why should we be concerned about which one is right? Many Christians have the notion that doctrine divides and is unimportant in the life of the individual or of the church. Nothing could be farther from the truth!

In his first letter to Timothy, the Apostle Paul emphasized repeatedly the importance of sound doctrine and teaching. He showed great concern for the truth of the message which Timothy was to preach and teach and spoke frequently of the imperative of holding to "**the faith**" as an objective body of essential truth. He encouraged Timothy to stay on in Ephesus to deal with false teachings in the churches there (1 Tim. 1:3-11). In emphasizing God's desire that all men might be saved, he makes their coming "**to the knowledge of the truth**" synonymous with this (2:3-4). Therefore it is essential that local church leaders be "**able to teach**" (3:2) and must hold "**to the mystery of the faith with a clear conscience**" (3:9), since the church of the living God is "**the pillar and support of the truth**" (3:15).

Paul warns that "**in the latter times some will fall away from the faith, paying attention to deceitful spirits and doctrines of demons**" (4:1), and that to "**be a good servant of Christ Jesus**" Timothy will not only have to be "**nourished on the words of the faith and of the sound doctrine**" but also have to point out this apostasy to the brethren (4:6). Paul exhorts him to "**prescribe and teach**" that "**the living God ... is the Savior of all men, especially of believers**" (4:10-11), and twice reminds him that by giving attention to his teaching he will insure salvation for his hearers (4:13, 16). In the concluding section, Paul shows a great concern that Timothy teach "**doctrine conforming to godliness**" and warns those whose lifestyle is moving them away from "**the faith**" (5:8, 17; 6:2-3, 10, 17). Paul's letter to Titus emphasizes these same concerns (1:1, 9-14; 2:1, 7, 10).

Based on the preceding, it is no overstatement to say that *biblical doctrine is foundational to the life, witness, and ministry of individual Christians, and to the life of the church.* Yet today, we see little concern for doctrine in most evangelical churches, and music is fast becoming doctrinally vapid. This situation is so serious that it must be called a crisis.

How Can We Be Sure to Get It Right?

The main emphasis of this book is upon the use of an inductive or bottom-up approach to the Bible, rather than a deductive or top-down approach. It is imperative to have an honest, scientific approach to the Bible, since Christ said that good, fruit-bearing soil are those with an "**honest heart**" (Lk. 8:15). The attitude of our hearts and our perspective must be right, as well as our methodology. An inductive approach must be primary.

The priority of inductive methodology. It should be axiomatic, both in science and theology, that inductive, empirical evidence is far more dependable than deductive reasoning. What do these terms mean? Induction is defined as "the process of reasoning from particular instances to general conclusions." In logic, it is "reasoning from particular facts or individual cases to a general conclusion." In science it is parallel to the empirical or scientific method, which involves gathering a large number of data points from many experiments and then drawing a general principle from this. The more data points the scientist has, the more certain the generalization derived from them. On the other hand, deduction is "reasoning from a known principle to an unknown, from the general to the specific, or from a premise to a logical conclusion;" and "from the general to the particular, or from the universal to the individual."[2]

Thus, the inductive theologian draws many data points from the careful exegesis* (interpretation) of many Scriptures and derives a general conclusion from them. The number, clarity, and relevance of those many passages is crucial to the certainty of the theological conclusions drawn. Building a doctrine on one or two passages, or passages which are unclear or not directly related to the issue, raises questions about the dependability of the results. This book gives priority to an inductive, exegetical methodology.

On the other hand, the deductive theologian starts with certain axiomatic general principles, such as the sovereignty of God or the depravity of man, and reasons logically to specific doctrines derived from them. This is essentially a scholastic approach* to doctrine common before the Reformation, but unfortunately carried over into Protestant theology.

An illustration from medical science may be helpful. For years the medical consensus was that eggs and nuts in our diet contribute to high blood cholesterol and therefore to heart disease, since they are high in fat and cholesterol. A decade ago an alternative approach caught my attention, since Christ confirmed that fish and eggs are good things to give to children (Lk. 11:11-13). Assuming that the Lord Jesus, the Creator, knew more about diet than doctors today, I included eggs and nuts in my low carbohydrate diet with dramatic results in correcting my blood cholesterol. In 1999 researchers reported a radical reversal of medical advice on eggs and nuts. The direct data now, coming from the medical histories of thousands of nurses, showed that the previous advice was based upon "hypothesis and indirect evidence rather than direct data."[3] The previous advice was deductive rather than inductive and empirical; it was *a priori* rather than *a posteriori*. And it was dead wrong!

Exegesis of the determining Scripture passages gives the particular facts, which must be the starting point of all theology. Only after the inductive process has been exhausted may the deductive method be used. Deductive reasoning is valid only in confirming and testing the results of induction or in filling in the gaps where the inductive data is missing or incomplete. It must never be given priority over induction.

An example of putting deduction before induction, is found in one writer's discussion of Hebrews 6:4-6.[4] He argues that this difficult passage must be interpreted in the light of the analogy of Scripture.* Since many other passages teach the eternal security of the believer, this passage cannot contradict this and must be interpreted in harmony with it. He admits, however, "as one who has always believed in the doctrine of eternal security, I must confess that this passage does indeed conflict with such a view."[5] Unfortunately he did not give a cogent interpretation harmonious with this view and thus left the problem unresolved. Although the principle of the analogy of Scripture is sound, all of the inductive data should have been explored more carefully before resorting to deduction (cf. Ch. 13).

Principles of normative interpretation. The Bible must be interpreted in the same way other literature is understood, but always being careful to ask the Holy Spirit, the divine Author, for guidance in understanding. This means that we must take it all literally, unless some recognizable figure of speech, such as metaphor, hyperbole, or simile, is used. Failure to recognize such figures would be 'crass interpretation.' Sound interpretation focuses on a few basic principles, which must never be ignored.

One of the most important is *the context of the passage.* This means not only the verses preceding and following the passage under consideration, but also the near paragraphs and flow of thought of the whole book as well. How does this passage fit into the near paragraphs, and how does it fit into the theme of the whole book? It may seem like an old platitude, but "a text out of context is a pretext." Avoid proof-texting* like the plague! This is what the cults do. It is also important to see the passage in its historical, sequential context. There is a development of ideas in the Bible, and if the progression is ignored, serious error can result.

Equally important is *the meaning of the words used.* This sometimes will require a careful word study of crucial words in the passage. Reference to a good Greek or Hebrew lexicon* (dictionary) may be adequate. In some cases all the usages of the word in the Bible should be examined. In a few cases the usage of a Greek word in the secular classical and common (koine) Greek as well as in the Septuagint Old Testament translation must be checked. This will give us a far better idea of the range of meanings from which to choose for the passage at hand. This is important, since the lexicons are not infallible! Here it must be emphasized that *word usage, not derivation, determines word meaning.* The derivation of a word from its root may be totally misleading, even though it is sometimes helpful.

It should be obvious that *the grammar and syntax* of the sentence* is also exceedingly important. The Greek language of the New Testament has a very precise and discriminating grammar, which is discernible from the many distinct forms of the words. Building upon this is the syntax* or relationship of the words in the sentence to be studied. Excellent Greek grammar books are constantly becoming available to help in this.

Many readers will plead ignorance of the Greek original: "Isn't this why we have translations?" Yes, the better modern translations can generally be trusted. In this book the New American Standard Version has normally been used as one of the most literal and dependable. However, there are times when the NAS translators do not give the best rendering, and then the most accurate of other translations will be quoted. On rare occasions, I will supply my own translation, when the above rules of interpretation lead to the conclusion that none of the existing translations are adequate.

Another widely used principle of interpretation is the *'analogy of Scripture'** (analogy of faith), which means looking for a parallel passage which teaches the same thing. This can be very helpful but can also be very misleading, especially if the other passages are not really parallel. This is a deductive method. Some interpreters fall into "parallelomania," which means, bringing in other passages which are not parallel and therefore irrelevant.

A healthy perspective. In science, the angle from which we look at the data is important. If a researcher looks at an instrument from other than a 90° angle there will be a parallax error. Approaching the Bible from a skewed angle gets equally false results. Belief in the *total inerrancy** of Scripture is a crucial starting point. Along with this the *sufficiency** of Scripture is also most important. If we look to human tradition, reason, or experience as a significant basis, we will probably fall into error.

Many people approach the Bible from the perspective of a denominational tradition. This is a skewed angle from which to study Scripture, since all human traditions come under the condemnation of the Lord Jesus when He warned the Pharisees: **"you invalidated the world of God for the sake of your tradition"** (Mt. 15:6). The Apostle Paul warned the Colossian Christians about the danger of being taken **"captive through philosophy and empty deception, according to the tradition of men,..."** (Col. 2:8). British scholar, F. F. Bruce warned: "There is a great danger, when once we have adhered to one particular school of thought or adopted one particular system of theology, of reading the Bible in the light of that school or system and finding its distinctive features in what we read."[6] It is spiritually perilous to get emotionally attached to a denominational tradition.

Human experience is another distorting factor. Although the evangelical faith is characterized by a strong emphasis upon our experiencing the truth of God's word personally, we must never interpret the Bible by our experience. *We must always interpret our experience by the Bible!* Scripture is the plumbline by which all human experience must be measured and evaluated. Otherwise, there cannot be one absolute truth of the word of God, denial of which is the major error of our contemporary culture.

A Personal Theological Pilgrimage

This book is the result of my personal theological pilgrimage. When I came to salvation as an engineering student, I was active in an Arminian church. I early became convinced of the doctrine of eternal security through inductive study. At seminary I accepted moderate Calvinism and in turn taught it for a score of years. However, dialogue with an extreme Calvinistic colleague and my study and teaching of the life of Christ and the book of Acts forced me to re-examine my Calvinism. A defining moment in my pilgrimage was a question posed to me on a radio call-in program about the relationship of foreknowledge and election. These things helped move me to my present mediate position between Calvinism and Arminianism.

An exploratory paper I presented at the Evangelical Theological Society annual meeting in Toronto in 1981 drew considerable interest. Since 1992 the results of in-depth research on sub-topics have been presented at various ETS meetings, which are the basis of this volume. It has been very exciting to see how all the pieces have come together, and it is astonishing how this mediate position resolves the supposed contradictions and paradoxes, which have plagued our theologies over the ages. But this really should not be surprising, since all Scripture has one Author, the Holy Spirit, and there should be no real contradictions in a biblical theology. In 2002 an academic presentation of this data was published under the title, *Beyond Calvinism and Arminianism: an Inductive, Mediate Theology of Salvation* (0-9624850-4-7). This present book seeks to make this study available to all serious Christians, not just theologians. If a reader wants to go into greater depth in looking into the biblical proofs of this position, the academic version is recommended and a revised edition is projected.

The Importance of Details

A major flaw in a deductive approach to any subject, whether it be science, medicine, or theology, is the tendency to make sweeping generalizations without adequate attention to the details of the data. Carl Sagan got plenty of undeserved media attention for his sweeping generalizations about evolution in the universe, but when we read the incredible detail from some writers, such as Michael Denton and Michael Behe, we see that evolutionists' sweeping generalizations get demolished by a host of details of fact.[7]

The major advantage of an inductive, empirical approach is that it forces us to pay attention to the details of the data. Indeed, in the preface of Michael Behe's *Darwin's Black Box*, this biochemist alerts his readers to the daunting task they will face in reading his book, because of the incredible multiplicity of details he must discuss in order to do justice to the subject. Many readers will face the same problem in theological studies. *I will be forced to go into great detail of linguistic, grammatical, syntactical, exegetical, and historical material to do justice to the subject.* Bear with it, if you really want to get to the bottom of these issues, even if the details at times get tedious. *There is no other way to get to the whole truth.*

1. I Howard Marshall, *Kept by the Power of God*, 3rd ed , (Carlisle, UK Paternoster, 1995), p 16

2 *Webster's New American Dictionary*, p 478, *Webster's New World Dictionary* (New York Prentice Hall, 1986), pp 368, 718, *Webster's Collegiate Dictionary* (Springfield, MA· G C Merriam Co , 1943), p. 262

3 Walter C Willett, "Old Beliefs Challenged by New Data," in *Nurses' Health Study Newsletter*, vol 6 (1999), p 5

4 Robert H Stein, *Difficult Passages in the New Testament* (Grand Rapids Baker, 1990), pp 348-55

5 Ibid , p 353

6 F F Bruce in Roger T Forster and V Paul Marston, *God's Strategy in Human History*, p vii

7 Michael Denton, *Evolution A Theory in Crisis* (Bethesda, MD Adler & Adler, 1985) and Michael Behe, *Darwin's Black Box* (NY Free Press, 1996)

PART ONE

THE FOUNDATIONS
OF SALVATION TRUTH

BALANCING THE ATTRIBUTES OF GOD

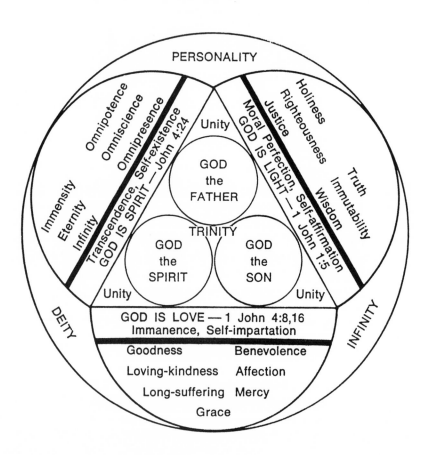

Evidently we must use greater care in formulating our concept of divine sovereignty than has sometimes been shown among theologians.... The moral seems to be that sovereignty is a more complex concept than we often imagine. Use of it requires some careful thinking rather than jumping to conclusions that seem intuitive. What seems intuitive for one theologian will be counter-intuitive for another. Intuition misleads us, because generally intuition does not make fine distinctions. Intuitively, we tend to formulate divine sovereignty by excluding anything that looks like it might be a limitation on God.   -John M. Frame

WHO IS THE GOD
WHOSE IMAGE WE BEAR?

Any attempt to develop an inductive theology of salvation must start with the character and attributes of the God who saves sinners. This is foundational. The main themes of the Bible all focus on God, mankind, sin, and salvation. Just a few verses into Genesis, God is described as creating humanity in His own image. An accurate biblical picture of God's character and in what ways humanity resembles God and in what ways mankind is different is essential to salvation truth. How Adam and Eve's fall into disobedience and depravity affects the image of God in humanity is another essential element. Our goal is to understand who God is, who we were created to be, and our own fallen human plight, as a sound basis for a balanced view of God's wonderful salvation.

Careful study of Scripture will show that none of the polarized views described in Chapter 1 gives a true picture. The key question then is: what is meant by the sovereignty of God and the depravity of mankind? All sorts of questions are raised by this diversity of viewpoints. Years ago, Doris Day used to sing, "Que Sera, Sera (What will be, will be)." Is this true? Is God the author of sin? Does God actually change His mind? Is God responsible for atrocities, such as the holocaust or nature's calamities? Has God really decreed before creation all that transpires on earth? Is life really a stacked deck? Does God really answer prayer, or does it just seem that way? If God doesn't control everything, how can the future be certain? Can *anybody* really get saved, or has God already decided the issue? Who is responsible to live the Christian life, God or me? And so the questions go. The ultimate question is: what kind of a god is God, and in what sense does humanity bear His image? Answering this first will help answer all the other questions.

It is imperative that sovereignty and depravity be defined biblically, using an inductive approach, drawing concepts *directly* from Scripture. This approach must begin in the first chapters of Genesis to get the whole picture of who God is in His relationship to mankind.

God Before the Foundation of the World

The earliest verses of Genesis imply that the God who created the heavens and the earth is not a solitary singleness, but an interpersonal Being. The word for God in the Hebrew is *ELOHIM*, which is a plural noun (3 or more) with a singular verb. Plural nouns and pronouns are frequently used to refer to God. Moses described the Spirit of God as involved in the work of creation (Gen. 1:2) and in striving with sinful humanity (Gen. 6:3). There are later references to a divine Messiah, who is called God's Son (Psalm 2:7; Isa. 9:6; 48:16; Micah 5:2). In the New Testament the Lord Jesus is depicted as the prophesied Messiah. He and His Apostles frequently explain His integral relationship to the Holy Spirit sent from the Father. The New Testament is more explicit in revealing that God is a Tri-Unity, that is, one God existing eternally in three persons. The Hebrew Scriptures emphasized the oneness of God because of humanity's early lapse into polytheism. However, all Scripture is consistent in affirming the Tri-unity of God.

This Tri-unity is an eternal reality, since in referring to the Lord Jesus, John wrote: "**In the beginning was the Word, and the Word was with God, and the Word was Himself deity. He was in the beginning with God.**" (Jn. 1:1-2, CGO). The grammar of this verse emphasizes that the Lord Jesus had the essential quality of deity in the pre-creation eternity.[A] This also comes out in His prayer: "**Now, Father, glorify Me together with Yourself, with the glory which I had with You before the world was**" (Jn. 17:5). The Scripture is also very clear that an essential attribute of God is love (1 Jn. 4:16). This is a glimpse into the eternal counsels of God from Christ's high-priestly prayer: "**...for You loved Me before the foundation of the world**" (Jn. 17:24). Augustine wrote: "If God is love, then there must be in Him a Lover, a Beloved, and a Spirit of love; for no love is conceivable without a Lover and a Beloved.... Where love is, there is a trinity."[1]

The New Testament gives other indications as to what God did before the foundation of the world. The Apostle Paul was chosen:

> ... to make clear how is to be carried out the trusteeship of this secret which has **for ages been hidden in God**, the Creator of all things, so that the many phases of God's wisdom may now through the church be made known to

---

A. Only the Williams translation comes close to bringing out the full meaning of the Greek: "The Word was God Himself," based upon the fact that the word *theos* is in the emphatic position at the beginning of the clause. Being without an article *theos*, connotes the quality of deity. However, Christ is not the only divine person, as Williams' rendering implies, thus my modification (cf. Wallace, *Greek Grammar*, p. 269).

the rulers and authorities in heaven, in accordance with the eternal purpose which **God** executed in the gift of **Christ Jesus our Lord** (Eph. 3:9-11, WILL).

Before creation God made a plan for the salvation of the world to be made known through Israel and the church. Paul, writing about the church, also revealed that "...**He chose us in Him before the foundation of the world, so that we would be holy and blameless before Him in love**" (Eph. 1:4). The future for all His saints is to participate in His future kingdom: "**Then the King will say to those on His right, 'Come, you who are blessed of My Father, inherit the kingdom prepared for you from the foundation of the world**" (Mt. 25:34). The only way God could prepare His church and His kingdom was to send His Son into the world:

...knowing that you were not redeemed with perishable things like silver or gold from your futile way of life inherited from your forefathers, but with precious blood, as of a lamb unblemished and spotless, *the blood* of Christ. For He was foreknown **before the foundation of the world**, but has appeared in these last times for the sake of you who through Him are believers in God, who raised Him from the dead and gave Him glory, so that your faith and hope are in God (1 Pet. 1:18-21).

God's eternal decrees. Unfortunately, theologians of past centuries developed elaborate notions of a comprehensive decree or decrees of God in the past eternity, by which He determined all that was to take place in the whole world throughout time. In letting their imaginations run, they got involved in sometimes bitter debate about the order of these supposed decrees of God. The New Testament is absolutely silent about any decrees of God, and there is only one reference to such decrees in the Old: "**I will surely tell of the decree of the LORD: He said to Me, 'You are My Son, Today I have begotten You**" (Ps. 2:7)[B] This is the unique event of human history upon which all of God's eternal plans were founded! Therefore, God was careful to implement His decree by raising Christ Jesus from the dead. There are five other references to God's decrees relating to His creation and judgments (Job 28:26; 38:10; Ps. 148:6; Prov. 8:29; Jer. 5:22).

God's Awesome Creation

Scientists are abandoning the idea of a steady-state universe, with matter and energy being eternal. A recent theory is the "big bang," which says that there was an incredibly massive explosion of matter and energy billions of years ago, resulting in our present rapidly expanding universe. Not only are scientists having to admit that the universe had a beginning, but increasingly many are recognizing an intelligence behind it all.[2] Although the Genesis account does not affirm a "big bang," it does indicate that scientists

B. Some cultists imagine that this speaks of the origin of the Messiah, the Lord Jesus, but the Apostle Paul made it clear that it speaks of His resurrection from the dead. Cf. Acts 13:33; Col. 1:18, Rev 1.5

are getting closer to the truth. It is clear that matter is not eternal, and the Bible clearly teaches that God created the universe out of nothing, *ex nihilo*. There is strong evidence that Genesis 1:1 is an absolute sentence affirming the creation of the heavens and earth in the beginning.[3]

The earth. There is considerable debate about the formation of the earth, plants, animals, and human beings in the six days spelled out in the rest of the chapter. What is clear is that the sovereign God wrought an incredible work of fiat creation. Erich Sauer affirms:

> Christ and the New Testament guarantee the historicity and literality of the opening chapters of the Bible. Everywhere the Lord and His apostles treat them as accounts of actual events; indeed they even draw from them dogmatic conclusions. Matt. 19:4-9; Rom. 5:12-21; I Cor. 15:21, 22; I Tim 2:13, 14; Jas. 3:9; 1 Jn.3:12; Rev. 20:2.[4]

Astronomers focus on God's macrocosm, and mind-boggling new discoveries about the vastness and complexity of our universe occur almost daily. There is a hint of the vastness of the expanding universe in Genesis 1:6-8, which speaks of the "expanse" of the heavens, a word which could well imply an expanding universe. Atomic physicists focus on the microcosm, and again knowledge of the incredible complexity of the building blocks of our universe is escalating. The universe almost seems infinite to us creatures, but we know that it is not infinite, nor could it be. But the majesty of this time-space universe is a growing testimony to the majesty of the infinite God Who created it all.

As we marvel at the immensity of the universe, the question arises: how could an insignificant planet like earth be the focus of God's cosmic plan of redemption? Geographically and spatially our planet is just one insignificant planet in the solar system of an insignificant star in an insignificant galaxy in an immense and expanding universe. Furthermore, human beings on this tiny earth seem to be an insignificant a part of its biomass. This question arises out of a confusion between spatial significance and spiritual significance. God, the Creator of all things, has invested our earth with a unique significance by creating man in His own image, setting man upon it, and sending His eternal Son to become incarnate among humans so that He might die and rise again to procure eternal life for them. The carrying out of this divine drama on earth makes it the most significant place in the universe. Waterloo is an insignificant village in Flanders, but the battle fought there to defeat Napoleon Bonaparte gave it incredible historical significance. Secular humanists are expending billions of dollars vainly searching for life on other planets because they do not believe in God and the centrality of His eternal plan for the earth. However, God has chosen to make human beings on earth the central focus of His eternal plan.

Angelic beings. Scripture tells us that God not only created the material universe, but also the angels, the first pair of human beings, and the animal and plant kingdoms. Scripture says very little explicitly about the creation of angelic beings. But there is a connection between the stars and these angels. Sauer observes this connection:

> The Word of God knows of thrones and lordships, of principalities and authorities (Col. 1:16), of sons of God and morning stars (Job 38:7), of the host of the high in the height (Isa. 24:21), of cherubim and seraphim (Rev. 4:6-8; Isa. 6:2, 3), of archangels and angels (Jude 9; Rev. 5:11; 12.7). And all these it describes by the same term, "host of heaven", *as it uses for the stars.*[5]

Probably the connection is best understood by identifying the universe as the dwelling place of these heavenly beings. In any case, there are indications that the angels take part in the history of human salvation.

Although little is said about the creation of angels in general, Ezekiel wrote about Lucifer's (Satan's) original created beauty and status in God's presence, symbolized in language addressed to the "king of Tyre" (Ez. 28:11-19). The language transcends that of any earthly prince (28:1-10).

> You had the seal of perfection, full of wisdom and perfect in beauty. You were in Eden, the garden of God; every precious stone was your covering:.... On the day that you were created they were prepared. You were the anointed cherub who covers, and I placed you *there*, you were on the holy mountain of God; you walked in the midst of the stones of fire. You were blameless in your ways from the day you were created until unrighteousness was found in you.... Your heart was lifted up because of your beauty; you corrupted your wisdom by reason of your splendor (Ez. 28:12-15, 17).

Similarly Isaiah prophesied about the "star of the morning, son of the dawn" under the rubric of the king of Babylon, another grossly idolatrous city (Isa. 14:12-14). Satan's revolt here described will be discussed later.

Humanity's Created Nobility

A unique creation

> Then God said, "Let Us make man in Our image, according to Our likeness; and let them rule over the fish of the sea and over the birds of the sky and over the cattle and over all the earth, and over every creeping thing that creeps on the earth." God created man in His own image, in the image of God He created him; male and female He created them (Gen 1:26-7).

Moses, in the usual Hebrew way, then gives a parallel explanation: "**Then the LORD God formed man of dust from the ground, and breathed into his nostrils the breath of life (*ruach hayyim*); and man became a living being (*nephesh hayah*)**" (Gen.2:7). Since the animals had been described in Genesis 1:30 as having *nephesh*, it is clear that *nephesh hayah* refers to physical life. However, since *hayyim* is the plural for 'lives' and since *ruach* can refer to 'breath' or 'spirit,' this expression could well indicate the unique spiritual qualities of mankind implied in the image of God emphasized in 1:26-7. What then is the meaning of that image?

The meaning of God's image in man

In the very act of creating human beings in His own image, God voluntarily limited the exercise of His own sovereignty. Christians have struggled to understand the meaning of that image of God in man. Some cults wrongly assume that it implies a physical image, but it is clear from the rest of Scripture that it involves the moral image of God. There are three common explanations. Some emphasize that the image of God enabled mankind to relate to God. Others focus on the rule over the animal, vegetable, and mineral domains of the earth which connects with that image. Others reject these ideas and focus on the constitutional nature of man as unique from the animals. There is probably truth in all three: What man does (relate to God and other people) and is able to do (exercise rule over nature) is dependent upon who he is (the substantive reality).

What is this substantive reality of the image of God? It should be self-evident that the major difference between man and the animals is in the eternality of man. God created mankind with an everlasting spirit, which animals do not possess. Since the Genesis context emphasizes humanity's distinctiveness from the animal creation over which he was given rule, immortality is clearly a major part of mankind's uniqueness.

God's moral attributes reflected in His image. Since Genesis does not explain the meaning of the image of God, we must derive its characteristics from three New Testament allusions, where this imagery is found in passages related to the restoration of the image through salvation in Christ. Paul referred to the knowledge of God being restored in the believer in Christ: "... **and have put on the new self who is being renewed to a true knowledge according to the image of the One who created him—**" (Col. 3:10). The context here makes it clear that Paul's focus goes beyond man's intelligence to his knowledge of God's revealed truth, which needs to be restored in fallen man through the new birth and the ongoing renewal process of the mind of the believer (Rom. 12:1-2).

In the same way the parallel passage in Ephesians 4:24 indicates that the moral qualities of righteousness and holiness are also part of the image of God: "... **and put on the new self, which in *the likeness of* God has been created in righteousness and holiness of the truth.**" It is widely understood that Adam was created in innocence with the possibility of attaining righteousness and holiness by continued fellowship with and obedience to God. Thus man was created as a moral being faced with moral choices, which animals are incapable of making.

Another clue comes from 2 Corinthians 3:18: "**But we all, with unveiled face, beholding as in a mirror the glory of the Lord, are being transformed into the same image from glory to glory, just as from the Lord, the Spirit.**" Can we infer from this that a certain aspect of God's glory was reflected in the highest example of His earthly creation, mankind? We see a pattern emerging from these references. Here is the basis for seeing *all* of the moral attributes of God are part of His image in man, even if a specific attribute is not explicitly referred to in Scripture. God's love, holiness, and spirit nature must have been a part of the original image (Isa. 6:3; Jn. 4:24; 1 Jn. 4:8). Thus, just as God is a personal God with intellect, emotions, and will, the image of God in man must involve intellect, emotions, and will. Seeing the many aspects of His image in man, the full spectrum of God's moral attributes should be included in our understanding.

God delegates limited autonomy. God is an autonomous being, totally sovereign over His creation. By creating Adam and Eve in His image, they became autonomous beings, with only one limitation to their autonomy, just one fruit which they could not eat. They were created to reflect His glorious attributes of holiness, love, righteousness, mercy, and justice and to remain in fellowship with Him. God created Adam with a human spirit, distinct from the soul. The spirit is the God-conscious part of man; the soul, the self-conscious part; and the body, the world-conscious part. The animals were created with only *nephesh*, which means soul-life (Gen. 1:30), but man was distinct in having a spirit (*ruach*) as well.

What is the evidence for distinguishing the human spirit from the soul? Those who don't make this distinction base it upon the interchangeable use of soul and spirit in describing fallen humanity. However, the nature of unfallen Adam and Eve is quite another question, and the nature of fallen man is not really direct evidence for the original condition of Adam and Eve or of regenerate believers.[C] Although the human spirit died in the fall, when we trust in Christ our spirit is actually made alive and functional again, so that we can relate to God personally. Before we look more into the implications of the fall, we should seek to understand Adam's created autonomy.

The creation account connects God's delegation to Adam of rule over the animal, vegetable, and mineral creation with his uniqueness as being in God's image, twice in Genesis 1:26-28. This delegated rule or dominion is in itself a further self-limitation of the exercise of God's sovereignty. Adam was to be God's regent over the earth. Although God was the ultimate authority,

---

C   The explicit evidence for the human spirit being distinct from the soul is found explicitly in two New Testament passages: **"Now may the God of peace Himself sanctify you entirely; and may your spirit [*pneuma*] and soul [*psuchē*] and body be preserved complete, without blame at the coming of our Lord Jesus Christ"** (1 Thess. 5:23); **"For the word of God is living and active and sharper than any two-edged sword, and piercing as far as the division of soul and spirit, of both joints and marrow, and able to judge the thoughts and intentions of the heart"** (Heb. 4:12). Even though the last passage does not speak of separating soul and spirit, it does imply a real distinction, just as we must distinguish joints and marrow. In addition, in 1 Cor. 2:11, 14-15 and 15:44-46 there is a contrast between the Greek adjectives *psuchikos* [natural=soulish] and *pneumatikos* [spiritual]. The connection of James 3:15 with Jude 19 is also supportive. (See Olson, *BCAA*, pp 88, 456.)

Adam was given a trusteeship of the world, further evidenced in that God told Adam to name the animals (Gen. 2:18-20). When we give a pet to a child, we usually allow the child to name the pet. Adam had free will in this and everything else, with the one exception of the fruit of the tree of the knowledge of good and evil. In these delegated areas God was no longer exercising His sovereignty. So when Adam and Eve disobeyed God's command, did they really exercise free will, or had God already decided what they would do, thus determining the outcome? Some Christians under the influence of Augustine's determinism would even deny that Adam and Eve had free will, thus making God the author of sin. Let us investigate the actual biblical teaching about God's sovereignty.

The Meaning of God's Sovereignty

The idea that God's eternal decrees dictate all that transpires in the universe, which Augustine and the Reformers developed, lacks any explicit biblical support. Reformed theologian John Frame has issued a warning:

> Evidently we must use greater care in formulating our concept of divine sovereignty than has sometimes been shown among theologians... The moral seems to be that "sovereignty" is a more complex concept than we often imagine. Use of it requires some careful thinking rather than jumping to conclusions that seem intuitive. What seems intuitive for one theologian will be counterintuitive for another. Intuition misleads us, because generally intuition does not make fine distinctions. Intuitively, we tend to formulate divine sovereignty by excluding anything that looks like it might be a "limitation" on God [6]

What explicit evidence is there for this decretal* view of God's sovereignty? A number of word studies and inductive investigation of the biblical data will help clarify the concept of God's sovereignty.

Key word studies

Although one modern translation renders *YHWH-ELOHIM* as "Sovereign LORD," there is no word for sovereignty in either the Old or New Testaments. Since sovereignty relates to political relationships of governance, the terms most directly related to it in the Old Testament are king, kingdom, decrees, and counsel, and in the New, counsel (*boulē*), purpose (*prothēsis*), and will (*thelēma*). Understanding in what sense God's governance over mankind is spelled out in the Scriptures is critical in defining sovereignty.

Kingdom. Four Hebrew terms for kingdom come from the same root (*melek*).[7] Usage concerning divine activity falls into three major categories: the Davidic Covenant promises, prophecies of the Messianic kingdom, and a few references to the general rulership of Yahweh over the nations of the earth (Ps. 103:19; Ps. 145). There are many more instructive references in the Psalms and prophets in which Yahweh is addressed as King. Some are references to the Messiah as King (Ps. 2 & 24), but most stress God's mighty acts as ruler of Israel and the nations, as manifested in His works of creation, judgment, deliverance, protection, and cleansing of sin (Ps. 2:7; 5:2; 9:10; 10:16; 20:9; 24:7-10; 44:4; 47:2,6,7; 68:24; 74:12; 84:3; 89:18; 95:3; 98:6; 145:1; Isa. 6:5; 33:22; Jer. 8:19; 10:7, 10). However, *there is not a hint in any of these passages of any exhaustive sovereignty* by which Yahweh decreed every event to transpire in the universe.

Indeed, the imagery of king and kingdom could not possibly communicate such an idea to ancient middle-eastern peoples, unless it were spelled out explicitly. These terms were not only used for the rulers of great empires, but also for the heads of small cities, and thus do not support such an idea.[8] Not even the greatest human kings' powers involved direct control of all events in their domain. Their decrees were carried out *indirectly* by their government functionaries. Therefore, there is no way that direct control of all events by a sovereign could be indicated by the cultural usage of the words 'king' or 'kingdom.' This is an exaggeration of the analogy of human kingly sovereignty: a notion which Calvinists imposed upon these words.

Counsel in the Hebrew ('etsah). The next word which relates to God's sovereignty is 'counsel,' for which there are frequent references in both testaments. The Hebrew *'etsah* is widely used on the human level for counsel or advice. On the divine level, there are a score of usages. In Psalm 33:11, in emphasizing the eternality of God's counsel in contrast to that of the nations, it is set in parallelism with "the plans of His heart." God has an eternal plan. Then the Psalmist looks for guidance from God's counsel (73:24) and rebukes Israel for not waiting for but rather spurning His counsel (106:13; 107:11). In Proverbs, 'Wisdom' gives her counsel (1:25; 8:14), and the permanence of God's counsel is highlighted (19:21).

The prophets speak of the Messiah's wise, Spirit-given counsel (Isa. 11:2) and of the greatness of Yahweh in His counsel and deeds, which are wonderful, omniscient, and abiding (Isa. 28:29; 46:10-11; Jer. 32:19). In Isaiah 46:10 the establishment of His counsel is linked with the accomplishment of His pleasure. However, there is not a hint that this involves any exhaustive efficacious decree in eternity past such as is held by Calvinists. The translators render it as "plan" in contexts which have to do with God's plans of bringing judgment (Isa. 25:1; 46:11; Jer. 49:20; 50:45). Therefore, the most that can be said about the revelation of Yahweh's sovereignty directly revealed in the Old Testament and warranted by inductive word studies of usage is that *an omniscient, omnipotent, omnipresent God sovereignly intervenes in human affairs according to His wise plan as He implements His general rule over the nations and His plan of redemption.*

Counsel in the Greek (boulē). It is even more astounding that the New Testament makes *absolutely no reference* to any of God's decrees. The Greek word which comes closest to 'decree' is *boulēma*, which is only used once. In Romans 9:19 Paul puts it in the mouth of an objector to what he says about God's sovereign dealings with the nation Israel. The weaker, related word *boulē* means 'counsel' or 'purpose' and has a secondary meaning, "resolution' or 'decision.' Luke uses it five times of the divine counsel. In His affirmation of John the Baptizer and rebuke of Israel's leadership, the Lord Jesus stated that **"the Pharisees and the lawyers rejected God's purpose (*boulē*) for themselves, not having been baptized by John"** (Lk.7:30). Is it not ironic that the very first (and only) connection of this term with God in the Gospels, not only does not imply some exhaustively efficacious implementation of God's eternal plan, *but quite the opposite brings out men's ability to frustrate God's plan for themselves?* Apparently God had a plan for the nation Israel, but over the centuries they failed to conform to that plan, and now their leaders outright rejected that plan for themselves and the nation.

The Book of Acts. First we find Peter's extremely relevant charge in his Pentecost sermon: **"... this Man, delivered up by the predetermined plan (*boulē*) and foreknowledge of God, you nailed to a cross by the hands of godless men and put Him to death"** (Acts 2:23). Peter (as quoted by Luke) used the strongest possible language to communicate divine sovereignty in the outworking of God's plan for the crucifixion. He used a participial form of *horizein* (ordain, appoint) to modify *boulē* (counsel). Peter, while acknowledging the out-working of God's pre-temporal plan by foreknowledge, placed full responsi-bility for the crucifixion upon the evil men who did it. There is no hint of implication that God forced the will of the Jewish leaders, Judas Iscariot, Pontius Pilate, King Herod Antipas, or the Roman soldiers. They were doing their own thing in their own sinful way.

For example, Harold Hoehner has shown how the political situation in AD 33 better explains Pilate's motivation than the situation in AD 30.[9] It would be no problem for an omniscient God to orchestrate events by His intensive knowledge of each of the players and circumstances. Indeed, Peter explicitly included God's prescience in the implementation of His plan (Acts 2:23). Since the cross is at the very center of God's plan, it is easy to understand God's most directive involvement in this event. However, the force of Peter's words must not be extended to other less central events.

In the synagogue of Pisidian Antioch Paul stated that David served the *boulē* (purpose) of God in his own generation (Acts 13:36) and reminded the Ephesian elders that he had declared to them the whole counsel (*boulē*) of God (20:27). If the *boulē* of God were all encompassing, how could Paul possibly have declared the whole of it to the Ephesian church in under three years? The writer of Hebrews argued that God showed the unchangeable-ness of his *boulē* by making an oath (6:17). So far there is no hint that this purpose, plan, or counsel of God exhaustively includes every event in the universe, including all the worst eruption of Satan's and mankind's evil over the centuries. This leaves just the one verse so crucial to the Calvinists.

The main proof-text. Ephesians 1:9-12 contains the last usage of *boulē* in reference to God's eternal plan and is the crucial proof-text used by

Augustine's Calvinistic followers to support their concept of sovereignty[10]:

> He made known to us the mystery of His will, according to His kind intention which He purposed in Him with a view to an administration suitable to the fulness of the times, that is, the summing up of all thing in Christ, things in the heavens and things upon the earth. In Him also we have obtained an inheritance, having been predestined according to His purpose <u>who works all things after the counsel (*boulē*) of His will</u>, to the end that we who were the first to hope in Christ should be to the praise of His glory (Eph. 1:9-12).

At this point, a reminder is needed concerning the *extreme cruciality of context in interpretation*. Has Paul been discussing anything relating to all-encompassing decrees of God in this context? Quite the contrary, Paul is focusing on God's glorious plan of salvation. The word 'decree' is not found here, or for that matter anywhere in the New Testament of God's decrees. In Ephesians 1:3-6 Paul is focusing on the Father's eternal plan of salvation, and then in 1:7-12 he surveys the Son's past work of redemption and the inheritance He purposes for us in the consummation ("the fulness of the times"). Verse 12 is a segue into vv. 12-13 in which the Spirit's work of applying salvation is described. Thus the total context before and after verse 11 is salvation oriented.

The grammar of this clause warrants closer examination. Note that the article *ta* with *panta* (all) probably has a demonstrative force, that is, "**He works all these things**."[D] This would make it clear that the "all things" of 1:11 has to do with the 'all *these* things' of the redemptive plan of God just alluded to, not with all human events. Any universalizing of the outworking of God's sovereignty in 'secular' events is totally absent from the context.

In sum, the weight of usage of this clause in Ephesians 1:11 militates for the demonstrative force, referring back to the outworking of the Father's eternal plan (1:3-6) as implemented by the Beloved Son through the blood-redemption of the cross (1:7-11).[E] All uses of this verse as a proof-text for the exhaustive sovereignty of God is crass Scripture twisting. If there were some

---

D "The Greek article was originally derived from the demonstrative pronoun *ho, hē, to*, and is clearly akin to the relative pronoun *hos, hē, ho*. It always retained some of the demonstrative force. This fact is evidenced by its frequent use in the papyri purely as a demonstrative pronoun" (Dana and Mantey, p 136) "The article was originally derived from the demonstrative pronoun That is, its original force was to *point out* something It has largely kept the force of drawing attention to something" (Daniel Wallace, *Greek Grammar*, p. 208) He states that the article intrinsically *conceptualizes*, also *identifies* an object, and at times *definitizes* (pp. 209-10) Cf A. T. Robertson, *Short Grammar*, p. 68.

E. In order to verify this interpretation of Ephesians 1:11 it is vital to do a study of the use of the article with the Greek word 'all' (*pas*), found 45 times in the New Testament, usually in the neuter plural (*ta panta*). A careful examination of the context of these usages shows that about 25 times the article has the demonstrative force mentioned by the grammarians, which restricts its meaning to some referent in the context. About 14 times the demonstrative force is absent, giving a more universal meaning to the expression (The remaining five are ambiguous or have a textual problem.)

antecedent development of such a notion in the usage of the terms, such proof-texting might be doubtfully justifiable, but there is not a shred of such development in either the Old or New Testaments!

While noting the importance of context, the same expression is used in the preceding verse (Eph. 1:10), where it is clear that Christ is to head up "**all these things**," that is, all believers in the Church (1:22), whether now in heaven or on earth. If its demonstrative force is ignored, universalism results. Thus, on what basis do Calvinists universalize it in verse 11?

It is also very important to note that Paul is referring to the objective work of the Son of God two millenniums ago as the antecedent of "all these things," and that he begins to make reference to the present subjective work of the Holy Spirit in applying salvation *after this* in verses 12-13. The cross was an eternally determined work of God; the same cannot be said about the application phase of the Spirit's work in the life of the individual, at least as far as this passage goes.

Thus the heavy weight which Augustine's followers put upon this one verse, after careful scrutiny leaves their viewpoint in serious doubt. Although it only takes one verse of Scripture to be a basis for truth, the correct interpretation of that verse is absolutely crucial, otherwise serious error results. Butler put it so well: "*We hold a few texts so near the eyes that they hide the rest of the Bible.*"[11] In this case, it is just one text!

The verb 'to will'. The verb *boulomai* ('to purpose,' 'to will') is used three times with God as the subject. In James 1:18 the participle *boulētheis* is used adverbially to describe the new birth. Although the translators tend to render it, "Of His own will," more literally it is, "purposefully" or "intentionally" that God gave us new birth. Does this verse clarify whether the new birth is implemented according to an unconditional or a conditional plan of God? Not at all! It is not explicit in this regard.

"The Lord is not slow about His promise, as some count slowness, but is patient toward you, not wishing (*boulomai*) for any to perish but for all to come to repentance" (2 Pet. 3:9). This verse has proved to be a major problem for the Calvinistic view. Indeed, it is in harmony with the whole tenor of Scripture concerning the eternal plan of God, which is, that the gospel of Christ be made available to every last human being before Christ returns.[12] This purpose of God, that all should come to repentance, makes the offer of the gospel a legitimate, bona fide offer. God's motivation is not ambivalent in this regard, lest He be accused of insincerity. God is in no way double-minded. (The third reference in Hebrews 6:17 is not relevant to the current investigation.)

Purpose (prothēsis). The word *prothēsis* occurs five times in reference to God's plan. The BAG lexicon gives: "plan, purpose, resolve, will,... design" as meanings.[13] Three usages have to do with God's plan of salvation (Rom. 8:28; Eph. 1:11; 2 Tim. 1:9) and two with His plan for the transition from national Israel to the Church in the general outworking of His plan of redemption. (Rom. 9:11; Eph. 3:11). There is no reference to a comprehensive plan for every event in human history. The question is how individuals come to be included in this salvation plan. In Romans 8:28 Paul first mentions **"those who love God, who are the called according to His purpose (*prothēsis*)."** Here God's salvation plan or design is seen as including those who love God. Paul makes it clear throughout the epistle that their calling to love God involves repentant faith. Their calling and justification are by faith. Faith must also be a prominent factor in his reference to foreknowledge and foreordination, since this is part of an unbroken sequence of five steps in Romans 8:29-30. In 2 Timothy 1:9, Paul confirms that salvation and calling are according to His own gracious plan or design (*prothēsis*). Whether this is worked out conditionally or unconditionally is not stipulated. (Rom. 9:11 will be discussed on pp. 298-303 as part of a broader discussion of Rom. 9-11.) Thus there is no explicit support for the Calvinistic view here either.

Will (THELĒMA). A study of the usage of *thelēma* is mostly marginal to the concerns of this investigation. It is used about eighteen times of the moral will of God in some regard, five times of God's salvation plan in some form, twice of God's guidance of a believer's walk, numerous times of Christ's own desire to fulfill the will of the Father, and a number of other general references. Again there is no revelation of a comprehensive determinative decree for the universe which is all-encompassing. However, determinists* take it that "God's decree is synonymous with God's will." This is based upon Theodor Beza's statement: "Nothing falls outside of the divine willing, even when certain events are clearly contrary to God's will."[14] Again the inductive data in the use of *thelēma* does not support this notion.

A Mediate Theological View

The solution to the serious polarization concerning who our God really is and how He relates to humans is found in a mediate view. Both extreme positions are in serious error, and the truth is in the middle (as it frequently is). These extreme positions in our understanding of God lead to extreme positions on His plan of salvation also, since all of the divisions of theology are interrelated. Therefore, it is absolutely imperative to develop a correct definition of God's sovereignty in order to grapple with the one-sided theology of salvation proposed by extreme Calvinists and open theists.* Likewise, the biblical teaching of God's absolute foreknowledge exposes the errors of open theism. A mediate position resolves the tension in a most satisfying way.

Even though J. O. Buswell, Jr. was a five-point Calvinist, he took issue with some of the concepts of God's attributes traditionally held by Augustine and the Reformers. His theology sensitized me to some of the problems with what has been called the "classic concept of God." He also alerted me to *a fundamental philosophical error in what I had been taught, which is, that God cannot foreknow that which He has not determined.* In reacting to such a notion held by extreme Calvinist Loraine Boettner, Buswell stated:

> But it is presumptuous for man to claim to know what kind of things God
> could or could not know. There is a mystery in knowledge which will
> probably never be resolved for us... For men to declare that God could
> not know a free event in the future seems to me sheer dogmatism.[15]

Buswell's most perceptive statement is a double-edged sword, since it also
cuts off the head of open theism as well. The biblical evidence for God's
infinite omniscience should be clear enough, without twisting its meaning.

There is another closely related error which is evident in the writings of
both opposing viewpoints. *A number of writers have confused the certainty
of a future event with the determination of that event by God.*[16] God knows
all future events as certain, whether He has determined them or not. His
omniscience is unlimited. Both Calvinists and open theists* err in making
the certainty of the future contingent upon God's determining it, but with
differing outcomes—the Calvinistic future being certain; the open theist's
future, partially open and uncertain. Both views are in error because God's
acts (decrees) must flow from His attributes (omniscience), not the reverse.

The mediate view affirms the essentials of the classic concept of God,
as modified by Buswell. The absolute foreknowledge of God is affirmed as
part of His omniscience, His absolute omnipresence, and His absolute
omnipotence, the exercise of which He has chosen to limit in significant
ways. The sovereignty of God is affirmed, but it must be defined in the light
of that self-limitation. The Greek philosophical concept of the simpleness of
God is rejected outright, since God reveals Himself as a Tri-unity, and His
works of creation are incredibly complex. The concept of a single all-
embracing decree of God must also be rejected, since it derives from the
notion of the simpleness of God and is totally without biblical support. Likewise, the impassibility of God (no passions) must be rejected as incompatible with the biblical narrative and is obviously derived from Greek philosophy. God certainly has revealed Himself as emotionally moved by the
human condition. Lastly, while affirming the immutability of God, we must
recognize His genuine dynamic interaction with humanity, which is not a
frozen immutability. His attributes are unchanging, but His relationships
with mankind are dynamic and changing.

Conclusions

God is the omnipotent Creator of the universe, who can do what He
pleases consistent with His attributes. In creating autonomous beings,
namely, Lucifer, the angels, and the human race, He has intentionally
limited the exercise of His own sovereignty. Like human sovereigns, God
exercises His sovereignty by punishing disobedience to His will at what
times and what ways suit His eternal plans. He further limits the exercise of
His sovereignty by delegating to mankind dominion over the earth, which is
intrinsic in the image of God with which He created man. Man was intended to reflect all of God's moral attributes in his relation to Himself and

to one another. There is no direct biblical evidence for the idea that in eternity past God decreed all that would transpire on the earth or that He irresistibly brings about the outworking of His will. Indeed, such a notion is contradictory to the creation of autonomous creatures who had free will. This notion is heavily derived from a misinterpretation of just one clause in Ephesians 1:11. There is absolutely no reference to God's decrees in the New Testament, and the Old Testament references are totally devoid of such a concept. But to get the whole picture, the impact of angelic revolt and human disobedience to God must be investigated in the next chapter.

1 Aurelius Augustine, cited by Erich Sauer, *The Dawn of World Redemption*, p 18-19

2 Michael Denton, *Earth's Destiny* and *Evolution a Theory in Crisis*.

3 Paul Copan and William Lane Craig, *Creation Out of Nothing*

4 Erich Sauer, *The Dawn of World Redemption*, p 38

5 Ibid , p 28

6 John M Frame, "The Spirit and the Scriptures," in D A Carson and John D Woodbridge, eds , *Hermeneutics, Authority and Canon*, pp 223-4

7 Francis Brown, *The New Brown-Driver-Briggs-Gesenius Hebrew and English Lexicon*, pp 574-5

8 R Laird Harris, Gleason L Archer, Jr , & Bruce K Waltke, eds , *Theological Wordbook of the Old Testament* (Chicago: Moody, 1980), I 507-9

9 Harold Hoehner, "Chronological Aspects of the Life of Christ Part V," *Bibliotheca Sacra* 524 (Oct '74) pp 340-8 (Also published in book form).

10 John S Feinberg is typical in the weight he puts on Eph. 1:11 in David and Randall Basinger, eds *Predestination and Free Will*, pp. 29-32 Also in Feinberg's, *No One Like Him*, pp 680-693

11 William F Butler, cited by Norman F. Douty, *The Death of Christ*, p 66.

12 C Gordon Olson, *What in the World Is God Doing?* 5th ed (2003), pp. 21-80

13 Arndt and Gingrich, p. 713

14 Patrick H Mell, *A Southern Baptist Looks at Predestination* (Cape Coral Christian Gospel Foundation, n d) P 53, Theodore Beza, cited by Vance, pp 479, 481.

15 J Oliver Buswell, Jr , *A Systematic Theology of the Christian Religion*, vol I, p 46

16 Gregory A Boyd, *God of the Possible*, p 32, Norman L Geisler, *Chosen But Free*, pp. 43, 45

I find, then that man was by God constituted free, master of his own will and power; indicating the presence of God's image and likeness in him by nothing so well as this constitution of his nature.... you will find that when He sets before man good and evil, life and death, that the entire course of discipline is arranged in precepts by God's calling men from sin, and threatening and exhorting them; and this on no other ground than that man is free, with a will either for obedience or resistance.

–Tertullian (AD 155–225)

PARADISE LOST: THE PLIGHT OF FALLEN HUMANITY

This inductive biblical investigation had to begin with an examination in the previous chapter of God's revelation about Himself and His creatures in the pristine period before the fall of mankind. Since most of human history has been lived under sin, it is now important also to look into the consequences of Satan's revolt and Adam's disobedience.

The Impact of Humanity's Fall
Universal depravity and spiritual death

Evangelical Christians and traditional Catholics are unique in believing that Adam and Eve's disobedience plunged the whole human race into a sinful condition. Although Judaism and Islam agree that Adam and Eve disobeyed God in Eden, they do not recognize that their descendants became sinners as a result. They, like followers of all other religions, hold that man is essentially good. However, the Genesis account is very explicit that God had warned them: "**From any tree of the garden you may eat freely; but from the tree of the knowledge of good and evil you shall not eat, for in the day that you eat from it you will surely die**" (Gen. 2:16-17). The immediate consequence of their sin was expulsion from the garden and from access to the tree of life, which represented the spiritual life they had enjoyed in fellowship with God.

Since they did not die *physically* when they disobeyed God's explicit command, the implication is that they died *spiritually*. Some suppose that this was just the beginning of the process of physical death, but the Bible is quite explicit about the spiritual impact of Adam's sin upon the whole human race. There was a constitutional change in Adam and Eve evidenced by several things: their attempt to cover their newly acquired sense of shame of nakedness (Gen. 3:7); their alienation from God seen in trying to hide from Him; and passing off the blame for their disobedience (Gen. 3:8-13). Although the account of God's judgments upon the snake as Satan's mouthpiece, the animals, Eve, Adam, plants, and the ground (Gen. 3:14-19) is very terse, the effects of those judgments are far reaching throughout human history (Rom. 8:18-23).

The immediate impact of their sin upon their first son reveals how quickly depravity spread throughout all humanity. This is evident in the way in which God confronted Cain for his deficient offering. Moses' account is brief and implies that God had told Adam and Eve that He required blood sacrifices to atone for their sins. Remember that God had covered the shame of their nakedness with the skins of sacrificed animals (Gen. 3:21). In faith and obedience Abel brought what was called "**a more excellent sacrifice**" (Heb. 11:4). But Cain, in his unrepentant pride, brought only vegetables, so "**for Cain and his offering [God] had no regard**" (Gen. 4:5). But God didn't give up on Cain. When God rejected his offering, he got angry. So God exhorted him: "**If you do well, will you not be accepted? And if you do not do well, sin is crouching at the door; its desire is for you, but you must master it**" (Gen. 4:7, RSV). God was well aware of the depravity of Cain's heart, but nevertheless gave him opportunity to repent and to come in faith with an acceptable offering. Cain's destiny had not been predetermined, and although he didn't repent and went on in envy to murder his brother, this was not inevitable. Even after Cain killed Abel, God continued to deal with him patiently.

Cain's depravity was passed on to his descendants. There was a devolution of the Cainite civilization morally, even while it was advancing by leaps and bounds technologically. The Apostle Jude spoke of the "**way of Cain**" (Jude 11) which was derived from Satan, the evil one (1 Jn. 3:12). This is a self-righteous religion by which Cain and his descendants sought to attain right standing with God by their own works, ignoring God's way of blood sacrifice. Cainite civilization developed rapidly since Cain built a city for the exploding population of his descendants (Gen. 4:17). It became a technologically advanced civilization as seen in Tubal-Cain, who developed iron and bronze technology, and Jubal, who developed music and the arts (4:21-22). Lamech violated God's original marriage plan with a bigamous relationship and used poetry to magnify his violent manslaughter (Gen. 4:23-4). This set the pattern for the civilization which magnified revenge to the extent that "**the earth was filled with violence**" (Gen. 6:11) by Noah's time. The number of true believers on earth declined because "**the sons of God [believers] saw that the daughters of [unbelieving] men were beautiful; and they took wives for themselves, whomever they chose**" (Gen. 6:2). The notorious *Nephilim* ("fallen ones") were renowned for their deeds of violence (Gen. 6:4). This pre-flood period shows human free will gone amok! Sin and depravity spread throughout the whole human race.

Paul later confirmed this understanding: **"There is none righteous, not even one.... For all have sinned and fall short of the glory of God.... Therefore, just as through one man sin entered into the world, and death through sin, and so death spread to all men, because all sinned"** (Rom. 3:10, 23; 5:12). Since in Romans 5:13ff Paul makes a contrast between the reckoning (imputing) of Adam's sin to all mankind and the reckoning (imputing) of Christ's righteousness to believers, it is clear that he is not just referring to our personal sins, but especially to universal guilt and depravity (Rom. 5:17). Then he summarized: **"For the wages of sin is death, but the free gift of God is eternal life in Christ Jesus our Lord"** (Rom. 6:23). In writing to the Ephesian Christians, Paul explains Satan's continuing involvement in man's spiritual plight:

> **And you were dead in your trespasses and sins, in which you formerly walked according to the course of this world, according to the prince of the power of the air, of the spirit that is now working in the sons of disobedience. Among them we too all formerly lived in the lusts of our flesh, indulging the desires of the flesh and of the mind, and were by nature children of wrath, even as the rest** (Eph. 2:1-3).

Personal sins, universal guilt, a sin nature derived from Adam and Eve, and universal spiritual death are all the clear consequences of Adam's sin.

Spiritual death carefully defined

A precise definition of spiritual death is now essential. Some are prone to use the illustration of the impossibility of evangelizing a corpse in a funeral parlor as a picture of spiritual death. How valid is this illustration?

In the last chapter the constituent nature of mankind was examined. If soul and spirit are not distinct, spiritual death has to be taken as a figure of speech. The soul=spirit could not have died literally because fallen man clearly retains a soul. But since the soul and spirit of man are distinct, spiritual death can be understood literally. Since the human spirit is distinct and especially the God-conscious part of man, spiritual death is best explained as the death of the human spirit, and the new birth as the literal making alive or resurrecting of the human spirit.

This is confirmed by Christ Himself in John 5:24-29. In vv. 24-27 He uses the imagery of the new birth as a spiritual resurrection: **"I tell you the truth, a time is coming and has now come when <u>the dead will hear</u> the voice of the son of God and those who hear will live. For as the Father has life in himself, so he has granted the Son to have life in himself"** (5:25, NIV). This is set in parallelism with the promise of bodily resurrection in similar language in vv. 28-29. Since the second is a literal resurrection (of the body), so also must the first be literal (of the human spirit). Note that the spiritually dead are able to hear Christ's voice and respond. Thus, neither spiritual death nor the new birth are figurative language. *The human spirit died literally in Eden, and the human spirit is made alive literally when we are born again.*

Our understanding of this truth is significantly dependent upon the definition of death. A comprehensive definition must fit spiritual, physical, and eternal death to be adequate. The common element of all three is separation. Spiritual death is separation from God (Isa. 59:1-2); physical death is separation of the soul and spirit from the body (as well as separation from loved ones); and eternal death is eternal separation from God (Rev. 19:20; 20:10, 14). As Paul explained in Ephesians 4:18: "**...being darkened in their understanding, excluded from the life of God because of the ignorance that is in them, because of the hardness of their heart....**" Resultant definition: *the rendering of the God-conscious part of man inoperative and, as a consequence, the separation of man from God.*

Delegation of sovereign control

The disobedience of Adam and Eve in the garden not only explains human depravity, it is most instructive about God in His relation to mankind. It should be obvious that, having created them as autonomous beings, God allowed, but did not cause them to sin. By granting them this autonomy, He thereby chose to limit the exercise of His sovereignty. Being sovereign, He could have prevented them from sinning or manipulated them to sin. But it is unthinkable that a holy God would in any way do such a thing, for this would make Him the author of sin. James made this very clear: "**Let no one say when he is tempted, 'I am being tempted by God'; for God cannot be tempted by evil, and He Himself does not tempt anyone. But each one is tempted when he is carried away and enticed by his own lust**" (Jas. 1:13-14). God created Adam and Eve to reflect the glory of His being, but they became fallen creatures, their offspring continuing and growing in their disobedience to Him.

Satan's limited autonomy. Satan's success in causing the fall of mankind in the garden is later seen as a usurpation of that rule previously given to man. The book of Job is the earliest indication of Satan's evil autonomy and authority (Job 1:6-12; 2:1-6). He was not acting as an agent of the sovereign God, but as an accuser working in opposition to God and His people. Again in Daniel 10 the heavenly conflict between God's angels and Satan's is worked out in conflict between people here on earth.[1] When Satan tested the Second Adam, the Lord Jesus, in the wilderness (Mt. 4:8-11) and offered Him the kingdoms of this world, He did not question Satan's authority. Later He called Satan "**the prince of this world**" (Jn. 12:31; 14:30; 16:11), and Paul called him "**the god of this world**" (2 Cor. 4:4) and "**the prince of the power of the air**" (Eph. 2:2). Most astonishing are the words of Hebrews 2:14: "**Since the children have flesh and blood, he too shared in their humanity so that by his death he might destroy him who holds the power of death—that is, the devil....**" Even the power of death was delegated to Satan. Obviously God's exercise of His sovereignty has been greatly limited thereby. God retains the ultimate sovereignty but has allowed Satan and fallen man to do their own thing in opposition to Him.

Humanity's rebellion. The violent behavior of the human race before the flood (Gen. 6:6) was just the culmination of God's allowing mankind to 'do his own thing.' Some have appropriately termed the pre-flood period "the dispensation of human self-determination." It was human free will gone amok! The period of Israel's judges was also a time when **"every man did what was right in his own eyes"** (Judges 21:25). Even though Israel was God's chosen people, He allowed them to go into apostasy for centuries, which implies that He limited the exercise of sovereign control.

Covenant promises. Every promise and covenant God made with mankind is an additional limitation of His sovereign freedom. He has thus bound Himself and will not go against His word. He made many covenants with mankind, with Noah, Abraham, Moses, David, and the New Covenant of Christ's blood. These are all really contracts God made with mankind. One is bilateral (the Mosaic); the rest are essentially unilateral (although they have some contingent features). In these covenant promises God limits the exercise of His sovereignty even more overtly.

Kingdom predictions. The Bible is full of prophecies about the future kingdom of Christ, by which the coming Messiah would personally rule in righteousness, justice, and peace over all humanity. Since the first-coming prophecies were fulfilled literally, we must take second-coming prophecies as literally true as well. These prophecies clearly imply that God's rule and dominion were not yet manifest on the earth, certainly not before Messiah's advent, and not literally in the two millenniums since then. Is this not a limitation in the exercise of His sovereignty at present? God is not exercising the fullness of His sovereign rule now. We have to wait for the coming kingdom glory to see the fulness of His sovereignty manifested. *This must be factored into a definition of sovereignty .*

The image of God defaced, not erased

One dimension of the fall which has been seriously overlooked is its impact upon the image of God in humanity. Many of the early church fathers expounded this important issue and connected it with free will.[2] It is very clear from Scripture that the image was not lost in the fall.

Genesis 9:6. Moses, inspired by the Spirit, gives an important clue at this strategic juncture in the history of revelation—immediately after the deluge. Before the flood, violence escalated into a vengeance syndrome bringing on God's judgment of a worldwide deluge. But God, in making the Noahic Covenant with a remnant humanity, affirms in Genesis 8:21 that Adam's sin nature had been transmitted to all mankind: **"I will never again curse the ground on account of man, for the intent of man's heart is evil from his youth; and I will never again destroy every living thing, as I have done."** Now a new provision for human violence and depravity must be initiated—the death penalty and attendant civil government necessary to implement it. **"Whoever** sheds man's blood, by man his blood shall be shed, for in the image of God He made man" (Gen. 9:6). In so doing, God affirms that man still retains the image of God, and thereby, offers some positive hope for mankind's future.

Further important insight about God's self-limitation emerges. Here God gave up the responsibility to directly punish murderers. That responsibility is now in the hands of judges and magistrates, whose God-like authority is confirmed in Psalm 82:6, Matthew 22:15-22, and in Romans 13:1-7. Even though the Roman government abused that authority in crucifying the Lord Jesus, that delegated authority has never been rescinded. This is a further self-limitation of the exercise of God's sovereignty.

Apostolic confirmation. Paul in his message on Mars Hill used the words of a Greek poet to reinforce the truth of Genesis (Acts 17:28):

> ... that they should seek God, if perhaps they might grope for Him and find Him, though He is not far from each one of us; for in Him we live and move and exist, as even some of your own poets have said, 'For we also are His offspring.'

Paul implies that men are able to seek God based upon the image of God, even though he doesn't use that language to the pagan Greeks. Deterministic theology's concept of depravity does not leave room for man to seek God, despite the dozens of injunctions in Scripture to do just that. Paul's exhortation to seek God is based upon the remnant image of God.

Some of the other supporting references are:"With it [the tongue] we bless our Lord and Father, and with it we curse men, who have been made in the likeness of God" (Jas. 3:9). Here is a straightforward passing reference to the retained image of God in fallen mankind. "For a man ought not to have his head covered, since he is the image and glory of God; but the woman is the glory of man" (1 Cor. 11:7). Again, this is a passing reference to man having been created in God's image as part of Paul's argument on a related subject, the relationship of men and women in the church.

Although the truth of the remnant image of God is nowhere directly developed in Scripture, it is an underlying presupposition of discussion of other doctrinal issues. Therefore, this foundational truth must be factored into the biblical doctrine of sin. It seems that most deterministic writers have not taken the image of God into account, but a balanced biblical view must include it. Although certain functional aspects of the image of God were damaged, it is clear that the reality survived the fall, and His image was not lost or erased. This implies that fallen mankind, still in God's image, is able to respond to God's entreaties. Depravity does not mean total inability!

The Fall and Human Depravity
Human depravity not in dispute

Many extreme Calvinists assume that they alone hold a biblical view of depravity. They insist on "total depravity," perhaps unaware that the Latin *depravare* is an intensive compound word already signifying "totally corrupt" or "completely crooked."[3] Thus, adding the word 'total' is an indication of a doubly intensified concept of depravity. But knowledgeable Calvinists recognize that Arminius and Wesley had a fully biblical view of depravity, even though many Arminians have a weakened and shallow understanding.[4]

Norman Geisler suggests that extreme Calvinism has an "intensive" view of depravity, in contrast to a biblical, "extensive" understanding. The intensive view, in effect, holds that the image of God and the human will are essentially destroyed.[5] The extensive view holds that the whole person of man was corrupted by sin, but that the image of God and the human will have not been destroyed but rather corrupted. This is essentially the semi-Augustinian view of the Synod of Orange (AD 529), not the semi-Pelagianism* of the later Roman church (cf. pp 321-22).

Does mankind retain any autonomy?

After the fall man retained some God-given autonomy, although limited by sin. Indeed, in his sin mankind continued increasingly to abuse that autonomy. God had not programmed humanity to play out the violence, concerning which Moses stated that **"The LORD was sorry that He had made man on the earth, and He was grieved in His heart"** (Gen. 6:6). The history of Israel is hardly more encouraging. Man was 'doing his own thing.' This is not only clear throughout the Old Testament narrative but stands out in boldface. It would be depressing to read of humanity's descent into progressive rebellion if we believed that God had programmed this in eternity past, and if we did not believe that God was working behind the scenes to accomplish His purpose in preparing His plan of salvation for lost mankind.

In the Gospels the rapidity with which Israel began to oppose and plot the demise of their Messiah is proof that mankind consistently and grossly abuses its autonomy. The Lord repeatedly warned His Apostles of the opposition they would suffer (Mt. 10:16-42), which began shortly after the day of Pentecost. Acts is a detailed chronicle of ongoing persecution. Not just in history, but also in apostolic prophecy there is testimony to its unmitigated continuance until Christ returns (Mt. 24-25; 1 Tim. 4:1ff; 2 Tim. 3:1ff; 2 Thess. 2:1-12; 2 Pet. 3:1-9). Not only did the church suffer severe persecution under the Romans for three centuries, but especially in recent years, severe persecution of true Christians around the world has become commonplace and escalating. Certainly this is not the record of man acting out some imagined eternal decree; it is man abusing the autonomy God gave him at creation by becoming Satan's instruments of hostility to God.

Does depravity mean total inability?

Human depravity in a real sense is affirmed by most evangelical theologians, even though there is significant semi-Pelagianism* at the popular fringe. On the other hand, there has been a subtle semantic shift or extrapolation in extreme Calvinistic circles from depravity to total inability. However, depravity does not imply inability. The biblical testimony is clear that humanity is totally unable to save itself. The new birth is one-hundred percent a work of the Spirit of God, as John 1:12-13 makes clear. Man cannot contribute one iota to his regeneration. But since repentant faith is the required condition of regeneration, then the whole question of whether fallen human beings can exercise repentance and faith must be examined (cf. Ch. 17).

One would never get the notion from the Old Testament narrative that mankind is totally unable to respond to God's confrontations. It gives a consistent picture of God confronting fallen man and expecting a positive response. God is portrayed as taking the initiative from the very beginning in confronting lost mankind. God confronted Adam and Eve in the garden. It is implied from His provision of shed-blood garments to cover their nakedness that they responded positively. Their expulsion from the garden, while denying access to the tree of life, had the positive impact of impressing their descendants with their alienation and spiritual need. Abel responded in faith and obedience, but Cain did not. One wonders why God would confront persistent rejecters like Cain, if the missing element was a repentant faith which God Himself gives only to some elect group? Enosh, the son of Seth, marked the beginning of men calling upon the name of the LORD (4:26). God then confronted mankind through prophets, such as Enoch and Noah (Jude 14; 2 Pet. 2:5). In the latter case none responded. The main point here is that God is not operating on the premise that man is totally unable to respond to His confrontation. The history of Israel makes it abundantly clear that God continued to confront the nation in many different ways, especially through the prophets, as to their need to seek Him, to repent, and to return to Him.

The New Testament record of John the Baptizer, Christ, and the Apostles, likewise, shows them adopting a very confrontational style, designed to bring about repentant faith in their hearers, indeed, *demanding* repentant faith from their hearers. All of this assumes the possibility of a positive response from their hearers. Thus those who argue that, apart from irresistible grace, evangelism is like preaching to corpses in a funeral parlor, have exaggerated the impact of the fall. Based upon a biblically accurate definition of spiritual death and the remnant image of God, such analogies are totally inappropriate. In any case, analogies prove nothing!

Does fallen man retain free will?

The first denial of free will. Free will is a dirty word among extreme Calvinists. But not with early church fathers, who not only coined the term but defended it against the determinism of Neo-Platonism, Gnosticism, and Manicheanism. *It is especially significant how many of them connected the image of God with free will.* For example, Tertullian (c. 155-225) writes:

> I find, then, that man was by God constituted free, master of his own will and power; indicating the presence of God's image and likeness in him by nothing so well as by this constitution of his nature... —you will find that when He sets before man good and evil, life and death, that the entire course of discipline is arranged in precepts by God's calling men from sin, and threatening and exhorting them; and this on no other ground than that man is free, with a will either for obedience or resistance.[6]

Novatian of Rome (c. 200-258), Cyril of Jerusalem (c. 312-386), and Gregory of Nyssa (c. 335-395), all made an explicit connection between the image of God and man's free will. "Not a single church figure in the first 300 years rejected it [free-will] and most of them stated it in works still extant."[7]

Who makes us do it?. Comedian Flip Wilson became famous for saying, "The Devil made me do it." Some theologians, in trying to explain how Adam with a good nature could perform an evil act, have pushed the problem back to Satan. But since it is clear that God did not create any sinful beings, this only pushes the problem back one step. Martin Luther, an Augustinian monk, pushed the problem back one more step to God by including Satan's sin in God's decrees. Extreme Calvinist R. C. Sproul is not willing to go that far, but admits that it is an "excruciating problem."[8]

Norman Geisler has argued quite effectively, both rationally and biblically, that self-caused actions are the best explanation for the origin of evil. God's creation of His creatures with free choice best explains the possibility of evil. God created Lucifer as a holy cherub, but unrighteousness was found in him and he became Satan. How did this happen? It is clear that Satan originated sin and rebellion against God (Isa. 14:12-15; Ezek. 28:12-17). Geisler suggests that there are only three options: "My actions are (1) uncaused; (2) caused by someone (or something) else; or (3) caused by my Self. And there are many reasons to support the last view." He shows that extreme Calvinists make a fundamental error in failing to distinguish between self-caused *being*, which is impossible apart from God, and self-caused *action*, which is the only way to explain Lucifer's sin.[9] Clearly, Lucifer's unrighteous pride was self-caused.

God's judgment of the sin of Satan (Ezek. 28:16-19; 1 Tim. 3:6; Rev. 20:10), of fallen angels (Jude 6-7; 2 Pet. 2:4; Rev. 12:4, 9), and of Adam and Eve (Gen. 3:1-19) makes it clear that God holds free creatures morally responsible for their free choices. Since God holds all mankind morally responsible for their moral choices, fallen people must have adequate freedom of the will to make moral choices; otherwise, He could not justly judge them for their deeds (Rev. 20:12). One of the most dominant ideas of Scripture, from Genesis to the Revelation, is that God judges the sins of individuals, families, and nations, and that He is just in His judgments.

Direct Scripture evidence. There is direct Scriptural evidence for the idea that fallen man continues to exercise his uncoerced will, not only in the ordinary decisions of life, but also in moral decisions relating to God. Moses challenged Israel: "**I call heaven and earth to witness against you today, that I have set before you life and death, the blessing and the curse. So choose life in order that you may live, you and your descendants, by loving the LORD your God, by obeying His voice, and by holding fast to Him;**" (Deut. 30:19-20a). A generation later, Joshua made the same challenge: "**And if it is disagreeable in your sight to serve the LORD, choose for yourselves today whom you will serve:...**" (Josh. 24:15). Isaiah similarly exhorted Israel: "**Come now, and let us reason together,... if you consent and obey,... but if you refuse and rebel,...**" (Isa. 1:18-19). (See also 1 Kings 18:21and Isaiah 45:22.) Didn't Moses, Joshua, and the prophets understand the doctrine of total inability and know that man cannot "choose life"? Some people think that expecting people to choose robs God of His glory and sovereignty. Not in the least!

Christ identified the problem of the Jewish leaders: "**You search the Scriptures because you think that in them you have eternal life; it is these that testify about Me; and you are unwilling to come to me so that you may have life**" (Jn. 5:39-40). At the Feast, He explained the contingent factor in our coming to the truth: "**If anyone is willing to do His will, he will know of the teaching, whether it is of God or whether I speak from myself**" (Jn. 7:17). This is capped off with the words of His final lament over Jerusalem: "**Jerusalem, Jerusalem, who kills the prophets and stones those who are sent to her! How often I wanted to gather your children together, the way a hen gathers her chicks under her wings, and you were unwilling. Behold, your house is being left to you desolate**" (Mt. 23:37-8). Many other direct invitations must be considered (Mt. 11:28; 22:3; Jn. 7:37-39). Judgment came upon those who were unwilling. *It is the will of man, not the will of God which is the problem.* So for those who positively respond and those who reject, Christ declared that the issue is the human will.

In Peter's warning about the end-time mockers: "**But they deliberately forget that long ago by God's word the heavens existed and the earth was formed out of water and with water**" (2 Pet. 3:5, NIV). Creation and the flood are two key issues that modern man does not want to accept, because then he would have to respond to God's claims.

Some may ask, why quote these familiar verses? Sometimes we miss the obvious force of the familiar. Norman Douty's comment is pointed:

> Moreover, in the Apostolic preaching of the Gospel, sinners were spoken to as if expected to act then and there—without any suggestion that, after all they were under some insuperable necessity of doing nothing It is simply a matter of record that the primitive preachers did not tell their hearers that they had absolutely no ability to do anything in response to God's call, invitation, command and threat [10]

Can mankind respond to general revelation?

God holds human beings responsible, not only for the special self-revelation in His word, but also for the revelation of Himself to all mankind in nature and conscience. Speaking of hard-core unbelievers, Paul wrote:

For the wrath of God is revealed from heaven against all ungodliness

and unrighteousness of men who suppress the truth in unrighteousness, because that which is known about God is evident within them; for God made it evident to them. For since the creation of the world His invisible attributes, His eternal power and divine nature, have been clearly seen, being understood through what has been made, so that they are without excuse (Rom. 1:18-20).

Then, in Romans 2:14-16 Paul explains the part that the human conscience, as the law of God written on the heart, has to play in helping people to respond to God's revelation in nature. Today the revelation of God in His creation is even clearer to us with our increased scientific knowledge. Whether in the macrocosm of astronomy or the microcosm of atomic physics, God's intelligent design is so manifest that many non-Christians are admitting that there must be an Intelligent Designer.

God has used this general revelation to prepare the minds of untold numbers of non-Christians for the gospel. For example, missionary surgeon Dr. Viggo Olsen and his wife were converted while he was an intern. As agnostics they first struggled with the question of the existence of a Creator God. Through apologetic literature they got a positive answer and then went on to the question of which book is a true revelation of that God. While struggling with this apologetic sequence, they both were saved.[11]

This all seems like an exercise in futility, if mankind is totally unable to respond to God's message. Why should God reveal Himself thus *to all mankind* and hold them accountable for it, if indeed He has already determined that only certain elect people can ever respond, believe, and be saved? Why should He write His law on human hearts, if people are totally unable to respond? It seems absurd!

Can mankind seek God?

The only time an extreme Calvinistic colleague ever admitted to any problem with his Calvinism was when he said that Isaiah 55:6 troubled him. However, if he had checked them out, he would have found a host of other passages which totally contradict the notion of inability simply by opening his concordance to "seek."

Many Christians base their view of inability on the English of Romans 3:10-11: "**There is none righteous, not even one; There is none who understands, There is none who seeks for God.**" In Paul's paraphrase of the Septuagint of Psalm 14, he was careful to use the intensified verb *ekzētein*, rather than the simple *zētein*. From its usage in Acts 15:17; Heb. 11:6; 12:17; and 1 Pet. 1:10, it is clear that Paul is not referring to an indifferent seeking, but a 'diligent seeking' for God. So Paul was not affirming that no one ever seeks God at all, but rather that *no one diligently seeks God*. It is also significant that this verb is a present participle, which likely has a customary force. This would refer to a regularly recurring action,[12] and thus, could be rendered, "**no one** customarily and diligently seeks God."[A] Otherwise, if neither of the above were true, Scripture would be in contradiction with itself. *There are only fifty verses which contradict a superficial reading of Romans 3:10-11!* Why do people ignore the fifty and focus on the one? William A. Butler got it right: *"We hold a few texts so near the eyes that they hide the rest of the Bible."*[13] In this case, it is just one text! Here are just a few of the fifty.

Consider God's predictive warning of exile to a disobedient Israel: "**But from there you will seek the LORD your God, and you will find Him if you search for Him with all your heart and all your soul**" (Deut. 4:29); God's rebuke to apostate Israel: "**I will go away and return to My place until they acknowledge their guilt and seek My face; in their affliction they will earnestly seek Me**" (Hos. 5:15); Amos's double exhortation: "**Seek Me that you may live**" (Amos 5:4, 6); and "**Seek the LORD, all you humble of the earth**" (Zeph. 2:3). (cf. 1 Chr. 22:19a; 28:9b; 2 Chr. 15:2b; Ps. 105:3b-4; Isa. 55:6-7; Jer. 29:12-13).

If someone naively responds that these are all part of the old dispensation, hear Paul, the Apostle of monergistic grace on Mars hill, Acts 17:26-28a (see quote on p. 31), and "**... to those who by perseverance in doing good seek for glory and honor and immortality, eternal life**" (Rom. 2:7). The remaining references can be found in any concordance.

The prodigal son. The parable of the prodigal son in Luke 15:11-32 is further evidence against inability. Some may be unclear as to whether it is referring to the restoration of a backslider or the salvation of a sinner. The Lord's language is clear: "**... for this son of mine was dead and has come to life again; he was lost and has been found**" (Lk. 15:24). The father repeats the same language to the older brother in v. 32. He was spiritually dead and lost. Yet the Lord makes the point that "**he came to his senses**" in the far country and repented of his sin and his unworthiness (15:17-19) and took the initiative to go to the father (15:20). This is in total harmony with the many other passages listed above and is impossible to reconcile with total inability. What is more, the Lord emphasized, in all three of the parables of lost things, the great joy in heaven when a sinner repents (15:7, 10, 25, 32)—there is even music and celebration! If sinners are saved by irresistible grace according to unconditional election by God in eternity past, what would be the point of rejoicing in heaven? The salvation of the 'elect' would be so cut and dried, there could be no surprise and rejoicing at what was a foregone conclusion.

Case studies. The New Testament supplies significant case studies. Consider Andrew and John, who sought the Lord after hearing the Baptizer's witness. Nathaniel was dubious about Philip's witness but took the trouble

---

A   The context of Psalm 14 is also very important, since Paul is quoting it. David is saying that the atheistic fool, who says in his heart that there is no God, does not diligently seek God. Although Paul expands the application of David's words somewhat, he is giving a generalized statement about the human race as a whole, extending to both Jews and Gentiles, but not intended to be all-inclusive.

to check out Jesus of Nazareth (Jn. 1:35-51). Nicodemus sought out the Lord, albeit by night, and ultimately came to faith in Him (Jn. 3:1-21; 19:39-40). The Ethiopian eunuch, although an excluded Gentile, had traveled to Jerusalem to worship and found the Lord through the other Philip on the Gaza road (Acts 8:26-38). The Roman centurion, Cornelius, prayed and worshiped the God of Israel, although yet unsaved (Acts 11:14). God honored his prayers and alms to Israel with the privilege of becoming the first Gentile convert in the church (Acts 10:1–11:17). Consider the noble-minded Berean Jews who examined the Scriptures daily to verify Paul's message and "therefore" believed (Acts 17:10-12).

In the early 60s, the young Maulvi (Mullah) of a mosque in a village in central Pakistan, where there were no Christians, became disillusioned with Islam. Ismail came to the Lahore railway station to inquire about Christianity or Hinduism by crossing over to India. Providentially, he was directed to a born-again Christian, who took him to the leaders of Bethany Assembly. They took him in and worked with him for some time. He attended worship each Lord's day until one day it was my turn to preach. The message from 1 Corinthians 13 was on love (something Muslims hear little about). Totally oblivious to this Muslim in the congregation, I didn't even give a gospel appeal, as I now habitually do. After half an hour of open prayer time, as the bread was being distributed during the Lord's supper, Ismail said out loud, "Give me some!" When one of the stunned elders gave a nod of approval, he was included. He shaved off his beard after the service, was baptized in the canal the next day, and changed his name to Timotheus. He began immediately to join us in witness for Christ.

Controverted Scripture passages

Calvinists base their idea of inability upon a number of Scripture passages, which are also discussed elsewhere (Ch. 23, pp. 309-313).

John 6:44, 65. - **"No one can come to me unless the Father who sent Me draws him; and I will raise him up at the last day.... And He was saying, 'For this reason I have said to you, that no one can come to Me unless it has been granted him from the Father."** Calvinists assume that apart from an irresistible drawing of the 'elect,' no one else (the 'non-elect') is allowed to come to Christ for salvation. However, this ignores the context, which is crucial.

The Lord is addressing those who have seen Him and yet have not believed (6:36), who are set in contrast with the believing remnant of Israelites who belonged to the Father, but now have been committed into Christ's hands. He refers to them in vs. 37 & 39 as **"all that the Father gives Me."** He keeps stressing faith as the distinguishing feature of this remnant (6:35, 40, 47), who were taught by the Father (6:45). *This is a reference to the early disciples, who had readily responded to Him when they met Him (cf. Jn. 1), because they were already regenerate.* This becomes clear in His high-priestly prayer in John 17:6, 9, & 24, where He clearly identifies them as His early disciples set in contradistinction from those who were to later come to faith through their word (17:20), thus not all the 'elect.'

Although John 6:65 is part of the same context, there are some additional considerations here. **"And He was saying, 'For this reason I have said to you, that no one can come to Me, unless it has been granted him from the Father.'"** Apart from the context, this might seem to refer to the 'non-elect.' However, many professing disciples had just been grumbling at His words (6:61), and then the immediately preceding verse is crucial, **"... 'But there are some of you who do not believe.' For Jesus knew from the beginning who they were who did not believe, and who it was that would betray Him"** (6:64). **"As a result of this many of His disciples withdrew, and were not walking with Him anymore"** (6:66). **"'Did I Myself not choose you, the twelve, and yet one of you is a devil?'"** (6:70).

Thus it is in reference to professing disciples, who had walked with Him for an extensive period of time and sat under His teaching and seen His miracles, especially to Judas Iscariot, that the Lord made the statement in John 6:65. They were rejecting the greatest light that anybody could reject. They had professed to believe, but they were counterfeits. These are the ones to whom God was not granting the privilege to come to Him. (For a fuller discussion of John 6 see pp. 310-313.)

John 8:43-44. Another similar statement comes in a similar context: **"Why do you not understand what I am saying? It is because you cannot hear My word. You are of your father the devil, and you want to do the desires of your father"** (8:43-44a). This statement cannot be generalized to all unregenerate people, since it is clear that the Lord Jesus is addressing some hard-core unbelievers who were planning to have Him killed. They were the ones who could not hear His word.

John 12:39-40. This same principle is operative in John 12:39-40: **"For this reason they could not believe, for Isaiah said again, 'He has blinded their eyes and He hardened their heart, so that they would not see with their eyes and perceive with their heart, and be converted and I heal them.'"** The context is the passion week, when the hostility of the rulers was reaching a peak and a hostile crowd had challenged Him (12:34) and was ignoring His miraculous works (12:37). He had spoken of impending judgment (12:31). The Isaiah quotation speaks of judgmental blindness upon those who closed their hearts to such great light, which was now being fulfilled especially in Israel's rejection of their Messiah. It has nothing to do with any supposed inability of all mankind to respond to the gospel.

Pauline passages. Although Romans 8:7-8 is frequently quoted by Calvinists to support their concept of inability, it affirms the inability of unregenerate man to fulfill the law or please God morally, but it says nothing about mankind's ability or inability to believe the gospel.

Romans 9:15-16 is a favorite proof-text of Calvinists, which will be taken up fully in Chapter 22. The antecedent of 'it' in v. 16 is God's sovereign purpose to choose Jacob over Esau as the progenitor of the nation Israel, as mentioned in v. 11. Thus, this passage also has nothing to do with human inability to believe the gospel message.

Similarly, 1 Corinthians 2:14-15 has nothing to do with the issue: "**But a natural man does not accept the things of the Spirit of God, for they are foolishness to him; and he cannot understand them, because they are spiritually appraised. But he who is spiritual appraises all thing, yet he himself is appraised by no one.**" In this context, Paul is speaking about the whole process of revelation and inspiration by which the Holy Spirit communicated even the "deep things of God" through the Apostles, which were ultimately written down in Scripture. It is in obvious contrast to the "spiritual man" who appraises all these deep truths. Thus he was not speaking of an inability of all the unregenerate to understand and believe the simple gospel message. The fact is that we were all 'natural' men once, but we did come to understand the simple demands of the gospel. Subsequent chapters explain how this happens.

Conclusions

Thus, it was seen that not only before the fall, but also after, God continued to delegate to mankind areas of authority, which are a self-limitation of the exercise of His sovereignty. The fall did not cause man to lose the image of God with which he was created, so he retained his free will, although now polluted by sin. Indeed, the spiritual death into which he was plunged involved alienation from the life of God, as symbolized by his exclusion from the tree of life. This most affected the human spirit with depravity. This is not to be understood as inability to respond to God, since humans are not only expected to respond to God's entreaties, but even to seek God, based upon the retained image of God and its consequent free will.

1 Roger T Forster and V Paul Marston,*God's Strategy in Human History* (Bethany House, 1973), ch 1.

2 Geisler, pp 145-54, Tertullian, Novatian, Cyril of Jerusalem, Gregory of Nyssa Many others could be found

3 Vance, *Calvinism* (2nd ed.), p. 185; D. A Kidd, *Collins Gem Latin Dictionary*, 2nd ed (Harper-Collins)

4. Sproul, *Willing to Believe*, p. 126, Cunningham, *Theology*, II:389; Jewett, *Election and Predestination*, p 17

5 Geisler, *Chosen But Free*, p 116; Hoitenga, *John Calvin and the Will*, p. 69-70, 73

6 Tertu lian, *Against Marcion*, Book II, ch 5, cited by Forster and Marston, p 250

7 Forster and Marston, pp 244ff, Geisler, pp 145-154.

8 Sproul, *Chosen by God*, p 31

9 Geisler, p 25, full discussion , pp 19-37

10 Norman F Douty, *The Death of Christ*, p 66

11 Viggo B Olsen, *Daktar Diplomat in Baqngladesh* (Chicago. Moody Press, 1973), pp 29-57

12 Daniel B Wallace, *Greek Grammar Beyond the Basics*, pp 521-3

13 Douty, *The Death of Christ*, p 66, citing the Schaff-Herzog Encyclopedia

He said to them, How unwise and slow you are to
believe in your hearts all that the prophets have spoken!
Did not the Messiah have to suffer these thing and
enter into His glory? Then beginning with Moses and
with all the Prophets, He interpreted for them in all the
Scriptures the things concerning Himself.
              - Luke 24:25-7, HCSB

Only by a *gradual* leading on has God made known His
plans in the history of salvation.... Nor did this leading on
take the form of a uniform progressive advance --
comparable to an ascending straight line; but in the form
of sections of time with fixed boundaries, like steps of
a staircase leading upward.   - Erich Sauer

THE DAWN OF WORLD REDEMPTION

The last chapter focused on the plight of fallen humanity from the Old
Testament narrative. This chapter will revisit that narrative to see the begin-
nings of the outworking of God's plan for the redemption of the whole world.
A chronological, sequential approach will prove to be the most helpful.[1]

Early Anticipations of the Gospel

Eden. When God judged Adam and Eve for their disobedience, He
gave the first hint of His wonderful plan to redeem lost mankind from sin. It
is found in His curse upon the snake as Satan's mouthpiece: **"And I will put
enmity between you and the woman, and between your seed and her seed; He shall
bruise you on the head, and you shall bruise him on the heel"** (Gen. 3:15). This
most remarkable statement is both a judgment and a prophecy about the
continuing conflict between God and Satan and their representatives. The
language is very terse and enigmatic. The Hebrew word 'seed' can be either
singular or plural, as in the English. However, it is not hard to understand the
reference to Satan's seed (or descendants) since so many people in the
world are under his power. It is seen in Christ's strong words to some
religious leaders: **"You are of *your* father the devil, and you want to do the desires of
your father. He was a murderer from the beginning, and does not stand in the truth,
because there is no truth in him"** (Jn. 8:44). In trying to understand the reference
to the seed of the woman, one wonders at this unique expression. The only
human being to whom it could accurately apply is the Lord Jesus, who was
virgin-born of a woman without a human father (Isa. 7:14; Mt. 1:20-25; Lk.
1:30-35). Biblical history confirms the enmity between Satan's people and
Christ. Although all of fallen humanity is under the sway of Satan, it is clear

41

that some key people are at the forefront of hostility against Christ and His people.

This understanding clarifies the last two clauses of Genesis 3:15. The symbolism of a snake is developed here: Satan, like a snake, will attack and bruise the unique seed of the woman, the Lord Jesus, the Messiah. Approaching His crucifixion He said, "**I will not speak much more with you, for the ruler of the world [Satan] is coming, and he has nothing in Me**" (Jn. 14:30). Satan had entered into Judas Iscariot to betray Him (Jn. 13:26-7). The cross was Satan's supreme attempt to destroy God's Messiah. When Christ died it seemed like a victory for Satan, but the resurrection turned the tables. It enabled Christ to bruise or crush the head of Satan. Note the apostolic clarification: "**...that through death He might render powerless him who had the power of death, that is, the devil,**" (Heb. 2:14). So here in veiled and symbolic language, God intimated that He was beginning to implement a plan of salvation for lost mankind.

God rejected Adam and Eve's futile attempt to cover the shame of their sin with a garment of fig leaves, since it did not involve the shedding of blood so necessary for forgiveness (Heb. 9:22). He Himself provided the garments of the skins of sacrificed animals. The expulsion from access to the tree of life had the positive impact of impressing Adam and Eve with their lost condition apart from the gracious salvation of God. They were now under the judgment of God and needed an atonement for their sin. Abel understood this; Cain did not! In his self-righteousness he tried to make a vegetable offering to God. Two others of the Sethite lineage who also clearly understood this were Enosh, who began to call upon God for salvation, and Enoch, who walked by faith in fellowship with God (Heb. 11:5).

Noah. This godly Sethite lineage became so corrupted that only Noah was left: "**But Noah found favor in the eyes of the Lord.... Noah was a righteous man, blameless in his time; Noah walked with God**" (Gen. 6:8-9). Moses does not tell us how Noah became a righteous man, but again there is an apostolic clarification (Heb. 11:6-7, NIV):

> **And without faith it is impossible to please God, because anyone who comes to him must believe that He exists and that he rewards those who earnestly seek Him. By faith Noah, when warned about things not yet seen, in holy fear built an ark to save his family. By his faith he condemned the world and became heir of the righteousness that comes by faith.**

After the flood Noah worshiped by making an altar and offering up animal sacrifices, as God had stipulated (Gen. 8:20-21). God blessed Noah and his family and made a covenant with them. An important part of it emphasized the sacredness of blood, which should not be eaten by man (Gen. 9:4). And the death penalty for murder emphasized the sacredness of human life. Instead of revenge, there must now be civil justice administered by governments operating under God's authority.

The incident of Noah's drunken nakedness confirms the indication in the garden of Eden that nakedness is a sign of the shame of sin. Note the carefulness of Shem and Japheth not to look on their father's nakedness (Gen. 9:20-23). Noah's prophecy over his sons seems to indicate that Shem had a deeper relationship to God, which was perpetuated in Abram's faith generations later. The terse statement, **"May God enlarge Japheth, and let him dwell in the tents of Shem"** (Gen. 9:27), predicts the widespread influence of Japhetic peoples and their coming under the influence of the faith of Shem. This was fulfilled in that faith in the Jewish Messiah has spread most widely among descendants of Japheth. Ham's indifference to the shame of his father's nakedness was passed on to his son Canaan, who came under God's curse. Centuries later the Canaanites became a corrupt and immoral people whom God judged through the Israelites.[A]

Idolatry. A most significant descendant of Ham and Cush was Nimrod, who became a powerful leader and hunter in his day. He was the founder of the city of Babel (Babylon) and of Nineveh in Assyria (Gen. 10:8-12). Moses gives a fuller account of God's judgment upon the builders of the tower of Babel in Genesis 11:1-9. This tower is easily identifiable as a ziggurat, remnants of which have been excavated in the Mesopotamian plain. Ziggurats had a religious significance as a place for idolatrous worship. So the indications are that Nimrod was the originator of idolatrous worship, out of which came the whole system of Babylonian idolatry, which spread throughout the Middle East.[2] This is the ultimate insult to the Creator God, yet continues to be a major problem in human culture over the millennia.

Gentile nations. Just before the record of the call of Abram, Moses gave the lineage of the seventy peoples who descended from Noah (Gen. 10). It is fascinating to connect them to nations in history and modern times.[3] However, a major point must not be lost that in calling out one special people to be the bearers of the promise of redemption, God has not forgotten the Gentile nations. Although from this point on, most of the rest of the Old Testament focuses on the nation Israel, the goal of it all was the salvation of all peoples. This is alluded to from time to time throughout the Old Testament, but only comes back into focus in the end of Christ's ministry.

The Call of Abraham, Isaac, and Israel

Over half of the human race is connected to a religion, whether Jewish, Christian, or Muslim, which believes that Abraham was an outstanding man of faith. God called Abraham from among the descendants of Shem, who

---

A. The curse on Canaan had nothing to do with race, since the Canaanites were not black. The descendants of the four sons of Ham are represented in Egyptian hieroglyphic friezes as having vastly differing racial characteristics. The issue here was moral failure, not race

had degenerated into idolatry in the Mesopotamian plain near Babel's idolatrous center, in order to start a new nation which would not only worship the one true God, but also spread the message of His coming Messiah and Redeemer among the pagan nations. Abraham wasn't the only true believer of his day. His nephew Lot, who accompanied him at first; Melchizedek, king of Salem, whom he encountered in the promised land; and Job, a likely contemporary, are others mentioned in Scripture. *So this was not a call to salvation.* It was a call to a land at the crossroads of the continents, from which the message of the one true God could easily go out to Africa, Europe, and Asia. God made the purpose of the call very clear: **"And I will make you a great nation, and I will bless you, and make your name great; and so you shall be a blessing; ... and in you all the families of the earth will be blessed"** (Gen. 12:2-3). *This was a call to be a witness and a missionary to the pagans living in the land.*

It was over forty years after God called Abraham to the promised land that He revealed *how* he would ultimately become the unique channel of blessing for the whole world. When he obeyed God in starting to offer up his son Isaac on Mount Moriah, God gave additional intimation of the coming Messiah: **"In your seed all the nations of the earth shall be blessed, because you have obeyed My voice"** (Gen. 22:18).[B] God's plan was that Abraham himself and his family were to be a blessing and channel of truth to the nations, which was only partially fulfilled, and moreover that His unique descendant would be the ultimate cause of salvation's blessings to the nations. A major part of God's plan for blessing the nations was to be the nation Israel itself. This is why most of the Old Testament focuses upon the Jewish nation and its successes and failures in being the recipients of God's blessing and therefore channels of blessing to the whole world. Ralph Winter has suggested that the common assumption which minimizes the call of Abraham himself and the Jewish nation to be witnesses, should be called the "Theory of the Hibernating Mandate," that is, that the mandate hibernated for two thousand years until Christ. In this connection he said, "The greatest scandal in the Old Testament is that Israel tried to be blessed without trying very hard to be a blessing."[4]

God made many promises to Abraham, most of which He confirmed with a covenant contract. Some of these were unconditional, such as the ultimate giving of the land to his descendants. Others are to be understood as having conditional elements to them, such as, the enjoyment of the land by each generation of his descendants (see Deut. 19). The most important feature of Abraham's life, which is reinforced by the New Testament, is the faith by which he believed God's promises and was put into right standing with God as a result. When Abraham was yet childless and God promised

---

B   This is the only one of the many times God made promises to Abraham which precisely fulfills the Apostle Paul's explanation in Galatians 4:15-16 of this as a promise of the Messiah.

him descendants as numerous as the stars and sand on the seashore, Abraham's trust in this incredible promise is declared to be the basis of his salvation: "**Then he believed in the LORD; and He reckoned it to him as righteousness**" (Gen. 15:6). Remember that Abraham was pushing one hundred and his wife Sarah, ninety. Two thousand years later, the Apostle Paul made this the basis for explaining the glorious truth of justification by faith alone in Romans 3:24–4:25. Paul makes it clear that faith in the salvation promises of God is the only condition for salvation.

Although his faith was the only condition for his right standing with God, Abraham continued in faith to worship God by building altars in different places in the promised land and making the stipulated blood sacrifices thereupon (Gen. 12:7, 8; 13:4, 18, etc.). The covenant God made with him was sealed with the shed blood of animal sacrifices to certify to Abraham that God would surely give him the land (Gen. 15:9-21). That this was unconditional is clear in that only God passed between the parts of the sacrificed animals in Abraham's dream while he was in a deep sleep. Unfortunately, Abraham and his descendants did not always walk in obedience to God and enjoy the purposed blessing in that land. Nevertheless the promise of ultimate Messianic blessing was secure.

Ishmael. Abraham and Sarah compromised with the local corrupt culture in the birth of Ishmael through her handmaid, Hagar. This was a carnal way of trying to help God out in providing an offspring for themselves as childless. Although Ishmael was not to be the channel of Messianic blessing, God did promise to bless him and his descendants (Gen. 17:20-21):

> **As for Ishmael, I have heard you; behold, I will bless him, and will make him fruitful and will multiply him exceedingly. He shall become the father of twelve princes, and I will make him a great nation. But my covenant I will establish with Isaac, whom Sarah will bear to you at this season next year.**

God's blessing upon Ishmael (whose name means 'God hears') is a clear indication that he was a believer. The covenant to be reaffirmed to Isaac and Jacob did not exclude Ishmael and his descendants from faith and salvation but was rather about the chosen lineage through whom the Messiah would come. When Sarah insisted that Hagar and Ishmael should be expelled from the family, Abraham did not do it in an ethical way, so God had to intervene to preserve his life (Gen. 21:9-21). In recounting this story, Moses reaffirmed: "**God was with the lad, and he grew; and he lived in the wilderness and became an archer**" (Gen. 21:20). Clearly the selection of Isaac over Ishmael was not an issue of salvation.[C] Unfortunately, the circumstances of Ishmael's expulsion must have negatively affected his walk with God and

---

C. It is significant that probably more Arab descendants of Ishmael today are believers in Christ than Hebrew Christians. Some misread Romans 9 to imply that God had sovereignly elected Isaac to salvation and Ishmael to go to hell. If God blessed him and "was with the lad," he must have been a believer

that of his descendants, who reverted back into paganism.

Birth and resurrection. There are two significant things about Isaac which in a wonderful way look forward to the salvation God was to provide through his descendant, the Messiah. The first was his miraculous birth. For Sarah to bear a child at the age of ninety, when she was long past the child-bearing age, was an incredible miracle. Her menopause of some forty years earlier had to be totally reversed! Although Isaac had a human father, this is anticipatory of the miraculous birth of the Lord Jesus of a virgin. God was conditioning the minds of Isaac's descendants to be open to a miraculously born Messiah. For Abraham it involved a tremendous step of faith:

> ... in the presence of Him whom he believed, *even* God, who gives life to the dead and calls into being that which does not exist. In hope against hope he believed, so that he might become a father of many nations according to that which had been spoken, "So shall your descendants be." Without becoming weak in faith he contemplated his own body, now as good as dead since he was about a hundred years old, and the deadness of Sarah's womb; yet, with respect to the promise of God, he did not waver in unbelief but grew strong in faith, giving glory to God, and being fully assured that what God had promised, He was able also to perform. (Rom. 4:17-21)

The second signal event in Isaac's life was his being offered up as a sacrifice by his father. Adherents of all three monotheistic world religions believe that Abraham offered up his son on Mount Moriah, even though the Muslims think it was Ishmael who was offered. Although God did not allow him to be actually sacrificed, by providing a ram as His own sacrifice, this anticipated the sacrifice of God's own Son two thousand years later on that same mountain (2 Chron. 3:1). It was not just in the sacrifice that this anticipated the passion of Christ, but also in the anticipation of resurrection. "Abraham said to his young men, 'Stay here with the donkey, and I and the lad will go over there; and we will worship and return to you'" (Gen. 22:5). Abraham expected to being the lad back with him. There is a New Testament explanation of this:

> By faith Abraham, when he was tested, offered up Isaac, and he who had received the promises was offering up his only begotten *son; it was he* to whom it was said, "In Isaac your descendants shall be called." He considered that God is able to raise *people* even from the dead, from which he also received him back as a type (Heb. 11:17-19).

In this connection Martin Luther said, "Faith reconciles contradictions." Thus Abraham had a resurrection faith, even though there was no actual resurrection necessary in this typological anticipation of Christ's resurrection two millenniums later. This indicates how God was laying the foundation for the ultimate realization and implementation of His plan of salvation through the cross and resurrection of Abraham's ultimate descendant, Jesus Christ.

Two nations. Isaac does not seem to have been a major player in the drama of the dawn of redemption. But when his wife Rebekah was barren, he prayed and God gave them twins, Jacob and Esau. When she asked the LORD about her difficult pregnancy, He answered, "**Two nations are in your womb; and two peoples will be separated from your body; and one people shall be stronger than the other; and the older shall serve the younger**" (Gen. 25:23). It is known from the subsequent narrative that God chose the younger son, Jacob, to be the father of the Jewish nation. But God's choice of Jacob over Esau did not pre-determine their salvation. God's word to Rebekah makes it clear that the issue was all about two nations, the Jews and the Edomites, since the unfolding story shows that Esau never personally served Jacob. Indeed, Jacob served Esau the lentil stew, by which he got him to give up his birthright, and years later he bowed down in obeisance to his brother. But Esau's descendants, the Edomites, did indeed serve the nation Israel from King David's time until the Babylonian captivity.[D]

Jacob's relationship with Esau went from bad to worse. Defrauding him of his father's blessing is an indication that Isaac and Rebekah had not nurtured their sons' faith in the LORD (Gen. 27). Rather there seems to be little indication of any faith until Jacob had the dream at Bethel of the ladder from heaven to earth and God's promise that the covenant would be perpetuated through him (Gen. 28:10-22). His understanding of God's ways at that point seems minimal, and until his wrestling with the Angel of the LORD at Peniel years later his lifestyle did not show much impact of his faith.

Before his death, Jacob's prophesying over his twelve sons was the high point of his life, especially since it included the clear Messianic reference to the Messiah coming through the line of Judah: "**The scepter shall not depart from Judah, nor the ruler's staff from between his feet, until he comes to whom it belongs, and to him,** *shall be* **the obedience of the peoples**" (Gen. 49:10, NAS, margin).[E] Although Jacob's eleventh son, Joseph, was not so honored, his life of faith and godliness was an outstanding testimony both to his own family and to the idolatrous Egyptians. There seems to be a disconnect between God's choice of Judah for the Messiah's lineage and Joseph's far superior faith and life. In Roman 9 the Apostle Paul argues for God's absolute sovereignty in His choice of the lineage of the chosen people of God and of the Messiah. This was a national issue.

D. Some Christians have misused reference in Romans 9 to this verse to teach that God sovereignly elected Jacob to salvation and Esau to hell. Although Esau was an unbeliever who despised his birthright (Heb. 12:16-17), his lack of faith is more attributable to the poor spiritual dynamic of Isaac's family life and the impact of the pagan culture surrounding their family.

E. The Lord Jesus was the last possible candidate to fulfill this messianic prophecy, because the scepter of government had already departed from Judah before He was crucified. Herod Agrippa did not have the authority to execute Christ, which was retained by the Romans through Pontius Pilate. By AD 70 with the destruction of Jerusalem, any shred of governmental authority had totally departed from Judah.

Israel's Redemption out of Egypt

The development of God's plan of redemption seemed to have been on hold for four centuries, while Israel was growing to be a great nation in bondage in Egypt and the circumstances in the promised land were ripening for Israel's conquest in judgment upon the polluted Canaanites (Gen. 15:16). But Egyptian religion and culture was due for God's judgments as well. As an idolatrous and naturistic religion was a continuing insult to the one true Creator God, His plan for emancipating Israel from slavery in Egypt had a double purpose. Egyptians worshiped the Pharaoh as divine and many animals as manifestations of their polytheistic deities. The ten plagues which God brought upon them were judgments upon the blasphemous divine claims of Pharaoh and also exposed the absurd worship of God's creatures by the Egyptians. The descendants of Abraham, Isaac, and Jacob were badly compromised by the polytheism of the Egyptians and were also subject to grinding slavery. Due to the rapid growth of the Hebrews, the Egyptians began a kind of genocide by killing the male Hebrew babies. God not only spared Moses, but also gave him an upbringing in Pharaoh's household. His abortive attempt to mitigate the slavery of his people forced him to spend forty years in the wilderness in preparation for leading Israel out of Egypt.

When the Hebrews cried out to the God of their fathers, He not only sent Moses to be the instrument of liberation (Gen. 2:23-25), but also began to reveal Himself more fully by His personal, covenant name, YAHWEH, the self existent One (Gen. 3:14-16; 6:2-8).[5] Redemption out of Egypt is a wonderful picture of our redemption in Christ. Israel had to recognize their need and cry out to God (Ex. 2:23-25). This is basic to our salvation as well.

Moses had to deal first with an arrogant Pharaoh. Five times Moses described Pharaoh's heart as being characteristically hard (Ex. 7:13-14, 22; 8:19; 9:7) and twice he said that Pharaoh hardened his own heart (8:15, 32). Since God had a purpose to bring judgment upon this idolatrous nation and its leader, He stated His intention beforehand, **"But I will harden Pharaoh's heart that I may multiply My signs and My wonders in the land of Egypt"** (7:3). God fulfilled this in the five times He hardened Pharaoh's heart judgmentally (Ex. 9:12; 10:1, 20; 11:10; 14:8). Note carefully that Pharaoh had hardened his own heart first! He later said to Pharaoh, **"But, indeed, for this reason I have allowed you to remain, in order to show you My power and in order to proclaim My name through all the earth. Still you exalt yourself against My people by not letting them go"** (Ex. 9:16-7). So God's purpose was clearly to make an example of Pharaoh and his idolatrous system as a testimony to a whole world of idolaters.[F]

F   Paul quoted this verse in Romans 9, not to prove that God reprobated Pharaoh to hell, but rather to make an example of this blasphemous leader of idolatrous religion as a testimony to the other nations, that they might see that He alone is the true God, the Creator. Paul had stated the principle in Romans 1.24, 26, 28 that God judgmentally gave the most hardened pagans over to a depraved mind

On the first confrontation with Pharaoh and his magicians, God demonstrated their impotence by the miracle of Aaron's rod. The ten plagues which God then poured out upon the Egyptians can be directly connected with their worship of the elements of nature. They worshiped the Nile river so God turned it into blood (Ex. 7:14-25). They worshiped the sun so the ninth plague was darkness over the land. The issue of each confrontation was the Hebrews' request that they be allowed to go out of the land to make animal sacrifices to the LORD (8:25-29).

Passover. The Passover judgment on the firstborn sons of Egypt most clearly foreshadowed Christ's redemption. The Hebrews applied the blood of sacrificed lambs to the doorposts and lintels of their homes so that their firstborn sons would be passed over by the angel of death (Ex. 12:1-32). God's commands emphasized the centrality of blood: **"The blood shall be a sign for you on the houses where you live; and when I see the blood I will pass over you, and no plague will befall you to destroy you when I strike the land of Egypt"** (Ex. 12:13). In all of the plagues, God stated that He had set a division or *ransom* between the Egyptians and the Hebrews (Ex. 8:23, see note). God made the Passover feast the central ritual of Israel's worship as a memorial to His powerful intervention.

When the herald of Christ, John, said, **"Behold, the Lamb of God who takes away the sin of the world"** (Jn. 1:29), the Jews should have understood the implications. The Lord Jesus was crucified on the Passover feast, and when He celebrated the Passover with His Apostles, He transformed it into a new memorial feast, the Lord's Supper. Paul confirmed the connection: **"For Christ our Passover also has been sacrificed"** (1 Cor. 5:7). Not only were the Jews to eat lamb each year in the Passover feast but also to observe the feast of unleavened bread. Christ claimed to be its fulfillment by saying, **"I am the bread of life; he who comes to Me will not hunger, and he who believes in Me will never thirst"** (Jn. 6:35).

It should be noted that the blood of the lamb had not only to be shed, but it had to be applied with hyssop to the lintel and doorposts to be effective. In a parallel way Christ's blood had not only to be shed two millennia ago, but it must be applied by faith in Him to be effective in our lives. Christ emphasized the imperative of believing to receive eternal life (Jn. 6:35, 40, 47). Then He used exaggerated symbolism to emphasize the importance of personal appropriation by faith: **"Very truly I tell you, unless you eat the flesh of the Son of Man and drink his blood, you have no life in you"** (Jn. 6:53, TNIV). This could not be a reference to the Lord's Supper, which had not yet been instituted. It rather emphasizes the necessity of appropriation of Christ's sacrifice personally by faith.

There are many details of the liberation out of Egypt which could be noted, but God wanted Israel to remember that He had ransomed them out of slavery in Egypt. Although not explained explicitly, it is understood that the blood of many lambs was the ransom price, and the main point is that they were liberated. This clearly is a picture of Christ's redemption, which liberates us from the slavery of sin. Indeed, in bringing them into the promised land, God was beginning the process of freeing Israel from the idolatry and sin with which they had compromised in Egypt.

When Israel grumbled against God in the wilderness, He judged them with poisonous snakes, killing many people. When they pled for mercy, Moses lifted up a bronze image of a snake on a pole and those who looked on it were spared from death. Christ referred to this: **"As Moses lifted up the serpent in the wilderness, even so must the Son of Man be lifted up; so that whoever believes in Him shall not perish, but have eternal life"** (Jn. 3:14-15). The bronze snake represents judged sin, as did the cross of Christ. Sin was judged in the cross, but just as the Israelites needed to look to that bronze snake to be healed, just so people must look by faith to the Crucified One to receive eternal life. There must be a personal appropriation by faith.

The Giving of the Mosaic Law

A rule of life. The Ten Commandments were the foundation of the moral code, which spelled out in great detail the rule of life for this new nation. It also provided judicial laws for providing justice among the people of the nation. An important purpose in the giving of the law was to bring the people under the conviction of their sin so that they might look to God and His Messiah for salvation (Rom. 3:19-20). At its heart is the system of Levitical sacrifices, which were to be offered by the Aaronic priests in the tabernacle, which was to be made according to God's pattern. This would provide a system of temporary atonement for the sins of the people until the coming Messiah could pay the full penalty for their sins (Rom. 3:24-6; Heb. 7). In addition, it provided a system of worship for God's people. Thus in a sense, *it was both a way of death and a way of life for the nation Israel.* (The gospel is also a way of death and a way of life, cf. 2 Cor. 2:15-16.) As the New Testament clarifies, one major purpose of the moral code was to help people see themselves as lost sinners. Thus, it pointed to the sacrificial system as the remedy for sin, albeit only temporarily. The law was only a shadow of the full reality to be provided ultimately in God's Messiah.

Why the Law? After seeing the glories of the covenant which God made with Abraham, one wonders why God gave the law. Abraham came into right standing with God by faith alone and had an inward, simple, and personal relationship with God. Why add the law with its complexity, outwardness, and seeming negativity? But the significant failures in the lives of the patriarchs, Abraham, Isaac, certainly Jacob, and especially his sons, demonstrate the need for more specific guidance in living a life pleasing to God. Only Joseph seemed to have been able to live an exemplary life of faith without the burden of the law. Their descendants fell into such deep compromise with the religions and cultures of the Canaanites and Egyptians, that it took centuries of living under the law to root out the worst compromises from the nation. Even in the golden age under Kings David and Solomon, the compromises were only too evident.

Symbols and types. Each feature of the Mosaic law had significance both for the Jews in their day and also as pictures of the coming realization of the plan of salvation in Christ. A most important part of the Mosaic system was the animal sacrifices because the shedding of blood is so important in the sight of God. As He emphasized to Noah, blood is sacred in His sight since it represents life. He made this clear in the law: "**For the life of the flesh is in the blood, and I have given it to you on the altar to make atonement for your souls; for it is the blood by reason of the life that makes atonement**" (Lev. 17:11). Just as the blood atoned for the sins of the Israelites by covering them, far more profoundly the blood of Christ provided a complete propitiation and redemption price for the sins of all mankind.

God gave Israel a tabernacle in the wilderness as the only place where sacrifices could be made. The pagans made their sacrifices on every high hill, but God emphasized that there was only one place acceptable sacrifices to Him could be made. That tabernacle was later replaced with the temple in Jerusalem. That tabernacle was called the 'tent of meeting' because it was the special place where a Jew could meet with God. The ark of the covenant in the 'holy of holies' in the tabernacle was the ultimate place where the sins of Israel were dealt with on the Day of Atonement (Yom Kippur) by the sprinkling of the blood by the high priest. Correspondingly, today we know that the fulfillment in the sacrifice of Christ is the only way of salvation for sinful mankind (Jn. 14:6; Acts 4:12; 1 Tim. 2:5-6).

The Aaronic priests were the only ones permitted to offer up sacrifices on the brazen altar in the tabernacle, and the high priest was the only one allowed to sprinkle the blood of the sacrifice on the ark of the covenant on Yom Kippur. Since Jesus Christ is the only one qualified as the supernatural Son of God, He alone could make the ultimate sacrifice for our sin.

It should be emphasized that the whole Levitical system, having been perfectly fulfilled in Christ's offering up of Himself, was therefore only temporary. We must not in any way perpetuate features of the Levitical system today. Indeed, forty years after the sacrifice of Christ, God shut off any possibility of restoration it by having the Romans destroy the temple in Jerusalem (AD 70). There are now no qualified Aaronic priests, and God is no longer impressed with the blood of animals, since the blood of His Son is far more precious. It should also be noted that the token of the Mosaic Covenant, which was the sabbath, was also a temporary sign given only to Israel (Ex. 31:17) and is no longer binding on the church today,[G] but was

---

G   There is a striking correspondence between the Levitical and Roman Catholic liturgical systems. Both have a priesthood, temples (cathedrals), and multiple sacrifices (the unbloody sacrifice of the mass). The New Testament church knows nothing of priests, temples, or sacrifices.

rather a picture of the coming salvation rest in the finished work of Christ.

Israel's Davidic Dynasty

After forty years in the wilderness, God brought Israel into the promised land under Joshua's military leadership and His supernatural power. Israel did very poorly in the land under a sequence of judges. They would forget the LORD and come under foreign domination. Then He would raise up a judge as deliverer from foreign oppression. The problem was that "**everyone did what was right in his own eyes**" (Jud. 21:25) and seemed ignorant of God's law. It was free will gone amok![H] God gave in to Israel's demand for a king, like the nations around them. In a sense it was a judgment upon them for rejecting Him as their king, since the first king, Saul, did not do well. His major sin was usurping the place of the priesthood in offering up sacrifices himself (1 Sam. 13:8-12).

God overruled their sin and disobedience by giving them a good king, David, who ultimately became the father of a kingly dynasty. David was in the prophesied lineage of Judah (Gen. 49:10). After David proved to be a man after God's own heart, God made a covenant with him which promised, not only a kingly dynasty for his descendants, but especially one unique descendant who would establish an eternal kingdom (2 Sam. 7:12-16). This was fulfilled in the Lord Jesus, who was from the lineage of David, both from His actual mother, Mary, and also from His legal father, Joseph. It had seemed that the Davidic dynasty came to an end when Jerusalem was destroyed and King Zedekiah was taken captive to Babylon in 586 BC. He was the last of a lineage of good and bad kings in the Davidic dynasty. Unfortunately, the priestly lineage of Aaron was also marred by many who were not faithful to God. *But God in His own time restored the kingly dynasty of David in a supernaturally born Son. He would not be just a king, but also our Great High Priest and the ultimate prophet of God.*

Prophecies of the Coming Messiah

At the end of his ministry Moses had alerted the nation Israel that: "**The LORD your God will raise up for you a prophet like me from among you, from your countrymen, you shall listen to him**" (Deut. 18:15). In the first instance, it is a reference to the true prophets who would speak God's message to the nation over the centuries. They were to be both fore-tellers of the future as well as forth-tellers of God's will for the present. The final fulfillment of this prophecy is the Lord Jesus Himself. The Messiah was to be both a prophet and the subject of prediction by the prophets.

His unique lineage. The prophesies of His unique lineage were seen

---

H   The extremely negative narrative of Israel in the time of the judges must not be explained as God's predetermination of their apostasies, but rather a failure of a leadership ignorant of the Mosaic Law.

in Genesis 3:15, 22:18, and 49:10, which limits it to the tribe of Judah. The prophet Nathan was sent to King David to give him God's promise of a perpetual dynasty (2 Sam. 7 & 1 Chron. 17). Additionally, God sent many other prophets to reaffirm the Davidic dynasty. Isaiah was the channel for many of the most graphic portrayals of the coming Messiah. In Isaiah 4 and 11 there is a striking description of the reign of the Messiah, God's branch from the roots of Jesse (David's father). Centuries later, Jeremiah prophesied at the time of the Babylonian conquest, that although King Jeconiah had come under a curse for his sin (Jer. 22:28-30), the Messiah would nevertheless still come through David: "'Behold, the days are coming,' declares the LORD, 'when I will raise up for David a righteous Branch, and He will reign as king and act wisely ... And this is His name by which He will be called, the LORD our righteousness'" (Jer. 23:5-6). The way in which God worked out this seeming contradiction was that the Lord Jesus' legal father, Joseph, although Jeconiah's descendant, was not his actual father (Mt. 1). His lineage through Mary came down through another son of David, Nathan (Lk. 3). Only a legal son of Joseph of Nazareth and one who was not physically his son could qualify as the Messiah without coming under the curse on King Jeconiah. The Lord Jesus is the only person in history who can qualify to be the Messiah of prophecy.

A virgin-born divine Messiah. The explicit virgin-birth prophecy, given over seven centuries beforehand (Isa. 7:14) and the miraculous births of Isaac and John the Baptizer should have opened the minds of the nation Israel to the possibility of an even more supernatural birth of the Messiah Himself. Both Matthew and Luke gave explicit testimony to this birth— Matthew from Joseph's perspective, and Luke from Mary's.

It was the prophet Micah who gave the place of Christ's birth, Bethlehem Ephrathah, which was David's hometown (Micah 5:1-5). In this remarkable prophecy a clear indication is given that the Messiah would be not merely human, but also divine. In Isaiah it is clarified that the Messiah, although born in Bethlehem, would arise in Galilee, where Nazareth is located. The child to be born was also to be the Son given by God, who Himself would be properly called the **"Mighty God, Progenitor of Ages, Prince of Peace"** (Isa. 9:6, Unger).[1] The way in which this would be accomplished was revealed when Isaiah confronted King Ahaz, a representative of the house of David, that the Messiah's birth would be an outstanding miraculous sign of a virgin birth, and that the child born would actually be Emmanuel, 'God with

---

I. My Hebrew professor, Merrill F. Unger, suggested that this is a more appropriate translation, which has the advantage of avoiding confusion of the persons of the Trinity. This is confirmed by Hebrews 1:1-2, where *aion*, speaks of the time-space universe.

us' (Isa. 7:10-14).[J]

King David himself also proved to be a prophet. Psalm 110 is quoted more times in the New Testament (7) than any other passage, and Peter used it on the day of Pentecost sermon as proof of the deity of the Messiah:

> The LORD says to my Lord: "Sit at My right hand until I make Your enemies a footstool for Your feet." The LORD will stretch forth Your strong scepter from Zion, *saying*, "Rule in the midst of Your enemies." ... The LORD has sworn and will not change His mind, "You are a priest forever according to the order of Melchizedek." (Ps. 110:1-2, 4)

The point is that David calls the Messiah his Lord, while we know that physically the Lord Jesus was his son (descendant) Two other Psalms indicate that Israel should have been looking for a divine Messiah. In Psalm 45:6-7, the Messiah is addressed as God:

> Your throne, O God, is forever and ever; a scepter of uprightness is the scepter of Your kingdom. You have loved righteousness and hated wickedness; therefore God, Your God has anointed You with the oil of joy above Your fellows.

His predicted passion. Psalm 22 is the most extensive Messianic prophecy from David's pen, which amazingly describes the crucifixion hundreds of years before that cruel form of execution was invented. The Psalm opens with Christ's words from the cross. In 22:6-8, the prediction of Messiah's rejection by His own people includes the words of mockery by the rulers; in vv. 11-18, the mob of enemies surrounding Him, the thirst, the nakedness, the stress on the body, even the piercing of His hands and feet are described in 22:14-17, and the Roman soldiers casting lot for his clothing (22:18). His prayer (Heb. 5:7) for victory out of it by His glorious resurrection is implied in 22:22-31; and in vv. 25-31, the consequent global evangelization and kingdom. Just as David described the physical realities of the crucifixion, just so Isaiah described its spiritual significance in Isaiah 52:13–53:12. Psalm 2:2, 7, 12 spoke of the glorious resurrection of Christ (cf. Acts 13:33):

> The kings of the earth take their stand and the rulers take counsel together against the LORD and against His Anointed [Messiah], ... I will surely tell of the decree of the LORD: He said to Me, 'You are My Son, today I have begotten You.' ... Do homage to the Son, that He not become angry, and you perish *in* the way.

J   The liberal translations, such as the RSV, sought to undermine this unique virgin birth prophesy by rendering *almah* as a young woman, but all seven usages of this word in the Hebrew are consistent with the translation 'virgin.' The Septuagint translators, over two centuries before Christ, rendered it into Greek as *parthenos*, which can only mean virgin. It is not a reference to a woman in Isaiah's day, as Hengstenberg showed over a century ago, but rather by prophetic perspective is distinguishing Shear-jashub, a sign for king Ahaz (7:16), from the sign for the future house of David, the virgin born Emmanuel.

Psalm 16:10-11 is the prophesy of the resurrection quoted by Peter on the day of Pentecost, which confirms the truth of Psalm Two: **"For You will not abandon my soul to Sheol; nor will you allow Your Holy One to undergo decay. You will make known to me the path of life; in Your presence is fullness of joy; in Your right hand there are pleasures forever."**

Two centuries after Isaiah, God gave Daniel many revelations concerning the Messiah, including the time of His triumphal entry into Jerusalem (Dan. 9:24-27). The angel Gabriel told him that "**... from the issuing of a decree to restore and rebuild Jerusalem until Messiah the Prince ...**" there would be a period of sixty-nine weeks or heptads of years. Although the calculation is complex, the best date for the decree of Artaxerxes Longimanus is 444 BC and for the crucifixion is AD 33. Understood rightly this is a remarkably accurate prediction.[6]

The Jewish nation puzzled for centuries about the two different and seemingly contradictory lines of Messianic prophesies. Peter gave, what seems obvious to us now, the answer of the two comings of the Messiah:

> **As to this salvation, the prophets who prophesied of the grace that *would come* to you made careful searches and inquiries, seeking to know what person or time the Spirit of Christ within them was indicating as He predicted the <u>suffering of Christ</u> and <u>the glories to follow</u>** (1 Pet. 1:10-11).

Conclusions

The Old Testament foundation for the New Testament gospel message has been surveyed. In response to the depraved plight of a sinful human race, God made preparations for the coming of a divine Messiah, who would deal with sin once and for all by the shedding of His own blood. But before sinful mankind can respond to the offer of salvation, they must first recognize their sinful, lost condition. A major purpose of the giving of the Mosaic law was to expose man's sinfulness.[7] The whole Old Testament looks forward to the coming Messiah, both in pictured anticipations and direct prophesies.

---

1 Erich Sauer, *The Dawn of World Redemption*

2 Alexander Hislop, *The Two Babylons.*

3 Arthur C. Custance, *The Three Sons of Noah.*

4 Ralph Winter, "The Long Look Eras of Missions History" *Perspectives* (1981 ed), p 168

5 Geerhardus Vos, *Biblical Theology*, pp 114-118

6. Sir Robert Anderson, *The Coming Prince* Anderson's calculation, made a century ago, was based upon 445 BC and 32 AD, but more recent research indicates that both should be adjusted by one year

7 Trevor McIlwain, *Building on Firm Foundations.* (Sanford, FL New Tribes Mission, 1988)

One of the most enduring errors, the root fallacy
presupposes that every word *has* a meaning bound
up with its shape or its components. In this view,
meaning is determined by etymology; that is, by
the root or roots of a word.

-D. A. Carson

The student should learn once and for all that
every single letter added to a Greek root adds
something to the idea expressed by the root.

-William Douglas Chamberlain

MORE THAN ATONEMENT: WORD PICTURES OF HIS PASSION

A major problem in getting the message of salvation straight is confusion in the terms used. Starting with erroneous definitions of terminology, will probably lead to erroneous conclusions. Much of the confusion and tension in contemporary theology stems from sloppy definitions, which have developed over centuries. Somehow, more recent linguistic work, massive as it has been, has not corrected many of these past errors.

Communists talked about "rectification of terms," but unfortunately they frequently distorted word meanings to their own nefarious ends. In biblical studies, honest and careful definition of crucial terms is imperative to arrive at sound results in doctrine. The Old Testament picture of atonement and New Testament terms, such as, sacrifice, propitiation, ransom-redemption, redemption-liberation, and reconciliation, require precise definition.

Old Testament Atonement

There is a serious anomaly in theological literature in the widespread usage of the word 'atonement' for the cross, when in fact, this word does not occur in the New Testament (except in the KJV). Its continued use has been justified on the basis of its overwhelming usage for centuries and the difficulty in changing at this stage of the game. However, there may also be some theological bias in its continued use. Many feel that the difference between atonement and the actual Greek New Testament words is so insignificant that change is not worthy of serious consideration.

It is clear that the three major New Testament terms, redemption, propitiation, and reconciliation, are not synonymous. Indeed, Lewis Sperry

Chafer, John Walvoord, and Robert Lightner have highlighted the distinctions between these terms and shown their importance in understanding the cross[1] Furthermore, there are eight different Greek words for redemption, and there is a significant difference of meaning between these words. Since this is so, it is irresponsible to continue to use a blanket term which obscures all of these distinctions. To continue to call the passion of Christ 'the atonement,' when in fact the word is never used in the New Testament, is not conducive to the kind of precision for which a science such as theology should be known. Such imprecision would be blameworthy in the physical sciences and ought to be also in the "queen of sciences" as well.

The term atonement is especially objectionable since it only describes the Levitical sacrifices, which were not a final dealing with sin and only anticipated the saving death of Christ. The anticipation clearly falls far short of the fulfillment, as the writer of Hebrews emphasized (Heb. 7:18-9; 8:6-13; 10:1-14). Therefore, it would be helpful to suggest another, better term for theological usage which would be both accurate and comprehensive enough to include the many New Testament words. Perhaps sacrifice, cross-work, and/or passion would be more helpful. The benefit of distinguishing distinct terms is to enable investigation of the distinction between objective and subjective aspects of salvation, so essential to a precise understanding of the cross. Most significant is the character of the one sacrificed. The Lord Jesus was not just a man–He was the God-man!

The Uniqueness of the One Sacrificed

Jesus the Messiah is not to be compared with the animal sacrifices, but rather contrasted starkly, even though they typified Him. He was not just a man, but God incarnate in human flesh. Many don't adequately emphasize His uniqueness in preaching and writing today. The unique Old Testament prophesies of His virgin birth, death, and resurrection have just been highlighted in the previous chapter. Missionary statesman, Patrick Cate, has shown how even the Qur'an gives testimony to some aspects of the unique and supernatural character of the Lord Jesus. This must be pursued.

His uniquely sinless life. Not only did the Lord Jesus claim to be without sin (**"Which of you convicts Me of sin?"** Jn. 8:46), but also the Gospel records portray Him as such. Both Paul and Peter affirmed His sinlessness (2 Cor. 5:21; 1 Pet. 2:21-4; 3:18), making it clear that for Him to be a sacrifice for our sins, He Himself had to be sinless. The Levitical sacrifices had to be without blemish or spot to portray Him adequately. Some skeptics, such as Bertrand Russell, have picked at imagined flaws, but without success. For example, he criticized the Lord for cursing the fig tree in frustration, when it is clear Christ was making an object lesson of the tree, as a picture of fruitless Israel. Could Russell cause a shrub to wither by his word? No other world religious leader claimed sinlessness. For example, although Muslims claim the sinlessness of all the prophets, Muhammad is said to have repented ninety-nine times a day.

His unique miracles of compassion. Most of the forty miracles of Christ recorded in the Gospels were interventions of love and compassion for hurting people. This stands in bold contrast to the purported miracles in the fabricated Gnostic gospels from centuries later, which had absurd miracles performed like a magic show. Giving sight to the man born blind, restoring the centurion's servant, the nobleman's son, the man with the withered hand, the ten lepers cleansed, and most of all raising the son of the widow of Nain, Jairus's daughter, and Lazarus– all come to mind. No other founder of a world religion claimed to have done anything like this.

His unique mastery over nature. Most of the rest of Christ's miracles show an incredible mastery over the forces of nature, starting with turning water into wine, the miraculous draft of fish, and walking on water. The multiplication of bread and fishes to feed great crowds happened twice, having Peter catch a fish to supply the coin for the temple tax, and most impressively, the stilling of the storm, are a few of the more significant miracles. No other founder of a world religion claimed to have done such.

His unique and penetrating teachings. The teachings of other founders of world religions are chaff compared with the Sermon on the Mount and the other significant teachings of the Lord Jesus. Even the great Hindu political leader, Mahatma Gandhi, thought that the Sermon on the Mount was the best, but did not become a Christian because of the exclusivity of the gospel. Just the Golden Rule alone stands above all their utterances.

His gentle, confrontational witness. Nothing in the life of any other religious leader compares with the witness of the Lord to Nicodemus, the Samaritan woman (and subsequently the people of Sychar), the rich young ruler, Matthew the tax collector, Zaccheus the extortioner, etc.

His bold confrontation of apostate religious leaders. Time and again the Lord Jesus came into conflict with the leaders of His own nation, who had fallen into the opposing errors of Phariseeism and Sadduceeism. He exposed their hypocrisy, externalism, and evil motives (Mt. 15, 23, etc.).

His unique prophetic ministry. Although Islam recognizes the Lord Jesus as one of the prophets, the Bible is very clear that He was much more than a prophet. Although they call Muhammad the capstone of the prophets, he did not make any predictions. But the Lord Jesus was not only a forth-teller of God's truth, but like the Old Testament prophets He was also a fore-teller. In His upper-room discourse, He predicted the coming of the Holy Spirit on the day of Pentecost. In the Olivet discourse, He predicted the destruction of the temple in Jerusalem, which happened in AD 70, and implied a longtime Gentile occupation of Jerusalem (Lk. 21:5-6, 20-24). Some of the end time prophecies are beginning to be fulfilled already:

earthquakes, plagues, famines, continuance of warfare, lawlessness, persecution of Christians, false Messiahs, love growing cold, etc. (Mt. 24:4-12; Lk. 21:8-19). Most striking is the persistence of the Jews and the restoration of Israel as a nation (Mt. 24:32-34, *genea* = race or nation). The catastrophic tsunami in 2004 fits the warning of Luke 21:25-6.

His predicted, intentional passion. Few Christians seem aware that the Lord Jesus predicted His own crucifixion and resurrection a dozen times in the last few months of His ministry. Here are the references for further study: Matthew 16:21; 17:9; 17:22-3=Luke 9:43-5; John 10:1-21; Luke 13:31-4; 17:25; Matthew 20:17-9=Luke 18:31-2; Mark 10:45=Matthew 20:28; 26:2; 26:12=Mark 14:8=John 12:7; John 12:20-36; Matthew 26:26-9.

His victorious resurrection and ascension. Muslims believe that Muhammad's body is in a tomb in Medina, but that the "prophet Jesus" has ascended to heaven (although they deny His death and resurrection). This is an embarrassment for Muslims to explain and illustrates how unique the resurrection and ascension of Christ is.

A Substitutionary, Expiatory Sacrifice

Pre-cross predictions. The most basic representation of Christ's death, both in Old Testament prophecy and New Testament fulfillment, is as a substitutionary sacrifice, to take away the sin of all mankind. The prophecies are so explicit that a basic theology of the cross can be developed from them alone. Although Psalm 22 mostly focused upon the physical details of His crucifixion, my tenth-grade English teacher explained why Christ cried out from the cross, **"My God, my God, why have You forsaken me?"** Although I was not yet a born-again Christian, her explanation stuck in memory that He was pointing the onlookers' attention to this marvelous prophecy of His crucifixion. Because He was bearing the sin of the world, the Father had to hide His face from Him.

But Isaiah 52:13–53:12 gives much more of the *significance* of His sacrifice, indeed, the word guilt-offering is used in 53:10. Nine times mention is made of His sacrifice being for sin, iniquity, and transgressions. Three times it was said that the LORD did it. The contrast between the reference to "all" in 53:6 and "many" in 53:11 & 12 is most significant. Since the identification of "all of us like sheep have gone astray, each of us has turned to his own way" (v. 6) is clearly a reference to the whole human race, the usage of the same expression must be the same: **"But the LORD has caused the iniquity of us all to fall on Him"** (53:6). Two truths emerge. His death was substitutionary, and He became a *substitute for all sinners*. But in 53:11 a limitation is found: **"By His knowledge the Righteous One, My Servant, will justify the many, as He will bear their iniquities."** Here the beginnings are seen of a contrast between the objective, historical aspect of His sacrifice and the subjective and personal.

Centuries later, the last prophet of the old order, John the Baptizer, gives testimony: "**Behold, the Lamb of God who takes away the sin of the world**" (Jn. 1:29). This allusion to the Passover lamb must have seemed enigmatic to the disciples who heard it, but in the light of subsequent revelation it is loaded with meaning. By the Holy Spirit, John confirmed the emphasis of Isaiah 53:6, that Messiah's death was substitutionary, expiatory, and universal in its availability.

Christ's own statement. The Lord Jesus dealt first with the highest priority issues in His ministry. Much of the Gospel accounts is taken up with the issues of human sin, His deity, and the demands of the proffered kingdom. He said little about the significance of His coming sacrifice and even less about the nature of the salvation which would be based on that sacrifice. Thus Matthew 20:28=Mark 10:45 stands out: "**just as the Son of Man did not come to be served, but to serve, and to give his life a ransom for many.**" He left it for the Apostles to explain the full significance of the cross doctrinally, but the word ransom implies substitution.

Apostolic testimony. The Apostle Peter's testimony is substantial. In addition to reference to redemption in 1:18-19, he gave three other descriptions in First Peter: "**And He Himself bore our sins in His body on the cross, that we might die to sin and live to righteousness; for by His wounds you were healed**" (2:24); "**For Christ also died for sins once for all, the just for the unjust, in order that He might bring us to God, having been put to death in the flesh, but made alive in the spirit**" (3:18); "**since Christ has suffered in the flesh,...**" (4:1). Here also the substitutionary aspect is undeniable.

Curiously, the Apostle Paul made little use of this picture, probably because he uniquely developed the two other pictures of redemption and reconciliation. His passing reference in 1 Corinthians 5:7 is most significant: "**For Christ our Passover also has been sacrificed.**" This builds upon John the Baptizer's Passover lamb allusion. Reminiscent of Isaiah 53, he wrote, "**He made Him who knew no sin *to be* sin[offering] on our behalf, that we might become the righteousness of God in Him**" (2 Cor. 5:21). Seeing Christ as a fulfillment of Levitical animal sacrifices he wrote: "**just as Christ also loved you, and gave Himself up for us, an offering and a sacrifice to God as a fragrant aroma**" (Eph. 5:2).

Predictably, the author of Hebrews made the most of this foundational understanding of the Messiah's death. In 1:3, he introduced the idea: "**When He had made purification of sins, He sat down at the right hand of the Majesty on high.**" Then in developing the idea of Christ's high priestly office, he contrasted Him with the Levitical high priest: "**who does not need daily, like those high priests, to offer up sacrifices, first for His own sins, and then for the *sins* of the people, because this He did once for all when He offered up Himself**" (Heb. 7:27). What a remarkable picture of *the high priest offering up himself* instead of an animal sacrifice!

As he developed the analogy of the symbolism of the Levitical temple and sacrifices, he reinforced the contrast:

> ... and not through the blood of goats and calves, but through His own blood, He entered the holy place once for all, having obtained eternal redemption.... how much more will the blood of Christ, who through the eternal Spirit offered Himself without blemish to God, cleanse your conscience from dead works to serve the living God? (Heb. 9:12, 14).

His blood obtained eternal redemption by cleansing the conscience of the believer from the sin which the dead works of Judaism could not expiate.

A single sacrifice. After developing the covenantal (or better testamental) nature of salvation as a basis for this (Heb. 9:15-21), the Apostle emphasized the singleness of the sacrifice, which he had brought into the previous passages, but now has highlighted:

> ...nor was it that He should offer Himself often, as the high priest enters the holy place year by year with blood not his own. Otherwise, He would have needed to suffer often since the foundation of the world; but now once at the consummation of the ages He has been manifested to put away sin by the sacrifice of Himself.... so Christ also, having been offered once to bear the sins of many ... (Heb. 9:25-28).

Then the climax of his development is reached:

> By this will we have been sanctified through the offering of the body of Jesus Christ once for all. . . . but He, having offered one sacrifice for sins for all time, sat down at the right hand of God, . . . For by one offering He has perfected for all time those who are sanctified (Heb. 10:10, 12, 14).

Notice the seven times here where He reinforces the once-for-all nature of the sacrifice. The consequence of this single sacrifice of the Savior is a once-for-all salvation for the ones who have been sanctified by it. If there were no other passage in the Bible to teach eternal security, these passages alone would be adequate. The book of Hebrews has more words for confidence, boldness, and assurance than any other book. Yet it has been so badly misunderstood as to deny assurance to so many believers. (See Chapter 13 for a fresh discussion of the warnings of Hebrews harmonious with this, especially Hebrews 6, which is so troubling to Arminians today.) When the Lord Jesus cried out on the cross, **"It is finished,"** He signaled the completion of the objective dimension of His sacrifice, by which a complete salvation is available to all sinners who come by faith.

The basis of substitution. The idea of substitution is clear in the Isaiah 53 prophecy. Although denied by many Arminians and all liberals, substitution in the cross is unambiguous in the New Testament. The use of the preposition *anti* in Matthew 20:28=Mark 10:45 and in 1 Timothy 2:5-6 should be adequate proof, since it clearly means 'instead of.' This makes irrelevant the false claim that the preposition *huper* does not mean "instead of" but merely "on behalf of." In any case, the very idea of Christ's death as a ransom price for sinners is undeniably substitutionary. Moreover, some of the clearer passages in which *huper* is used in a substitutionary sense are: Romans 4:25; 8:3; 1 Corinthians 15:3; 2 Corinthians 5:14; Galatians 1:4; 2:20; 3:13. Clearly the Levitical and Passover sacrifices were substitutionary, and the book of Hebrews makes clear that Christ's death was a fulfillment of those sin offerings (cf. 1 Cor. 5:7). Christ died both for our benefit and as a substitutionary sin offering.

Propitiation

The New Testament words for propitiation or satisfaction (*hilaskomai, hilastērios, hilasmos*) come from the word for mercy, which is infrequently used in the New Testament. The connotation of mercy comes out very clearly in the prayer of the publican in Christ's parable as Luke used the verb *hilaskomai*: **"God, be merciful to me, the sinner"** (Lk. 18:13). Take note that this parable was given before the cross, so the same words must not be used in our prayers. God is merciful and has proven His mercy in the cross. This also comes out clearly in the description of the Lord Jesus as a **"merciful and faithful high priest"** (Heb. 2:17).

Hebrews 9:5 is the link to the mercy seat on the Ark of the Covenant in the Levitical system: *hilastērion* is used here of the mercy seat. Then Paul uses this same word for Christ's sacrifice as the fulfillment of the mercy seat:

> ... being justified by His grace through the redemption which is in Christ Jesus; whom God displayed publicly as a <u>propitiation</u> in His blood through faith. *This was* to demonstrate His righteousness, because in the forbearance of God He passed over the sins previously committed (Rom. 3:24-5).[2]

Although Christ's death is thus linked to the Levitical mercy seat, its efficacy goes far beyond it. Paul alluded to this in his reference to God passing over the sins previously committed, ie. of pre-cross saints (cf. Heb. 9:15). Now God has displayed the cross as the new mercy seat by which He declares that He is satisfied with the blood of Christ as a full satisfaction for sin and a basis for justification. This is where He demonstrated His mercy.

The Apostle John used the noun *hilasmos* twice:

> And if anyone sins, we have an Advocate with the Father, Jesus Christ the righteous; and He Himself is the <u>propitiation</u> for our sins; and not for ours only, but also for *those of* the whole world (1 Jn 2:1-2); In this is love, not that we loved God, but that He loved us and sent His Son *to be* the <u>propitiation</u> for our sins (1 Jn. 4:10).

For whom is Christ the propitiation? John's use of the word 'world' clearly indicates that he is referring to all mankind. This would be harmonious with the truth of Isaiah 53:6, just examined. This is the objective, historical aspect of Christ's death, which is available to all mankind. Chafer had argued that propitiation is a God-ward work of Christ.[3] How wonderful to know that God is perfectly satisfied with the sacrifice of Christ for the sins of the whole world.[A] *God is indeed propitious!*

Two Distinct Dimensions of Redemption

The tendency of translators and theologians to lump together the diverse ideas behind the eight Greek words related to redemption obscures a significant distinction. These words fall into two categories, one with an emphasis upon the objective, historical payment of the ransom price which the Lord Jesus paid through His passion, and the other, upon the subjective liberation of the individual captive from sin.

The usage of the different words must be examined. It should not be assumed that because they are all derived from two roots the usage relates to their derivation. Contemporary linguists emphasize the importance of *usage over derivation.* Carson warns of the danger of the root fallacy: "One of the most enduring of errors, the root fallacy presupposes that every word actually *has* a meaning bound up with its shape or its components. In this view, meaning is determined by etymology; that is, by the root or roots of a word."[4] The usage of *agoradzein, lutron,* and *antilutron* refer to the objective ransom price paid by Christ's death. On the other hand, *exagoradzein, lutrotes,* and *apolutrosis* most clearly refer to the subjective liberation of the captive. The verb, *lutroein,* from which four of the nouns are derived, and the noun, *lutrosis,* are general words encompassing both concepts.

Both aspects undistinguished

Lutroein and lutrosis. The usage of the verb *lutroein* includes both dimensions, the objective and the subjective. Indeed, the BAG lexicon lists both: "1. *free by paying a ransom, redeem...* 2. gener. *set free, redeem, rescue*". They cite 1 Peter 1:18 under the first and Luke 24:21 and Titus 2:14 under the second.[5] This is confirmed by Buchsel's study of the secular usage. The Septuagint and Jewish usage, however, only minimally have the idea of the ransom price and stress the liberation phase.[6] The same is true of the abstract noun *lutrosis* as well. The BAG lexicon lists the two phases separately, but list the three scriptural usages (Lk. 1:68; 2:38; Heb. 9:12) under the liberation locus and cite the Didache under the ransom aspect.[7]

Focus on the objective, historical aspect: ransom

Three of the Greek words focus on the objective, historical dimension, that is, a purchase by the payment of a ransom price.

Lutron. The noun *lutron,* in secular usage, meant "price of release, ran-

---

A. Some extreme Calvinists claim that John is referring to the sins of Jewish Christians and then to Gentiles as well. However, no New Testament introduction says that First John was written to Hebrew Christians. There is no hint of this in the epistle which is part of the "general epistles," so clearly universal by having been written from Ephesus in the 90s.

som"[8] It especially referred to money paid for prisoners of war or slaves. The Septuagintal usage is the same, especially as an equivalent to a forfeited life. Thus it is clear that the focus of Christ's usage in Mk. 10:45 and Mt. 20:28 is on the substitutionary ransom price: "**just as the Son of Man did not come to be served, but to serve, and to give His life a ransom for many**." There is no basis for thinking that the consequent meaning of the release of the prisoner is in view. This is totally objective, historical, and general.

Antilutron. Paul's usage of *antilutron* in 1 Tim. 2:6 is clearly based upon Christ's ransom statement, except that instead of using the preposition *anti* separately, Paul follows the Hellenic Greek liking for compounds: "**For there is one God, and one mediator also between God and men, the man Christ Jesus, who gave Himself as a ransom for all, the testimony *borne* at the proper time**." "Materially *antilutron* is the same as *lutron*."[9] Thus understanding the focus to be upon the objective payment of the ransom price helps to explain how this ransom can be for "all". There would be a serious theological problem if the focus were to be on the liberation of the captive, since obviously all have not been liberated. Extreme Calvinists have tried to solve the problem by insisting that 'all' does not mean 'all' in this and other contexts. A much simpler solution is simply to note the objective focus of this word. There is no theological incongruity to the idea that the objective ransom price Christ paid was sufficient for all without exception, even though not all have been liberated.

Agoradzein. Least controversial would be the meaning of the verb *agoradzein* since it has a vast secular usage, "to buy, to purchase."[10] Clearly the overwhelming focus is upon the active purchase, and it is frequently used in this sense in the Gospels. Paul's usage in 1 Corinthians 6:20 and 7:23 mentions the price *(timē)*: "**For you have been bought with a price...**" This helps to explain how Peter could use this word in reference to unregenerate false teachers in 2 Peter 2:1: "**... just as there will also be false teachers among you, who will secretly introduce destructive heresies, even denying the Master who bought them, bringing swift destruction upon themselves** " Christ paid the objective price, but Peter does not have the liberation of the captive in view. This is confirmed by his later reference to the false teachers in 2:19 as "slaves of corruption." The usage in Revelation 5:9 and 14:3, 4 might possibly include the liberation dimension, but its basic meaning makes perfect sense in the context.

Focus on the subjective, experiential aspect: liberation

The remaining three words focus upon the emancipation of the slave.

Apolutrosis. The abstract compound noun *apolutrosis* shows a clear semantic shift caused by the prefix *apo*, from the ransom price to the release of the captive. Thus the BAG lexicon only lists "release", both literally and figuratively.[11] Buchsel in *TDNT* confirms this understanding most explicitly:

> How far is the idea of a *lutron*, a ransom or the like, still implied in *apolutrosis*? Are we to assume that whenever *apolutrosis* is used there is

also a suggestion of *lutron*? In none of the *apolutrosis* passages is there any express reference to a ransom.. . **They think only of the act of emancipation itself, and of what it implies. ... The true rendering, then, is "redemption" or "liberation," not "ransom." "Release" is also possible in Hb. 11:35 and "remission" in Hb. 9:15** (emphasis mine).[12]

Thus it is clear that the addition of the prefix *apo* has resulted in a very significant semantic shift from the usage of *lutron*. Chamberlain's statement in his grammar is very important, *"The student should learn once and for all that every single letter added to a Greek root adds something to the idea expressed by the root."*[13] Chamberlain's point again is very relevant.

Lutrotēs. The one New Testament usage of the personal noun of agency *lutrotēs* (redeemer, liberator) in Acts 7:35 also focuses upon the liberation phase by referring to Moses as the liberator. Moses did not pay any ransom price to liberate Israel from Egypt. It is not used in the secular Greek, and its Septuagintal usage is harmonious with this.[14]

Exagoradzein. Paul's usage of the compound verb *exagoradzein* is harmonious with this. It is used in secular Greek in reference to the manumission of a slave. All of the New Testament usages are by Paul. "**Christ redeemed us from the curse of the Law, having become a curse for us.... in order that He might redeem those who were under the Law, that we might receive the adoption as sons**" (Gal. 3:13, 4:5). Paul's emphasis in Galatians on the liberation of the Christian from the slavery of the Mosaic Law makes it is clear that he had the liberation dimension in mind. Buchsel confirms this: "The predominance of an objectivising understanding of *exegorasen* has led most of the exegetical and biblico-theological work on the passage astray." He goes on to clarify, "*exagoradzo* also means, in accordance with the sense of the *ek* in many composites, an 'intensive buying,' i.e., a buying which exhausts the possibilities available." He sees the usage in the prison epistles as harmonious with this (Col. 4:5; Eph. 5:16).[15] In conclusion, the addition of the prefix *ex=ek* ('out of') radically shifts the emphasis of the word from the price paid to the liberation of the slave. *Agoradzein* and *exagoradzein* must be seen as two distinct words, with distinct, even contrasting ranges of meaning. Chamberlain's point is equally relevant here also. Therefore, *exagorazein* is a subjective, personal term.

Clarification of the contrast

Thus it is clear, not only that the linguistic evidence supports a distinction between the objective ransom phase of Christ's death and the subjective liberation phase in the life of the Christian, but also that such a distinction is of great value theologically. It helps to explain how the ransom price could be connected with unregenerate false teachers (2 Pet. 2:1) and all mankind (1 Tim. 2:5-6), when the liberation has been effective for only a limited number. Thus, it helps resolve the tension between these two truths. Christ's ransom price was sufficient for all mankind and provisionally available to all, but the liberation has been effectual only for those who believe.

An illustration helps to understand the importance of this distinction. When heiress Patty Hearst was kidnapped by the Symbionese Liberation Army some years ago, her father paid a ransom price of two million dollars. However, Patty, having been brainwashed into sympathy with her captors, even joined them in a bank robbery and refused to be liberated. The *lutron* (ransom price) had been provided, the act of *agoradzein* (paying the ransom) had been fulfilled, but there was no *apolutrosis* or *exagoradzein* (liberation) effectuated. The objective provision was made, but the subjective release did not occur because of the will of the captive. Just so the objective ransom price for the sins of the whole human race was provided on Calvary, but the subjective release of the majority of the captives has not taken place because of their own willful rejection of the redeemer.

Reconciliation

Paul uniquely developed the picture of reconciliation through the cross, using three related words: *katallassein, katallagē, & apokatallassein*. There is little controversy about the meaning of these words, the first word means "to change, exchange, reconcile" and is used twice in Romans 5:9-11:

> Much more then, having now been justified by His blood, we shall be saved from the wrath *of God* through Him. For if while we were enemies, we were reconciled to God through the death of His Son, much more, having been reconciled, we shall be saved by His life. And not only this, but we also exult in God through our Lord Jesus Christ, through whom we have now received the reconciliation.

This basic context makes it clear that reconciliation is directed at man's alienation from God, and that believers are said to have been reconciled to God, even from a state of total enmity toward Him. Since Paul designates our prior state as enemies of God, it is clear that this is subjective and individual rather than objective and historical. This happens in the life and experience of the believer as a part of the conversion process. It is also clear that the idea that God was somehow historically reconciled is not supported here or in any of Paul's other passages. Reconciliation is always manward. Believers have received this reconciliation.

This passage is also a wonderful basis for the security of the believer, since Paul made it clear that if God was able to reconcile us when we were at enmity, He is even "much more" able to complete that salvation through Christ's resurrected and ascended life now interceding for us at the Father's right hand (Heb. 7:25). *Amazingly, he said that our future salvation is even more sure than the present.*

The interpretation of 2 Corinthians 5:18-20 is not as straightforward:

> Now all *these* things are from God, who reconciled us to Himself through Christ, and gave us the ministry of reconciliation, namely that God was in

Christ <u>reconciling</u> the world to Himself, not counting their trespasses against them, and He has committed to us the word of <u>reconciliation</u>. Therefore, we are ambassadors for Christ, as though God were entreating through us; we beg [sic. you] on behalf of Christ, <u>be reconciled</u> to God.

Paul's use of an aorist* participle in 5:18 in reference to the believer's reconciliation as a past event is harmonious with Romans 5. But Paul's use of a periphrastic* present participle in 5:19 in reference to the reconciliation of the world is more difficult. The finite verb 'was' is imperfect and together they have an imperfect force.[16] Thus it could be fairly said that, *in the cross, God was in the process of reconciling the world.* Obviously the world has not yet been reconciled. But the cross was the foundation of that *process* of reconciliation, which has been going on since that day, as sinners one by one respond to the good news.[17] This is confirmed by Paul's statement that God gave to believers a ministry of reconciliation and a word of reconciliation. Then he explained in 5:20 how this works— God entreats the world through us, His ambassadors, as we plead with sinners to be reconciled to God (note that the 'you' in v. 20 is not in the Greek). From this it is clear that the work of reconciliation is subjective and personal, not objective and historical.

Paul used the stronger compound word *apokatallassein* in Ephesians 2:16, speaking of the goal of the cross to thoroughly reconcile Jew and Gentile together in one body, the Church. Abbott-Smith suggests that the prefix *apo* signifies a more complete and thorough reconciliation.[18] Then in the parallel passage in Colossians 1:20-22, Paul expanded the purview to "all kinds of things" to be thoroughly reconciled in the end time, including the reconciliation of the Colossian believers in their day (cf. discussion on p. 58, *BCAA).* This is harmonious with his earlier use of these words.

Conclusions

With so many distinct Greek words used to portray the cross of Christ, it is fuzzy thinking which perpetuates the use of the Old Testament term 'atonement' in theological literature, especially since it only refers to the prefiguring of the Christ's sacrifice in the Levitical system, which was far short of the reality. However, the pre-cross predictions are most instructive, coupled with the apostolic references to His death as a substitutionary expiatory sacrifice. The book of Hebrews especially contrasted the Levitical offerings with the ultimate efficacy of Christ's sacrifice, an efficacy which guaranteed eternal redemption to the believer.

In the focus upon the words for propitiation, an objective universality is revealed, which confirmed the picture of sacrifice. The work of propitiation thus was God-ward in that Christ's death was a perfect satisfaction to the Father for the sins of the whole world.

Two dimensions in the broad concept of redemption emerged: ransom-redemption, focusing upon the objective ransom price paid; and liberation-

redemption, focusing upon the subjective liberation of the sinner from slavery. Ransom-redemption, like propitiation, is potentially universal in its intent. However, liberation-redemption consistently is limited to believers, as also is reconciliation. These terms portray a subjective application of the merits of Christ's sacrifice to those who claim it in repentant faith.

For centuries there has been endless debate over limited atonement vs. general redemption.* The whole debate is beside the point. Atonement is not a New Testament word! The best terms are an 'unlimited or general ransom price or purchase' and a 'limited or particular liberation'. The whole question arose because of failure to do the careful word studies needed as a basis for sound theology. Chapter 16 builds upon this linguistic foundation to examine the view of extreme Calvinists that Christ died only for the elect.

---

1   Lewis Sperry Chafer, *Systematic Theology,* III, pp 86-96, 190-93, Robert P Lightner, *The Death Christ Died A Case for Unlimited Atonement,* pp 73-91; *Sin, the Savior, and Salvation,* pp 117-27, John F Walvoord, *Jesus Christ, Our Lord,* pp. 163-90

2   The NIV has reverted back to the erroneous use of 'atonement' here

3   Chafer, III, 93-96.

4   D A Carson, *Exegetical Fallacies,* p. 26

5   Arndt and Gingrich, *Lexicon,* p 484.

6   Buchsel, in *Theological Dictionary of the New Testament,* IV 349-50

7   Arndt and Gingrich, p 484

8   Ibid , p 483

9   Buchsel, p 349

10   Arndt & Gingrich, p. 12

11   Ibid , p 95

12   Buchsel, pp 354-5

13   William Douglas Chamberlain, *An Exegetical Grammar of the Greek New Testament,* p 11.

14   Buchsel, IV 351

15   Ibid , I 125-8

16   Wallace, *Grammar,* pp 647-48

17   There is exegetical criticism of the KJV and NAS translation that "God was in Christ" in favor of the NIV that "God was reconciling the world to himself in Christ " However, it doesn't affect the conclusions significantly

18   Abbott-Smith, *Lexicon,* en loc

... Jesus came into Galilee, preaching the gospel of God, and saying, "The time is fufilled, and the kingdom of God is at hand; repent and believe in the gospel." (Mk. 1:14-5)

... how I did not shrink from declaring to you anything that was profitable, and teaching you publicly and from house to house, solemnly testifying to both Jews and Greeks of repentance toward God and faith in our Lord Jesus Christ.

- the Apostle Paul
(Acts 20:20-1)

WHAT MUST I DO TO BE SAVED?

"What must I do to be saved?" This was the question of the Philippian jailor to Paul and Silas. It is also the question of the ages, which demands a clear answer. Although the Bible gives a very clear answer in simple terms, people have incredibly confused and complicated the issue, because the biblical answer seems too simple.

Some say, "Believe and be baptized!" Others, "Believe and follow Christ!" "Repent and confess all your sins, believe in Christ, be baptized, and join the church!" still other insist. "Let go and let God!" "Pray through!" "Surrender to Christ!" "Repent and live a life of obedience to Christ!" Still others say that there is nothing you can do to be saved; just wait on God to give you the faith and assurance that you are among the elect! Some say "Deny yourselves and take up your cross in order to be saved." Others yet insist that we must keep the Mosaic Law, especially the sabbath. But the largest church organization in the world says it isn't so simple: "One must be christened, participate regularly in the mass, keeping on doing penance for sins, have a priest perform extreme unction just before death, and have relatives pay for masses to get out of purgatory." The late Pope was trusting in Mary's intercession.

The watchword of the Protestant Reformation was that salvation is by grace through faith alone. What is meant by faith and what about all these other conditions added onto faith according to various 'Christian' groups? Did the Apostle Paul oversimplify the issue? Did Martin Luther?

The answer to all these questions is found in just one authoritative source–the Bible. Human opinion is useless, human reasoning hopeless, tradition even more confusing, and the varieties of human experience even more misleading! The only source for salvation-trutht is God's perfect self-revelation recorded in His inspired word.

From all the above confused and contradictory answers one might think that the Bible itself is confused and self-contradictory. However, the Bible's answer is clear, harmonious, and simple–if only we can rid ourselves of our presuppositions, biases, and traditions, and come to God's word with an open and "**honest heart**" (Lk. 8:15). A sequential journey through the New Testament helps to see what the text plainly indicates. The best inductive study is to go chronologically to see the progress of the revelation of God's truth. It is best not to jump around from passage to passage, which frequently obscures the context.

John the Baptizer's starting point (John 1:29)

The herald of the Lord Jesus was given insight to sum up the essential foundation of salvation in one statement as he introduced the Messiah to the Israel, by saying, "**Look, the Lamb of God, who takes away the sin of the world.**" In just one sentence he made clear that the Lord Jesus would be the fulfillment of all the Old Testament blood sacrifices. However, the fulfillment far exceeded the sacrifices pointing to Him. The shedding of blood to provide garments for Adam and Eve (Gen. 3), the Passover lambs slain to redeem the firstborn in Egypt (Ex. 12), the blood of the sacrificial animals sprinkled on the Mercy Seat– all were temporary provisions (Heb. 10:1-4). But John announced that *Christ's sacrifice would completely take away the sins of the whole world.*

John tersely focused upon the two main issues of the ministry of Christ—*who He is and what He came to do.* Some people wonder why the Gospels say so little about what He came to do until the last months before His crucifixion. One answer is that the first issue, *who He is,* had to be made absolutely clear first. Only then, just before the cross He spelled why He came: "**just as the Son of Man did not come to be served, but to serve, and to give his life as a ransom for many**" (Mt. 20:28). Was this man just a prophet, a miracle worker, a human Messiah, a deceiver, an egomaniac, or was He really God incarnate? Israel had to face this issue *first.*

In the course of His ministry the Lord Jesus also focused upon the reality of sin in the nation Israel and among all peoples. Until the chosen people realized how sinful and apostate they had become, there was little point in His explaining the nature of His future sacrificial work on the cross.

Repentance and faith

Mark describes the beginning of His ministry in this way: "**After John was put in prison, Jesus went into Galilee, proclaiming the good news of God. 'The time has come,' he said. 'The kingdom of God is near. <u>Repent and believe</u> the good news'**" (Mk. 1:14-5). This twofold demand of the Lord relates to the two issues just mentioned. Although there is much discussion about the nature of the kingdom of God, one thing that is sure is that it centers on the King, the Lord Jesus Christ Himself. The kingdom was at hand because the King had arrived (cf. Lk. 17:20-25). In the light of His arrival and the impending kingdom, Israel's sin had to be faced and repented of. But they would not see any need to repent unless they believed in the Lord and His message, nor could they really believe in Him in the true sense unless they had repented of their sin, their false views of God, His word, and His Messiah. Repentance and true faith go hand in glove. Perhaps a better analogy is the two sides of a coin: repentance is tails, the negative side, and faith is heads, the positive side of the coin. The two sides make one coin. Years later Paul spoke of the essence of his message as, "**repentance toward God and faith in our Lord Jesus Christ**" (Acts 20:21 NAS). His message was the same! These two sides of the coin should be examined separately and then put back together. There is just one condition of salvation, one coin with two sides.

The message of repentance

The Lord's forerunner, John, after many silent centuries, had again voiced God's demand to Israel for repentance: "**<u>Repent</u>, for the kingdom of heaven is near**" (Mt. 3:1). He spoke much about God's judgment upon sin by exposing Israel's sinful, hypocritical, and externalistic ways. His bold rebuke of King Herod's adultery brought about his imprisonment. At that point the Lord Jesus took up John's message in virtually identical language (Mt. 4:12, 17). But what does repentance mean? There are many misconceptions about its meaning current today, as in that day.

The Greek for repentance is *metanoia*, which means a change of mind, heart, will, attitude, or mind-set. The Jewish people needed to change their minds about themselves, both individually and corporately as a nation, about their sin, and about God and His demands upon the human race. It is obvious that coming to faith in Christ must involve a real change of attitude.

The Sermon on the Mount was the Lord's first major effort to change the mind and attitude of the Jewish nation. In Matthew 5, He exposed the false Rabbinic misinterpretations of the Mosaic Law by the contrasting expression, "**You have heard that it was said ... but I say to you**" (Mt. 5:21-2; 27-8; 31-2; 33-4;38-9;43-4). He exposed the hypocritical externalism of publically giving alms, praying, and fasting so as to be seen of men. He exposed their 'theologically correct' materialism (Mt. 6:19-34). He warned especially about the false prophets and leaders of Israel, who used God's name but were counterfeits (Mt. 7:15-23). Throughout His teaching the Lord warned about the arrogant, self-righteous religious leaders, who were leading the nation astray (Mt. 23). Thus, the Sermon on the Mount was a true, higher exposition of the Mosaic Law to help the Jewish people see themselves as sinners before God and in need of His salvation. The most shocking indictment he made was: **"For I tell you that unless your righteousness surpasses that of the Pharisees and the teachers of the law, you will certainly not enter the kingdom of heaven"** (Mt. 5:20).

There were very few really righteous in Israel and only a small godly remnant of believing, righteous Jews, such as Mary and Joseph, Elizabeth and Zechariah, etc. The majority were unregenerate sinners who needed to repent. Through the ministry of John the Baptizer, Christ's early disciples, such as Peter, Andrew, James, John, and Nathaniel, had become part of this godly, repentant remnant (Jn. 1). But even the pre-eminent teacher in Israel, Nicodemus, needed to be born again (Jn. 3:1-36). When the Pharisees and Scribes grumbled at the Lord's connection with sinners at Matthew Levi's feast, He said: **"*It is* not those who are well who need a physician, but those who are sick. I have not come to call the righteous but sinners to <u>repentance</u>"** (Lk. 9:31-2). Using two incidents in which people were tragically killed as an example, He later pressed His point, **"But unless you <u>repent</u>, you too will all perish"** (Lk. 13:3, 5). When Zaccheus, the crooked tax collector, came to repentance, He affirmed, **"For the Son of Man came to seek and to save what was lost"** (Lk. 19:10). Thus, repentance involves a radical change of mind or attitude about sin, self, and the Savior.

One misconception about repentance which developed in the church after the time of the Apostles was that it meant a change of direction in one's lifestyle, turning over a new leaf in life. Instead, repentance is a change of *mind*, and conversion is a change of *direction or lifestyle*. When one is driving down the interstate, repentance is the realization that one is going in the wrong direction. Conversion is when one finds an exit and make a u-turn. They are related, but distinct. This is important because the Pharisees had the idea that as long as things looked good on the outside, one was all right with God. But the Lord Jesus was more concerned with the issues of the heart (Prov. 4:23), as the starting place for dealing with the external lifestyle. Unfortunately, many legalistic scholars today have fallen into the same confusion by equating repentance and conversion.[A] This same mindset eventuated in the Roman Catholic Douay translation, "do penance." It implies that repentance is something done externally.

Another erroneous notion is that repentance means sorrow for sin. This emphasizes the emotional dimension, whereas the Greek word puts the emphasis upon the mind and will of mankind. Paul exposes the error of this notion in writing to the Corinthian church: **"Godly sorrow brings repentance that leads to salvation and leaves no regret, but worldly sorrow brings death"** (2 Cor. 7:10). Although *godly sorrow* can bring true repentance, sorrow in itself is

---

A   Unfortunately, two major theological dictionaries have fallen into this error by skewing the data, probably because of a legalistic, externalistic mind-set of the article authors See Appendix G in *BCAA*.

not repentance. This error is also connected with the confusion between repentance and remorse. Remorse is essentially being sorry for getting caught in sin. This is what happened to Judas Iscariot. When things didn't work out the way he had planned, he was remorseful and went out and hung himself. Quite in contrast, Simon Peter repented of his denial of the Lord Jesus and was restored (Jn. 21). Weeping and mourning is not a condition for being saved, since God is ready to save any sinner who comes in repentant faith.

The appeal to believe the good news by trusting Christ

The positive side of the coin is to believe the good news, which in essence is to trust Christ. Just as repentance is emphasized in the Synoptic Gospels (Matthew, Mark, and Luke), just so believing is emphasized in John's Gospel. The active verb *pisteuein* (to believe) is found 96 times in this Gospel, but the noun *pistis* (faith) does not occur, although frequently found in the epistles. Unfortunately, in English, the noun (faith) and the verb (believe) are from two different roots, but the Greek words come from the same root. Their meaning in Greek is a lot stronger than the words belief and believe, which have been badly watered down in English– "I believe it will rain today." It would be far better to use the word 'trust' both as a noun and verb to more faithfully render the meaning of the original.

John gives a clear picture of the meaning. In the prologue of his Gospel, he equates it with 'receiving' Christ: "**Yet to all who received him, to those who believed in his name, he gave the right to become the children of God–**" (Jn. 1:12, NIV). Speaking to Israel's premier teacher, the Lord made trust in Himself the condition for receiving eternal life (Jn. 3:15-16). John concludes the narrative with the words: "**Whoever believes in the Son has eternal life, but whoever rejects the Son will not see life, for God's wrath remains on him**" (Jn. 3:36, NIV). There is another Greek word used in this verse which has caused some discussion, the verb, *apeithein* (rejects) is translated "believeth not" in the KJV and "does not obey" in the NAS translation. Since the positive verb, *peithein* has the idea of being persuaded, one authoritative Greek lexicon rightly supports the KJV and NIV against the NAS. John is not talking about obedience here, but faith and rejection. This indicates that true faith involves persuasion.[B]

The Jewish leaders began to oppose the Lord early in His ministry, eliciting this wonderful claim from His mouth: "**In very truth, anyone who gives heed to what I say and puts his trust in him who sent me has hold of eternal life, and does not come up for judgement, but has already passed from death to life**" (Jn. 5:24, NEV). Note the wonderful assurance which true faith engenders in the heart. It is the assurance of a present reality (**has hold of eternal life**), a confi-

---

B. The BAG lexicon states, p 82: " Since, in the view of the early Christians, the supreme disobedience was a refusal to believe their gospel, *apeitheo* may be restricted in some passages to the meaning. *disbelieve, be an unbeliever.*"

dence for the future (**does not come up for judgement**) based upon a past event (**has already passed from death to life**). This is the verse the Spirit used in my life over fifty years ago to bring me into the assurance of eternal life, which has never left me.

The narrative of the Samaritan woman helps: "'**Everyone who drinks of this water will thirst again; but whoever drinks of the water that I will give him shall never thirst; but the water that I will give him will become in him a well of water springing up to eternal life**'" (Jn. 4:13-14). Christ used the symbolism of drinking living water to explain that believing is like drinking, or appropriating the living water for one's self (Jn. 4:10, 13-4). He used this same symbolism extensively in the bread of life discourse:

> **I am the bread of life. He who comes to me will never go hungry, and he who believes in me will never be thirsty. ... I tell you the truth, unless you eat the flesh of the Son of Man and drink his blood, you have no life in you. Whoever eats my flesh and drinks my blood has eternal life, and I will raise him up at the last day** (Jn. 6:35, 53-4).

This is the same symbolism as with the Samaritan woman. 'Eating' symbolizes coming to Christ, and 'drinking' portrays saving faith. One must appropriate or partake of Christ; it is not just mere intellectual assent to certain truths. Later at the feast of Tabernacles, in that most dramatic scene, He reinforced this essential idea: "**On the last and greatest day of the Feast, Jesus stood and said in a loud voice, 'If a man is thirsty, let him come to me and drink. Whoever <u>believes in me</u>, as the Scripture has said, streams of living water will flow from within him**'" (Jn. 7:37-8).

Matthew recorded a unique invitation, which amplifies the Lord's reference in Jn 6:35 to coming to Him as an aspect of believing: "**Come to me, all you who are weary and burdened, and I will give you rest**" (Mt. 11:28). Notice the universality of this invitation. In the context, He had just denounced the towns of Israel which were unrepentant despite the flood of light of His presence to which they had been privileged (Mt. 11:20-24). This implies that the invitation is now extended to the Gentiles as well as the Jews, which means the whole world of people burdened with sin. This brings us back to where we began– John 1:29, "**the sin of the world.**"

Earlier in the Sermon on the Mount, He had exhorted the nation to "**Enter through the narrow gate. For wide is the gate and broad is the road that leads to destruction, and many enter through it. But small is the gate and narrow the road that leads to life, and only a few find it**" (Mt. 7:13-14). John records His words in a later discourse about the gate to the sheep pen: "**I am the gate; whoever enters through me will be saved. He will come in and go out and find pasture**" (Jn. 10:9). Note the universality of the invitation, but also its exclusivity. Christ is the only gate or door to eternal life. Just before this He had made it plain to the Pharisees: "**I told you that you would die in your sins; if you do not <u>believe</u> that I am the one I claim to be, you will indeed die in your sins**" (Jn. 8:24, NIV).

Conversion is the result of
repentant faith and the new birth.

The Greek words for conversion (*strephein, epistrephein*) refer to a change of direction, used in the literal sense of "turning oneself around" (Mk. 5:30; 8:33) or metaphorically of a spiritual turning toward God. It can refer to both a change of the direction of one's life and of a change of lifestyle. Conditioned on repentant faith, God gives the new birth as a total work of the Spirit in imparting new, divine life to the spiritually dead. The outward result of this is conversion. God's way is to start on the inside with the new birth, which then begins to impact the outward life in conversion.

The major error of the Scribes and Pharisees of Christ's day was externalism, without a change of heart. Many legalistic professing Christians today have fallen into the same tragic error. The Lord Jesus did not actually say much about conversion; He left that to His Apostles to clarify. The major issue throughout most of His ministry was— who is He?

The centrality of the cross and the resurrection

It was not until the last months of His ministry that the Lord Jesus began to speak explicitly about the cross. Beginning at Caesarea Philippi, He began to predict a dozen times that He must go up to Jerusalem, suffer, be killed, and rise from the dead (Mt. 16:21; Lk. 9:22). He only explained its significance in Mt. 20:28: "**Just as the Son of Man did not come to be served, but to serve, and to give his life a ransom for many.**" This makes it clear that the cross is the basis of the salvation He had been offering.

However, before the Lord could talk about the cross, He first had to deal with Israel's sin by explaining the true meaning of the Mosaic Law and His higher standard of morality (in the Sermon on the Mount) for the impending kingdom of righteousness which He was offering to Israel in fulfillment of Old Testament prophecies. Then He had to help them to understand who He was—God incarnate in human flesh. Only then, upon their rejection of Him as righteous king and His righteous kingdom, could He press on to Jerusalem and the cross. This helps to explain why the form in which His message was proclaimed over most of His ministry, especially as recorded in the Synoptic Gospels, seems quite different from the message as proclaimed by the Apostles in Acts and the epistles. But the core of the message is the same: people must repent and then turn to Him as God's Messiah in faith, that is, as King and Savior. But before the proffered kingdom could be inaugurated, first He must suffer and die according to God's eternal plan.

As a consequence of His deity, the Lord also claimed to be the only way of salvation, contrary to the pluralistic ideas in vogue today: "**Jesus answered, 'I am the way and the truth and the life. No one comes to the Father except through me**" (Jn. 14:6).[C]

C. Two prominent evangelical leaders, when challenged on the Larry King program in the summer of 2005, waffled about Christ being the only way of salvation, and thus "gave away the store."

John recorded a number of incidents and teachings which pointed to the cross and resurrection, first in more symbolic language, and later more explicitly. At the first cleansing of the temple at the first Passover of His ministry the Lord Jesus said to the Jewish leaders: "**Destroy this temple, and I will raise it again in three days**" (Jn. 2:19). At the second Passover, after feeding the multitude He said, "**I am the bread of life; ... This bread is my flesh, which I will give for the life of the world**" (Jn. 6:35a, 51c).

At the feast of Dedication (Chanukah) four months before the cross, the Lord described Himself as the Good Shepherd who lays down His life for His sheep (Jn. 10:11-18). Then, as the last Passover and the crucifixion approached, in connection with the raising of Lazarus, He said to Martha, "**I am the resurrection and the life. He who <u>believes in me</u> will live, even though he dies**" (Jn. 11:25). Then during passion week, in reference to the Gentiles who wanted to see Him, He said, "**I tell you the truth, unless a kernel of wheat falls to the ground and dies, it remains only a single seed. But if it dies, it produces many seeds. ... But I, when I am lifted up from the earth will draw all men to myself**" (Jn. 12:24, 32). In addition, there are about a dozen explicit predictions the Lord made of His passion.

The gospel in the Lord's final orders

The Lord Jesus had laid the foundation for the "Great Commission" in His exhortation to the fishermen: "**Come, follow me and I will make you fishers of men**" (Mt. 4:19). During the forty days after His resurrection and before He ascended on high, He commanded: "**Therefore go and make disciples of all nations, baptizing them in the name of the Father and of the Son and of the Holy Spirit, and teaching them to obey everything I have commanded you**" (Mt. 28:18-20a). The incident later in Jerusalem, which Luke recorded, explains how they were to make disciples:

> This is what is written: The Christ will suffer and rise from the dead on the third day, and <u>repentance and forgiveness of sins</u> will be preached in his name to all nations, beginning at Jerusalem. You are witnesses of these things. I am going to send you what my Father has promised; but stay in the city until you have been clothed with power from on high (Lk. 24:47-9).

The gospel in apostolic preaching

Another excellent way to get at the heart of the salvation message is to examine the apostolic preaching in Acts. Most of the proclamation is in the words of Peter or Paul, and in Luke's explanations along the way.

Peter's messages to Israel. After explaining the phenomena connected with the gift of the Holy Spirit, Peter moved right on to the cross (Acts 2:23), the resurrection, and ascension as proof that Jesus is both Lord and Messiah (2:24-36). Many in the crowd came under conviction as Christ had promised in John 16:8-11: "**When the people heard this, they were cut to the heart**

and said to Peter and the other apostles, 'Brothers, what shall we do?'" (Acts 2:37). Peter's response needs to be translated more clearly from the Greek:[D] "**All of you [pl.] must imperatively <u>repent</u> (and let him [sing.] be baptized in the name of Jesus Christ), for the forgiveness of your [pl.] sins; and you [pl.] will receive the gift of the Holy Spirit**" (Acts 2:38, Olson translation). Verse 41 makes clear that only those who had received the word were baptized; baptism of itself was of no saving value. It is God who does the saving, and nothing man does can contribute to our salvation: "**And the Lord was adding their number daily those who were being saved**" (2:47b).

As Peter's second opportunity came through the healing of the lame man, he focused on the cross and resurrection (Acts 3:13-18) and then exhorted: "**<u>Repent, then, and turn to God</u>, so that your sins may be wiped out, that times of refreshing may come from the Lord...**" (3:19). They were on the verge of a great revival, if only the nation would repent and turn to God. Tragically, instead they arrested the Apostles. Still Luke says, "**But many who heard the message <u>believed</u>, and the number of men grew to about five thousand**" (4:4, NIV). Notice how repentance and faith are used interchangeably, and there is no mention of baptism here. Note also that repentance is prior to conversion. Some wrongly assume that because repentance and conversion are connected by 'and,' they are synonymous.

It is exceedingly important in this pluralistic age to note that the Apostle Peter confirmed the Lord's claim to be the only way of salvation: "**Salvation is found in no one else, for there is no other name under heaven given to men by which we must be saved**" (Acts 4:12, NIV). When brought before the Sanhedrin, Peter did not waver from the same message:

> **God exalted him to his own right hand as Prince and Savior that he might give repentance and forgiveness of sins to Israel. We are witnesses of these things, and so is the Holy Spirit, whom God has given to those who obey him** (5:31-2).

Some have misused this verse to teach that God gives repentance as a gift to some elect individuals. However, the context is clear that Peter is talking about God giving the nation Israel the *opportunity* to repent and be forgiven. Others have misused this verse to claim that only obedient Christians receive the Holy Spirit after their conversion. A unique verb, *peitharchein* is used here, speaking of the submission to Christ's authority implicit in repentant faith. Obviously, the Jewish rulers were not submitting to Christ's authority as Prince and Savior, whereas all true believers have submitted.

At his martyrdom, Stephen raised the same issue: "**You stiff-necked people, with uncircumcised hearts and ears! You are just like your fathers: You always resist the Holy Spirit**" (Acts 7:51). Salvation is not through some irresistible

---

D. The standard translations have not made clear the marked shift from the second person plural imperative (repent) to the third person singular imperative (let him be baptized), which is sometimes called a cohortative Since the verb 'to repent' is in the plural, as is the forgiveness and the gift of the Spirit, these connect and are not conditioned upon baptism, which alone is in the singular.

work of the Spirit upon some elect group. Human beings have a free will to resist the work of the Spirit, as most do.

Luke records how Philip went down to the Samaritans to follow up the ministry of the Lord Jesus there (Jn. 4): "But **when they believed** Philip as he **preached the good news of the kingdom of God and the name of Jesus Christ, they were baptized, both men and women**" (Acts 8:12).

The importance of human response to the message as the key factor in conversion is confirmed by Peter's miracle in Lydda of healing a paralytic named Aeneas: "**All those who lived in Lydda and Sharon saw him and turned to the Lord**" (Acts 9:35). This kind of astonishing result has sometimes been experienced by missionaries even to the present, as whole tribes and villages come together to Christ. Missiologist Donald McGavran has termed this phenomenon "people-movement conversion." There are some humanly caused circumstances which usually lead up to such mass responses. This is hard to harmonize with ideas of God only saving some few sovereignly elect people. These ideas will be studied subsequently (Chaps. 20 - 23).

Most significant is Peter's message to the first Gentile converts after Pentecost, Cornelius and his household. After bearing witness to the cross and resurrection, Peter said, "**All the prophets testify about him that everyone who believes in him receives forgiveness of sins through his name**" (Acts 10:43, NIV). It should be noted that all these Gentile relatives and close friends, having been prepared by Cornelius' influence (v. 24), received the gift of the Holy Spirit at the point at which they came to faith, neither before nor afterward, as some erroneously teach. Extreme Calvinists teach that the regenerating work of the Spirit precedes faith, and Pentecostals deny that we receive the Spirit *when* we believe (cf. 1 Cor. 6:19-20; Rom. 8:9). Peter based his conclusion, that even these Gentiles should receive baptism, on the fact that they had already received the Holy Spirit (Acts 10:44-8). Clearly, baptism did not qualify them for salvation or the gift of the Spirit.

In Jerusalem when Peter defended his baptism of Gentiles he reaffirmed that their faith was the condition of receiving the Spirit of God:

> 'So if God gave them the same gift as he gave us, who **believed** in the Lord Jesus Christ, who was I to think that I could oppose God!' When they heard this, they had no further objections and praised God, saying, 'So then, God has even granted the Gentiles **repentance** unto life' (Acts 11:17-18, NIV).

Note that believing and repenting are used here interchangeably as the condition of receiving the Spirit, the giver of eternal life. In their response, the Apostles and elders were indicating that now God was giving Gentiles the *opportunity* to repent and receive eternal life.[E]

Accordingly, Luke follows this up with the narrative of the incorporation

---

E. Some suppose that this shows that repentance is a direct gift of God to the elect, but this ignores the context of the passage. The issue was Jews and Gentiles. God didn't give all Gentiles repentance.

of Gentiles into the church in the great cosmopolitan city of Antioch of Syria: "... men from Cyprus and Cyrene, went to Antioch and began to speak to Greeks also, telling them the good news about the Lord Jesus. The Lord's hand was with them, and a great number of people believed and turned to the Lord" (Acts 11:20-21, NIV). This unique character of the church was manifest through the incorporation of Gentile converts, so much so that it was there that the disciples were *first* called Christians (11:26).

Paul's missionary tours. Luke then narrates the progress of the gospel out into the broader Gentile world under the ministry of Paul and Barnabas on their first missionary tour. Their sermon in the synagogue of Pisidian Antioch is recorded at length. After preaching the ministry, death, and resurrection of Christ, the Apostles said, "Therefore, my brothers, I want you to know that through Jesus the forgiveness of sins is proclaimed to you. Through him everyone who believes is justified from everything you could not be justified from by the law of Moses" (Acts 13:38-39, NIV). Both Jews and devout Gentile converts to Judaism responded to the message and the Apostles were invited back. On the next Sabbath, when a crowd gathered to hear the message, the leaders of the synagogue opposed them, causing the Apostles to say: "'It was necessary that the word of God be spoken to you first; since you repudiate it and judge yourselves unworthy of eternal life, behold, we are turning to the Gentiles....'" Luke reports, "When the Gentiles heard this, they began rejoicing and glorifying the word of the Lord; and all who had devoted themselves to eternal life believed" (13:46, 48, Olson translation).[F] As the Apostles moved on to Iconium, Luke again contrasts the great number of Jews and Gentiles who believed with the Jewish leadership, "who refused to believe..." (14:2).

At the Jerusalem church council, in defending Gentile salvation by grace through faith alone, Peter was very explicit (Acts 15:7-9, 11, NAS):

> Brethren, you know that in the early days God made a choice among you, that by my mouth the Gentiles would hear the word of the gospel and believe. And God, who knows the heart, testified to them [by] giving the Holy Spirit, just as he also did to us; and He made no distinction between us and them, cleansing their hearts by faith.... But we believe that we are saved through the grace of our Lord Jesus, in the same way they also are.

On the second missionary tour, Paul and Silas got a positive response in Philippi. God opened the heart of Lydia, who was already worshiping Him by customarily meeting with Jewish women at a place of prayer.[G] After

---

F. The perfect participle, *tetagmenoi*, can be either middle or passive voice. Since the Apostles had just referred to the Jews' rejecting and considering themselves unworthy of eternal life, the middle voice reflexive meaning makes much better sense here. The verb *tassein* is used in 1 Cor. 16 15 in the sense of being devoted to something BAGD, p. 991, and Alford. *Gk Testament*, II, 153-4.

G. This is not an indication of irresistible grace, as some suppose, because her heart was already right with God, and she like other godly Jews just needed to be moved into the New Testament church through the hearing of the gospel message.

baptism she called herself **"a believer"** (Acts 16:15). The story of the conversion of the Philippian jailor has rightly been emphasized in gospel presentations. The incredible testimony of the Apostles praying and singing hymns at midnight in prison with their feet in stocks, must have brought conviction to the jailor, reinforced by the earthquake, causing him to cry out, **"Sirs, what must I do to be saved?"** Since he had already had a change of mind, their response did not leave anything out: **"Believe in the Lord Jesus, and you will be saved, you and your household,"** (Acts 16:30-31, NAS). They told the whole truth. Note that it was *after* they had believed and were saved, that those who had believed were also baptized (16:32-34).

When the Apostles came to Thessalonica, they went into the synagogue, **"...and for three sabbaths reasoned with them from the Scriptures, explaining and giving evidence that the Christ had to suffer and rise again from the dead"** (Acts 17:2-3). Luke says that **"some of them were persuaded,"** in describing the conversion of many devout Greeks and prominent women. Human persuasion plays a significant part in people coming to faith. After the success of this persuasive evangelism had caused a riot, the Apostles arrived in the Jewish synagogue in Berea. Luke records:

> Now these were more noble-minded than those in Thessalonica, for they received the word with great eagerness, examining the Scriptures daily *to see* whether these things were so. **Therefore** many of them **believed**, along with a number of prominent Greek women and men (Acts 17:11-12, NAS).[H]

As Bible teachers have long stressed, we must always ask what 'therefore' is *there for.* Luke is clearly showing cause and effect. There is a connection between the Bereans' mind-set and the fact that many of them came to saving faith. In making this connection, Luke is simply reflecting the Lord Jesus' own explanation of His parable of the four soils (Lk. 8:15).

When forced out of Berea, Paul left Silas and Timothy there and found a great opportunity for witness on Mars Hill in Athens among the Greek philosophers. He reminded them that God created mankind **"that they would seek God, if perhaps they might grope for Him and find Him.... Therefore having overlooked the times of ignorance, God is now declaring to men that all *people* everywhere should repent,..."** (Acts 17:27, 30). Luke goes on to tell how only a few believed there, possibly because of their proud philosophical mind-set (17:32-34).

Finding a synagogue in the cosmopolitan city of Corinth, Paul again reasoned with the people there and tried **"to persuade Jews and Greeks"** (18:4). The results were most encouraging. **"Crispus, the leader of the synagogue, believed in the Lord with all his household, and many of the Corinthians when they heard were believing and being baptized"** (Acts 18:8). Toward the end of his eighteen-month ministry there Paul also saw the conversion of the new synagogue leader, Sosthenes (Acts 18:17; 1 Cor. 1:1).

H. The NIV translation carelessly omits the 'therefore,' although the word *oun* is clearly in the Greek text.

With such great success in Corinth it is no surprise that Paul continued the same persuasive approach in the great religious center of Asia, Ephesus (18:19). He left Priscilla and Aquila there, whose witness was greatly reinforced by the arrival of Apollos, an eloquent and zealous man, who had only a rudimentary knowledge of Christ's person and work. After Priscilla and Aquila 'brought him up to speed' on the whole Christian message, he went over to Corinth and **"greatly helped those who had believed through grace, for he powerfully refuted the Jews in public, demonstrating by the Scriptures that Jesus was the Christ"** (Acts 18:27-28).

Sometime later on his third missionary tour Paul, coming back through Galatia and Phrygia to strengthen the churches, arrived in Ephesus. His interaction with a dozen disciples of John there reinforces the same pattern. Since they had even less understanding of New Testament salvation than Apollos had, Paul had to move them into the full New Testament reality of the Church-age message and experience: **"John baptized with the baptism of repentance, telling the people to believe in Him who was coming after him, that is, in Jesus"** (Acts 19:4).[1] When they received the Holy Spirit through the laying on of Paul's hands, they were transitioned from being godly Jews to becoming part of the New Testament body of Christ. Paul re-baptized them to signify this transition (19:5-6). Since they were already saved people, baptism did not contribute to their salvation in the least, but God confirmed it by giving them the Holy Spirit at this point. Since they were part of this decades-long transition to the full New Testament church, their experience was an exception to the normal order, which is the giving of the Spirit at conversion.

Luke again emphasizes Paul's confrontational witness: **"And he entered the synagogue and continued speaking out boldly for three months, reasoning and persuading _them_ about the kingdom of God"** (Acts 19:8). After completing his ministry in the two Greek provinces, Paul returned to Asia and met with the elders of the Ephesian church. His summary of his method and message in Acts 20:20-21 totally confirms this:

> **... how I did not shrink from declaring to you anything that was profitable, and teaching you publicly and from house to house, solemnly testifying to both Jews and Greeks of repentance toward God and faith in our Lord Jesus Christ.**

As we journeyed through the Gospels and Acts, we saw repentance and faith linked in Mark 1:15 and _continuously used almost interchangeably throughout_, and now Paul confirms that both are integrally connected. Thus when Ryrie speaks of "repentant faith," it is an accurate representation of the biblical message. This seems so obvious that one wonders how some can emphasize one to the exclusion of the other.

---

1 Dispensationally speaking, these men were still in the pre-Pentecost epoch as godly Jews and needed to hear the complete message of the cross and resurrection in order to receive the Holy Spirit and be baptized into the Church

Perhaps one further point will help to clarify the existing confusion. It seems clear that while the message was being proclaimed to Jews (as in the Synoptic Gospels and early chapter of Acts), the emphasis was upon repentance. As the message went out to the Gentiles (John's Gospel, later Acts, Romans, etc.), the emphasis is upon faith, trust, and believing. The Apostles contextualized* the message for their differing hearers. Missionaries have learned that as they go into diverse cultures, the way of communicating the message must be adapted for the particular culture.

Clarifying other issues

It becomes clear through our journey that the message is totally consistent and simple, that repentance and faith are the two aspects of the one condition for the receiving of forgiveness of sins, the new birth and its concomitant eternal life, all based upon the death and resurrection of Christ. *Baptism, when it is mentioned, is always subsequent to salvation and a part of full discipleship.* This pattern is also confirmed in the message which the Apostles preached and wrote (cf. Ch. 18). However, some question whether the Lord's very stringent discipleship teachings are not conditions for salvation. Chapter 11 is an examination of the three major contexts to answer this more controversial question: Matthew 10:37-38; 16:24-8=Luke 9:23-7; and Luke 14:25-34.

Conclusions

This journey through the Gospels and Acts should make it abundantly clear that repentance and faith are both necessary for salvation, but *not as separate conditions.* They are always integrally connected like the two sides of a coin, as confirmed by the constant interchangeability of terminology .

It should never be thought for a moment that water baptism should be added to simple repentant faith as necessary for salvation. If that were so, the biblical writers were guilty of constant, serious errors in omitting reference to baptism in the overwhelming majority of passages.

Nor may any other condition be added to the simple New Testament condition of repentant faith. If it seems too simple to many, it is because they are 'hung up' on the legalistic human desire to make a material contribution to their own salvation. But as this investigation will show, salvation is not in the least dependent upon human performance. It is solely by the gracious, unmerited favor of God through Jesus Christ.

I know not how the Spirit moves
    Convincing men of sin,
Revealing Jesus through the word,
    Creating faith in Him.
But I know whom I have believed,
    And am persuaded that He is able
To keep that which I've committed
    Unto Him against that day.
             -Daniel W. Whittle

HOW CAN THE DEAD BELIEVE?
THE SPIRIT'S CONVICTION

How can Evangelicals retain a divine initiative in understanding the plan of salvation? Since mankind is spiritually dead, an explanation is needed as to how *any* spiritually dead sinner can come to faith in Christ. Calvinists go back to Augustine's doctrine of irresistible grace, which involves the new birth preceding faith. Arminians, on the other hand, have a doctrine of universal prevenient (preceding) grace to enable all sinners to respond to God's message. Those in the middle do not find either solution satisfying, because neither is inductively* derived. The answer is in the explicit teaching of the Lord Jesus in the upper room, just before the cross and preparatory to the Pentecost event. This is a neglected key to the problem.

A neglected key

It is tragic that in the discussion of these issues a vital key to its resolution has been overlooked, even though clearly taught in the Upper Room Discourse (Jn. 16:7-11) and exemplified on the day of Pentecost and afterward. The only theologians who have given serious attention to the truth of the convicting work of the Spirit are Lewis Sperry Chafer and James Oliver Buswell, Jr. Few others have given more than a passing notice to this truth, if at all. In 1948, Chafer wrote, "Within the whole divine enterprise of winning the lost, there is no factor more vital than the work of the Holy Spirit in which He convinces or reproves the *cosmos* world respecting sin, righteousness, and judgment."[1] In 1962, Buswell wrote: "The doctrine of conviction as a work of the Holy Spirit prior to either regeneration or faith, it seems to me, solves this problem..."[2]

The core of the issue is how *any* spiritually dead sinner can hear the gospel, believe, and be saved. In order to solve this problem, starting from their concept of total inability, extreme Calvinists have reversed the biblical order and put the new birth before faith. On the other hand, Arminians seem to put too much emphasis upon human factors. An inductive study of the convicting or convincing work of the Spirit will lead to a mediate solution to the problem and is a vital key to resolving the centuries-old controversy between Calvinists and Arminians.

Calvinists put a great stress upon objective truth: the objective decrees of God in eternity and objective realities in redemption history. But they struggle in the subjective realm. That is, how can one be included among the elect, and how can one know if one is among the elect? What can unregenerate people do while waiting for God's irresistible grace to strike? Many Calvinists have made lists of things sinners can do to prepare themselves for God's irresistible grace in the event that they may happen to be among the elect (preparationism*). This is a bad solution to their intractable problem. It was the Anabaptists,* Moravians and pietistic* Lutherans who began to try to balance off the strong objective slant with a more personal, experiential and subjective approach. Arminians and moderate Calvinists have sought to balance the objective and subjective dimensions of salvation. Today the Pentecostal and charismatic movements have overemphasized the subjective aspect. Albeit, pietistic[A] subjectivism is an important dimension of mainstream evangelicalism today. The restoration of the doctrine of the conviction of the Spirit provides a necessary balance and is a key to this whole conundrum.

In making this proposal a vital distinction must be made, which has not been recognized in the literature. *This is the distinction between the means by which people come to saving faith in Christ, which is a process having heavy human involvement, and on the other hand, the new birth itself, which is one-hundred per cent the work of the Holy Spirit, accomplished instantaneously without any human participation.* Thus, there is a process in which the Holy Spirit works mediately through human instrumentality to bring the sinner under conviction leading to faith, which then triggers the Spirit's work of regeneration. This is a simple, but overlooked distinction.

The Determining Scriptures

The context of John 16:7-11

But I tell you the truth, it is to your advantage that I go away; for if I do not go away, the Helper [*Paraklētos*] will not come to you; but if I go, I will send Him to you. And He when He comes, will convict the world of sin and righteousness and judgment; concerning sin, because they do not believe in Me; and

---

A. Pietism was an evangelical movement in the Lutheran churches of northern Europe starting about 1675 with an emphasis upon a personal experience of the new birth and conversion, Bible study, personal prayer, and a godly lifestyle. Philip Spener and August Francke were key leaders.

concerning righteousness, because I go to the Father and you no longer see Me; and concerning judgment, because the ruler of this world has been judged.

The watchword, "Context is king!" is totally appropriate here. One of the main themes of the Upper Room Discourse (John 14 to 16) is the prophecy by our Lord of the coming of the Holy Spirit, which was to be fulfilled about fifty days forward on the day of Pentecost. Not only did Christ state this explicitly, but He reaffirmed it in many different ways:

And I will ask the Father and He will give you another Helper, that He may be with you forever, that is the Spirit of truth, whom the world cannot receive, because it does not behold Him or know Him, but you know Him because He abides with you, and will be in you (John 14:16-17).

Then, He identified a specific day in which the Spirit would be *given* (14:20), which is obviously Pentecost. In subsequent chapters, He kept weaving this idea into the rest of the discourse. In 14:26 and again in 15:26, He spoke of the Father *sending* the Spirit and also about the Spirit *coming* from the Father, a word He used again in 16:7, 8, & 13. In 15:26, He also spoke of the Spirit *proceeding* from the Father in the present tense, a reference which has occasioned the controversial and dubious notion of the eternal procession of the Spirit. However, it seems likely in the context that this is a futuristic use of the present tense, thus reinforcing the other statements. Lastly, in 16:7 He reiterated the verb 'send.' Thus, 'give' is used once, 'send' three times, 'come' four times, and 'proceed' once. *It is clear that the Lord Jesus is predicting Pentecost as an advent of the Holy Spirit equally as earthshaking as His own at Bethlehem.* Frank Bottome was not off target in penning the hymn, "The Comforter Has Come."

Of course, we all believe in the omnipresence of the Holy Spirit and might wonder how Christ could predict the advent of an omnipresent Person. Although the Son of God Himself shares the omnipresence of the Trinity, He had an advent through incarnation. Therefore, Charles Ryrie's clarification that the Holy Spirit came to reside in the newborn church is very cogent.[3] In any case, it is clear from the context that the Holy Spirit was to begin His special ministry of conviction on the day of Pentecost. Thus, it is astonishing that few, if any, writers have made the connection between the convicting work of the Spirit and the events recorded in Acts 2. First, the meaning of the key words must be carefully examined.

The meaning of *elegchein* (to convict, convince)

Elegchein and its cognates are mostly used in the writings of Greek philosophers in the intellectual realm of the controverting of propositions. Epictetus used it in an ethical sense, of the cure of souls. In the Septuagint, it translates Hebrew words meaning, 'to rebuke,' 'to shame,' 'to punish,' 'condemn,' 'convict,' 'to test,' and 'to examine.' Buchsel concluded that:

.. it denotes the disciplining and educating of man by God as a result of His judicial activity. This embraces all aspects of education from the conviction of the sinner to chastisement and punishment, from the instruction of the righteous by severe tests to his direction by teaching and admonition.

It is used seventeen times in the New Testament and means "to show someone his sin and to summon him to repentance." The means used to bring this about are: the prophet, conscience, the self-revelation of light, divine instruction, and the Law. *Elegchos* has the sense of 'proof,' 'convincing,' 'refutation,' 'investigation,' and 'account.' The abstract noun *elegsis* means 'persuasion,' 'refutation.'[4] The BAG lexicon lists four meanings: "1. *bring to light, expose, set forth.... 2. convict or convince someone of someth., point someth. out to someone....* 3. *reprove, correct....* 4. heightened, punish, discipline...."[5] (Current English dictionaries indicate that the older usage of 'convict' has been replaced by 'convince' except in the legal sphere.)

Most of the New Testament usages have to do with confronting and reproving moral error, whether in unbelievers (Lk. 3:19) or believers (most). Paul used it twice to encourage Titus to refute and correct the doctrinal errors of Christians (1:9, 13). Only in 1 Corinthians 14:24 is it used in the sense of John 16 to refer to convicting or convincing an unbeliever to repent and believe the gospel. Jude used it of the return of Christ in final judgment upon the godless (15). The abstract noun *elegchos* is used in Hebrews 11:1 of faith as a conviction of the unseen, that is, in a subjective sense.

The meaning of *kosmos* (world)

It should go without saying that John's usage of *kosmos*, which is so replete at about a hundred times, must be determinative as to the Lord's meaning here. Abbott-Smith lists four connected usages:

1 *order* ... 2. *ornament, adornment* ... 3. Later, the *world* or *universe*, as an ordered system ... 4. In late writers only, *the world, i.e. the earth*;... hence by meton., (a) of the human inhabitants of the world ... (b) of worldly affairs or possessions ...; (c) in ethical sense, of the ungodly, the world as apart from God and thus evil in its tendency....[6]

John overwhelmingly uses it in the fourth sense, especially 4.(c). This is not controversial, and thus in the exegesis of the passage, the focus must be on the Holy Spirit's ministry to the unregenerate people of this evil world-system, who need salvation. This is made even more striking by Christ's reference to Satan as the **"prince of this world"** in John 12:31, and again even more significantly here (Jn. 16:11).

The meaning of *paraklētos* (One who entreats, exhorts, encourages)

Translators have struggled to come up with the right word to render this multifaceted term. *Paraklētos* is used by John alone, four times here of the Lord's description of Himself and the coming Holy Spirit (as well as in 1 John 2:2). To get the meaning of this word in this context it is important to connect it with its verb, *parakalein*, which many scholars have failed to do. The BAG lexicon mentions how the active idea of the verb became more prominent in the meaning of the noun, thus "equating *paraklētos* with *parakalein*." They continue: "The Gk. interpreters of John's gosp. understood it in the active sense=*parakalon* or *paraklētōr* ..."[7] Abbott-Smith lists as prominent meanings of the verb, 'beseech,' 'entreat,' 'admonish,' 'exhort,' 'encourage,' and for the abstract noun, *paraklēsis*, 'appeal,' 'entreaty,' 'exhortation,' 'encouragement.' These connotations greatly open up the meaning of *paraklētos* in John 14-16, since they directly connect with the ministries of Christ and the Holy Spirit.[B]

The development of Christ's thought

Christ, the first Paraklētos. When Christ promised the coming of the Holy Spirit on the day of Pentecost, one of His significant ministries would be the convicting, convincing, exposing, and reproving of mankind. The verb is a simple future which would imply that this ministry of the Spirit had not yet begun, and thus, that Pentecost was to be its beginning. Indeed, there is no reference to any such activity of the Spirit in the Old Testament or Gospel accounts. Christ Himself was the first *Parakletos*, who, while He was in the world, sought to bring people under the conviction of sin, righteousness, and judgment by His entreaty and exhortation.

The Lord implied that He is the first *paraklētos* in referring to the Holy Spirit as **"another."** Clearly, Christ's ministry was full of urgent entreaty, admonishing, exhorting, and encouraging of unbelievers and disciples. He also is represented as believers' advocate before the Father (Rom. 8:34; Heb. 7:25; Mt. 10:32; 1 Jn. 2:2). Similarly, the Holy Spirit's ministries include urgent entreaty, admonishing, exhorting, and encouraging, especially in John 16:8-11. But the meaning 'advocate' just doesn't fit in *this context*.

There are many examples. In the Sermon on the Mount, Christ used the Mosaic Law to bring Pharisaic Jews under the conviction of their sin and recognition of their need of His righteousness. His sinless character and supernatural works brought conviction to the Apostles, such as in Luke 5:8, when Peter saw the miraculous draft of fish. His interview with the self-righteous rich young ruler shows His use of the Law to bring conviction (Mt. 19:16-26). He sought to show him that he did not love his neighbor as himself, which made him a sinner. Now, as Christ was to depart, and His personal ministry of conviction must necessarily end, He promised the Holy Spirit as another *Paraklētos*. The Spirit would begin to take the responsibility for this important ministry and would not be limited to a human body.

B. The problem is the rare extra-canonical usage as 'advocate' or 'counsel' does not seem to connect with the verb *parakalein* and the noun paraklēsis *TDNT* erroneously separates discussion with separate articles by different scholars (Behm,, v: 801; Schmitz, v: 773-6, 793-7) Since the Luther and KJV rendering of "comforter" is the least common usage of the verb, it is the least helpful translation Many modern translations use "counselor," "helper," or "advocate," which miss the main point in this discourse

Christ's clarification. The Lord Jesus gave a clarification of the three-fold convicting ministry of the Spirit. Although His explanation in John 16:8-11 is not transparent, by drawing upon the broader context the meaning is clarified. In 16:9, He explained that the conviction of sin especially relates to the world's unbelief in Him: "... **concerning sin, because they do not believe in Me.**" Earlier John referred to mankind's sin as the key issue with which Christ had to deal (John 1:5, 29) and the main obstacle for people to come to Christ (1:5, 10-11, 3:19-21). More specifically, He focused upon the one sin which is the central issue in order to be saved—rejection of the Messiah Himself (3:18, 36). This highlights the uniqueness of *unbelief as the only unforgivable sin.* People need to be convinced that they are sinners, but especially, of the seriousness of unbelief in Christ.

John used the symbolism of the spiritual blindness of mankind repeatedly in his Gospel. Christ is the light come into the world, and men were so spiritually blind that God had to send John the Baptizer to point people to the light (1:6-9).[C] The Apostle Paul confirmed the spiritual blindness of the unregenerate as not being just a natural problem of man's sin, but also a satanic blindness as well (2 Cor. 4:3-4):

> But even if our gospel is veiled, it is veiled to those who are perishing, in whose case the god of this world has blinded the minds of the unbelieving, that they might not see the light of the gospel of the glory of Christ, who is the image of God.

Chafer clearly emphasized this connection with spiritual blindness.[8]

Since mankind is spiritually dead, a significant issue arises. The extreme Calvinistic scenario is that since man is spiritually dead and unable to believe, therefore, sinners must be born again in order to believe. They have got it backward since Christ said in reference to the new birth: "**Very truly I tell you, a time is coming and has now come when the dead will hear the voice of the Son of God and those who hear will live**" (Jn. 5:25, TNIV). He did not say that the *regenerate* shall hear, but that the *dead* shall hear and come to life spiritually. The convicting, convincing work of the Spirit is a key as to how this can happen.

The second focus of conviction is in verse 10, "... **and concerning righteousness, because I go to the Father, and you no longer behold Me.**" While He was in the world, Christ brought conviction of righteousness, since He was the perfect example of absolute righteousness. Just the presence of His sinless person brought conviction about the source of true righteousness; He was full of grace and truth. Also consider that He went back to the Father by way of the cross and resurrection, thus, providing the basis for sinners to be declared righteous. Therefore, based upon Christ's going to the Father in

C. It should be noted that John 1:9 does not make the enlightenment of Christ's advent universal, as held by the Quakers, but rather general. Few translators have recognized that *panta anthropon* can easily be rendered "all mankind," that is, Christ's enlightenment reaches out to all mankind, not just Jews.

this way, Paul could expound this doctrine of justification in Romans, the theme of which is the righteousness of God, or more exactly, a righteousness from God. Therefore, Christ is the ultimate source of righteousness for unrighteous mankind (Rom. 10:4). This is the heart of the gospel about which the Spirit came to convince mankind.

The third focus of conviction is in verse 11, "**... and concerning judgment, because the ruler of this world has been judged.**" Again, the connection is not transparent. This is a reference to Satan's judgment in the cross, and connects with John 12:31-32: "**Now judgment is upon this world; now the ruler of this world shall be cast out, and I, if I be lifted up from the earth, will draw all men to Myself.**" Satan's doom was sealed in the cross, even though he is now a usurper at large, prowling about like a roaring lion (1 Pet. 5:8). Most relevant to the lost people of this world-system is the fact that their doom has also been sealed, as long as they have not been liberated from Satan's power by faith in Christ. The Lord Jesus made this logical connection of the judgment of Satan through the cross and His drawing all mankind to Himself in faith. The convicting work of the Spirit is the means by which He is drawing all mankind to Himself. Satan's power was broken in the cross, as Paul later affirmed in Colossians 2:15: "**When He had disarmed the rulers and authorities, He made public display of them, having triumphed over them through Him.**" Satan's condemnation and expulsion from God's presence in heaven makes it imperative that those who are under his sway claim the Messiah's finished work to experience redemption-liberation. *Since the Spirit's ministry focuses on these three area, our witness for Christ must be brought into harmony with the Spirit's strategy in pointing people to Christ.*

Its Historical Actualization

Pentecost

With the context of the Upper Room Discourse and His promise to send the Spirit in mind, it is now obvious that the fulfillment of that promise in the events of Acts 2 must be examined. Indeed, the Lord Himself confirmed this fulfillment a week before Pentecost (Acts 1:4-5, 8):

> Gathering them together, He commanded them not to leave Jerusalem, but to wait for what the Father had promised, 'Which,' *He said,* 'you heard of from Me; for John baptized with water, but you will be baptized with the Holy Spirit not many days from now.' ... but you will receive power when the Holy Spirit has come upon you; and you shall be My witnesses ...'

As the historical record is examined, Acts 2:37 stands out. After Peter completed his sermon, boldly proclaiming the risen Messiah and charging Israel with His death, Luke records: "**Now when they heard *this*, they were pierced to the heart, and said to Peter and the rest of the apostles, 'Brethren, what shall we do?'**" Thousands of Jews were evidently under the conviction of the Spirit, although not yet saved were asking how they could be. The verb *katanussein* used here occurs only once and means, "1. *to strike or prick violently.* 2. *to stun.* 3. of strong emotion, pass., *to be smitten: tēn kardian*, Ac 2^{37}."[9]

The answer comes immediately: **"And Peter *said* to them, 'Repent, and let each of you be baptized in the name of Jesus Christ for the forgiveness of your sins, and you shall receive the gift of the Holy Spirit'"** (Acts 2:38). They needed to repent as a condition of receiving the Holy Spirit. Thus, in the brief time between v. 37 and their actual repentance, they were the recipients of the Spirit's convicting ministry, but not yet of His regenerating work. Conviction precedes repentance, which precedes the gift of the Spirit's indwelling and new birth. The Spirit used the supernatural gift of languages and Peter's sermon as the means of bringing them under conviction. Conviction is a mediate or indirect ministry of the Spirit, as contrasted with the work of regeneration, which is direct.

Luke did not record whether the three thousand who were saved were the only ones who had come under conviction. Presumably, others came under conviction but did not repent at that time. Perhaps many of them were among the thousands who were saved subsequently. Perhaps many never came to repentance and faith. Luke does not say.

Other examples

Positive examples. There are other incidents in Acts which connect with this. Some are explicit statements of a positive response to the Spirit's working. Moreover, every time people are being saved, it implies the Spirit's convicting work is involved, whether Luke is explicit or not. In connection with the healing of the lame man outside the temple gate, the Apostles' witness caused thousands more to believe (3:11–4:4). Luke consistently connected the disciples being Spirit-filled with their boldness and the resulting fruitfulness of their witness (4:8, 31, 33; 5:32; 6:10; 7:55; 9:17; 11:24; 13:9, 52; etc.). In Samaria, Philip saw crowds come to Christ (8:5-8).

Even when Saul of Tarsus was persecuting Christians, the Holy Spirit was convicting him through the witness of Stephen and other Christians' testimonies, as he dragged them into court. The risen Lord said to him, **"It is hard for you to kick against the goads"** (Acts 26:9-14). Up to that point he had been resisting the conviction of the Spirit. But after his conversion and subsequent filling with the Spirit, he immediately proclaimed Christ boldly in Damascus (9:17-22). Peter's ministry in Lydda, Sharon, and Joppa got a massive response (9:35, 42), which was connected with outstanding miraculous signs by the Holy Spirit.

Cornelius and his household were not saved people before Peter preached to them (11:14), but the Spirit must have been working in their lives before they heard the gospel from Peter. The outstanding follow-up of the conversion of these first Gentiles took place in Antioch of Syria, where a large number of Gentiles were saved through Jewish believers from Cyprus and Cyrene, and later, through the Spirit-filled ministry of Barnabas (Acts 11:19-26). The Spirit continued working there as Paul and Barnabas were sent out as the first cross-cultural missionaries among the Gentiles (13:1-3).

On their first stop in Cyprus, Barnabas and Paul were the instruments of the Spirit in persuading the proconsul, Sergius Paulus, who had summoned them to share the gospel (13:6-12). After Paul's sermon in the synagogue of Antioch of Pisidia, Luke records: "**And as Paul and Barnabas were going out, the people kept begging that these things might be spoken to them the next Sabbath**" (Acts 13:42). Many were under conviction and some were being saved. Many were convicted but not yet saved. Responding to the Jewish opposition, the Apostles announced: "**It was necessary that the word of God should be spoken to you first; since you repudiate it and judge yourselves unworthy of eternal life, behold, we are turning to the Gentiles**" (Acts 13:46). Many of these convicted Gentiles rejoiced at the opportunity and believed (13:48). This verse has been a major Calvinistic proof-text, but the translation needs to be corrected to (cf. Ch. 23, pp. 313-15): "**And as many as had been devoting themselves to eternal life were believing.**"

On Paul's second missionary journey, the account of Lydia's conversion stand out: "**... and the Lord opened her heart to respond to the things spoken by Paul**" (Acts 16:14). Although Calvinists see this as an example of irresistible grace, it can equally be understood as a reference to the convincing, enlightening work of the Spirit. It is our responsibility to be the instruments of the Spirit in opening sinners' eyes to the truth (Acts 26:18). Subsequently, the Philippian jailer also was certainly under conviction to have cried out, "**Sirs, what must I do to be saved?**" (Acts 16:30). He had heard the testimony of Paul and Silas in prison and being overwhelmed by the extraordinary circumstances, recognized his own need of eternal salvation. Paul's response was similar to that of Peter on the day of Pentecost, except that he used the imperative "believe" instead of "repent."

The language Luke used to describe Paul's witness at Thessalonica ('**reasoned**,' '**explaining**,' '**giving evidence**') indicates that he sought to be the Spirit's instrument in persuading the Jews and devout Gentiles in the synagogue, which resulted in many conversions (Acts 17:1-4). This is harmonious with the meaning of *elegchein*, as seen above. Again at Athens and Corinth, Luke used similar words related to convincing and persuading, i.e., '**reasoning**,' '**trying to persuade**' (17:17; 18:4). Especially at Corinth, this convincing ministry of the Spirit through Paul was effective in the conversion of two synagogue rulers, Crispus and Sosthenes, during his eighteen-month ministry there, as well as many other Jews and Gentiles (18:8, 17). The example Calvin gave from 1 Corinthians 14:24-25 is also relevant: "**But if all prophesy, and an unbeliever or an ungifted man enters, he is convicted by all, he is called to account by all; the secrets of his heart are disclosed; and so he will fall on his face and worship God, declaring that God is certainly among you.**" Note that the unbeliever is convicted by the instrumentality of people, not by some 'irresistible grace.'

Negative reactions. There are also some accounts which might be understood as negative reactions to the Spirit's conviction. After the second arrest of the Apostles and Peter's defense, there is a negative reaction in Acts 5:33: "**But when they heard this they were <u>cut to the quick</u> and were intending to slay them.**" After Stephen's defense and charge, a similar reaction is seen using the same word, *diapriein*: "**Now when they heard this they were <u>cut to the quick</u>, and they began gnashing their teeth at him**" (Acts 7:54). They were almost surely under the conviction of the Holy Spirit. Stephen had just accused them of always resisting the Holy Spirit (7:51). If so, it would indicate that not all who are convicted come to faith. Related to this is the account of governor Felix's reaction to Paul's forthright witness in which he was under conviction: "**And as he was discussing righteousness, self-control and the judgment to come, Felix became frightened and said, 'Go away for the present, and when I find time, I will summon you'**" (Acts 24:25).

Human instrumentality. Since the cognates of *elegchein* have the sense of 'proof', 'refutation', and 'persuasion', it is relevant to consider accounts where the Holy Spirit was using the Apostles in related activity. Luke records in Acts 14:1: "**And it came about that in Iconium they entered the synagogue of the Jews together, and spoke <u>in such a manner</u> that a great multitude believed, both of Jews and Greeks.**" In Acts 18:28 there is a similar emphasis upon the human instrumentality in reference to Apollos's witness: "**... for he powerfully refuted the Jews in public, demonstrating by the Scriptures that Jesus was the Christ.**" There are also a number of allusions to Paul's use of reasoning and persuasion in his evangelism, such as 18:4: "**And he was reasoning in the synagogue every Sabbath and trying to persuade Jews and Gentiles.**" Human instrumentality comes through very clearly in Paul's testimony about Christ's apostolic charge to him: "**... to open their eyes so that they may turn from darkness to light and from the dominion of Satan to God, in order that they may receive forgiveness of sins and an inheritance among those who have been sanctified by faith in Me**" (Acts 26:18). It is clear that the above enumerated things are the work of the Holy Spirit, but Christ mandated Paul to do them. The issue is the Holy Spirit's use of human instrumentality in His ministry of conviction. Extreme Calvinists tend to see all of the Spirit's ministries functioning directly and immediately, thus minimizing human instrumentality.[10] It is of interest that Berkhof mentions that Lutherans use this passage in constructing an *ordo salutis* (plan of salvation), but as a Calvinist, he apparently did not feel comfortable in doing so.[11]

The epistles. The epistles also shed some light on this ministry of the Spirit: "**And it is the Spirit who bears witness, because the Spirit is the truth. For there are three that bear witness, the Spirit and the water and the blood; and the three are in agreement**" (1 John 5:7-8). Here the focus is on objective witnesses to the gospel message by his reference to the water and the blood. Thus, the Spirit uses objective witnesses in His work of conviction. Hebrews 10:29 also refers to those who are convicted but never really come to repentance and faith, counterfeit believers: **"How much severer punishment do you think he will deserve who has trampled under foot the Son of God, and has regarded as unclean the blood of the covenant by which he was sanctified, and has insulted the Spirit of grace?"** Since these had never been regenerated, apparently they were convicted by the Spirit and in failing to believe had insulted the Holy Spirit by rejecting so much light (cf. Ch. 13). Jude 15 also speaks of Christ in His coming convicting the ungodly, but it will be too late for repentance then.

The Extent of Conviction

One question that has been minimally discussed is the extent of the Spirit's ministry of conviction. Is it universal, is it general, or is it limited only to the elect? The answers to this question from Chafer and Buswell are puzzlingly inconsistent. Chafer, as a moderate Calvinist, held that it is limited to the elect.[12] Since he had always stressed the world-system of the unregenerate as hostile to God and taught general redemption, this is inconsistent; his Calvinistic leanings bleed through. On the other hand, Buswell, as a five-point Calvinist, posited a universal ministry of conviction.[13] He arrived at this through misunderstanding of John 1:9 and his belief that the witness of nature is part of the witness used by the Spirit in conviction. His conclusion, however, is more consistent with Arminian theology. Much more satisfying, in the light of the biblical examples of conviction noted above, is the view of John Walvoord: "The fact is that the Spirit of God brings conviction and understanding to many who never believe, who turn from the gospel even after the way of salvation is made plain to them."[14] This is in harmony with the mediate nature of many of God's workings in relation to world evangelization. This is also in harmony with Calvin's understanding: "Under the term *world* are, I think, included not only those who would be truly converted to Christ, but hypocrites and reprobates."[15]

The Nature of Conviction

One outstanding question then, is whether conviction is objective or subjective, external or internal. From the evidence given above, conviction seems to work both internally through believers and externally though objective evidence. The emphasis of the secular and Septuagintal usage of *elegchein* was objective. Since the Holy Spirit came to indwell the Church, it follows that He works through the members of Christ's body as they proclaim the word of God. This is the clear pattern of the book of Acts. In any case, He uses human instrumentality.

There is another remaining question. Since the Spirit's ministry of conviction was clearly said to have begun at Pentecost, how did pre-Pentecost saints come to saving faith? Apparently the work of conviction was *an enhancement* given to the church for a more effective impact of the gospel after the day of Pentecost. But as seen in earlier chapters, a balanced view of depravity does not preclude sinners from exercising repentant faith on their own. This may sound shocking to Calvinists, but it is what the inductive biblical data leads to.

Conclusions

In making a distinction between the means that the Holy Spirit uses in bringing spiritually dead sinners to saving faith and the direct work of the Spirit in the new birth, a key emerges as to how the spiritually dead can believe prior to regeneration. The Spirit's conviction of the sinner through the human instrumentality of ministry of the word of God best explains all the Scriptural data. Since we are to be the instruments which the Holy Spirit uses to bring conviction, we must follow the apostolic example by focusing on the three areas which Christ emphasized.

Limiting it to the elect moves the focus back to a deterministic view of God's decrees. Universalizing it to all men at all times does not do justice to Christ's use of the future tense and the rest of the evidence. Although Calvin's references to it are harmonious with this, it does not fit into the system of extreme Calvinism, especially their doctrine of irresistible grace.

---

1   Lewis Sperry Chafer, *Systematic Theology* (Dallas. Dallas Seminary Press, 1948), VI, p 88

2   Buswell, *Systematic Theology*, II, p 163.

3   Since Dr Ryrie made this point in class, there is undoubtedly documentation somewhere in his many books

4   Friedrich Buchsel in Gerhard Kittel, ed , *Theological Dictionary of the New Testament*, II, pp 473-476.

5   William F Arndt and F Wilbur Gingrich, *A Greek-English Lexicon of the New Testament*, pp 248-9

6   G Abbott-Smith, *A Manual Greek Lexicon of the New Testament* (Edinburgh: T & T. Clark, 1937), p. 255

7   Arndt and Gingrich, *Greek-English Lexicon*, pp 623-4.

8   Chafer, VI, p 90

9. Abbott-Smith, p 237

10   Charles Hodge, *Systematic Theology*, II, p 663.

11   Berkhof, *Systematic Theology*, p 416

12   Chafer, VI, p. 94

13   Buswell, II, p 160

14   John F Walvoord, *The Holy Spirit*, p. 111, also Ryrie, *Basic Theology*, pp 324-5

15   John Calvin, *Commentary on the Gospel According to John*, p. 138, see also *Institutes* , 3.24 8

Then I grasped that the justice of God is that righteousness by which through grace and sheer mercy God justifies us through faith. Thereupon I felt myself to be reborn and to have gone through open doors into paradise. The whole of Scripture took on a new meaning, and whereas before the justice of God had filled me with hate, now it became to me inexpressibly sweet in greater love.

-Martin Luther

INSTANT SALVATION: RIGHT STANDING AND NEW BIRTH

One might think that for evangelical Christians justification by faith alone would be a 'slam dunk,' a universally accepted doctrine. Recent events, such as the *Evangelicals and Catholics Together* (*ECT*) and the document signed in Augsburg on Reformation Day, 1999, between Lutherans and Catholics, required this chapter. But then there are many other compromises of this glorious truth, which make it clear that the gospel is not just under eclipse but also under siege as well. According to surveys of George Barna, James Hunter, and others, 77% of Evangelicals say that mankind is basically good by nature and 87% say that in salvation God helps those who help themselves.[1]

This is not unimportant or marginal truth. The Apostle Paul saw the compromises of this truth by the legalists in the Galatian churches as a major threat to the gospel of Christ. He accused them of deserting Christ for another gospel and twice repeated the warning that anyone who preaches a contrary gospel is accursed (Gal.1:6-9). Paul made very clear that law-works neither justify us before God nor matures us in the Christian life. Paul feared that he had labored over the Galatians in vain because of their legalistic reversion to mere observances (4:9-11). He told the legalists that they had cut themselves off from Christ and had moved outside of the pale of His grace (5:4).

As Paul later wrote his theological expansion of this to the church in Rome, he emphasized that the righteousness which comes from God in the gospel is available to sinful man only **"by faith from first to last"** (1:16-17 NIV). He went on to expound that glorious truth of *justification by faith alone*, which was the watchword of the Reformation.

The Reformers' concerns. Martin Luther said that justification by faith alone is the "article upon which the church stands or falls."[2] It was the

95

material principle of the Reformation, because it was the essential difference between the Romanist concept of salvation and the great biblical
doctrine. He found the legalisms into which the Galatians had fallen closely
akin to the legalisms of the Roman Catholic church.

Although it was the grossness of the sale of indulgences which triggered
Luther's ninety-five theses against Romanist errors, the heart of his concern
was the denial of justification by faith alone. Not only did Roman Catholics
have an erroneous definition of justification as 'to make righteous,' and a
serious confusion of justification and sanctification, but the whole Roman
system itself was a denial of the faith-alone principle of Galatians and
Romans. Their understanding of the sacraments as the means by which
merit is distributed to the faithful from the Church's treasury of merit was
totally opposed to the biblical doctrine.

The Reformers saw this as the essence of the gospel of Christ. 'Evangelical' comes from the Greek word for gospel, *euangelion*. Since the
modernist-fundamentalist controversy (early 20th cent.), this word is used to
describe those who hold to the inerrancy of Scripture, because the essence
of the gospel is dependent upon the trustworthiness of the Bible. Too
frequently the word Evangelical is used merely as a synonym for Protestant,
but it is clear that most Protestants no longer hold to the trustworthiness of
the Scripture or the essence of the gospel— justification by grace through
faith alone.

The Reformers saw Romanism as an eclipse of the true gospel. R. C.
Sproul explains, "An eclipse of the sun does not destroy the sun. An eclipse
obscures the light of the sun. It brings darkness where there was light. The
Reformation sought to remove the eclipse so that the light of the gospel
could once again shine in its full brilliance, being perceived with clarity."[3]

Since the Reformation, a number of other movements have also
eclipsed the gospel: dead orthodoxy's minimizing the personal dimension,
modernism's outright denial, neo-orthodoxy's philosophical word-juggling,
postmodernism's relativism, and the cults' use of proof-texting* and
extrabiblical authorities. Even within evangelicalism there are a number of
theological movements which compromise the purity of justification by
grace through faith alone.

Justification defined

First, the heart of Paul's statement in Romans must be set out:

"... being justified as a gift by His grace through the redemption which is in
Christ Jesus" (Rom. 3:24); "For we maintain that a man is justified by faith
apart from the works of the Law" (Rom. 3:28); "But to the one who does not
work, but believes in Him who justifies the ungodly, his faith is reckoned as
righteousness" (4:5); "But the free gift is not like the transgression. For if by
the transgression of the one the many died, much more did the grace of
God and the gift by the grace of the one Man, Jesus Christ, abound to the

many" (5:15); "**For the wages of sin is death, but the free gift of God is eternal life in Christ Jesus our Lord**" (6:23).

A major problem in the dialog between Catholics and Evangelicals over the centuries has been the definition of terms. In the *ECT* dialogue, this is obviously a major sticking point. Chuck Colson admitted to R. C. Sproul in a private conversation that the two sides do not always agree on the meaning of statements in the *ECT* document.[4] So it is imperative to focus upon the definition of terms used in the discussion.

The truth of justification has been obscured by the perpetuation of Latin-origin words in theological discussion. This goes back to the dominant use of the erroneous Latin Vulgate for over a millennium, by both Catholics and Protestants. Luther struggled with the righteousness of God as an attribute of God, since it seemed to mock him in his great sense of sinfulness. But when through his study of Romans he grasped for the first time that God makes righteousness available to the sinner by justification, he was born again and began to love God.

Since the Greek word which Paul uses (*dikaioein*) means "to declare righteous," it would have been clearer if the translators had simply translated it this way.[A] But translators and theologians have stuck to the more obscure and ambiguous word, 'to justify.' The Greek word clearly has a forensic, legal connotation and was in the language of the courts. Paul presented the truth of God's declaration of the sinner as righteous in His sight based on faith alone, without works of any kind. Following Paul's teaching, the Reformers stressed that it was an *alien* righteousness, that is, alien to the sinner before conversion. Romanism stubbornly clung to the error of a prior, infused righteousness, that is, that God declares the righteous to be righteous.[5] They objected to the 'legal fiction' of the evangelical doctrine. But Evangelicals have understood justification as an early step in the process of transforming a godless sinner into a saint, the last phase of which is our transformation by the resurrection at Christ's return.

Thus, although God's plan of salvation has many aspects, which include conversion, regeneration, sanctification, and ultimately glorification, God's declaration of repentant sinners to be righteous is distinct from, and not to be confused with, these other aspects. It is important to grasp the force of Paul's phrase, "the righteousness of God," throughout Romans.

It is not just the meaning of the Greek word, but the whole flow of Paul's thinking in Romans, which makes this concept abundantly clear. The Catholic Douay version, by translating the noun, *dikaiosune*, as the "justice of God," obscured the truth. The King James and subsequent translations partially clarified the idea by translating "the righteousness of God." But it

---

A. Abbott-Smith, *Manual Lexicon*, p. 116: "cl. to deem right, to do one justice; .   in NT, as LXX (1) to show to be righteous, (2) to declare, pronounce righteous."; The BAG *Lexicon*, p. 196: "2. To justify, vindicate, treat as just; . . . 3a. Be acquitted, be pronounced and treated as righteous."

was for the NIV to properly render the phrase **"a righteousness from God"** (Rom. 1:17; 3:21-22).[B] The correctness of this translation is confirmed by Paul's whole explanation in Romans 4 that justification involves God counting sinners like Abraham and David to be righteous by faith. Paul builds upon Genesis 15:6: **"And Abraham believed God, and it was reckoned to him as righteousness"** (Rom. 4:3), and upon Psalm 32:1-2: **"Blessed is the man whose sin the Lord will not take into account"** (Rom. 4:8).

This truth of imputation becomes even clearer when seen in the light of the appropriate synonyms, as 'reckon, count, account, or charge.' Paul refers to a two-fold imputation: of the believer's sin to Christ the sin-bearer, and of Christ's righteousness to believing sinners (Rom. 4:1-8; Col. 2:13-14). Thus, not only are all believers' sins charged to Christ's account when He bore them on the cross, but also His righteousness is accounted to believers to give perfect standing with God. The whole argument of Romans is based upon this truth. A study of the development of Paul's thought shows that this is exactly the main theme: a righteousness of which mankind is totally devoid (Rom. 1:18–3:23); a righteousness which God reckons to sinners by faith (3:24–5:21); a righteousness which God works in the life of the believer through the Holy Spirit (6:1–8:39); a righteousness which Israel missed and which is available to all humanity by faith (9:1–11:36); a righteousness which is worked out in human relationships (12:1–15:13); and a righteousness which is to be made known to the nations (15:14–16:27).

Based on faith alone

From Paul's explanation of the justification of Abraham and David, it is obvious that they were not consistently righteous in their conduct. For that matter, neither were most of the other Old Testament saints like Lot, Solomon, Jehoshaphat, or Manasseh,. Even New Testament saints, such as Peter and the Corinthian Christians, manifested considerable inconsistencies which would destroy salvation, if it were not based upon faith alone.

During the Reformation, Roman Catholics objected that the Apostle Paul did not use the word 'alone' in his discussion of justification. This is technically true, but when we see the flow of his thought, it is obvious that his meaning is 'by faith *alone*,' since he contrasted faith with law-works, with circumcision, and with works of righteousness in general. Surveying Paul's other letters reveals the same clarity: Galatians 2:16; 3:2-14; Ephesians 2:8-10; Titus 3:5, etc. Paul arrived at that clarity, humanly speaking, through his conversion out of Pharisaic legalism, as the Holy Spirit revealed the gospel message in its bas relief, as described in Galatians 1:11-24

B   It could be the attribute of God which Paul has in mind, if he were using the genitive case. However, in the Greek the same form is also used for the ablative case, which would be translated, **"a righteousness from God,"** as in the NIV translation. Thus Paul would not be speaking about God's attribute, but rather a righteousness which God makes available to sinful men.

Not uniquely Paul's doctrine. Some have claimed that Paul put his own spin on the gospel, standing in contradiction to the message of the Lord Jesus and the other Apostles, especially James. However, in the Gospels, the strong emphasis upon repentance and faith started right with John the Baptizer (Mt. 3:2) and was constantly reiterated by the Lord Jesus Himself (Mt. 4:17; 8:10, 13; 9:12-13, 22; 11:28-30; 18:3; 19:25-26; 20:28; 21:31-32; Mk. 1:15; 6:12; Lk. 5:20, 31-32; 13:3; 23:42-43; 24:45-49). The Lord Jesus did not choose to spell out the doctrine of justification by faith, since during His ministry the key issue was Himself and Israel's relationship to Him. Many years after Christ's resurrection and ascension, the Apostle John wrote his Gospel to focus on the necessity of believing on or receiving Him. The verb 'to believe' is found 96 times in this Gospel, with much teaching about the nature of that faith. In addition, all four Gospels record the Lord's consistent opposition to Judaism's traditionalism, externalism, and legalism, which is the basis upon which Paul built his theology. The survey of the apostolic preaching, (*kērugma*) in Acts also confirms that Paul's doctrine was in total harmony with this (Acts 2:28; 3:16; 5:31; 10:43; 11:17-18; 13:38-9; 15:11; 16:31; 17:11-12, 30; 20:21; 22:16; 24:24; & 26:18-20; cf. Ch. 7 & 18).

Harmony with the Apostle James. The major problem in the minds of many opponents of this is James' teaching in his epistle: "**You see that a man is justified by works, and not by faith alone**" (Jas. 2:24). This requires clarification. It is clear that James did not write to contradict Paul, since James wrote before Paul. On the other hand, it is highly unlikely that Paul was writing to contradict James, since Paul wrote much about the importance of good works in the life of the believer (cf. Titus). Paul was not an antinomian in denying absolutes of morality, since he wrote about being under "the law of Christ" (1 Cor. 9:21). Luther wrongly thought to resolve the apparent contradiction by denigrating James' epistle.

The first clarification comes from the proper translation of 'to justify': 'to declare righteous.' The difference between Paul and James is clarified when the subject of this verb is considered. In Paul's writings it is God who declares the sinner righteous by faith alone. James, however, is concerned about how *other people* view a professing believer, and the necessity of showing faith to others so that *they* will declare the believer righteous: "**But someone may well say, 'You have faith, and I have works; show me your faith without the works, and I will show you my faith by my works'**" (Jas. 2:18). In that case, others are the subject of the verb 'to declare righteous.'

A second consideration is the differing usage of the verb 'to believe' by Paul and James. Paul is obviously referring to genuine faith or trust in Christ, whereas James may be using it in the sense of a mere profession of faith. There is a clue in James 2:19: "**You believe that God is one. You do well; the demons also believe, and shudder.**" Here believing could mean intellectual assent to the truth, rather than trust in Christ as Savior. Other examples of such usage are: John 2:23-25; 6:64-66; 8:32 and Acts 8:13, 18-24. However, other good scholars have pointed out that even if James refers to true faith, the other considerations resolve the problem. Alternatively, James could be referring to ongoing faith in the Christian life, since the rest of the letter is addressed to believers.

Thirdly, recognize the differing definitions of 'works,' as both use the same word but with different terms in mind. By works Paul speaks of law-works or works by which people are trying to earn merit before God. James, on the other hand, means the fruit of true faith in the life of the believer. Believers are justified in the sight of men by leading consistent lives.

Both Paul and James use Abraham as an example to make differing points. Paul refers to Genesis 15:6, near the beginning of Abram's life of faith, even before his name was changed. James refers to the triumphant pinnacle of his life of faith about forty years later, when he offered up Isaac on Mount Moriah. It is significant that almost half of the human race today believes that he offered up his son there (even though Muslims believe it was Ishmael). Thus, Abram was declared righteous by God based on his faith alone, as attested to by Genesis 15, but he was declared righteous by people based upon the fruit of his faith in the offering of his son.

Thus, Luther should not have denigrated the book of James in order to maintain the purity of Pauline doctrine. Indeed, Luther was so over-whelmed with the rediscovery of the marvelous truth of justification by faith alone that he reacted too far in the opposite direction by making the dichotomy between faith and works too sharp. Some today are doing the same.

The harmony of grace and faith

Paul made a special point of the perfect harmony of the principle of grace with a faith-alone salvation:

> **For this reason it is by faith, that *it might be* in accordance with grace, in order that the promise may be certain to all the descendants, not only to those who are of the Law, but also to those who are of the faith of Abraham, who is the father of us all ...** (Rom. 4:16).

This is especially important because of the misconceptions of the meaning of the word 'grace.' It is clear from Paul's usage that he means 'the unmerited favor of God,' because of the way he sets faith and works in contradistinction. He sets faith in opposition to law-works (Rom. 3:19-31; 4:13-15), to confidence in circumcision (4:9-12), and ultimately to any works of righteousness (Rom. 4:1-8; Eph. 2:8-9; Tit. 3:5).

The human race is so bent on self-salvation that even religions which parrot the word grace don't have a clue to its real meaning. Roman Catholics abundantly use the word grace, but seem clueless as to its biblical meaning. They endlessly quote the erroneous translation, "Hail, Mary, full of grace," and then go about trying to establish their own righteousness by their own works, including devotions to Mary, which is pagan.

This was true of the Pharisees in Christ's day as well (Rom. 9:30-32). The crowd of works-oriented Jews who had followed the Lord Jesus across the lake of Galilee asked, **"What shall we do, that we may work the works of God?"** His answer was incisive: **"This is the work of God, that you believe in Him whom He has sent"** (John 6:28-29). Some have mistakenly thought He was saying that faith is a work. Nothing could be farther from the truth! Rather, He was seeking to wean them away from their works-obsessed mindset. Faith is to be set in contradistinction to works in order to maintain the grace principle of salvation (Rom. 4:16).

The gracious nature of salvation

The Lord Jesus and His Apostles had to constantly struggle with the legalistic mind-set of the Jewish nation out of which they had come. The issue came into special focus as the gospel went out into the Gentile world. Hebrew Christians struggled with the idea that these pagans could be directly saved through repentant faith without first becoming Jewish through circumcision and obedience to the Mosaic Law (Acts 15:5). At the conference of the Apostles with the elders of the Jerusalem church on this issue, Peter defended the gracious nature of salvation (Acts 15:8-11):

> And God, who knows the heart, testified to them giving them the Holy Spirit, just as He also did to us; and He made no distinction between us and them, cleansing their hearts by faith. Now therefore why do you put God to the test by placing upon the neck of the disciples a yoke which neither our fathers nor we have been able to bear? But we believe that we are saved through the grace of the Lord Jesus, in the same way as they also are.

Unfortunately the decision of the council did not satisfy those legalistic teachers, because they followed Paul's missionary itinerary and promoted legalism in the churches of Galatia and in Corinth. On his third missionary tour, while in western Asia Minor, Paul heard of the Galatian situation and wrote his fiery epistle to those churches to alert them to the serious problem of undermining the gracious nature of salvation:

> I am amazed that you are so quickly deserting Him who called you by the grace of Christ, for a different gospel;... But even if we, or an angel from heaven, should preach to you a gospel contrary to what we have preached to you, he is to be accursed! (Gal. 1:6, 8).

After reminding them of the outcome of the Jerusalem Council (2:1-10), Paul quoted the words he had used to correct Peter's inconsistent behavior when some of the legalists came down to Antioch of Syria:

> We are Jews by nature and not sinners from among the Gentiles; nevertheless knowing that a man is not justified [declared righteous] by the works of the Law but through faith in Christ Jesus, even we have believed in Christ Jesus, so that we may be justified by faith in Christ and not by the works of

the Law; since by the works of the Law no flesh will be justified.... I do not nullify the grace of God, for if righteousness *comes* by the Law, then Christ died needlessly (Gal. 2:16, 21).

What Peter needed to be reminded of was that even Jewish Christians had been saved by grace through faith alone, in the same way Gentiles are saved. Although the specific issue there was circumcision and the works of the Mosaic Law, any additional requirement which people add to simple repentant faith is a serious lapse into legalism, whether it be baptism (which corresponds to circumcision) or any other human performance.   Paul summarized his point so aptly in Galatians 3:22: **"But the Scripture has shut up everyone under sin, so that the promise by faith in Jesus Christ might be given to those who believe."**

Some months later in Corinth, Paul had more leisure to pen his more reasoned theological explanation of the issue in his epistle to the church in Rome, which he hoped to visit.   These two letters became the key to the Reformation, fifteen centuries later.   In his later epistles Paul continued to emphasize the gracious nature of salvation.   After reminding the Ephesian Christians of their previous depravity he contrasted a grace-through-faith salvation with human works in 2:4-10, and clarified the trusteeship of the newly revealed message of God's gracious salvation given to him (Eph. 3:1-7).   He even reminds his missionary protégés of this crucial aspect of the message (Titus 3:4-7; 2 Tim. 1:9).   Peter and the other Apostles also wrote in harmony with this, although they did not emphasize it the way Paul did.

Instantaneous new birth by faith

Simultaneous with justification, or being put into right standing with God, is the work of the Holy Spirit in giving new birth to the sinner dead in sin. Both are contingent upon the sinner looking in faith to Christ for salvation. Since the Reformation, evangelical Christians have professed to believe in faith as a condition of justification. However, extreme Calvinists do not believe that faith is a condition for the new birth. Rather, they reverse the order to say that since those dead in sin cannot exercise faith, God must *first* give them new birth so that they may be able to believe. The inductive Scriptural data is very clear that they have got it backwards. There is a full examination of the biblical data in Chapter 17.

The term 'born again' is used so loosely today that we must be careful to define it biblically. There are half a dozen Greek words for it in the New Testament. The most common is *gennaein*, a word for either begetting or being born, which is used only by John (Jn. 1:13; 3:3, 4, 5, 6, 7, 8; 1 Jn. 2:29; 3:9; 4:7; 5:1, 4, 18). In His dialog with Nicodemus, the Lord Jesus twice used the word *anothen* with it, which has the idea of being born "from the top down," meaning "all over again." Three times He spoke to Nicodemus about being "born of the Spirit." In his first epistle, John consistently refers to "being born of God." Peter twice uses the same word with the prefix *ana* ('again') in 1 Peter 1:3 & 23, where the new birth is seen as effected by the word of God. James uses a narrower term (1:18) which refers to the successful delivery of the baby at the end of pregnancy.[6] In Titus 3:5 Paul used a compound noun, *palingenesia*, which is usually translated as 'regeneration.' In 2 Corinthians 5:17 and Galatians 6:15 he speaks of a new creation; and uses the verb, 'to create,' in Ephesians 2:10. Lastly in that context he also uses a compound verb, "to make alive with" (Eph. 2:5). Thus we might define the new birth as *God imparting new divine life by the Holy Spirit through the word of God to spiritually dead sinners* (Eph. 2:1-5).

By the analogy with human birth, it seems clear that it is not a process, but an event at a point in time. Although human birth is not quite instantaneous, spiritual new birth must be so understood.[c] Although the new birth is not expressly stated to be conditioned on faith, the eternal life which is its result is consistently said to be by faith (cf. Ch. 17).

Justification and sanctification

One most significant issue over the centuries has been the relationship of justification and sanctification. This was an issue between the Catholic church and the Reformers, between the Reformers and other Protestants, between Evangelicals with differing views of salvation truth, and even among Calvinists. Again, fuzziness of definition contributes significantly to the confusion. Therefore, the focus should be on definitions and relationships.

Definitions. Since justification is a declaration by God that the believing sinner is counted righteous in His sight, it must be a once-for-all declaration of God, not a continuing process (Rom. 4:5). Justification must be distinct from, but simultaneous with regeneration (the new birth), since both are conditioned upon faith. Believers are justified by faith and born again by faith. *Both are instantaneous and initial.*

Sanctification, however, is used in two tenses in the New Testament. It is used in the past tense of *positional sanctification* and in the present tense of our *progressive growth* in holiness. The translation into English is somewhat confusing, although not at all controversial. Both the Hebrew and Greek words have to do with being 'separated from, set apart unto something', and in that sense becoming holy or sanctified. Holy is the Anglo-Saxon word; sanctified is Latin-derived.

Believers are called "saints" sixty-one times in the New Testament, reflecting the truth that at the point of initial faith, they were *positionally* set apart for God. This term was used irrespective of the degree of holiness attained in their lifestyle. Paul said that the Corinthian believers "**had been sanctified**" (1 Cor. 6:11), even though some of them were "**yet carnal**" (3:3),

---

C. A major error which Augustine passed down to Luther is the notion that justification and the new birth are a *process*. This has been the root of much confusion. See David Anderson, "Regeneration. A *Crux Interpretum*." *JOGTS*, 13:25 (Aug 2000).

and there were serious moral problems in the church there.

On the other hand, believers are continually exhorted to progress in the ongoing process of *experiential sanctification*. Paul's exhortation in 2 Corinthians 7:1 uses the word holiness: **"Therefore, having these promises, beloved, let us cleanse ourselves from all defilement of flesh and spirit, perfecting holiness in the fear of God."** Many other terms and images communicate the same idea throughout Scripture. Theologically, this is the way the term sanctification is most commonly used, but positional sanctification must also be recognized and distinguished. It is appropriate to use the contrasts: position versus condition; standing versus state.

Relationships. Thus while positional sanctification, like regeneration, is simultaneous with, yet distinct from, justification, progressive sanctification must be kept far more distinct in our thinking. The new birth and positional sanctification begin the lifelong process of progressive sanctification. Although it is called 'progressive,' it is not always continuously up hill in the lives of all believers. Indeed, we all stumble and fall from time to time. But God's goal is that believers should be continuously separated from the world, the flesh, and Satan's forces, and set apart for the things of God.

The question that has troubled Christians over the ages is, does lack of progressive sanctification in the life of a believer in any way condition or cancel one's justification? Since justification is a declaration by God, the answer must be a resounding, NO! Lack of holiness in the life of a professing believer may raise serious questions in the minds of other Christians, but ultimately only God has the final answer as to the status of the individual. A fruitless believer may be challenged and questioned, but no one has the authority to write them off and condemn them, as many tend to do.

Many would object to the above by quoting the words of the Lord Jesus, **"You will know them by their fruits"** (Mt. 7:16). Here, as always, it is imperative to check the context. In the whole context He is warning about false prophets who come **"in sheep's clothing, but inwardly are ravenous wolves"** (Mt. 7:15). These can be and must be discerned by their fruits, but there is not a verse of Scripture which states or implies that anyone can know for sure about a professing Christian who does not show the kind of fruit which should be manifested. Peter used a whole chapter of his second epistle to instruct the churches how to deal with false teachers. But there is neither example nor exhortation to write off fruitless or problem believers.

Fruitless believers may be disciplined and/or excommunicated for some of the more serious sins. But they must not be assumed to be unbelievers. God disciplined Ananias and Sapphira (Acts 5), and the Corinthian church was to excommunicate the unrepentant immoral man (1 Cor. 5), but it must not be assumed, as many do, that they were not true believers. On the other hand, Peter discerned from the words of Simon, the baptized magician, that he was not a real believer (Acts 8:20-23). When some of the Galatians fell into denial of justification by faith alone, Paul began to have doubts about their salvation and challenged them (Gal. 4:9-11). But any doctrinal understanding which backloads justification by faith alone with a particular legalistic standard of progressive sanctification must be avoided. Does not God know ahead the outcome of each individual's life? He could not possibly justify a sinner and then later change His mind based upon lack of sanctification.

It is true that the New Testament does challenge us with tests of eternal life (as in 1 John), by which we can examine our own lives to see those lifestyle problems which seriously raise questions about our salvation. But we should also be concerned about the way that legalistic Christians write off problem believers, and the way that some fall back into an extreme introspection, which seriously undermines their own assurance.[7]

Repentance, faith, and conversion

There has been long-standing confusion about the relationship and definitions of repentance, faith, and conversion. Perhaps it started with the Roman Catholic mistranslation in the Douay Version of repentance (*metanoia*) as 'penance,' which implies some works on the part of man. Although this was corrected by Martin Luther, in the Protestant versions, and even in the contemporary Catholic versions, there still are a number of serious misconceptions about these key words and their relationships.

Repentance and conversion. Perhaps the most persistent error arises from the confusion of repentance and conversion since they are frequently linked together in Scripture. Although repentance and faith are the necessary conditions for conversion, it should be recognized that conversion goes far beyond initial repentance and faith. *Simply put, repentance is a change of mind or attitude, whereas conversion is a change of direction in lifestyle.* Before a person can change the direction of life, there must first be a change of mind or attitude. This can be illustrated by driving down an interstate highway in the wrong direction. First, there must be the realization that one is headed in the wrong direction, which is repentance. Only then can one look for the first exit to make a U-turn and get going in the right direction, which is conversion.

The danger of confusing the two is that conversion does not always, or even usually, occur overnight. It frequently involves *a process*, first of coming to repentant faith and then, after being born again, through progressive sanctification the lifestyle begins to turn around. In some cases it is sudden and radical, but in others it is slow and gradual. For example, the latter was the case with Abraham, Jacob, and many other saints in both testaments. The linguistic data does not at all support any equivalency between repentance and conversion. However, there is considerable confusion in the lexicons, theological dictionaries, and theologies, and even critical misstatements of fact (cf. App. G, *BCAA*)

Contributing to the confusion is the assumption on the part of many that since these two terms are frequently coordinated by connecting them with a conjunction, they must be synonymous, such as, "repent and return." Many examples can be given in both testaments. However, just because two terms are so associated does not imply that they are synonyms. This is as illogical as saying that apples and oranges means that apples equals oranges. Indeed, there is a logical progression of thought from repentance (a change of mind or attitude) forward to conversion (a turning around of the lifestyle). It is worth noting that many of the scholars who are guilty of this false assumption are part of a more legalistic, sacramental wing of Christendom. No, the Lord Jesus would have spoken out bluntly against any such confusion of internal change of heart with mere external change. Indeed, He frequently did so in excoriating the Pharisees.

There is some confusion in Calvinistic writings on this important distinction. Some define repentance as "a turning from all sin." This is totally without linguistic foundation in the usage in Greek literature up to New Testament times. If this definition were correct, then no one will get to heaven, because no one has turned from all sin. Even conversion cannot be so defined without serious implications.

Repentance and remorse. Another area of confusion in the minds of many is failure to distinguish repentance from remorse. The first is the consistently correct rendering of *metanoia*; the second comes from the usage of *metamelomai*. The distinction can be best illustrated by contrasting Peter and Judas. After Peter denied the Lord, he repented and was restored into fellowship with Him. After Judas' betrayal of the Lord did not work out the way he intended (He apparently hoped that the Lord would slip through the hands of His arrestors, as He had many times before), he went out, returned the money (Mt. 27:3), and committed suicide. This was remorse! Paul made the distinction clear in 2 Corinthians 7:10: "... **For the sorrow that is according to** *the will of* **God produces a repentance without regret,** *leading* **to salvation; but the sorrow of the world produces death.**" Although the usage of *metamelomai* is not always consistent, Thayer says that *metanoia/metanoein* is the "fuller and nobler term."[8]

The compromises of faith alone

The Roman Catholic compromise. The Roman Catholic compromise of biblical doctrine has already been noted. The Council of Trent (1547-8) unfortunately hardened their opposition to the Protestant position by hurling anathemas at those who affirmed the Reformation view. Rome has never retracted those anathemas. Ironically, *Evangelical and Catholics Together* did not make any reference to the teaching of justification by faith *alone*, either in the points agreed upon or in the points of disagreement for further study. *Thus they swept it under the rug!* It is clear that the sacramental system of salvation totally contradicts a by-grace-through-faith-alone salvation. No matter what word games such signatories play, Rome would have to scrap its whole merit system to be consistent with a gracious conception of salvation. This involves the notion of a treasury of merit which Christ bestowed on the Catholic Church to distribute to its people in a piecemeal fashion by means of the five relevant sacraments and the other merit-earning devotions advocated by the Church. Sproul rightly says that the contradiction is foundational and systemic.[9] It implies that the sacrifice of Christ was not sufficient for salvation, but that we must add to it.

To make the situation even worse, the fact is that now since Vatican Council II (1962-65) many Catholics do not hold to traditional Catholicism any more. There is a major liberal element in the Roman church, which holds to the evolutionary philosophy of Father Tielhard de Chardin. They retain Catholic symbolism, but the teaching is radically liberal and therefore rejects the evangelical gospel as well.

The Arminian compromise. It is not clear to what extent Jacob Arminius compromised the grace principle, but contemporary Arminianism does tend to do so by its denial of the eternal security of true believers. In their view, the believer's future salvation is contingent upon his own perseverance in faith and good works, involving a significant compromise of the by-grace-through-faith-alone principle.

The Puritan back-loading of the gospel. Recent studies, mostly coming out of Great Britain, reveal a strong tendency among the Puritans* or extreme Calvinists to back-load experiential sanctification into the salvation message. Michael Eaton observed a strong pattern of introspection and legalism, which he found unsettles the believer's assurance of final salvation. Given the Calvinist's doctrine of unconditional election, the burning question continues on through life, "How do I know whether I am among the elect, or not?" This causes them to look inward to their sanctification rather than Christward. Indeed, many great Puritan preachers went to their deathbed unsure of their elect status.[10]

This has been perpetuated to the present as manifest in the confusion of salvation and discipleship in the writings of Reformed Baptists,and others of reformed tradition. The "lordship salvation" teaching of John MacArthur also fails to distinguish salvation from discipleship.[11] In this sense it also back-loads the gospel with the works of sanctification (Cf. Ch. 11).

The sacramental compromise. Hundreds of millions of Protestants hold to a sacramental concept of salvation, which compromises the purity of gracious salvation. It starts with baptismal regeneration (cf. Ch. 18) and a sacramental concept of the Lord's supper adds to this, that is, the notion that in some magical way grace is communicated to the participant through the elements. This comes from the later church fathers, was perpetuated by the Roman Catholic Church, carried over into Protestantism, and is found especially among Lutherans, Anglicans (Episcopalians), and others.

The liberal denial. Since the end of the nineteenth century there has been a modernistic takeover of the major denominations in the western world. Kenneth Kantzer once stated that in 1890 all of the Protestant theological seminaries in the USA were evangelical except Harvard. By 1920 they had all become liberal, some more and some less. The control of these denominations fell into the hands of the liberals. (More recently the Southern Baptists alone have succeeded in reversing that trend by the Evangelicals regaining control of most of their institutions.)

The point is that liberalism, which denies the inspiration of Scripture, almost inevitably also denies the gospel of Christ. In the early twentieth century the "social gospel" replaced the salvation message in those denominations. Since then various forms of neo-orthodoxy, modernism, and now post-modernism have been in vogue in those denominations, all of which tend to undermine the gracious nature of salvation.

The charismatic de-emphasis. There is also a great danger in the charismatic movement (and to some extent in Pentecostalism as well) in shifting the emphasis away from the Reformation doctrine of justification by faith alone and the finished work of Christ, to the present subjective experience of the believer. Charismatic experiences become the focus, not the cross of Christ and the Pauline theology of the cross.

Conclusions

From all of this it is plain that the gospel of Christ is under siege in this present day. The human tendency to want to earn salvation has seriously compromised the gospel, even among professing evangelical believers.

1   As quoted by R C Sproul, *Faith Alone: The Evangelical Doctrine of Justification*, p 12

2   Martin Luther, as quoted by R C Sproul, *Faith Alone*, p 18

3   Sproul, p 19

4. Ibid, p 37

5   Alister E. McGrath, *Institia Dei A History of the Christian Doctrine of Justification*, I·31.

6   Abbott-Smith, pp. 51-2

7   Michael Eaton, *No Condemnation A New Theology of Assurance*, pp. 23-25.

8   Joseph Henry Thayer, *A Greek-English Lexicon of the New Testament*, p, 405

9   Sproul, p 68

10 Michael Eaton, *No Condemnation A New Theology of Assurance*, p 4

11 John F MacArthur, *The Gospel According to Jesus*

Blessed assurance, Jesus is mine,
Oh, what a foretaste of glory divine,
Heir of salvation, purchase of God,
Born of His Spirit, washed in His blood.

Perfect submission, all is at rest,
I in my Savior am happy and blest;
Watching and waiting, looking above,
Filled with His goodness, lost in His love.

-Fanny J. Crosby

THE SEARCH FOR FULL ASSURANCE

Over the centuries Christians have struggled with the issue of assurance. Despite the widespread proclamation of the gospel and Bible teaching today, many true Christians still struggle with this extremely important issue. Those in the Arminian tradition tend to say that we can be sure of our present salvation, but we cannot be sure of ultimate salvation. Those of the extreme Calvinistic tradition tend to say that we cannot be sure that we are among the elect and ultimately saved, but those who are the elect can never lose their salvation. Most would agree with Michael Eaton: "I find neither doctrine very encouraging. In fact, both seem rather terrifying."[1]

Evangelical Christianity is unique in affirming that assurance of ultimate salvation is possible here in this world. Muslims believe the only way to be sure of paradise is to become a martyr for Islam. Many medieval Christians also thought that martyrdom was the only sure way to salvation. Catholics believe that even the Pope himself cannot be sure! Is there a middle way which gives evangelical Christians a firm and genuine assurance of ultimate salvation based upon biblical truth? There are millions of Christians who can give a resounding "YES" to this question. However, both extreme Calvinism and Arminianism tend to undermine assurance.

Since the time in 1949 when I put my name in the promise of the Lord Jesus in John 5:24, I have had that assurance. Christ promised eternal life to those who have heard and believed His word, that they shall not come into condemnation, and have already passed out of death into life. Like millions before me, I just took Him at His word and personalized His wonderful promise. Many would respond that this is a naive and superficial under-

109

standing, and there are other complicating factors which make such an assurance dubious or even impossible. Let us sort out these issues.

Do all real Christians have assurance?

The question really should be, "should all real Christians have assurance?" The fact is that many genuine Christians do not have perfect or even substantial assurance. A fly in the ointment has been misinterpretation of Hebrews 11:1 to imply that saving faith is equal to assurance: **"Now faith is the assurance of *things* hoped for, the conviction of things not seen."** This would seem to teach that saving faith is equivalent to assurance, wouldn't it? Just a minute! A basic rule of interpretation is to see every verse in its context. What is the context of this whole eleventh chapter of Hebrews, the great faith chapter? Is it saving faith or ongoing faith in the life of the believer? Very clearly, the Apostle describes the ongoing faith of Abel, Enoch, Noah, Abraham, Sarah, and their descendants, especially focusing on Moses. These are the heroes of faith held up as examples to Hebrew Christians of victorious faith, but this does not speak of the way of salvation.

So we must not rule out the possibility, even the probability of true Christians not having a solid assurance of ultimate salvation. We must not write off Christians who lack assurance, but rather instruct, encourage, and exhort them to claim it. An intriguing biblical example of a believer who lacked assurance would be John the Baptizer in prison as recorded in Matthew 11:1-14. He sent his disciples with the question: **"Are You the Expected One, or shall we look for someone else?"** Since the Lord Jesus was not inaugurating His kingdom as John had announced, now even he is questioning the identity of the Lord, which he had proclaimed so boldly. Despite John's temporary lack of faith, the Lord commended him: **"there has not arisen *anyone* greater than John the Baptist"** (Mt. 11:11).

Certainly assurance is a major goal of all the Apostles' writings. John is very explicit as to his purpose: **"These things have I written to you who believe in the name of the Son of God, so that you may <u>know</u> that you have eternal life"** (1 Jn. 5:13). Some may quibble as to whether eternal life includes an assurance of ultimate salvation or not (a subject for four chapters in Part II), but as to the present assurance there can be no doubt. Simon Peter's exhortation is also very clear: **"Therefore, my brothers, be all the more eager to make your calling and election sure. For if you do these things, you will never fall, and you will receive a rich welcome into the eternal kingdom of our Lord and Savior Jesus Christ"** (2 Pet. 1:10-11, NIV). That he is speaking about the subjective realization of assurance is clear from the preceding exhortation to manifest Christian virtues in our lives. Since the gracious nature of salvation is clear elsewhere, as already observed, this could not be about how to get salvation.

Much full assurance. A unique Greek word is used in Paul's epistles and Hebrews which confirms the above. It is *plērophoria*, which means "full assurance, confidence."[2] Unfortunately, the full force of this word is lost in many translations. Paul used it in 1 Thessalonians 1:5 to describe the way he brought the gospel to them: "**for our gospel did not come to you in word only, but also in power and in the Holy Spirit and with** full conviction**; just as you know what kind of men we proved to be among you for your sake.**" Although this is an intensified compound word, Paul added the adjective "much" (*pollē*) to further intensify it, "**much full assurance.**"

He also prayed that the Colossians might attain "**... to all the wealth that comes from the full assurance of understanding, resulting in the true knowledge of God's mystery, that is, Christ Himself,...**" (Col. 2:2). This parallels Hebrews: "**And we desire that each one of you show the same diligence so as to realize the full assurance of hope until the end,**" and the exhortation: "**let us draw near with a sincere heart in full assurance of faith, having our hearts sprinkled clean from an evil conscience and our bodies washed with pure water**" (Heb. 6:11; 10:22). Since this was the Apostles' purpose for their disciples, there must be a reasonable expectation of its realization in life. Such assurance does not come automatically upon exercising saving faith. Words like 'eagerness,' 'diligence,' and 'attain,' put responsibility upon the believer. Although we are saved by grace through faith alone, assurance of that salvation clearly involves human participation. What are the hindrances and basis for this assurance?

What misunderstandings hinder assurance?

Subjective introspection. There are many obstacles to assurance. Instead of focusing on the promises of the word of God, many have looked within themselves for some feelings or experience as a basis of assurance. A relevant saying is attributed to Martin Luther: "Feelings come and feelings go, and feelings are deceiving. My trust is in the word of God; naught else is worth believing." Evangelicalism is distinguished by seeking to balance the objective truths of the historic Christian faith with the subjective experience of salvation in the life of the believer. Essential to that balance is starting with the objective realities of the person and saving work of Christ. We must not start with subjective experience either for salvation itself or for its assurance.

To start with our subjective personal experience is to put the cart before the horse. For example, Andrew Fuller was raised in an extreme Calvinistic tradition in the midlands of eighteenth-century England (cf. p. 347). As a teenager he struggled to come into assurance because he was looking within himself for some warrant that God would accept him. At the age of sixteen, he cast himself upon Christ and became an outstanding pastor, missions proponent, and theologian. Later he wrote, "I now found rest for my troubled soul; and I reckon that I should have found it sooner, if I had not entertained the notion of my having no warrant to come to Christ without some previous qualification."[3]

Passive waiting. Related to this is the idea that the sinner cannot take any initiative in salvation and must wait passively for God to give salvation like a lightning bolt. Jonathan Edwards (1703-58), one of the key evangelists of the First Great Awakening in America, struggled with this problem. Although almost everyone in town was anxious concerning eternity, some came into assurance rather quickly, but others found it ten times more difficult to come into assurance, going through soul agony for extended periods of time. Edwards struggled to balance the implications of his Calvinism, which said that there was nothing they could do but "lie at God's feet and wait His time," against the need to actively help them to come to faith. But his direct knowledge of biblical truth told him that he must guide them with steps they could take to prepare themselves for the gift of salvation, which is called 'preparationism.'*[4] A century later D. L. Moody struggled with a similar problem personally. He thought that God gives salvation arbitrarily like a lightning bolt, but then his Sunday School teacher showed him Romans 10:17: **"So faith comes from hearing, and hearing from the word of Christ."** He turned to the Bible, faith developed, and he got assurance of his salvation.

Knowing the time. Others are confused about knowing *when* they were saved. They think that one has to know exactly *when* one was born again in order to know *that* one has really been saved. Although spiritual rebirth must be an event in time and space, there is no Scripture indicating that one must know the exact time and place of being born again. Indeed, the parallel with physical birth shows that just as a child doesn't remember the time and place of its own birth, just so a Christian may not be aware of the exact circumstances of one's own new birth. The important thing for a child is to know that one is alive now; just as the important thing for a child of God is to know that one is alive spiritually now. Just because some Christians can identify the exact moment when they trusted Christ and were saved, does not mean that all genuine Christians must have the same awareness. I know I was saved in the summer of 1949 and that I had been a lost sinner before that. However, I cannot be sure exactly when it happened. Some genuine Christians have even less understanding of a time and place. On surveying my Bible college classes as to how many knew the time and place of their new birth, usually only about half knew when. It is a serious error to write off such Christians as not really being saved. It is a legalism to add additional stipulations for salvation to what has been explicitly revealed in the word of God.

What is the basis of assurance?

Assurance is not some vague and mystical thing reserved for only some elite Christians. It is the clear will of God for all true Christians. Since the basis for this full assurance is clearly spelled out in God's word, no one need guess or keep wondering about it. Just checking out and understanding what the Bible says is a sure path to full assurance of faith. There are a number of clear factors which enter into attaining biblical assurance.

The person of Christ. Clearly, the objective facts of the deity and saving work of Christ are the essential foundations of assurance. From our survey of the Gospels, the identity of the Lord Jesus as God incarnate is vital. It is impossible to have good assurance if one is not clear on the full deity of Christ. The Lord Jesus was not just a good teacher, prophet, miracle worker, or whatever, He was God come to dwell in human flesh (Jn. 1:14-18). After D. James Kennedy gave a great message at Ocean Grove, NJ on the uniqueness of Christ, a lady said to him, "I have been a faithful Congregationalist for over fifty years and have never heard what you preached today." He asked, "What did I preach?" She responded, "That Jesus is God incarnate." Thereupon he counseled both husband and wife and led them to faith in Christ. This was the central issue that Christ had to get clarified with His own nation Israel, and it is the central issue that professing Christians need to face up to today. The person whom we have received by faith and to whom we relate today is God incarnate.

The work of Christ. Coupled with the unique person of the Lord Jesus is the foundation of His unique work of salvation in His sacrificial death and resurrection. There can be no assurance apart from this! Christ's finished work on Calvary must be the object of our faith. Unless we understand the basis of forgiveness and justification, we will continue to struggle with the guilt of our sin. The more we understand of the ransom-redemption and the propitiation provided on the cross, the more we can be assured that "Jesus paid it all." These are the objective historical facts upon which our assurance is based. When the Lord Jesus cried out, "**It is finished**," we understand that God had done everything which was necessary for the full and free salvation of the repentant sinner.

It is also important to understand the subjective, internal dimensions of salvation. When we understand that justification means that God charges our sins to Christ since He bore them on the cross, and now God declares us perfectly righteous in His sight by charging Christ's righteousness to us– only then can we experience the sense of release from the guilt of our sin. This is the redemption-liberation aspect of salvation and the full reconciliation with God which was seen in Chapter 5.

The Word of God. These wonderful truths just surveyed are widely available. How do we access them and make them our own? Most people in the world are totally ignorant of these realities. How do we appropriate them for ourselves? We enter into these salvation realities through trusting in the salvation promises in the word of God. Lack of assurance is frequently caused by a fuzzy perception of these promises. But the promises in the Bible are the necessary channel to access Christ's saving reality.

Perhaps a contemporary illustration will be helpful. There is a wealth of information and help available to the whole human race on the internet. However, most are not getting the benefit of it for a number of reasons.

First, one must have a computer or similar device. Secondly, one must have software in the computer which connects with the internet through a phone or cable connection. The message of the Bible is God's appointed means to access His salvation, just as a computer and its software is the appointed way to access the internet. Yet many who have the computer and software don't get much help from the internet because of ignorance of how to use it. They may have learned how to access a few websites and get a little help, but they are very insecure and lost as far as the rest of it is concerned. Just so, many Christians who understand enough of God's message of salvation to be saved, don't have assurance because of ignorance of most of what the Bible teaches. The more one understands, believes, and obeys the word of God, the more likely one will have good assurance of salvation.

Personal trust. Hundreds of millions of people in the world have Bibles. Two billion people are professing Christians, but only a small percentage have assurance of salvation in Christ. What is missing? The clear answer is–a personal trust in the finished work of Christ. The gospel must be personally appropriated by each individual. It is not enough to intellectually assent to the truths of the historic Christian faith. Each individual must personally claim for oneself the merits of the sacrifice of Christ and receive the gift of eternal life.

My experience is typical. I had attended Sunday School in an evangelical church faithfully from childhood and always believed that Christ died for the sins of the world. But it wasn't until as an engineering student at the age of nineteen that I claimed salvation for myself and was born again into the family of God. I put my name into the promise of John 5:24. This is why evangelical Christians speak of "accepting Christ as your personal savior."

It is most important to understand the two dimensions of the Christian faith. The first is the objective, historical facts of God's plan of salvation—universal sin and depravity, and the virgin birth, deity, sacrificial death, and bodily resurrection of Christ. These are all foundational. But these objective, historical realities do not automatically save anyone, as important as they are. This is because there is also a subjective, internal, and personal dimension to the Christian faith as well. It takes place right now in our personal lives. It requires a human response to the gospel message—the repentance and faith emphasized in Chapter 6. Failure to grasp these two dimensions of the good news of Christ has been a problem for billions.

An essential part of the foregoing discussion is to put these two elements together— the promises of the word of God and our personal trust in Christ and His saving work. This involves claiming those promises for ourselves and taking God at His word. If we don't take God at His word and claim His promises, we are making God out to be a liar. In the book of Hebrews the Apostle shows that this was the nation Israel's problem: "**For indeed we have had good news preached to us, just as they also; but the word they heard did not profit them, because it was not united by faith in those who heard. For** we who have believed enter that rest ..." (Heb. 4:2-3a). One of the clearest such salvation promises in Romans 10:8b-10 also emphasizes that trust in Christ is a matter of the heart:

> ... the word of faith which we are preaching, that if you confess with your mouth Jesus *as* Lord, and believe in your heart that God raised Him from the dead, you will be saved; for with the heart a person believes, resulting in righteousness, and with the mouth he confesses, resulting in salvation.

The witness of the Spirit. Although repentant faith is the responsibility of mankind to exercise, immediately upon man's believing, the Holy Spirit begins a whole new series of ministries in the life of the new believer. Before a person comes to faith, the Holy Spirit had been actively convicting him of sin, righteousness, and judgment, according to the promise of the Lord Jesus in John 16:8-11. Now the Spirit begins to work in the life in a number of significant ways. Not only is the believer born again, but is also indwelt by the Holy Spirit (Rom. 8:9-11), baptized by the Spirit into the body of Christ (1 Cor. 12:13), sealed by the Spirit until the day of redemption (Eph. 4:30), and the Spirit becomes a witness to the new believer that he is saved: "**For you have not received a spirit of slavery leading to fear again, but you have received a spirit of adoption as sons by which we cry out, 'Abba! Father!' The Spirit Himself testifies with our spirit that we are children of God,...**" (Rom. 8:15-16). Here is the divine confirmation of the reality of faith and salvation. The Spirit begins to give assurance that sins have been forgiven and that one is now a child of God. That assurance may develop immediately or gradually, dependent upon the life situation of the individual. Some people, such as Saul of Tarsus, grasp the implications of salvation more readily and come into full assurance very quickly (Acts 9:19-22). Others struggle to grasp important dimensions of salvation truth, and thus their assurance may be weak at first. We must be careful not to put everybody in a mold and insist that everyone's experience of salvation should fit a pattern.

The witness of the life. Our salvation does not depend in the least upon human performance. It is totally by the unmerited favor of Christ that we are saved. However, *our assurance* of salvation is heavily conditioned upon human factors. Peter, after speaking of God's wonderful provision for a life of godliness (2 Pet. 1:2-4) and exhorting us to apply all diligence in showing godly qualities in our lives (1:5-9), goes on to speak about assurance: "**Therefore, brethren, be all the more diligent to make certain about His calling and choosing you; for as long as you practice these thing, you will never stumble;...**" (2 Pet. 1:10). Although human performance does not contribute one iota to our salvation, Peter is very explicit that our *subjective assurance* of that calling to salvation is very dependent upon our diligence to grow in the Christian life and develop Christian character. Besetting sins and backsliding in the Christian life can be very destructive of the certainty and assurance that God wants us to have. This is one of the main points of John's first epistle, which has as its goal that **"you may know that you have eternal life"** (1 Jn. 5:13). Along the way to that goal John emphasized many aspects of the Christian life and character which contribute to or else undermine our certainty.

Life Factors which Undermine Assurance

There are two aspects of the problem of assurance. Some Christians may just question the reality of their own salvation, even though they may have no doubts about the truth of the Christian faith. Others, however, may have more deep-seated doubts about the very veracity of the faith itself. Let us sort out the diverse problems which Christians face.

Sin and backsliding. Any pastor or evangelist can testify to the fact that sin and backsliding in the Christian life can seriously undermine an individual's assurance of salvation. Actually it should be a no-brainer for any Christian to realize how sin undermines assurance. However, some new Christians might have thought that getting saved would liberate them from all sin in their lives, not realizing that while we are saved from the penalty of sin, the old sin nature within us remains. Unfortunately there has developed within the Arminian tradition a whole movement of a number of denominations called the holiness movement, which teaches that total experiential sanctification is possible here on earth. This would mean that it is possible for a Christian to live a sinless life. However, the Apostle John writing to those saved individuals who believe in the Son of God (1 Jn. 5:13) said, **"If we [believers] say that we have no sin, we are deceiving ourselves and the truth is not in us. ... If we say that we have not sinned, we make Him a liar and His word is not in us"** (1Jn. 1:8, 10). John uses some pretty strong language to warn us of the seriousness of this error, since if we deny the problem, we are far from the biblical solution.

Therefore, it is very common for Christians who struggle with sin, especially serious sins, to wonder if they were really born again. They may even think that they need to get born again all over again, since they think that maybe it didn't take the first time. This was the problem of the Christians alluded to in Hebrews 6:4-7, discussed in detail in chapter 13.

Sometimes Christians who fall into sin stop attending church services and seriously backslide. In such a condition it is no wonder that they lose the assurance of salvation. They need to claim the promise of God, which is sandwiched between the two verses above: **"If we confess our sins, He is faithful and righteous to forgive us our sins and to cleanse us from all unrighteousness"** (1 Jn. 2:9). This is not a salvation verse for unbelievers, but a way of restoration for the sinning and backslidden Christian.

Life's calamities and discouragements. Remember the doubts which John the Baptizer experienced in prison, when things did not turn out the way he expected. A significant number of Christians today are stumbled by negative circumstances in their Christian lives. They may have had unrealistic expectations as to what the Christian life entails. Perhaps they had been influenced by the contemporary vogue of the "prosperity gospel" to think that every Christian has the right to prosper financially, and when they struggle financially, they question the reality of the gospel. Others may have thought, along with many Pentecostals and Charismatics, that every Christian has the right to be healed. When they or some loved one falls into chronic illness or even dies, their faith and assurance are undermined.

Many may blame God when calamities come into our lives. If God is sovereign, He is to blame! Such thinking overlooks the fact that Christians are not exempted from life's calamities, which go back to the sin of our first parents and the consequent judgment of God upon the creation, which was originally good (see especially Genesis 3:14-19). Additionally, God judged the earth a second time through the worldwide deluge because of the universal violence, vendettas, and murder permeating the whole human race (Gen. 6). Worldwide weather as we now know it was a consequence of that flood (Gen. 2:5-6; 8:22), and many natural calamities today, such as tornadoes and tsunamis spring from that.

We must also remember that Satan usurped the rule of the earth from Adam in the Garden and now is the "**prince of this world,**" "**the God of this world,**" and the "**prince of the power of the air.**" He has a host of evil angels helping him to keep most of the human race under his control. So we should not be astonished that calamities come in the Christian life.

Doubts about the authority of Scripture and/or the deity of Christ. Since our salvation promises are in the Bible, the word of God, Satan has made the inspiration of the Bible a major target for his attacks. While he sometimes uses atheists and agnostics to attack the veracity of Scripture, he frequently uses religious people, as in Christ's day. Not only do attacks come from Muslims, Hindus, and other religionists, but also from professing Christians. Christ warned about the "**wolves in sheep's clothing**" who would seek to undermine the faith of God's people (Mt. 7:15). Sometimes it is pastors who dishonestly feign belief in the Bible but in their hearts don't believe it. They preach ethical teaching, but they omit the necessary essentials of salvation truth. Some of them are more honest to make their denials forthrightly, but that still doesn't make it right.

Frequently it is a religion professor in a college, university, or seminary who attacks the Bible and the Christian faith. Before 1890, all of the Protestant theological seminaries in America, except Harvard, held evangelical views. Due to the impact of destructive higher criticism of the Bible coming from Germany and the United Kingdom and also of Darwinian evolution, virtually all the Protestant seminaries became liberal or modernistic by 1920.[5] The denominational control of the old-line denominations was taken over by these liberals with few exceptions. This means that they did not believe that Moses wrote the Pentateuch, or that Daniel wrote the book of

Daniel, or that the Apostles wrote the Gospels and all of the epistles. Today if you take a religion course in a university or mainline denominational seminary, you will hear denial of the Bible as the word of God on every hand. This has been true also in many Roman Catholic institutions, since Catholic scholars have borrowed critical views from liberal Protestants, as well as from the evolutionary philosophy of the Jesuit, Teilhard de Chardin. Even in professedly evangelical institutions, there is frequently serious compromise with these liberal views. The faith of the students can be seriously undermined by this, as well as their assurance of salvation.

These days such attacks are not limited to the educational sphere. The media is constantly bombarding people with such denials. The "Jesus Seminar" of liberal scholars in Chicago a few years ago concluded that very little of the Gospel records record authentic information about the Lord Jesus. This was not only widely reported in the media, but unbelieving scholars of this type are constantly being used as resource people in the documentaries aired on television, whether done by Peter Jennings, or the Discovery, or History channels. Rarely do they honestly interview evangelical scholars who believe that the Bible is the inspired word of God.

In addition, many evangelical scholars have begun to compromise their evangelical faith with these liberal denials. After graduating from an evangelical seminary, I got permission to audit classes for a few days in my own denominational seminary. In the first class attended the professor denied that Moses wrote the Pentateuch and gave out the liberal destructive higher critical view as truth. A number of Arminian denominations do not have any doctrinal statement on the inspiration of Scripture. Their professors can teach any unbelief that suits their fancy. But even many denominations and educational institutions which have a clear statement on the inerrancy of the Bible are tolerating compromise by their leaders and teachers.[A]

All of this weakens the confidence of Christians in His deity and saving work. Some denial comes from direct unbelief in what the Bible says; some from ignorance of the Bible's own claims for its inerrancy; some from ignorance of Christ's own claims about His deity; and some from the fuzzy thinking of those who use a number of subtle interpretive devices to obscure the clear meaning of Scripture.[6] Sometimes scholars can get so immersed in the writings and views of other scholars that they don't spend time studying the Bible itself.[B] The result is that they have doubts about the full deity of Christ, which in turn undermines confidence that He really is able to

---

A. The widespread nature of this problem became clear when the Evangelical Theological Society membership voted in 2003 not to expel two members whose writings have consistently denied the inerrancy of Scripture. It seems that the mindset of tolerance so prevalent in our culture has greatly influenced the thinking of many evangelical scholars. See Harold Lindsell, *The Battle for the Bible.*

B I recently heard a sermon by an Old Testament professor in an evangelical seminary of Reformed tradition, in which he twice stated that he rarely reads the New Testament. Needless to say, there was no explicit explanation of salvation in his message

provide the full salvation which He promises.

In an exit interview with a departing professor, he expressed surprise when I said that I had close to 100% certainty of the deity of Christ. When I asked him what percentage he could affirm, he replied, "Oh, about sixty percent." This explained student reports that his teaching raised too many questions, which he did not answer. Over half a century that I have been studying the Bible, my conviction has continually grown that the Bible is absolutely true and is absolutely clear on the full deity of Christ.

The most concerted attack on the deity of Christ comes from Muslims, who believe that it is blasphemous to call any man God. This is the major obstacle for Muslims to become Christians. As a missionary to Muslims in the metro New York area Dick Bailey was counseling a Muslim background believer (MBB) who had been struggling with issues of assurance and victory over sin for years. When Dick asked him, "Is it possible that you still have a problem with the deity of Christ?" he responded, "Yes, that's it! I still struggle with this issue." This was the root of his problem! There are other doctrinal errors which also undermine assurance of ultimate salvation.

Doctrinal Errors Which Undermine Assurance

The unforgivable sin. In serving as a Bible answerman on Christian radio, one of the most frequent questions we got was, "What is the unforgivable sin?" Many were confused and feared that they had committed it! However, there is absolutely no need for anybody today to worry about "the unforgivable sin." As usual, it is so important to see the context in which Christ uttered these words (Mt. 12:24-32). Some of the Pharisees had accused Him of casting out demons by Satan's power, when actually it was by the power of the Holy Spirit. After showing them the absurdity of this accusation, He said,

> Therefore I say to you, any sin and blasphemy shall be forgiven people, but blasphemy against the Spirit shall not be forgiven. Whoever speaks a word against the Son of Man, it shall be forgiven him; but whoever speaks against the Holy Spirit, it shall not be forgiven him, either in this age or in the *age* to come (Mt. 12:31-32).

His words have come true in that over the ages many who have blasphemed His name have later been saved, such as Saul of Tarsus. But since the Holy Spirit is the person of the Triune God who applies salvation to the human heart, those whose hearts were so callous and closed to the Spirit's working could not be saved. This was an outrageous, wholehearted hostility toward God, since they saw the incomparable divine Son of God heal the sick, exorcize demons, and even raise the dead. Since no one today has literally seen Christ do such things, probably no one today can commit this sin. In any case, a person who is concerned about such a possibility certainly does not have such a callous heart and should no longer fret about this. We should focus instead on our Lord's positive statement, **"any sin and blasphemy shall be forgiven people."**

Ignorance of the gracious nature of salvation. Most human beings would like to contribute to their own salvation, even if only a little. Evangelical Christianity is totally unique in affirming that salvation is absolutely by the unmerited favor of God and not dependant in the least upon human performance. Every other major religion insists that salvation is achieved by the works of mankind. Islam is the most hard-core in this regard. According to Islamic traditions (*hadith*), when Muhammad was dying, his daughter Fatimah asked him to pray for her salvation. His response was, "Daughter, my prayers will do you no good! Only your own good works will save you!" It is salvation by human merit. The most important word in Hindu philosophy, familiar by now to many westerners, is *karma*. It is a noun of agency coming from the Sanskrit verb "to do," in short it means "works." The second most important word is *dharma*, which means, "custom, religion, etc." Hindus try to achieve *moksha* (liberation) by the mental and physical discipline of yoga and by following cultural and religious customs. The same is true of all the other world religions.

Most of the two billion professing Christians are trying to be saved by human works, even though the Bible is so clear on this. Catholicism had deteriorated so badly in the medieval period that the Reformers' emphasis upon salvation by grace through faith alone was totally rejected by the Roman hierarchy in the Council of Trent (1547-8). Although some Catholics today for the first time are reading the Bible and coming to a more evangelical view of salvation, their accumulated dogmatic system is hostile to salvation by God's unmerited favor. Five of the sacraments, which all Catholics must fulfill for salvation, constitute a system which is at core dependent upon human performance and merit. Although many priests water down the way they communicate to people, as if salvation is only through christening, the other four general sacraments are commonly understood to be essential to ultimate salvation. Since it is never quite clear which sins are mortal and which are venial, and how faithfully one must go to mass, the Catholic is always uncertain about salvation. Even the Pope cannot be sure. There is no real assurance for the Catholic!

Neither can liberal Protestants have any assurance, since they too are in a works salvation. The social gospel of the last century did not even affirm eternal salvation; it was only concerned with human society here and now. Neo-orthodoxy talked about an existential encounter with Christ, but was not clear about who He was, or just what that encounter involved. Now post-modernism denies that there are any absolutes of truth or morality, so there cannot be any absolute truth about salvation either.

Even among Evangelicals we find that extreme Calvinists have real problems knowing for sure whether they are among the elect. If God's election is based upon some secret counsel known only to Him, then how can we know for sure? The answer to this question is complex and a major portion of the rest of this book will be devoted to answering it. The uncertainty of Christians over the centuries about their elect status arises from the doctrine of absolute predestination. Careful examination of all the passages relating to election and predestination will show that they are conditioned upon God's foreknowledge of who will come to repentant faith. Actually the biblical material is quite simple, but over the centuries theologians have brought in philosophic considerations which have muddied the waters. There is also some confusion about the translation of key words and the interpretation of key passages, which all must be seen in their contexts. We should not allow human philosophy to color our understanding of Scripture or scholarly rationalizations to undermine the simple promises of the Bible.

On the other hand, Arminians can be sure about the present, but not about future salvation. In their view some sin or failure of faith could send them to hell, . This also seems like a complex issue and some chapters will focus upon clarifying it (cf. Chapters 12-15). It mostly arises from failure to understand who are being addressed in certain warnings in the Bible and exactly what the nature of those warnings really are. There has been a tendency to be satisfied with a superficial read of what these and other passages actually say, without careful study of the context, the exact words used, and the grammar and syntax of the passages. But one does not have to be a Greek scholar to resolve these problems. Over the centuries, misinterpretation of the warning of Hebrews 6 has been a major hangup for many. On the telephone call-in program, this was the number one question which was asked, month after month.

Why have so many struggled with assurance?

It is shocking to read Archibald Alexander's case studies of conversion experiences from the eighteenth and early nineteenth centuries as collected by this early Princeton theologian. It is so distressing to read page after page of people's struggles to come into the assurance of eternal life, with so little clear biblical guidance given them. It reminded me of the long struggle[c] John Wesley, although an Anglican priest, had to come to salvation and its assurance. Alexander's anecdotes are probably from among his own Reformed tradition. From his narratives it seems that most Christians had little clue as to how to lead a distressed soul into the assurance of salvation. If many of the Reformed preachers of the day had as little assurance as evangelist Asahel Nettleton (cf. pp, 152-3), it is no wonder that lay people were in confusion. On his deathbed he said, "The most that have ventured to say concerning myself is, that I think it possible I may get to heaven."[7] In discussing this book with the pastor (of Calvinistic convictions), we wondered together whether it was D. L. Moody (1837-1899)[8] here in America and

---

C. Wesley was heavily into asceticism, mysticism, legalism, & Platonic philosophy in the many years of his struggle. See Robert G. Tuttle, Jr., *John Wesley: His Life and Theology*, pp. 143-155.

C. H. Spurgeon (1834-1892) in Great Britain who set evangelicalism on a better course in the last half of the nineteenth century. Since that conversation, my research has indicated that Andrew Fuller (1754-1815) in Great Britain and the New Divinity theologians of the Second Great Awakening in America had earlier laid the foundation for Spurgeon and Moody (Chaps. 24-25).

Alexander's anecdotes from the early nineteenth century are no better. There seemed to be such ignorance of the simple gospel message and such a prevalence of legalism in both the Calvinistic and Arminian camps that many people struggled for years to come into assurance of salvation. Alexander gives a general impression: "It is a lamentable fact that in this land of churches and of Bibles there are many who know little more of the doctrines of Christianity than the pagans themselves."[9] It is probable that George Whitefield, Andrew Fuller, the New Divinity preachers, Charles Finney, Moody, and Spurgeon may really be key figures in moving Protestants back to a more simple gospel presentation.

Conclusions

Assurance of salvation is foundational to a stable and victorious Christian life. How can we live in victory and blessing if we are not really sure whether we have been saved or not, or if we are not sure whether God will ultimately send us to hell? It is absolutely imperative that every professing Christian settle these issues related to assurance so as to come into the **"much full assurance," "the full assurance of faith," "the full assurance of understanding,"** and **"the full assurance of hope."**

1 Michael Eaton, *No Condemnation A New Theology of Assurance*, p. 4.

2 G Abbott-Smith, *Manual Lexicon of the Greek New Testament*, p 365

3 Andrew Gunton Fuller, *The Complete Works of Andrew Fuller*, 2 vols (Boston, 1833), I, 20

4 Archibald Alexander, *Thoughts on Religious Experience*, p 28

5. Kenneth Kantzer, Staley Lecture at Northeastern Bible College, Essex Fells, NJ, 1970s.

6 See Robert L. Thomas, *Evangelical Hermeneutics· The New Versus the Old*

7 Eaton, *No Condemnation*, p. 3.

8. "No man has ever done more for the Christian cause in his generation. He had recruited for Christ many who were leaders in the next." (J. C. Pollock in Woodbridge, ed. *Great Leaders of the Church*).

9 Archibald Alexander (1772-1851), *Thoughts on Religious Experience*, pp 67-71, 28

PART TWO

CRUCIAL

SALVATION

ISSUES

THE SEQUENCES OF SALVATION

Special
Revelation

THE GOSPEL
GOD'S LAW

General
Revelation

CONSCIENCE
REVELATION
IN NATURE

CONVICTION → REPENTANT
FAITH

JUSTIFICATION
REGENERATION
SPIRIT BAPTISM &
INDWELLING
POSIT. SANCTIFICATION

A HUMAN PROCESS

INSTANTANEOUS
WORKS OF GOD

My hope is built on nothing less
  Than Jesus blood and righteousness
I dare not trust the sweetest frame,
  But wholly lean on Jesus name.

His oath, His covenant, His blood
  Support me in the whelming flood;
When all around my soul gives way
  He then is all my hope and stay.

On Christ the solid Rock I stand;
  All other ground is sinking sand.

-Edward Mote (1834)

GOSPEL PROCLAMATION
ON GOD'S TERMS

One of the most misunderstood, abused, neglected, and yet vital portions of Scripture is the dialogue of the Lord Jesus with His Apostles as He got them apart at Caesarea Philippi for teaching, as recorded in Matthew 16 and more briefly in Mark and Luke. Many vital issues arise from this passage since it not only includes Peter's divinely revealed confession of the Messiah's deity, the first mention of the church and its foundation, the investing of Peter with the keys, the binding and loosing, and the first of a dozen predictions of His passion. Not only has Romanism usurped this passage as the basis for its cultic heresy, but Protestants seem to have only dimly grasped its monumental significance. Critically, many of the commentators have not been helpful in getting to the truth of the passage.

The evidence is really one-sided that the Lord Jesus taught that He Himself is the rock upon which the church was to be built, certainly not Peter. Furthermore, the symbolism of the gates of Hades refers to the Messiah's victory over death and the church's subsequent offensive attack against Satan's grip on the human race, which is moving on the broad road to eternal death. Peter was commissioned by the giving of the keys to lead the charge against Satan's domain by opening the door of faith to Jews, Samaritans, and Gentiles. He was to do this by proclaiming forgiveness on heaven's terms, not on the legalistic terms of the Pharisees, nor the rationalistic terms of the Sadducees, but only on the basis of God's word, which is settled forever in heaven. Lastly, the building of the church was to be based upon His predicted passion.

The Bedrock, Christ Himself

The first gross misinterpretation by many scholars is the identity of the rock upon which Christ was to build His church: **"But I also say to you that you are Peter, and upon this rock I will build My church; and the gates of Hades will not overpower it"** (Mt. 16:18). This is a case where the hymn writers are correct and the majority of scholars are dead wrong. We sing, "On Christ the solid rock I stand, all other ground is sinking sand," "Jesus is the rock of our salvation," and "Rock of ages cleft for me." But many Bible scholars don't believe it! Although the most popular Protestant view identifies Peter's *confession* of Christ's deity or his *faith* as the rock, some ironically join with Roman Catholics in identifying *Peter himself* (although without all the Romanist implications). Others associate *all the Apostles* with Peter as the foundation-rock of the church.

In 1997, I was sharing a series of meetings in Pakistan with a British brethren scholar. At the last breakfast before we parted, he asked me what I had preached on the previous evening. When I told him, he replied incredulously, "Gordon, you don't *really* believe that Jesus is the rock, do you?" He referred to the 'Aramaic problem'. Unfortunately, there was no time to respond before I had to leave, but that dialogue forced me to dig deeper into the evidence. My discoveries have been astonishing!

The Old Testament background

It is unthinkable to claim to interpret this passage without researching the Old Testament symbolism of the rock (which few have done) and doing a word study of the Hebrew and Aramaic words related to this (which *virtually none* have done!). The symbol of God as Israel's rock is pervasive, starting from the repeated allusions in the song of Moses (Deut. 32), right on through. Two Hebrew words (*tsur* and *sela'*) are used 39 times of the true God and once of false gods. This provides the background for understanding the two different Greek words used in Matthew 16. Incredibly, many commentators pontificate about the Aramaic, but none surfaced who mentioned the Hebrew/Aramaic words *tsur/tur*, *sela'*, or *shu'ah*, and few noted the dominant symbolism of God as the Rock in the Old Testament.

The passage and its context

The geographical context of this passage is dramatic. Caesarea Philippi is at the headwater of the eastern branch of the Jordan River, where water gushes out of the side of a cliff. When the Lord Jesus had elicited the confession of His deity from Peter and said, **"You are *Petros* (Πέτρος), and upon this *petra* (πέτρα) I will build My church"** (Mt. 16:18), the distinction between these two Greek words is very significant. Since *petra* means 'bedrock' or 'cliff,' the cliff from which the Apostles were seeing the Jordan waters gush certainly brought to mind the cliffside out of which God brought water twice in Moses' day. The Old Testament symbolism cannot be ignored in this most Jewish Gospel in which is found the record of the Jewish Messiah instructing His twelve Jewish Apostles to the Jewish nation (Mt. 10:5-8) based upon the Old Testament kingdom promises.

My Greek professor, S. Lewis Johnson, Jr., suggested in class that Matthew used the contrast of these two distinct Greek words to indicate what he saw with his eyes, that is, the Lord's gesture with His hand toward His own chest when He uttered the word πέτρα (*petra*), thus indicating that He Himself is the Rock upon which the church was to be built. Matthew did not have a camera to record that gesture. He was limited to the use of words to communicate the whole picture and did this by using the genius of the Greek language to its fullest advantage. The sequence of ideas is consistent since Peter had just affirmed the Lord Jesus as deity. Therefore, *the divine Messiah alone is qualified to be the foundation of the church.* What is the contextual and linguistic basis for Johnson's suggestion?

Two major lexicons give helpful definitions of *petra* (πέτρα):

> [in LXX chiefly for סלע, צור;] *a rock* , i.e. **a mass of live rock as distinct from πέτρος [*petros*], a detached stone or boulder.** ...; of a hollow rock, *a cave, ...* Metaph., Mt 16[18]... (emphasis mine)[1]

> 1. *rock*—a. lit., of the rock in which a tomb is hewn ... *rocky grotto ...rocky ground.* ... It forms a suitable foundation for the building of a house. ... The rock at various places in the desert fr. which Moses drew water by striking it . b. in a play on words w. the name Πέτρος [*petros*]; ...[2]

Some object to making a distinction since the difference is just a matter of gender between these two words, *petros* (m.) and *petra* (f.). However, the usage of these words is in total contrast. There is a principle in the Greek word-building process which Chamberlain emphasized: "The student should learn once and for all that every single letter added to a Greek root adds something to the idea expressed by the root."[3] A strong case can be made for a difference in gender having significant impact upon connotation as well since *these are two distinct and different words*. In addition, there is Christ's usage in the Sermon on the Mount (Mt. 7:25) of a rock foundation upon which a building can be permanently erected. Here it clearly does not mean stone, or even boulder, but cliff or bedrock.

Matthew's demonstrative emphasis. Note well that Matthew used a demonstrative with attributive force with the articular noun *petra* (πέτρα), thus indicating that Christ is pointing to something. The construction is: ἐπὶ ταύτῃ τῇ πέτρᾳ (*epi tautē tē petra*). Examination of usage of the same construction indicates that there is a strong emphasis in all.[4] It comes out only in the translation of Acts 1:11: "**This same Jesus shall come**" (KJV, NIV, Amplified). But the context of all other usages confirm this that the words 'same' or 'very' could well be used in every case to bring out the full meaning. Thus, this is essentially a *double demonstrative*, that is, an actual demonstrative plus the article which still retains some of that force.[A] The question arises, whether the Lord is pointing to Simon Peter to identify him, or whether He is pointing to Himself. One authoritative grammar states that the article with nouns tends to designate persons, while the article is usually lacking with abstract nouns.[5] So *petra* is not to be seen as an abstract noun since it has an article. This further militates again the common Protestant 'confession' view. This could be well paraphrased, **"You, Simon are a stone; but upon this very bedrock [pointing to Himself] I will build my church."**

The Aramaic question. Some evangelical scholars deny that the Lord Jesus is the Rock, based upon the supposed Aramaic original. 'Supposed' is appropriate because there is no assurance that the Lord was speaking Aramaic here. Greek was widely spoken and used by first-century Jews along with Aramaic and Latin.[6] However, even if He were speaking Aramaic, the argument is pointless. There is no language on earth which cannot distinguish between bedrock or a cliff and a detached stone, even if the speaker has to use an adjective or other device. However, as already seen, in Aramaic as in Hebrew, *the distinct words were readily at hand. Kaipha* (Cephas) is the name the Lord Himself gave to Simon, and it *never* refers to a boulder, bedrock, cliff or mountain. It consistently refers to smaller stones. Quite in contrast, *tsur* in Hebrew and its Aramaic equivalent (*tur*) consistently refer to mountains, bedrock, cliffs, etc. and *shu'ah* refers to smooth bedrock. Thus, this objection is patently specious. Remember that we do not have the Aramaic of Matthew, if it ever existed, and after all, it is the original Greek manuscripts which are the inspired word of God.

The analogy of Scripture. Since the Apostle Peter was the one being addressed, it is important to ask how Peter understood the Lord's words. In Peter's first witness before the Sanhedrin, he quoted Psalm 118:22 in reference to Christ being the stone which they, the builders, had rejected, and who is the unique way of salvation (Acts 4:11-2). Peter used *lithos* (stone) since that is the word used in the Septuagint Greek translation.

Years later, in his first epistle, Peter quoted Isaiah 28:16, Psalm 118, and Isaiah 8:14 in reference to Christ (1 Pet. 2:4-8):

And coming to Him as to a living stone which has been rejected by men, but is choice and precious in the sight of God, you also as living stones, are being built up as a spiritual house for a holy priesthood, to offer up spiritual sacrifices acceptable to God through Jesus Christ. For *this* is contained in Scripture: "Behold, I lay in Zion a choice stone, a precious cornerstone, and he who believes in Him will not be disappointed." This precious value, then, is for you who believe; but for those who disbelieve, "The stone which the builders

A. Robertson and Davis explain that the article in the Ionic and Attic originally was a demonstrative pronoun and is common in the New Testament as such and then refer to Broadus's statement that the Greek article is a pointer in three ways, and that the most common of these is to distinguish one individual from other individuals (Robertson and Davis, *Short Grammar*, 10th ed., p. 275.) Wallace agrees.

rejected, this became the very corner stone," and, "A stone of stumbling and a rock of offense."

Again, Peter mostly used *lithos* (λίθος) as in the Septuagint. But notably he used *petra skandalou* (πέτρα σκανδάλου) in the Isaiah 8:14 quote, as did the Septuagint in rendering *tsur*. The first two quotations use the symbolism of Messiah as the foundation cornerstone of the church, the spiritual temple of God. These are Messianic prophecies in their own context, and Peter so confirms this. Although the Isaiah 8:14 symbolism is different, the reference is also clearly Messianic, and Peter significantly quotes the Septuagint rendering of *tsur* as *petra* (πέτρα). Peter gives an unambiguous inspired commentary that the Lord Jesus is the bedrock.

Although the Apostle Paul was not present at Caesarea Philippi, in 1 Corinthians 3:10-15 he confirms the symbolism of the divine Messiah Himself as the rock. Although Paul is not referring to the church universal, he makes it clear that the foundation for the Corinthian church, which he laid, is Christ: **"For no man can lay a foundation other than the one which is laid, which is Jesus Christ."** He picks up the symbolism again in 10:1-4: **"and all drank the same spiritual drink, for they were drinking from a spiritual rock which followed; and the rock was Christ"**[B] Obviously Moses did not strike a small stone or even a boulder, but undoubtedly it was a cliff rockface from which the water gushed. This is clear from the usage of the two Hebrew words used there. The Apostle Paul, knowing that the Lord Jesus had invited sinners to drink of the living water of which He was the source (Jn. 4:10-14; 7:37-9), drew from the symbolism of water from the rock in the wilderness to point to Christ. Jeremiah also alluded to this symbolism, that God is the fountain of living waters (Jer. 2:13; 17:13).

Paul gave another relevant reference. Opposing views depend heavily upon one interpretation of Ephesians 2:20 without recognizing a viable alternative view: **"... having been built on the foundation of the apostles and prophets, Christ Jesus Himself being the corner *stone*, ..."** Many assume from the English that the apostles and prophets are the foundation, but the Greek idiom here can be translated in two ways. It is more probably a genitive of reference, which refers to the apostles and prophets as those *who laid the foundation.*[C] In the following context he emphasizes his own unique involvement in that process and that of the other apostles and prophets (Eph. 3:1-10). This fits with his earlier statement to the Corinthians that he had laid the foundation of their church, and others were building upon it. He then makes the unambiguous statement of Christ as the foundation (1 Cor. 3:10-11). Paul is presumably consistent in his symbolism. Peter was privi-

---

B. I have omitted the word 'them' from the NAS since it is not in the Greek. The rock did not follow the Israelites, but rather followed in the biblical account. J. Sidlow Baxter, *Studies in Problem Texts*, pp. 27-8.

C This involves a grammatically ambiguous genitive. Since Paul is referring in the context to the building of the church, God's temple, upon the foundation, the question arises as to who the subject of the action is. A subjective genitive would supply the answer: the apostles and prophets *laid the foundation.*

leged to lay the foundation of the Jerusalem church. He could not be the foundation and also lay it, unless he were God. *Only the divine Messiah could be both the foundation and the builder as well.*

The cultural gap factor. Western Christians question: "If the Lord intended to say that He Himself is the rock, then why did He not come out and say directly, 'I am the Rock'?" This reveals the cultural gap between us and the Lord Jesus as a first-century Jew. Perusal of the Synoptic Gospels shows that the Lord Jesus rarely used the first person. He normally referred to Himself in a third person manner with the expression 'the son of man.' Even His question here in the KJV ("Whom do men say that I, the Son of man, am?" 16:13) has to be corrected to: **"Who do people say that the Son of Man is?"** (NAS).

Most revealing is our Lord's dialogue with the Jerusalem leaders in Matthew 21:41-44. After quoting the Psalm 118:22 passage, He said, **"And he who falls on this stone will be broken to pieces; but on whomever it falls, it will scatter him like dust."** Note the off-handed third person way in which He refers to Himself. This clarifies where Peter got the idea of quoting Psalm 118 in 1 Peter 2. Contemporary Americans have the most 'up front' culture in human history in that we unabashedly use the big 'I' so frequently; first-century Jews did not. Certainly the Lord Jesus did not. We should not expect Him to speak like a contemporary American.[D]

There is another cultural consideration here. It is probably accurate to describe the way of thinking (cognitive process) in ancient Hebrew culture as concrete and relational, much like animistic tribal and Chinese cultures.[7] This 'concrete-relational thinking' is pervasive in the Old Testament and the Synoptic Gospels, in contrast with Western culture, which is more conceptual and abstract (from the Greeks). The common Protestant interpretation, that the rock is Peter's confession, is a clear example of this abstract, conceptual way of thinking. It is highly unlikely that the Jewish Messiah would be referring to so abstract a concept as a confession by the symbolism of a rock. Remember, this is a culture which did not even have an abstract word for 'sex.' It is always made concrete and relational, i.e., **"Adam knew his wife."** Westerners couldn't communicate without an abstract word like 'sex.' That interpretation is improbable on this basis alone.

Was Peter rock-like? Another question must be asked about the 'Peter' view. What was rock-like about Peter? As has been shown, *Kaipha* in the Aramaic does not mean 'rock.' 'Stone' is a more accurate rendering. He was one of the first living stones to be incorporated into the temple of God. But his character was hardly rock-like. He is the only one of the eleven who denied Christ overtly, even though the others deserted Him. He failed to

---

D Having lived eight years in a culture greatly influenced by middle-eastern Arab and Persian cultures has sensitized me to the different cognitive process of various cultures. I continue to come across linguistic and cultural connections with the Aramaic and Hebrew OT

initiate the mission to Samaritans, as commissioned by the Lord in Acts 1:8. God had to use two striking visions to convince him to bridge the cultural gap to the Gentiles (Acts 10), and even then he struggled with the integration of Gentiles into the church (Gal. 2). We have no record of his being involved in fulfilling the last part of the Greatest Commission in pioneer evangelism among the Gentiles. Indeed, Paul's statement in Galatians 2:8-9 indicates that Peter continued to see himself as an Apostle to the Jews.

The church fathers. We need not be overly concerned to try to find a consensus of the church fathers, especially since the records accessible today are most probably distorted and fragmentary. Nevertheless, it is of some interest to examine their views. Dr. Lannoy of the Sorbonne in Paris has tabulated, that of the seventy-seven most authorized fathers and doctors of the church who have commented on this verse, only seventeen interpret it as Peter, forty-four see it as Peter's confession (including Justin, Cyril, Hilary, Chrysostom, Ambrose, etc.), and sixteen affirm it as Christ Himself (Athanasius, Jerome, Augustine, etc.).[8] Although there is no agreement, a significant number of major fathers confirm this thesis. It is in no way a modern, Protestant, or obscurantist interpretation, as some claim.[9]

Building the Church

Our Lord's dialogue with His Apostles at Caesarea Philippi came three years into His ministry and a couple of months before His passion. For three years, John the Baptizer, the Lord Himself, the twelve Apostles, and then the seventy-two (or 70) disciples had been proclaiming the impending Messianic kingdom. However, now that His enemies are set on His death, He announces a radically new program, but related to the old, that is, His *ekklesia*, His assembly. Its uniqueness is signaled by this first reference and the simple future of *oikodomein*, "**I will build my church [assembly].**" It is not coincidental that this context also contains the first explicit reference to His upcoming passion, the first of a dozen such predictions which come in those few months before their fulfillment: "**From that time Jesus began to show His disciples that He must go to Jerusalem, and suffer many things from the elders and chief priests and scribes, and be killed, and be raised up on the third day**" (Mt. 16:21). There were three veiled symbolic allusions to His passion prior to this, nothing explicit (John 2, the Jonah allusion, and the good shepherd). There could be no *ekklesia* until He should first die and rise to provide the basis for the church. There is no reason to depart from the normal understanding of a simple future, that the church was not yet in existence and would not be until after His passion. Indeed, the foundational bedrock had not yet been laid to be able to start construction. Furthermore there could be no church (assembly) until He had gained victory over death and Hades. How was this to be accomplished?

The Gates of Hades

Most Christians visualize the word picture which the Lord Jesus gave here in a reverse way: they see the church as under demonic attack and somehow resisting and triumphing. Christians often have a fortress mentality. But the Lord said nothing about the gates of the church, nor about Satanic attack. The symbolism is straightforward and needs no sophisticated discussion. The gates of hades cannot uproot themselves and attack the church. Gates are always defensive!

What are the gates of Hades? Hades is, of course, a transliteration of ᾅδης, which is almost always a rendering of *sheol* in the Septuagint, and before the resurrection of Christ refers consistently to the abode of the dead, both in pagan and Scriptural conception. King Hezekiah wrote about his experience of being spared from entering the gates of Sheol (Isa. 38:10), and the idea of death's association with Hades is virtually a given among interpreters. (Its use in the story of the rich man and Lazarus is not clear as to whether Abraham was in a different part of Hades or in a distinct place.)

In any case, the post-resurrection conception is clear that Hades is the temporary prison of the unsaved dead, and that the saved are in "everlasting habitations" (Lk. 16:9), in Paradise (23:43), with the Lord (2 Cor. 5:8), united with Christ (Phil. 1:23), in the heavenly Jerusalem (Heb. 12:22), etc. Since Satan is to be cast into the lake of fire at the end of the millennium (Rev. 20:10), it seems he has no direct connection with Hades. But the indirect connection is with the unsaved, who are under his sway and are on the broad road to death (Mt. 7:13-14), Hades (Mt. 11:23; Lk. 10:15; 16:19-31), and ultimately the lake of fire (Rev. 20:13-5).

Thus, the battle between Satan and the church is for the eternal souls of mankind, and as Christians win the lost to salvation, they are snatched from entering the gates of Hades as 'brands from the fire.' The issue is not Satan's attack against the church, but rather *Christ through His church snatching the souls of mankind from eternal death, Hades, and the lake of fire*.

The way that *katischusousin* is usually rendered as 'prevail, overcome' raises a problem. It does seem to imply that the gates of Hades are on the attack. The problem is in the translation of the verb *katischuein*, since in the secular literature it is usually intransitive, "be strong, powerful, gain the ascendancy."[10] (The two other usages in Luke do not help significantly.) This context logically requires the rendering 'withstand' to fit the obvious symbolism. Louis Barbieri's suggestion is the most cogent of all. He points out that since the Lord's passion is mentioned subsequently in the context, the Lord "Jesus was thus telling the disciples His death would not prevent His work of building the church."[11] His resurrection was the ultimate victory over the gates of Hades, and assures the believer's victory over death as well. As Peter and the Apostles were to proclaim this victory, the gates of Hades would not be able to withstand the attacks of the church as lost people are delivered from Satan's grip and eternal death.

The Keys of the Kingdom

The Lord Jesus then linked the gates with the keys: "**I will give you the keys of the kingdom of heaven; and whatever you bind on earth shall have been bound in heaven, and whatever you loose on earth shall have been loosed in heaven**" (Mt. 16:19). The Roman-Catholic-generated misconception that Peter was given the keys of heaven should be obviously wrong, an error perpetuated in the plethora of jokes about Peter at heaven's gates deciding admission criteria. This sort of thinking assumes that Peter is here given papal authority with the powers of absolution, inherent in the keys and the binding and loosing. This springs from the simple observational error which overlooks that it is the keys of the *kingdom*, not of heaven itself.

The issue is complicated by the fact that the keys are not to open the gates of Hades, so there is a metaphor shift here. Keys have a twofold significance: they open or shut doors, and they are symbols of authority. The Lord Jesus used the term 'key' in the first sense in Luke 11:52, that the scribes had taken away the key of knowledge, not entering in themselves and hindering those entering in. In a similar context of Matthew 23:13 the Lord used the verb from which *kleis* (key) is derived *kleiō* to make a similar accusation: "**you shut off the kingdom of heaven from men; for you do not enter in yourselves, nor do you allow those who are entering to go in.**" The second meaning relates to the first and seems evident in Revelation 1:18 and 3:7-8, where Christ has the keys of death and Hades, and since He has the key of David, when He opens no one can shut, and when He shuts, no one can open. Furthermore He sets before the Philadelphia church an open door, presumably of evangelism.

It becomes clear that syntax, word study, and even immediate context alone cannot clarify the Lord's meaning here. The broader context of the progressive fulfillment in the book of Acts is necessary to clarify His meaning. The most viable scenario which fulfills all the data was suggested by Alford over a century ago:

> Another personal promise to Peter, remarkably fulfilled in his being the first to admit both Jews and Gentiles into the Church; thus using the power of the keys to open the door of salvation.[12]

It was Peter who preached the Pentecost sermon through which three thousand Jews were saved. He had the keys to open the door of faith for the nation Israel to enter into the kingdom of God (and more explicitly the church). The Lord Jesus had commanded the Apostles to be witnesses to Samaria also (Acts 1:8), but Peter failed to take the initiative, which caused a dilemma. Philip's preaching resulted in converts and baptisms. But the converts could not receive the Spirit in the normative way (at the time of exercising faith) because Peter had not officially opened the door of faith to *the Samaritans*. The belated receiving of the Spirit through the laying on of the hands of Peter and John was an anomaly caused by Peter's failure. God made sure that it was Peter who opened the door of faith to *the Gentiles* by giving visions both to him and to Cornelius to make it happen. Peter thus is pictured as a trustee (*oikonomos*), holding and using the keys, thus fulfilling a temporary trusteeship until he completed the task.

It is noteworthy that the gift of languages (tongues) was a supernatural sign probably given to the nation Israel on all three occasions to attest this official opening of the doors of faith. (Although not explicitly mentioned in Samaria, there was undoubtedly some external divine phenomenon to attest the gift of the Spirit.) Later as Paul and Barnabas followed through on that opening into the Gentile world, Luke used that very language: "**how He had opened a door of faith to the Gentiles**" (Acts 14:27). In the Jerusalem Council Peter testified on that exact point: "**Brethren, you know that in the early days God made a choice among you, that by my mouth the Gentiles should hear the word of the gospel and believe. And God, who knows the heart, bore witness to them, giving them the Holy Spirit, just as He also did to us**" (Acts 15:7). Thus Peter used the authority he had been given on three occasions to open doors of faith. Having fully utilized the keys to open doors of faith to all humanity, he relinquished any related authority. There was no continuing primacy or even leadership in the subsequent record.[E] But the question of the content of Peter's preaching needed to be addressed, and this is the subject of the rest of Matthew 16:19.

Proclamation on God's Terms

After many years of wrestling with this text a major neglected factor emerged: the context of preceding events going back to the beginning of Matthew 16. On the other side of the sea of Galilee Christ had a confrontation with the Pharisees and Sadducees. Then His warning follows about the leaven of the Pharisees and Sadducees, their false doctrines (Mt. 16:11-12). Later in Caesarea Philippi this narrative develops. Since the language of the binding and loosing is widely recognized as rabbinic language, the relevance of the context comes into focus. Because later in Matthew 23, Christ essentially accused the Pharisees and scribes of binding on earth what God had not bound in heaven, we can see the relevance (esp. 23:4 & 13). On the other hand, we know that the Sadducees were the rationalists of Judaism, who loosed on earth what God had not loosed in heaven. Robertson affirmed: "Rabbis of the school of Hillel 'loosed' many things that the school of Schammai 'bound'."[13] Robert Gundry also noted the "leavenlike teaching of the Pharisees and Sadducees in v. 12."[14]

Focusing on the syntax of 16:19, the periphrastic* future perfect passives in this statement are most significant. The problem is intensified by the failure of most translators to represent its full force in English. Charles Williams put emphasis upon bringing out the full force of verb tenses into his translation: "**and whatever you forbid on earth must be what is already forbidden in**

E   After Acts 11 we see no real leadership or primacy by Peter, or for that matter by James. Many wrongly assume that James was the lone pastor of the Jerusalem church.

heaven, and whatever you permit on earth must be what is already permitted in heaven."[15] The Amplified Version followed his lead, as did the New American Standard Version.[F] Chamberlain's grammar states:

> There are a few future perfect periphrastics: *estai dedemenon* and *estai lelumenon* (Mt. 16:19). This is wrongly translated 'shall be bound' and 'shall be loosed,' seeming to make Jesus teach that the apostles' acts will determine the policies of heaven. (Moulton, *Prolegomena*, p. 149f.) They should be translated 'shall have been bound' and 'shall have been loosed'.... Cf. Mt. 18:18. This incorrect translation has given expositors and theologians a great deal of trouble.[16]

Robertson's brief comment is in agreement: "All this assumes, of course, that Peter's use of the keys will be in accord with the teaching and mind of Christ.... Every preacher uses the keys of the kingdom when he proclaims the terms of salvation in Christ."[17] This is a rare construction in the New Testament, which implies that Matthew must have had a clear intent to use it. Blass and DeBrunner state: "Periphrasis occasionally provides a rhetorically more forceful expression."[18] Gundry's comment gives further confirmation:

> The passives "will have been bound" and "will have been loosed" imply divine action "In heaven" is a reverential substitute for God's name and also implies divine action The periphrastic future perfect tense does not mean "will be . ," but "will have been ..." (see J R. Mantey in *JETS* 16 [1973] 129-38). Thus God will not ratify at the last judgment what Peter does in the present age, but Peter does in the present age what God has already determined. In other words, Peter has received direction from God for his scribal activity. This direction consists in Jesus' teaching.[19]

One wonders why the translators have been so timid in giving full force to this rare construction. We can understand why the Anglican King James translators, many of whom were just one step out of Rome, would give a connotation supportive of the Anglo-Catholic viewpoint, which dominated the translation process.[20] But why do contemporary translators fall into the rut of past poor translations, when doctrinally it is so harmful?

Psalm 119:89 affirms: **"Forever, O LORD, Thy word is settled in heaven."** This is the standard which Peter and the Apostles were to use in proclaiming the terms of entrance into the church. They had been taught by Christ Himself, but did not yet understand His death, burial, and resurrection and its implications (16:21ff., cf. Lk. 9:44). So the Holy Spirit had to give them further revelation as to its meaning for accurate proclamation, as was fulfilled in the apostolic preaching (*kērugma*). So really Christ was charging Peter and the Apostles to make sure they did not fall into Pharisaic legalism in proclaiming the message, that is, making salvation's terms harder than heaven's standard. Nor were they to fall into Sadducean rationalization, that is, making salvation too easy and the door too wide. *They must 'tell it like it is.'*

F.   Although the NAS committee waffled in between (1971), they ultimately realized the strong grammatical evidence and corrected the 1995 edition.

Conclusions and Implications

Conclusions. The most significant conclusion is that the evidence is one-sided that the Lord Jesus the Messiah indicated that He would build His assembly upon His own divine person. The Old Testament background symbolism of God as the Rock, the availability of several Hebrew and Aramaic words for Him to have used in the wordplay (if indeed He was speaking Aramaic), the consistent distinction of usage of Πέτρος (*petros*) and πέτρα (*petra*), the wordplay parallels in the literature, Peter's own understanding, the cultural context, the broader context, and the analogy of Scripture—all militate toward this conclusion. The most shocking aspect of this is the absolute failure of most scholars to check out the other Aramaic options before pontificating against this view.

The Lord further ensured the victory of the church over the gates of Hades by His own entering into death and His victorious resurrection, assuring likewise the church's victory over death.

He then delegated to Peter the responsibility to open the door of faith by proclaiming the message of this victory, first to their own nation, then to the Samaritans, and lastly to the Gentiles. With this He gave a charge that Peter and the church must proclaim it *only on God's revealed terms*, not corrupting the message by legalism or rationalization.

Finally, He gave the first of a dozen predictions of His imminent death, burial, and resurrection as the only basis for that church and its victory.

Implications. We should not draw our conclusions motivated by trying to arrive at certain implications. However, we must not shrink from declaring bluntly the clear implications of these conclusions. Exegesis and theology must have their 'so what?'

In this day of rapprochement between Evangelicals and Roman Catholics, the 'Peter' view facilitates these dangerous compromises. It is very difficult to hold that view without in some way magnifying Peter and denigrating the Messiah Himself, despite the insistence of its evangelical advocates. The 'confession' view at least does not have that objection, and yet the focus is still too much upon a man, not the divine Messiah Himself. The 'Peter and Apostles' view, with slim Scriptural basis, also opens the door for compromise with Rome.

The common connection of the gates of Hades with Satanic attack on the church has led to a fortress mentality, by which many have failed to see that the Church is to be on the offensive, not in a defensive posture.

Recognizing the unique, but temporary nature of Peter's stewardship of the keys is significant also in avoiding Roman Catholic pretensions. It also helps to clarify the anomaly of the belated reception of the Spirit by the Samaritan believers in Acts 8.

Recognizing the normative force of the future periphrastic perfect passive participles in the binding and loosing is additionally crucial in avoiding compromise with Rome and also in avoiding making salvation's terms either too hard by legalisms or too easy by modernistic rationalizations. It also helps us understand the charge of Matthew 18:18 for the church's ethical standards to avoid legalism and permissive rationalizations.

Finally, recognition of the integral connection of this first reference to the church with the first of a dozen predictions of His passion, helps us to grasp the uniqueness of the church as set in contrast to the kingdom offer to Israel.

1. G. Abbott-Smith, *A Manual Greek Lexicon of the New Testament* (Edinburgh, T. & T. Clark, 1937), p 359

2   Arndt and Gingrich, *Greek-English Lexicon*, p 660

3. William Douglas Chamberlain, *An Exegetical Grammar of the Greek New Testament*, p. 11

4   Daniel B. Wallace, *Greek Grammar Beyond the Basics* (GR: Zondervan, 1996), pp. 241-2   (Mk. 1 9; 15 39; Lk 7:44; Jn 4:15; Acts 1 11, 1 Cor 11 25, Tit. 1·13, 2 Pet 1.18; Jude 4; Rev. 11 10.)

5   Blass and DeBrunner, *A Greek Grammar*, trans. Robert W Funk, pp 133-4.

6   Robert H Gundry, "The Language Milieu of First-Century Palestine " *Jour of Bib. Lit.*, 83 (1964) 404-08.

7   David J Hesselgrave, *Communicating Christ Cross-Culturally* (GR Zondervan, 1978), pp 223-34

8   Luis Padrosa, "The Roman Catholic Church" in Howard F Vos, *Religions in a Changing World*, p 376.

9. D A. Carson, *The Expositors Bible Commentary*, ed Frank E Gaebelein, vol 8, (1984), p 368

10 Arndt & Gingrich, p. 425.

11 Louis A Barbieri, Jr. in John F. Walvoord and Roy B. Zuck, eds , *The Bible Knowledge Commentary*, pp 57-8.

12 Henry Alford, *The Greek Testament* , originally 4 vols (Chicago Moody, 1958 [1849]), I 173-4.

13 A T Robertson, *Word Pictures in the New Testament* , 6 vols (Nashville Broadman, 1930), I 134

14 Gundry, *Matthew*, p 334

15 Charles B Williams, *The New Testament in the Language of the People* (Chicago Moody, 1963 [1937])

16. Chamberlain, p. 80

17. Robertson, I 134   See also his *A Grammar in the Light of Historical Research*, pp 826, 878f, 887-889, 906.

18 Blass, et al, p 179

19 Gundry, p. 335.

20 Gustavus S Paine, *The Men Behind the King James Version* (GR: Baker, 1977).

Absolutely free! Yes, it is absolutely free.
God's grace has made salvation
    Absolutely free!
Tell again the story
    Of His wondrous love to me,
How God has made His great salvation,
    Absolutely free.

                                   -Author Unknown

ARE WE SAVED BY DISCIPLESHIP?

As a new Christian half a century ago, I struggled with the passages in the Gospels which recorded the Lord Jesus' most rigorous teaching about discipleship (Mt. 10:32-39; Mt. 16:13-28=Mk. 8:31-37=Lk. 9:22-25; Lk. 14:25-35). I knew for sure that we are saved by grace through faith alone, based upon wonderful Pauline passages, such as Ephesians 2:8-9. But reading Christ's demands for discipleship, there seemed to be a serious tension, indeed apparent contradiction. I struggled with this until the distinction between salvation and discipleship was clarified. This resolved the problem, and over the years this distinction proved to be not only helpful, but also essential and foundational to the whole doctrine of salvation. Failure to understand this may be a root of the modernists' claim that Paul's gospel is different from Christ's. Of more immediate concern, however, is the absolute confusion caused among Evangelicals, whether Calvinistic or Arminian, who don't recognize this simple distinction.

In short, the Lord Jesus seemed to be saying that it would cost us something to become saved, while the Apostle Paul made clear that it is by His unmerited favor through faith alone. If the Lord were speaking about salvation, then we could identify a number of essential conditions for becoming saved: take up one's cross and follow Him to martyrdom, self-denial, severance from one's family, counting a significant cost and paying this price, giving all our possessions to the poor, and following Christ whole-heartedly. Indeed, this is the way that many evangelical Christians understand Christ's words. If this is correct, extremely few people will be saved! Probably very few readers will make it. There are legions who have sacrificed significantly, who by this standard will not make it either. Obviously, something doesn't compute!

It is amazing how writers at opposite ends of the spectrum of viewpoints ignore this fundamental distinction. Arminian Robert Shank has as a premise of his whole argument against eternal security that in these passages Christ is telling us how to be saved.[1] At the opposite end we find the neo-Puritans,* such as Walter Chantry and Harold Camping. Camping wrote, "A true saving faith in the Lord Jesus Christ involves the act of self denial."[2] Chantry, in decrying the easy-believism and "cheap grace" of contemporary evangelical doctrine and evangelism, states, "It is an essential demand of the gospel that he [the rich young ruler] forsake his wealth." He goes on to say that we "have to sell all in obedience to Christ."[3] John MacArthur's view has been termed "lordship salvation," but because he bases his understanding upon a denial of the distinction between salvation and discipleship, 'discipleship salvation' is a better description.[4] He stated, "... no distinction has done so much to undermine the authority of Jesus' message."[5] On the other hand, Charles Ryrie has stated, "No distinction is more vital to theology, more basic to a correct understanding of the New Testament, or more relevant to every believer's life and witness."[6] How *do* these teachings of the Lord Jesus relate to that of the Apostles?

Christ's Discipleship Teachings

Before turning to the three key discipleship discourses, attention must first be paid to the meaning of the word 'disciple' (*mathētēs*), the most common New Testament description of a Christian: "*learner, pupil, disciple.* 1. gener. *Pupil, apprentice* (in contrast to the teacher)."[7] We become disciples through coming to Him in repentant faith (John 6:35) and begin to learn of Him. This is the symbolism of that great gospel invitation: "**Come to Me, all who are weary and heavy-laden, and I will give you rest. Take My yoke upon you, and learn from Me**, for I am gentle and humble in heart; and you shall find rest for your souls. For My yoke is easy and my load is light" (Mt 11:28-30). In the culture of the day, the disciple sat at the feet of the teacher (rabbi) to learn from his instruction and also to live with Him and learn from his lifestyle. To 'take up a yoke of discipleship' was an expression reflecting this culture. It is not simplistic to suggest that Christ's first command is to *come to Him*; only then is it possible to follow Him (Mt. 16:24). We are not saved by walking on the narrow road. In the Sermon on the Mount He commanded people to "**enter by the narrow gate**" (Mt. 7:13), which is, of course, Himself (Jn. 10:9), in order to get onto the narrow road. It is only a legalistic mindset which ignores these simple distinctions, to the eclipsing of the simple gospel message.

Later in the Bread of Life discourse, Christ used the symbolism of eating and drinking to picture coming to Him and believing on Him: "**I am the bread of life; he who comes to Me shall not hunger, and he who believes in Me shall never thirst**" (Jn. 6:35). In short, coming to Him in faith makes us His disciples. In His discipleship teachings, to avoid confusion *it is imperative to examine the contexts sequentially, considering the dynamics of His ministry.*

Sending out twelve ambassadors

The first passage chronologically is found in Matthew 10:32-39, in connection with sending the Twelve out to the towns and cities of Israel at the end of the second full year of His ministry. (Mark and Luke record the sending, but do not include the discourse.) After the immediate brief instructions for the venture at hand, He launched into an extended discourse about the persecution His ambassadors will experience up to the end of the age (Mt. 10:16-37). He spoke about their being delivered up to courts, being scourged, brought before rulers, family members betraying them, being hated for His sake, not fearing those who kill the body, bringing a sword, not peace, and loving Him more than family. Against this background in Matthew 10:37-9 He charged:

> He who loves father or mother more than Me **is not worthy of Me**; and he who loves son or daughter more than Me **is not worthy of Me**. And he who does not take his cross and follow after Me **is not worthy of Me**. He who has found his life shall lose it, and he who has lost his life for My sake shall find it.

Then He went on to speak about the reward which comes to those who go out to serve in His name (10:40-42).

Note that He said nothing about being saved or becoming His disciple here. Rather, He spoke about *being worthy of Him* (37, 38). It would have been inordinate for Him to charge His twelve Apostles with the need for salvation at this point, since most of them had been His disciples for over two years (cf. John 1), and had been selected from among a much larger band of disciples to be His Apostles. In giving them a charge to go out to the people of Israel to confront them with the message of repentance (Mk. 6:12), He warned them of the severe persecution that would attend their representing Him as His Apostles (sent ones). After charging them regarding cross-bearing, He alluded to the *rewards* for their worthy service (Mt. 10:40-42). *Thus to read into His words a message of salvation would be to ignore what He actually said and the context in which He said it.*

The context rather indicates that He is telling His born-again Apostles (except for Judas) that to be worthy of Him as they represent Him (10:40), they will have to face persecution, even death. The key phrase is: **"he who has lost his life for My sake."** They must give their lives over to the Lord, and that is the only way they will really find a true purpose in life and thus really "find" it (Gk: 'gain for oneself'). The word translated 'life' is *psuchē*, which is never used of the eternal life (*zoē*) received in salvation. The Apostles already had eternal life; now they needed to find the abundant, meaningful life in the center of God's will. The exhortation is for true disciples to follow Christ in persecution in order to be *worthy of Him*.

Facing His passion

A year later, a few months before the cross, the Lord took His Apostles north to Caesarea Philippi at the headwaters of the east branch of the Jordan.   There He elicited Peter's famous confession of His deity and announced a new direction for the remaining weeks of His ministry —Jerusalem and the cross (Mt. 16:13-28=Mk. 8:31-37=Lk. 9:22-25). This is the occasion for the first of a dozen prophecies of His impending passion which He made at the end of His ministry.   This was also the first intimation to His Apostles about the church, which He was now planning to build, based upon that predicted passion.   After Peter's misguided attempt to dissuade the Lord, Mark's Gospel indicates that the Lord summoned a crowd of other disciples and gave the second of His discipleship discourses in words similar to the first occasion (Mt. 16:24-27, ESV):

> If anyone would come after me, let him deny himself and take up his cross and follow me. For whoever would save his life will lose it, but whoever loses his life for My sake will find it. For what will it profit a man if he gains the whole world and forfeits his life? Or what shall a man give in return for his life? For the Son of Man is going to come with His angels in the glory of his Father, and then he will repay each person according to what he has done.

From the previous discourse, the Apostles would have understood that now that the divine Messiah is committed to go up to Jerusalem to die, their lives would be at risk, and at the least they would suffer the persecution which would undoubtedly follow. It is in the light of this that He emphasized self-denial and a willingness to take up a cross to follow Him to death.

Thus, even though the Lord had summoned a crowd of other disciples who had apparently followed Him there (cf. Mark), there is no more basis for assuming that He is giving salvation truth here than in the previous context.   That this crowd had followed Him way up to Caesarea Philippi in Gentile territory would indicate that these were strongly motivated disciples. They also needed to hear this discipleship challenge.   Those in the crowd who had less sincere, perhaps political, motivations needed to be alerted to the fact that a cross, not a throne, was in the offing.   So any assumption that the presence of the crowd would imply that the Lord must be speaking about salvation is misguided.   There is no invitation here to *come to Him*, but rather an exhortation to *follow after Him* to possible death in Jerusalem. *This simple distinction is not simplistic.*

Luke added one word to his record which makes a salvation interpretation absurd: "'If anyone wishes to come after Me, let him deny himself, and take up his cross **daily**, and follow Me'" (Lk. 9:23).   It is the little word "daily" which totally destroys the legalistic interpretations.   We are to take up our cross *daily*.   If salvation were the subject, we would have to get saved daily, and salvation then would become the piecemeal dispensing of merit a little at a time based on works, as Roman Catholicism advocates.   The epistle to the Hebrews obliterates this possibility by emphasizing that Jesus Christ died once for all, that we might be saved once for all (Heb. 7:25-27; 9:12, 24-26; 10:10-14).   *The interpretation of this passage hinges upon this one word*

'daily,' which must on no account be overlooked.[A]
The rest of the passage (Mt. 16:25-27), as in the previous context, has also been widely misunderstood as referring to eternal salvation. As in Matthew 10:30 the word *psuchē* should be consistently translated here as 'life.' The verb, 'to save,' *(sōdzein)* is used in secular Greek of salvation "from peril, injury, or suffering."[8] The relevance to the immediate context is seen as the Lord warned His disciples of the cost of following Him to His passion in Jerusalem. So He was really warning them that if they try to save their lives from peril, injury, or suffering, they will in reality lose their lives, which then would count for nothing in the light of eternity. Then He reinforced this with the next clause of Matthew 16:25, "**... but whoever loses his life for My sake will find it**"(ESV). From the world's point of view they are losing their lives, but in reality they will find life's true significance. In verse 26, He reinforced this one step farther, by emphasizing the absolute profitlessness of gaining even the whole world (of money, fame, and power) and forfeiting one's own life. Such a life is a total waste in God's sight.

The issue here relates to salvaging our lives for Christ's sake. If we believers try to save our lives for ourselves by clinging to them and using them for our own agenda, they will be lost or wasted as far as the program of Christ is concerned. On the other hand, if we lose our life in the sense of giving it up to Christ, only then will we really salvage it.

As in Matthew 10, the Lord concluded by promising to reward faithful service when He returns (16:27-28) and to judge the believer's works (cf. 1 Cor. 3:10-15; 2 Cor. 5:9-11). The issue is not salvation but true discipleship. Mark and Luke use almost identical words in their accounts, and the slight differences are of minimal significance (except for the word 'daily').

In Perea shortly before His passion

Luke alone recorded this third significant discipleship discourse given to a great crowd of His followers in Perea across the Jordan in the last stage of His final trip up to Jerusalem to be crucified (Luke 14:25-35). It is fair to assume that a significant part of the crowd following along with Him had come to believe in His messiahship. In a few weeks many of them would be welcoming Him to Jerusalem with shouts of Hosanna. Their presence does not imply that He is explaining the way of salvation to them at this point.

Only one verse here closely parallels the other discipleship passages: "**Whoever does not carry his own cross and come after Me cannot be My disciple**" (Lk. 14:27). Verse 26 is similar to Matthew 10:37, but is put more bluntly, using hyperbole: "**If anyone comes to Me, and does not hate his own father and mother and wife and children and brother and sisters, yes, and even his own life, he cannot be my disciple.**" Comparing this with the Matthew 10 statement helps understand the hyperbole of His language. Reference to the cost of discipleship being

---

A. However, it should be noted that MacArthur makes only passing reference to Luke 9:23 in his *Gospel According to Jesus* (p 202) and does not recognize the significance of this very important word.

likened to counting the cost of building a tower or of winning a battle is a new emphasis. Again, as in Matthew 10 and 16, He is talking about being a *worthy disciple* in the face of persecution, a disciple in the fullest sense of the word. He is also warning insincere followers that they need to anticipate persecution and a high cost of discipleship and to settle the issue beforehand. He might have intended to sort out the true from the false, but this is quite different from setting out a cost as a precondition for salvation.

If He had been speaking about how to become saved, His rigorous demands would be absolutely out of the question for any spiritually dead person to fulfill. In demanding that an inquirer count a cost, He would have been totally contradicting any offer of salvation as a free gift. The two are totally incompatible. To cap it off, the Lord required that His disciples give up all their own possessions (Lk. 14:33). If this is a precondition for salvation, there would be extremely few Christians in the world, and it is transparent that salvation would cost us financially and materially. In that case salvation could hardly be a gift of His unmerited favor, could it?

Christ's Salvation Witness

Now that we have distinguished salvation from discipleship in our Lord's most explicit teachings to His disciples, let us see how this understanding is confirmed in the way he dealt with individuals. Did He use discipleship language in dealing with unregenerate inquirers or not?

The progressive discipleship of His first disciples. John tells the story of the Messiah's recruiting of the first four of His disciples from among the disciples of John the Baptizer (Jn. 1:35-51): Andrew, Simon Peter, James and John. They promptly switched their allegiance to Christ and became His disciples. Since they had been John's disciples, we can understand that they had already repented and been baptized. Thus, we can understand them to be regenerated Israelites. The same would be true of Philip and Nathaniel. Clearly the Lord attested the regenerate state of Nathaniel, as his own declaration of Jesus' deity and messiahship confirms. His message to them is to follow Him as disciples (1:43). Apparently they were joined subsequently by a larger number of believing disciples, who followed the Lord on a more casual, intermittent basis.

It was some months later that the Lord recruited the four fishermen, as *full-time disciples*, causing them to leave their family fishing business to fish for people (Mt. 4:18-22; Mk. 1:16-20; Lk. 5:1-11). This was the second stage in their progressive commitment to His person and program. Then it was well over a year later that He commissioned the twelve out of many disciples to be His Apostles (Mt. 10:1-15; Mk. 6:7-11; Lk. 9:1-5), as the third stage. They made a progressively deeper commitment to him after their conversion. *Please note that all of the above discipleship teaching (Mt. 10 & 16; Lk. 9 & 14) came long after this.*

Nicodemus, the distinguished teacher of Israel. Nicodemus had not yet made any significant commitment to Christ, although he sincerely acknowledged the Lord's teaching ministry as from God. So the Lord immediately exposed his ignorance as the distinguished teacher of Israel, who had no clue as to the Old Testament teaching of the necessity of a new birth (Ezek. 36:25-27). God had spoken about cleansing Israel from their sin with clean water and putting His Spirit within them to enable them to do His will. MacArthur says that the Savior's demand for a new birth was "shocking to Nicodemus (John 3:9). Don't miss that point or minimize Jesus' challenge to this man. Our Lord's strategy in witnessing was to go for the throat, and He established His direct, confrontational approach in this first encounter."[9] The legalism and externalism of Pharisaic rabbinic teaching had blinded Nicodemus as to the heart of God's previous revelation.[B]

After pointing Nicodemus to Himself (Jn. 3:10-13), the Lord used the symbolism of the brass snake which Moses erected in the wilderness as a picture of His coming crucifixion. It was also a reminder of the rebellious sin of Israel and God's judgment which occasioned that incident. Even though the word 'repentance' is not used here, it would take a vast change of mind or attitude for Nicodemus to take this look of faith at the Messiah. Apparently he did not do so at this point in time, but three years later when he saw the Lord Jesus being lifted up in crucifixion, he summoned up the courage to commit himself by helping to embalm the Lord's body (Jn. 19:39). He must have remembered the Lord's words of John 3:14.

MacArthur, however, distorts the implications of this account by focusing upon the 'does not obey' in the NAS translation of John 3:36: "Real faith results in obedience." There is a serious issue of the translation of *apeithein* here and elsewhere. Although in secular Greek it normally means "to disobey, be disobedient," most modern translators follow the BAG lexicon: "... **but the one who refuses to believe in the Son will not see life; instead, the wrath of God remains on him**" (Jn. 3:18, HCSB). To read obedience into this word is an unjustified legalistic spin.[C] How much obedience must result from genuine faith? How immediately must that obedience begin? This is front-loading obedience into the definition of faith.

B. Although there are many interpretations of the water of 3:5, it is simplest and best to understand it as a symbol of the Holy Spirit, and it can be translated, "water, even the Spirit." This is confirmed by the same symbolism in Jn. 4:14 and 7:37-39. It certainly does not refer to baptism, which only symbolizes Spirit baptism and cleansing from sin (cf. Ch. 18).

C So KJV, NKJV, NIV, TNIV. " . since, in the view of the early Christians, the supreme disobedience was a refusal to believe their gospel, ἀ[*apeithein*] may be restricted in some passages to the meaning. *disbelieve, be an unbeliever.* This sense, though greatly disputed (it is not found outside our lit.), seems most probable in Jn. 3 36; Ac14:2, 19·9, Ro 15:31, and only slightly less prob. in Ro 2·8, 1 Pt 2:8, 3:1, perhaps also vs 20; 4·17; 1 Mg 8.2." (BAG, p. 82). Since the positive verb *peithein* has the meaning, "*convince, persuade,* etc." (BAG, pp. 644-5), and since John sets the negative *apeithein* in opposition to *pisteuein*, it seems clear that "disbelieve" is John's meaning.

An immoral Samaritan woman (John 4). There is nothing supportive of discipleship salvation in the Lord's witness to the Samaritan woman. However, MacArthur suggests that His invitation to her to drink of the living water conveys commitment as well as appropriation. By quoting Matthew 20:22 (**"Are you able to drink the cup that I am about to drink?"**) and John 18:11 (**"The cup which the Father has given Me, shall I not drink it?"**) he seems to have made a point. However, in moving beyond commitment to obedience, he has gone beyond the data by pushing a dubious translation of *apeithein*, as just discussed.[10] Commitment and obedience are two different things!

A turncoat tax-collector. A major issue related to discipleship salvation in the account of Matthew's conversion is the issue of a new convert's sense of sinfulness (Mt. 9:9-13; Mk. 2:13-17; Lk. 5:27-32). MacArthur correctly emphasizes the importance of an inquirer having a sense of sin in coming to Christ. Matthew as a tax-collector was indeed a despicable sinner in the eyes of the Jews and in the eyes of God. After Matthew had left his tax office to follow the Lord and invited other notorious sinners to meet the Lord Jesus at a banquet, the Lord responded to the Pharisaic criticism with the most significant statement: **"I have not come to call the righteous but sinners to repentance"** (Lk. 9:32). The self-righteous Pharisees did not recognize their sin; Matthew certainly had. The question arises as to how immediate and deep must that sense of sin be for a person to be genuinely saved? We must not extrapolate Matthew's story as a notorious sinner to be a paradigm for all conversions, especially of children raised in Christian homes.

MacArthur does so: "It is impossible to suggest that a person can encounter the holy God of Scripture and be saved without also coming to grips with the heinousness of his own sin and consequently longing to turn from it."[11] He then gives examples of Peter, Paul, Job, and Isaiah coming to a deep sense of their own sinfulness (Lk.5:8; 1 Tim. 1:15; Job 42:6; Isaiah 6:5). The major problem with this is that none of these examples express the heart condition of these men at the point of their conversion; indeed, for some it was years after God's first dealings with them.

Furthermore we don't know the actual point of Matthew's conversion. When the Lord Jesus walked by his tax-office and called him in two words to **"Follow Me,"** this was not the first contact they had made. Almost certainly Matthew had been in the crowd hearing our Lord's teaching at least once and probably many times before. He was presumably converted on one of those occasions, since he couldn't *follow* Christ until he had first *come* to Him for salvation (Mt. 11:28). So this account says nothing about Matthew's sense of sinfulness at the point of his conversion. This usually grows as we grow in the Lord, and growing Christians ought to have a strong sense of repugnance for sin in their lives.

A self-righteous synagogue ruler. Not too long after the discipleship discourse of Luke 14, a works-oriented synagogue ruler came to the Lord with his revealing question, as all three Synoptics record it: "**Teacher, what good thing shall I do that I may obtain eternal life?**" (Mt. 19:16-26=Mk. 10:17-27=Lk. 18:18-27). This passage has also been misused by those who put a legalistic spin on salvation, since they have missed the main point of the story.[12] The Lord Jesus was seeking to wean him step by step away from this mindset. First, He pointed him to the Mosaic Law, which Paul later explained was to bring people under the guilt of sin (Rom. 3:19-20; 1 Tim. 1:8-11). This must have been Christ's motivation also, but the man supposed that keeping part of the Law was adequate, since he asked, "**Which ones?**" The Lord pointed him to the Leviticus 17:18 summary of the second tablet of the Law: "**You shall love your neighbor as yourself**" (Mt. 19:19). This was to get him to see, as a rich man, that he did not love his neighbor as himself. In his self-righteousness, however, he responded, "**Teacher, I have kept all these things from my youth up; what am I still lacking?**" (Mk. 10:20; Mt. 19:20). In order to bring this young man into an awareness of his own sinfulness, the Lord instructed him to sell his possessions, give to the poor, and come and follow Him. This was the ultimate test of whether he had kept the intent of the Law. He apparently didn't get the point, since he went away sorrowful. *The Lord was trying to get him to see that he didn't love his neighbor as himself and therefore that he hadn't really kept the Law.*

The truth of this understanding is confirmed by the following dialogue with His disciples. After pointing out the obstacle which riches present to people in getting saved (which Paul confirmed in 1 Cor. 1:26-28), the Lord resorted to hyperbole to emphasize His point: "**... it is easier for a camel to go through the eye of a needle, than for a rich man to enter the kingdom of God**" (Mt. 19:24). Legions of legalistic commentators have tried to make a camel's passage through the eye of a needle a human possibility by the supposition that the eye of the needle is a reference to some postern gate, which a camel could conceivably negotiate. This is not only without a scintilla of evidence, but also totally at odds with the point Christ made in the next interchange. The disciples understood the incredibility of His hyperbole by crying out in astonishment, "**Then who can be saved?**" His answer is clear: "**With men this is impossible, but with God all things are possible.**" When will legalists learn that, humanly speaking, salvation is an impossibility? Salvation must be a work of God's unmerited favor, else no one would be saved. But since the contemporary Jewish view was that riches are a sign of God's favor, Christ's point was astonishing to the disciples: that riches predispose people away from the gospel.

Note in passing a point made elsewhere, that there are many human factors which predispose people against the gospel (e.g. materialism, Islam, evolutionary humanism). This hardly fits with unconditional election. We should also note that Mark recorded the observation, "**And looking at him, Jesus felt a love for him,...**"(10:21). We wonder, does God love the non-elect? We don't know whether this man ever came to faith in the Messiah.

In reference to the cost of salvation, it should be obvious to any Evangelical that the only cost is that which Christ paid, as Peter expressed so clearly, "**... knowing that you were not redeemed with perishable things like silver or gold from your futile way of life inherited from your forefathers, but with precious blood, as of a lamb unblemished and spotless, *the blood* of Christ**" (1 Pet. 1:18-19).

So we must not take our Lord's words to this self-righteous religious ruler as a basis for saying that an inquirer has to sell his property and give to the poor in order to be saved. Walter Chantry has built most of his case for discipleship salvation upon his misunderstanding of this passage. Chantry himself probably did not forsake his wealth in order to be saved. When he says that we "have to sell all in obedience to Christ," presumably he does not mean this to be taken literally. But he does not clarify.

John MacArthur, although much of his discussion about this ruler is helpful, also misses this key point: After wrongly connecting this with the discipleship teaching of Luke 14:33, he states:

> Our Lord gave this young man a test. He had to choose between his possessions and Jesus Christ. He failed the test. No matter what he believed, since he was unwilling to forsake all, he could not be a disciple of Christ. Salvation is for those who are willing to forsake everything.[13]

If this dialogue is to be understood as a paradigm for salvation of all, then this is the only place in Scripture that an unbeliever was challenged with this option. Did MacArthur forsake everything at the time of his conversion? Does he lay this demand upon all the inquirers he seeks to lead to Christ? Let's be real. If salvation is a matter of passing or failing such a test, the gospel is not a gospel of grace, as MacArthur has sought to proclaim. In that case, it would be a thoroughly legalistic corruption of the gospel.

The subsequent clarification by the Lord to His Apostles of His intent in Matthew 19:23-26 is significantly not expounded by MacArthur, except in passing in his next chapter. As noted above, the Lord is making it clear that if salvation depends upon man, it is an absolute impossibility; it is possible only with God. Certainly this case study should not be extrapolated as a general rule for all, since this man's self-righteousness was uniquely hardcore. This was not the case with the next example.

Zaccheus, the crooked tax-collector. The account of the conversion of Zaccheus is quite terse and concluded with one main point which the Lord stated: "**The Son of Man has come to seek and to save that which was lost**" (Lk. 19:1-10). As with Matthew, we don't know how much prior teaching of the Lord he had heard or what the Lord Jesus told him in his house about being saved. We can only reconstruct a hint of the extortionate methods of his practices from his admission of fraud and his ready willingness to give half (not all) of his goods to the poor. We do well to understand this, as most do, as the fruit of his conversion, certainly not the condition, as MacArthur recognizes.[14] Thus this example proves very little for or against 'discipleship salvation.'

Two significant parables.

Two of the ten parables of the kingdom which the Lord Jesus gave us are most relevant to this: "**The kingdom of heaven is like a treasure hidden in the field, which a man found and hid; and from joy over it he goes and sells all that he has, and buys that field. Again, the kingdom of heaven is like a merchant seeking fine pearls, and upon finding one pearl of great value, he went and sold all that he had, and bought it**" (Mt. 13:44-46). Parables are the most difficult part of our Lord's teaching to interpret, especially when there is no introductory explanation, as here. We must interpret parables in the light of Christ's clear teaching elsewhere. Far too many interpreters take it that the sinner is represented by the man who sells all to buy either the treasure or the pearl. However, who has sold all that he had to buy something of great value? The answer is obvious that the Lord Jesus sold all that He had to redeem us from sin. The basic word for redemption is the ordinary word 'to buy.' Christ purchased us with His own blood. What could be clearer? Can we purchase salvation? Absolutely not! We are bankrupt; we don't have anything to sell by which we might purchase it, even if it were for sale. It is God's gift of free grace (Rom. 3:24; 6:23; Eph. 2:8-9). How then can all these interpreters say that we have to sell all in order to be saved? *This shows the depth to which a legalistic concept of salvation has spread among Protestants since the Reformation.*

One might wonder about the identity of the treasure and the pearl in these parables. This is not central to my point, but Israel is portrayed as God's treasure, and the church can be seen as the pearl of great value.

The Issues of Discipleship Salvation

Salvation and rewards. The distinctions between salvation and rewards was made by C. I. Scofield and emphasized by dispensationalists.* On the other hand, there is a strong reticence on the part of some from the Reformed* tradition to acknowledge this distinction. For example, Harold Camping says that any acknowledgment of God's rewarding of the faithful service of believers would undermine the gracious character of salvation. There is no logical contradiction between the two, and there is so much Scripture to support both truths. Part of the problem for Camping may be his failure to distinguish between the judgment seat of Christ and the great white throne judgment of the lost (Rev. 20:15), which is a consequence of his amillennialism.*[15] A clear passage here is 1 Corinthians 3:10-15, which pictures Christians building the church upon the rock Christ Jesus. Paul is very explicit that if our work for Christ survives the fire of the day of Christ, we shall receive a reward. On the other hand, concerning the one whose work is burned up as being wood, hay, or stubble, "**he himself shall be saved, yet so as through fire**"(1 Cor. 3:15). Clearly the judgment seat (*bēma*) of Christ is an examination of a believer's works, which could hardly be a description of the issue of salvation by grace through faith alone.

Are there carnal Christians and fruitless believers?. It is useless to try to deny that carnal Christians existed in the Corinthian church or for that matter today, as some neo-Puritans* have done. Paul was very explicit in contrasting spiritual Christians from two other varieties:

> **And I, brethren, could not speak to you as to spiritual men, but as to men of the flesh, as to babes in Christ. I gave you milk to drink, not solid food; for you were not yet able *to receive it*. Indeed, even now you are not yet able, for you are still fleshly. For since there is jealousy and strife among you, are you not fleshly, and are you not walking like mere men?** (1 Cor. 3:1-3)

Some fleshly believers (*sarkinos*) were identified as babes in Christ, new Christians who have not yet grown (1 Cor. 3:1). But he directly confronted others as being more acutely fleshly (*sarkikos*) in behaving as the unregenerate in regard to party politics in the church (3:2-4). This is not to say that they were totally given over to a pagan lifestyle. However, later when Paul addressed the problem of the incestuous man in the church, the discipline he counseled was so **"that his spirit may be saved in the day of the Lord Jesus"** (1 Cor. 5:5). Even though Paul had some very positive things to say about the Corinthian church (1:4-9), there were many other evidences of carnality among them. Much as some would like to legislate carnal Christians out of existence by insisting that such people are not really Christians, this is a legalistic solution to the problem. *One form of legalism is in legislating the ideal among God's people*. This is an erroneous solution.

What was this discipline of the incestuous professing believer **"to deliver such a one to Satan for the destruction of the flesh,..."** (1 Cor. 5:5)? Of the two major interpretations, the most viable is that the church should excommunicate him, if unrepentant, and pray for his premature physical death. This is confirmed by the parallel situation of those abusing the Lord's table: **"For this reason many among you are weak and sick, and a number sleep"** (1 Cor. 11:30), which he described as a disciplinary judgment on those believers, so that they **"may not be condemned along with the world"** (11:32).

We already have the striking example made of Ananias and Sapphira, who although they were willing to make a substantial gift to the church, lied about it (Acts 5:1-11). There is absolutely no basis for questioning the reality of their salvation. John confirmed this principle in 1 John 5:16-17 in speaking about a sin of a brother unto death. Although Arminians have the 'luxury' of saying this is the loss of salvation, more Calvinistically minded interpreters would have to lean to it being premature physical death. I am also convinced that this was also a danger for some of the Hebrew Christians addressed in Hebrews 6:1-9 (cf. Ch. 13).

Whenever we raise the issue of the fruitless Christian, we hear the protest misquoted from Matthew 7:16, **"You will know them by their fruits."** Apparently the protestors never bother to look at the context, which is about the false prophets, the ravenous wolves in sheep's clothing, whom we can identify by their fruits. But the fact is that it is sometimes hard to tell the difference between a carnal Christian and a counterfeit believer. Paul was not always sure. But we can see the evil fruits of that liberal preacher who denies the salvation message or that legalistic priest who is distributing piecemeal salvation by human merit.

Two other passages of Scripture which are relevant but are discussed elsewhere should be studied. Some of the believers described in Hebrews 6:4-8 were bearing "thorns and thistles" (cf. Ch. 13). Also in Christ's parable of the four soils, the third-soil type people were believers who "**brought no fruit to maturity**" (Lk. 8:14). This is not to condone the lifestyle of believers described in these many passages. Each of us will have to give account at the judgment seat of Christ. There are also temporal consequences for our sins and failure to do the full will of God. But the Scriptures are very realistic in portraying life as it is, not as we might idealize it.

Conclusions

As the three major discipleship teachings of the Lord Jesus have been examined in chronological sequence and context, it has become clear that He is not declaring the way of salvation but is putting demands of discipleship upon those who had already been converted. *The word 'daily' in Luke 9:23 is crucial.* Upon examining Christ's salvation witness to a number of unbelieving individuals, there is no evidence that He laid discipleship teaching upon them. The so-called 'lordship salvation' issue would be better recognized as a 'discipleship salvation' issue. At bottom the distinction between salvation and discipleship is clear and important in avoiding legalism, even if the legalism be promoted under the name of 'grace.'

---

1 Robert Shank, *Life in the Son*, p 18.

2 Harold Camping, in *Family Radio News*

3 Walter Chantry, *Today's Gospel Authentic or Synthetic?*, p 47

4 Charles Ryrie refers to it as "so-called lordship/discipleship/mastery salvation " in *So Great Salvation*, p 29

5. John F. MacArthur, Jr , *The Gospel According to Jesus*, p 30

6 Charles C Ryrie in the foreword to Zane C Hodges, *The Hungry Inherit*, p 7

7 Arndt and Gingrich, *Greek-English Lexicon*, p 486

8 Abbott-Smith, *Lexicon*, p 436

9 MacArthur, pp 37-47, esp 39, his treatment here is quite helpful

10 Ibid , pp 46-47, 52-53.

11 Ib.d , p 60

12 I am indebted to Alan A McRae, the founder of Biblical Seminary, for the main ideas of this exposition, given in a popular lecture in Dallas, attendant to his Griffith-Thomas Lectures at Dallas Seminary in the early 1950s

13 MacArthur, p. 78

14 Ibid., p 95

15 Although Harold Camping is not a trained theologian, as a most vocal spokesman for his extreme form of Reformed theology, it is appropriate to reference him Since such statements are repeatedly aired on Family Radio, it is extraneous to try to document an exact quotation

... unless one understands and accepts the doctrine of eternal security, one can not accept without a great deal of reservation the doctrines of the grace of God. The whole body of grace truth loses very much of its meaning to those who reject the doctrine of eternal security.

—J. F. Strombeck

WHY THE STRUGGLE WITH ETERNAL SECURITY?

As a new believer in an Arminian church, the first doctrinal issue I faced was the security of the believer. I came to Christ through my childhood buddy, Herb Hage. Together we began to look up every passage relevant to the issue and check key word usage in a concordance. We were also greatly helped by John F. Strombeck's fine book, *Shall Never Perish.*[1] Within some months we both became convinced that salvation is eternal, not probationary. Half a century of study has confirmed that conclusion.

Although James Arminius never did deny eternal security, his Remonstrant followers and the Wesleyans did. Thus it is commonly thought that the dividing line between Calvinism and Arminianism is eternal security. But even in reference to eternal security, it is clear that we must go "beyond Arminianism and Calvinism" to get the whole truth, since there is a tendency in both camps to intrude human performance into the ultimate salvation of the believer. It is ironic that Arminians are joined by extreme Calvinists in rejecting 'eternal security.' As a result, we should not be surprised that there is a lot of confusion of definition and interpretation of relevant Scripture.

The focus of this chapter will be on an accurate definition, the significance, some implications, and a summary of the positive biblical evidence. Subsequent chapters will require a detailed investigation of controverted passages, foremost of which is Hebrews 6. During a decade as a Bible answerman on Christian radio, the most frequent question we got related to Hebrews 6. It was most troubling to Arminius and Arminians (and Calvinists, for that matter). There is a unique contribution to resolving this problem text in Chapter 13.

151

Clarification of the Doctrine

Since there is so much confusion as to what eternal security means, it is imperative to define it clearly: *Whoever once truly trusts Christ's finished sacrifice and resurrection for eternal life and is born again can never be lost, no matter what work (or lack of work) may accompany that faith.*[2]

First, it is clear that the truth of eternal security is *not identical* to the traditional Calvinistic doctrine of the *perseverance* of the saints. The *preservation* of the saints better describes it, because the emphasis is upon the work of God, not upon the works of man. This is not just a semantic difference; there is a significant conceptual difference as well. Many extreme Calvinistic writers recognize this and reject the term eternal security and the phrase, "once saved, always saved." The nub of the difference is that they generally put the onus upon the saints to persevere, while a biblical concept of eternal security puts the responsibility upon God to preserve the saved. This means that, in the final analysis, the extreme Calvinistic view is that the good works of the saints are necessary to ultimate salvation. Laurence Vance's careful study and extensive documentation are important. He says: "But by confounding God's *preservation* of the believer with the believer's *perseverance* in the faith, Calvinists have contradicted their entire system of theology."[3] John Murray represents this view: "But let us appreciate the doctrine of the perseverance of the saints and recognize that we may entertain the faith of our security in Christ only as we persevere in faith and holiness to the end."[4] Arthur Pink is even more explicit: "Those who persevere not in faith and holiness, love and obedience, will assuredly perish."[5] Although Calvinists admit that true believers can fall temporarily, most hold that a true believer will come back to Christ before death. However, Charles Hodge, a nineteenth-century Calvinistic theologian, commented on Paul's words in 1 Corinthians 9:27, "... this devoted apostle considered himself as engaged in a lifestruggle of his salvation."[6] This is astonishing!

Calvin's doctrine of temporary faith is an enigma, inconsistent with his other doctrines. He spoke of a "false work of grace," and in like manner, R.C. Sproul says that "we may think that we have faith when in fact we have no faith." Over the centuries, Calvinists have consistently believed that those who do not persevere in a godly lifestyle until the end of life were never really saved in the first place. How could Charles Hodge even entertain the idea that Paul had to struggle to keep himself saved and might not succeed? He could hardly say that Paul was not saved in the first place, could he?

Most serious is the common Calvinistic notion that one cannot know whether one is among the elect or not. This affected much of Puritan thinking and is still rife among the Reformed.* Asahel Nettleton, a nineteenth-century Calvinistic evangelist, represents the problem: "The most that I have ventured to say respecting myself is, that I think it possible I may get to heaven."[7] Michael Eaton describes from personal experience another serious consequence of this kind of theology: "... an ossified legalism, a crippling introspection, and a harshness of spirit that seemed nothing like the Jesus of the Bible."[8]

Eaton has chronicled the contemporary seriousness of the problem and shows how critical a matter it has been for what he calls "Developed Calvinism," as well as for Arminianism. Speaking as a long-term high-Calvinist pastor, he states: "Is it not a fact of history that the Calvinist has tended to have less assurance of salvation than the Arminian? The Arminian is at least sure of his present salvation. As a result of the high Calvinist doctrine the Calvinist often doubts his present salvation and thus has a less contented frame of mind than his evangelical Arminian friend."[9]

Parallels between Arminianism and extreme Calvinism

Extreme Calvinism seems to be very similar to the Arminian view of insecurity. Robert Shank, a representative Arminian, wrote: "There is no saving faith apart from obedience.... There is no valid assurance of election and final salvation for any man, apart from deliberate perseverance in faith."[10] Eaton has demonstrated the irony of the weak assurance of "developed Calvinists" and Arminians alike. He compares Nettleton with John Fletcher, a friend of John Wesley, and shows that neither had any assurance of ultimate salvation:

> These great men exemplify a theological problem that has troubled evangelical churches and preachers since the 17th century, if not before On the one hand, Nettleton's doubts relate to the *genuineness* of salvation. On the other hand, Fletcher said no Christian could be absolutely sure about the *permanence* of their salvation. Nettleton's teaching has been popularly summarized in the phrase 'Once saved, always saved' - but he was not quite sure that he was even once saved! John Fletcher taught 'Once saved, maybe lost'! I find neither doctrine very encouraging. In fact, both seem rather terrifying.[11]

The point is, that as long as human performance intrudes into the issue of ultimate salvation, there can be no **"full assurance of faith"** (Heb. 10:22) or full assurance of any kind, it matters not whether one be a Calvinist or an Arminian. Both in effect make human performance until the end of life an essential condition of ultimate salvation. The premise of Shank's defense of conditional security is that Christ's major discipleship passages (Mt. 10 & 16; Lk. 9 & 14) are salvation truth.[12] About the time I read Shank, I also interacted with Calvinist John MacArthur's "lordship salvation" view in which he does the same thing. Both are tragically wrong! (Cf. Ch. 12)

There is another striking parallel between extreme Calvinists and Arminians. Both assume that there is no such thing as fruitless or carnal believers. Arminians say that any Christian who is fruitless or carnal has lost his salvation; extreme Calvinists say that such a person was never really saved in the first place. But Scripture is explicit in describing carnal, fruitless believers (1 Cor. 3:1-3, 15; 5:1-13; 11:17-34; Mt. 13:22; Heb. 6:7-8; 2 Pet. 2:7).

The parallels go even farther. Both make fear of ultimate perdition a major motivation for moral behavior. Arminians say that we all must fear falling into sin, because sin causes a Christian to lose salvation. Extreme Calvinists say that a sinful lifestyle is proof that a professing Christian is not among the elect, and that the only proof of election is perseverance in holiness until the end. Fear of ultimate condemnation is the motivation for holiness here also. Charles Stanley aptly comments, "Fear and love do not mingle well. One will always dilute the other. Furthermore, fear spills over into worry. Let's be realistic for a moment. If my salvation is not a settled issue, how can I be anxious for nothing (see Phil. 4:6)?"[13] It is true that fear of loss of rewards at the judgment seat of Christ is a biblical motivation for godliness (2 Cor. 5:10ff), but not fear of condemnation.

Another parallel is that both viewpoints are fuzzy about distinguishing salvation and rewards. Christ and the Apostles clearly taught that there are rewards in the kingdom for godly living, which are over and above simply being saved. Many extreme Calvinists and Arminians deny this. Words like rewards and crowns are sprinkled throughout the New Testament and need to be given adequate consideration.[14]

Understanding Arminian thinking

I have never really been an Arminian, since after my conversion I quickly distanced myself from conditional security. However, Charles Stanley was a convinced (and probably convincing) Arminian for a decade, until, as a seminary student, he restudied the issue from scratch. He attributes his shift of viewpoint to two factors:

> First, I was guilty of ignoring the context of many verses I quoted to defend my view. As I began digging deeper into the events and discussions surrounding these passages, they took on a different meaning. Second, I discovered through my study that the concept of salvation through faith alone cannot be reconciled with the belief that one can forfeit his or her salvation. If I must do or not do something to keep from losing my salvation, salvation would be by faith and works.

Early on I learned the truth of Stanley's appraisal. My Arminian pastor asked me to lead the mid-week Bible study and prayer meeting in his absence. As a 20-year-old college student, I naively selected eternal security as my subject. I began by asking the group of two dozen believers, "When you get to heaven, on what basis will you be able to say that you got there?" Everyone responded in a similar vein, that it will be by faith in Christ *plus* faithfulness and obedience to Him. There were different ways of expressing it, *but not one said it was by faith in Christ alone*! This was a vivid lesson.

Stanley describes how when he first began to grasp security, it was as if a light came on and he was freed from prison. He had the awesome thought, "I had been eternally secure since the day as a twelve-year-old when I prayed, asking Jesus to save me." As a result he began to experience the true meaning of unconditional love, and words like 'grace,' 'peace,' and 'joy' took on new meaning in his experience. There was a new intimacy with Christ as he felt secure in love and acceptance and release from the bondage of guilt and fear that had dominated for a decade (Jn. 8:32).

He explains the two Arminian scenarios as to how a Christian can lose salvation. Some say it is only through apostasy, quoting Heb. 6:4-6, the parable of the four soils, and "falling from grace" (Gal. 5:4). Others focus on the illogic of a holy God allowing sinful behavior in a Christian's life with impunity. The latter say, "God is merciful, but not a fool!" "It would be unfair for God to give equal salvation to faithless and faithful Christians alike." " Eternal security is just a license to sin." "There must be a point of no return in the life of the sinful Christian."[15]

R. T. Kendall was a fervent Arminian for even longer than Stanley and thought eternal security was a devilish doctrine. However, one day driving from his student pastorate in an Arminian church to his Arminian college, the Holy Spirit gave him a strong conviction that he was eternally saved. This experience opened up the Scriptures to him to see that actually all truly born-again believers are eternally secure, not just himself! The irony is that all true believers are eternally secure, whether or not they believe it. Indeed, many extreme Calvinists do not have the assurance that they are really saved and secure in Christ.[16]

Earl Radmacher was also taught in his youth that eternal security was a doctrine of the devil. What so confused him was the conflicting counsel as to how to get saved: "hang onto God," "let go and let God," "pray through," or "surrender to God." After he was saved at age fourteen, because he was untaught in the truths of the grace of God, he was on a spiritual roller coaster until he came to the truth of eternal security.[17]

Let it be absolutely clear that we are not advocating the eternal security of all professing Christians, no matter how orthodox or evangelical they might seem to be. The Bible is clear that there are counterfeit Christians who make a false, superficial profession of faith in Christ, but have never been genuinely born again. It is also clear that there are backslidden, carnal Christians, whose lifestyle is not glorifying to God. They will lose rewards at the judgment seat of Christ, but they themselves will be saved "so as by fire" (1 Cor. 3:15). Sometimes it is hard to distinguish the counterfeits from the backslidden. But the Lord knows their hearts and He is the ultimate judge.

Thus, it is a challenge to develop a position on security which maintains the truth of justification by faith alone without lapsing into the legalistic addition of works found both in Arminianism and extreme Calvinism. Approaching it inductively from a mediate position will avoid the confusion of the polarized views.

The Positive Biblical Basis

I have believed in eternal security for over half a century for one simple reason: *God says it in His word.* Since learning Greek and Hebrew in seminary, I have learned many reasons why that early concordance study might have been defective. However, continued research and interaction with other Christians have only confirmed those conclusions.

The positive biblical evidence for the eternal security of the believer is so overwhelming, that one is amazed that Christians who struggle with security don't seek more assiduously to resolve the tension with controverted passages. The next few chapters address this. First, the positive biblical rationale for security must be fixed in mind, which is so unambiguous that none need struggle. Louis Chafer suggested a simple outline for discussion, which is hard to improve. There are substantial and extensive Scriptures which relate security to each of the members of the Trinity. Here is only a brief overview of a few passages.

The Father's Preservation of His Choice People
The age-spanning purpose of God

Moving away from a Calvinistic view of predestination in no way weakens the force of Paul's chain of logic in Romans 8:28-30. Paul starts with a wonderfully assuring promise to believers, which many Christians have found a great encouragement in times of contrary circumstances: "**And we know that God causes all things to work together for good to those who love God, to those who are called according to *His* purpose**" (Rom. 8:28). If a true believer could lose salvation and go to hell, this promise is meaningless! Paul does not set up loving God as a condition, but rather a description of those who are called by God to salvation. Then he gives the reason that verse 28 is true, as clearly rendered by the NEB translation:

> For God knew his own before ever they were, and also ordained that they should be shaped to the likeness of his Son, that he might be the eldest among a large family of brothers; and it is these, so fore-ordained, whom he has also called. And those whom he called he has justified, and to those whom he justified he has also given his splendour (Rom. 8:29-30, NEB).

There is an unbreakable chain of five links in this promise. It starts with God's foreknowledge and finishes with glorification. If anyone should become lost along the way, Paul's logic and the faithfulness of God to His promises are destroyed. 'Calling' is that work by which a sinner comes to faith in Christ by responding to the universal invitation of the gospel. Those who are called are those who love God, in other words, true Christians. Paul is very explicit that God has pre-appointed them to be conformed to the likeness of His Son, and not only declares them to be righteous in His sight, but has already counted them to be glorified (aorist,* not future tense).

Then in Romans 8:31-35, Paul raises seven unanswerable questions. His mind is boggled by God's overwhelming grace in that God is now for us, He will freely give us all things with Christ, no one can lay any charge against God's elect since God Himself declares us righteous, Christ now intercedes for us, and no one or thing can separate us from His love. One hundred percent of those whom God foreknew, He will glorify by conforming them to Christ's image. This is outrageously true, whether or not those who want to intrude human performance into the sequence can believe it. Those who hold to conditional security must assume an implicit condition here of continued human performance, which would stand in total contradiction to the gracious nature of salvation expressed in Romans 4:16:

> For this reason *it is* by faith, in order that *it may be* in accordance with grace, so that the promise will be guaranteed to all the descendants, not only to those who are of the Law, but also to those who are of the faith of Abraham, who is the father of us all.

God's unbounded love provides a much-more salvation.

In Romans 5:5-10 the Apostle Paul amplified the statement of Christ in John 3:16 regarding the greatness of God's saving love:

> ... the love of God has been poured out within our hearts through the Holy Spirit who was given to us. For while we were still helpless, at the right time Christ died for the ungodly.... But God demonstrates His own love toward us, in that while we were yet sinners, Christ died for us. Much more then, having now been justified by His blood, we shall be saved from the wrath *of God* through Him. For if while we were enemies we were reconciled to God through the death of His Son, much more, having been reconciled, we shall be saved by His life (Rom. 5:5-10).

Paul's Spirit-inspired logic here is inexorable. If God could love us and reconcile us to Himself when we were hostile to Him, now that He has already reconciled us to Himself, is it not even more sure that He will complete this work of salvation? Paul turns the tables on human logic by saying that our future salvation is even more sure than our present salvation. Is it not easier for God to complete the saving of saints than it was to save us from His wrath in the first place when we were sinners? The answer is a resounding 'yes' because of the saving life of Christ– His present intercession for us at the Father's right hand, which he refers to again in 8:34, and is confirmed in Hebrews 7:25 and in 1 John 2:2.

If this were not enough, Paul lists every entity in the universe which might be able to separate us from the love of God, and affirms that none of them can do so (Rom. 8:38-39). This certainly must include Satan, the demons, the world-system, and our own sinful flesh. This is how Paul can affirm that "**God causes all things to work together for good**" for His saints. Thus, there is a synergism between the Father and the Son since Christ's intercessory work contributes to our security.

God's infinite power to keep us saved

The Lord Jesus mentioned another synergism of the members of the Trinity in His promise in John 10:27-29:

> My sheep hear My voice, and I know them, and they follow Me; and I give
> eternal life to them, and they will never perish; and no one will snatch them
> out of My hand. My Father, who has given *them* to Me, is greater than all;
> and no one is able to snatch *them* out of the Father's hand.

As a new Christian fifty years ago, I was astonished by an Arminian book in which the writer inserted conditional 'ifs' into Christ's unconditioned promise: "**If** My sheep hear my voice," and "**If** they follow Me." The Lord makes six parallel statements about His sheep, and to insert a condition in two of them to suit one's theology or predilections is to violate the word of God. This is a simple case of tampering with Scripture. Once we become His sheep through the new birth, these six things are characteristic of His sheep. The promise He makes to His sheep is a promise of absolute protection.

Some Arminians rationalize that we can wriggle out of His hand and lose salvation, but the burden of proof is upon them to show that this is possible. The fact is that all sheep will stray. The Lord chose this symbolism intentionally to communicate that He will keep sheep who are prone to wander. He reinforced this promise by stating that His omnipotent Father will protect His sheep. Not only do all the other positive promises contradict the possibility of wriggling out of His hand, but the warnings Arminians consider as warnings to sheep of hell, are not really such. His real sheep need not ever fear going to hell. Writing to those who have been born again, Peter reaffirmed this truth which he heard from the lips of the Lord: "... **to obtain an inheritance which is imperishable and undefiled and will not fade away, reserved in heaven for you, who are** <u>**protected by the power of God through faith**</u> **for a salvation ready to be revealed in the last time**" (1 Pet. 1:4-5). Peter understood Christ's promise in absolute terms.

Although Paul did not hear Christ's words directly, he claimed the truth for himself: "**... for I know who I have believed and I am convinced that He is able to guard what I have entrusted to Him until that day**" (2 Tim. 1:12). He believed this, not just for himself, but for all who have responded to God's call, based upon Abraham's conviction of God's omnipotence, that "**being fully assured that what God had promised, He was able also to perform**" (Rom. 4:21). Christ's brother had the same conviction: "**Now to Him who is able to keep you from stumbling, and to make you stand in the presence of His glory blameless with great joy,...**" (Jude 24).

The Son's Preservation of His Sheep
His great and precious promises

The promises in the bread of life discourse are even more explicit:

> Jesus said to them, "I am the bread of life; he who come to me will not
> hunger, and he who believes in Me will never thirst. ... All that the Father
> gives Me will come to Me, and the one who comes to Me I will certainly not
> cast out. ... This is the will of Him who sent Me, that of all that He has given
> Me I lose nothing, but raise it up on the last day. For this is the will of My

> Father, that everyone who beholds the Son and believes in Him will have eternal life, and I Myself will raise him up on the last day. (Jn. 6:35-40)

If one who came to Christ and believed on Him could ever again spiritually hunger and thirst in hell, then Christ misled us! To avoid any ambiguity, not only did He assert that a new believer will not be rejected upon coming to Him, but that He will not reject such a one at any future time. This understanding of 6:37 is supported by the assurance of future protection and resurrection in 6:39-40. How could the Lord Jesus have made it any more explicit than He did? Thus the promise of John 10:27-29 must likewise be understood in absolute terms.

His intercessory prayers

Calvinists have long pointed to the impossibility that the Father should not respond to the prayers of the Son since He was sinless and in total harmony with the will of the Father. Christ's prayer for Peter (Lk. 22:32) was efficacious. His high-priestly prayer in the upper room must be efficacious as well: "I am no longer in the world; and *yet* they themselves are in the world, and I come to You. Holy Father, <u>keep them in Your name</u>, *the name* which You have given Me, that they may be one even as We *are*" (Jn. 17:11). This prayer was not just for the Eleven but for all subsequent believers: "I do not ask on behalf of these alone, but for those also who believe in Me through their word" (17:20). The loss of one sheep would imply that Christ's prayer went unanswered. Unthinkable! This is even more unthinkable because of Hebrews 7:25, Romans 5:10; 8:34 (already discussed), and 1 John 2:1-2: "And if anyone sins, we have an Advocate (Intercessor) with the Father, Jesus Christ the righteous; and He Himself is the propitiation for our sins ..." As discussed in Chapter 6, propitiation means a total satisfaction for the Father's offended holiness by the cross of Christ. This then is the basis of Christ's high-priestly ministry for His children at the Father's right hand. For the children of God the sin issue was totally settled on the cross when He cried, "It is finished."

His completed propitiation, redemption, and reconciliation

Paul clearly showed how the justification of the ungodly is based upon the propitiation of Christ's shed blood on the cross in Romans 3:24-25. One phase of His redemptive work, better called ransom-redemption, like propitiation, was the objective basis for forgiveness for any who claims it by faith. He paid the ransom price for the sins of all mankind. However, some of the Greek words for redemption focus on the liberation of the captive, both the present possession and the future liberation of the body: "In Him we have redemption through His blood, the forgiveness of our trespasses, according to the riches of His grace" (Eph. 1:7). We now have redemption as a present possession, but await the final liberation of our bodies. Since the Lord Jesus fully paid for all our sins, if a Christian should go to hell, God would be getting double payment for our sins, first from Christ, and then from that condemned Christian. But our just God would never do such a thing! Paul tied the completion of redemption in with the sealing work of the Spirit.

The Spirit's Preservation of His Saints
The sealing and earnest of the Spirit
Paul's connection of the certainty of the future redemption of the body with the sealing and earnest of the Spirit provides a segue into all the relevant ministries of the Spirit (Eph. 1:13-14):

> In Him, you also, after listening to the message of truth, the gospel of your salvation–having also believed, you were sealed in Him with the Holy Spirit of promise, who is given as a pledge of our inheritance, with a view to the redemption of *God's own* possession, to the praise of His glory.

His earlier reference to the sealing and earnest (pledge) in 2 Corinthians 1:21-22 did not make that connection explicit but rather with the anointing of the Spirit: "**Now He who establishes us with you in Christ and anointed us is God, who also sealed us and gave *us* the Spirit in our hearts as a pledge (earnest).**" There is a common misconception (especially in Pentecostal circles) that God specially anoints a few for ministry. But Paul made it clear that all believers have been anointed, since all have been set aside for ministry, which John confirmed in 1 John 2:20, 27. The Graeco-Roman cultural concept of the sealing of a purchase until the day of redemption and of the giving of earnest money as a down payment until making full payment on that day is most vital. The Holy Spirit Himself is God's seal and earnest pledge that the transaction of salvation which He began at our conversion will be consummated on that day. God's integrity as an 'honest dealer' is at stake. With apology to native Americans, we could say that God is not an 'Indian giver.'[A] This is reinforced in Ephesians 1:13-14 and is the basis of Paul's later exhortation: "**Do not grieve the Holy Spirit of God, by whom you were sealed for the day of redemption**" (Eph. 4:30).

Irreversibly born again by the Spirit
Christ's words to Nicodemus about the new birth in John 3:1-15 and John's reference to it in his prologue (Jn. 1:12-13) must be the starting point: "**But as many as received Him, to them He gave the right to become children of God, *even* to those who believe in His name, who were born, not of blood nor of the will of the flesh nor of the will of man, but of God.**" Clearly, we become children in the family of God by the new birth. The new birth is a supernatural and irreversible work of the Spirit, not just a reformation or turning over a new leaf. Not only did Peter understand that God "**has caused us to be born again to a living hope through the resurrection of Jesus Christ from the dead**" (1 Pet. 1:3), but also

---

A. This expression, common among children in my childhood, arose when one child gives something to another, and then changes his mind and takes it back. Perhaps the colonists saw native Americans as fickle, since they did not have the same concept of property rights in their culture.

that "you have been born again not of seed which is perishable but imperishable, *that is,* through the living and enduring word of God" (2:23). Paul's unique use of the word regeneration (*palingenesia*) in Titus 3:5 is reminiscent of Christ's use of it in Matthew 19:28 to refer to that end time transformation of all of creation. Both are certainly irreversible transformations.

Neither before my conversion or after did I hear the new birth preached in my Arminian church. It seems that my pastor's concept of salvation was more a work of man, and thus was reversible. When Jimmy Carter was elected President and said that he was a born-again Christian, the media people, who had never heard of it, went scrambling to get a definition from supposed authorities, such as a Baptist seminary professor. Unfortunately his definition was very fuzzy and man-centered, probably because his doctrine was not clearly evangelical. However, the biblical portrayal of the new birth as the impartation of divine life by the Spirit into a spiritually dead sinner, thus constituting him as a new creation in Christ (2 Cor. 5:17), would imply the irreversibility of this as a work of God, not of man.

Permanently indwelt by the Spirit

One of the major subjects of the Upper Room Discourse is the promise of the giving, sending, and coming of the Holy Spirit on the day of Pentecost and its implications. Although the Lord had alluded to the opportunity to pray for the Holy Spirit in Luke 11:13, there is no indication that any of the Apostles did so. In the light of their failure to do so His words in John 14:16-17 are more meaningful: "**I will ask the Father, and He will give you another Helper, that He may be with you forever;** *that is* **the Spirit of truth, whom the world cannot receive, because it does not see Him or know Him,** *but* **you know Him because He abides with you and will be in you.**" A study of the Hebrew text of the whole Old Testament reveals an almost total absence of the preposition 'in' in reference to the Holy Spirit and believers. Thus David could pray, "**Do not cast me away from Your presence and do not take Your Holy Spirit from me**" (Ps. 51:11). Christ's clear implication was that the Holy Spirit abode *with* pre-Pentecost saints, *not in them.* David was not afraid of losing his salvation, but rather of losing the presence of God in the person of the Spirit *with him.* Accordingly he prayed: "**Restore to me the joy of Your salvation**" (Ps. 51:12a). But now in this new dispensation of the Spirit, the Lord promised His Apostles that "**in that day**" (Jn. 14:20) the Spirit "**will be in you.**" Ryrie's explanation is most satisfying that on the day of Pentecost the omnipresent Holy Spirit came to dwell in the Church, both individually and corporately.[18] He was not only to regenerate believers as He had done previously, but also to indwell them permanently: "**... that He may be with you forever.**"

In this discourse the Lord continued to emphasize the new order which would be inaugurated in the age of the Holy Spirit: "**But the Helper, the Holy Spirit, whom the Father will send in My name, He will teach you all things, and bring to your remembrance all that I said to you**" (Jn. 14:26; also see 15:26; 16:7-8, 13a). It is mind-boggling how some theologians, because of their commitment to a theological system, can deny that the Holy Spirit came on the day of Pentecost to inaugurate a number of new ministries, and that there are essential differences between His ministries before Pentecost and after. Paul later affirmed this new reality of the indwelling Spirit in as essential to being a Christian: "**Or do you not know that your body is a temple of the Holy Spirit who is in you, whom you have from God, and that you are not your own?**" (1 Cor. 6:19-20); "**But if anyone does not have the Spirit of Christ, he does not belong to Him**" (Rom. 8:9). He thus assured the Roman Christians that "**... He who raised Christ Jesus from the dead will also give life to your mortal bodies through His Spirit who dwells in you**" (Rom. 8:11b). The present permanently indwelling Spirit is the guarantee of our final salvation.

Immersed in/ identified with Christ's body by the Spirit

Since it is clear that *baptizein* refers to immersion and identification, one wonders if the usual transliteration as 'to baptize' (and 'baptism') has obscured the truth, rather than helped it. In any case, just before His ascension, the Lord promised that the disciples would "**be baptized with the Holy Spirit not many days from now**" (Acts 1:5). One does not need a Ph.D. in mathematics to see this also as a reference to the Pentecost event about a week later, as recorded in the next chapter. Although the word *baptisma* is not used in Acts 2 in reference to the Spirit (only water), Peter so understood it when he gave testimony about the first Gentile conversions: "**And as I began to speak, the Holy Spirit fell upon them just as *He did* upon us at the beginning. And I remembered the word of the Lord, how He used to say, 'John baptized with water, but you will be baptized with the Holy Spirit**" (Acts 11:15-16).

Thus Paul's later doctrinal clarification is most important: "**For by one Spirit we were all baptized into one body, whether Jews or Greeks, whether slaves or free, and we were all made to drink of one Spirit**" (1 Cor. 12:13). Since the context is all about the church as the body of Christ, Paul had no hesitation in affirming that even those carnal Corinthians had been immersed into the Church, the body of Christ by this ministry of the Spirit. It is that ministry which constitutes the Church. By his use of the word 'all' Paul made it clear that even the most backslidden believer in Corinth was still indwelt by the Spirit and part of the body of Christ. Thus there is not one warning of the loss of the Spirit in the New Testament after Pentecost. Rather Paul's exhortations to Christians are positively to "**keep in step with the Spirit**" (Gal. 5:16, NIV); "**ever be filled with the Spirit**" (Eph. 5:18, Williams); "**Do not quench the Spirit**" (1 Thess. 5:19); and "**Do not grieve the Holy Spirit of God**" (Eph. 4:30). These should be the concern of the Christian today, not the fear of losing the Holy Spirit and eternal life with Him.

Conclusions

Eternal security is properly defined as God's work of preservation of true Christians, totally by God's unmerited favor, apart from any human performance. Both Arminians and extreme Calvinists reject this truth. This denial undermines the gracious nature of salvation as a gift of God received by faith alone. There are major and extensive lines of biblical teaching upon which eternal security can be inductively based. The Scriptures which seem to pose problems for security will be examined in the next chapter.

1   John F Strombeck, *Shall Never Perish* (Moline, IL Strombeck Agency, 1936) Excellent books have been written by Charles Stanley, R T Kendall, Robert Gromacki, Joseph Dillow, Harry Ironside, and others

2. R T. Kendall, *Once Saved, Always Saved*, p 19. Kendall's definition was helpful in formulating mine

3   Vance has documented Mathison, Gerstner, Pink, Rose, Hoekema, and Talbot and Crampton as Calvinists who object to these terms, p 562, quotation, p 566, cf. Kendall, pp 19-21

4   Murray, *Redemption*, p 155.

5   Pink, *Eternal Security*, p 28.

6   Charles Hodge, *Commentary on First Corinthians*, p. 169.

7   B Tyler and A. A Bennett, *The Life and Labours of Asahel Nettleton* (Banner of Truth, repr 1975), p. 30, quoted by Michael Eaton, *No Condemnation A New Theology of Assurance*, p. 3

8   Eaton, *No Condemnation*, p. 6

9   Ibid, p 20

10 Robert L. Shank, *Life in the Son* (Springfield, MO Westcott, 1960), 2nd ed., p 219, 293

11 Eaton, pp 3-4, 9.

12 Shank, p. 18

13 Charles Stanley, *Eternal Security Can You Be Sure?* pp 9-11

14 Joe L Wall, *Going for the Gold Reward and Loss at the Judgment of Believers* (Chicago Moody, 1991)

15 Stanley, pp 4-5, 16-22

16 Kendall, pp. 15-16.

17 Earl D. Radmacher, *Salvation* (Nashville: Word, 2000), pp. 188-9.

18 Charles C Ryrie, *Basic Theology*, pp 362-5, There are other more explicit passages I cannot locate at present

More secure is no one ever
   Than the loved ones of the Savior –
Not yon star on high abiding
   Nor the bird in homenest hiding.

God His own doth tend and nourish,
   In His holy courts they flourish;
For His love and deep compassion
   Comforts them in tribulation.

Neither life nor death can ever
   From the Lord His children sever,
Rest secure with this Defender –
   At His will all foes surrender.

Lina Sandell Berg

IS THE BIBLE AMBIGUOUS ABOUT ETERNAL SECURITY?

In a seminary chapel message years ago, Wally Howard, a youth evangelist, suggested that eternal security was a paradoxical truth, that although the Bible's promises of eternal security are clear, the warnings and our experiences of true Christians losing their salvation must be held in tension. There are both Calvinists and Arminians who would agree. However, this is most definitely an unnecessary concession to contradiction in the biblical text since both sides of the tension cannot possibly be true. Either God's promises of security are true and all true Christians are eternally secure, or else all of the promises have some unstated conditions implied, as Arminians believe. If the inerrancy and integrity of Scripture are true, there cannot be any real contradiction. Those who hold to such serious paradoxical tension cannot explain how this is logically possible.

Those passages which are perceived by many as 'problem passages' will be shown to be in total harmony with the promises of security, *if each passage is approached inductively in its own integrity and context, and if faulty presuppositions are expunged*. Two foundational parables are first examined, which show that Christ distinguished more kinds of human response to his word than many acknowledge. The book of Hebrews will be taken as a paradigm of how best to deal with controverted passages. Many are examples, exhortations, and warnings to true believers relating to the consequences of the Christian life, both temporally and for rewards at the judgment seat of Christ. Other passages relate to superficial professors of faith, counterfeit Christians, or in a most acute form, those who apostatize into rank denial and corruption of the faith. A few passages are best understood as relating to corporate Israel or the Church. Finally, some in the Olivet Discourse are in the context of the unique future Great Tribulation.

Two Foundational Parables

Parables are notoriously difficult to interpret. Many Christians suppose that Christ used parables uniformly throughout His ministry to simplify and clarify the truth. Upon examining His first use of parables in the last half of His ministry (Mt. 13), the Apostles are questioning why He was beginning to use parables (13:10). His answer was that parables are given to hide the truth from those who were rejecting His person and message: "...'To you it **has been granted to know the mysteries of the kingdom of heaven, but to them it has not been granted.... Therefore I speak to them in parables; because while seeing they do not see, and while hearing they do not hear, nor do they understand'**" (Mt. 13:11, 13). Through cavalier use of parables many Christians have jumped to erroneous conclusions about the truth which the Lord was communicating.

The parable of the sower and the four soils

This parable is foundational, both because it occurs in all three Synoptic Gospels, and because Christ gave us its interpretation. The first soil is not controversial: it is those who do not respond at all to the gospel. Arminians presume that the second soil refers to believers who lose their salvation. This is a possible but not necessary interpretation. See the explanation: "**The one on whom seed was sown on the rocky places, this is the man who hears the word and immediately receives it with joy;** yet he has no *firm* root in himself, but is *only* temporary, and when affliction or persecution arises because of the word, immediately he falls away**" (Mt. 13:20-21). Note that the word of God had not taken root in this individual's heart. There was a thin layer of soil on a rocky pan, which kept any root from developing ("**no root**" 13:6). It is a presumption that this describes a truly saved individual. They are counterfeits.

On the other hand, the third type of soil is misunderstood by many Calvinists: "**And the one on whom seed was sown among the thorns, this is the man who hears the word, and the worry of the world and the deceitfulness of wealth choke the word, and it becomes unfruitful**" (Mt. 13:22); "**... bring no fruit to maturity**" (Lk. 8:14). In this case the plant did grow up and survive ("**... and the thorns grew up with it, and choked it out**" (Lk. 8:7). There may have even been some stunted fruit, which would be useless since it did not mature. For example, a corn stalk may grow a few feet and produce an ear of corn with no edible kernels. Few interpreters have considered the option that this represents the fruitless Christian. Otherwise, if both refer to counterfeits, there would be little difference between soils number two and three. In that case, Christ would have been illustrating only three kinds of soil in the parable, not the four as He presented it. He intended us to distinguish *four* types of responses, not *three*. Many glibly quote Matthew 7:20, "**by their fruits you will**

know them," failing to recognize that in that context the Lord is speaking about false prophets, not about ordinary believers. Yes, there are many true Christians who are leading fruitless lives, whether it fits our theology or not.

The fourth category clearly represents the fruitful Christian: **"And the seed in the good soil, these are the ones who have heard the word in an honest and good heart, and hold it fast, and bear fruit with perseverance"** (Lk. 8:15). Those who believe that the only saved people in this parable are those in the fourth category have a serious theological dilemma. If that were true, Christ would seem to be ascribing their salvation to having **"an honest and good heart."** This would be a problem for the doctrine of total depravity. However, if the Lord is describing the difference between two different categories of believers due to the difference in their mindset and heart attitude, there would be no contradiction to the doctrine of depravity before conversion. The Lord is explaining why some believers **"bear fruit, thirty, sixty, and a hundredfold,"** while other equally saved people **"bring no fruit to maturity."** Interpreters who deny the existence of fruitless Christians are not dealing fairly with all Scripture testimony. Paul called them carnal (1 Cor. 3:3), and Christ identified them clearly in the second foundational parable.

The parable of faithful and faithless trustees

Those who object to distinguishing two categories of believers in the previous parable must consider a neglected parable in Luke 12:41-48, coming after the Lord's parable of teaching readiness for His return:

> Peter said, "Lord, are You addressing this parable to us, or to everyone *else* as well?" And the Lord said, "Who then is the faithful and sensible steward, whom his master will put in charge of his servants, to give them their rations at the proper time? Blessed is that slave whom his master finds so doing when he comes. Truly I say to you that he will put him in charge of all his possessions. But if that slave says in his heart, 'My master will be a long time in coming,' and begins to beat the slaves, *both* men and women, and to eat and drink and get drunk; the master of that slave will come on a day when he does not expect *him* and at an hour he does not know, and will cut him in pieces, and assign him a place with the unbelievers. And that slave who knew his master's will and did not get ready or act in accord with his will, will receive many lashes, but the one who did not know *it*, and committed deeds worthy of a flogging, will receive but few. From everyone who has been given much, much will be required; and to whom they entrusted much, of him they will ask all the more.

Notice Peter's great question. We must clearly identify the kinds of people to whom the Lord is referring. There are four in this parable also. Here fruitful believers come first (12:42-44) and counterfeits second (**"assign him a place with the unbelievers"** 12:45-6). Thirdly, a disobedient believer is described, who will suffer loss at the judgment seat of Christ (12:47; cf. 1 Cor. 3:15), and the fourth is a carelessly ignorant believer, whose loss will not be as great (Lk. 12:48). It is essential to sound interpretation that we accurately identify the answer to Peter's question and thus carefully distinguish counterfeits from these three categories of believers. This is what we must also do in examining the other controverted passages.

The Real Thrust of Hebrews

The most problematic passages are found in the Epistle to the Hebrews. Careful inductive study of these warnings becomes a paradigm or model of how to approach the others. Certainly a major obstacle to belief in eternal security is the apparent force of the five warnings in the book of Hebrews (2:1-4; 3:12--4:13; 6:1-9; 10:26-39; 12:25-29). Arminians assume that they are all addressed to born-again Christians and warn of their ultimate eternal lostness. On the other hand, Calvinists tend to see all five as addressed to counterfeit Christians. These assumptions need to be examined most carefully in the various contexts. *This can not be resolved as long as it is assumed that they were all addressed to the same kind of people.*

Diverse spiritual needs. It is essential to see that the Apostle is addressing at least *three different kinds of people* in those Hebrew Christian congregations, the same kinds of people we find attending church today: inquirers who have not yet professed faith, false professing Christians, and genuinely born-again Christians, some of whom have a serious spiritual problem. Each possibility must be considered in each context. These warnings must not be forced into the same mold based upon certain presuppositions. This is a lapse into deductive methodology based on theology, rather than giving priority to an inductive* approach.

In this connection, observe the Apostle's use of the term "people of God." Just as Old Testament Israel was the "people of God" without every individual being a true believer, just so the Apostle refers to the "people of God" in a general professing sense. As a matter of fact, there is nothing in the address of the letter which states it was written to churches. It is a message "to Hebrews" pure and simple, whatever their spiritual state. But when he refers to them as "brethren" or "we," it must not be implied that they are necessarily true believers (cf. Rom. 9:3). The main burden of the author is that every individual in the Hebrew Christian community, whether an interested inquirer, a counterfeit Christian, or a genuine believer, comes into a mature Christian life with assured faith as its basis.

Some of these Jews had not personally claimed this full forgiveness and assurance of faith: inquirers were in danger of drifting away from the message (2:1-4), and counterfeit believers with an evil heart of unbelief were in danger of apostasy by reverting back to Judaism (3:6–4:12; 10:26-31), thus refusing this final message of God from heaven (12:14-29). Some true believers were spiritually immature because of a poor grasp on these central truths of the New Testament message of grace (5:11–6:2). Indeed, a few were so confused by the overhang of Judaism's multiple sacrifices that they thought that whenever they fell into sin, they needed to get saved all over again. By so doing, they were making a shambles of the Christian life and were not only fruitless, but in danger of premature physical death as the most extreme form of spiritual discipline (6:3-8). *Thus the writer's many exhortations and warnings are targeted to individuals with diverse spiritual needs and problems, just as we find in any congregation today.*

A superior priesthood. The Apostle emphasizes the finally revealed reality (1:1-2) that the divine high priest of the New Testament (covenant) offered Himself once-for-all on the cross to provide a once-for-all salvation for those who trust Him. To this end he demonstrates that because Christ is fully God and fully man (ch. 1 & 2), He is perfectly qualified for a high priestly ministry far superior to the Aaronic priesthood of the obsolete Mosaic covenant (4:14–5:10; 7:1-8:13), which could not finally and perfectly deal with sin and its guilt (9:1–10:18).

The emphasis on certainty and assurance. Far from undermining the eternal security of the true believer, this epistle is freighted with many words, expressions, and concepts which affirm this truth in no uncertain terms, as well as to encourage all Hebrews to personally enter into its full reality. The great irony of these misinterpretations of Hebrews is that this book has more words like confidence/boldness (*parresian* 4t), assurance (*plerophoria 2t, hupostaseos 4t*), confirmation (*bebaios* 8t), access (3t), promises (*epangelia* 17t), hope (6t), than any other Bible book. The Apostle not only speaks of Christ's eternal redemption (9:12), eternal salvation (5:9), eternal inheritance (9:15), but furthermore that He saves us forever (7:25), and that we are perfected for all time (10:14). *In sum, He was sacrificed once-for-all that we might be saved once-for-all* (7:25-27; 9:12, 25-6; 10:10-14).

He not only wants all to enter into full assurance of hope (6:11) and faith (10:22), but speaks much of the true believer having confidence (3:6; 4:16;10:19, 35), boldness, and perfect access into the very throne of God through a new and living way (7:19; 10:19-22). He speaks of God's promises being confirmed by an oath (6:16), a New Testament contract sealed by Christ's blood (9:15-22), providing salvation rest (4:1-11), a strong encouragement (6:18), a hope which is the anchor of the soul because of the unchangeableness of His purpose (6:19), the guarantee of a superior covenant (7:22), and the faithfulness of God to His promises (6:13-17). He caps it off by saying that faith is the assurance of things hoped for (11:1). The believer can live in the reality of a totally cleansed conscience (9:14; 10:22) and a firm hope (3:6; 6:11, 18, 19; 7:19; 10:23).

The first exhortation/warning (Heb. 2:1-3)

For this reason we must pay much closer attention to what we have heard, so that we do not drift away *from it.* For if the word spoken through angels proved unalterable, and every transgression and disobedience received a just penalty, how will we escape if we neglect so great a salvation?

Upon examining the first warning (2:1-3), there is no hint that those addressed have even made a profession of faith. They have heard the message (2:1) and were in danger of neglecting and drifting away from it. Inquirers frequently get interested and then drift away. This warning reminds them that this message is the word of the living God (1:1f), spoken by the divine Messiah (Hebrews 1 is proof of His deity), and confirmed by miracles. *Thus there is no escape for inquirers who neglect the message.* This exhortation is relevant to counterfeit Christians as well.

The second exhortation/warning (Heb. 3:12–4:13)

Take care, brethren, that there not be in any one of you an evil, unbelieving heart that falls away from the living God. But encourage one another day after day, as long as it is *still* called "Today," so that none of you will be hardened by the deceitfulness of sin. For we have become partakers of Christ, if we hold fast the beginning of our assurance firm until the end (3:12-14).

Since the context of this warning is quite different, see the force of the whole context. In 3:1-6 we have a comparison between Moses' house (Israel) and Christ's house (the professing church). In 3:7-11 the Apostle quotes extensively from Psalm 95, which deals with the problem of unregenerate Israelites in the wilderness, who"did not know My ways" (3:10). Against this background he warns his readers, "that there not be in any one of you an evil, unbelieving heart that falls away from the living God" (3:12). Note that he nowhere implies that they had faith now and might lose it. He is concerned about those who *now* have evil, unbelieving hearts. Although he calls them "brethren" since they are professing believers, just as with the Hebrews of 1500 years earlier, this does not guarantee that they are true believers. In 3:14 we see a conditional statement describing true believers set in contrast to the preceding: "For we have become partakers of Christ, if we hold fast the beginning of our assurance firm until the end,..."

In 4:1-2 he is concerned lest having the promises of salvation, any of them should come short in the sense that the word of God "was not united by faith in those who heard." Then positively he affirms, "For we who have believed do enter that [salvation] rest" (Heb. 4:3). Then he speaks about the Sabbath rest available for the "people of God" (4:9-10), and that those who rest from their self-effort do enter this salvation rest.[A] Just as Paul warns about the Pharisees who were trying to establish their own righteousness by their works in Romans 9:30--10:4, just so, the author of Hebrews makes a similar point. Note that he uses an aorist tense* in 4:3 to refer to their believing, which normally would be point or non-durative action in past time, as contrasted with the continuous action of the present tense. It is those who

---

A Although many interpreters understand "rest" to be a reference to a higher level of victorious Christian living, there are many reasons to understand it to be the rest of salvation The context is all salvation-oriented. The passage itself contains much salvation language, but no clear reference to victorious living The writer fears that the Hebrews will fail to enter that salvation-rest.

have already come to true faith who do enter salvation rest. *So the exhortation is for those who have not yet really exercised saving faith to do so and enter in*: "**Let us labor therefore to enter into that [salvation] rest, lest any man fall after the same example of unbelief (*apeitheias*)**" (Heb. 4:11, KJV). Thus, careful examination of the passage in its context makes it clear that it is a warning to counterfeit Christians to make sure of the genuineness of their faith.

The third exhortation/warning (Heb. 5:11–6:9)

The *context* of the third warning is different yet from the previous two and extremely significant, so the reader must turn to the passage. The section from 5:11–6:2 is an exhortation to genuine Christians who are spiritually immature to go beyond elementary gospel teaching and "**press on to maturity**" (6:1). Although they had been Christians for some time, they were still babes in Christ and needed to grow to maturity (5:11-14). However, there was a hindrance to their spiritual growth. This is seen in the negative qualifier of 6:2, the danger of trying to relay the foundation: "... **not laying again a foundation ...**" A key interpretive element is to decide the identity of this foundation which some were trying to relay. Many interpreters have identified it as Judaism. *However, when we examine the six characteristics of the foundation, it becomes clear that the foundation is salvation. Their problem was that they were not making progress in the Christian life because they were trying to lay salvation's foundation all over again (which is impossible).* One cannot successfully build the superstructure if one is absorbed in relaying the foundation. A Christian who thinks he needs to get saved over and over again will not make progress in growth.

The foundation (Heb. 6:1-2). Observe carefully the six-fold description of the foundation: 1) "**Repentance from dead works**": Note that it does not say that the foundation *is dead works*, but rather *repentance from* dead works. This means that when they heard the gospel they repented from the dead works of the apostate and obsolete Jewish religion and trusted Christ.[B] 2) "**Faith toward God**": Before their conversion to Christ, most of the Hebrew Christians did not have genuine faith in the true God. It was only through Christ that they came to know and trust in the true God. Throughout Israel's history it seems clear that a majority of Jews did not have saving faith. When Christ came, Israel was at a spiritual low point of demonism and unbelief. The Apostle Peter confirms this in writing to Hebrew Christians: "**who through Him [Christ] are believers in God, who raised Him from the dead, and gave Him glory, so that your faith and hope are in God**" (1 Pet. 1:21). It was through *faith in Christ* that they first became believers in God. 3) "**of instruction about baptisms**": The word baptism is in the plural since there are two baptisms in the New Testament, water and Spirit-baptism. Both relate to salvation truth.

B. Not that the Old Testament set out a religion of dead works, but that the Judaism of the first century had become an apostate, externalistic, and legalistic religion of the traditions of men (Mt. 15 & 23).

Spirit-baptism is coincident with salvation (1 Cor. 12:13), and water baptism is to follow immediately as a public witness of salvation.

4) "**laying on of hands**": To the Jews the laying on of hands meant identification with the sacrifice upon which they laid their hands. In the early church new converts had hands laid upon them to show identification with the church (Acts 8:12-17; 9:17; 19:1-7, as in identification with the first missionaries, 13:1-3). This aspect of the foundation was also salvation-related. 5) "**the resurrection of the dead:**" This is also foundational to the Christian and not to the Israelite. The Sadducees rejected resurrection outright (Acts 23:8), and other Jews did not accept the most important resurrection—that of Jesus Christ. Although resurrection is seen in the Old Testament, it was not a significant part of the Judaism of New Testament times, nor of today. 6) "**eternal judgment**": Although eternal judgment is also seen in the Old Testament, Jews then, like Jews today, focus on this present life, not on judgment and eternal life.[1] Obviously eternal judgment relates to salvation truth. Thus the foundation is not Judaism but salvation in Christ. True believers must build their lives upon that foundation.

Some not permitted to go on to maturity (Heb. 6:3-5). The Apostle then makes the devastating statement: "**And this we shall do if God permits**" (6:3). He implies that God does not permit some to go on to maturity (if they keep trying to relay salvation's foundation). Then he switches from the first person 'we' to the third person 'they'. Clearly, this is a smaller category of people with a serious problem. A number of cases where God did not allow believers to go on to maturity can easily be identified: Ananias and Sapphira are a dramatic example of this (Acts 5:1-11). There are other examples of believers who were dying prematurely because of certain sins (1 Cor. 11:28-34; 5:1-8; Rom. 8:13, Gk.), and John speaks about "**a sin unto death**" (1 Jn. 5:15-17). It must not be assumed that he is referring to eternal death. This analogy of Scripture indicates premature physical death as the issue.

Were these people really believers? Although Calvinists tend to see them as counterfeit Christians, one commentator has said that, if the Apostle had wanted to describe genuine believers, he could hardly have found a clearer way to do it (Heb. 6:4-5). They have "**once for all been enlightened**" (6:4). This is the same word (*photizein*) used in 2 Cor. 4:3-6 to describe the enlightenment of the gospel as it breaks through the Satanic blindness of the perishing: God "**is the One who has shone in our hearts to give the light of the knowledge of the glory of God in the face of Christ.**" It is also used it in Eph. 1:18, with the same symbolism in Eph. 5:8-11.

Then they are said to "**have tasted of the heavenly gift**" and "**have tasted the good word of God and the powers of the age to come.**" The force of the Greek word 'taste' (*geuomai*) is obviously crucial here, much stronger than in the English. It frequently means 'to eat' or metaphorically, 'to experience.' This becomes clear by comparing its closest usage in 2:9: "**... Jesus, because of the suffering of death crowned with glory and honor, that by the grace of God He might** taste (*geuomai*) death for everyone." Christ actually experienced death to the full, and He himself actually used this verb four times of tasting death. He didn't merely sample its flavor, as the English word might imply. A millennium earlier David wrote, "O taste and see that the Lord is good" (Ps. 34:8), and Peter also used it in this sense (1 Pet. 2:3). Thus these people had really experienced the heavenly gift, the good word of God, and the powers of the coming age. They were also said to "have been made partakers (*metochoi*) of the Holy Spirit." Although some try to weaken the force of this word, usage will not allow that. It is used five times in Hebrews, three of which (beside 6:4) are used in a vital and deep sense. Go back to 3:14: "For we have become partakers (*metochoi*) of Christ, if we hold fast the beginning of our assurance firm until the end." This is clearly referring to true believers; so also must 6:4 be. They were really saved! Robert Stein has put it well: "With regard to Hebrews 6:4-6 it is clear that any one of the six characteristics found in these verses can be interpreted as referring to someone who is not a true Christian, but when all six are grouped together, such an interpretation becomes much more difficult, if not impossible."[2] But what happened to these genuine Christians to justify the strong language of 6:6?

Falling away (Heb. 6:6). What is meant by "fallen away"? (6:6). There is no 'if' in the Greek since *parapesontas* is a participle, as were the preceding verbs. Discerning the meaning of the word *parapiptein* is made more difficult because it does not occur anywhere else in the New Testament. It is a compound of the preposition *para* ('beside') and the common verb *piptein* ('to fall'). Williams translated it, "fallen by the wayside" with the footnote, "Picture of runners falling beside the race track."[3] Hal Harless has done an exhaustive study of the usage of the word in the classical, Koine, and Septuagintal Greek and shown that it never refers to apostasy and confirms the Williams' rendering. Another way to get at its meaning is by looking at the noun derived from this verb. *Paraptoma* occurs a score of times in the New Testament and means, "Ethically, a *misdeed, trespass* (LXX)"[4] Thus it is the picture of a Christian falling into a trespass. There is no hint of falling away from salvation in the meaning of this word.[5]

Indeed, this picture and the rest of the sentence clarify the whole meaning of the passage. Upon falling into sin, these Christians thought they had to go back to the starting line of the race and get saved all over again. When runners in a race stumble and fall by the wayside, they would never think of going back to the starting line, but just get back on the track and keep running. Donald Barnhouse used to say that when you stumble in the Christian life, the place to get back on the track is by dealing with the sin that caused the stumbling, alluding to 1 John 1:9. These Hebrew Christians had never heard of 1 John 1:9, mainly because it hadn't yet been written. So the Apostle warns them that "it is impossible to renew them [all over again] to [the first, salvation (6:1)] repentance, since [by so doing] they again crucify to themselves the Son of God and put Him to open shame" (Heb. 6:6). By trying to get saved all over again, they were in effect recrucifying Christ. Note the emphasis upon repetition here as contrasted with the once-for-all (*hapax*) death of Christ: "not laying **again** (*palin*) a foundation" (6:1); "**renew** them **again** unto repentance, crucifying **again**" (*palin anakainizein eis metanoian anastaurountas*, 6:6).

Why would a Christian want to get saved repeatedly? These Hebrew Christians came out of a background in which every time they sinned they had to bring a new sacrifice. From childhood the principle of multiple sacrifices had been etched on their minds. Now as Christians they didn't understand that Christ died once-for-all that we might be saved once-for-all. Since this is the major theme of the next four chapters, it is imperative to examine the following passages: 7:25-27; 9:11-12; 9:24-28; 10:1-4; 10:10-14:

> Therefore He is able also to <u>save forever</u> those who draw near to God through Him, since He always lives to make intercession for them. For it was fitting for us to have such a high priest, holy, innocent, undefiled, separated from sinners and exalted above the heavens; who <u>does not need daily</u>, like those high priests, to offer up sacrifices, first for His own sins and then for the sins of the people, because this He did <u>once for all</u> when He offered up Himself.... But when Christ appeared as a high priest of the good things to come, He entered through the greater and more perfect tabernacle, not made with hands, that is to say, not of this creation; and not through the blood of goats and calves, but through His own blood, He entered the holy place <u>once for all</u>, having obtained <u>eternal redemption</u>.... By this will we have been sanctified through the offering of the body of Jesus Christ <u>once for all</u>. And every priest stands <u>daily</u> ministering and offering <u>time after time the same sacrifices</u>, which can never take away sins; but He, having <u>offered one sacrifice</u> for sins <u>for all time</u>, sat down at the right hand of God,... For by <u>one offering</u> He has perfected <u>for all time</u> those who are sanctified.

What could be clearer than that *Jesus Christ died once for all that we might be saved once for all*? This was the glorious truth which these Jewish believers had not really grasped, failure of which was the cause of their lack of spiritual growth. They thought that we must be born again, and again, and again. But the new birth is a once-for-all work of the Holy Spirit of God.

Actually, the main point that the Apostle affirms here is that it is impossible to get saved all over again. The inconsistency of the Arminian interpretation has been pointed out by many Calvinistic interpreters. That is, if this is speaking about losing salvation, then Arminians ought never to invite people to be re-saved. Thus this would become a message of absolute despair. Indeed, I have counseled those who thought that they had lost it for good and were in despair. However, when a Christian sins, we are to claim 1 John 1:9 and have our fellowship restored.

The illustration (Heb. 6:7-8). Some object that the illustration of the field does not fit the above interpretation. However, upon closer examination it is most appropriate and harmonious. The ground which yields thorns and thistles is said to be "worthless", "rejected", "disapproved", "disqualified," etc., depending upon which translation is read. The Greek word *adokimos* is the negative of *dokimos* and five other related words, all of which have to do with trial, test, proving, for which the result is approval. Thus *dokimē* is used in this sense in Rom. 5:4; 2 Cor. 2:9; 13:3; Phil. 2:22. *Dokimos* is used in the sense of 'tested', 'accepted', 'approved', in Rom. 14:18; 16:10; 1 Cor. 11:19; 2 Cor. 10:18; 13:7; 2 Tim. 2:15; and Jas. 1:12. *Thus the essential idea of the negative is disapproval, not rejection.*

This also applies to 1 Corinthians 9:27, where Paul is concerned lest through indiscipline he should become "disapproved" after having preached to others. Certainly the KJV is wrong in translating "castaway," and the NIV is far superior: "disqualified." The issue is not salvation, but approval at the judgment seat of Christ, when service for Christ will be judged.

The references to "cursed" and "burned" raise a problem. There is a vast difference between actually being cursed and being **"close to being cursed."** One can be close to being killed in an accident and yet be 100 percent alive. Paul used the same symbolism when he wrote that the works of those who build with wood, hay, or straw will be burned up at the day of Christ. **"If any man's work is burned up, he shall suffer loss, but he himself shall be saved, yet so as through fire"** (1 Cor. 3:11-15). M. R. DeHaan rightly understood Hebrews 6 as the sin unto death, that is, premature physical death.

The reassurance (Heb. 6:9). How do the Apostle's words of reassurance to the majority of the Hebrew Christians relate to the preceding? He was convinced of better things about most of them, and that they manifested the appropriate accompaniments of salvation, even though he is giving such a strong warning to a minority. He goes on in subsequent verses to describe those accompaniments. However, those who have been living a roller coaster Christian life by trying to get saved repeatedly will inevitably not manifest the **"things that accompany salvation."** Realistically, not all genuine Christians manifest the appropriate fruit, the accompaniments.

Thus, it is a fair conclusion that this warning is to truly born-again Hebrew Christians who, because of their upbringing in a religion of multiple sacrifices for sins, thought that whenever they fell into sin they had to get saved all over again. Although there are no Hebrew Christians in exactly the same circumstance today, there are many professing Christians who fall into the same erroneous way of thinking. Roman Catholics and Arminians do not know that Jesus Christ died once for all that we might be saved once for all. Sometimes children do not understand that we only need to accept Christ once. Some Christians with besetting sins keep post-dating their time of conversion to put their last fall into sin before their conversion (in their own thinking). Thus, in effect, they are trying to get saved over and over again. This is not some theory. It is sad to report that a close colleague, who suddenly died young had a serious deceit problem in his life. Upon further investigation it became clear that his story fits the pattern described above. But the Lord Jesus died once for all that we might be saved once for all![6]

The fourth exhortation/warning (Heb. 10:26-39)

This passage is similar to the second warning. Here the Apostle is concerned about those who have forsaken meeting with other Christians, because they might be counterfeit Christians. As in chapter 3, he uses "we" to refer to all professing Hebrew Christians and is concerned lest they return to Judaism with its colorful pageantry and begin again to offer up animal sacrifices for sin. Thus he warns that if they turn away from the sacrifice of Christ, "there no longer remains a sacrifice for sin" (Heb. 10:26). In the plan of God the sacrifice of Christ has replaced the whole Mosaic system.

Much has been made by Arminian interpreters of the use of *epignosis* (knowledge), as if the prepositional prefix requires the meaning 'full knowledge'. However, usage rather than etymology is much more significant in determining meaning of words, and the usage does not bear this out. It is used 20 times in the New Testament and sometimes does mean 'full knowledge', but a number of times it is equivalent to *gnosis* (Rom. 1:28; 1 Tim. 2:4; 2 Tim 2:25; 3:7; 2 Pet. 2:20 - the last passage is exactly parallel). The BAG lexicon lists "knowledge, recognition" as the meaning. The verb *epiginoskein* from which this noun is derived is important. While the BAG lexicon lists many instances in which "1. with the preposition making its influence felt--a. know exactly, completely, through and through" they also list, "2. with no emphasis on the prep., essentially = *ginoskein*... a. know... b. learn, find out... c. notice, perceive, learn of... d. understand, know... e. learn to know."[7] Thus these professing Christians could well have had a merely intellectual knowledge of the gospel without being genuinely born again.

The use of the word 'sanctified' in 10:29 seems to contradict this. However, it must be remembered what the root meaning of the word *hagiazein* is (and of the Hebrew *qodesh*): 'to set apart.' Inanimate objects were 'set apart' for God's use. Clearly Paul uses the word of the unbelieving spouse and children of a mixed marriage in 1 Corinthians 7:15. Professing Christians were 'set apart' at their baptism, whether they were genuinely saved or not.

The expression "His people" (Heb. 10:30) was puzzling until it was realized that the Apostle, in paralleling Israel and the church and quoting from the Old Testament passages about Israel, is referring to God's professing people corporately, without specifying whether they have genuine faith or not. Thus he can speak in most severe language of the fate of those of "His people," who come under the judgment of God: "a certain terrifying expectation of judgment and the fury of a fire which will consume the adversaries" (10:27); "vengeance" (10:30); "it is a terrifying thing to fall into the hands of the living God" (10:31). These people are clearly going to Hell.

The language of 10:29 also is much too severe to be describing a backslidden Christian: "trampled under foot the Son of God, and has regarded as unclean the blood of the covenant by which he was sanctified, and has insulted the Spirit of grace." Thus the evidence is all consistent that the Apostle has counterfeit Christians in mind in this passage.

The fifth exhortation/warning (Heb. 12:25-29)
In this passage the address shifts back to that of the first warning, inquirers into the faith. There is nothing in the context which implies that the addressees had even made a profession of faith. And the language of the warning is reminiscent of the first one. The danger was of refusing Him who is speaking from heaven, of turning away from Him. Of course, it is equally relevant to counterfeit Christians within the church. Thus there is nothing in the last warning which in any way conditions the eternal security of the truly born-again believer in Jesus Christ.

Conclusions
Thus, there are at least three different spiritual conditions represented in these passages, conditions which are common in churches today. Of the five warnings only the third (5:11--6:9) is referring to truly born-again Christians, and it in no way compromises their eternal security in Christ. Indeed, the book of Hebrews was intended to give assurance to true believers, while unsettling counterfeit Christians and complacent inquirers. The principle of distinguishing different categories of people is vitally important in biblical interpretation, especially of parables. This gives us the key for distinguishing other examples, exhortations, and warnings *addressed to true believers* related to blessings and rewards, from those *addressed to counterfeits and apostates.* Not only does the letter to the Hebrews provide a paradigm for approaching other biblical material, but it is loaded with positive language to encourage the true believer to enjoy full assurance based on the finished work of Christ alone. Nothing in these passages undermines the eternal security of the truly born-again believer. Other problems and issues of security will be examined in the next chapter, by distinguishing exhortations and warnings to true believers from those to counterfeits and apostates.

---

1 Jakob Jocz, "Judaism," in Howard F. Vos, *Religions in A Changing World* (Chicago Moody, 1959), p. 53

2 Stein, Ibid, p. 353

3 Charles B Williams, *The New Testament* (Chicago Moody Press, 1958), p. 489.

4. G Abbott-Smith, *A Manual Greek Lexicon of the New Testament* (Edinburgh T & T Clark, 1937), 3rd Ed , p. 342.

5 Hal Harless, "*PARAPIPTO* in Hebrews 6," pp. 6-15, (a paper given at the ETS annual meeting in San Antonio, Nov 2004). Harless found over 200 usages in the classical Greek, 8 in the Septuagint O T translation, and 57 in the Koine Greek. The word clearly does not mean 'to apostatize' but rather 'to fall into sin, to fall by the wayside '

6 The view expounded above is a minority interpretation, to which I was first introduced 50 years ago by a seminary classmate, the late Dr. Phillip R Williams, who pointed out to me his observations in the Greek text Over the years I have developed this approach more rigorously Of previous commentators I could only find one who hints in this direction, M R DeHaan, who in his commentary refers to the sin unto death More recently Walter A Henrichsen, *After the Sacrifice* (Zondervan, 1979), pp 76-81, took a similar position to mine

7 Arndt and Gingrich, *A Greek-English Lexicon of the New Testament* pp 290-1.

First, I was guilty of ignoring the context of many verses I quoted to defend my view. As I began digging deeper into the events and discussion surrounding these passages, they took on a different meaning. Second, I discovered through my study that the concept of salvation through faith alone cannot be reconciled with the belief that one can forfeit his or her salvation. If I must do or not do something to keep from losing my salvation, salvation would be by faith *and works.*

-Charles Stanley

RESOLVING SECURITY PROBLEMS

Since September 11, 2001 homeland security has become a major issue around the world. Far more important is the issue of eternal security for Christians. Previous chapters focused on the importance of discerning the identity of addressees of a particular passage, whether inquirer, genuine believer, or a counterfeit believer. Now it is important to press this distinction of passages addressed to true believers from passages of exhortation and warning to counterfeits and apostates.

Issues Relating to True Believers

Besides Hebrews 6 there are many other exhortations and warnings to true believers unrelated to any notion of loss of salvation. There are other examples of true believers who had a serious problem or concern. Peter's denial of His Lord, John the Baptizer's doubt and disillusionment in prison, and Paul's concern in 1 Corinthians 9:24-27 have already been discussed.

John Mark and Demas were both drop-out missionaries (Acts 13:13; 2 Tim. 4:10), but we have no basis for assuming that they lost their salvation because of missionary failure. Indeed, the Holy Spirit afterward used John Mark to be the author of the second Gospel. He was a 'kosher Jerusalem boy' who found the idolatrous pagan culture of Perga too much for him and became the first missionary to experience culture shock. It seems that Demas backslid badly, but there is no hint that he lost his salvation because of this. The world in many different ways presses into the life of far too many true Christians today as well.

The sin unto death

Early in the history of the church, Luke gave us a striking account of extreme divine discipline, the story of Ananias and Sapphira (Acts 5:1-11).

It is gratuitous to assume that they were believers who lost their salvation, just because they were struck dead physically. There was evidence of dedication to Christ in giving part of their estate to the church. But Peter confronted them for lying to the Holy Spirit. There is an Old Testament precedent in the death of Uzzah, who reached out his hand to steady the ark of the covenant and was struck dead (2 Sam. 6:6-8). It is just as presumptuous to assume that Uzzah lost his salvation. Neither the chronicler nor Luke have provided an explanation, so we must turn to the epistles.

There are two parallels in the church of Corinth. Paul exhorted the church to excommunicate an immoral man in extreme language: "*I have decided* **to deliver such a one to Satan for the destruction of his flesh, so that his spirit may be saved in the day of the Lord Jesus**" (1 Cor. 5:5). The most straightforward understanding is that 'flesh' refers to his body and thus, as with Ananias and Sapphira, to premature physical death. The only significant alternate interpretation is to take the 'flesh' as his sin nature. This hardly makes sense, since it is difficult to grasp how Satan could help a Christian deal with his sin nature. Paul probably intended more than excommunication from the church by the use of such strong language, but he did not question the genuineness of the man's ultimate salvation. In the second epistle it seems that the man had repented, and Paul encouraged the church to restore and forgive him (2 Cor. 2:5-11). Those who deny the existence of carnal Christians, not only ignore 1 Corinthians 3:1-3, but also 5:5 and 11:27ff.

Paul was also concerned about some who were desecrating the observance of the Lord's table, when he wrote (1 Cor. 11:29-32):

> **For he who eats and drinks, eats and drinks judgment to himself if he does not judge the body rightly. For this reason many among you are weak and sick, and a number sleep.... But when we are judged, we are disciplined by the Lord so that we will not be condemned along with the world.**

It is clear that sleep is a euphemism for physical death, and that Paul is not concerned about their ultimate salvation since he is quite explicit. Both of these passages help us to understand the Ananias and Sapphira account.

Paul made an enigmatic statement in his letter to the Romans: "**So then, brethren, we are under obligation, not to the flesh, to live according to the flesh—for if you are living according to the flesh, you must die; but if by the Spirit you are putting to death the deeds of the body, you will live**" (Rom. 8:12-13). Arminians conclude from this that carnal Christians, who are living according to the flesh, will lose their salvation.[1] However, there is a serious translational issue here. Most translations do not take into account the word *mellein* in 8:13,[A] for

---

A   It has long puzzled me as to why the major translations virtually ignore the word, although it is granted that *mellein* is frequently used as a periphrasis* for the future tense of the verb. Why not render it according to its first listed usage since it avoids both a serious interpretive and theological problems?

which the BAG lexicon lists a primary meaning when used with a present infinitive as: "*be about to, be on the point of.*"[2] Rotherham translates it, "**ye are about to die;**" Moffatt, "**you are on the road to death;**" Weymouth, "**If you so live you are on your way to death;**" F. F. Bruce, "**you are bound to die;**" Knox, "**you are marked out for death.**" These renderings are closer to the mark. Here also Paul is referring to premature physical death as God's extreme discipline of some carnal Christians. They were in imminent danger of physical death.

The Apostle John gave us the last clarification:

> If anyone sees his brother commit a sin that does not lead to death, he should pray and God will give him life. I refer to those whose sin does not lead to death. There is a sin that leads to death. I am not saying that he should pray about that. All wrongdoing is sin, and there is sin that does not lead to death (1 Jn. 5:16-17, NIV).

The main issue is whether the death is physical or spiritual. Arminians opt for spiritual and eternal death but then have the problem of finding a scriptural stipulation as to which are venial and which are mortal sins. There is no such biblical legislation. On the other hand, the clear pattern seen in Corinth should inform our interpretation. John also is concerned about premature physical death. To this we must also add the force of Hebrews 6:7-8. None of this conditions the eternal security of true believers.

The vine and the branches

The fruit-bearing vine. The Lord's extended metaphor of the fruit-bearing branches of the vine in John 15:1-16 needs careful examination in this light. Verses 2 and 6 are taken by Arminians to show loss of salvation by Christians, represented as branches in Christ, the true vine: "**Every branch in Me that does not bear fruit, He takes away; and every *branch* that bears fruit, He prunes it so that it may bear more fruit**" (15:2). Two pressing questions here are: What does the Lord mean by "**every branch in Me**" and "**He takes away**"? Joseph Dillow has an excellent discussion of "**in Me**" in which he suggests that, in Christ's usage in the Gospel of John, it refers to a close personal relationship:

> A review of the sixteen usages in John seems to suggest, that when He used this phrase, the Lord referred to a life of fellowship, a unity of purpose rather than organic connection. It should be noted that this is somewhat different from Paul's usage. While Paul did use the phrase 'in Christ' in this way, he often used it in a forensic (legal) sense referring to our position in Christ or to our organic membership in His body (e.g., 1 Cor. 12:13). John never does this.[3]

He then shows how this is especially clear in John 10:38; 14:20, 30; 16:33; and 17:21-23. Thus when the Lord spoke about abiding (remaining) in Him (15:4, 5, 6, 7, 8, 9), he meant that believers must remain *in fellowship* with Him in order to bear fruit. This helps in understanding that salvation (or loss of it) is not the issue here, but that believers maintain continual fellowship with Him so as to be fruit-bearing Christians (15:2, 4, 5, 8, 16). Backslidden

Christians, who are out of fellowship with Him, cannot bear fruit. On the other hand, just remaining in union with Christ positionally does not guarantee fruitfulness. In the parable of the sower there are genuine Christians who don't bear fruit to maturity. Also in the paradigm of Hebrews 6, the ultimate issue was the fruitfulness of true believers (6:7-8).

Restorative husbandry. This understanding of the passage is confirmed by a closer examination of the verb *airein* used in the clause, "**He takes away.**" Although 'take away' is a possible rendering since it is listed third in our two best lexicons, both Abbott-Smith and the BAG lexicon list the *first meaning* as, *"lift up, take up, pick up"*; *"to raise, take up, lift or draw up."*[4] In grapevine husbandry it is a regular practice to lift up a marginal branch or a fallen vine off the ground with meticulous care to allow it to heal. Dillow references R. K. Harrison and his own experience in Austria in this regard. Harrison further shows that *airein* has this meaning in 10 out of 24 usages in the Gospel of John.[5] Translators should give this first consideration, and thus the NIV rendering "cuts off" is clearly unjustified. Does it not make sense that first the Lord should speak of His restorative dealings with His branches before mentioning His more stringent dealings? This leaves the Arminian interpretation on shaky ground.

Stringent husbandry. Arminians then hasten to verse 6: "**If anyone does not abide in Me, he is thrown away as a branch and dries up; and they gather them, and cast them into the fire and they are burned.**" If the issue in the passage relates to remaining (abiding) in fellowship with Christ, then the symbolism should be understood in that light, since this is an extended metaphor. Calvinists have long suggested that this is a case of extreme divine discipline of a backslidden believer. It is not God who throws the branches into the fire, but men.[6] The passage parallels Hebrews 6:8 and 1 Corinthians 3:11-15.

Jim Bakker of the infamous PTL is a graphic example. When the scandal erupted, many assumed that Jim was a counterfeit Christian. But upon reading his book, *I Was Wrong*, my opinion changed. In prison as he re-examined the tragic events, he realized that his life and ministry had been all wrong. The world trashed his life and testimony big-time. He was cast out as a branch and thrown into the fire of severe chastisement. Presumably his theology was Arminian, but there was no mention of loss of salvation, even though he lost everything else.[7] An illustration proves nothing but does help us to understand the severity of Christ's language.

Exhortations and warnings to true Christians

Discipleship exhortations. In Chapter 11 it was seen that the Lord's three main discipleship exhortation contexts are not related to the salvation issue, but rather to worthy discipleship (Mt. 10:34-39; 16:24-28=Lk. 9:22-27; Lk. 14:25ff). Both Arminians and extreme Calvinists have failed to observe the contexts and the word 'daily' in Luke 9:23 and have assumed that we must deny self and take up our cross in order to be saved: "**If anyone wishes to come after Me, he must deny himself and take up his cross daily and follow Me.**" We cannot be saved daily. Worse yet, it would end up being a human-performance salvation, in contradiction to a by-grace-alone salvation.

The unforgiving slave. The parable of the unforgiving slave, which the Lord told in response to Peter's question about how many times to forgive one's brother, poses some difficulty of interpretation (Mt. 18:21-35). Since Christ spoke about the lord of the slave handing him "**over to the torturers until he should repay all that was owed him,**" many think that it speaks about believers losing salvation and going to hell. However, care must be taken with parables not to make too literal a transfer of detail to real life. Just as in the parable of Luke 12 where the lashes are probably represent pain, so in this parable the reference to the torturers probably speaks of pain in the life of the unforgiving Christian. Unforgiving Christians really torture themselves emotionally and spiritually and will face anguish at the judgment seat of Christ. Salvation is not the issue here.

Ensuring election. Peter's exhortation is the solution to the assurance problems of both Calvinists and Arminians. It is the solution to extreme Calvinists' hesitancy to affirm that we can be sure that we are among the elect, and to the Arminian notion that human performance can affect our ultimate salvation (2 Pet. 1:10-11):

> **Therefore, brethren, be all the more diligent to make certain about His calling and choosing you; for as long as you practice these things, you will never stumble; for in this way the entrance into the eternal kingdom of our Lord and Savior Jesus Christ will be abundantly supplied to you.**

Peter's first concern is that every believer enter into assured certainty about ultimate salvation. Then there are two consequences of diligence in gaining an assured Christian life: we shall never stumble in our walk, and our entrance into the kingdom will be abundant. His reference to 'stumbling' is not a reference to losing salvation, but to those falls and stumbles common to all Christians. He is not referring to mere entrance into the kingdom, which is by God's grace, but to *abundant entrance,* as we are rewarded for faithfulness at the judgment seat of Christ.

Arminian Guy Duty understands Peter to be speaking about the objective fact of election being conditioned on our diligence in the ways described. He has not considered the probability that Peter is alluding to the subjective experiential assurance that is so foundational to a stable Christian life.[8] However, this is the option which fits the context and the rest of biblical truth. On the other hand, extreme Calvinists need to recognize that Peter's exhortation implies that Christians can and must do what they can to gain full assurance of present salvation. There is absolutely no need for them to live in uncertainty as to whether or not they are among the 'elect'. There are many in Calvinistic churches today who do not believe it is possible to know whether one is among the elect or not.[9]

Working out salvation. It should be superfluous to discuss Paul's exhortation in Philippians 2:12-13, but some Arminians get hung up on it:

> **So then, my beloved, just as you have always obeyed, not as in my presence only, but now much more in my absence, work out your salvation with fear and trembling; for it is God who is at work in you, both to will and to work for *His* good pleasure.**

Obviously Paul is not exhorting them to work *for* their salvation. They were already saved, and Paul had great confidence in the Christians at Philippi, for there was neither heresy nor immorality among them, and the whole epistle is exceedingly positive. He is addressing **"my beloved,"** who have always obeyed. The reference to **"fear and trembling"** is not a reference to hell, but to our life and service being examined at the judgment seat of Christ. Notice how Paul connects the reverential fear of the Lord with that judgment seat in 2 Corinthians 5:10-11. Yes, God was at work in the lives of those Philippian believers, so there was no question about their ultimate salvation.

The overcomers. Christ's letters to the seven churches of Asia in Revelation 2 and 3 are not so straightforward to interpret. Lehman Strauss argued that all true believers are the 'overcomers' whom the Lord is addressing.[10] Joseph Dillow identifies the overcomers as faithful Christians who will be especially rewarded in the kingdom. Arminians take it that these are true Christians who persevere to the end, the rest losing salvation.[11] Calvinists tend to see them as the true Christians who persevere to the end, the rest being counterfeits.[12] We must not argue from a theological position, but seek to examine these letters in their own integrity and context. This is a broader issue than there is space to develop here. Let us simply focus on the 'problem verses' in this passage, noting carefully that individuals in the churches with different spiritual conditions are addressed.

Warnings to Asia's churches. In the letter to the church in Ephesus the Lord threatens to remove their lampstand unless they repent (Rev. 2:5). This must be understood corporately of the church, not a threat to individuals. In the Smyrna letter the Lord Jesus promises those who remain faithful under persecution **"a crown of life"** (2:10). The distinction between salvation and rewards is very important, and the various crowns promised to the faithful are an important part of these promises. In the letter to the Pergamum church Christ's promise to judge the Nicolaitans within the church does not relate to eternal security (2:14-16). Whatever the exact nature of the Nicolaitan heresy, such apostates were never true Christians. But the Lord has a charge against the corporate church.

The warnings to the corrupt Thyatira church are quite severe, especially to the Jezebel figure and her children. The Old Testament antecedent of Jezebel would not indicate a true believer (2:20-23). In the Sardis church there were some who had not soiled their garments and are promised reward, "**for they are worthy**" (Rev. 3:4). This seems to be distinct from the promise to all believing overcomers. Special comment is necessary regarding the promise "**I will not erase his name from the book of life**" (3:5). It is a basic law of logic, often violated by interpreters, that the converse of a true statement may or may not be true (not necessarily true or false, thus undetermined). Christ affirms that he will not erase their names, with no implication that he does or does not erase anybody else's name. Any such implication is to insert an idea into Christ's words which He did not say.

Believers in the faithful Philadelphia church are exhorted not to lose their crown, which is a reward with no reference to loss of salvation (3:11). Lastly, to the true believers in the apostate Laodicea church the risen Lord speaks of church discipline and rewards (3:19-21). A warning comes to the church corporately that since it nauseates Him, Christ will spit this church out of His mouth (3:16), with no reference to individual true believers.

Issues Relating to Apostates and Counterfeits

Examples of counterfeits

While examining the question of whether a true Christian can lose salvation, it isessential to factor the reality of counterfeits in the church into the discussion. Counterfeits can then become apostates to the faith. We are not talking about the eternal security of mere professing Christians. Judas Iscariot is the classic example of an extremely plausible counterfeit. None of the Apostles suspected that Judas was a counterfeit even after Christ's overt identification of him by giving him the choice morsel of food (Jn. 13:23-30). The Lord knew all along that he was a counterfeit—not that he was a true believer who lost his salvation (Jn. 6:64-71; 12:4; 13:2).

Judas was one of a number of counterfeit disciples to whom Christ alluded: "'**But there are some of you who do not believe.**' **For Jesus knew from the beginning who they were who did not believe, and who it was that would betray Him**" (6:64). It was already noted (p. 39) that He was referring to them in saying, "**For this reason I have said to you, that no one can come to Me unless it has granted him from the Father**" (6:65). Judas and those professing disciples had been bathed in the greatest light of God's truth that any humans had ever experienced and yet were rejecting Christ. He knew that their hearts were so set against the truth, that even His personal ministry could not penetrate.

Another less clear example is Simon the sorcerer (Acts 8:9-24). Although Luke says he believed and was baptized, in a number of other contexts *pisteuein* (to believe) is used of something less than saving faith (Jn. 2:23-24; 8:31). Apparently Simon had not really repented of his sorcery and magic and wanted to use the Holy Spirit for his own ends, perhaps supposing that the Holy Spirit was an impersonal force. Peter discerned him to be an unregenerate person, for he said,

'May your silver <u>perish with you</u>, because you thought you could obtain the gift of God with money! You have <u>no part</u> or portion in this matter, for <u>your heart is not right</u> before God. Therefore repent of this wickedness of yours, and pray the Lord that, if possible, the intention of your heart may be forgiven you. For I see that you are in the gall of bitterness and in the bondage of iniquity' (Acts 8:20-23).

Peter understood that Simon would perish, that he had no part in the work of the Spirit, and that forgiveness was improbable. If he had only stumbled, Peter could not have said any of this. Even worse was his response to Peter's exhortation to repent by asking Peter to pray for him. This sounds pious, but *he himself* needed to pray a prayer of repentance, which he apparently did not do. This is another paradigm of a counterfeit believer.[B]

A prominent example is Chuck Templeton, who was an early associate and friend of Billy Graham. In 1949 Templeton began to share his intellectual doubts about the truth of the Bible with Graham, causing him to go through a spiritual crisis. They moved in opposite directions, Graham to full commitment to the Bible as the word of God, and then to his worldwide evangelistic ministry, while Templeton moved into skepticism, claiming that Graham had committed intellectual suicide. In that timeframe I heard Templeton preach on Absalom, a very eloquent and dramatic sermon. I don't remember any gospel in it or even what the main point was. Lee Strobel interviewed him in connection with his book, *Farewell to God: My Reasons for Rejecting the Christian Faith*.[13] Reading the account of his 'conversion' and having heard just one sermon, I have no difficulty taking him to have been a counterfeit, who later became an apostate. John was clear in his analysis of anti-Christian apostates: "**They went out from us, but they were not** *really* **of us; for if they had been of us, they would have remained with us; but** *they went out,* **so that it would be shown that they all are not of us**" (1 Jn. 2:19).

Exhortations and warnings to counterfeits and apostates

We have already examined the warnings of Hebrews, four of which are addressed to inquirers into the faith and/or counterfeit, superficial professors of faith. Because those Jews were addressed as 'brethren' and the 'people of God,' does not imply individual, personal faith any more than it did for national Israel before Pentecost. A number of other exhortations and warnings addressed to counterfeits must be examined.

Corinthian immorality. One of Paul's strongest warning arose because of the immorality in the church of Corinth, to which he wrote: "**Or do you not know that the unrighteous will not inherit the kingdom of God?**" (1 Cor. 6:9). After a list of the grossest sinners, he reaffirms that such shall not inherit the kingdom and reminds Christians that some were such before they came into

B. Since the Holy Spirit is a person, He can use us, but it is unthinkable that we can use Him. This is the error of many today who abuse the gifts of the Holy Spirit.

right standing with God (1 Cor. 6:9-11). So although he is warning true Christians who have fallen into serious sin that this is characteristic of the old life, now that they are believers they must flee immorality. This warning is a double-edged sword. For true believers *compromising* with immorality, it was a wake-up call, but for counterfeits it is a direct warning that if one's life is *characterized* by such one cannot expect to inherit the kingdom. Distinguishing backslidden believers from counterfeits is not easy. God knows; an individual himself may or may not know, so Paul covers both possibilities.

Corinthian syncretism. At several points in his epistles, Paul expressed doubts about the genuineness of some of the people in churches he had founded. Hearing that some of the Corinthian Christians were influenced by Greek philosophy to question the bodily resurrection, he wrote: "Now I make known to you, brethren, the gospel which I preached to you, which also you received, in which also you stand, by which also you are saved, if you hold fast the word which I preached to you, <u>unless you believed in vain</u>" (1 Cor. 15:1-2). By the use of the conditional 'if' Paul is entertaining some doubt about the genuineness of the salvation of some, because he saw the bodily resurrection of Christ as an essential part of the gospel, as expounded in the rest of the chapter and later in Romans 10:9: "that if you confess with your mouth Jesus *as* Lord, and believe in your heart that God raised Him from the dead, you will be saved."

Guy Duty argued that all conditional statements in Scripture show that salvation is conditional until consummated in glory.[14] We agree that the initial reception of salvation is conditioned on repentant faith, but disagree that in the ongoing Christian life it is no longer conditional. The new birth, the sealing and earnest of the Spirit, and God's keeping power have put the believer in a radically different position from the inquirer or counterfeit. Thus Paul is not expressing doubt that some of the true Corinthian Christians would persevere, but whether some of them were genuine. This is presumably the same concern he expressed later in 2 Corinthians 13:5: "Test yourselves *to see* if you are in the faith; examine yourselves! Or do you not recognize this about yourselves, that Jesus Christ is in you—unless indeed you fail the test?" He is concerned about their present state, not some future contingency.

Galatian legalism. Paul also expressed a concern for the some of the Galatian Christians who had reverted back to "the weak and worthless elemental things" of legalism: "I fear for you, that perhaps I have labored over you in vain" (Gal. 4:11). That this favorite Arminian proof-text has been pulled out of context is clear when we see that concern in 5:4 as well: "You have been severed from Christ, you who are seeking to be justified by law; you have fallen from grace." Here he is addressing hard-core legalists who are not just trying to be sanctified by legalism, but justified as well. By putting themselves outside of the pale of God's saving grace, any connection they might have thought they had with Christ was nullified. We could turn the tables at this point. Those who deny eternal security are intruding human performance into salvation and are in danger of being described in Paul's terminology as "fallen from

grace." Paul is not talking about those whose faith is wavering or who are being overcome by sins, but rather about legalists, and this is a subtle form of legalism. This is not to imply, by any means, that all Arminians are fallen from grace, but we must face up to the implications of Paul's warning.

During a decade on a radio call-in program, we were inundated with questions on the sabbath by sabbatarian legalists, who would even lie to the operator to push their point of view on the air. During extended conversations with many, it became clear that a great many of them didn't have a clue about salvation by grace through faith in Christ alone. They were trusting in their sabbath-keeping and indeed were "**fallen from grace.**"

Colossian heresy. The Colossian church was threatened by an incipient Gnostic heresy and Paul hastens to include such a conditional warning early in his epistle (Col. 1:22-23a):

> ... yet He has now reconciled you in His fleshly body through death, in order to present you before Him holy and blameless and beyond reproach— if indeed you continue in the faith firmly established and steadfast, and not moved away from the hope of the gospel that you have heard.

It seems that some of those in the church in Colossae were falling prey to a denial of the incarnation, so after reminding them that the Lord had a fully human body, which actually died to provide salvation, he warns them not to move away from this essential salvation truth. Although he does not clarify the spiritual status of those who were in danger of moving away from the hope of the gospel, the most likely candidates would be the counterfeits. It is an unjustified assumption of Arminians that a true Christian could do so.

Prophetic warnings. Paul's warning to the Ephesian elders is similar: "**I know that after my departure savage wolves will come in among you, not sparing the flock; and from among your own selves men will arise, speaking perverse things, to draw away the disciples after them**" (Acts 20:29-30). Although the context does not clarify the spiritual state of these false teachers before their apostasy, the Lord Jesus had clarified this years earlier. After using similar language in the Sermon on the Mount to describe the false prophets (Mt. 7:15-21), the Lord explained: "**Many will say to Me on that day, 'Lord, Lord, did we not prophesy in Your name, and in your name cast out demons, and in Your name perform many miracles?' And then I will declare to them, 'I never knew you; depart from Me, you who practice lawlessness'**" (7:22-23). The Lord will not say, "I knew you, but you departed from Me;" He said, "**I never knew you.**" They were *never* true believers! This is undoubtedly true of other apostates prophesied in 1 Timothy 4:1-3 and 2 Peter 2:1-22, where Peter's concluding words are confirmatory: "**It has happened to them according to the true proverb, 'a dog returns to its own vomit,' and, 'A sow, after washing, *returns* to wallowing in the mire'**" (2:22). Peter does not say that sheep can regress into becoming dogs or pigs.

In writing this section, I am struck with the fact that all these passages focus upon professing Christians who depart into heresy and denial of the gospel. None speak about true Christians losing salvation because they lost their faith or were overwhelmed with sins. There are no such passages to which Arminians can point! Yet these are the usual Arminian scenarios as to how true Christians can supposedly lose their salvation.

James questions the faith of some. The reconciliation of James 2:14-26 with justification by faith alone has already been discussed (pp. 99-100). James is mainly concerned with believers showing their faith to the world. In so doing, it seems as if James raises a question about the reality of the faith of fruitless professing believers. Although we cannot lightly dismiss the faith of the fruitless believer, we may question its reality, as we have seen (1 Cor. 15:2, Gal. 4:11, Col. 2:13; Acts 20:29-30; etc.). However, the context of the whole book leads many good interpreters to understand James as speaking about the profitlessness of the life of the fruitless Christian.

Individualizing Corporate Entities

One pitfall Arminians fall into is individualizing passages referring to a corporate entity, such as Israel or the Church. The parable of the demon-possessed man (Mt. 12:43-45), like all parables, is difficult. Even if it refers to an individual, it really says nothing about eternal security since exorcizing a demon is not necessarily to gain salvation. But the context shows that it refers to the nation Israel. In the exile, the demon of idolatry was exorcized, only to have Phariseeism, Sadduceeism, and other corrupt teachings come into the nation. The use of the word *genea* in 12:39 & 45, when correctly translated as 'race, stock, or nation' makes the national analogy clear. Christ's contrasting of Israel with Gentiles in 12:41-42 confirms this.

Paul's extended metaphor of the branches of the olive tree in Romans 11:17-24 is a similar example. If he had individuals in mind, it might be helpful to the Arminian cause. However, Romans 9–11 is a section which deals with the dispensational transition in God's dealings with the nation Israel to His dealings with the corporate Church. Is God just in His dealings with national Israel? Paul's main point is that God was fair in cutting off the natural branches from the olive tree of blessing and grafting in the Gentiles. Similarly God can be fair in grafting in the natural branches of Israel again. None of this implies that individual Jewish or Gentile Christians have been, or ever will be cut off. This passage has nothing to do with eternal security.

Similarly, in the letters to the seven churches of Revelation 2–3 some expressions refer to the whole church. This is especially relevant for the letter to Laodicea (3:14-22). Warner Salman's famous painting of Christ knocking at the heart's door notwithstanding, the word picture is of a church so apostate that Christ is knocking at the door of the *church* to gain entrance and to have fellowship with individuals in the church. Thus when He says in 3:16, "**I will spit you out of My mouth**," He is not referring to individuals but to the church corporately. This is a church which nauseates the Lord Jesus! Christ would never spit a true believer out of His mouth (Jn. 6:37).

Passages Pulled out of Context

The issue of dispensational* context arises mostly in the Olivet Discourse of Matthew 24 and 25. Christ's prophetic discourse has a very Jewish tone, which He connected with a unique, future great tribulation period ("**the time of Jacob's trouble**"- Jer. 30:7) before He returns to earth. This helps us understand Matthew 24:13 and the parables of the ten virgins and the talents as not contradicting eternal security. No mater what view of prophecy one holds, all must recognize the importance of context here in this prophetic sermon of the end times connected to a unique great tribulation period (Mt. 24:21) and the glorious return of Christ to earth (24:29-31). Throughout the passage the Lord is talking about such difficult times that physical survival is tenuous (vv. 9, 16-20, 28). Thus when He said: "**But the one who endures to the end, he will be saved**" (24:13), it must be considered whether he is referring to physical deliverance or to spiritual salvation since *sozein* frequently refers to physical deliverance. In any case, this could not refer to the hundreds of millions of Christians who have already died before the rapture, since the 'end' He refers to is the end of the great tribulation and His return to earth. Thus if one takes Christ's teaching at all literally (and we must), this verse says nothing about the eternal security of most Christians in past centuries. Then why should end-time believers' eternal security be more jeopardized than that of believers throughout the ages just because the times will be more perilous?

Even though we ought to focus on the unique great tribulation context of the parable of the ten virgins (25:1-13), let us just examine the parable itself. First off, we note that all were virgins, none prostitutes, or for that matter, none even married. They all had oil. It doesn't sound like these were counterfeit believers or apostates, does it? The problem was that some did not have the foresight to bring extra oil. Arminians assume here that oil is a symbol of the Holy Spirit, and that they lost the Holy Spirit and eternal life. But these are all gratuitous assumptions. Go back to the foundational parable of the faithful and unfaithful trustees in Luke 12, and remember that the third and fourth type of slaves were believers who were punished for failing to be ready for the Master's return. Some of the virgins had the same problem, lack of preparedness for the Lord's return. They were excluded from the wedding feast, but some assume that this means exclusion from the kingdom itself. Dillow makes a major case for all true believers being in the kingdom, but only faithful ones will receive rewards, such as symbolized in this parable as a wedding feast. Albeit, it is highly irresponsible to deny the security of church-age saints based upon the interpretation of very difficult parables set in a unique end-time context.

The same can be said for the parable of the talents (Mt. 25:14-30). The main point is the rewards Christ will give to his servants. There are three categories of servants distinguished here. The first two are rewarded for faithfulness when the Master returns. The third was characterized as wicked and lazy and not only did he miss out on reward, but was thrown into outer darkness, where there will be weeping and gnashing of teeth. Dillow argues that the outer darkness outside of the wedding feast is not to be assumed to be hell for unbelievers, but could be a place of temporary anguish during the feast. Many believers will experience extreme anguish at the judgment seat of Christ for their lazy unpreparedness for His return and will be deprived of the rewards which are given to the faithful.[15] Perhaps the severity of Christ's language can be taken as hyperbolic emphasis. But even if Dillow is wrong and the third category represents counterfeits, there is nothing in the parable which says that a true Christian loses eternal life. Parables are indeed difficult!

Conclusions

Careful examination of the many 'problem passages' shows that many are addressed to true believers and relate to the consequences of sin and not to loss of salvation, while others are addressed to counterfeits and apostates and warn of the condemnation that they are facing unless they become genuine believers. In every case we must be clear as to what the exact spiritual condition of the individual is and precisely what the consequences are spelled out to be. Failure also to distinguish individual from corporate warning, and failure to see each passage in its proper dispensational context also contribute to the confusion. There are false presuppositions which add to the confusion in the minds of many.

1   Guy Duty, *If Ye Continue*, p 101. Duty refers to Rom 8 13 only in passing and does not discuss the passage.

2. Arndt and Gingrich,*Lexicon*, pp 501-2.

3   Joseph C. Dillow, *The Reign of the Servant Kings* (Miami Springs, FL· Schoettle Pub , 1992), pp. 402-3

4   Arndt and Gingrich, p 23-4, Abbott-Smith,*Lexicon*, p 13

5   Dillow, p. 409, R K Harrison, "Vine" in *NISBE*, 4:986

6   Lewis Sperry Chafer, *Systematic Theology*, III·298-300, VII:4.

7. Jim Bakker, *I Was Wrong* (Nashville: Thomas Nelson, 1996)

8   Duty, p 139

9. Years ago a reporter from the Newark Star-Ledger interviewed the leaders of a Dutch Reformed church in Bergen County, NJ, all of whom said that they did not know whether or not they were among the 'elect.' Historically this has been a major problem in the Reformed tradition D L Moody found the problem to be rife in Scotland

10 Lehman Strauss, *The Book of the Revelation* (Neptune, NJ. Loizeaux Bos , 1964), pp. 107-24

11 Ibid, pp 146-56

12 Dillow, pp 469-86

13 Charles Templeton, *Farewell to God* (Toronto McClelland and Stewart, 1996), Lee Strobel, *The Case for Faith* (GR Zondervan, 2000), pp. 9-23

14 Duty, *If Ye Continue*.

15 Dillow, pp 389-96

Before the throne my Surety stands --
    My name is written on His hands.
Five bleeding wounds He bears,
    Received on Calvary;
They pour effectual prayers,
    They strongly plead for me:
The Father hears Him pray, His dear Anointed One;
    He cannot turn away the presence of His Son.
    ... ...
No condemnation now I dread,
    I am my Lord's and He is mine;
Alive in Him, my living Head,
    And clothed in righteousness divine.
                                    -Charles Wesley

WHY *NOT* BELIEVE IN SECURITY?

One would think that there must be some powerful reasons not to believe in eternal security since roughly half of Evangelicals do not believe it, and many more have compromised this biblical truth in various ways. In Chapter 12 the positive biblical evidence for security was reviewed. In Chapter 13 the parable of the four soils and the warnings of Hebrews, which have been badly misunderstood as negating security, were clarified. In Chapter 14 we saw how other 'problem passages' have been misinterpreted by failing to recognize the difference between warnings to true believers of spiritual loss and warnings of condemnation to counterfeits and apostates. Since Arminians give two different scenarios describing how a true Christian can lose salvation, these must be dealt with also. There is a critical need to pull together the key issues at stake in denial of eternal security.

False Presuppositions of Denial
In understanding why both Arminians and extreme Calvinists struggle to accept the simplicity of eternal security and its concomitant assurance of ultimate salvation, there are a number of common presuppositions in their thinking which hinder them from taking Scripture at face value.

All warnings imply loss of salvation. It is a presumption that every warning in Scripture is a threat of loss of salvation unless the believer toes the line. This is not only gratuitous, but totally false. Yes, there are warnings to inquirers and counterfeit believers of ultimate condemnation unless they come to Christ in reality. There are also warnings to believers relating to temporal consequences and at the judgment seat of Christ for spiritual failure, but not of loss of salvation.

All exhortations imply that failure results in loss of salvation. Many also presume that failure to respond properly to all exhortations in Scripture may result in loss of salvation. Exhortations are addressed to a diversity of spiritual conditions, none of which imply that believers who fail to respond may condition their ultimate salvation.

All conditions demand continued performance for salvation. Guy Duty is representative of this kind of thinking as he traces all the conditional statements from Genesis to Revelation and argues that, even after our conversion, continuance in meeting all those conditions is necessary for ultimate salvation. Duty is correct that salvation is conditional, but there is just *one* condition at *one* point in time. Once we have been born again through **"repentance toward God and faith in our Lord Jesus Christ"** (Acts 20:21), all other conditional statements relate to temporal blessing or rewards at the judgment seat of Christ. *Salvation is conditional in its initiation, but unconditional in its continuation, since God has promised to preserve true believers.*

Can Sin Negate Salvation?

Some people who reject eternal security feel that they themselves are secure in Christ, but they suspect that not all true Christians are. What about the converted drug addict, the alcoholic, the homosexual, the sexually promiscuous, etc.? They are dubious about them. It is clear that there is more than a little self-righteousness in this line of reasoning. No, either all true Christians are eternally secure or none are.

Others, however, turn the issue upon themselves. They will say, "My sin is so great that I have lost my salvation." What they have really lost is the assurance of salvation. Let us try to get to the bottom of this confusion.

What about sins committed after conversion?

A root error of multitudes of Christians has been to think that salvation only provides forgiveness for sins committed before conversion. Some of the church fathers fell prey to this kind of erroneous thinking, and the case of the emperor Constantine is a classic example. He postponed his baptism until just before his death in the hopes that there would be few or no post-baptismal sins for which he would have to personally answer. This kind of thinking is still endemic in the Roman Catholic system. To press the issue back one more step, we could say that it springs from the error of baptismal regeneration—that baptism actually does wash away our sins (cf. Ch. 18).

All sin forgiven. The notion that only pre-conversion sins were forgiven through the sacrifice of Christ is so clearly unbiblical that it should be called a root error. It is the source of incredible confusion. Partial forgiveness is totally foreign to the Bible; there is no hint of any time limitations in the biblical declarations of forgiveness. King Hezekiah prayed after God extended his life by fifteen years, "**It is You who has kept my soul from the pit of nothingness, for You have cast** <u>all my sins</u> **behind Your back**" (Isa. 38:17). King David did not think it presumptuous to pray,"**And forgive** <u>all my sins</u>" (Ps. 25:18). Micah had the same conviction about the nation Israel: "**Yes, You will cast** <u>all their sins</u> **into the depths of the sea**" (Mic. 7:19).

The Lord Jesus uses such all-inclusive language, with one exception: "**Truly I say to you,** <u>all sins shall be forgiven</u> **the sons of men, and whatever blasphemies they utter; but whoever blasphemes against the Holy Spirit never has forgiveness, but is guilty of an eternal sin**" (Mk. 3:28-9). The context makes it clear that this was a very specific form of acute unbelief in attributing Christ's miracles to the devil.

Even the blasphemies of Saul of Tarsus were forgiven (Act. 9:1; 1 Tim. 1:12-15). Paul's own doctrinal statement is unambiguous: "**. . . He made you alive together with Him,** <u>having forgiven us all our transgressions</u>, **having canceled out the certificate of debt consisting of decrees against us, which was hostile to us; and He has taken it out of the way, having nailed it to the cross**" (Col. 2:13-14). We should also note the many references to "sin" as a totality concept, which includes Adam's sin imputed to us (Rom. 5:12ff), the sin nature inherent in us (Eph. 3:1-3), as well as individual personal sins. The singular "sin" refers to all three aspects of sin, all of which were dealt with at the cross.

When Christ paid for our sins, all of our sins were yet future. When Christ died for the sins of Old Testament saints, all of their sins were past and only temporarily covered until He should provide the redemption price. This is the point of Paul's statement in Romans 3:24-25:

> ... being justified as a gift by His grace through the redemption which is in Christ Jesus; whom God displayed publicly as a propitiation in His blood through faith. *This was* to demonstrate His righteousness, because in the forbearance of God He passed over the sins previously committed.

Some have erroneously thought that this was a reference to the sins they committed before they were converted, but this is not the case. As discussed in Chapter 3 (and confirmed in Hebrews), the Levitical sacrifices and sprinkling of blood on the mercy seat only provided a temporary covering for the sins of pre-cross saints. Nothing in the context of Romans 3 or the rest of the New Testament would support this misinterpretation.

It should be emphasized that eternal life is not a lifetime of probation, as some cultists teach. When God says "eternal life" He means **eternal** life, not probationary life. The book of Hebrews speaks about "**eternal salvation**" (5:9), "**eternal redemption**" (9:12), and an "**eternal inheritance**" (9:15).

Three aspects of forgiveness. It is essential to recognize that there are at least three different dimensions or aspects of forgiveness in the Bible. Basic is the salvation-forgiveness through trust in Christ's finished work. It is total. The second is the fellowship-forgiveness which John referred to in 1 John 1:1-10. The issue is the believer's fellowship with God and fellow believers. This, he makes clear, is contingent upon our walking in the light (1:7) and confessing our sins to the Lord (1:9). Lewis Sperry Chafer used to use this illustration: Salvation is like a steel band connecting the believer to Christ; fellowship with Christ is like a thin thread, broken so easily by sin, but restored so easily by confession. The third dimension is the horizontal—our fellowship with other believers being contingent upon keeping short accounts with them (Mt. 5:23-24;18:15). Failure to distinguish these distinct aspects has caused untold confusion.

Is full forgiveness a license to sin?

One of the major reasons people reject eternal security is they feel that it is a license to sin. Some years ago I preached on the warning of Hebrews 6 (cf. Ch. 13) in a church where a friend from my Arminian home church was active. After the message he said with great agitation, "Gordon, you are just preaching a license to sin!" I responded, "Brother, I believe you are living the Christian life for the same reason that I am—because of your gratitude for His free gift of salvation and your love for God in response. Neither of us is living for God because He threatens us with hell if we don't shape up." This ended the discussion, as it should. Just as my Arminian friend thought grace to be a license to sin, so also Paul's opponents in Rome misunderstood his message of grace: **"What shall we say then? Are we to continue in sin so that grace may increase?"** (Rom. 6:1). Paul went on to show that our union with Christ makes that unthinkable. But a similar reaction from opponents of eternal security shows that we have got the gospel of grace straight.

Motivation. However, this raises a most important question: what is the true motivation for living a godly life? There is not one passage in the New Testament, rightly understood, which threatens a true believer with hell, if he does not shape up. God doesn't hold a club over our heads, threatening to squash us if we don't get in line. No, the Bible is full of many other higher motivations for obedience. Most parents are smart enough to use positive motivations in the lives of their children before they resort to spanking and negative reinforcement (the board of education on the seat of learning). However, they would never threaten to disavow their child's sonship, except under the most extreme conditions. I take it that God knows far better how to motivate His own children. There are many positive as well as negative motivations which God sets before us.

Clearly the highest motivation is gratitude for the gift of eternal life. **"For the love of Christ controls us, having concluded this, that one died for all, therefore all died; and He died for all, so that they who live might no longer live for themselves, but for Him who died and rose again on their behalf"** (2 Cor. 5:14-15). Our love for Christ in response to His love for us is the ultimate motivation for living for

Him. In the same context, Paul had just mentioned another positive rein-forcement in the rewards of the judgment seat of Christ: **"For we must all appear at the judgment seat of Christ, so that each one may be recompensed for his deeds in the body, according to what he has done, whether good or bad"** (5:10). This clearly is the reward seat (*bēma*) described in 1 Corinthians 3:11-15 and Romans 14:1-12, not the great white throne judgment of the unsaved dead (Rev. 20:11-15). The many crowns promised to faithful believers are clear examples of such rewards (Jas. 1:12; 1 Thess. 2:19; 1 Pet. 5:4; 1 Cor. 9:24-27; 2 Tim. 4:6-8; Rev. 2:9). Concomitant with this is the fear of loss of rewards which Paul mentions in this connection: **"Therefore, knowing the fear of the Lord, we persuade men, but we are made manifest to God; and I hope that we are made manifest also in your consciences"** (5:11). Although *phobos* is frequently a strong word for fear, the context shows it should not be rendered "terror" as in the KJV, but rather refers to reverential fear. Paul built this teaching upon the clear statements of the Lord Jesus (Mt. 16:27; 19:27-30).

Even more serious are warnings to believers of the temporal conse-quences of a sinful lifestyle. There are many examples of God's chastise-ment in Israel's history, such as King David's sin and explicit New Testament references as well (Heb. 12:3-13). Paul uses very strong language about those who destroy the church (the temple of God in 1 Cor. 3:16-17), and his language in 1 Corinthians 5:5 & 11:27-32 is the doctrinal explanation of the premature death of Christians like Ananias and Sapphira (Acts 5:1-11), which truth John described as the "sin unto death" (1 Jn. 5:16-17). There is no hint in the text that they lost their salvation. There are also a number of other incentives which God uses in our lives. Some extreme Calvinists deny rewards, somehow thinking that it compromises the doctrines of grace. Unfortunately some of our Arminian friends do not seem to have been able to distinguish salvation and rewards either. Failure to make this important distinction has led to untold confusion in the interpretation of Scripture.

Denial of security colors our view of sin and holiness.

There is much confusion about the meaning of holiness and sanctifica-tion, which causes both Arminians and Calvinists alike to insist that a holy lifestyle is a condition for ultimate salvation. Passages such as Hebrews 12:14 have been grossly misunderstood: **"Pursue peace with all men, and the sanctification without which no one will see the Lord. See to it that no one comes short of the grace of God;..."** The misinterpretation arises because of failure to understand that the core meaning of sanctification (*hagiosmos*, used only here in Hebrews) derives from its verb "1. *to dedicate, separate, set apart for God;...* 2. *to purify*, make conformable in character to such dedication: forensically, to free from guilt."[1] There are five uses of the verb in this sense in Hebrews (2:11; 10:10, 14, 29; 13:12), which make it clear that the Apostle is using the verb *hagiozein* and the noun *hagiosmos* in the sense of *posi-tional* sanctification, not *experiential* holiness. Paul's usage, however, is quite different. Although he uses *hagiazein* and related nouns (*hagiosmos*, *hagiosunē, hagiotēs*) in both the positional sense (1 Cor. 6:11; Eph. 5:26) and in the experiential sense (2 Cor. 7:1), he usually uses the word 'justification' to refer to our forensic or legal position in Christ. Since the writer of Hebrews does not use this group of words in the experiential sense, we must not import Paul's quite different usage into Hebrews.[A] Most Evangelicals recognize that the use of the word 'saint' (*hagios*) is consistently positional all through the New Testament. Although the Catholic failure to recognize the positional nature of the usage of 'saints' is the most extreme error and is really semi-Pelagianism,* any other attempt to intrude human holiness into our ultimate salvation also seriously compromises salvation by grace alone through faith alone in Christ. The legalistic, pumped-up human holiness of Romanism is bankrupt, witness the pedophile priest scandal, as is any other legalistic attempt, whether it be in the Galatian church or any church today.

What degree of human holiness is necessary to guarantee our ultimate salvation? If one accepts the premise that some human holiness is necessary, then the answer would have to be, "total holiness." Unless we lapse back into a Muslim mindset or that of street philosophers, who hold that God weighs good deeds against bad works and judges on this basis, there is no other answer! Does God have some sort of a sliding scale with a cut-off point? Romanism has at least attempted to classify mortal and venial sins. However, Catholics give fuzzy answers to which sins and how much fall into each category. Nevertheless, James totally contradicts such thinking: **"For whoever keeps the whole law and yet stumbles in one *point*, he has become guilty of all"** (2:10). Paul is just as clear in seeking to relieve the legalistic Galatians of such muddled thinking: **"For as many as are of the works of the Law are under a curse; for it is written, 'Cursed is everyone who does not abide by all things written in the book of the law, to perform them'"** (Gal. 3:10). Since Paul affirms that Christians are under the law of Christ (1 Cor. 9:21), this principle would apply to all Christians as well. Any man-made sliding scale would in reality become a slippery slope which would dump every last one of us into the lake of fire. None of this kind of thinking has the least biblical basis.

What degree of human sinfulness will nullify a Christian's salvation? Those who deny eternal security, whether from an Arminian or an extreme Calvinist perspective, have a poorly developed doctrine of sin. I learned this early in my Christian life when I gave a testimony in a youth meeting at my church, thanking God for victory over a particular sin, which I had confessed to the Lord by claiming 1 John 1:9. Afterward my Arminian pastor got me aside and told me that this was not a sin, it was a mistake! His theology informed him that if it had been a sin, I would have lost my salvation.

It is not clear as to how the Wesleys developed their doctrine of sinless perfection, but it may have been the overhang from their pre-conversion

---

A. This is one of many indications that Paul is not the author of Hebrews. I have a dozen compelling reasons why Paul could not be the author of Hebrews, but space does not allow elaboration.

background in a very legalistic, ascetic, and mystical form of Anglicanism.[2] But their Arminianism has been described as "evangelical Arminianism" in contrast to the Arminianism of the Remonstrant followers of Arminius, over a century earlier. Most intriguingly, one doctoral dissertation argues that Wesley was so influenced by Calvin that his theology was as close to that of Calvin as was that of the Puritan,* John Owen, if not closer.[3] In any case, despite Wesley's denial of security and affirmation of sinless perfectionism, the fact that untold multitudes came into assurance of salvation through him shows how many other things he got right. Calvinists the world over are blessed by singing the great hymns of the Wesley brothers. Nevertheless, sinless perfectionism and denial of eternal security were twin errors of the Wesleyan movement which have far reaching consequences.[4]

The sentiment that "real Christians don't sin" is expressed in various forms in both Arminian and extreme Calvinistic circles. It shouldn't take much study of Scripture to see how simplistic and false this is. The biblical narrative is full of believers who sinned, sometimes egregiously.[B] Even if we set aside sins of commission for a moment and consider sins of omission, it becomes obvious that all Christians continuously sin. The Apostle James was so down-to-earth realistic: **"Therefore, to one who knows *the* right thing to do and does not do it, to him it is sin"** (3:17). Most Christians throughout the centuries have been guilty of the sin of failing to fulfill the great commission, at the very least, and it should be unnecessary to enumerate the many sins of omission of which most Christians are guilty. R. T. Kendall, as pastor of a major London church, gives a list of sins common among Christians which is over a page in length, and he affirms that the list is "ridiculously long."[5] For any Christian to say that he has never committed such sins since his conversion is absurd. Just ask his/her spouse! Even when we don't sin overtly, sin is frequently in the motives and thoughts of the heart, as the Lord Jesus emphasized in the Sermon on the Mount (Mt. 5).

Can Failure of Faith Negate Salvation?

Another major concern of Arminians is that those who stop believing in Christ must necessarily lose their salvation. They argue that the verb 'to believe,' when used in reference to salvation, is mostly used in the present tense or in a durative or linear usage of the aorist.*[6] Although it is true that the verb is frequently used in the present tense, there are a multitude of usages in the aorist* and perfect tenses which relate to salvation. Although John uses the present tense of *pisteuein* about three-quarters of the time, and Luke about half the time in Acts, Paul uses the present sparingly in his epistles. Most strikingly, when Paul told the Philippian jailor how to be

---

B.   e.g. Abraham, Lot, Jacob and his sons, Saul, David, Solomon, Amaziah, Uzziah, Peter, Ananias/Sapphira, 1 Cor 3, 5, & 11 and many others.

saved, he used the aorist* imperative (Acts 16:31), which is usually action at a point in time in the past. So the whole foundation of this argument is false. Furthermore, there are two diverse uses of the present tense, the present habitual and the present continuous. The use of the present does not always imply continuous action.[c] Indeed, we find that there are clear biblical examples of true believers who did not continuously believe and confess Christ. We should hardly have to mention Peter's name to bring recall of his triple denial of Christ. Did he lose his salvation at that point? The burden of proof is on Arminians to show that he did. No, when the Lord restored him to fellowship (Jn. 21:15-17), Peter's lack of faith or salvation was not an issue. Indeed, the Lord had assured Peter: **"But I have prayed for you, that your faith may not fail; and you, when once you have turned again, strengthen your brothers"** (Lk. 22:32).

On the other hand, few readers might think to examine the account of John the Baptizer in prison (Mt. 11:1-15): **"Now when John, while imprisoned, heard of the works of Christ, he sent *word* by his disciples and said to Him, 'Are You the Expected One, or shall we look for someone else?"** Zane Hodges makes a significant point here:

> It is hard to believe one's eyes when this passage is first encountered. Here is the great prophet and forerunner of God's Christ calling into question the very person to whom he had once given bold testimony.... Clearly then, this great servant of God is asking a question he presumably had settled decisively long ago. His inquiry is manifestly an expression of doubt about the very truth by which men and women are saved.[7]

There is no question that John was a believer, for the angel told his father that he would be **"filled with the Spirit from his mother's womb"** (Lk. 1:15). Yet now he is having second thoughts about who Jesus is; his faith seems very weak, virtually extinguished.[D] However, rather than rebuking his lack of faith, the Lord gives him commendation in the strongest terms imaginable: **"Truly I say to you, among those born of women there has not arisen *anyone* greater than John the Baptist!"** Certainly his salvation was not in jeopardy. From these two examples it becomes crystal clear that continuous faith is not a condition of ultimate salvation. What if Peter or John had died in that state of denial or unbelief? Would they have gone to hell? Unthinkable!

The Lord's promise to pray that Peter's faith would not fail raises a significant point. Can a true believer's faith fail in the ultimate sense of apostasy from the faith? Was Peter unique in this regard? Later he testified that the believers to whom he wrote were kept (protected) by the power of God (1 Pet. 1:5). Did not the Lord Jesus pray the same prayer in the upper

---

C   In the Sanskrit-derived sister languages to Greek of North India (such as Hindi), there actually are different forms for the present habitual and present continuous tenses.

D.   John's disillusionment is easily explainable in terms of his Spirit-given expectation of Messiah's coming in judgment to deliver and reign over Israel (Mt. 3:1-12). We now know what John did not, that this had to come after passion and death.

room for the rest of the Eleven and also for those who should believe through their word (Jn. 17:11-12, 20-21)? Is He not right now at the Father's right hand interceding for all believers, by which **"He is able also to save forever those who draw near to God through Him"** (Heb. 7:25)?

Peter himself provided the key as to how God sustains the faith of true believers: **"for you have been born again not of seed which is perishable but imperishable, *that is*, through the living and enduring word of God"** (1 Pet. 1:23). With the Samaritan woman Christ used the symbolism of drinking to communicate the act of believing: **"but whoever drinks of the water that I will give him shall never thirst; but the water that I will give him will become in him a well of water springing up to eternal life"** (Jn. 4:14). First, the verb 'drinks' is an aorist* subjunctive, not a present tense. Second, the promise is that those who drink will *never* thirst again, which is a very explicit promise of eternal security, reinforced in the bread of life discourse (Jn. 6:35). Third, the "well of water" is an obvious reference to the Holy Spirit, which is confirmed by His further reference at the feast of Tabernacles, when He cried out,

> If anyone is thirsty, let him come to Me and drink. He who believes in Me, as the Scripture said, 'from his innermost being will flow rivers of living water.' But this He spoke of the Spirit, whom those who believed [aorist tense] in Him were to receive; for the Spirit was not yet *given*, because Jesus was not yet glorified (Jn. 7:37-9).

This is the foundation of His promise of the permanent indwelling of the Spirit to all believers: **"I will ask the Father, and He will give you another Helper, that He may be with you forever; *that is* the Spirit of truth,... *but* you know Him because He abides with you and will be in you"** (Jn. 14:16-17). The Lord's express affirmation of the permanence of the Holy Spirit's indwelling is reinforced by Paul's three references to the earnest and sealing of the Holy Spirit (2 Cor. 1:21-22; Eph. 1:13-14; 4:30). The Holy Spirit is an ever-flowing well springing up to eternal life, who keeps true believers in faith. The irreversible nature of the new birth also needs to be emphasized in this connection. True believers may be extremely weak in their faith at any point in the Christian life without jeopardizing their ultimate salvation.

Even John Calvin, through a misunderstanding of Hebrews 6:4-6 (cf. Ch. 13, pp. 170-4), taught a doctrine of temporary faith: "Experience shows that the reprobate are sometimes affected in a way so similar to the elect, that even in their own judgment there is no difference between them. Hence it is not strange, that by the Apostle a taste of heavenly gifts, and by Christ Himself a temporary faith, is ascribed to them." He also spoke of an "ineffectual calling" and an "inferior operation of the Spirit."[8] These are unbiblical notions!

Many might so misunderstand a number of references to believers who stop believing as a cessation of genuine saving faith. In the parable of the four soils the Lord Jesus explained the second category: **"The one on whom seed was sown on the rocky places, this is the man who hears the word and immedi-**

ately receives it with joy; yet he has no *firm* root in himself, but is *only* temporary, and when affliction or persecution arises because of the word, immediately he falls away" (Mt. 13:20-21). Note well that the word of God did not have a firm root in the person himself. It did not involve the whole personality: intellect, emotions, and will. There are examples in John 6:64-66; 8:31; Acts 8:13ff; and James 2:19 of those whose faith was not genuine. Perhaps it did not meet the criterion which Paul stipulated in Romans 10:9, to **"believe in your heart that God raised Him from the dead."** I always liked the tract entitled, "Missing Heaven by 18 Inches," because all through my teen years people thought I was a Christian, but there was no personal heart trust in Christ's finished work. Since I have already shown that it is people who have to do the trusting, we need not blame counterfeit faith on an "inferior work of the Spirit," as Calvin does. The Spirit neither strikes people with genuine or inferior faith.

Is security based upon the Calvinistic notion of election?

For those of us who repudiate the Calvinistic notion of unconditional, individual election, is the case for eternal security thereby undermined? Not in the least! Most Calvinists depend heavily upon their doctrine of election as a basis for "perseverance of the saints." But since this argument is totally deductive, there is a far stronger inductive basis for eternal security in the direct statements of Scripture. Thus, our confidence in eternal security is not weakened one iota by a strong rejection of unconditional election.

What Is at Stake? Why Believe It?

Many renowned scholars, both Calvinistic and Arminian, have confessed to a very real tension between the positive promises of the Bible and the exhortations, warnings, and problem passages. Howard Marshall, an outstanding Arminian scholar, has confessed that the tension has to be left unresolved.[9] Robert Stein, as one who holds to eternal security, confessed that he had no satisfying interpretation of Hebrews 6. However, the tension is certainly resolvable. Indeed, for believers in the inerrancy of Scripture, *it must be resolvable.* Moderate Calvinistic and mediate writers have made substantial progress in resolving this tension.

An essential reason for believing in eternal security is its integral connection with the great Pauline doctrine of justification by grace through faith alone, so important to the Reformation. This was a significant factor in Charles Stanley's "conversion." Years earlier J. F. Strombeck wrote, *"The whole body of grace truth loses very much of its meaning to those who reject the doctrine of eternal security"* (italics his).[10] In one of his excellent books, Strombeck used the illustration of the way color printed on one side of a fabric "bleeds through" to the other side. In a similar way, denial of security bleeds through all the other teachings of the those who deny it, whether Arminian or extreme Calvinist. The full forgiveness of sin through the cross and the unconditional love of God for His children are compromised with human performance by denial of security.

Kendall points out another issue at stake in the denial of eternal security. He suggests that many Arminians are really hedging their bets. "Their view is that, even if the doctrine of once saved, always saved is true, they still prefer to play it safe and live the Christian life as though this doctrine might not be true. After all, if it is true, they will be saved anyway—if it is not true, they hope to be sure they have enough good works to cushion their security." It is like people who lift their feet as the jetplane takes off to help it along, rather than fully trust the plane. It is like the man who got baptized thirteen times, by every conceivable mode, just to cover all the bases. Kendall urges such people to "go for broke"—stake your whole case on the finished work of Christ alone.[11]

Furthermore, I can confirm Kendall's experience that coming to believe in security opened up the Scriptures in a new way for me. Although, unlike Kendall, I did not have the erroneous theological baggage to clear out of my thinking, I did begin to sense a wonderful harmony of Scripture, both as I first wrestled with the issue and in my studies over these years. Indeed, the unresolved tension perceived by many honest interpreters like Marshall would be a great obstacle to belief in the inerrancy of Scripture. Perhaps this explains why many evangelical Arminian denominations do not have any traditional belief in the inerrancy of Scripture.[12] Appreciation for the wonderful doctrinal harmony of the Bible is a great reinforcement of faith in the verbal, plenary inspiration of Scripture.*

The last reason for believing in eternal security relates to the quality of our fellowship with the Lord and the motivations for godly Christian living. Shortly after coming to understanding of security I was greatly blessed by Strombeck's second book, *Disciplined by Grace*. There I learned for the first time the implications of Paul's words to Titus: "**For the grace of God has appeared, bringing salvation to all men, instructing us to deny ungodliness and worldy desire and to live sensibly, righteously and godly in the present age,...**" (2:11-12). How thrilling it was to see, as Strombeck worked through Paul's epistles, how all of his appeals for godly living were based, not on the Mosaic Law, but upon the gracious salvation God has freely given us (Rom. 12:1-2; Eph. 4:1-3; Col. 3:1-4, etc.).

Both Kendall and Stanley have described the frustrating legalism they experienced among those who deny security, and Michael Eaton has described the legalism he experienced in "developed Calvinism" and found in the writings of the Puritans.* The goal of these writers is to show that intruding human performance into the issue of our ultimate salvation, not only compromises the clear biblical teaching of salvation by grace alone, through faith alone, by Christ alone, but it compromises the biblical basis for a godly Christian life under the gracious hand of a loving God.

We who are parents understand the importance of showing unconditional love to our children as a basis for a healthy, positive relationship. "If abandoning the faith or falling into sin short-circuits salvation, I have the ability to demonstrate unconditional love to a greater extent than God."[13] How can we trust a heavenly Father whose love for us is conditioned upon our performance until the last breath of life? How can we experience true fellowship with such a God? How can we have peace in our Christian life if there is always uncertainty about where we *really* stand with Him? How can we live a stable Christian life if we constantly fear that God will ultimately disown us? Kendall goes so far as to say that legalistic morality is not true biblical godliness. When we understand Christ's constant exposure of the legalism of the Pharisees' morality, we would have to agree with Kendall.

Conclusions

The bottom line of God's plan of salvation is the confident assurance that we will get to glory and can live a fruitful life here in this sinful world with that confidence. How tragic that so many of both Calvinists and Arminians do not experience this joy and peace in believing! It is to be hoped that the preceding four chapters will contribute to many such Christians entering into this full assurance which God has purposed for us.

This is not only vital for every believer's own personal life, but also for our witness and service for Him. If the gospel we communicate and the lifestyle we model are legalistic, the impact of our life and witness will be far short of what God expects from us. God saved us to bear abiding fruit.

---

1 Abbott-Smith, *Lexicon*, p 5.

2 Robert G Tuttle, Jr , *John Wesley His Life and Theology* (GR Zondervan, 1978), pp. 143-55

3. S Lewis Johnson, Jr made this statement in tapes on "Particular Redemption" made at Believer's Chapel in Dallas TX, for which I do not have present access or information Alan C Clifford published his dissertation as *Atonement and Justification* (Oxford: Clarendon, 1990).

4 Harry Ironside dealt very effectively with this error from Scripture and his early years in the Salvation Army. *Holiness the False and the True* (Neptune, NJ: Loizeaux Bros)

5 Kendall, *Once Saved, Always Saved* (Moody, 1985), pp 149-50.

6 Robert Shank, *Life in the Son*, 2nd ed (Springfield, MO. Westcott, 1960), pp. 75-82 Stanley, in referencing Shank's argument, oversimplifies it, p 73. Shank, however, limits his discussion to a few contexts in John.

7. Zane Hodges, *Absolutely Free*, p 105

8. John Calvin, *Institutes of the Christian Religion*, 3 2.11-12; *Commentary*, Lk 17 13.

9 I Howard Marshall, *Kept by the Power of God*, 3rd ed (Carlisle, UK Paternoster, 1995), p 278, Robert H. Stein, *Difficult Passages in the New Testament* (GR Baker, 1990), p 353

10 Strombeck, p. 7

11 Kendall, p 61-2

12 This is true of the Evangelical Mission Covenant Church, in which I was raised Indeed, this has been a significant issue at North Park Theological Seminary over the years A former colleague of mine, who graduated from a Nazarene seminary, informed me that the Church of the Nazarene does not have any tradition or affirmation of inerrancy More recently I visited the campus of a college of the Church of God (Anderson, IN), and found no such commitment to inerrancy by their faculty.

13 Stanley, p 11

It is incontestable that Christ came for the expiation of the sins of the whole world. But the solution lies close at hand, that whosoever believes in Him should not perish but should have eternal life (John 3:15).... For although there is nothing in the world deserving of God's favour, He nevertheless shows He is favourable to the whole world when He calls all without exception to the faith of Christ, which is indeed an entry into life.

-John Calvin

CHRIST REALLY DIED FOR *EVERY* SINNER!

What about Limited Atonement?

This chapter on 'general redemption'[1] should not be necessary, since examination of the Greek words for Christ's passion and salvation in Chapter 5 clearly showed the basis for believing that Christ died for each and every sinner. However, since the error of 'limited atonement' has dogged the church for four centuries, it must be responded to in more detail.

A uniquely held doctrine. Extreme Calvinism *alone* holds to limited atonement, which means that Christ died only for the elect and not in any real sense for all mankind. It is clear from their statement of the issue that it derives from their premise of unconditional election, and that the issue would never have arisen apart from that doctrine. Limited atonement is peculiarly a view of extreme Calvinists and is rejected by moderate Calvinists, Arminians, Lutherans, Pietists,* and those who hold to a mediate view—in short, all other Christians.

A new doctrine. The doctrine of limited atonement is relatively recent. It was not held until Theodor Beza (1519-1605) and does not appear in any creed until the Canons of Dort (1618-9). Neither Augustine nor any first generation Reformer held it.[2] There has been a strong reaction against it from a majority of Christians ever since it was first touted. Since it is clear that Calvin himself did not hold to it, in all honesty, we cannot refer to those who hold it as Calvinists (cf. App. E in *BCAA*). Many terms have been used: Ultra-Calvinists, Hyper-Calvinists, Developed Calvinists, Scholastic Calvinists, etc. For historical accuracy they should be designated as 'Beza-ites.' Norman Geisler uses the term extreme Calvinists, and it seems accurate.

Two dimensions of salvation truth. Inductive study of the various Greek words referring to Christ's saving work reveals two major dimensions: on the one hand, an objective, historical, universal aspect, and on the other hand, a subjective, individual, and limited aspect (cf. Ch. 5). The truth is two-sided. Taking one side and forcing all other Scripture to fit in with that is a reductionist error. The truth must be grasped with both hands. It is not that there is any contradiction, paradox, or antinomy in these two aspects of His work on the cross. Both are perfectly in harmony. Christ frequently set forth two-sided truths (cf. His explanation about Elijah in Mt. 17). It is mainly Westerners, with our Greek-derived way of thinking (cognitive process), who so easily fall into this reductionist error.

The View Clarified

Definition and terminology. The best term for the view defended here is 'general redemption,'* since 'universal redemption' might imply universalism, that is, that all will be saved. Many extreme Calvinists prefer other terminology than 'limited atonement,' such as "definite atonement," "particular redemption," or "effective redemption." The terminology does not change the issue, so the common usage, limited atonement, will be retained. Since this doctrine first surfaced in the Synod of Dort (1618-9), consider a clear definition in the Canons of Dort (emphasis mine):

> For this was the sovereign counsel, and most gracious will and purpose of God the Father, that the quickening and saving efficacy of the most precious death of his Son should extend to all the elect, for bestowing <u>upon them alone</u> **the gift of justifying faith**, thereby to bring them infallibly to salvation: that is, it was the will of God, that Christ by the blood of the cross, whereby he confirmed the new covenant, should effectually redeem out of every people, tribe, nation, and language, all those, and <u>those only</u>, who were from eternity chosen to salvation, and given to him by the Father; that he should confer upon them faith, which together with all the other saving gifts of the Holy Spirit, he purchased them by his death;[3]

Attempted clarifications. Over the centuries the catch phrase, "sufficient for all, but efficient only for the elect" has been used, but it resolves little or nothing. Calvin attributed it to medieval scholastics and saw it as unhelpful.[4] Since all can accept it, it does not clarify the issues. However, if Christ's death is sufficient for all but has no applicability to all, then its sufficiency for all is meaningless. The sufficiency of the cross for all is only meaningful if all can somehow benefit from it.

Another catch phrase Calvinists have used is, "Christ died for all without distinction, but not for all without exception." This *does* express the view of extreme Calvinists, but does not do justice to all Scripture, which teaches that Christ died for all without exception, as well as for all without distinction– the 'general redemption' view affirmed in this book.*

The Exegesis of Key Scriptures
Restrictive passages

Those who hold to general redemption do not deny that Scripture frequently focuses the extent of the death of Christ upon believers. In acknowledging this common ground with extreme Calvinists, it should be noted that even some of the passages usually adduced in favor of a limitation have some ambiguity. A number of the passages claimed by extreme Calvinists do not specifically mention the death of Christ, and being irrelevant will not be discussed here: Matthew 1:21, John 1:9; 5:21. *Note that nowhere does the Bible explicitly say that Christ died for the 'elect,' per se.* Expressions such as 'sheep,' 'the church,' etc. are used in these passages, but without any restrictive language which would in any way contradict the other more general passages. Lightner aptly points out, "All men, including the elect, are lost until such time as they individually and personally exercise faith in Christ as their own Savior. There simply is no distinction in the Bible between elect and nonelect sinners in their unregenerate state."[5]

Matthew 20:28; 26:28; Mark 10:45. "**... just as the Son of Man did not come to be served, but to serve, and to give His life a ransom for many.**" Extreme Calvinists assume that the many for whom Christ paid the ransom price are the elect. They read into our Lord's words a theological concept of election in limiting its focus. Calvin himself did not so interpret it: "'Many' is used, not for a definite number, but for a large number, in that He sets Himself over against all others. And this is its meaning also in Rom. 5:15, where Paul is not talking of a part of mankind but of the whole human race."[6]

John 10:11, 15. "**... and I lay down my life for the sheep.**" Edwin Palmer is typical of extreme Calvinists who add the word 'alone' to Christ's statement. "He lays down His life for His sheep, and His sheep alone."[7] He assumed that sheep is equivalent to elect, but that equivalency is indefensible. The definition of sheep is clarified by Christ's statement in 10:26, "**But you do not believe, because you are not of my sheep.**" Christ did not exclude the possibility that any of the unbelieving Jews He was speaking to would subsequently believe and become His sheep. As a matter of fact, John describes in 10:40-42 how many of them followed Him down to Perea and believed on Him there. At the time the Lord made the above statement, they were *not* His sheep, and yet subsequently, became such, and thus are also among the elect of God. Therefore, at a given point in time those who are His sheep are not all of the elect. These two terms, sheep and elect, are not equivalent. At a given moment His sheep are a subset of the elect of all ages. So if Christ died for His sheep alone, then He did not die for all the elect. Consider the logical tangles one gets into in conceptualizing elect sinners who have not yet come to faith in Christ. The Bible never deals with such a category of people; but Calvinists must do so constantly.

John 17:9. "**I pray for them. I am not praying for the world, but for those you**

have given me, for they are yours" (NIV). Extreme Calvinists affirm that there is a parallel between Christ's refusal to pray for the world and their teaching that Christ did not die for the whole world. However, first it must be asked *why* Christ did not pray for the world. Was it because He did not want the world to be saved and knew, as the sinless Son, that the Father would have to answer His prayer? No, for He wept for unbelieving Israel (Mt. 23:37). Was it because as a matter of principle He did not pray for unbelievers? No, on the cross He prayed for those who were crucifying Him (Lk. 23:34), that the Father would refrain from immediate judgment upon them.

First, it should be noted that He did not say, "I pray not for the non-elect." In the world (*kosmos*) of unregenerate sinners for whom He did not pray at this time, was a host of people who subsequently believed and evidently were among the elect, and for whom He *did* pray in v. 20: "**I do not ask on behalf of these alone, but for those also who believe in Me through their word; that they may all be one;...**" Note also that this prayer was not a prayer for the *salvation* of the disciples—they had already been saved. He is praying for the Father to keep them, protect them from Satan, sanctify them, unify them, and glorify them. This would not have been an appropriate prayer for those who did not believe in Him. So when the nature of our Lord's motivation and prayer is understood, it is clear that it is not at all relevant to this issue.

Acts 20:28. "**Be on guard for yourselves and for all the flock, among which the Holy Spirit has made you overseers, to shepherd the church of God which He purchased with His own blood.**" Paul's words to the Ephesian elders appropriately focus the efficacy of Christ's blood in acquiring (*peripoiein*) His church. Since this verb has a broader connotation, it apparently doesn't speak only of His death, but has both the objective and subjective aspects of the salvation of the corporate church in view. Thus, it in no way compromises the truth of general redemption.

Romans 5:15, 19. "**For if by the transgression of the one the many died, much more did the grace of God and the gift by grace of the one Man, Jesus Christ, abound to the many.... For as through the one man's disobedience the many were made sinners, even through the obedience of the One the many will be made righteous.**" Extreme Calvinists typically take the word 'many' to be a reference to the elect and not to all mankind, contrary to Calvin's view quoted in his comment on Matthew 20:28 above.

Galatians 3:13. "**Christ redeemed us from the curse of the Law, having become a curse for us—for it is written, 'Cursed is every one who hangs on a tree'**" Paul focused upon believers here, and the context clearly limits his meaning to believers, since the unregenerate are never said to have been released from the Mosaic Law, as believers have been (Rom. 7:6; 2 Cor 3:6-11). Having noted this contextual limitation, it should also be noted that Paul does not use *agoradzein*, as he does in passages with a more general reference, but he used *exagoradzein*, which focuses on the redemption-release aspect of the cross. This is not contradictory to, but rather harmonious with, general ransom-redemption taught in other passages. Lightner is helpful here: "If references such as this, in which the writer includes himself in the death of Christ, may be used to prove limited atonement, then when writers of Scripture use similar phraseology in speaking of man's sin, it could be said that they teach limited depravity or sin."[8] Then he references Isaiah 53:6 and 64:6. Where is consistency?

Ephesians 5:25-6. **"Husbands, love your wives, just as Christ also loved the church and gave Himself up for her; that He might sanctify her, having cleansed her by the washing of water with the word,..."** Extreme Calvinists assume that the focus of Christ's love upon the church excludes all other humans. But in the context it is totally appropriate in discussing marriage for Paul to focus on that special love of Christ for His church. Norman Geisler put it well:

> There are good reasons why the fact that Christ loves the church does not mean He did not love the world as well. For one thing, the fact that I love my wife does not logically mean that I lack love for other persons. It simply puts special focus on my love for someone who is special in my life.[9]

1 Peter 3:18. **"For Christ also died for sins once for all, *the* just for *the* unjust, in order that He might bring us to God, having been put to death in the flesh, but made alive in the spirit."** Significantly, we observe that Peter describes Christ's substitution being for the **"unjust."** This hardly is a synonym for the 'elect.' It describes the whole human race. The goal of that substitution, Peter says, is to **"bring us to God."** So actually this passage gives both the objective aspect (substitution for the unjust) and the subjective aspect (bringing believers to God) together in one statement, as does 1 Timothy 4:10. Although quoted as a proof-text, this passage actually affirms both aspects: the first part is general; the second, limited. No contradiction here!

Unlimited passages

Christ died for the 'whole world.' There are many passages which extend the intent of Christ's death and salvation to the whole world. Note that most of the references are in John's writings. In all these cases John followed Christ's consistent usage of the word *kosmos* in the negative sense of the unregenerate, hostile satanic world-system of sinners. The BAG lexicon is explicit: "*the world*, and everything that belongs to it, appears as that which is at enmity w. God, i.e. lost in sin, wholly at odds w. anything divine, ruined and depraved" (supporting refs.: Jn. 8:23; 12:25, 31; 13:1; 14:30; 16:11; 18:23; 1 Jn. 4:17; 5:19; 1 Cor. 3:19; 5:10).[10] In the following references also, according to John's consistent usage, it must have a similar meaning, certainly not 'elect.' Norman Douty's extensive survey of lexicons, Bible encyclopedias, and dictionaries shows that none support the convoluted meanings read into this word by extreme Calvinists.[11]

John 1:29. The words of John the Baptizer: "**Behold, the Lamb of God who takes away the sin of the world!**" - Extreme Calvinists implausibly try to divert the issue by stating that *kosmos* has a geographic sense in other contexts, and thus refers to the elect in all the world. The rule for determining word meaning is always to see how *the same author* uses the word first before going elsewhere. They violate this important word-study principle.

John 3:16-19. "'For God so loved the world, that He gave His one and only Son, that **whoever believes in him** shall not perish but have everlasting life. For God did not send his Son into the world to condemn the world, but to save the world through him. **Whoever believes in him** is not condemned, but whoever does not believe stands condemned already **because he has not believed** in the name of God's one and only Son'"(NIV). Note Puritan John Owen's outrageous rewording of it: "God so loved the elect throughout the world, that he gave his Son with this intention, that by him believers might be saved."[12] Not only does this passage speak of Christ's death for the whole unregenerate world of mankind, but it also stipulates its meaning by the clarifying phrase "whoever believes," which Owen unconscionably omits. This passage could not be clearer that faith, not election, is the condition of salvation.

John 4:42; 1 John 4:14. "**They said to the woman, 'We no longer believe just because of what you said; now we have heard for ourselves, and we know that this man really is the Savior of the world.**'" Although these are the words of the Samaritans, the second reference shows that John quotes it approvingly: "**And we have seen and testify that the Father has sent his Son to be the Savior of the world**" (NIV). In what clearer way could he state general redemption?

John 12:46-47. "**I have come *as* a light into the world, that everyone who believes in Me may not remain in darkness. And if any one hears My sayings, and does not keep them, I do not judge him; for I did not come to judge the world, but to save the world.**" The meaning of 'world' in verse 47 is the same as in verse 46. There the picture is of a world of unregenerate humans in spiritual darkness, upon which the light of Christ has begun to shine. This is the same world which He came to save. To put a spin on it and make it the world of the elect, as extreme Calvinists do, is an unconscionable distortion.

1 John 2:2. "... and He Himself is the propitiation for our sins; and not for ours only, but also for *those of* the whole world." - Extreme Calvinists, such as R. C. Sproul, find the greatest difficulty in explaining this verse: "On the surface this text seems to demolish limited atonement."[13] Arthur Pink gives the usual extreme explanation, (as does Harold Camping on Family Radio):

When John says, 'He is the propitiation for *our* sins' he can only mean for the sins of *Jewish believers....* When John added, 'And not for ours only, but also for *the whole world* he signified that Christ was the propitiation for the sins of *Gentile* believers *too,* for as previously shown, 'the world' is a term *contrasted* from Israel

How outrageously Pink stated that "to insist that 'the whole world' in 1 John 2:2 signifies the entire human race is to undermine the very foundation of our faith."[14]

There is not a shred of evidence that John was writing his epistles to Jewish Christians. A consensus of scholars identify the recipients as both Jewish and Gentile believers. As a matter of fact, John is quite explicit in 5:13: "**These things I have written to you who believe in the name of the Son of God, in order that you may know that you have eternal life.**" Why do extreme Calvinists try to limit John's clear declaration to just *Jewish* believers? Only their doctrinal bias forces them to such a distortion. A few verses farther John gives an unambiguous picture of the meaning of 'world' (*kosmos*): "**We know that we are of God, and the whole world lies in *the power* of the evil one**"(5:19). Certainly John is not saying that only the Gentile world is in Satan's grip, nor the world outside of Asia Minor. It is the world of unregenerate mankind, set in contrast to believers. Thus John simply affirmed that Christ's death is a satisfaction for the sins of believers and also for a lost world of sinners.

2 Corinthians 5:19. "**... namely, that God was in Christ reconciling the world to Himself, not counting their trespasses against them, and He has committed to us the word of reconciliation.**" Reconciliation is a subjective, experiential dimension of Christ's cross-work, based upon verse 18. In order to relate verse 19 to this, it is essential to note the differing tenses of the two participles. In verse 18 it is an aorist participle,* thus indicating a completed action—God reconciled us to Himself. But in verse 19 it is a present participle, thus indicating an ongoing action—God was in Christ *in the process* of reconciling the world to Himself. The world has not been reconciled to God, but His sacrifice was the beginning of the process of reconciling a world of unregenerate sinners to Himself.

Christ died for all, the lost, the ungodly, for sin.

There are a host of references to Christ's death for all mankind or every man. The meaning of general availability of salvation is confirmed by the additional connection of His death for the ungodly and for the lost, with no contextual basis for limiting any of these expressions to the elect in any of these passages. It is freely granted that there are contexts in which according to common Greek usage, the word 'all' does not mean all without exception. For instance, in 1 Timothy 6:10, the NAS translation reads: "**For the love of money is a root of all sorts of evil.**" It is obvious that not all evils spring out of the love of money. Additionally, in John 12:32 there is a contextual basis in 12:20 for understanding the Lord's reference to all kinds of men being drawn to Christ, that is, Gentiles as well as Jews

Having noted this, it must be insisted that in at least one of the following references, and probably in all of them, the allusion to 'all' must be a reference to all mankind without exception. The same extreme Calvinists who deny that all ever means all without exception, interpret the 'all' in Ephesians 1:11 as having an all inclusive meaning: **"who works all things after the counsel of His will**." As shown in Chapter 3, this all-inclusive interpretation is the sole proof text for their view of the outworking of the sovereignty of God and ignores the context and grammar. They must insist upon it here, at the very least, even if it were a totally unique usage. But, of course, it is not a unique usage. 'All' must mean all at least occasionally, if words are to have any meaning. This reminds us of Bill Clinton answering evasively, "that it all depends upon what the meaning of 'is' is." Extreme Calvinists are guilty of the same sort of obfuscation. Let us examine each context.

Isaiah 53:4-12. **"All of us like sheep have gone astray, each of us has turned to his own way; but the LORD has caused the iniquity of us all to fall on Him"**(53:6). Although the prophet speaks continually in the first person in vv.4-6, which extreme Calvinists might take to refer to the elect, the context indicates he is referring to the nation Israel as a whole, not just the elect of Israel. Not only does he refer to those who **"have gone astray"** and **"turned to his own way"**, but also in v. 8 to **"my people to whom the stroke was due."** However, in vv. 11-12 there is a shift to third person, **"He will bear their iniquities ... He Himself bore the sin of many**." This shift may be an early indication of the two-sidedness of Messiah's passion. *Calvin, however, comments that 'many' is equivalent to 'all,' contrary to the extreme Calvinistic interpretation.*[15]

2 Corinthians 5:14, 15. **"For the love of Christ controls us, having concluded this, that one died for all, therefore all died; and <u>He died for all</u>, that they who live should no longer live for themselves, but for Him who died and rose again on their behalf."** Paul's point here is straightforward in his use of 'all' three times in the universal sense of 'all mankind,' set in contrast with **"they who live,"** the limited group of born-again ones. Nothing in the context or the syntax of the Greek raises any question about the prima facie interpretation.[16]

Romans 5:18. **"So then as through one transgression there resulted condemnation to all men, even so through one act of righteousness there resulted justification of life <u>to all men</u>."** Paul closely parallels Adam's one transgression with its universal consequences and the one sacrifice of Christ with its universal intent. He does not say that all men were justified but that Christ's sacrifice did have this as a potential goal. This is implied in the use of the preposition *eis* (unto). One of the less frequent usages of *eis* makes it even clearer: "*For the purpose of...*"[17] Thus, we could rightly translate by slightly improving on the NIV: **"even so the purpose of one act of righteousness was justification that brings life for all mankind."** The purpose for which Christ died is to make justification available to all mankind. Although the Greek construction is difficult, Paul's intent is clear–a provision for all mankind. Extreme Calvinists overlook Paul's logic, that just as Adam's integral connection with the whole human race condemned all mankind, just so Christ's identification with all mankind as the Son of Man, dying as a man, had as its goal bringing justification of life to all mankind.

1 Timothy 2:1-6. "First of all, then, I urge that entreaties *and* prayers, petitions *and* thanksgivings, be made on behalf of all men, for kings and all who are in authority, so that we may lead a tranquil and quiet life in all godliness and dignity. This is good and acceptable in the sight of God our Savior, who desires all men to be saved and to come to the knowledge of the truth. For there is one God, *and* one mediator also between God and men, *the* man Christ Jesus, who gave Himself as a ransom for all ..." Paul's use of 'all' three times in this context gives a solid base for taking all three in their normative sense of 'all without exception.' His exhortation to pray for "**all men**" (*huper pantōn anthrōpōn*) could not be limited to all without distinction, but must also imply all without exception. No restriction to the 'elect' is possible here since Calvinists admit we don't know who the 'elect' are. Although Paul desired that we especially pray for those in authority, it is clear that he was concerned about the salvation of all mankind as well (2:4), all without exception. Paul used the same Greek expression in the plural in both verses. There is no way to restrict our prayer focus to the 'elect' who are still unregenerate. So the reference to Christ's "**ransom for all**" (2:6) must also be taken in a universal sense. As shown in Chapter 5, *lutron* is used of the objective ransom price and not of the subjective application to the individual, so the same must be true of the unique word here, *antilutron*.

1 Timothy 4:10. "For it is for this we labor and strive, because we have fixed our hope on the living God, who is the Savior of all men, especially of believers." Apart from the last phrase, Paul's statement might seem to promote universalism, which would be a problem for all Evangelicals. Take note that *anthrōpos* is sometimes used generically, that is, "all mankind."[18] This might be adequate, but Paul significantly added the last phrase "especially of believers" so that there might be no misunderstanding. Was this a mental lapse on Paul's part, which he patched up with the last phrase? No, he could have gotten his scribe to redo the sentence. There must be intrinsic truth in the first part of the sentence, that God is the Savior of all mankind in some real sense, that is, in the objective, potential sense. All can agree that Paul's clarifying phrase narrows the truth down to the ultimate reality—that only believers will be saved. Here, as frequently, the truth is two-sided.

Titus 2:11. "For the grace of God has appeared, bringing salvation to all men,..." Although the syntax of the sentence is difficult, modern translations have followed a host of scholars in correcting the KJV by connecting "**salvation**" with "**to all men.**"[19] Since this Pauline concept is seen in the above passages, his reference here can also be understood generically, salvation's availability to all mankind. Lightner identifies the key issue:

> The question is, "*Is it scripturally and logically sound always to restrict every usage of the words 'all,' 'whosoever' and 'world' when they occur in a salvation context?*" This is precisely what the limited redemptionist

always does and must do. There may not be a single exception if the limited viewpoint is to stand.[20]

Hebrews 2:9. "But we do see Him who was made for a little while lower than the angels, namely, Jesus, because of the suffering of death crowned with glory and honor, so that by the grace of God He might taste death <u>for everyone</u>." The context stresses the identification of the Lord Jesus with the whole human race in His incarnation (2:6-8, 14-18), so it is appropriate that His death should be for all mankind. It is noteworthy that the Apostle uses the singular here, and Alford comments: "If it be asked, why *pantos* (each) rather than *pantōn* (all), we may safely say that the singular brings out, far more strongly than the plural would, the applicability of Christ's death to each individual man."[21]

Luke 19:10. "For the Son of Man has come to seek and to save that which was lost." There is no better term than 'lost' to describe all mankind without exception, which certainly cannot be narrowed to the elect only. This clear statement of Christ as to the intent of His coming should end all discussion.

Romans 5:6. "For while we were still helpless, at the right time <u>Christ died for the ungodly</u>." Paul was in good company with Christ for clarity in affirming His death for the ungodly, whom he characterized in 5:10 as "**enemies of God**." Did Christ die for just the ungodly 'elect,' whoever they may be? The integrity of language and the word of God is at stake. If Paul didn't mean to say that Christ came to save all the lost, why didn't he plainly say so?

1 Corinthians 15:3. "For I delivered to you as of first importance what I also received, that Christ died for our sins according to the Scriptures,..." The question is, for whose sins did Christ die? The context of 15:1-2 settles it. The gospel which Paul preached was to all his Corinthian hearers, not just those who responded at any time. This is the way he had preached it on Mars Hill: "**all men everywhere**" (Acts 17:30-1).

Salvation is offered to "whomever". Appropriate to the fact that Christ died for a whole world of sinners, lost and ungodly people, that is, all mankind, are the 110 references to the gospel being offered to "whomever" without restriction. The apostolic preaching is the best effort of the Apostles to announce it unambiguously. Hear Peter: "**And it shall be that <u>everyone who calls on the name of the Lord</u> will be saved**" (Acts 2:21); "**Of Him all the prophets bear witness that through His name <u>everyone who believes in Him</u> receives forgiveness of sins**" (Acts 10:43). Hear Paul: "**... and through Him <u>everyone who believes</u> is freed from all things, from which you could not be freed through the Law of Moses**" (Acts 13:39); "**... for '<u>Whoever will call on the name of the Lord</u> will be saved**" (Rom. 10:13). Hear John: "**And let the one who is thirsty come; let <u>the one who wishes</u> take the water of life without cost**" (Rev. 22:17b). If Christ did not die for all human beings, and if the majority of human beings can never ever respond to these invitations, then such invitations are an absolute mockery!

Serious Implications of a Limited View
Limiting God's love
It is significant that Calvinists tend to emphasize the holiness of God as His foremost attribute, while Arminians emphasize His love. On what basis is such a judgment made? Is not God infinite in all His attributes? Why pick one attribute above another? Are they not all in perfect harmony with one another? Was not Jesus Christ, the God-man, the most perfectly balanced and integrated man who has ever walked this planet?

Any attempt to limit the love of God is a gross distortion of His infinite character. However, the doctrine of limited atonement does just that, in that it denies that God loves the non-elect, since it was by His choice that they are non-elect. They have been excluded from the pale of God's love since Christ did not die for them. Jerom Zanchius, one of the early advocates of limited atonement, in surveying God's attributes makes *no mention of the love of God*.[22] R. C. Sproul defends the limitation of God's love only to the elect: "Is there any reason that a righteous God ought to be loving toward a creature who hates him and rebels constantly against his divine authority and holiness?"[23] Would no extreme Calvinists before their conversion have fitted this description? Let's face it, many Christians, including Paul and Luther, once were such! Do we detect self-righteousness here? Christ's words in the Sermon on the Mount are an adequate answer to Sproul: "**But I say to you, love your enemies and pray for those who persecute you**" (Mt. 5:44). Does God ask us to do something He Himself is unwilling to do? Some extreme Calvinists distribute tracts with titles such as, "Does God Love You?" or "God May Not Love You!" However, if we communicate to sinners a picture of a less than gracious and loving God, we not only present a caricature, but also an additional obstacle to their repentance and faith.

According to 1 John 4:16 love is the very essence of God, and God's character cannot change (Heb. 1:11-12; Jas. 1:17). Scripture is clear that God loves sinners but hates their sin, and as long as they remain unrepentant the wrath of God is upon them. But God's love through the cross extends potentially to all mankind. God loved Israel (Deut. 7:7), even though not all were among the elect, and Christ loved the young ruler although he turned away from Him (Mk. 10:21).

The universal offer of the gospel
The universal offer of the gospel is freely admitted by most Calvinists and is biblically clear (Acts 17:30; Mt. 28:18-20). Robert Lightner states the problem: "Why does God invite all men if Christ did not provide for all?" Richards answers: "To us, no maxim appears more certain *than that a salvation offered implies a salvation provided*; for God will not tantalize his creature by tendering them with that which is not in his hand to bestow."[24]

Leading advocates of limited redemption admit a "great difficulty" and plead paradox. Moreover, all who believe in unconditional election *do have the problem*, but the general redemptionists have it to a lesser degree. If extreme Calvinists were totally honest with inquirers, they would have to say, "Unless you are one of the elect, Christ did not die for you, and indeed you cannot exercise saving faith to be saved." If moderate Calvinists were totally honest, they would have to admit, "My friend, Christ died for you, but unless you are one of the elect, you cannot exercise saving faith to be saved." Those holding a mediate position can honestly say, "My friend, Christ died for you, and no matter who you are, if you exercise repentant faith you will definitely be saved." W. Lindsay Alexander put it so aptly: "On this supposition [of limited atonement], the general invitations and promises of the Gospel are without an adequate basis, and seems like a mere mockery; an offer, in short, of what has not been provided."[25]

The personalization of the gospel

Lightner noted the tendency of limited redemptionists to advocate presentation of the gospel only in general terms. However, he focuses on three essentials that must be included: "(1) something about personal sin; (2) the substitutionary death of Christ for the sinner; and (3) faith or trust in Christ's finished work." In emphasizing that the gospel must be personalized, he makes it clear that the limited redemptionist cannot personalize #2 without misleading a non-elect sinner.[26] Those who hold unconditional election cannot really personalize #3 since it would be misleading to tell a non-elect sinner that if one will only trust Christ he will be surely saved, assuming that the "non-elect" cannot trust Christ.

I am personally very sensitive to this, since all through my teen years I believed that Christ died for the sins of the world, but did not know that He died for *my sin*. No doubt I was spiritually dead in that condition. Over fifty years ago I put my name into John 5:24 and personalized it. As missionaries to Pakistan, we found untold thousands in the Christian community who believed that Christ died for sin, but had no personal relationship with Christ. They were orthodox in their doctrine, but unregenerate. They also desperately needed to have the gospel personalized. Hundred of millions of professing Christians worldwide are lost because they have never personalized the gospel in their own life. This is not a marginal issue!

Lightner shows how J. I. Packer made a deliberate switch from the personalization of the sinner's sin (#1) to an explicit denial of the personalization of His substitutionary death (#2):

> . . the New Testament never calls on any man to repent on the ground that Christ died specifically and particularly for him. The basis on which the New Testament invites sinners to put faith in Christ is simply that they need Him, and that He offers Himself to them, and that those who receive Him are promised all the benefits that His death secured for His people.[27]

Lightner questions what Packer's biblical basis is for such a pronounced shift. Why must one be personalized, when the other may not?

Years ago, Rona, a Jewish co-worker of my daughter came for a Bible study. Joyce had been witnessing to her about the deity of Christ. When no one else showed up for the study, we began to go through Isaiah 53, showing her that **"all we like sheep have gone astray"** and that **"the Lord has laid on Him the iniquity of us all."** I will never forget the look on her face when she exclaimed, "Now I see it, Jesus is *my sin-bearer*." She has gone on in her walk with the Lord and has won her husband to Christ.

Other Evangelicals are absolutely right to insist that there must be a personalization of the whole gospel. Extreme Calvinists must prove from Scripture that the death of Christ may not be so personalized, and explain why we can't sincerely assure any and every sinner that if one will trust Christ, salvation will surely result. The lack of assurance among so many Calvinists is a result of their lack of personalization of the death of Christ.

The requirement of faith obviated

Extreme Calvinism, in effect, denies that faith is the required condition for salvation. If "Christ purchased faith for the elect," then faith cannot be a required condition for salvation. Indeed, they hold that faith is a consequence of regeneration, not a condition. Thus, there would be no point in telling the unregenerate to believe, since they cannot do so. Since by irresistible grace God regenerates the elect, faith becomes an afterthought, a mere extraneous appendage. *This is confirmed by the omission of any mention of faith in the five points of Calvinistic theology, the TULIP.* This was not accidental or inconsequential. Lightner sees this as a most serious problem with the limited view and asks:

> If the cross applies its own benefits and is God's only saving instrumentality, what place does faith have? When are man's sins forgiven—at the cross, thus before multitudes of men are ever born, or when man believes and thus appropriates what Christ has done?[28]

Dozens, yes, hundreds of references can be given to support the latter, that faith is the condition of justification, regeneration, eternal life, etc.

John Owen complicated the issue by arguing that since unbelief is a sin for which Christ died, then unbelief is no more hindrance than other sins in partaking of the fruit of his death.[29] Not only does this eliminate the need to actively exercise faith but is directly contradictory to all appeals for faith in Scripture. Owen's premise is clearly wrong; unbelief is a unique sin, one which, if persisted in, will lead to condemnation (Jn. 3:18). When Christ accused the Pharisees of "unforgivable sin," the context indicates that He was referring to hard-hearted unbelief. Unbelief must be distinguished from other sins, lest the necessity of faith be totally obviated.

Christ's ministry to the 'non-elect'

If Christ only died for the elect, what was the point in Christ bothering to deal personally with 'non-elect,' whoever they might be. Calvinists say that since we do not know who the elect are, we must deal with all men. But Christ was not so limitated. He did not get the rich young ruler to see his sinfulness. He went away sorrowful, and there is no hint that he ever came to faith in Christ. Didn't Christ know that he was non-elect, or to put it more bluntly, "reprobate"? Why did He patiently deal with him step by step?

Conclusion

Since the inductive biblical basis for general redemption is overwhelming, it is clear that the only support for limited atonement comes from scholastic, deductive, and faulty logic.

---

1. The expression 'universal redemption,' used in the past, is misleading in possibly implying universalism.

2. See the appendix of Calvin quotations on general redemption in my *Beyond Caslvinism and Arminianism.*

3 Canons of Dort, II, 8.

4. John Calvin, *Commentaries,* 1 John 2.2 , *en loc.*

5 Robert P. Lightner, *The Death Christ Died A Case for Unlimited Atonement,* p. 48.

6 Calvin, *Commentary on John,* en loc

7 Edwin H Palmer, *The Five Points of Calvinism,* p 43

8. Lightner, pp. 60-61.

9 Geisler, *Chosen, but Free,* p. 76

10 William F Arndt and F Wilbur Gingrich, *Greek-English Lexicon,* p. 447

11 Norman F. Douty, *The Death of Christ,* pp 41-45

12 John Owen, *The Death of Christ,* p 214

13 Sproul, *Grace Unknown,* p 176

14 Pink, *Sovereignty,* p 259-260

15 Calvin, *Sermons on Isaiah,* en loc

16 Douty, pp 94-106, Lightner, pp 64-6, Leon Morris, *The Cross in the New Testament,* p.220

17 Dana and Mantey, p. 104.

18 Arndt and Gingrich, p 67

19 John Peter Lange, *Titus,* p 16, Arndt and Gingrich, p 809, F F Bruce, *The Letters of Paul,* p 293

20 Lightner, p 69

21 Alford, *Greek Testament,* p. 1459.

22 Zanchius, pp 44-76 It should be noted that in the next section (Chapter I) he does discuss the love of God, not as an essential attribute of God, but only in reference to the elect.

23. R. C. Sproul, *Chosen by God,* p. 33.

24 James Richards, *Lectures on Mental Philosophy and Theology* (1846), p. 322, cited by Lightner, pp 114-5

25 W. Lindsay Alexander, *A System of Biblical Theology* (1888), II, p 111

26 Lightner, 2nd ed , pp 149-53; Some of this material is only in the 2nd edition in an appendix.

27 J I Packer, *Evangelism and the Sovereignty of God,* p 68

28 Lightner, pp 124-30 .

29 John Owen, *The Works of John Owen,* X, p 174

His grace has planned it all,
    'Tis mine but to believe,
And recognize His work of love
    and Christ receive.
For me He died,
    For me He lives,
And everlasting life and light
    He freely gives.

-Norman J. Clayton

17

THE PRIORITY OF REPENTANT FAITH

One of the most outrageous examples of theologians favoring a deductive, rationalistic approach over an inductive, exegetically based methodology is seen in the question of whether faith is a prior condition or a consequence of the new birth. From the beginning we have warned about the danger of giving a deductive methodology priority over inductive exegesis of the Scriptural data. This is especially relevant to this pivotal salvation issue.

This crucial issue is rarely discussed. My theological pilgrimage started when an extreme Calvinistic colleague shocked me by emphasizing its importance to Calvinistic theology, since the inductive data is so clearly opposite. It is a major premise of extreme Calvinism that because man is spiritually dead, he must be regenerated *before* he can repent and believe.[1]

Faith Prior to the New Birth

The historical background. Calvin struggled with the problem of the order of faith and regeneration. In his commentary on John 1:12-13 he directly addressed the problem.[2] It seems that Calvin's successors are far less aware of the problem and tend to just refer to the "Calvinistic order" of regeneration prior to faith. John Murray was one.[3] James M. Boice is more explicit: "We know from Paul's teaching elsewhere that justification presupposes faith (Rom. 5:1), so we can insert faith before justification, but after regeneration."[4] R. C. Sproul also affirms the maxim that "Regeneration precedes faith" is "a cardinal point of Reformed theology."[5]

The direct inductive data

Can the dead believe? First off, the question arises as to the seeming impossibility of unregenerate sinners, who are spiritually dead, ever respond-

216

ing to the word of God in faith. Starting with John's Gospel the answer comes early in the words of Christ, **"Very truly I tell you, a time is coming and has now come when the dead will hear the voice of the Son of God and those who hear will live"** (Jn. 5:25, TNIV). Evangelical interpreters agree that this is a reference to sinners being born again. Notice that Christ did not say that *the regenerate* shall hear His voice, but that *the dead* shall hear his voice and come to life. They are dead when they hear! As to *how* those who are spiritually dead can hear, believe, and be born again, there is room for discussion, but as to the *fact*, Christ's own words are clear. In Chapter 3 it was seen that a balanced biblical understanding of depravity and spiritual death does not contradict the exercise of repentant faith on the part of sinful mankind. In Chapter 7 the convicting ministry of the Spirit was seen as helping remove obstacles to faith.

   The Gospel of John. Tracing through the New Testament reveals that the new birth and those truths related to it are always conditioned on repentant faith. **"Yet to all who received him, to those who believed in his name, he gave the right to become the children of God—..."** (Jn. 1:12, NIV). Notice that it is those who receive Him (those who believe on His name) who are given the right (*exousia*) to become the children of God. Faith first; then new birth. The NIV rendering makes the sequence even clearer, since the relationship of believing on His name to receiving Christ is obscured in the KJV and NAS, since it is tacked onto the end of the sentence in common Greek word order. But *tois pisteuousin* (those believing) is clearly an attributive participle and in the NIV is rightly put immediately after those who received Christ, in apposition to it.[6] Thus, receiving is synonymous with believing, and both describe the condition upon which God gives the right (*exousia*) to become His children. The intervention of the word *exousia* before the description of new birth makes it impossible to reverse the order here. Thus we have:

received/believed—> given the right to become —> children of God

The word '**received**' (*elabon*) is an aorist,* which is usually described as non-durative usually in past time, and the present participle, '**believed**,' with the article *characterizes such people as believers*. Extreme Calvinists claim that the participle indicates the continued action of believing, but this does not negate the validity of all the contemporary translations and is irrelevant.
   Unfortunately the NIV takes liberties with 1:13 in rendering *oude ek thelēmatos sarkos* as "nor of human decision," which reveals a decided Calvinistic bias. They may call it "dynamic equivalence" but it really is a paraphrase, not translation. Here the KJV, NAS, ESV, HCSB, etc. are more literal and leave the interpretation up to the reader, as they ought: "... **who were born, not of blood, nor of the will of the flesh, nor of the will of man, but of God"** (1:13, NAS). All agree that we cannot will ourselves to be born again; it is totally a work of the Spirit. But in John's sequence, just noted, faith is the clear condition upon which God gives sinners the right or authority. Here the

analogy with human procreation and birth breaks down. Sinners, created in God's image, can claim that right by faith to be born into God's family! How astonishing! Whatever spin we may put on this passage, *faith comes first*.

The most famous verse of the Bible is only a little less clear. In John 3:16 it is those who believe who get eternal life, not the reverse. Few would argue that having eternal life does not imply the new birth since the result of the new birth is by definition the impartation of new, eternal, divine life to a sinner dead in sin. The verb 'believing' is a substantival participle which is "both gnomic [descriptive] and continual."[7] In any case, this does not in any way affect John's sequence since the verb 'have' (*echēi*) is subjunctive. The beginning of the believing must precede the having of eternal life.

"... but whoever drinks of the water that I will give him shall never thirst; but the water that I will give him will become in him a well of water springing up to eternal life" (Jn. 4:14). Christ told the Samaritan woman first to drink (by faith); then she would have a well of water (the Holy Spirit) springing up to eternal life. The order is the same. Throughout this Gospel, drinking is symbolic of the initial act of faith. In this symbolism, drinking obviously has to precede the water springing up in the individual to eternal life by the Spirit. There is no ambiguity in the Greek tenses here. It is the sinner who drinks or exercises faith.

A similar symbolism is used in the bread of life discourse:

> Jesus said to them, 'I am the bread of life; he who comes to Me shall not hunger, and he who believes in me shall never thirst.... For this is the will of My Father, that everyone who beholds the Son and believes in Him, may have eternal life;... he who eats this bread shall live forever (Jn. 6:35, 40, 58).

Although the symbolism of 6:35 should be adequately clear, the future tense of verses 40 and 58 shows that the believing is antecedent to the possession of eternal life. Some have contended that the order is not clear in statements like verse 47 and that the possession of eternal life presupposes the believing. This is not possible in the above verses. Note the same symbolism also in His dramatic tabernacles feast claim:

> Now on the last day, the great day of the feast, Jesus stood and cried out, saying, "If any man is thirsty, let him come to me and drink. He who believes in Me, as the Scripture said, 'From his innermost being shall flow rivers of living water.'" But this He spoke of the Spirit, whom those who believed in Him were to receive; for the Spirit was not yet give, because Jesus was not yet glorified (John 7:37-39).

Christ clearly set believing as a condition of receiving the Spirit, as further clarified by John's comment in v. 39, where the substantival participle is in the aorist tense. Although John usually uses the present participle,[8] the aorist here confirms the priority of the disciples' faith, since the indwelling Spirit was not yet received until John 20 or Acts 2 (as variously understood).

Although this sampling of this Gospel should be adequate, allusion to the key verse should cap it off nicely: "... but these have been written that you may believe that Jesus is the Christ, the Son of God; and that believing you may have life in His name" (20:31). Here John clearly used an instrumental participle 'believing', which modifies the action of the main verb, 'to have' life. The instrumental force of the participle could be better translated, "and that <u>by</u> believing you may have life." First faith, then life.

Acts. It is to be expected that the apostolic preaching (*kērugma)* of the early church as recorded in Acts would give us crystal clear data on this sequence. Such is the case. In Acts 2:37-38 the fulfillment of Christ's prediction about the Spirit's convicting work (Jn. 16:8-11) is seen:

> Now when they heard this, they were pierced to the heart, and said to Peter and the rest of the apostles, 'Brethren, what shall we do?' And Peter said to them, 'Repent,... for the forgiveness of your sins, and you shall receive the gift of the Holy Spirit.'

First they were convicted ("pierced to the heart") and said, "What shall we do?" Peter told them to repent, apparently on the presupposition that the conviction of the Spirit enabled them to do so. Only then would they receive the gift of the Holy Spirit—what could be clearer?

Subsequently, in replying to the Jewish leaders, Peter said that God gives the Holy Spirit "to those who obey Him (*peitharcheo*='to obey authority,' 'to be persuaded') " (5:32). A positive response must precede the new birth.

In Philip's ministry in Samaria the sequence is undeniable:

> But when they believed Philip preaching the good news about the kingdom of God and the name of Jesus Christ, they were being baptized, men and women alike.... they sent them Peter and John, who came down and prayed for them that they might receive the Holy Spirit. For He had not yet fallen upon any of them (Acts 8:12, 14b-16a).

The Samaritans believed and were baptized but did not receive the Spirit until later. Although the delay is exceptional, the sequence is normative.

In Peter's brief to the Jerusalem church about the conversion of Cornelius and his household, we note: "if God gave them the same gift [the Spirit] as He gave us, who believed in the Lord Jesus Christ..." (11:17). Note that here *pisteusasin* is an aorist* participle with instrumental or temporal usage, most probably expressing the means by which the Apostles and the Gentiles received the gift of the Spirit: "<u>by</u> believing in the Lord Jesus."

Likewise, in the Jerusalem Council Peter used the same sequence: "cleansing their hearts by faith" (15:9), and Paul conditioned another ministry of the Holy Spirit upon faith in 26:18: "sanctified by faith." Thus every relevant context indicates the same sequence: first faith, then regeneration or a related ministry of the Spirit. See also Acts 10:43 and 13:39.

The epistle to the Romans. Although the Apostle Paul makes little reference to the new birth in this great theological treatise, since Luther's time there has been little dispute among Evangelicals that faith is the condition for justification. The centrality of faith in salvation is seen in the key verse: "**For in it [the gospel] the righteousness of God is revealed from faith to faith; as it is written, 'But the righteous man shall live by faith'**" (1:17). The NIV renders *ek pisteōs eis pistin* even more forcefully: "**For in the gospel a righteousness from God is revealed, a righteousness that is by faith from first to last.**" Faith cannot be made an appendage to our theological system; it is at the core. *It is ironic that faith is not even mentioned in the five points of Calvinism, especially since justification by faith had become the governing principle of the Protestant Reformation.* There is no need to show the consistent order in Romans of justification by faith, but simply list the many references: 3:22, 25, 26, 28, 30; 4:3, 5, 9, 16, 24; & 5:1, 2 (18 in total).

The significance of Romans 4:16 must be reinforced: "**For this reason it is by faith, in order that it may be in accordance with grace, so that the promise will be guaranteed to all the descendants.**" Faith is not in any way meritorious or to be thought of as a work. That faith should be understood as a *condition* of salvation in no way undermines the gracious nature of salvation.

Another passage also requires special comment: "**... through whom also we have obtained our introduction by faith into this grace in which we stand**" (Rom. 5:1-2). If the new birth precedes faith, how can Paul say that faith was the means of our introduction into God's grace? By Calvinistic lights, regeneration is that which introduces us into God's grace.

Later, in discussing the circumstances of Israel's being set aside dispensationally, Paul came back to his theme in Romans 9:30-32:

> **What shall we say then? That Gentiles, who did not pursue righteousness, attained righteousness, even the righteousness which is by faith; but Israel, pursuing a law of righteousness, did not arrive at that law. Why? Because they did not pursue it by faith, but as though it were by works.**

Then he amplified the instrumentality of faith: "**... righteousness based on faith...**" (10:6); "**... believe in your heart that God raised Him from the dead, you shall be saved; for with the heart man believes, resulting in righteousness...**" (10:9,10); "**So faith comes from hearing, and hearing by the word of Christ**" (10:17).

If regeneration precedes faith, we have the incongruent sequence of: **regeneration—> faith —> justification and salvation.** This would certainly imply that logically it is possible to be born again without justification. Note here that it is man who does the believing in his heart. God does not believe for us, nor does he even say that God puts the faith in our hearts. L. Berkhof was clearly wrong in denying the mediacy of the word of God in regeneration. Let it be emphasized that *calling (the circumstances by which we come to faith) is mediate through the word of God, but that regeneration itself is immediately and directly, one hundred percent the work of the Spirit.* This crucial distinction has been lost in much of the discussion.

The epistles to the Galatians and Ephesians. In Galatians 3 there is an additional dimension in that Paul was more explicit about the relationship of faith to the receiving of the Spirit: "**... did you receive the Spirit by the works of the Law, or by hearing with faith?**" (Gal. 3:2); "**Does He then, who provides you with the Spirit and works miracles among you, do it by the works of the Law, or by hearing with faith?**" (3:5); "**... so that we might receive the promise of the Spirit through faith**" (3:14); "**For you are all sons of God through faith in Christ Jesus**" (3:26). There are no subtleties of interpretation needed here since the sequence is self-explanatory. In understanding how this sequence is possible, it is important to distinguish the conviction of the Spirit (which precedes faith) from the indwelling and regenerating works of the Spirit, which are subsequent to faith (cf. Ch. 7). The sequence in Paul's thought is consistent throughout.

By the time of the first Roman imprisonment, Paul had not changed his mind: "**In Him, you also, after listening to the message of truth, the gospel of your salvation—having also believed, you were sealed in Him with the Holy Spirit of promise,...**" (Eph. 1:13). Here an aorist* participle, *pisteusantes*, ('having believed') modifies the main verb *esphragisthēte*, ('you were sealed'). It could be either a temporal or an instrumental participle. Both options establish the point that faith precedes and is instrumental in the sealing ministry of the Spirit. Is it possible to say that regeneration precedes the faith and sealing? This is highly improbable– virtually impossible.

Passages on the relationship of faith and the word of God. The Lord Jesus, in His parable of the four soils, established the priority of the word of God in the process of people coming to faith and salvation. The Lord attributed the differing responses to His word to differences in the soil, not to any sovereign work of irresistible grace. The devil also gets into the picture: "**When anyone hears the word of the kingdom, and does not understand it, the evil one comes and snatches away what has been sown in his heart**"(Mt. 13:19). Luke adds: "**... so that they might not believe and be saved**" (Lk. 8:12). The sequence here is clear: hearing the word of God —> believing —> being saved. It is hard to imagine how it might be possible for the new birth to precede "being saved." Christ does not even intimate that the differentiating factor between the soils is God's elective choice. There is an intrinsic difference between the soils themselves. The second category of soil is explained thus: "**... yet he has no firm root in himself, but is only temporary, ...**" (Mt. 13:21). There is a difference in the soil. The fourth category is described: "**And the seed in the good soil, these are the ones who have heard the word in an honest and good heart, and hold it fast, and bear fruit with perseverance**" (Lk. 8:15). There is apparently a difference in the soil here also. The Lord Jesus attributes the difference to a mindset of the heart. Many people have their hearts closed to the gospel by their religious or cultural background. Witnesses to Muslims experience that the hearts of most have been poisoned against the gospel by the brainwashing of Islamic teaching. In Western society there are increasingly more people brainwashed with relativistic and evolutionary dogmas, which close their minds to the gospel. The universal spiritual blindness of the whole human race is overcome by the convicting work of the Spirit as diverse antecedent factors in the individual's life come into play. Here the pattern set by our Lord is faith in the word of God is prior to being saved.

The Calvinist's reaction to the above is: "Doesn't this attribute salvation to human merit?" However, a mindset is not something meritorious. Since the Lord Jesus taught it, theology must adjust to His teaching.

Peter understood the words of Christ in this way: "... **obtaining as the outcome of your faith the salvation of your souls**" (1 Pet. 1:9). Then in the same context he linked faith in the word of God in the same order: "... **for you have been born again not of seed which is perishable but imperishable, that is, through the living and abiding word of God**" (1:23). It is as people believe the word of God that they are born again. The word of God does not become operative by itself. The issue is faith in the word of God. The extreme Calvinistic scenario separates faith from the word of God thus: *the word of God proclaimed —> regeneration —> faith*. But faith must be in the word of God before regeneration can possibly take place.

The writer of Hebrews made a direct link between the word of God and faith: "**For indeed we have had good news preached to us, just as they also; but the word they heard did not profit them, because it was not united by faith in those who heard. For we who have believed enter that [salvation] rest,...**" (Heb. 4:2-3a). We must not insert regeneration in between the word of God and faith.

Extreme Calvinistic proof-texts

Extreme Calvinists do try to come up with proof-texts. James White came up with one in his debate with Dave Hunt: "**Whoever believes that Jesus is the Christ is born of God,...**" (1 Jn. 5:1a). White claimed that since the verb *gennaein* is in the perfect tense, the birth must have preceded the believing. However, he misunderstands the perfect tense. Wallace explains: "The force of the perfect tense is simply that it describes an event, that completed in the past, has results existing in the present time."[9] Thus the perfect tense says nothing about whether or not the action precedes or follows the believing and none of the translations imply such.

What Is the Source of Faith?

Is faith the gift of God?

Part of the extreme Calvinistic reversal of faith and the new birth is their supposition that repentance and faith are the direct gift of God, an immediate or direct work of the Holy Spirit in the human heart. This is another unexamined presupposition of Calvinistic theology.

Roy Aldrich, in a germinal article, objected to the Calvinistic reversal, not only because of its lack of Scriptural support, but also because, although this viewpoint intends to maintain the purity of grace, it actually undermines it. Since the sinner cannot believe until he becomes the object of irresistible grace, W. G. T. Shedd, for example, instructs the sinner to 1) read and hear the divine Word; 2) give serious application of the mind to the truth; and 3) pray for the gift of the Holy Spirit for conviction and regeneration.[10] Jonathan Edwards actually listed thirteen steps of preparation. Aldrich continues:

> A doctrine of total depravity that excluded the possibility of faith must also exclude the possibilities of "hearing the word," "giving serious applica-tion to divine truth," and "praying for the Holy Spirit for conviction and regeneration." The extreme Calvinist deals with a rather lively spiritual corpse after all [11]

Preparationism* is a problem Calvinists have made for themselves. Another pivotal issue is the question of the source of faith. Is faith directly the gift of God? Or is it developed in the sinners heart indirectly or mediately?

Misused proof-texts

Ephesians 2:8-9. Calvinists have a ready arsenal of proof-texts for the idea that faith is the direct, immediate gift of God. By far the most frequently referred to is Ephesians 2:8-9: **"For by grace you have been saved through faith; and that not of yourselves, *it is* the gift of God; not as a result of works, so that no one may boast."** What is the gift of God, faith or salvation? In the Greek original it is clear that it cannot be faith, since the relative pronoun *touto* (this) is neuter and *pistis* (faith) is feminine and cannot serve as its antecedent.[12] Many church fathers, Calvin, and a host of the greatest scholars reject this misinter-pretation, and although Calvin doesn't explain the grammar, he is very explicit about this error:

> And here we must advert [refute] to a very common error in the interpretation of this passage. Many persons restrict the word *gift* to faith alone. But Paul is only repeating in other words the former sentiment His meaning is, *not that faith is the gift of God, but that salvation is given to us by God*, or, that we obtain it by the gift of God (emphasis mine).[13]

Thus it is clear that the demonstrative *touto* refers to the whole concept of salvation by grace. Gregory Sapaugh reinforces this by noting that:

> This position is further supported by the parallelism between *ouk hymon* ('**and this not of yourselves**') in 2.8 and *ouk ex ergon* ('**not of works**') in 2:9. The latter phrase would not be meaningful if it referred to *pisteos* ('**faith**'). Instead, it clearly means salvation is '**not of works**.'[14]

This is exactly what Paul affirmed in Romans 6:23: **"... but the free gift of God is eternal life in Christ Jesus our Lord."** Vance makes a most important point here: "But by its very nature a gift has to be received or rejected. There is no such thing as an irresistible gift."[15] Is there any question that all those who con-tinue to ignore the unambiguous grammar and scholarly opinion of even Calvin himself are rightly called hyper-Calvinists? R. C. Sproul is entrenched in his deductive dogmatism when he says: "This passage should seal the matter forever. The faith by which we are saved is a gift of God."[16]

Acts. In a number of cases, such as Acts 5:31 ("**... to grant repentance to Israel,...**") and 11:18 ("**... Well then, God has granted to the Gentiles also the repen-tance *that leads* to life.**") the context indicates that God is giving *the opportunity* for repentant faith to a class of people, not that God is giving faith directly on an individual basis. Acts 5:31 obviously cannot be an irresistible gift of repentance to individuals since in the main Israel did not repent. Acts 11:18, when seen in its context, clearly is a reference to the dispensational* opportunity now being offered to the Gentiles based upon the conversion of Cornelius and his household, not to God giving repentance to individuals directly. The other Apostles and the Judean church had not yet understood that Gentiles could be saved directly, so this response to Peter's defense of his actions obviously is a reference to *the opportunity to repent.*

Calvinists claim three other proof-texts. Acts 13:48 and 16:14 say nothing directly about repentant faith being the gift of God. Starting with Calvinistic presuppositions, these verses might seem to support their case, but see the full discussion, pp. 313-5. However, Acts 18:27 requires comment here: "**... he [Apollos] greatly helped those who had believed through grace.**" Calvinists read into this, "believed through irresistible grace." Of course, non-Calvinists believe that it is through God's grace that we have opportunity to believe in Christ. When we exercise repentant faith, we are affirming the gracious nature of salvation, the harmony of which Paul emphasized in Romans 4:16: "**For this reason *it is* by faith, in order that it *may be* in accordance with grace,...**"

Other proof-texts in Paul's epistles. Although the language of 2 Timothy 2:25 ("**... with gentleness correcting those who are in opposition, if perhaps God may grant them repentance leading to the knowledge of the truth,...**") does not so obviously exclude repentance as the immediate gift of God, it is clear from the context that God uses His servants to correct those in opposition, specifically Timothy's gentle and patient correction. Note also that the broader context refers to heretical teachers (2:17-18, 23), not to ordinary unsaved people. Timothy is to be kind in trying to teach them the truth, in the hope that they will repent of their doctrinal error and cease being the devil's tool in disrupting the churches.

Calvinists also misuse Philippians 1:29 to make their claim: "**For to you it has been granted for Christ's sake, not only to believe in Him, but also to suffer for His sake,...**" However, it is clear that we are given faith only in the same sense in which we are given suffering, that is, mediately through circumstances. No one would argue that suffering is an immediate and irresistible work of grace. As in the two Acts passages above, Paul refers to the privilege and opportunity given to the Philippian Christians to believe, while alerting them to the fact that suffering for Christ comes with that privilege.

Some proof-texts like Romans 12:3 ("**... as God has allotted to each a measure of faith.**"); 1 Corinthians 12:8-9 ("**For to one is given the word of wisdom through the Spirit,... to another faith by the same Spirit,...**"); 1 Corinthians 4:7 ("**What do you have that you did not receive?**"); and Philippians 2:13 ("**... for it is God who is at work in you, both to will and to work for *His* good pleasure.**") are blatantly pulled out of context. They have to do with *the spiritual gift* of 'faith' or the ongoing work of the Holy Spirit in the life of the believer, rather than saving faith for the sinner. *They are not at all about how sinners believe and are saved!*

Two other Pauline passages seem relevant only to those who read the KJV alone: Galatians 2:20 and Philippians 3:9 have the "faith of Christ," which some Calvinists assume is a reference to faith which Christ gives. However, these are obviously objective genitives and should be translated "**faith in Christ**," as rendered by most of the modern translations, supported by most commentaries. Christ is to be the object of our faith.

There are a number of other passages referred to by Calvinists which apart from Calvinistic presuppositions seem totally irrelevant to the issue at hand. They are: 1 Thessalonians 1:4-6; 1 Corinthians 2:4-5; 7:25 (adduced by Augustine); 2 Corinthians 4:6; Romans 10:17 (affirms the opposite); and Ephesians 1:17-18. The connection of all these passages to faith as a gift from God is so obscure that one can't imagine how to try to respond. This is the worst form of proof-texting.

Proof-texts from Peter's epistles. Two passages from Peter are adduced by Calvinists. The first is easily clarified: "... **who through Him [Christ] are believers in God,...**" (1 Pet. 1:21). For the Christian it is a axiomatic that it is through Christ that we really became believers in the true God in a real sense. Even if they had been religious Jews, as were many of the recipients of this letter, most did not really know God until they trusted in Christ.

In 2 Peter 1:1 the believers addressed are said to have obtained (*lachousin*) a like precious faith: "**To those who have obtained a faith of equal standing with ours,...**" (RSV). Since the verb (*lachousin*) is an aorist *active* participle, it should be translated as in the KJV, RSV, ESV, HCSB, and Williams, 'obtained' rather than 'received,' which would be passive.[17] The point is that faith must be actively exercised by people, not passively received as a gift. Thus, careful examination of the grammar has turned a Calvinistic proof text against their view. Additionally, use of the adjective *isotimon* ('of the same kind') would militate for the objective connotation of the faith (*pistis*), that is, the body of truths which we believe, rather than our individual faith. If this is true, this passage proves to be irrelevant to the issue. In any case, Peter does not explain how they obtained that faith, which is the point under discussion, except that he used the active voice.

Proof-texts from John's writings. Three references in the bread of life discourse (John 6:37, 44-45, 65) are also misused in this connection and say nothing directly about faith as a gift of God. Calvinists read into them the idea of irresistible grace. However, Christ is not saying in 6:37 that all the elect shall infallibly come to Christ, but the context indicates that He is rather speaking about the remnant of regenerate Israelites who had belonged to the Father. Now the Son has come, and that remnant is being turned over to Him by the Father and will certainly come to Him. But most in that multitude were not a part of that remnant. (For full discussion see pp. 310-13.)

Careful consideration of these proof-texts in their contexts shows that there is no basis for seeing faith as a direct gift from God. It is salvation which is the gift of God, and faith is the means by which we receive it.

Faith develops mediately in human hearts.

Since God is never represented in Scripture as striking people with faith as a direct gift, where then does faith come from? A number of Scriptural observations are relevant to this important question:

Faith comes mediately through the word of God. The word of God is clearly a means of producing faith in the heart according to Romans 10:17: "**So faith comes from hearing, and hearing by the word of Christ.**" D. L. Moody wrote, "I used to think that faith would strike me like a lightning bolt, but then somebody showed me Romans 10:17. I turned to the word of God, and faith came and has been growing ever since."[18]

The conviction of the Spirit prepares the heart for faith. The solution to the conundrum faced by extreme Calvinists is found in the convicting or convincing ministry of the Spirit (Jn. 16:8-11). Clearly Acts 2:37ff was the first fulfillment and a graphic case study among the many examples in Acts. The Spirit works through human instrumentality to convict sinners of the sin of unbelief, man's total lack of righteousness, and God's sure judgment upon sin. Conviction is neither universal or limited to the elect (cf. Ch. 7).

Faith is always ascribed to man, not God. It is not incidental to the Gospel record that Christ commented on the faith of individuals in such a way to make clear that faith is a human phenomenon. There are nine different individuals, as recorded in fourteen different Gospel passages, whose faith is highlighted. Christ responded to the faith of the palsied man and his bearers (Mt. 9:2; Mk. 2:5; Lk. 5:20) by healing him. He told many like the immoral woman, "**Your faith has saved you**" (Lk. 7:50). The woman with the flow of blood was told, "**Your faith has made you well**" (Mt. 9:22; Mk. 5:29,34; Lk. 8:48). Two blind men who received their sight were told, "**It shall be done to you according to your faith**" (Mt. 9:28-29). A synagogue ruler whose daughter was raised from the dead was told, "**Only believe, and she will be made well**" (Lk. 8:50). The cleansed leper who returned to thank the Lord was told, "**Your faith has made you well**" (Lk. 17:19). Bartimaeus and his companion were told, "**Receive your sight; your faith has made you well**" (Mk. 10:52; Lk. 18:42).

Paul says that the faith of the ungodly is reckoned as righteousness (Rom. 4:5). This is out of sequence if man has no participation in faith! The noun *pistis* ('faith') and the verb *pisteuein* ('to trust') occur sixty times in Romans, the theme of which is a righteousness by faith "**from first to last**" (1:17, NIV). Calvin was not reticent about calling faith a human means:

> The next question is, in what way do men receive that salvation which is offered to them by the hand of God? The answer is, *by faith*; and hence he concludes that nothing connected with it is our own. If on the part of God, it is by grace alone, and **if we bring nothing but faith,** which strips us of all

commendation, it follows that salvation does not come from us.... When, **on the part of man**, the act of receiving salvation is made to consist in faith alone, **all other means**, on which men are accustomed to rely, are discarded. Faith, then, brings a man empty to God, that he may be filled with the blessings of Christ (bold mine).[19]

Christ constantly pointed out the faith of those who possessed it. If faith is immediately the gift of God, it would not have been consistent or appropriate for Christ to commend the Centurion and the Syrophoenician woman for the greatness of their faith (Mt. 8:10, 13; Lk. 7:9; Mt. 15:28).

Some conversions are attributed to antecedent conditions. The parable of the four soils indicates some antecedent differences in the soils of peoples' hearts which account for their coming to faith (Lk. 8:11-15). Cornelius' prayer (and his alms) are mentioned by the angel in reference to the opportunity given him to hear the message of faith (Acts 10:4). Lest anyone say that he was already regenerate, remember Peter's recitation of the angel's words to Cornelius that "**he [Peter] shall speak words to you by which you will be saved**" (Acts 11:14). Luke records that the noble-minded Bereans examined the Scriptures daily and that "**many of them <u>therefore</u> believed**," (Acts 17:12). Luke's "therefore" does not fit Calvinistic theology. The Apostle Paul stated that although he was the chief of sinners, he was shown mercy *because* he acted ignorantly in unbelief (1 Tim. 1:13-16). Calvinistic theology says that the basis of God's saving mercy is an unrevealed mystery.

God uses people to bring unbelievers to faith. Christ commanded His disciples to become "**fishers of men**" and contrasted the great harvest field with the lack of laborers to reap a harvest (Lk. 10:2; Mt. 9:37-8; Jn. 4:35). In the Great Commission He commanded them to "**make disciples.**" In commissioning Paul, He sent him to the Gentiles "**to open their eyes so that they may turn from darkness unto light and from the dominion of Satan to God,**" (Acts 26:17-18). Observe the *heavy human involvement* in all of these passages. The Spirit normally works mediately through His servants. This is axiomatic!

The many commands to repent/believe imply response is possible. Not only so, but Paul stated that the command is to all men everywhere (Acts 17:30-31). The "all" here must refer to all without exception since the "everywhere" implies all without distinction.

Why are people commanded to seek God? Was Isaiah also ignorant of the Calvinistic doctrine that men are spiritual corpses and cannot seek God in any way (Isa. 55:6)? See a full discussion, pp. 36-8.

God gives people opportunity to believe in answer to our prayer and witness. In 1 Timothy 2:1-6 Paul links our prayers for "**all men**" (v. 1) with the desire of God that "**all men**" might be saved (v. 4), and the fact that Christ "**gave Himself as a ransom for all**" (v. 6). Frequently God uses the witness of other Christians unknown to us in answer to our prayers. As an example, students at my college especially prayed one night for the salvation of a student's brother on the west coast. He was saved the very next day through other Christians' witness to him. Frequently God uses human instrumentality in answering our prayers.

Problems with a direct gift of faith

Why did Christ bother to witness and persuade the non-elect? He would certainly know that they were non-elect and would not come to faith. This is clearest in His dealings with individuals like the rich young ruler.

Why should Paul bother to use persuasion at all? Luke highlighted the fact so frequently in Acts (17:3-4,17; 18:4; 19:8-9) that Paul used a confrontational and persuasive approach. One would think that the elect would believe upon hearing the gospel merely stated. Indeed, why should the elect not believe the first time that they hear the gospel? Buswell cited Calvinistic missionaries who would preach only once in each village under that supposition.[20] Apparently the human element of persistence and persuasion are important factors in people coming to faith in Christ. To press this line of thought one step further, one could raise the question about the validity of any sort of human methodology at all in preaching the gospel, if indeed faith is the immediate gift of God. Some extreme Calvinists pursue this to its logical conclusion and deny any use of means. But most acknowledge the validity of *some means* and resort to paradox or antinomy to explain the inconsistency. Some object to more direct use of means, such as a public invitation. However, on the day of Pentecost, the Apostles must have had some means to separate out the inquirers so that they could baptize them and incorporate them into the new-born church.

Why did Christ marvel at unbelief? If faith is the immediate gift of God, Christ should not have been astonished at the unbelief of the people of Nazareth (Mk. 6:6). Didn't Christ know what every Calvinist knows—that they were spiritually dead and could do no other than disbelieve?

How can unbelief be judged? Donald Grey Barnhouse once raised the question as to how God could judge unbelief as sin, if indeed faith is the gift of God? If it is God who has withheld the gift of faith, unbelief cannot be called a sin.

How can we explain degrees of unbelief being judged more sorely? If it is God who chooses not to give the non-elect the gift of faith, how can God justly judge some more severely than others? (cf. Mt. 11:20ff.)

How can demonic activity hinder a direct work of the Spirit? In the parable of the soils the Lord Jesus made it clear that Satan can intervene in the process of sinners coming to faith: **"And those beside the road are those who have heard; then the devil comes and takes away the word from their heart, so that they may not**

believe and be saved" (Lk. 8:12; also 2 Cor. 4:4). If Satan had the power to intervene in a direct, irresistible work of the Holy Spirit, then he would be more powerful than the Spirit.

Why are some classes of people harder to win than others? Paul identifies the Cretans as a problem people (Titus 1:12-13), and we could identify Muslims and upper-caste Hindus today as such. Natural factors and the extent of Satan's activity need to be taken into account. If the Spirit immediately produces faith in the heart of the elect, cannot the Spirit break through a Muslim's heart with equal ease as with an American nominal Christian? Since the church growth initiative of Donald A. McGavran beginning in the 50s, missiologists have been engaged in very fruitful study of the human factors (religious, sociological, anthropological, etc.) which contribute to people coming to faith in significant numbers. There was a negative response from Calvinists at first, but Calvinistic missiologists have had to ignore the theological problems and agree with the validity of these factors in human conversion since it is so obvious to missionaries.

Why does God give the gift of faith to so many Americans and to so few Libyans, Mongolians, Tibetans, Afghans, Tunisians, Turks, etc.? If one starts with Calvinistic premises, one is forced to the conclusion that God is partial and loves Americans more than others.

Coming to faith is a process.

While the new birth itself is an instantaneous work of the Holy Spirit in which man has no participation, the process by which humans come to faith may take years and involve spiritual struggles. Indeed, Satan's agents try their worst to sidetrack inquirers to keep them from coming to faith. Ignorance of the real nature of the gospel is a major hindrance, as are all the smokescreens the godless world-system raises. And certainly the sinful nature and depravity of the inquirer is a major obstacle. The Spirit keeps on using Christian witness to break down these obstacles until the person comes to genuine repentant faith. *But the process must be clearly distinguished from the new birth itself, otherwise confusion results.* This simple distinction does not fit in with Calvinistic doctrine at all.

Faith is not meritorious.

Nothing stated under these headings is profound; these points should be obvious to all. Yet they directly contradict the deterministic theology which sees the Holy Spirit as immediately and irresistibly 'zapping' the elect with faith and leaving the non-elect in reprobation. They may plead paradox and antinomy, but the conflict and contradiction goes far beyond antinomy.

Calvinists accuse other Christians of synergism,* but that term is pejorative and begs the question. Its derivation from *ergein* implies that works are involved (man working with God). However, faith is not a work! Christ told a works-oriented multitude to believe in the Son: "**This is the work of God, that you believe in Him whom He has sent**" (Jn. 6:29). His words could be paraphrased, "If you works-oriented legalists want to do something to be saved, just simply believe in Him whom He has sent." Evangelicals must agree that Christ is not calling faith a meritorious work. It is simply responding to God's gift. Otherwise Christ would contradict Paul's argument in Romans 4:16 "**that it is by faith that it might be by grace.**"

Conclusions

This study leads to the following conclusions: 1) Contemporary Calvinists have gone far beyond Calvin and show a serious lapse into scholastic deductionism rather than giving preference to direct Scriptural inductive study, which is overwhelmingly consistent in showing that faith precedes and is the condition for the new birth. 2) Repentant faith is not the immediate, direct gift of God, but comes mediately through the proclamation of the word of God and human instrumentality. 3) We must distinguish the means of coming to faith, which is a mediate process, from regeneration itself, which is a direct, immediate, and instantaneous work of God.

---

1 Samuel Fisk, *Calvinistic Paths Retraced*, Norman Geisler, *Chosen But Free*, appendices 5 and 10

2 John Calvin, *Commentary on the Gospel according to John*, trans Wm Pringle, p. 44.

3 John Murray, *Redemption Accomplished and Applied* (GR Eerdmans, 1955), pp 98, 103

4. James Montgomery Boice, *Awakening to God*, p. 53

5 R C Sproul, *Chosen by God*, p 72.

6 Daniel B. Wallace, *Greek Grammar Beyond the Basics* (GR: Zondervan, 1996), pp. 617-9.

7 Ibid , p 620.

8. Ibid , p 621, footnote.

9 Ibid , p 573 (omitting parenthetical amplifications for brevity)

10 W G T Shedd, *Dogmatic Theology* (Nashville Thomas Nelson, 1980), II, p. 472ff

11 Roy L Aldrich, "The Gift of God," *Bibliotheca Sacra*, vol 122 p 248

12 Henry Alford, *The Greek Testament* (Chicago Moody, 1958), III, p. 94

13 John Calvin, *Commentaries*, trans. Pringle, vol XXI, pp 228-9.

14 Gregory Sapaugh, "Is Faith a Gift? A study of Ephesians 2:8, " *Journal of the Grace Evangelical Society* 7, no. 12 (Spring 1994), pp 39-40

15 Laurence M. Vance, *The Other Side of Calvinism*, pp. 516-7.

16 R C. Sproul, *Chosen by God*, p. 119

17 A T. Robertson, *Word Pictures*, VI, p 147, Cleon L. Rogers, Jr , and Cleon L Rogers, III, *Linguistic and Exegetical Key to the New Testament* (Zondervan, 1998), p. 581.

18 D L Moody, paraphrased since exact reference unavailable

19 Calvin, *Commentaries on the Epistles of Paul to the Galatians and Ephesians*, trans Wm Pringle (GR Baker, 1979 reprint), XXI.227 (see also footnote by Bloomfield, pp 227-8).

20 James Oliver Buswell, Jr., *A Systematic Theology of the Christian Religion*, II, p. 132ff

Is it Thy will that I should be
Buried, in symbol, Lord, with Thee;
Owning Thee by this solemn sign,
Telling the world that I am Thine?
Gladly I yield obedience now;
In all things to Thy will, I'd bow;
I'll follow where my Savior led,
And humbly in His footsteps tread.
This emblematic, watery grave
Shows forth His love - Who came to save;
And as I enter it, I see
The price my Savior paid for me.
                              - Anon.

IS BAPTISM ESSENTIAL FOR SALVATION?

One of the earliest errors to enter the church was to make the ordinances into sacraments. Water baptism and the Lord's Supper began to be viewed as efficacious in the early centuries and were subsequently crystallized in the developing Roman Catholic Church as its doctrine of baptismal regeneration and the mass. In some almost magical way, when an individual is baptized, they think the process of regeneration begins. One question which naturally arose from that viewpoint was how to deal with post-baptismal sin, since presumably these had to be dealt with separately. The root of the problem was thinking that baptism was an essential condition for salvation, which in effect made it a substitute for faith. The Catholic Church today is the major advocate of baptismal regeneration. On the popular level, the average priest affirms that Roman Catholic baptism assures ultimate salvation.

The Reformers did not make a total break with a sacramental view of the ordinances. Luther continued to hold to Christ's mystical presence in the elements of the Lord's supper and saw some efficacy in infant baptism. Thus, Lutherans and Reformed over the centuries have come to believe in baptism as having some effect upon the infant, whether in regeneration or in inclusion in the covenant. The Anglican Church (Episcopalian in the USA) has always held differing degrees of efficacy in the sacraments, depending upon which segment of the Church is considered (Anglo-Catholic, Liberal, or Evangelical).

In America, the scene was complicated by the Restoration or Stone-Campbell Movement (Churches of Christ and Christian Churches). Additional millions here moved toward understanding baptism as effecting the forgiveness of sins. Some within the Restoration Movement churches are very aggressive in convincing people that one must be baptized by them for the forgiveness of sins. What is the biblical data in answer to this most important question?

The arguments for baptismal regeneration usually derive from the Gospel accounts of John's baptism being a **"baptism of repentance for the forgiveness of sins,"** from Christ's words to Nicodemus in John 3, from the Mark 16:16 wording of the Great Commission, from Peter's Pentecost sermon (Acts 2:38), from Ananias' words to Paul in Acts 22:16, and Paul's doctrinal statement in Titus 3:5. These are the 'proof-texts,' but there are also certain presuppositions held by baptismal regenerationists which need to be examined. Another significant factor is inaccurate translation of several of the passages in the King James Version, since the translators were all Anglicans and mostly held to baptismal regeneration. This obscures the meaning of these passages, and subsequent translators have, unfortunately, not given a more precise rendering to clear up the problem. *The issue is not whether baptism is commanded of believers, but whether it is a necessary condition for becoming a genuine Christian.* What is the inductive evidence?

The Inductive Biblical Development
The Old Testament background

The antecedent of the Lord's supper was the Passover remembrance of Israel's exodus. This is clear, since it was at a Passover celebration that the Lord Jesus modified and simplified the Passover seder (order) and commanded Christians to remember His death by its observance. Before Christ, when Jews observed the Passover, there was no indication that they viewed it as efficacious or other than a simple memorial of a mighty intervention of God. Indeed, Moses explained that the meaning of Passover was **"in order that you may remember all the days of your life the day when you came out of the land of Egypt"** (Deut. 16:3).

In a similar way, circumcision was the antecedent of baptism. It was initiatory into the people of God, whether for a Jewish male or a Gentile convert. Moses also explained its symbolism to a new generation of Jews about to enter the promised land, **"Moreover the LORD your God will circumcise your heart and the heart of your descendants, to love the LORD your God with all your heart and with all your soul, in order that you may live"** (Deut. 30:6). He exhorted them, **"Circumcise then your heart, and stiffen your neck no more"** (Deut. 10:16). Israel was not to trust in external circumcision but in a work of the Spirit on the sinful human heart. Seeing the New Testament linkage of circumcision and baptism, it is not surprising to find that there are frequent warnings about trusting in physical circumcision and outward religious observances (Matt. 5:8; 6:1; 23:27; Acts 15:1-29; Gal. 5:2-3; 6:12-15; Rom. 2:25-29; 4:9-16; Col. 2:11-13). Paul's connection of circumcision and baptism is of a **"circum-**

cision wrought without hands," by the Spirit of God on the human heart (Col. 2:11-12). The baptism he refers to must also be a spiritual baptism (1 Cor. 12:13). This is crucial background in understanding water baptism.

The Gospel accounts

The ministry of John the Baptizer. John was called the Baptizer because he initiated the ritual of water baptism. Proselyte baptism practiced by Jews was not really baptism at all, but a self-immersion. John was the first person who immersed *another* person, and thus, he was called the Baptizer, that is "the one doing the immersing."

As John the Baptizer came announcing the coming of the Messiah-King and His impending kingdom, his ministry of preparation emphasized the absolute necessity for Israel to repent or be judged (Matt. 3:2). When many hypocritical Pharisees and Sadducees came to make a show by being baptized, he warned them sternly that unless their repentance was genuinely from the heart, they would be cut off from the kingdom (Mt. 3:5-10). To reinforce his point he stressed that the coming Messiah would not just perform external water baptism, but an efficacious baptism of the Spirit and of fire (Mt. 3:11-12). One could put on an outward show of repentance in water baptism, but one could not get away with externalism when the Messiah comes. Unfortunately, many have misinterpreted John's words in verse 11 to imply the opposite by ignoring the context, **"As for me, I baptize you with water for *(eis)* repentance."** Understood in its context, there is no way that John could be implying that baptism causes repentance. The Greek preposition *eis* could imply this when taken alone, but in the context, grammarians have recognized that *eis* can mean 'because of' in a number of contexts, such as Mt. 12:41.[1] Thus, John said, **"I baptize you with water because of (your) repentance."**

Similarly in Mark's Gospel: **"John the Baptist appeared in the wilderness preaching a baptism of repentance for the forgiveness of sins"** (Mk. 1:4). Luke also uses the same phrase in 3:3 to describe John's ministry: *"baptisma metanoias eis aphesin hamartion."* The question is whether the forgiveness is conditional upon the baptism or the repentance? Baptismal regenerationists assume erroneously that it is conditioned upon baptism as well as repentance. What is the relation between *baptisma* and *metanoias,* since *metanoias* is in the genitive/ablative case? It could be a genitive of reference, which would be translated, **"a baptism with reference to repentance for the forgiveness of sins."** It could also be an ablative of source, which is defined as a noun that "owes its existence in some way to that which is denoted in the ablative."[2] Thus, it would be a **"baptism derived from repentance for the forgiveness of sins."** In neither alternative does it imply that forgiveness is contingent upon baptism. Therefore, it is the repentance which brings forgiveness of sins, and this accords with John's warning to hypocrites.

Note well John's own stated purpose: **"but in order that He might be** manifested to Israel, I came baptizing in water" (Jn. 1:31). He had the great privilege of baptizing the Messiah Himself. It should be clear that Christ was not baptized for forgiveness or new birth, since He needed none. *He was baptized to identify with the repentant remnant of Israel.* It was to be an external witness of His messiahship to John, as God had told him, "**'He upon whom you see the Spirit descending and remaining upon Him, this is the one who baptizes in the Holy Spirit.' And I have seen, and have borne witness that this is the Son of God**" (Jn. 1:33-34). This identification with the godly remnant of Israel is further confirmed by the secondary, metaphorical meaning of the word *baptizein,* that is, "to be overwhelmed by something, to be identified with someone." This is clear from Christ's own usage in Mark 10:38f, "**Are you able to drink the cup that I drink, or to be baptized with the baptism with which I am baptized?**" referring to His death. Paul speaks of Israel's identification with Moses as they escaped from Egypt (1 Cor. 10:2). Christ's own baptism was an identification, not efficacious. Likewise, our baptism is an identification with Christ, not an efficacious ritual (1 Cor. 12:13, etc.).

The ministry of the Lord Jesus Christ. After John was imprisoned, Christ began His public ministry by preaching, "**The time is fulfilled, and the kingdom of God is at hand; repent and believe in the gospel**" (Mk. 1:15). In our survey in Chapter 6, this same message was found in the Gospel accounts of Christ's preaching with absolutely no reference to baptism at all. Repentance and faith (trust) are emphasized over and over again, but there is total silence about baptism in His preaching. Indeed, the only hint that Christ practiced baptism at all are the three references in John 3:22,26; and 4:1-2. In fact the word *pisteuein* (to believe, trust) is used 96 times in John's Gospel without ever being linked to baptism.

There are numerous incidents where the Lord declared an individual's sins forgiven before there was any possibility of baptism. In the story of the paralytic who was let down through the roof, Mark says that Jesus, seeing their faith, said to the paralytic, "**My son, your sins are forgiven**" (Mk. 2:1-12). Clearly, his sins were forgiven apart from baptism. In the account of the woman with the flow of blood: "**Daughter, your faith has made you well; go in peace, and be healed of your affliction**" (Mk. 5:34). Shortly thereafter, He told the synagogue official, "**Do not be afraid any longer, only believe**" (5:36). When the Lord commissioned the twelve Apostles and sent them out to the lost sheep of the house of Israel, Mark states, "**And they went out and preached that men should repent**" (Mk. 6:12). None of the Gospel writers mentions baptism at this important point in Christ's instructions to the Apostles. The last such case is the thief on the cross. The Lord took the genuine expression of repentant faith on his part as an adequate condition for promising him, "**Today you shall be with me in paradise**" (Lk. 23:42-3).

Christ's words to Nicodemus. In Christ's interview with Nicodemus, the interpretive possibilities of His imperative to be "**born of water and the Spirit**" (Jn. 3:5) must be examined carefully. Many hastily assume a reference to water baptism and do not seriously consider other interpretations which are more supportable from the context and the analogy of other Scripture. There are three other commonly-held views.

Some good interpreters have held that 'water' is a reference to natural birth and 'Spirit' to the contrasting new birth of the Holy Spirit. This view builds upon the fact that natural birth is a watery birth in the bursting of the amniotic sac. This finds strong support from the immediate context. Nicodemus's reaction to Christ's first statement about being born again (3:3) showed the limitation of his thinking to mere physical birth (3:4). Thus, to correct his thinking the Lord said in effect, "you must not only be born naturally, but you must also be born of the Holy Spirit." This is further reinforced by Christ's clarification in verse 6, **"That which is born of the flesh is flesh, and that which is born of the Spirit is spirit."** This is an obvious contrast of the first, physical birth with the second, spiritual birth. This interpretation must surely be given serious consideration.

Two other interpretations see the word 'water' as symbolic. One builds upon the other references to the Holy Spirit's use of the word of God to produce regeneration, such as James 1:18 and 1 Peter 1:23-4. Ephesians 5:26 speaks of Christ cleansing the church by **"the water of the word."** The weakness of this view is that it has to go far afield to find support.

A more cogent interpretation sees 'water' as a symbol representing the Holy Spirit, and the reference to 'Spirit' as clarifying the meaning of the symbol. The *kai* (and) is better translated 'even' and is explanatory. This view receives strong support from the broader context of the fourth Gospel since the Lord used water as a symbol of the Spirit in his witness to the Samaritan woman (Jn. 4:10-14), and again at the feast of Booths when He gave that most dramatic invitation, **"If any man is thirsty, let him come to Me and drink. He who believes in Me, as the Scripture said, 'From his innermost being shall flow rivers of living water.'"** John clearly tells us that the Lord was speaking of the Holy Spirit (7:37-39). Another grammatical indication supportive of this view is the fact that neither 'water' nor 'spirit' in the Greek have an article. This would seem to indicate that these are not two distinct entities. As Charles Hodge emphasized over a century ago: "the sign and the thing signified are often united, often interchanged, the one being used for the other." He bases this statement upon the strong Old Testament symbolic usage of water. For example, Isaiah 12:3: **"Therefore you will joyously draw water from the springs of salvation."** (cf. Isa. 35:6; 44:3; 55:1; Ezek. 36:25; Jer. 2:18; Zech. 14:8.)[3] It would be absurd to read baptism into all of these passages. The Lord Jesus, speaking to a very knowledgeable teacher of the Old Testament, built upon a familiar symbol in explaining salvation.

Mark 16:16. Mark's form of the Great Commission read superficially might seem to indicate that baptism is a necessary condition: **"He who has believed and has been baptized shall be saved; but he who has disbelieved shall be condemned"** (Mk. 16:16). The key is to avoid reading into the statement what

Christ did not say. This is a common failure of interpretive logic. *Christ did not say that those who are not baptized will be condemned.* Those interpreters take the converse of His positive statement to be true, that is, that those who are not baptized will be condemned. But an axiomatic rule of logic, found in all the basic textbooks, is that the converse of a statement is not necessarily true. The only way it can be proved whether the converse of a true statement is true or false is from other data. In this case, data from other Scripture indicates that the converse is false—that those who are not baptized are not necessarily condemned. Note also that some other interpreters do not see this as a reference to water baptism at all, but to Spirit baptism. Thus, the Lord did not make baptism an essential condition of salvation.

The book of Acts

The book of Acts is crucial, since it records the early preaching and practice of the gospel message.

Peter's Pentecost sermon. The invitation which Peter gave at the end of his Pentecost sermon is very significant. Thousands of Jews were under the conviction of the Spirit because of his preaching of the word of God (Acts 2:37). Peter's command was twofold: **"Repent, and let each of you be baptized in the name of Jesus Christ for the forgiveness of your sins, and you shall receive the gift of the Holy Spirit"** (Acts 2:38). What is the relationship between repentance and baptism? Are forgiveness and the gift of the Spirit contingent upon repentance alone or upon baptism as well? The careless rendering of the KJV is partially corrected by the NAS translators quoted above, who showed a break in thought between the two imperatives. *Metanoesate* (Repent) is a second person plural active imperative and could be paraphrased, **"All of you must imperatively repent!"** *Baptistheto* (**"let each of you be baptized"**) is a third person singular passive imperative, which is radically different in thrust. The shift from second to third person, from plural to singular, and from active voice to passive, is extremely significant. The third person singular imperative is a much weaker hortatory form, as the NAS has rendered it.[4] Because of that break in the grammar, the phrase about baptism should really be viewed as parenthetical: **"Let each of you who repents be baptized."** Note also that the promise of forgiveness and the gift of the Holy Spirit are both phrased in the plural, so that they connect with repentance, not baptism. Thus, the force of Peter's words in the Greek is: **"All of you (pl.) must imperatively repent (and let him [s.] be baptized) for the forgiveness of your (pl.) sins, and you (pl.) will receive the gift of the Holy Spirit."** Three thousand converts were baptized that day, but it is clear from the grammar of the passage that they were not saved through that baptism.

The ministry of Peter and others. This is confirmed by the subsequent pattern of gospel preaching in the Acts narrative. In Peter's second sermon, faith, repentance, and conversion are stressed, but there is no mention of baptism (Acts 3:16, 19). In the Apostles' second confrontation with the Sanhedrin, Peter emphasized repentance and forgiveness without mentioning baptism (5:31). When Philip first preached to the Samaritans, he baptized those who believed, but they did not receive the Holy Spirit until Peter and John came down from Jerusalem days later, when Peter used the keys to officially open the door of faith to the Samaritans. Even though this is an anomaly explained by the dispensational* transition involved, it clearly shows that baptism was not at all efficacious, even when true faith was present (8:12-17). The conversion of Cornelius and his household became a clear paradigm of salvation truth for Gentiles (10:43-48). Yet Peter's sermon concludes, **"that through His name everyone who believes receives forgiveness of sins"** (10:43). Immediately, *before* being baptized, they received the Holy Spirit. Indeed, Peter took the manifest reception of the Spirit as proof that they were fit candidates for baptism, although they were Gentiles. When Peter defended his actions before the Jerusalem church, he made that same point in quoting the words of Christ from Acts 1:5, which contrasts water baptism with Spirit baptism (11:15-17). Further, in describing the founding of the Antioch church, Luke says that those who believed turned to the Lord, but does not mention baptism at all (11:21).

Paul's ministry. In the preaching of Paul and Barnabas in the synagogue of Antioch of Pisidia they speak of forgiveness through faith with no mention of baptism (Acts 13:38-39). When Luke describes the subsequent response, he mentions believing as connected to eternal life, without reference to baptism (13:48). Thus, Paul really did tell the Philippian jailer the whole truth when he said, **"Believe in the Lord Jesus, and you shall be saved and your household"** (16:31). They did get baptized in obedience to Christ's command, but Paul very significantly left baptism out of the gospel message. In subsequent narratives, Luke refers several times to converts believing, without reference to baptism (17:12, 34; 19:18). Most significant is Paul's charge to the Ephesian elders, where he describes his preaching as, **"repentance toward God and faith in the Lord Jesus Christ"** (20:21)-- again, no mention of baptism.

The account of Paul's meeting a dozen disciples of John the Baptizer in Ephesus is very significant (19:1-7). He specifically asked them whether they had received the Spirit. Their answer was negative. Why did Paul rebaptize them? Clearly, John's baptism was not Christian baptism of the New Testament church, founded on the day of Pentecost. John was the end of the previous dispensation or age (Mt. 11:11). So Paul needed to rebaptize these Jewish Old Testament believers from the previous legal dispensation to incorporate them into the New Testament body of Christ. An anomaly was caused by the absence of those men from Judea at the Pentecost event. But if baptism is for the forgiveness of sins, then Paul erred greatly. If John's baptism were efficacious, Paul had no need to baptize them over again.

Some interpreters might say that John's baptism was ineffective and had to be repeated, but the inconsistency of this becomes clear in that they claim Mark 1:4 as a proof-text for baptism being for forgiveness of sins. They can not have it both ways; either John's baptism was efficacious or it was not. Those disciples were genuine in their repentant faith as seen in their immediate reception of the Spirit at the laying on of hands.

Paul's testimony before the Sanhedrin has occasioned much discussion because of the translation of Ananias' words to the newly converted Paul, "'And now why do you delay? Arise, and be baptized, and wash away your sins, calling on His name'" (Acts 22:16). Many wrongly understand Saul to be yet unsaved and needing to wash away his sins by baptism. If this were true, it would be a serious anomaly and contradict the rest of the New Testament. First of all, it is clear that Saul was already converted on the Damascus road three days earlier. His first response to Christ shows that he was instantaneously born again: "'What shall I do, Lord?'" (22:10). He called Jesus his Lord and submitted to His instruction! However, Ananias had every right to be suspicious of this chief persecutor of the church and assumed that he was yet unconverted.

The main difficulty with Ananias' words is translational. The participial phrase at the end of the sentence has been badly mistranslated by the KJV and other translations. *Apolousai tas hamartias sou epikalesamenos to onoma autou* ("wash away your sins, calling on His name"). This is a dangling participle, which is poor English, but good Greek. The relationship and force of these adverbial participial phrases are spelled out in the grammars. It is clear that this is an instrumental participle, which indicates "the means by which the action of the main verb is accomplished."[5] Therefore, to make good English out of it, it should be properly translated: "**Wash away your sins by calling on His name.**" The addition of the one little word 'by' corrects the abominably poor grammar of the English and fairly represents the force of the Greek. This is in perfect accord with the truth of Joel 2:32 quoted by Paul in Romans 10:12-14, "'**Whoever will call upon the name of the Lord will be saved.**'" It is clear that sins are washed away by calling on His name, not by getting baptized!

Lastly, note Paul's summary of his commission as he recounts it to Herod Agrippa, "**... to open their eyes so that they may turn from darkness to light and from the dominion of Satan to God, in order that they may receive forgiveness of sins and an inheritance among those who have been sanctified by faith that is in Me**" (Acts 26:18). Again, the significant omission of baptism is seen in this summary of salvation. Likewise, with Paul's statement, "**... that they should repent and turn to God, performing deeds appropriate to repentance**" (26:20).

The New Testament epistles

Non-Pauline epistles. Both James and Peter give definitive statements about the place of the word of God in bringing about the new birth. "**In the** exercise of His will He brought us forth by the word of truth, so that we might be, as it were, the first fruits among His creatures" (Jas. 1:18). "For you have been born again not of seed which is perishable but imperishable, that is through the living and abiding word of God" (1 Pet. 1:23). Neither mentions baptism. Peter's reference to baptism in 1 Peter 3:20-21 requires closer examination: "**And corresponding to that, baptism now saves you—not the removal of dirt from the flesh, but an appeal to God for a good conscience—through the resurrection of Jesus Christ,...**" Here the Greek word *antitupon* is very significant. Transliterated, it is 'antitype'. Thus, Peter is clearly stating that he is speaking figuratively. The flood of Noah was a type; baptism is the antitype. Then Peter, having stated this, realizes that his readers might interpret it crassly. So he breaks his line of thought to explain that he is not speaking of water baptism cleansing the body, but of the work of God upon the conscience. This is to follow the example of Moses. Crass interpretation fails to recognize figurative language where it is so obvious.

Pauline epistles. Paul supplies theological clarification in his letters. He reflects on his early ministry in Corinth: "**I thank God that I baptized none of you except Crispus and Gaius, that no man should say you were baptized in my name. Now I did baptize also the household of Stephanus; beyond that, I do not know whether I baptized any other. For Christ did not send me to baptize, but to preach the gospel,...**" (1 Cor. 1:14-17a). It is extremely hard to see how Paul could write these words if he really believed that people are born again through baptism or that baptism was an essential condition of being saved. If so, Paul would certainly have made it a point to keep a roll of those he had baptized. Now just a few years later, he can not even remember whom he had baptized. How could he thank God for so few he had baptized? How could he set baptism and preaching the gospel in such strong contrast, if baptism is really an essential part of the gospel of salvation?

Paul's letter to the Galatians is extremely relevant to the issue. Legalists had sneaked into the Galatian churches to try to counteract Paul's gospel of grace (2:4-5). They insisted that circumcision and obedience to the Mosaic Law were necessary for both salvation and Christian morality. After refuting their viewpoint conclusively in the first four chapters, Paul warned them about the spiritual danger of those who trust in external rituals: "**Behold I, Paul, say to you that if you receive circumcision, Christ will be of no benefit to you. And I testify again to every man who receives circumcision, that he is under obligation to keep the whole Law. You have been severed from Christ, you who are seeking to be justified by law; you have fallen from grace**" (Gal. 5:2-4). It is not that circumcision in itself was wrong, for Paul had had Timothy circumcised so that he might join them in witness to the Jews (Acts 16:3). It is trusting in the external ritual of circumcision which is spiritually dangerous. *In a very real way trusting in baptism for salvation is the very same sort of externalistic legalism that Paul so clearly warned about.* One would have to say that trust in an efficacious ritual of baptism for salvation puts one in the very same spiritual danger that Paul warns about. This is to sever one's self from Christ, rather than trusting in a personal relationship with Him. As Paul concludes his letter, **"For neither is circumcision anything, nor uncircumcision, but a new creation"** (6:15). It is not far afield to substitute the word 'baptism' for the word 'circumcision' in this verse and yet retain its main point.

After writing Galatians, Paul wrote the more reasoned theological statement, the book of Romans. He makes exactly the same point: **"But he is a Jew who is one inwardly; and circumcision is that which is of the heart, by the Spirit, not by the letter, and his praise is not from men, but from God"** (Rom. 2:29). In defending justification by faith alone, Paul makes a major point that circumcision is just a sign and seal of faith, not in the least efficacious (4:9-16). His argument is based upon the fact that Abraham was a believer for many years before he was circumcised. His conclusion establishes an essential principle, **"For this reason it is by faith, that it might be in accordance with grace, in order that the promise may be certain to all the descendants"** (4:16).

Those who might question the connection between circumcision and baptism need to take note of Paul's words to the Colossians, written years later: **"And in Him you were also circumcised with a circumcision made without hands, in the removal of the body of the flesh by the circumcision of Christ; having been buried with Him in baptism, in which you were also raised up with Him through faith in the working of God, who raised Him from the dead"** (Col. 2:11-12). Since the circumcision was wrought **"without hands,"** it is clear that the baptism referred to must be the Spirit baptism of the heart, not ritual water baptism. Only this could be efficacious. Yet water baptism is the New Testament counterpart of circumcision for the nation Israel.

Finally, note Paul's words to Titus in his last years of ministry: **"He saved us, not on the basis of deeds which we have done in righteousness, but according to His mercy, by the washing of regeneration and renewing by the Holy Spirit, whom He poured out upon us richly through Jesus Christ our Savior"** (Tit. 3:5-6). Based upon all the previous investigation, it is unthinkable that Paul is referring to baptism here. The grammatical connection between 'washing' and 'regeneration' is most likely a genitive of apposition, indicating that the washing is the internal washing of regeneration by the Holy Spirit. Indeed, **"renewing by the Holy Spirit"** must be explanatory. Otherwise it is redundant.[6] One is biblically naive to think that baptism is an efficacious washing or more than a symbolic act.

The Doctrinal Crystallization

The conclusions drawn from the inductive study must be summarized:

Repentant faith is the only condition of salvation. Over 150 times in the New Testament, repentant faith is stipulated as the only condition of salvation.[7] If baptism were an essential condition, it is clear that it should have been emphasized in these 150 contexts. Otherwise God is guilty of misleading communication on this central issue.

A few controverted passages have been mistranslated. It was seen how some passages were mistranslated because of theological bias of the King James translators, such as Matthew 3:11, Mark 1:4, Luke 3:3, Acts 2:38 and 22:16. A serious logical fallacy was noted in reading efficacious baptism into Mark 16:16. There are a number of promising interpretative possibilities in Christ's words to Nicodemus in John 3:5 which are much more cogent than the assumption that 'water' is a reference to baptism. That same assumption that Paul is referring to baptism in Titus 3:5 is totally unwarranted. Thus, there is total consistency in Scripture on this point.

Many got salvation without baptism. A number of examples in the ministry of Christ and the Apostles were noted where an individual was unquestionably saved without any possibility of baptism. In some cases they were baptized subsequently.

Some baptized individuals did not receive the Spirit. Two cases were observed where individuals who had repented/believed did not receive the Holy Spirit until subsequently. These are serious anomalies for baptismal regenerationists, and are best understood as being part of the dispensational* transition from Israel to the New Testament church.

The new birth is a work of the Spirit through the word. A number of definitive statements about the new birth were examined: John 3:3-18; James 1:18; and 1 Peter 1:23. All of them refer to the word of God and/or the Holy Spirit of God as the active agents. None mention water baptism. Salvation is frequently referred to in both testaments as a washing, but this washing is never accomplished by baptism (Jn. 13:1-20). Salvation is the bath; the believer needs to cleanse his walk by confession of sin (1 Jn. 1:9), symbolized by washing only the feet (Jn. 13). Further study showed Ananias' use of this symbolism (Acts 22:16); Peter's vision of the unclean food speaking of Gentile salvation as a cleansing (10:15; 11:9); Paul's references to Christians as having been washed (1 Cor. 6:11; Eph. 5:26; Tit. 3:5); John's speaking of forgiveness as a cleansing (1 Jn. 1:7,9); and martyrs described as having **"washed their robes and made them white"** (Rev. 7:14). This is always accomplished by the Spirit through the word without any reference to baptism

Water baptism is contrasted with Spirit-baptism. Both John and Christ set water baptism in bold contrast with Spirit-baptism as to efficacy. Paul gave the doctrinal explanation of Spirit-baptism in many contexts, which are erroneously assumed to be reference to water baptism. In both 1 Corinthians 12:13 and Colossians 2:11-13, Paul makes it clear that he is speaking of Spirit-baptism, not water baptism. The other passages (Rom. 6:3-4) must be interpreted in the light of these clear doctrinal statements. Spirit-baptism is efficacious for salvation; water baptism is not.

Paul minimized the cruciality of baptism. Paul's thanksgiving to God that he baptized so few in Corinth, his lack of memory of whom he baptized, and his statement of his commission to evangelize—all are incomprehensible if baptism is in some way effective in accomplishing salvation, or even a part of it (1 Cor 1:14-17). Baptism must be seen as a command to believers, not a means to become believers.

Requiring baptism for salvation is equal to legalism of Judaizers. The Pharisees were legalists because they believed that salvation is contingent upon ritual circumcision and law keeping. The Judaizers whose teaching fomented the Jerusalem Council insisted that circumcision was essential for salvation (Acts 15:1). The Council concluded that these people "**unsettled the souls**" of believers (Acts 15:24). In a similar way, the legalism of requiring the external rite of baptism as a condition for salvation unsettles the souls of Christians today. In so doing, they radically change the whole nature of the Christian message. They also make it dependent upon ritualism and law-works. Today's legalists draw from the New Testament command to be baptized, but by giving it undue importance in salvation, they have re-established the same principle as the Judaizers. Only now it is a different rite. This makes salvation no longer of grace (unmerited favor), and puts them in the same camp as the Galatian legalizers, who Paul says were bewitching the people (Gal. 3:1). Paul calls it a slavery and expresses concern for the salvation of those so deceived (Gal. 4:9-11, 5:1-4).

---

1. F Blass and E. DeBrunner, *Greek Grammar,* trans. Robert W. Funk, p 112; A. T Robertson and W Hersey Davis, *A New Short Grammar of the Greek Testament,* p. 256

2. H E Dana and Julius R Mantey, *A Manual Grammar of the Greek New Testament* , p 76; also p. 82

3. Charles Hodge, *Systematic Theology* (Grand Rapids. Eerdmans, 1968), III. p. 593

4   William D. Chamberlain, *An Exegetical Grammar of the Greek New Testament* (NY: Macmillan, 1952), p. 86.

5. Dana and Mantey, p 228

6. Hodge, III, pp. 595-9

7. Lewis Sperry Chafer, *Systematic Theology* (Dallas: Dallas Seminary Press, 1948), III, p 376.

Behind the shameful apathy and lethargy of the church, that allows one thousand millions of human beings to go to their graves in ignorance of the Gospel, there lies a practical doubt, if not denial, of their lost condition.

-A. T. Pierson (1886)

THE ONLY LIGHT IN THE DEADLY NIGHT: IS CHRIST THE ONLY WAY OF SALVATION?

The central issue in the biblical basis and motivation for Christian missions is the uniqueness of Jesus Christ and the gospel He gave His Apostles to proclaim throughout the world. If Christ is not uniquely the Savior of the world, then there is little point to Christian missions! If other religions have a true knowledge of God and salvation, then why bother to send missionaries to them? If there is salvation to be found apart from the sacrificial death of Christ, then missions is a tragic mistake—indeed, Christ's death itself was a tragic mistake! So the essential basis of world missions is the uniqueness of Christ, His gospel, and the lostness of the unevangelized.

However, with the massive immigration of third-world peoples, western culture is becoming increasingly pluralistic. In our society we must defer to the sensibilities of not only Roman Catholics, Jews, atheists, and agnostics, but now Muslims, Hindus and others as well. "In a pluralistic world it is becoming increasingly difficult to maintain the uniqueness of the Christian faith." Herbert Kane went on to highlight the problem:

> When we move into the non-Christian world, where the missionary has to operate, we find that the exclusive claims of Christianity are vigorously challenged by the non-Christian religions now undergoing an unprecedented resurgence It is safe to say that the most offensive aspect of twentieth-century Christianity is its exclusiveness. Such a claim does not make sense to the Hindu, the Buddhist, or the Confucianist.[1]

The problem is not just outside the church. Even among evangelical Christians there is a serious erosion of biblical teaching in this regard. A number of surveys taken in the 80s and 90s indicate that a shockingly large percentage of Christians do not believe that Christ is the only way of salvation, and that the unevangelized are lost and will go to hell. A survey of Christian collegians attending the Urbana '67 missionary conference indicated that less than forty percent of the students, who were mostly from secular colleges, believed that the unevangelized are lost. Although in Christian colleges the picture is much better, there still is cause for concern. Richard Bailey's 1971 study showed that twenty-seven percent of students in Christian liberal arts colleges and nine percent in Bible colleges did *not* believe that the heathen are lost.[2] Our own surveys of freshman Bible college students confirm that the situation in our post-modern culture has not improved in the intervening years, but has undoubtedly gotten worse.

How can Christians hold such views? Actually the problem has a long history. Origen, an early Alexandrian church father, advocated universalism, which is the view that all men will ultimately return to God and be 'saved.' His view did not gained popularity, since his doctrine was deviant in other areas and so obviously contrary to the Bible. Although the authority of the Bible was not seriously questioned then, in the last few centuries, with the widespread attacks upon the authority of the Bible, universalism has revived. Because of the connection between unitarianism (with its denial of Christ's deity) and universalism, the merged Universalist-Unitarian denomination is the major overt representative of this viewpoint. But there are many universalists in the old-line liberal denominations. Even among those who claim a more orthodox theology, such as Karl Barth, (father of Neo-orthodoxy) there has been a revival of universalism, which Robertson McQuilkin calls the "New Universalism." However, it also is not based upon full acceptance of the authority of the Bible, as might be expected.

But even among those who more consistently acknowledge the authority of Scripture, there are those who, while admitting that not all will be saved, hold that the sincere seeker after truth who has not heard the gospel will not be condemned by God. McQuilkin calls this the "Wider Hope Theory." Even more recently some have adopted a variant of this, the "New Wider Hope Theory," which states that:

> Those who live by the light they have will be saved on the merits of Christ's death. We recognize that this is a more conservative version of the New Universalism. It doesn't say that all will be saved on the merits of Christ, but that some may be saved on the merits of Christ through general revelation, apart from the special revelation of Scripture.[3]

A number of supposedly evangelical scholars have expressed such sentiments from time to time, but without any substantial defense of their viewpoint. It would seem to be fuzzy thinking arising from an emotional reaction rather than biblical fact. More recently Clark Pinnock and John Sanders have written and spoken extensively in support of this view, calling it "inclusivism."[4] It is very harmful in distorting Scripture and seriously undermining the missionary program of the church. Indeed a century ago a missions-minded pastor put it well: "Behind the shameful apathy and lethargy of the church, that allows one thousand millions of human beings to go to their graves in ignorance of the Gospel, there lies a practical doubt, if not denial, of their lost condition."[5] Since then the number of unevangelized people has escalated to over three billion, but the root cause of the church's apathy has not changed. So it is imperative that the uniqueness of the Christian faith, the lostness of non-Christian peoples, and the inclusivistic denials of these foundations be carefully examined.

The Uniqueness of Christ and His Gospel

When the Bible's statements are compared with other 'sacred books,' we find that Christ's claims are unique. Christ's person and work are also unique in backing up His unparalleled claims. The salvation He procured has no equal in the religions of the world—nothing even comes close!

The unique claims of Christ and His Apostles

The Lord Jesus claimed to be a unique person. He claimed to have come from eternal existence with God the Father in heaven. He claimed equality with God. He used titles of Himself which are appropriate only for God. He claimed to have the attributes, offices, and prerogatives of deity. He accepted worship as God. The Apostles also referred to Him in the same unique ways. The Apostle John used the title translated in the KJV as the **"only begotten Son of God."** The Greek word used here is *monogenēs* which means "'in a class by himself,' 'the only one of his kind,' or in other words 'unique.'"[6] The NIV translates it as **"His one and only Son."**

In addition, Christ claimed to be the *only* Savior of the world. His most direct statement is in John 14:6, **"Jesus said to him, 'I am the way, and the truth and the life; no one comes to the Father, but through Me.'"** The Apostle Peter confirmed this in his words to the Jewish leaders, **"And there is salvation in no one else; for there is no other name under heaven that has been given among men, by which we must be saved"** (Acts 4:12). Later the Apostle Paul also added his testimony: **"For there is one God, and one mediator also between God and men, the man Christ Jesus"** (I Tim. 2:5). If people can be saved apart from Christ, then Christ and his Apostles made false claims.[7]

Sometimes we overlook the obvious. The astounding fact is that no founder of any world religion ever made *claims* that compare with Christ's. Thomas Schultz's statement stands out boldly:

> Not one *recognized* religious leader, not Moses, Paul, Buddha, Mohammed, Confucius, etc., have [sic] ever claimed to be God; that is, with the exception of Jesus Christ. Christ is the only religious leader who has ever claimed to be deity and the only individual ever who has convinced a great portion of the world that He is God.[8]

Although this statement is mind-boggling, it could have been made even stronger. Some of the founders of world religions didn't even have much to say about God at all. It seems that Gautama the Buddha, Confucius, and Lao Tse were essentially agnostics in the sense that they did not claim to know God or concern themselves with Him. Some of the religions, like Hinduism and Shinto, do not have identifiable founders.

The two who came closest to a biblical concept of God were Zoroaster (Zarathustra) and Muhammad. Although Zoroaster may have gotten some concepts of God correctly passed down from Noah's day, his teachings were not written down until after Christ and those writings were undoubtedly influenced by the Christian view. In any case, Zoroastrianism is a dying religion today with few followers.[9] It is a well known fact that Muhammad borrowed heavily from Jews and Christians and modified the concept of God considerably. In any case, no founder of a world religion claimed sinlessness, deity, or the ability to save mankind. Even if any had, none of them would have been able to make their claims stick! Only Jesus the Messiah's claims are substantiated by His person and work.

His life supports His claims.

A careful study of the religions of mankind reveals that there is no parallel to the person and work of Christ. There are over a hundred detailed prophecies of His first coming fulfilled in His ministry.[10] Even though Isaac and John the Baptist were miraculously born of aged parents to prepare humanity's minds for the virgin birth, He was the only one in human history born of a virgin. He alone lived a sinless life and revealed a loving, personal and holy Father-God with whom He had fellowship eternally. He confirmed His claims to deity by His unique miracles of love and compassion. God had confirmed the ministry of the Old Testament prophets by wonderful miracles, but none of them compares with Christ's. He alone made predictive prophecies which are continuing to be fulfilled, including a dozen about His own death and resurrection. He alone died as a sinless sacrifice for sin, which was sealed by His bodily resurrection from the tomb. This was not just a restoration of physical life, but His post-resurrection appearances in a glorified body made it unique. He alone ascended into heaven bodily with the promise to return in the same way to establish His rule upon the earth. *Not one of these things can be said for Zoroaster, Gautama the Buddha, Lao Tse, Confucius, Guru Nanak, or Muhammad.*

His unique salvation

The uniqueness of the fall. Just as remarkable as the unparalleled person of Christ is His plan of salvation. Careful study of other religions uncovers nothing like it in any of its major features. Indeed, none of the world religions have any plan of salvation at all from sin and the fall. This is understandable since none, including Judaism and Islam, have any concept of man as a fallen creature under the sway of sin. All religions view mankind as essentially good, imagining that salvation by God is not necessary. Hinduism's *moksha* (realization) has to do with release from the cycle of life. Buddha's *nirvana* (oblivion) has to do with release from the sufferings of life. Zoroastrianism and Islam do have a concept of paradise after death, but it is attained by human merit, not by the work of God.

The uniqueness of grace. The key difference between evangelical Christianity and all other religions is salvation by grace. All other religions are based upon human merit, not the grace of God. Grace means 'unmerited favor.' We cannot earn it! Only biblical Christianity teaches that God reaches down to save sinful man. All the other religions see man struggling upward to God (if one even exists). The Sikhs of India use the word for grace (*parshad*), but they, like adherents of other religions, are striving to please God by their own works. Even the cultic corruptions of Christianity depart from the truth in this essential point, whether it be Mormons, Jehovah's Witnesses, or other cults. Roman Catholics also overwork the word 'grace' but do not understand salvation by grace alone. Catholics try to merit God's grace by baptism, confirmation, confession, attendance at mass, good works, and last rites. But salvation is not by human merit: **"For by grace you have been saved through faith; and that not of yourselves, it is the gift of God; not as a result of works, that no one should boast"** (Eph. 2:8-9).

Forgiveness and assurance. All systems of meritorious salvation undermine two important things: the forgiveness of sin and the present assurance of eternal life. No one can know for sure about salvation as long as it is based upon human merit. Indeed, unless it is claimed by faith in Christ, any sense of forgiveness is a deception. Although various religions differ in details, they are all alike in striving to merit God's favor. For example, a tradition of Islam states that when Muhammad was dying, his daughter Fatimah asked him to pray for her salvation. His reply was, "Daughter, my prayer will do you no good! Only your own works will save you!" Muslims deny the cross of Christ and His redemptive sacrifice as a basis for forgiveness. This is typical of all other religions. Erich Sauer has well summarized the confused diversity of man's religions:

> Heathenism as a whole rests not only on error and deceit, but at the same time also on a spiritistic foundation . . Through all this the heathen, under demon influence, became the "creator of his gods." . . .
>
> | The Grecian says | . Man, know thyself |
> |---|---|
> | The Roman says | : Man, rule thyself. |
> | The Chinese says | · Man, improve thyself. |
> | The Buddhist says | : Man, annihilate thyself. |
> | The Brahman says | : Man, merge thyself in the universal sum of all. |
> | The Moslem says | : Man, submit thyself. |
> | But Christ says | : **"Without Me ye can do nothing,"** |
> | and in HIM | |
> | the Christian says | : "**I can do all things through Christ Who makes me mighty**". |
>
> "In his religion the heathen expresses his *godlessness*. Religion is *the sin*, namely, the sin against the first command, the replacing of God by the gods;" "the most powerful expression of the opposition of man against God and contradiction within himself "[11]

An historical salvation. Christian salvation is also without equal in being based upon real, historical events that God wrought among men. Most of the oriental religions are filled with myths and legends about their many man-like gods. Shinto has its creation-myth. Hinduism has legends about Krishna and many other deities. We are not sure *whether* Lao Tse even existed. We really can't know *when* Zoroaster lived. But Christianity is an historical faith, based upon what God did in human history in the incarnation, ministry, and passion of Christ and the work of the Holy Spirit through the church. The human authors of the Bible frequently tied their narratives in with secular history. Archaeology confirms the essential historicity of many events in the Bible. Islam makes the strongest claims of historicity among the religions. That doesn't matter much, however, since Muhammad claimed to be neither God nor Savior. He didn't claim to work any miracles or to have risen from the dead. Even more astonishing is that Muslims believe that Muhammad is buried in a tomb in Medina, whereas they believe that the 'prophet Jesus' is in heaven. Paradoxical, isn't it?

Are the Unevangelized Really Lost?

Previous generations referred to the unevangelized as the 'heathen,' but the term, 'heathen' must be defined first. The dictionary definition is, "an unconverted member of a people that does not acknowledge the God of the Bible; a pagan."[12] Actually the definition could be broadened to include any unchurched person in any country since there are pagans everywhere.

What do we mean by 'lost'?

People can be lost in many senses—geographically, intellectually, emotionally, etc. What really counts is what God means by the word 'lost.' The Lord Jesus said that the basic purpose of His coming was **"to seek and to save that which was lost"** (Luke 19:10). The biblical picture, as discussed in Chapter 3, is that man is lost in reference to God. In Adam's fall all mankind became separated from God. Not only did Adam and Eve die spiritually when they sinned (Gen. 2:17), but they caused the whole human race to be born spiritually dead and under God's wrath, without hope and without God in the world, and alienated from the life of God (Eph. 2:1-3, 12; 4:18).

Eternally lost. Mankind is not only lost in that he is now without God, but apart from Christ's salvation that separation becomes eternal death (Rom. 3:23; 6:23). It is the Lord Jesus Himself who had the most to say about eternal punishment. Herbert Kane summarized well:

> The Bible clearly teaches that there are two destinies open to man. One involves everlasting happiness in the presence of God and the holy angels (Lk 15:10; Rev 22:3-5; 1 Thess 4:17), the other involves everlasting misery in the company of the devil and his angels (Mt 25.41). The New Testament speaks of two gates—one strait and the other wide; two ways—one broad and the other narrow; two destinies—one life and the other destruction (Mt 7:13-14). In the day of judgment the sheep will be separated from the goats (Mt 25:31-46), and the wheat from the

tares (Mt 13˙36-43), the good from the evil (Jn 5˙29). And in the resurrection there will be a separation between the just and the unjust (Acts 24.15)[13]

Universal spiritual and physical death. The Bible is clear about the universality of man's lost condition—none are exempt. Paul writes that God's law shuts every person's mouth, that all the world is guilty before God, and that **"death spread to all men, because all sinned"** (Rom. 3:19-20; 5:12). People are not becoming lost—they are already lost! **"Whoever believes in Him is not condemned, but whoever does not believe stands condemned already because he has not believed in the name of God's one and only Son"** (John 3:18, NIV). This is true both of people who reject the gospel and of those who have never heard it. Unless people are saved through Christ, they will stay lost for eternity.

All mankind's need of salvation

The Lord Jesus made it abundantly clear that all men need to be saved. This was true of both God's chosen people, the Jews, and Gentiles. In commenting on people who had died suddenly and tragically, Christ said, **"Unless you repent, you will all likewise perish"** (Luke 13:5). Christ even told a very religious Jewish leader, Nicodemus, that he needed to be born again in order to enter the kingdom of God (John 3:5). If that was true of Nicodemus, it is certainly true of pagans. The book of Acts records the conversion of the first pagan Gentiles, the Roman centurion Cornelius and his household (Acts 10:1—11:18). Even though Cornelius had already given up his Roman idolatry and prayed to the true God of Israel, the angel told Cornelius that when the Apostle Peter came, he would speak words by which they would be saved (11:14). Even though this devout and sincere heathen's prayer was answered, he was not yet saved until he heard the message of salvation from Peter. The inclusivists would have us believe that Cornelius was a "pagan saint," already saved through general revelation. They ignore Cornelius' contact with the word of God through Judaism and the angel's explicit statement that they were to be saved through Peter's message of God's word.

On his second missionary journey Paul had opportunity to preach to some very civilized and intellectual Greek philosophers in Athens. Universalists rationalize that Greek philosophy was as good a preparation for the gospel as the Old Testament, and the inclusivists claim that the Greeks had the truth of God through the Greek writers to which Paul alludes. However, Paul told them bluntly that, **"God is now declaring to men that all everywhere should repent, because He has fixed a day in which He will judge the world in righteousness through a Man whom He has appointed, having furnished proof to all men by raising Him from the dead"** (Acts 17:30-31). Later, he explained that repentance in a limited Christian context when he described his ministry as **"solemnly testifying to both Jews and Greeks of repentance toward God and faith in our Lord Jesus Christ"** (Acts 20:21). He did not mean repentance within the context of any pagan religion, but only as it is linked with faith in Christ.

What about those who have never heard?

We have gone into considerable detail to show the clarity of Bible revelation about the universal and eternal nature of man's lostness apart from Christ, because these are exactly the points that the various kinds of universalism and inclusivism deny. Scripture is clear that God's condemnation comes to all men until they are saved by faith in Christ. The universalists and inclusivists have to contradict the Bible to hold to salvation outside of personal faith in Christ. Indeed, most do not hold to inerrancy of Scripture. However, many would raise the valid question, "What about those who have never heard the gospel of Christ and had opportunity to believe and be saved? It isn't really fair of God to condemn them to hell, is it?"

The unevangelized have a revelation of God. It is not as if the heathen did not have any knowledge of God. The Apostle Paul mentions two kinds of revelation of God that all men have by nature, which are referred to as 'general revelation'. In Romans 1:18-25 he traces the reason for God's wrath falling upon the heathen. He points out that the heathen were not always heathen. They, like all of us, descended from Adam and Noah, who knew God. But they suppressed the truth in unrighteousness (1:18), didn't honor Him as God or thank Him, but in the pride of their own wisdom indulged in foolish speculations (1:21-22). So generation after generation, they got farther away from the true knowledge of God and ultimately fell into idolatry and immorality (1:23-25) (probably at the Tower of Babel). Indeed, a number of pagan tribes have a tradition about once knowing God and His book, but having lost that knowledge.[14]

Paul also emphasized the fact that all humanity has been given a revelation of God in nature, when he wrote:

Because that which is known about God is evident within them; for God made it evident to them. For since the creation of the world His invisible attributes, His eternal power and divine nature, have been clearly seen, being understood through what has been made, so that they are without excuse (Rom. 1:19-20).

There are a number of impressive arguments philosophers have used over the millenniums for the existence of God. The cosmological argument reasons from the fact that this universe clearly had a beginning and therefore a Creator (Aristotle's "Unmoved Mover"). The teleological argument reasons from design and order in creation to show that there must have been a 'Designer God'. God's hand in creation is obvious! The more we learn about nature through modern science, the more we see design and order. But we don't need modern science to see this. David saw it three millenniums ago: "The heavens are telling of the glory of God; and their expanse is declaring the work of His hands. Day to day pours forth speech, and night to night reveals knowledge.... Their line has gone out through all the earth, and their utterance to the end of the world" (Ps. 19:1-4). The heathen "are without excuse," Paul concludes, because they repress the truth about the true God and don't worship Him.

A second type of revelation is the human conscience—the law of God written on human hearts. Paul argues that men do not have to possess the written law of God to come under condemnation:

> **For all who have sinned without the Law will also perish without the Law; and all who have sinned under the Law will be judged by the Law; . . . For when Gentiles who do not have the Law do instinctively the things of the Law, these, not having the Law, are a law to themselves, in that they show the work of the Law written in their hearts, their conscience bearing witness, and their thoughts alternately accusing or else defending them, on the day when, according to my gospel, God will judge the secrets of men through Christ Jesus** (Rom. 2:12-16).

Although the human conscience is a weak testimony to God and His Law, nevertheless man is responsible for its light. By it all men are condemned as sinners, since no one lives up even to his own conscience. Although God's general revelation in nature and human conscience is adequate to condemn men, there is no hint in the Bible that it is adequate for salvation. It tells man nothing about God's plan of salvation. It is the responsibility of believers to tell them. Inclusivists claim that general revelation is adequate for salvation without any explicit Scriptural proof of this notion.

God's holiness and judgment. Those who rationalize away God's judgment on heathen who have not heard usually appeal to God's love. "Could a God of love condemn the unevangelized?" they ask. They forget God's holiness and wrath. Yes, God in His love gave His unique Son that whoever believes on Him should not perish (John 3:16). But the Bible has much to say about God's wrath and judgment upon sinners. Indeed it was Christ Himself who gave the fullest revelation about God's wrath and judgment (see the Kane quotation above). Remember that God's judgment is not based upon relative merit—as in the Muslim's concept of God's scales. One sin is enough to condemn us to hell. No man, heathen or nominal Christian, can be holy and righteous enough to escape condemnation (cf. Hab. 1:13). The inclusivists totally ignore the mass of Scripture which emphasize God's signal judgments upon mankind, such as the Noahic deluge which destroyed the whole human race, the judgment upon the idolatrous worship of the tower of Babel, the ten judgmental plagues upon the idolatrous worship of Egypt, the order to exterminate the idolatrous and immoral Canaanites, and the many prophecies of God's coming judgments upon the pagan nations surrounding Israel.

However, it should also be pointed out that there are degrees of judgment in hell. The moral heathen will not be judged as severely as those who sin against greater light (Matt. 11:20-24). The parallel truth is that for believers there are degrees of reward for faithfulness (over and above salvation, which is by grace). God is fair and just!

Reductio ad absurdum. One useful way to examine the logic of a proposition is called *reductio ad absurdum,* which means reducing it to the absurd. If one starts with the premise that only those who consciously reject the gospel will go to hell, see how absurd the conclusion comes out. If that were true (and it isn't), then missionaries would be bringing condemnation to most heathen who have not heard before their arrival. The fact is that the majority of the unevangelized who hear do not believe and get saved. Most reject the gospel. If that majority was not lost before the missionary came, then the missionary would have brought condemnation to more people than he brought salvation to. As missionaries to a Muslim country, when we preached and witnessed to Muslims, very few accepted Christ. Thus, we would have brought condemnation to most to whom we witnessed. How absurd the whole missionary enterprise then becomes! Indeed, if many unevangelized were really seeking for the truth (as some maintain), why don't missionaries experience them believing upon the first hearing of the gospel. The fact is that most unevangelized have to hear time and again before they believe and are saved. This shows the effects of sin and depravity. The Apostle Paul spelled it out quite clearly, **"And even if our gospel is veiled, it is veiled to those who are perishing, in whose case the god of this world has blinded the minds of the unbelieving, that they might not see the light of the gospel of the glory of Christ, who is the image of God"** (2 Cor. 4:3-4).

This brings us to another dimension of the problem—Satanic and demonic involvement. Not only are man's religions a hindrance to knowing God, religion is something Satan uses to keep men from really knowing God. Paul expands on this: **"But I say that the things which the Gentiles sacrifice, they sacrifice to demons, and not to God"** (1 Cor. 10:20). Even apostate forms of Christianity are the Devil's tool to keep men from the true knowledge of God. In the Sermon on the Mount Christ put it bluntly (Matt. 7:15, 21-23):

> Beware of the false prophets, who come to you in sheep's clothing, but inwardly are ravenous wolves. . . . Not everyone who says to Me, "Lord, Lord," will enter the kingdom of heaven; but he who does the will of My Father who is in heaven. Many will say to Me on that day, "Lord, Lord, did we not prophesy in Your name, and in Your name cast out demons, and in Your name perform many miracles?" And then I will declare unto them, "I never knew you; *depart from me, you who practice lawlessness.*

Objections answered

Isn't sincerity enough? It is granted that there are many sincere followers of other religions, and from the human point of view it might seem that God would honor that sincerity. The fact is that the Bible gives no hint that God is at all impressed with so-called sincerity in other religions. Our God is a God of truth. Other religions do not lead to the One God—they are all false. Both Cain and Abel may have been sincere in their worship, but God rejected Cain's offering because it wasn't made according to truth. Cornelius, the Roman Centurion, was sincere, but he wasn't saved before Peter shared the gospel.

The medical and engineering world provide helpful illustrations. A patient may be given the wrong medicine very sincerely, but may die nevertheless. This is very personal, because my brother died of polio because of the wrong advice of a doctor. He may have been well trained and very sincere in telling my sister-in-law to keep him in bed at home, but he was sincerely wrong! The engineers who built those bridges which collapse in the wind or flood were probably very sincere. But people who die in such tragedies get no solace from their sincerity. If sincerity isn't enough in medicine or engineering, what indications do we have that it is enough in the far more important sphere of man's eternal destiny?

Is it really fair of God to condemn those who've never heard? Our problem so often is that we look at things from man's point of view and fail to see God's perspective—and that's the only one that counts! Remember that God could justly condemn all men to Hell. We are all by nature children of wrath. It is only by God's grace that any of us are saved. We with our limited perspective and knowledge may deign to criticize the justice of the omniscient God. But our criticisms arise from ignorance of all the facts. On what basis is man judged? The word of God is very clear: "**Now we know that God's judgment against those who do such things is based on truth**" (Rom. 2:2, NIV). When God's judgment came upon Sodom and Gomorrah, Abraham's words of intercession for Lot expressed the truth: "**Shall not the judge of all the earth deal justly?**" (Gen. 18:25).

Doesn't God apply the merits of Christ's death to pious heathen apart from hearing and believing the gospel? Inclusivists have suggested the possibility that the heathen might be considered like the Old Testament saints, who were saved apart hearing the gospel. First of all, it should be noted that the Old Testament saints did believe the promises of the revelation God had given them concerning the coming Messiah. Thus, this parallel breaks down, since the heathen do not have such a special revelation. It should also be noted that not only is there no indication in Scripture that such is the case, but also this would contradict direct statements in the Bible. Some have misunderstood Paul's statement in Romans 3:25: "**... because in the forbearance of God He passed over the sins previously committed.**" However, it is clear that Paul is talking about the sins of Old Testament saints being forgiven in anticipation of the cross (cf. Heb. 9:15).

There are many specific statements in Scripture which exclude those who don't personally believe in Christ, such as John 3:5,16-18, etc. Christ was even more explicit in John 8:24 when He said, "**... for unless you believe that I am He, you shall die in your sins.**" Paul also left no room for doubt in referring to the second coming of Christ: "**...dealing out retribution to those who do not know God and to those who do not obey the gospel of our Lord Jesus**" (2 Thess. 1:8). This is not an easy doctrine; indeed, it is difficult! But we must never allow our feelings to dictate what we determine to be truth. Simply believe what God has said and act upon it!

A Critique of Contemporary Inclusivism

It has been in the last few decades that inclusivists, such as Lesslie Newbiggin, Clark Pinnock, and John Sanders, while claiming to be Evangelicals, have become increasingly vocal about their denial of the lostness of the unevangelized. Some who have not examined their lack of evangelical credentials have become their followers. My own research has shown, for example, that Newbiggin, while called an ecumenical Evangelical, was neither evangelical nor a friend of Evangelicalism.[A] There are a number of responses from evangelical writers, who give a more thorough refutation of inclusivism than is possible here.[15]

It has been clear for a score of years that Clark Pinnock has moved away from the inerrancy of Scripture, and Ramesh Richard has shown that his view of Christ's deity is also very defective[16]. Pinnock, despite his claim to have a high view of Christ, says that Christ's uniqueness and finality belong to Jesus *only derivatively*. He also rejects an incarnational Christology as the norm.[17] Thus the foundation for his doctrine of salvation is exceedingly weak, even heretical.

Richard shows how one of the axioms of Pinnock's inclusivism is his optimistic view of the universal love of God based upon global covenants, like that with Noah, the so-called "pagan saints" outside of Israel before Christ, and God's continuing dialog with the nations. His second "particularity" axiom is that salvation is only through the cross of Christ, and that explicit faith in Jesus Christ is not a necessary condition of salvation. Indeed, salvation is not to be so narrowly defined as merely individual, spiritual salvation from hell, but is to be understood more holistically and corporately. Sanders speaks about the "faith principle" in the unevangelized world, which does not necessarily require explicit faith in the Lord Jesus. He sees this exemplified in pre-messianic believers, like Enoch, Noah, Job, Melchizedek, and ultimately Cornelius, among others. He believes that these "pagan saints" had faith in the general revelation found in nature, not explicit faith in Christ. This would rightly seem to undercut any motivation for missions. However, Sanders suggests that the restrictive view is not the only motive for missions, and that there are other legs upon which the table can stand: the great commission and the needs of those who have only "implicit faith" (not explicit) and therefore *haven't experienced the fullness of salvation* we can share with them. The Bible, however, knows nothing of

A. In 1980 I wrote "An Evaluative Review of *The Open Secret* by Lesslie Newbiggin" (1978), in which I showed his non-evangelical view of inspiration, Christology (many Christologies in the NT), and his almost universalist soteriology. He takes offense at the idea that we can have assurance of ultimate salvation, and carries his concept of "surprise" in the teachings of Christ to lead to the possibility that God is working through atheists, humanists, and Marxists and that they will be "surprised" to be included, while those who presume to think they are in will be surprised to find themselves excluded from salvation (pp. 196-8).

such halfway Christians, who just need to be brought to a higher level of salvation. If the unevangelized are not already lost, biblical motivation for missions evaporates.

A critique. Many of the key issues have already been addressed in this chapter. Furthermore, the inclusivists' weak view of Scripture allows them to be very selective in the passages they treat. Their overly optimistic spin on the universal love of God manifest before Christ significantly omits the very obvious judgments of God already mentioned. They also fail to take into account the substantial special revelation given to the so-called "pagan saints" of earlier dispensations and the almost direct passing down of the knowledge of the true God to the descendants of Noah, such as Job and Melchizedek. They were not dependent upon natural revelation alone. Their faith was in the true God, Yahweh, and in the messianic expectation of salvation yet to be provided. Granted that they did not have a clear understanding of the person and work of the Messiah, as predicted and promised. Indeed, the prophets themselves searched to understand this salvation (1 Pet. 1:10-11). However, Charles Ryrie suggests that the content of faith required for salvation necessarily grew with each successive revelation and dispensation. In any case, the New Testament clearly testifies that in this present age faith has to be put in Jesus the Messiah *explicitly.* Sanders objects: "A single statement by our Lord Jesus could have settled the controversy before it began."[18] The fact is that He did, and it is in the best known verse in the Bible, John 3:16. There is a legion of other passages which stipulate that saving trust has to be **"in Him"** (His one and only Son). They cannot separate the objective, historical reality of the person and work of Christ from the subjective appropriation of that salvation by repentant faith in this divine Messiah. To do so is to violate the whole tenor of the New Testament proclamation.

The inclusivists deal with generalities. What about the specifics? What about sincere religious Muslims, undoubtedly millions out of the one billion nominal Muslims in the world today? Muslims believe that to call the 'prophet Jesus' God incarnate is the greatest of all sins, a blasphemy. Therefore, the doctrine of the Tri-Unity of God is also blasphemous. They believe that the 'prophet Jesus' was not crucified, and that to see His substitutionary sacrifice as the basis for forgiveness of sin is heresy. Now what kind of "implicit faith" can a sincere Muslim have which might save him?

Or consider sincere Hindus, who worship 33 million idolatrous gods and as pantheists deny the personality of God. They worship cobras, monkeys, rats, elephants, and especially cows. Remember what God did in judgment upon the religion of Egypt, where it was frogs, ibises, crocodiles, cats, and especially bulls which were worshiped, which worship was judged in the ten plagues. Or consider the hundreds of millions of Buddhists. At the end of the Congress of World Religions, which convened in Chicago in 1993, as they drew up a joint ethical statement, they had to leave out the word 'God' lest they offend the Buddhists, who do not believe in a personal God. Just who are these "pagan saints" of the inclusivists?

In conclusion, inclusivists have failed to be honest with the biblical text, mostly because they do not believe in the inerrancy of Scripture.* God has spoken clearly and distinctly in His word on this issue, and we must just have honest hearts to believe what He says (Lk. 8:15).

Note: Taken from *What in the World Is God Doing? The Essentials of Global Missions*, 5ᵗʰ ed. 2003.

---

1   J Herbert Kane, *Understanding Christian Missions*, p 105.

2   Richard Bailey, "Missions--Christian Collegians' Concepts," *Eastern Challenge*, 7 (July 1971), p. 3; MARC, *Christian Collegians and Foreign Missions* (1968).

3   J Robertson McQuilkin, "The Narrow Way," in *Perspectives*, p 128

4   Clark H Pinnock, *A Wideness in God's Mercy. The Finality of Jesus Christ in a World of Religions* (1992), "Toward an Evangelical Theology of Religions," JETS, 33 (1990) 359-368; John Sanders, *No Other Name. An Investigation into the Destiny of the Unevangelized* (1992), Sanders, ed., *What About Those Who Have Never Heard? Three Views on the Destiny of the Unevangelized* (1995)

5   A T Pierson, *Evangelize to a Finish*, p 12 Cf also *The Crisis of Missions*, p. 291.

6. James Oliver Buswell, Jr., *A Systematic Theology of the Christian Religion*, 2 vols. (1962), 1 111

7. For a good summary of these claims see Henry C. Thiessen, *Lectures in Systematic Theology*, revised by Vernon D. Doerksen (1979), pp 92-96.

8   Josh McDowell, *Evidence That Demands a Verdict* (1972), p. 92, citing Thomas Schultz, "The Doctrine of the Person of Christ with an Emphasis upon the Hypostatic Union" (Dissertation, Dallas Theological Seminary, 1962), p. 209.

9   John B Noss, *Man's Religions*, 4th ed (1969), p. 344. Paul C Haagen on Zoroastrianism in Howard F Vos, *Religions in a Changing World*, pp 207-12, naively shows parallels between Christ and Zoroaster, without clarification, apparently unaware that Zoroaster had a human father and that the *Zend Avesta* was not written down until centuries after Christ, thus allowing Zoroastrians to invent such comparisons.

10 McDowell, *Evidence*, pp 147-84.

11 Erich Sauer, *The Dawn of World Redemption*, trans. by G H Lang (1951), p. 85 (quotations from unattributed German sources)

12 *Webster's Collegiate Dictionary*, 5th ed., s v "heathen "

13 Kane, *Understanding*, p. 130

14 Don Richardson, *Eternity in their Hearts* (1981), pp 28-120

15 Ramesh P. Richard, *The Population of Heaven* (1994), Millard J Erickson, *How Shall They Be Saved? The Destiny of Those Who Do Not Hear of Jesus* (1996); Ronald H Nash, "Restrictivism," in John Sanders, ed., *op cit* (1995), also, Ajith Fernando, *Crucial Questions about Hell* (1991), Larry Dixon, *The Other Side of the Good News Confronting the Contemporary Challenges to Jesus' Teaching on Hell* (1992), William V. Crockett and James G Sigountos, eds , *Through No Fault of Their Own? The Fate of Those Who Have Never Heard* (1991), Edward Rommen and Harold Netland, eds , *Christianity and the Religions A Biblical Theology of World Religions* (1995).

16 Richard, pp 47-55.

17 Pinnock, *Wideness*, p. 53-62

18 John Sanders, *No Other Name An Investigation into the Destiny of the Unevangelized* (1992), p 19

PART THREE

UNSCREWING

INSCRUTABLE

DOCTRINES

The Resultant Plan of Salvation

As relates to the application phase of salvation the following plan of salvation (*ordo salutis*) emerges:

A. *God's eternal plan for the cross, the church, and the kingdom*

B. *God's foreknowledge of repentant believers*

C. *Election in Christ to salvation and service based upon foreknowledge*

D. *Conviction wrought mediately by the Spirit through human instrumentality and the word of God*

E. *Sinners responsible to repent toward God and trust in Christ for salvation*

F. *Justification and regeneration conditioned on repentant faith*

G. *Outward conversion resulting from regeneration and justification*

H. *The truly regenerate and justified believer's salvation is eternal.*

I. *Sanctification and discipleship are the believer's responsibility by walking in the Spirit and will be rewarded in the kingdom.*

The election of God will be a fatal labyrinth
for anyone who does not follow the clear road
of faith. Thus, so that we may be confident of
remission of sins, so that our consciences
may rest in full confidence of eternal life, so
that we may boldly call God our Father, under
no circumstances must we begin by asking
what God decreed concerning us before the
world began.

20

~John Calvin

THE CHURCH'S GLORIOUS
FUTURE PREAPPOINTED

The Apostle Peter was an uneducated fisherman, who admitted that he struggled to understand some of the difficult teachings in Paul's letters (2 Pet. 3:15-16). Apparently election and foreknowledge were not among those "hard to understand" teachings, since Peter himself referred to election four times (1 Pet. 1:1-2; 2:6, 9; 2 Pet. 1:10) in his epistles and foreknowledge three times (1 Pet. 1:2, 20; 2 Pet. 3:17) and is quoted twice in Acts (2:23, 4:28) touching on these ideas. That the election of Hebrew Christians scattered among the Gentiles in the diaspora was "**according to the foreknowledge of God**" did not seem hidden or hard to understand for Peter. He addressed them as: "**Elect according to the foreknowledge of God the Father, through sanctification of the Spirit, unto obedience and sprinkling of the blood of Jesus Christ:**" (1 Pet. 1:2, KJV). Later, writing to the Romans, Paul confirmed Peter's understanding of the relationship of foreknowledge to the related truth of foreordination: "**Because those whom He knew beforehand He appointed beforehand to share the likeness of his Son, so that He might be the First-born among many brothers**" (Rom. 8:29, NBV). *Both Peter and Paul clearly affirm that election and foreordination are conditioned on God's foreknowledge.*

Four centuries later, Augustine was the one who made it hard to understand and accept, by denying that election and foreordination are conditioned on God's foreknowledge, contrary to the only two passages which relate these ideas (1 Pet. 1:1-2; Rom. 8:29). The majority Western Latin church struggled with his view of unconditional election for a century until the Synod of Orange set it aside in AD 529. A millennium later the Reformers

259

revived this doctrine, but even Calvin called it "a horrible decree." It was Augustine's innovation which caused the problem.

Someone may say, "Didn't Peter use a reverse order in the Pentecost sermon when he said, "this **Man, delivered over by the predetermined plan and foreknowledge of God, you nailed to a cross by the hands of godless men and put Him to death**" (Acts 2:23)? Please note, however, that Peter was *not speaking about our individual election*, but about God's plan for the crucifixion of the Messiah. There is a massive difference between the two! Additionally, the syntax of the sentence demands careful investigation, given below.

Unconditional election means that in eternity past God decided who would be saved or lost totally apart from any condition man can meet. It should be superfluous to emphasize how crucial the issue of conditional or unconditional election is to all of salvation truth. Unconditional election was the key point of Augustine's system; for Calvin's; and it is still for contemporary Calvinists. It is widely recognized that the other points of Calvinism are ancillary to unconditional election.

Outstanding questions

In the light of sixteen centuries of theological controversy over election since Augustine, there are many problems to be resolved and questions to be answered. Since the definition of terms is crucial, word studies must be done of the Greek terms for foreknowledge, foreordination, and election.

How does foreknowledge differ from election? Does it have a pregnant meaning? At issue are the questions as to whether election is conditional or unconditional; whether individual or corporate. Is God's foreknowledge contingent upon His will? Can a future event be certain in the mind of God without Him having determined it? What do the Greek words for election and 'predestination' really mean? Are election and foreordination synonyms, and if not, how do they relate? How does the Hebrew cultural emphasis upon corporate solidarity color the issue? How much emphasis does the Bible put upon election, after all? How do the context and the grammar of key passages, such as Romans 8–11, impact our understanding? Nothing can be assumed.

Two crucial passages are found in the heart of Romans: 8:28-30 and 9:1-29. The latter will be examined in Chapter 22. To unpack the truth of 8:28-30, we must study two key Greek words in the flow of Paul's thinking: *proginoskein* ('to foreknow') and *proorizein* ('to foreordain' or 'to pre-appoint'). *Our word study of the first indicates that it has its normal primary meaning of 'foreknow' in this and all other contexts. On the other hand, the second, which is a very rare word, has been grossly misunderstood and mistranslated and has nothing to do with 'predestination.'* In the next chapter we shall look at election in the flow of the election of Israel, Christ, the Apostles, and the Church, especially focusing upon Ephesians 1:3-14.

A Word Study of Foreknowledge

Calvinistic claims. A major premise of Calvinism is that the Greek verb 'to foreknow' (*proginoskein*) and the noun 'foreknowledge, prescience' (*prognosis)* have a pregnant meaning of "making one the object of loving care or elective love."[1] This is based upon their claim that the Hebrew word 'to know' (*yada'*) has this pregnant meaning in a few contexts, and the simple Greek word 'to know' (*ginoskein*) has this connotation in three places. Thus, when they come to the seven usages of *proginoskein* and *prognosis* in the New Testament, they claim that this selective pregnant meaning is to be understood there as well. However, there is *no linguistic basis* for this idea of a pregnant meaning, and these words must be taken in their normative sense, 'to foreknow' and 'foreknowledge.'

Conditionality. If these words are taken in their normative meanings, the two key passages clearly confirm the conditionality of God's foreordination and election: 1 Peter 1:1-2 and Romans 8:28-30. If there were a pregnant meaning, then it would weaken the case for election being conditioned upon the foreknowledge of God, since foreknowledge and election would become essentially synonymous. This then undermines the prima facie reading of these passages, which both make election and foreordination contingent upon God's foreknowledge. It also raises the question as to how Peter can speak of being **"elect according to the foreknowledge of God"** and how Paul can write, **"whom He foreknew, He also foreordained to be conformed to the image of His Son,"** if indeed these terms are virtually synonymous and redundant. Calvinists cannot answer this question. There must be an essential difference between these terms!

Methodology. Thomas Edgar has done careful research on the meaning of *proginoskein* and objects to the procedure of building the meaning of this word upon the meaning of a Hebrew word or even upon a supposed meaning for *ginoskein.* Even though I had gone into considerable detail to show that there is no such pregnant meaning in either *yada'* or *ginoskein*,[A] Edgar's point is well taken, and the Calvinists' methodology is highly questionable.[2] Even if the Hebrew did have such a pregnant meaning (and it does not), it says little or nothing about the meaning of *proginoskein.*[B]

A. Thus these less relevant details are found in an Appendix F in *BCAA*.

B. This is confirmed by Don Carson's reference to another category of word-study errors: "14. Problems related to the Semitic background of the New Testament." While recognizing that the Septuagint has influenced the meaning of New Testament Greek words to some extent, he goes on to warn: "But it is to say that it is methodologically irresponsible to read the meaning of a Hebrew word into its Greek equivalent without further ado. The case must be argued." (D. A. Carson, *Exegetical Fallacies*, pp. 62-64) Those who read a pregnant meaning into *ginoskein* put heavy dependence upon their spin on *yada'*. (See Bertram and Bultmann in Kittel, *TDNT*, I, p. 700, text and footnotes.)

Proginoskein, prognosis

How are are the verb *proginoskein* and the noun *prognosis* used outside of the New Testament? There is no pregnant connotation of elective choice hinted at in the Septuagint, in classical Greek usage, in the Koine Greek as found in the papyrii and inscriptions, in Philo or Josephus, nor in the church fathers before Augustine.[3] The verb simply means, *"to know beforehand, foreknow"* and the noun, *"foreknowledge,"*[4] or 'prescience.'

The lexicons. Thus the determinists' only argument comes from reading this supposed pregnant meaning into the seven usages in the New Testament. Thayer's lexicon doesn't give any such meaning but does refer to Meyer, Philippi and Van Hengel as opposing it. Neither Liddell-Scott-Jones nor Abbott-Smith's lexicons hint at any such meaning. The BAG lexicon does list a secondary meaning, "choose beforehand" but give no *linguistic* support. They only refer to the two Romans usages (8:29 &11:2) and four German theological articles for support[5]. However, theology must be built upon linguistic and exegetical data, not the reverse. Support is totally lacking from the New Testament usage. Lexicographers are fallible and have their biases, so we must check out their work at every stage.[C]

Complete New Testament usage. Some writers only examine the usages where God is the subject. Thomas Edgar objects to this defective methodology, which implies that a verb changes its meaning dependent upon who the subject is.[6] Other verbs do not change meaning when God is the subject.[D]

The first question on use of these words in Acts 2:23, 1 Peter 1:1-2, 20, and in Romans 8:29-30; 11:2 is: does this well established primary meaning makes sense in these contexts also? We must not switch to some supposed pregnant secondary meaning for theological reasons. For a score of years I had bought into this theological spin on these words, but upon re-examining the evidence, I realized that the mind is a slippery thing, and that most of us can easily be persuaded of something which has little or no basis in fact. Edgar points out that none of the commentators on Romans who claim a pregnant meaning give even one example of such usage to support their claim.[7] Consider the five contexts where this word refers to God as the subject, starting with the earliest.

God's foreknown plan for the cross. On the day of Pentecost the Apostle Peter announced to Israel that the Messiah's death and resurrection

---

C   See especially my exposé of the outrageous distortions of data in *TDNT* in the word studies of repentance and conversion, found in an Appendix G in *BCAA*..

D.   All the usages of these words must be examined, and in Acts 26:5 and 2 Peter 3:17 the verb is used with exactly the same meaning as in the rest of Greek literature. In Acts 26:5 the meaning is simply to know something about a person beforehand. In 2 Peter 3:17 Peter refers to his readers' prior knowledge of the distortions of Scripture by unprincipled men. There is neither the possibility nor the claim in either of these passages that the word means anything other than its primary, well-established meaning.

were according to God's foreknown plan as prophesied by David:

> ... this *Man*, delivered up by the predetermined plan and foreknowledge of God, you nailed to a cross by the hands of godless men and put *Him* to death. And God raised Him up again, putting an end to the agony of death, since it was impossible for Him to be held in its power (Acts 2:23-4).

The Greek reads: "*Touton tē hōrismenē boulē kai prognosei tou theou ekdoton,...*" We must come to Luke's use of *prognosis* here straightforwardly, that if the primary meaning fits, we must look for no other. Peter's meaning is transparent: that our omniscient God worked out His eternal plan for the cross by means of His absolute foreknowledge of all the human factors which went into it —the motivations and situations of Judas, the Jewish leaders, Herod, Pontius Pilate, the Roman soldiers, the mob, etc.

Calvinists, such as S. M. Baugh, subvert the simplicity of Peter's statement by claiming that God's "appointed purpose" and His "foreknowledge" are essentially synonymous. He claims that the syntactical construction here is 'hendiadys' but does not quote any grammar or lexicon to support his claim: "By using one article for the two nouns *purpose* and *foreknowledge*, Peter is expressing a close interconnection between the two.... In point of fact the two nouns are expressly united."[8] However, 'hendiadys' is an obscure, controversial figure of speech, and Baugh is really stretching to make this claim. Thus, to say that the "**determinate counsel**" and the "**foreknowledge of God**" are synonymous or "united" is as wrong as saying that 'apples and oranges' means that apples are the same as oranges.

Unless we believe that God coerced Judas, the Jewish leaders, Pilate, and the other participants to do what they did, the straightforward way for God to work out His appointed purpose was to accomplish it by His foreknowledge. Thus the *prima facie* understanding of Peter's words is perfectly comprehensible as it stands. Based on a syntactical study of the Greek, the translation could be fine tuned accordingly: "**This man was handed over to you by God's appointed purpose through His foreknowledge.**"[9] The syntax of this sentence not only leads us to reaffirm the primary meaning of foreknowledge, but also supports the point that God's foreknowledge cannot be contingent upon His will (cf. pp. 23-24 & *BCAA*, pp. 159-60).

Elect according to foreknowledge. In 1 Peter 1:1-2 the noun *prognosis* is used in its primary sense, with absolutely no contextual reason to shift to a disputed secondary meaning, except for a theological bias:

> Peter, an apostle of Jesus Christ, to the elect who are sojourners of the dispersion in Pontus, Galatia, Cappadocia, Asia, and Bithynia, according to the foreknowledge of God the Father, in sanctification of the Spirit unto obedience and sprinkling of the blood of Jesus Christ: Grace to you and peace be multiplied (ASV).

Although the phrase, "**according to the foreknowledge of God the Father**" is separated in the Greek from the word **"elect"** by the geographical locations of the dispersed Christians (best represented by the ASV), most commentators take them as connected. The meaning is straightforward that Peter is writing to **"the elect according to the foreknowledge of God."**

One wonders how the meaning could be other than this simple statement, for certainly God's foreknowledge must be the basis for everything He does. God the Father does not turn off His omniscience. The meaning of 'elect' and 'election' must still be investigated, but whatever they do mean, it makes perfect sense that it is according to His foreknowledge. If we may put it bluntly, God does not close His eyes and throw darts.

There is one philosophical objection to Peter's simple statement and another attempt by some interpreters to undermine the simplicity of Peter's statement, both of which are discussed below.[E]

Those who give *proginoskein* a pregnant, elective force have another serious problem. If 'election' and 'foreknowledge' both have an elective idea, then Peter is guilty of redundance, that we are elect according to the elective choice of God. This spin insults Peter and the Holy Spirit.

God's foreknown plan for His Messiah. Peter's third reference to foreknowledge is in the same context as the previous. He echoes the language of Acts 2:23-4 in speaking first of the sacrifice of Christ and then of the resurrection, according to God's foreknown plan (1 Pet. 1:18-21):

> For **He [Christ] was foreknown** before the foundation of the world, but has appeared in these last times for the sake of you who through Him are believers in God, who raised Him from the dead and gave Him glory, so that your faith and hope are in God.

Since this passage is just a few verses away from the preceding use of the word, it is a fair to say that Peter uses the verb here with the same primary meaning as he had used it earlier and as consistently found in all Greek usage hitherto. Only if the context should *demand* another meaning may we stray from this. The context of the verse clearly indicates that the primary meaning of 'foreknowledge' makes perfect sense.

E   Many hold that God cannot know that which He has not decreed. Not only does that notion contradict Peter's simple statement, but it also makes God's omniscience a contingent attribute, subject to the activity of His decretive will. This is highly objectionable in that it denies the infiniteness of one of God's essential and necessary attributes. *God's actions always flow from His attributes, never the reverse.* Some others claim that the Greek preposition *kata* ('according to') with the accusative case can be watered down to mean "in agreement with" (Buswell, II, p 140). But the uses of *kata* with the accusative are well understood and explained in the standard lexicons and grammars. The one category which best fits the context is. "5. of the norm ... *according to, in accordance with, in conformity with, corresponding to.* a. to introduce the norm which governs something—" (BAG lexicon, p. 408). Thus God's foreknowledge can be understood as the norm or standard which governs His elective work. So the prepositional phrase, "according to the foreknowledge of God," clearly governs the verbal noun *eklektois*. This is simple, straightforward, and clear, that is, as long as we don't come to this verse with a philosophical or theological agenda (Wallace, p. 377; Chamberlain, *Exegetical Grammar*, p. 123).

The broader context is also so important. The persecuted Christians to whom Peter was writing needed to know that the salvation-hope of which they had become partakers is rooted in the plan of God, foreknown from before creation, which therefore will surely be consummated **"at the revelation of Jesus Christ"** (1 Pet. 1:7, 13), that it is a **"salvation ready to be revealed in the last time"** (v. 5), and that the prophets not only predicted the sufferings of Christ, but also **"the glories to follow"** (v. 11). In other words, the omniscient God, who knows the end from the beginning, has a foreknown plan for His Messiah, which He is working out in the cross (vv. 11, 18-19) and resurrection (vv. 3, 21), and He will keep believers by His power (vv. 4-5) until Messiah's return. Although they are suffering, their hope for the future is not in vain. Since the context is focusing upon the death and resurrection of Christ, it is unlikely that Peter is referring to any 'elective choice' of Christ.

Additionally, those who would like to see some elective choice here in Peter's usage, need to face a serious Christological problem their spin raises. If 'forechoice' is assumed to be in this verse (as the NIV erroneously renders it), a conflict arises with the concept of who Jesus Christ actually is. He was not a first-century Jewish man chosen by God from among many to be the Messiah. Indeed, as James Daane pointed out, like Isaac of old, the Lord Jesus was supernaturally brought into being to be the Elect (Choice) One of God. Isaac, the ancestor of God's first chosen people, was supernaturally prepared by a miraculous birth (Isa. 43:1, 6, 7, 20, 21). There was no pre-existing nation of Israel, which God then chose from among other nations.[F]

In a parallel way, there was no extant man named Jesus of Nazareth whom God chose to be His elect Messiah. Through the virgin birth He was supernaturally prepared to be His Elect (Choice) One. In the next chapter the implications of calling the Lord Jesus the Elect One (Lk. 9:35) will be examined. But it cannot mean that He was one extant individual chosen from among many to be the Messiah, which notion was the basis of more than one ancient heresy. Therefore, to read some elective choice into 1 Peter 1:20 is to lead to heresy about the person of Christ. Far better to simply take the word in its primary meaning. But how does Paul use the word?

Israel's failure anticipated. To understand Paul's use of *proginoskein* in Romans 11:1-3, consider the immediately preceding context:

> I ask then, Did God reject his people? By no means! I am an Israelite myself, a descendant of Abraham, from the tribe of Benjamin. God did not reject his people, whom he foreknew. Don't you know what the Scripture says in the passage about Elijah—how he appealed to God against Israel: 'Lord, they

---

F   "On the basis of the Old Testament narrative concerning Abraham and the birth of his son, and Paul's New Testament interpretation of this Old Testament narrative, it must be said that the nation of Israel is not viewed as one extant nation among many, which is then selectively chosen by God as his elect people. Rather, Israel as the object of God's election not only does not exist but even has no possibility of existence apart from God's elective and creative action" (Daane, *The Freedom of God*, p. 101).

have killed your prophets and torn down your altars; I am the only one left, and they are trying to kill me'? (Rom. 11:1-3)

This is a major context in which Calvinists see a pregnant meaning in *proginoskein*, and a few modern translations (not the NIV or the NAS) have translated it that way. Although it is true in a sense that God chose Israel, *the urgent question is whether this is the point that Paul is making here.* The context shows that it is not!

In the broader context of Paul's argument of Romans 9–11, we see that although God sovereignly chose the nation Israel, He also acted justly and righteously in setting Israel aside temporarily because of their unbelief in the Messiah (9:6-29). They missed the way of faith, and now God is turning to the Gentiles as well with a universal message (9:30–10:15). In 10:16-21 Paul makes the point very forcefully that both Moses and the prophets had said that Israel had God's word, rejected it, and would be set aside in favor of another people. First Paul quoted Isaiah's prediction (Isa. 53:1) that Israel would not believe the Messiah. Then he quoted Moses' prediction that God would make Israel **"jealous by that which is not a nation"** (Deut. 32:21). Finally in 10:21 he quoted Isaiah's prediction: **"'I was found by those who sought me not, I became manifest to those who did not ask for me,' but as for Israel he says, 'All the day long I have stretched out my hands to a disobedient and obstinate people'"** (Isa. 65:1-2).

So not only did God foreknow that Israel would fail and be supplanted by other people in His plan, but He had Moses (the Law) and Isaiah (the Prophets) explicitly predict this. So when we cross that artificial divider into Chapter 11 and find Paul stating that God foreknew Israel, *we cannot depart from the primary meaning of the word without doing violence to the preceding context.* Many interpreters have totally missed this.

Someone may respond that Paul did not say that God foreknew something about Israel, but that He foreknew Israel. However, in connection with Romans 8:29, Tom Edgar has pointed to the parallel syntax of Acts 26:5, where Paul testified to Festus and Agrippa: **"So then, all Jews know my manner of life from my youth up, which from the beginning was spent among my *own* nation and at Jerusalem; <u>since they have known about me</u> for a long time previously, if they are willing to testify, that I lived *as* a Pharisee according to the strictest sect of our religion."**

> The most significant thing is the syntax. The object of the verb *proginosko*, "foreknow," is the personal pronoun, "me," *me*. Paul says, "they knew *me* before from the beginning." The passage is clear. The Apostle Paul says very specifically, "foreknowing me ... that I lived according to the strictest sect of our religion, a Pharisee." Thus, *to foreknow a person* means to *know something about that person beforehand....* Often, Greek verbs take an object where some prepositional idea such as, "about, or something about," seems to be "built into" the Greek term but must be supplied in English.[10]

Thus in Romans 11:2 the Greek idiom signifies that God knew something about Israel beforehand. No unforeseen event disrupted God's plan!

Then Paul raised the question as to the permanence and totality of that setting aside and goes on to argue that it is not total (Rom. 11:4-10) and it is not final (11:11-32). If *proginoskein* is taken in its primary sense, Paul's argument makes perfect sense in the flow of his thought. God knew ahead of time and predicted that Israel would fail to fulfill His purpose for them, indeed, that they would reject their Messiah and be replaced by another people. But this has not upset His plan and purposes in the least or nullified the word of God (9:6) since He foreknew all along what would transpire. He foreknew that after the rejection of the Lord Jesus there would be a remnant of true Jewish believers (Rom. 11:4-10) and that Gentile wild branches would be grafted into the root of Abraham (11:11-24). He foreknew and had His prophets predict an end-time restoration of Israel (11:23-32). In the meantime, God's main thrust is to save Gentiles through the church and the ministry of apostolic missionaries to the Gentiles like Paul's team (11:11-24). Since God foreknew the whole future of Israel when He chose them, the word of God has not failed (9:6). Thus, the primary meaning makes perfect sense in the context. This is not to deny that God chose Israel in a sense, but this is not the point in Romans 11:2.

A Word Study of *Proorizein*

No predestination in the Bible. Through the influence of the Latin Vulgate translation, *proorizein* has been translated mainly as "to predestinate." However, this is a very rare Greek word, and there is a serious question as to how it should actually be translated. It never occurred in the Septuagint Greek Old Testament. It is found only once in the classical Greek literature before the New Testament (Demosthenes) and a few times in secular Greek from the third to the fifth centuries AD. From an examination of its six occurrences in four contexts in the New Testament and the meaning of its cognates *horizein* and *aphorizein*, as well as these rare secular usages, a meaning like 'to preappoint' emerges. *Since the idea of "destiny" is not at all present in this group of words, the translation "to predestinate" is totally erroneous.* Perhaps Jerome was influenced by Augustine's theology in his Vulgate translation. Albeit, a clean break from a clearly erroneous translational tradition is needed. Erasmus, the Catholic humanist scholar, said that the "Vulgate swarmed with errors."[11]

Procedure. A serious methodological problem arises in determining the meaning of this word because of its rarity. Although the "root fallacy" that Carson warns about must be avoided, he points out that in the case of rare words, there is no other alternative but to check out the root and other related words.[12] It is astonishing that there is so very little serious investigation of *proorizein* in the literature. Amazingly, Schmidt in *TDNT* does not even give the secular Greek references, but simply refers to "this comparatively late and rare word."[13] We must do what Schmidt has failed to do, examine those references.

Secular usage. First, the one pre-Christian classical usage in Demosthenes (IV BC; 31, 4) must be examined. This is in the context of a court case in which Demosthenes was trying to recover an inherited house from Onetor, who had defrauded him. In court he stated: "To prove that these statements of mine are true, that he [Onetor] even now declares that the land is mortgaged for a talent, but that he laid claim to two thousand drachmae more on the house,..." The word translated "laid claim" is *prosōrisato*.[14] When I first observed this, I wondered, "what in the world has this got to do with predestination?" Later it occurred to me that it is wonderful to know that God has laid claim to us. But this hardly relates to predestination. Classical scholar Arthur Way took note of Demosthenes' usage in his paraphrased translation of Romans 8:29: "**Long ere this He knew our hearts, long ere this He claimed us (as a man claims property by setting his landmarks thereon) as those whom He should mould into the very likeness of His own Son,...**"[15] The noun *proorismos* was used by Hippocrates of the early determination of a disease (Hp praec. 3). In a romance novel of Egypt by Heliodorus in the third century AD, there is a reference to appointing the day of a wedding beforehand (7, 24, 4).

Cognates. It is most instructive to examine the root word *horizein* in the secular, the Septuagint, and the eight occurrences in the New Testament. According to *TDNT* it "means 'to limit,' 'to set the limit,' and then fig. 'to fix,' 'to appoint'." Five of the usages refer to Christ: Luke 22:22; Acts 2:23; 10:42; 17:31; and Romans 1:4. In each of Luke's usages Christ was **appointed** by the Father to a ministry, either of the cross or as judge. In Romans 1:4 Christ was "**designated the son of God with power by the resurrection**." The compound *aphorizein,* used 10 times in the New Testament, means 'to separate,' and is frequently used of God separating, marking off, or appointing someone for His service (Rom. 1:1; Gal. 1:15; Acts 13:2). Schmidt confirms: "In connection with what was said about *horizō*, it seems that at the heart of the NT we find the principle of God separating, i.e., marking off for His service."[16]

New Testament usage. Thus, moving on to consider the possible impact of these meanings upon the usage of *proorizein* in the New Testament, consider that in Acts 4:28 the main idea is that God's power and counsel had *previously appointed* the crucifixion to happen. In 1 Corinthians 2:7 Paul refers to the wisdom of God in the gospel of the cross, which although previously hidden and now revealed *was previously appointed* for the Church's glory. In Romans 8:29-30 the main idea is that God has *previously appointed* those who love God "**to be conformed to the image of His Son.**" In Ephesians 1:5 a very similar meaning emerges that God has *previously appointed* His elect Church "**to adoption as sons.**" In Ephesians 1:11 it is seen that the Church has been *previously appointed* to obtain the inheritance which God has planned for it. Thus, in all four contexts the meaning harmonious with the root meaning "previously appointed" makes perfect sense. This also fits with the extrabiblical usage. But as mentioned earlier, the idea of destiny is not found in *horizein, aphorizein,* or in the limited secular use of *proorizein,* and therefore *should not be imposed upon the six New Testament usages.*

The church fathers. Lampe has given over thirty references to *proorizein, proorisis, proorismenos, proorismos, prooristikos* from the early church fathers. None of them gives any indication of "predestination" as a likely meaning. All simply can be understood of 'preappointment.'[17]

Lexicons. Since this exhausts the primary sources, the secondary ones should be checked. John Parkhurst's 16th century lexicon does not list 'predestinate' among the meanings: "II. To decree or ordain before-hand, to fore-ordain, fore-appoint."[18] A century ago, Thayer, although noting the Vulgate rendering, did not list 'predestinate' among the meanings in English: "*to predetermine, decide beforehand,* Vulg. [exc. In Acts] *praedestino,... to foreordain, appoint beforehand,* Ro. viii.29 sq.; *tina eis ti,* one to obtain a thing. Eph. i.5..." Similarly, Abbott-Smith did not include 'predestinate' among the meanings. Only the BAG lexicon, after referencing the limited secular usage, lists "*decide upon beforehand, predestine* of God" among the meanings. They give the biblical references and seem not to have investigated the usage of the church fathers, other than Ignatius.[19] The references given above suggest that "preappoint" is a more appropriate meaning of the word.

Modern translations. It is significant that a number of other modern translations besides Arthur Way have abandoned "predestinate," in breaking free from the rut of the Vulgate. Reference Romans 8:29 in the New English Bible: **"For God knew His own before ever they were, and also ordained that they should be shaped in the likeness of His Son, ..."** Charles B. Williams has "**marked off as His own,**" J. B. Rotherham "**fore-appointed,**" A. T. Robertson has "**pre-appointed,**" William F. Beck has "**appointed long ago,**" and the New Berkeley Version, "**appointed beforehand.**" The English Revised Version (1886), American Standard Version (1901), James Denney, Alfred Marshall, and F. F. Bruce all have "**foreordained,**" not significantly different from 'preappointed.' Ordained has to do with God's order and appointment to service, as does the use of *horizein* in reference to Christ's ministry, where appointment is a more appropriate rendering.

Thus, generation after generation of translators should have recognized the extreme theological significance of this word and researched back before the Latin Vulgate to its primary usage. Apparently only the above translators really did their homework on this. The others were in a translational rut or else were so biased theologically that they were not open to other possibilities. This has done great damage to the truth.

Implications. Some might feel that we are making too fine a point of all of this. Does it matter whether the Bible speaks of being 'predestined to salvation or condemnation' or whether it speaks of being 'preappointed to the image of Christ and His service?' The difference has vast theological and personal significance. The word 'predestination' carries with it strong overtones of Augustine's notion of unconditional election. Albeit, Calvinists and Arminians alike can agree that God has preappointed believers to be conformed to the image of His Son and to His service.

A glorious future for His children

> But we know that for those who love Him, for those called in agreement with His purpose, God makes all things work together for good. Because those whom He knew beforehand He appointed beforehand to share the likeness of His Son, so that He might be the First-born among many brothers (Rom. 8:28-29, NBV).[20]

The translation quoted, done by predominantly Calvinistic translators, fairly represents the original of both *proginoskein* and *proorizein*. Here we need to see how the context impacts any possible pregnant meaning of *proginoskein* other than the primary one, 'to foreknow.'

The broader context of Romans. The key verse of Romans is widely recognized to be 1:17: **"For in the gospel a righteousness from God is revealed, a righteousness that is by faith from first to last, just as it is written: 'The righteous will live by faith'"** (NIV). Paul then goes on to show how God makes that righteousness available to mankind, which totally lacks it (1:18–3:20), through justification by faith alone (3:21–5:21) and sanctification by faith (6:1–8:39). That it is all **"by faith from first to last"** is attested by the fact that the words 'faith' and 'to believe' occur a total of 60 times and 'disbelieve' 9 times in this book, punctuating Paul's major arguments.

Since Martin Luther recovered the glorious truth of the fourth link in Paul's five-link sequence, which is justification by faith alone, evangelical Christians have sought to emphasize the cruciality of faith in God's whole plan of salvation. This is seen in the rest of Paul's sequence in Romans 8:30 (ASV): **"... and whom he foreordained, them he also called: and whom he called, them he also justified: and whom he justified, them he also glorified."** Certainly the calling to salvation is by repentant faith. The final glorification also has to be by faith. Is it possible that faith can be left out of the foreknowledge which is the "first" of the process? It is unthinkable that God in His foreordination (better, 'preappointment') turns off His omniscient foreknowledge.

In order to get the full flow of Paul's thinking here, go back ten verses: **"For I consider that the sufferings of this present time are not worthy to be compared with the glory that is to be revealed to us"** (Rom. 8:18). In the rest of this chapter, Paul moves on to focus upon the certainty of the future glory of God's children, which he first mentioned in 8:17-18. In Romans 9–11, he even raises the question of the future for Israel, even though for a while Israel has failed and been set aside. It is with this future focus in mind that Paul speaks of the goal of our glorification in 8:30 and the four stages which precede it. *This future focus must be kept in mind as this sequence of five steps in God's plan of salvation is interpreted.*

It is so striking, that theologians have developed an *ordo salutis* (plan of salvation) from these verses.[21] It all starts with God's foreknowing His people, who are identified as those who love God. Next in the sequence is foreordination, or more precisely preappointment (*proorizein*), then calling, then justification, and lastly, glorification. There is some discussion as to whether the sequence is logical or chronological, or both. Probably it is both. In any case, it must start with foreknowledge before and distinct from *proorizein*, just as *proorizein* must precede and be distinct from 'calling', and calling distinct from justification, and justification distinct from glorification, which logically and chronologically comes last.

Thus, any definition of *proginoskein* (foreknowledge) which would make it in any way synonymous with *proorizein* (preappointment) would absolutely destroy the logic of Paul's (and the Spirit's) sequence. This would reduce it to a mere redundancy and totally undo the symmetry of the development. This is the final refutation of any pregnant connotation for *proginoskein.*

Note also that there is nothing in the context which would say anything about any unconditional decrees in eternity past as to who will be saved and who will be consigned to hell. Paul is starting with God's foreknowledge of us and stating that God has preappointed us to be conformed to the image of His Son, which is glorification. God does work all things together for good for those who love Him since our future is certain and glorious. God is for us, and nothing can separate us from His love in Christ. The focus is not on any presumed past 'predestination,' but on the certainty of a glorious future. So the Calvinists are half right on this one. Right about eternal security, but wrong on unconditional election.

Calvinistic response. One way Calvinists have dealt with this self-evident contradiction in their system is to ignore it, as seen in John Murray, who very subtly *omits any reference to foreknowledge* in his discussion:

> It is not by any means likely that Paul in Rom 8:28-30, in setting forth the outlines of the order followed in the application of redemption, would begin that enumeration with an act of God which is other than the first in order. In other words, it is altogether likely that he would begin with the first, just as he ends with the last. This argument is strengthened by the consideration that he traces salvation to its ultimate source in the election of God. Surely he traces the application of redemption to its beginning when he says, "whom he did predestinate them he also called."[22]

We presume that this very serious omission of the actual first term (fore-knowledge) was not intentional dishonesty on Murray's part, but resulted from his assumption that the two terms are synonymous. However, in giving him the benefit of the doubt, note that *this is nevertheless a very serious mishandling of God's word*, whether intentional or not!

In Romans 8:29 it is probable that God's foreknowledge of something about "those who love God" is "built into" the Greek, although not obvious in English. *But it is the context, not just in these verses, but the context of the whole book, which strongly suggests that faith is that which God foreknows about His people.* Since the subject of Romans is "**a righteousness that is by faith from first to last**" and since 'faith' and 'believing' occur sixty times in Romans, it becomes clear the repentant faith is that which God foresees as the basis of the pre-appointment of His saints. He foreknows *our faith*, pre-appoints *those who believe*, calls us *by faith*, justifies us *by faith*, and glorifies us *by faith.* It is a faith process "**from first to last.**" God does not close His eyes and throw darts.

Conclusions

Now the results of these two major word studies and the interpretation of Romans 8 must be pulled together . There is absolutely no linguistic basis for seeing an elective meaning in God's foreknowledge. The secular usage, the Septuagint, and the early church fathers contain no hint of this imagined pregnant meaning. The seven usages in the New Testament, examined carefully in context, cannot be forced into supporting it either. The claims all come from theologians. *Not one unambiguous, incontestable linguistic example can be given for an elective connotation.*

It also seems that very few translators and linguists, and virtually no theologians, have bothered to dig more deeply into the meaning of *proorizein*. The rare secular Greek usage raises overwhelming doubt about the traditional rendering 'to predestinate.' Since the verb from which it is derived, *horizein*, is used of being appointed to service or responsibility, a good case can be made for the rendering of *proorizein* as 'preappointment.' This meaning makes better sense in the four New Testament contexts in which it is used and is confirmed by the early church fathers' usage of the word. Although the older lexicons do not even mention 'to predestinate' as a meaning, some of the more recent lexicons and theological works, having been influenced by deductive theological considerations, do list that meaning. Although a majority of the translations have blindly followed the Vulgate rendering, a dozen translators and Greek commentators have broken away from this translational rut. *Thus the word 'predestinate' should have never gotten into any Bible translation.* The consequence of this is clear since the word 'predestinate' itself carries strong overtones of unconditional election.

Therefore, there is absolutely no basis for denying the clearly conditional force of both 1 Peter 1:1-2 and Romans 8:28-30, conditioned on what God foreknew about His saints, especially their faith. It is absolutely irresponsible to build the doctrine of absolute predestination upon the dubious rendering of such a rare Greek word!

1. Berkhof, *Systematic Theology*, p. 111-2.

2 Thomas Edgar, "The Meaning of *PROORIZO*," a paper given at the ETS, March 30, 2001 at Langhorne, PA

3 Bultmann in *TDNT*, I, pp. 715-6; also Liddell, Scott, and Jones, *Lexicon*, 9th ed , p 1473, Moulton and Milligan, *Vocabulary*, p. 538; and G W H Lampe, *A Patristic Greek Lexicon* (Oxford, 1961), p. 1141. I have personally checked the LXX and Josephus usages

4 G Abbott-Smith, *Lexicon*, p 379.

5. Thayer, p. 538; Abbott-Smith, p 379, Arndt and Gingrich, p 710.

6 Edgar C. James, "Foreknowledge and Foreordination," in *Bibliotheca Sacra* (July 1965), p. 217, S M Baugh, "The Meaning of Foreknowledge," in *Still Sovereign*, eds Thomas R Schreiner and Bruce Ware, pp. 183-200, Douglas Moo, *Romans*, p 522 Refutation in Thomas R. Edgar, *op. cit.*

7 Thomas R Edgar, p. 1 He refers to commentaries by Dunn, Fitzmeyer, Moo, Morris, Murray, and Schreiner.

8 S M Baugh, "The Meaning of Foreknowledge," in Schreiner & Ware, *Grace of God, Bondage of the Will*, I, p 190

9 There is extensive discussion of the syntax of 'hendiadys' in my *Beyond Calvinism*, pp 159-160.

10 Edgar, p. 3

11. Erasmus, *The Praise of Folly*, cited by Hunt, p. 171.

12 Carson, pp 31-32.

13 K L Schmidt in Kittel, *TDNT*, V, pp. 452-56

14 Demosthenes, 31,4, *Against Onetor*; This is, of course, the classical Greek form of the word..

15 Arthur Way, *The Letters of St Paul* (London. Macmillan, 1926), p 129

16 Schmidt, p 452-5.

17 G W H Lampe, p 1161.

18. John Parkhurst, *A Greek and English Lexicon of the New Testament*, new edition by Hugh James Rose (London many publishers, 1829), pp 727-28

19 Thayer, p 541, Abbott-Smith, p 382; Arndt and Gingrich, p. 716

20 Gerrit Verkuyl, ed , *The Modern Language Bible: The New Berkeley Version* (rev. 1969). Of 20 scholars on the revision committee only 2 or 3 are not identifiably of Calvinistic tradition

21 L Berkhof, *Systematic Theology*, pp. 415-17

22 John Murray, *Redemption Accomplished and Applied* (GR· Eerdmans, 1955), p 94

What predestination means, in its most
elementary form, is that our final destination,
heaven or hell, is decided by God, not only before
we get there, but before we are even born.
                                    –R. C. Sproul

You will be saved or damned _for_ all eternity
because you were saved or damned _from_ all
eternity.
–George Bryson's characterization of Calvinism

WHO ARE GOD'S CHOICE PEOPLE?

Having carefully examined the meanings of foreknowledge and foreordination, the biblical teaching on election must now be investigated. In order to get an accurate picture, it is essential to trace the concept of election through the Old Testament and, since our current translations are deficient, do an in-depth word study of the three Greek words for election (*eklegomai, eklektos, eklogē*) in the New. These word studies may seem tedious but are essential. Only then can the key passages about election be rightly understood (Lk. 9:35; Mt. 22:14; 1 Pet. 1:1-2; 2 Pet. 1:10-11, and Eph. 1:3-14).

Old Testament Election

The patriarchs. The biblical concept of election begins with the calling of Abram, the progenitor of God's ancient 'chosen people,' into the promised land. The details of his conversion from an idolatrous background in Ur of the Chaldees to faith in the true God have not been revealed. It is clear that God called him to settle in the less-populated land of Canaan to begin a separated nation dedicated to the service of the true God. As Abram matured in his faith, God made wonderful promises to him (Gen. 12:1-3) and then sealed them with a covenant of blessing (Gen. 15). This covenant was reiterated and expanded on a number of occasions, culminating in the promise of his ultimate descendant, the Messiah (Gen. 22:16-18).

Abram was not the only believer of his time, but rather was chosen from among other believers to begin a whole new program of God. His nephew, Lot, is identified as a believer, as was Melchizedek, who is described as being greater than Abram (Heb. 7). Job was a believer probably in the same general time frame. So there is nothing in Scripture which even implies that

God's choice of Abram and his descendants was unto his salvation, but rather unto the service of God.[1] . Although Isaac, his legitimate son, was to be the heir and bearer of the promise, there is no hint that Isaac was chosen to salvation and Ishmael reprobated to Hell. Indeed, God promised Hagar that Ishmael would be blessed (Gen. 16:10-12; 21:17-20). If Ishmael was reprobated, then God lied!

When God told Rebekah that there were two nations in her womb, and that the Edomites would serve the Israelites (Gen. 25:23), it is remarkable how this prophecy was fulfilled by Jacob's cunning and deceit. Although Esau is later characterized as a profane man, this was not by God's choice, even though determinists* misinterpret Romans 9 to imply that. God's choice had to do with the *nations* coming from Rebekah's womb and did not determine the personal salvation of the twins. Indeed, it is transparent that physical descent from Isaac did not guarantee salvation for anyone. This is not only clear in the Old Testament narrative, but also in Paul's later explanations in Romans 2 and 9 through 11. In the next chapter a careful examination of Romans 9 will be made, considering the Old Testament texts which Paul quotes. From this it becomes clear that Paul is not at all referring to an unconditional election of individuals to salvation, but of His dealings with the nation Israel corporately.

The point is that Israel was to be a witness to the one true God in an idolatrous, polytheistic world. Even when they failed God, they were to be a "crucible nation,"(Deut. 4:20).[2] Both the blessings for obedience and the judgments for disobedience were to be a testimony for the truth of God. Abraham, Isaac, and Jacob's witness was relatively feeble, but Joseph's was outstanding. When God brought Israel out of Egypt under Moses, that witness was exceedingly powerful, as was attested to by the many Psalms which refer to it. David, Solomon, Jonah, Daniel, and many others continued that witness in diverse circumstances. *So Israel was made God's elect or chosen nation, but that choice was not automatically to salvation.*

The superlative servant of God. The servanthood of Israel comes into particular focus in the latter part of Isaiah's prophecy (Isa. 41:8-9). However, in that context Isaiah sees the ultimate fulfillment of Israel's ministry in the Messiah, Yahweh's Servant (Isa. 42:1-7): **"Behold, My Servant, whom I uphold; my chosen one in whom My soul delights. I have put My Spirit upon Him; He will bring forth justice to the nations.... and I will appoint you as a covenant to the people, as a light to the nations, to open blind eyes,..."** (42:1, 6b-7a). The Hebrew noun used here is *bāchir*, 'elect,' which is derived from the common verb *bāchar* ('to choose, elect, decide for'). Schrenk in *TDNT* explains,"It is important to note, however, that it always involves a careful, well thought-out choice.... In all of these cases serviceability rather than simple arbitrariness is at the heart of the choosing." The derived noun *bāchûr*, sometimes refers to young men, "in that the picked or chosen men in a military context are usually the young men." The derived adjective *mibhār* means 'chosen,' or 'choice': "As such it is often translated as a superlative."[3] The Septuagint Greek translation of the Hebrew has the same meaning and emphasis on 'choiceness.' It is clear that the translators should have referred to Christ as the "choice One" in harmony with its frequent usage in the Hebrew. *This is the key to understanding election in the New Testament.*

A Word Study of Election

It is surprising that the meaning, 'the choice of the excellent,' found in the Hebrew and the Greek of the Septuagint, is not adequately carried over into our New Testament translations, especially since this idea is predominant in secular Greek as well.

Pre-New Testament usage. The verb *eklegomai* has a basic meaning in the middle voice, "to choose something for oneself," "to make one's choice." The secular and Septuagint Greek predominantly shows a derived meaning of the selection of the best or the choice, such as "the most beautiful of what is to be praised" or "something good from literary treasures," "that which is choice or excellent," "what is desired, or costly," "what is costly in the concept of the pure," "emphasizes the choice or excellent element...." The adjective *eklektos* means 'chosen,' or 'select.' In the secular and Septuagint Greek the predominant meaning is 'choice' or 'selected,' "choice, select, costly, sterling, purified, profitable, best of its kind, of top quality." This meaning is also clearly seen in Romans 16:13 and 1 Peter 2:4, 6. The meaning of the noun *eklogē* in secular Greek is predominantly 'selection', also having a qualitative meaning, and in Jewish writings, human free choice.[4] *Thus, the New Testament meaning must be based upon the predominant usage in both secular and Septuagintal Greek.*

New Testament Usage

In the New Testament, the verb *eklegomai* ('to choose') is used 21 times, three of which refer to human choice, most to God's choice of Israel, Christ's choice of the twelve Apostles, the end-time elect, God's choice by principle of the poor and weak (1 Cor. 1), and two theologically significant references (Lk. 9:35; Eph. 1:4).

The adjective *eklektos* ('chosen,' 'choice,' 'elect') is found 22 times, nine of which are in end-time contexts of tribulation saints. It is used in Christ's aphorism in the parable of the king's wedding feast (Mt. 22:1-14), the words of Israel's rulers as Christ hangs on the cross (Lk. 23:35), Peter's references to Christians (1 Pet. 1:1-2 & 2 Pet. 1:10), his reference to Christ, the 'choice' One of God (1 Pet. 2:4, 6), to the church as the 'elect' of God (1 Pet. 2:9); and the references in 2 John 1, 13, probably to churches. In addition to Paul's reference to elect angels (1 Tim. 5:21) and "**Rufus, the choice man in the Lord**" (Rom. 16:13), he surprisingly used it theologically only four times (Rom. 8:33; Col. 3:12; 2 Tim. 2:10; and Tit. 1:1), all plural. *There is never any reference to a singular 'elect' individual.*

Of the seven usages of the abstract noun *eklogē* ('election'), four are Paul's references to Israel (in Rom. 9-11), and only one to Christians (1 Thess. 1:4). God told Ananias that Saul of Tarsus was His 'chosen' instrument for witness to Gentiles (Acts 9:15). Peter's only use refers to the assurance of the believer's election (2 Peter 1:10).

Christ, the Choice One. Of the three references to Christ as the elect of God, the starting point is the Father's affirmation on the Mount of Transfiguration (Lk. 9:35): **"This is my Son, My Chosen One (ho eklelegmenos); listen to Him!"** This language identifies Him with God's Elect Servant in Isaiah 42:1-7. The parallel with **"beloved Son"** in the other Gospels (Mt. 17:5=Mk. 9:7) makes it clear that this means '**Choice One,**' since they quote it as: **"This is My beloved Son, with whom I am well pleased; listen to Him!"** *Thus 'beloved' and 'choice' are equivalent.* Luke shows how His being the Choice Messiah was the heart of the issue with the Jewish rulers throughout His ministry, reaching its acme as they mocked Him as He hung on the cross: **"And even the rulers were sneering at Him, saying, 'He saved other; let Him save Himself if this is the Christ of God, His Chosen One [His Choice One]"** (Lk. 23:35).

Peter explicitly confirms this understanding in his usage in 1 Peter 2:4, 6: **"And coming to Him as to a living stone, rejected by men, but choice and precious in the sight of God.... 'Behold I lay in Zion a choice stone, a precious corner *stone.*'"** In 1 Peter 1:20, there is no way that Jesus of Nazareth is to be considered as chosen by God from among other Jews to be the Messiah. Clearly, the connotation of 'choice' or 'select,' seen in the secular and Septuagint usage, *is absolutely demanded* in both of these contexts, which is confirmed by the close connection with '**precious.**' The Lord Jesus was in no way chosen by God; He is the '**Choice One.**' The notion that Jesus of Nazareth was chosen to be the Messiah at His baptism is the heart of two ancient heresies, the Cerinthian form of Gnosticism and the Ebionite heresy. As James Daane pointed out, like the nation Israel, He was formed by a miraculous birth:

> God's election must produce what it elects. And it does. Isaac is a son of miracle.... the nation of Israel is not viewed as one extant nation among many, which is then selectively chosen by God as his elect people. Rather, Israel as the object of God's election not only does not exist but even has no possibility of existence apart from God's elective and creative action.[5]

In the similar way, through the virgin birth, Jesus of Nazareth was uniquely brought into being to be the '**choice One**' of God. Thus the pre-New Testament usage of these words is not only helpful, but *mandatory* to understand the real meaning of election.

Christ's decisive parable and aphorism. In examining the few doctrinally significant passages, the parable of the king's wedding feast in **Matthew 22:1-14** is basic. (Because of length of this passage, the reader should open the Bible here.) Note in 22:3 that those who were first invited to the wedding feast **"were unwilling to come."** They even mistreated and killed the messenger slaves (22:6). The king emphasized that those invited "**were not worthy**" (22:8) and sent judgment upon them. Then he had his slaves invite people from the highways indiscriminately, "**both evil and good**" (22:9-10). Even though wedding garments were surely provided for the guests, when a guest was found without them, he was ejected into outer darkness (22:11-13). At that point the Lord Jesus gave this enigmatic aphorism: "**For many are called, but few chosen**" (22:14). If Christ were speaking in here about unconditional election, there would be *a radical disconnect with the parable* to which this aphorism is attached. Some interpreters recognize this and see this as a "non-technical use" of *eklektoi*. Whatever way some may try to dismiss the relevance of the parable and aphorism to this issue, *it is obligatory to interpret the aphorism in harmony with the parable.* Otherwise, the logical acumen of our Lord Jesus is insulted.

For fifty years I struggled with the obvious contradiction the standard translations raise. But the secular and Septuagintal usage of this word and usage in Luke 9:35, 1 Peter 2:4, 6, and Romans 16:13 give an easy solution to an extremely serious interpretive problem. *It must be translated*: "**Many are invited, but few are choice.**" This now make sense, since those who did not respond to Christ's invitation are described as "**unwilling to come**" and "**not worthy.**" This is not attributed to God's choice! On the other hand, those who ended up in the feast were not chosen either; they had merely responded to the open invitation.

Some think that this makes salvation a matter of human merit. The answer is clearly found in the fact that in salvation it is God who makes the believer "choice" by His grace. This is the point of the provision of wedding garments for the guests, who would have had no opportunity to get them on their own. Justification by faith involves God's provision of the wedding garments. This symbolism was anticipated in Isaiah 61:10: "**I will rejoice greatly in the LORD, my soul will exult in my God; for He has clothed me with garments of salvation, He has wrapped me with a robe of righteousness, as a bridegroom decks himself with a garland, and as a bride adorns herself with her jewels.**" Believers are elsewhere called "saints," without undermining the gracious character of salvation, since this is positional truth. *Being 'choice' is also positional truth.*

The broader context of this parable and its aphorism confirms the appropriateness of this translation. It is one of a group of parables Christ gave after His triumphal entry, in all of which He declared His rejection by His own 'choice people,' Israel. In accusing God's choice nation of being unwilling to accept the invitation He had been extending to them for over three years, He made it clear that the invitation is going out to all, whom the king will then qualify to be His select guests, although their previous condition was both "**evil and good.**" Thus, in effect He set in contrast God's ancient choice nation and the new "choice people" to whom the kingdom of God would be given. This idea was explicitly declared in the previous context: "**Therefore I say to you, the kingdom of God will be taken away from you, and be given to a nation producing the fruit of it**" (Mt. 21:43). There is strong irony in Christ's aphorism: the choice nation is being set aside and indiscriminate invitees ("**evil and good**") become choice by God's gracious plan.

The chosen Apostles. The Gospel writers also used the verb *eklegomai* a number of times in reference to the Lord's choice of His twelve Apostles, which, of course, included Judas Iscariot (Lk. 6:13; Jn. 6:70; 13:18; 15:16, 19). None of these says anything about a doctrine of election to salvation, since the Eleven were already saved before He chose them as Apostles, and Judas was clearly a counterfeit. The Lord even referred to this fact in John 6:70. It is outrageous, therefore, that some Calvinists use John 15:16 as a proof-text for the notion of unconditional election: "**You did not choose Me, but I chose you, and appointed you, that you should go and bear fruit, and that your fruit should remain,...**" To extrapolate the address and meaning of this verse to all believers in a doctrinal way is seriously misguided and irresponsible, even though *by application* we can affirm that all believers have been appointed to bear abiding fruit, which is not automatic.

Peter's simple explanation. Now the simple statement of Peter, that philosophically naïve fisherman, must be examined again: that believers are "**...elect (*eklektoi*) according to the foreknowledge of God the Father, by the sanctifying work of the Spirit, that you may obey Jesus Christ and be sprinkled with His blood:**" (1 Pet. 1:1-2). From the predominant usage of *eklektoi* in secular and Septuagintal Greek, it has become clear that Peter is addressing the Christians as 'choice ones,' just as Paul addressed Christians in his letters as '**saints.**' Peter's explanation that this was accomplished by the "**sanctifying work of the Spirit**" confirms that this happens when sinners are saved by putting faith in Christ, not in past eternity. What God foreknew in eternity is now being implemented by the Holy Spirit.

Thus, reading a pregnant determinative meaning into *prognosis* (foreknowledge) contradicts Peter's simple explanation that our becoming God's choice ones is by the sanctifying work of the Spirit. It is implemented by the preaching of the gospel and the "**sanctifying work of the Spirit.**" This is clarified by the root idea of sanctify as 'to separate, to set apart.'

It is significant that after Peter referred to Christ as the "**choice stone**" (1 Pet. 2:4, 6), he went on to refer to the Church as "**an elect [choice] race, a royal priesthood, a holy nation, a people for *God's* own possession, that you may show forth the excellencies of him who called you out of darkness into his marvelous light: who in time past were no people, but now are the people of God:**" (2:9 ASV). Peter borrowed language used of Israel to refer to the Church, thus indicating that the Church's election, like Israel's, was corporate. *Peter indicated in 1 Peter 1:1-2 that election is conditional and in 2:4-9 that it is corporate.*

Peter's single use of the abstract noun 'election' (*eklogē)* is very supportive of this understanding: "**Therefore, my brothers, be all the more eager to make your calling and election [choice] sure. For if you do these things, you will never fall, and you will receive a rich welcome into the eternal kingdom of our Lord and Savior Jesus Christ**" (2 Pet. 1:10-11, NIV). Here the issue is quite simple: if individual election is unconditional, how can anything which those professing believers do change that eternal reality? Unconditional election means that there is *no condition* which any person can meet in order to become or remain elect. But clearly Peter, thinking of careless professing believers, affirms that they must be **"diligent"** (NAS) to make it sure. This exhortation is in contradiction to the notion of unconditional election foisted upon the church by Augustine.

Paul's usage. Paul's use of the noun *eklogē* (election) is more complex. He used it four times in the Romans 9-11 discussion of Israel's election. The first usage is: "**... knowing, brethren beloved by God, *His* choice of you; for our gospel did not come to you in word only, but also in power and in the Holy Spirit and with full conviction;**" (1 Thess. 1:4). The point is simple: if this is a reference to individual election, how could Paul know that of every individual in the Thessalonian church? He spoke of the manifest work of God in their corporate conversion, not only, as in Acts, that in just a month or so some Jews and many Gentiles were converted before his untimely departure, but also the radical change in their lifestyle (1:3, 6-10). Since the New Testament consistently warns of counterfeit believers in every church, Paul could not have known this about every individual in the church there. But Paul is convinced that there is an *elect company of believers* in Thessalonica. There is no basis for going beyond this, because there is nothing in the context which indicates individual election. He saw that they had met the condition of repentant faith and had come into **"much full assurance"** (*plērophoria pollē*) by the powerful working of the Spirit. They became God's choice people by the work of the Spirit in conviction, regeneration, and sanctification, not by an eternal decree.

Paul uses the verb *eklegomai* in speaking about the principles of God's chosen plan, contrary to the things the world values (1 Cor. 1:26-29):

> **For consider your calling, brethren, that there were not many wise according to the flesh, not many mighty, not many noble; but God has <u>chosen</u> the foolish things of the world to shame the wise, and God has <u>chosen</u> the weak things of the world to shame the things which are strong, and the base things of the world and the despised, God has <u>chosen</u>, the things that are not, that He might nullify the things that are, that no man should boast before God.**

This context is perfectly understandable in terms of the general principles which operate in the way people respond to God's calling through the gospel. The Lord Jesus explained this principle after dealing with the rich young ruler: **"Truly I say to you, it is hard for a rich man to enter the kingdom of heaven"** (Mt. 19:23). It is not the world's intellectuals, power brokers, millionaires, and 'beautiful people' who are responding in significant numbers to the gospel. This is human nature and hardly based upon some mysterious unconditional election. Indeed, Paul tells how the open secret of God's wisdom has now been revealed through the Apostles (1 Cor. 2:6-7). Thus, it is astonishing that J. I. Packer stated that this passage is one of the five major passages upon which the Calvinistic doctrine of election is based.[6] Here is a clear case of reading one's theology into a passage.

Romans. There are five doctrinally significant passages in Romans. **"He who did not spare His own Son, but delivered Him up for us all, how will He not also with Him freely give us all things? Who will bring a charge against God's elect [choice ones]? God is the one who justifies; who is the one who condemns?"** (Rom. 8:32-34). This is the wonderful consequence of the five-linked chain of vv. 28-31. Now that believers have been foreknown, pre-appointed to be conformed to the image of Christ, called, justified, and glorified, there can be no condemnation (Rom. 8:1). Certainly justification and glorification, put in a past tense, must be understood as positional truth. Since we are positionally God's 'choice ones' (*eklektoi*), the idea of God allowing a condemnatory charge against us is unthinkable. Which possible rendering, 'chosen' or 'choice,' makes better sense in the flow of Paul's logic? He had identified us as **"those who love God"** in v. 28. Either is possible in this context, but 'choice' is to be preferred: **"Who will bring a charge against God choice ones?"** In this case Paul's usage in Romans 16:13 would be the same as here.

Paul's use of the abstract noun *eklogē* in Romans 9:11 refers to the selection of Jacob over Esau to be the progenitor of His choice nation. Salvation is not at all the issue here, nor are Jacob and Esau in view as individuals. Paul's other three uses of 'election' or 'choice' in Romans 11 all relate to the same issue. **"In the same way then, there has also come to be at the present time a remnant according to God's gracious choice"** (11:5). In the preceding verses, Paul referred to God's reserving a remnant of 7000 in the days of Elijah and has made a comparison with the remnant of Jewish believers in his day according to a principle of God's gracious choice. This he explained involved a hardening of unbelieving Israel, as part of that transition from Israel to the Church: **"What then? That which Israel is seeking for, it has not obtained, but the election obtained it, and the rest were hardened"** (11:7 NAS, margin). From the strong corporate context of this passage, it is obvious that Paul is not speaking of the selection of individual Jews to be that remnant, but rather is dealing with the Jewish people corporately. In the preceding chapters he made it abundantly clear that faith is the principle upon which that remnant came into being (9:30–33; 10:2-4, 8-17).

The third use here is even more obviously corporate: **"From the standpoint of the gospel they are enemies for your sake, but from the standpoint of God's choice they are beloved for the sake of the fathers;"** (11:28). The antecedent of 'they' are Jews who are enemies of the gospel, and yet, Paul says that corporately they are still God's elect nation, which will ultimately be converted in the end time at the return of the Deliverer (Rom. 11:11-27). Most transparently here, the abstract noun *eklogē* could not refer to individual election to salvation. *Thus there is a consistent corporate usage of this term in these four places.*

Paul's later references. The context of Colossians 3:12 is also helpful:

"Therefore, as God's chosen people, holy and dearly loved, clothe yourselves with compassion, kindness, humility, gentleness, and patience" (NIV). With the prior usage in mind, it must be retranslated accordingly: "Therefore, as God's choice people, holy and dearly loved, clothe yourselves with compassion, kindness, humility, gentleness, and patience." In many of Paul's letters he extensively describes the believer's exalted position in Christ, and then immediately bases his exhortations for godly living upon that position (Rom. 12:1-2; Eph. 4:1; Col. 3:1-3). Since believers have been exalted to become God's choice people, holy and dearly loved, how appropriate that these moral qualities should be seen in us. On the other hand, being chosen by God with no revealed conditions would not be nearly as solid a base for a moral appeal. Some who see themselves as 'the elect of God' are arrogant, self-righteous, and proud. Certainly Israel, so conscious of their being the chosen people of God, had become arrogant, self-righteous, and proud in Christ's day. In this light, a strong case can be made for the rendering "choice ones."

Consider the context of Paul's usage in Titus 1:1: "Paul, a servant of God and an apostle of Jesus Christ for the faith of God's elect and the knowledge of the truth that leads to godliness—a faith and knowledge resting on the hope of eternal life, which God, who does not lie, promised before the beginning of time" (NIV). Here Paul is writing to Titus, his missionary colleague, for the benefit of God's eklektoi, with a view to strengthening their faith and enhancing their godliness. As in Colossians 3:12, the appeal to godliness is more harmonious with Paul's usual appeal based upon believers' exalted position in Christ as God's 'choice ones.' In other epistles, he more frequently addresses the recipients as 'saints' (Rom. 1:7; 1 Cor. 1:2; 2 Cor. 1:1; Eph. 1:1; Phil. 1:1; Col. 1:2), but here those to whom Titus is ministering are called 'choice ones.' This rendering simply takes note of the predominant meaning in the secular and Septuagintal Greek. It is worth noting how he links their being elect to their faith, which truths cannot be separated.

Paul's reference to the eklektoi in 2 Timothy 2:10 brings out an aspect which is reflected in other contexts. "... for which I am suffering even to the point of being chained like a criminal. But God's word is not chained. Therefore I endure everything for the sake of the elect [choice ones], that they too may obtain the salvation that is in Christ Jesus, with eternal glory" (NIV). If God's people have been unconditionally elected to salvation, how can Paul say that his suffering in prison in Rome could contribute in any way to their ultimate salvation? On the other hand, Paul's propagation of the word of God even from prison could impact the lives of many believers, if they are understood to be God's choice people, not just some privileged class of 'elect.' There is also an overtone of suffering here and in Christ's frequent reference in His prophetic discourse to the eklektoi in the great tribulation (Mt. 24:22, 24, 31; Mk. 13:20, 22, 27; & possibly Lk. 18:7). Suffering saints are far more appropriately described as 'choice ones,' rather than some 'unconditionally elected ones.'

Election Only in Christ: Ephesians 1:3-14

Apart from 1 Corinthians 1:26-29, already discussed, Paul used the verb *eklegomai* only once and that in the most doctrinally significant passage:

> Blessed be the God and Father of our Lord Jesus Christ, who has blessed us with every spiritual blessing in the heavenly *places* in Christ: even as he chose us in him before the foundation of the world, that we should be holy and without blemish before him in love: having foreordained us unto adoption as sons through Jesus Christ unto himself, according to the good pleasure of his will, to the praise of the glory of his grace, which he freely bestowed on us in the Beloved: (ASV).

The major question is whether the meaning, 'choosing the choice' is carried over into this context, as well. Another question which must be raised is whether Paul is speaking about individual selection or God's choice of the corporate church. Nothing can be assumed!

Election is in Christ. Israel was God's choice servant, and Isaiah parallels the Messiah as God's ultimate elect, or 'choice' servant. Now that He has risen and ascended on high, the corporate church is God's choice servant, chosen from the foundation of the world. It is not incidental that Paul wrote that we are chosen "**in Him.**" This idea is strongly reinforced by the *twenty times* in the first two chapters of Ephesians that Paul used the expressions, "**in Him**," "**in Christ**," "**in Christ Jesus**," "**in the Beloved One**" (1:1, 3, 4, 6, 7, 9, 10 (do), 12, 13 (do), 15, 20; 2:6, 7, 10, 13, 15, 21, 22; Paul's total usage=160 t.). Since He is the elect one, it follows that the only possible election is "**in Him**," and there is no election apart from Him. He did not write that we are chosen *to be* in Him, but that we are "**chosen in Him.**" Our election or chosenness is in Christ. Thus, it is only those individuals who are connected to Him by faith who are the elect. He is the corporate head of the Church and only those who have a relationship with Him can in any sense be called the elect. Therefore, there can be no direct or individual election apart from union with Him. This should be virtually axiomatic.

The basis of election must be factored in as well. The only two passages which relate election, or its related truth of pre-appointment, to God's foreknowledge both put foreknowledge first (Rom. 8:29; 1 Pet 1:1-2). In Christ's parable of the wedding feast, God foreknew who would respond to the open invitation given on the highways of life. The conditionality of it, based upon our relationship to the Elect One by faith, becomes paramount. The foundational truth is the corporate election of the Church "in Christ." Individual election, if it may be spoken about it at all, is secondary and ancillary and comes only through a faith-connection with the Head. Therefore, it is conditional, as both Peter and Paul have affirmed so simply and clearly. The only basis for not accepting this truth is a prior theological commitment.

Relationship to foreordination/preappointment. Ephesians 1 is the only passage in which election is directly connected with foreordination or 'preappointment.' In the relationship of the verbs here the adverbial function of the participle is possibly that of means, manner, or result.[7] Thus, foreordination or preappointment is clearly distinct from election, but closely related. The exact relationship is hard to define with certainty, but most likely preappointment to adoption as sons results from election. Paul's other references to adoption are threefold: in Galatians 4:5-7 he uses a cultural illustration of our present liberated sonship; in Romans 8:14-15 he refers to the Spirit of adoption believers have received; and in Romans 8:23 he speaks about the future liberation of our bodies from the curse, as the final stage of that adoption to sonship. Paul's use of *huiothesia*, as the Greco-Roman appointment of a child as the son and heir, fits in well with the rendering of *proorizein* as 'preappointment' and confirms this meaning.

Appointment to a future inheritance revealed. Since *proorizein* is used again in Ephesians 1:11, this context must also be examined:

> ... making known to us the mystery of his will, according to his good pleasure which he purposed in him unto a dispensation of the fulness of the times, to sum up all [these] things in Christ, the things in the heavens, and the things upon the earth: in whom also <u>we were made a heritage</u>, having been <u>foreordained</u> according to the purpose of him who works all [these] things after the counsel of his will: (Eph. 1:9-11, ASV).

The adverbial participle of *proorizein* modifies the aorist tense of *klēroein*, a verb which occurs only here in the New Testament and in the secular Greek and the church fathers means 'to appoint' or 'to apportion', as *TDNT affirms*:

> *Klēroō* does not denote a pre-temporal act. It is an 'appointment' or 'determination' which affects men in their being. It is also the goal which is assigned to them in their calling. Materially, then, it is related to *eklēthēmen* ['we were called'], but with the nuance, implicit in *klēros* ['a lot'], that the call imparts something to the called, namely, a life's goal."[8]

This meaning supports the understanding of *proorizein* as 'to preappoint.' Since *klēroein* is so rare, the exact meaning is difficult to verify. Paul's reference twice in the passage (Eph. 1:14, 18) to our inheritance (*klēronomia*) and to our adoption as sons (1:5) confirms the idea of our being appointed to an inheritance. So the participle of *proorizein* probably explains that this was done by preappointing us according to God's purpose or plan.

Paul is here focusing upon God's intentions and purposes (Eph. 1:9) for His 'choice ones' in the consummation (1:10) to preappoint them to a guaranteed inheritance (1:11), the seal and pledge of which is the promised Holy Spirit (1:13-14). Notice how this *focus on the future* continues on in 1:18, in 1:21, and in 2:7 where he refers to God's grace to His saints in the coming ages. In discussing Romans 8:28-30 in Chapter 20, that same futuristic perspective in Paul's use of *proorizein* was noted there as well. *The focus is not upon eternity past, but upon the glorious future for those who are now "in Christ."* The same futuristic perspective in 1 Peter 1 was observed in connection with *eklektois.* All three of these definitive Scripture passages are in harmony in focusing on the future glory of God's choice church, with only a passing allusion to its beginning before creation (1:4).

　　Passages not using *eklegomai.* One favorite proof-text of Calvinists is 2 Thessalonians 2:13-14: "**because God has chosen you from the beginning (*ap archēs*) for salvation through sanctification of the Spirit and faith in the truth. It was for this He called you through our gospel, that you may gain the glory of our Lord Jesus Christ.**" This verse does not use the verb *eklegomai* but rather *hairein,* which means, 'to take,' or 'to choose.'[9] It presents significant difficulty for translation since there is a textual problem. The UBS text has the preferred reading as *aparchēn,* which means 'firstfruits.' Although the majority of manuscripts read *ap' archēs,* which means 'from the beginning,' the committee had good reasons for their decision to prefer the other reading. Since in the secular Greek the verb is used in the sense of 'picking fruit,' Knox renders it: "**God has picked you out as the firstfruits in the harvest of salvation.**" The TNIV and the ESV also opt for "firstfruits": "**God chose you as firstfruits....**" This makes much better sense in the context since it was accomplished by, "**the sanctification of the Spirit and faith in the truth.**" This is not some pre-temporal election by God, but a historical event recorded in Acts 17. God's picking them as firstfruits alludes to the fact that the Thessalonian church was one of the early churches planted by Paul and was the recipient of his earliest epistles. Unfortunately this is another example of the majority of translators continuing on in the rut of past misjudgments. Now we have better tools and should sharpen the focus.

　　John's usage. The elder Apostle John's use of the adjective twice in 2 John to refer to a church as the "**elect lady**" and to his own church as the "**elect sister**" (vv. 1, 13) is a euphemism in a time of growing persecution, to obscure his meaning to hostile eyes. Mission agencies working today in restricted countries have developed a similar code to communicate with our "workers." The corporate implications of his usage are quite transparent.

Other considerations

　　Slight doctrinal emphasis. Is it not amazing that out of 51 usages of this group of words in the New Testament, only ten could possibly refer to a doctrine of election of individuals, whether conditional or unconditional? Three are in Peter, six in Paul, and the one enigmatic aphorism of Christ. It is also striking that beyond this there is no other theological reference in the four Gospels, Acts, James, Hebrews, Jude or John's writings (cf. Ch. 23 regarding John 6). Considering the centrality of unconditional election in Augustine's system and the theological controversies his view has engendered, this is a flimsy basis for a whole theological system.

The open secret of election. A key theme of Paul's theology, referred to in Ephesians 1:9 and initiated by the Lord Jesus in Matthew 13, is the truth of the "**mysteries of the kingdom of God.**" It is important to understand that *mustērion* should never have been merely *transliterated* as "mystery." From Paul's consistent usage elsewhere (Rom. 16:25-6; Eph. 3:4-5; and Col. 1:26-7), it clearly has the connotation of "**open secret,**" as Williams has rendered it.[10] The open secret was hidden from past ages, but now has been revealed. This *mustērion* is a complex of truths related to the Church, the body of Christ: the union of Jew and Gentile in the Church (Eph. 3:4-5), the organic body nature of the Church itself (Col. 1:24-26); the indwelling Christ as the riches of the open secret (Col. 1:27); and the transformation of our bodies at the rapture of the Church (1 Cor. 15:50-54).

This is relevant to the nature of election in two regards. First, it is clear that the basis of God's election is not a mystery today, but has been revealed. Second, since Paul keeps connecting these open secrets related to the church with God's choice of His people through the gospel, there is substantiation that Paul has in mind a corporate election in Ephesians 1:4.

Since God has revealed the open secret of the basis upon which people can be saved, the criteria which contribute to people coming to repentant faith in Christ should not be hard to find. Indeed, the Lord Jesus had a lot to say about these criteria. Calvinists hold that the basis of God's foreordination is a part of God's secret counsel, frequently quoting Deuteronomy 29:29: "**The secret things belong to the Lord our God, but the things revealed belong to us and to our sons forever, that we may observe all the words of the law.**" However, God really *has revealed* the basis of His foreordination and calling to salvation. Since Christ explained its basis on a number of occasions, the basis of God's foreordination is a mystery no longer.

Christ the revealer. In the Sermon on the Mount Christ made it clear that it was not the arrogant and self-righteous, but "**the poor in spirit**" who would be blessed to possess the kingdom of God (Mt. 5:3), those who recognize their spiritual poverty and need. After reproaching the towns of Israel which had sinned against such great light in rejecting Him (Mt. 11:20-24), He said, "**I praise Thee, O Father, Lord of heaven and earth, that Thou didst hide these things from the wise and intelligent and didst reveal them to babes. Yes, Father for thus it was well-pleasing in Thy sight**" (Mt. 11:25-26). The next verse (11:27) is a favorite proof-text of those who believe in a hidden and arbitrary sovereign election. However, from the context we see that the "babes" can be identified as "**anyone to whom the Son wills to reveal *Him*,**" and He follows this up immediately with His universal invitation: "**Come to Me, all who are weary and heavy-laden, and I will give you rest**" (Mt. 11:28). The connection of the "poor in spirit" to the "babes" is straightforward.

The crucial place of the parable of the four soils is seen not only in its repetition in all three Synoptic Gospels, but also in the interpretation supplied by the Lord Himself. A main point is in Luke 8:15: **"And the *seed* in the good soil, these are the ones who have heard the word in an honest and good heart, and hold it fast, and bear fruit with perseverance."** Apparently a person who has a heart which is honestly open to the truth is the one who responds to the gospel message. No mystery here! There are many occasions on which the Lord commended those who had faith and rebuked those who had closed their hearts in unbelief. Many more examples are given in Chapter 17.

The apostolic revelation. In 1 Corinthians 1:26-29, in expanding on the teaching of the Lord Jesus, Paul reminded the arrogant Corinthian Christians, proud of their sophisticated Greek philosophical knowledge and their liberated lifestyle, of the broad principles which have governed the selective process by which people come to faith in Christ. There are many other clear human factors which enter in prominently, which are identified in Chapter 23. One of those factors which Paul identifies as operative in his own conversion was ignorance: **"I thank Christ Jesus our Lord, who has strengthened me, because He considered me faithful, putting me into service; even though I was formerly a blasphemer and a persecutor and a violent aggressor. And yet I was shown mercy, because I acted ignorantly in unbelief"** (1 Tim. 1:12-13). Paul has taken us into the supposedly secret counsels of God to identify the factor of *ignorance* as a basis upon which God showed him mercy.

In 2 Thessalonians 2:9-11 he contrasts this with the basis upon which in the end time God will close the door of salvation in a judgmental delusion:

> **... *that is*, the one whose coming is in accord with the activity of Satan, with all power and signs and false wonders, and with all the deception of wickedness for those who perish, because they did not receive the love of the truth so as to be saved. And for this reason God will send upon them a deluding influence so that they might believe what is false,...**

His reference to **"those who did not receive the love of the truth"** seems to be the converse of the good soil of Christ's parable and the language of Paul's colleague, Luke in Acts 17:11-12, in reference to the Berean Jews: **"Now these were more nobleminded than those in Thessalonica, for they received the word with great eagerness, examining the Scriptures daily, *to see* whether these things were so. Many of them therefore believed, along with a number of prominent Greek women and men."** Note the extreme significance of Luke's **"therefore"** in verse 12. The Bereans were those who had **"honest hearts"** (Lk. 8:15) to check out Paul's message in the Scriptures. There really is some revealed basis for God's election and calling. It is not mysterious and unconditional, certainly not arbitrary or capricious!

Corporate Solidarity

The concept of corporate solidarity is not an abstract idea in Middle and Far Eastern cultures. During World War II thousands of Japanese pilots were willing to become Kamikaze (divine wind) by crashing their bomb-laden planes onto the decks of American aircraft carriers. Even today the Japanese are famous for their loyalty, not only to their extended families, but even to the business corporations to which they devote their lives. More recently, hundreds of thousands of Iranian young men went into battle against Iraq (and Saddam Hussain), with the full expectation that they would become martyrs. Some of this may be explainable in terms of Islamic theology, but, since they were fighting other Muslims, much of it has to relate to ideas of national corporate solidarity. Today, the Palestinian young men who become suicide bombers in the Intefadeh in Israel must be doing so under some concept of corporate solidarity. After years living in Asia, one only begins to grasp the importance of corporate solidarity to the cultures.

But this is not just a cultural notion. It is a biblical concept rooted in Genesis and in New Testament theology based upon the fall. Certainly the Pauline doctrine of the imputation and transmission of Adam's sin to the whole race (Rom. 5:12ff) establishes the principle of corporate solidarity from the very beginning of the human race. William Klein summarizes R. P. Shedd's Old Testament data for corporate or ethnic solidarity:

> (1) The personality of the group transcended time and space so a family could be identified with its ancestor (Ge 13:15-17; Isa 41:8; Hos 11:1; Mal 1:3-4). (2) Punishment and blessing extended beyond the specific individual responsible. As for punishment see the account of Achan's sin (Jos 7) or Korah's rebellion (Nu 16), as well as the statements in Ex 20:5-6. As for blessing note Ge 12:3 and Ex 32:13. (3) Regarding the covenant Shedd states, "All the members of a covenantal community are subordinate to the whole. To sever oneself from the group is to be cut off from the covenant and thereby from the covenant-making God." (4) The high priests, on the Day of Atonement, sacrificed for the sins of the people (Lev 16:15, 19, 21). The sins of the community, seen as a unity, could be transferred to the scapegoat. (5) Certain prayers expressed the intercessor's sense of corporate guilt (Ne 9:33; Da 9:5-19).... In parallel to Shedd's points, any reader notices that the writers of the Old Testament commonly treat the entire people of Israel as a unit (Isa 5.1-7; Jer 12:10).[11]

Klein went on to cite H. Wheeler Robinson as a strong advocate of the idea of "corporate personality" in the Old Testament, and, after alluding to his discussion of 2 Samuel 21:1-14 regarding King Saul's sin of the slaughter of the Gibeonites and David's judgment upon his family as a consequence, quotes Robinson's most apt statement:

> Corporate personality means for us the treatment of the family, the clan, or the nation, as the unit in place of the individual. It does not mean that no individual life is recognized, but simply that in a number of realms in which we have come to think individualistically, and to treat the single man as the unit, e.g., for punishment or reward, ancient thought envisaged the whole group of which he was part.[12]

Missionaries have also seen the extreme importance of understanding the diverse cognitive processes or ways of thinking in Asian and African peoples, much of which is characterized by corporate solidarity.

The new choice people of God. It should be noted that Ephesians is pre-eminently Paul's epistle of the Church, the body of Christ. Other than reference to Tychicus, the bearer of the letter, there are no personal references in the letter. The key issue of the oneness of both Jew and Gentile in the one body is a major theme. Klein and others have argued for the corporate nature of election. A number of cogent arguments are given:

1. Israel's election by God was clearly corporate and did not guarantee salvation to anybody; it was for service.

2. The concept of corporate solidarity is not only essential to the cultures into which the Old Testament came, but is an essential component of the Old Testament itself. Corporate solidarity is still today integral to Asian and African cultures. With Western cultural emphasis upon individualism, this has been lost in the thinking of Western scholars. It is not surprising that the notion of individual election to salvation arose in the Western, Latin church and is totally absent from Eastern Christianity. The Greek churches, which presumably understood Greek better, have no concept of individual election.

3. Peter unequivocally confirmed the corporate nature of election in 1 Peter 2:9, as we have seen. Paul's heavy corporate-solidarity emphasis in Romans 5 and 9–11, strongly colors the rest of his epistles. The idea of Adam, as corporate head of the human race, affecting the whole race by one sin (Rom. 5:12ff.), both transmitted and imputed, is hard for Westerners to grasp. We more easily accept that Christ was our representative head, suffering for our sins. That Israel should corporately be set aside and cut off from the root of Abraham is another major issue in Romans. The references to churches in 2 John is further confirmation.

4. There are many New Testament symbols of the church which have strong corporate overtones: the vine, the body, the temple of God, the flock, the bride, the household, and the people (nation) of God.

5. Church ordinances are corporate in nature. The Lord's table is more obvious, but when we relate water baptism to spirit-baptism putting us into the corporate church, its corporate dimension is also clear.

6. Election (chosenness) is functional. Israel was chosen to be God's servant nation. The twelve Apostles were chosen to be messengers to Israel, and this did not guarantee their salvation (i.e. Judas).

7. The use of the adjective 'elect' is always in the plural, except in Rom. 16:13 and 2 John, where it does not refer to individuals as elect.[13]

Taking these considerations into account, it becomes clear that God elected the corporate church in eternity past to become His choice people, not specifically the individuals who are a part of it.

Conclusions

The understanding of Christian election must be founded upon the election of Israel and of Christ. In neither case was there an unconditional election to salvation. The Church succeeded Israel as the choice people of God in this present age of grace and only exists because of its connection by faith with its Head, Jesus Christ, the Choice One of the Father. The predominant meaning of 'choice' and 'choice of the best' in secular Greek and the Septuagint carries over into the New Testament very significantly, and opens up the meaning of key passages. Although traditional translations are meaningful in most other passages, the translators have not given adequate consideration to the predominant usage of these key words before New Testament times.

In considering all the theologically relevant passages, there is no basis for a doctrine of individual, unconditional election. The corporate nature of election is clear enough in numerous contexts to lead to the probability that the whole doctrine should be taken corporately. This is difficult to prove or disprove with absolute certainty. There are a significant number of contexts in which conditional election is also clear. Conversely, there is no clear, unambiguous evidence of unconditional election in any context. Therefore, unconditional election must not be read into ambiguous passages. The presumption in those cases is in favor of a consistent picture of election being conditioned upon the sinner's response to the gospel message in repentant faith.

Is election corporate or is it conditional? It is probably both and, whichever way one slices it, unconditional individual election is in error. At the very least, it is hoped that enough doubts about Augustine's novel doctrines have been raised to cause Calvinists to stop building their whole theology of salvation upon the sparse, indeed, nonexistent biblical data.

---

1   Sauer, The Dawn of World Redemption:, pp. 89-90.

2   Ibid, pp 108-120

3   John N Oswalt in Harris, Archer, Waltke, *Theological Wordbook of the Old Testament*, pp 100-101

4   G Schrenk and G. Quell in *TDNT*, IV, p. 144-5; 176-182; Arndt and Gingrich, pp. 241-242.

5. James Daane, *The Freedom of God*, p. 101.

6   From the debate between Clark Pinnock and J. I Packer on Calvinism and Arminianism

7   Wallace, *Grammar*, pp 624-6 Note chart #82 on p 626

8. Werner Foerster in *TDNT*, III, pp 764-5.

9   Arndt and Gingrich, *Lexicon*, p. 23 They reference an ancient source, "if you pick fruit "

10   Charles B. Williams, *The New Testament*, p. 445. Curiously Williams has only used this rendering in Colossians and not in the parallel passages in Ephesians He should have been consistent

11   William W Klein, *The New Chosen People*, p 37, referencing R P Shedd, *Man in Community*, pp. 3-41.

12   H Wheeler Robinson, as cited by Klein, p. 39.

13   Klein; *Chosen People*; Daane, *Freedom of God*; Forster and Marston, *Strategy*. Ideas drawn from many sources.

Calvinism emphasizes divine sovereignty and free grace; Arminianism emphasizes human responsibility. The one restricts the saving grace to the elect; the other extends it to all men on the condition of faith. ... The Bible gives us a theology which is more human than Calvinism, and more divine than Arminianism, and more Christian than either of them.
                                    -Philip Schaff

22

HAS GOD DETERMINED EACH PERSON'S DESTINY?

The most pressing question is, has God determined each individual's destiny before creation? In Chapter 2 we discovered a total lack of reference to any such decrees, or any wall-to-wall exhaustive exercise of God's sovereignty. What are the implications of those Augustinian notions. The investigation must be narrowed to the basis of salvation for the individual, especially in Romans 9, since this has been a major basis for the notion of individual unconditional election. Since the study of predestination and unconditional election in the last two chapters was totally unsupportive of such notions, the focus must now be sharpened .

Problems with All-inclusive Decree(s) of God
There are many serious problems raised by such a concept of sovereignty to be faced by Augustinian Calvinists. Their view is so dependent upon this notion of decrees that James Daane calls it "decretal theology."

Such decrees are an extreme extrapolation of biblical data.
Extrapolation is a word used by scientists and engineers in making graphs of data. They attempt to draw smooth curves to connect the dots on graphs. There is a certain amount of guesswork in constructing the line between the points, which is *interpolation*. Any point on that estimated line is an interpolation, which may or may not be an accurate estimate. But an *extrapolation*, on the other hand, is to go beyond the data, off to the right or left on the graph. This is extremely risky! In going beyond the data, one has no idea which way the data might lead the curve. Extrapolation of graphs of stock performance in the financial world is even more risky, since the market can turn on a dime. Theological extrapolation is riskier yet!

Augustinian theology is an extreme extrapolation of the biblical data; it is not only risky but dangerous. Since the Old Testament says so little about God's decrees and the New even less (zero), *the decrees of Calvinistic theology are pure speculation!* All discussion about the logical or chronological order of God's decrees in eternity past is absolute nonsense. It is worse than the medieval theologians' discussions about the number of angels which can dance on the head of a pin.

The investigation in Chapter 2 of other related terms, such as king, kingdom, counsel, and will, yielded no basis for defining God's sovereignty in such a way. Ephesians 1:11 has been grossly pulled out of its context and extrapolated to make it a reference to an all-inclusive decree(s), when actually the subject at hand is God's gracious plan of salvation, planned by the Father and implemented by the Son of God.

Such decrees make God the author of sin.

The most serious other problem of an all-encompassing decree is that it must include all sin, including Satan's original rebellion against God, the fall of Adam and Eve in the garden, and ultimately, all the rest of the sin of mankind throughout the ages. The more extreme writers, such as Gordon Clark, Herman Hoeksema, Cornelius Van Til, and B. B. Warfield, are at least consistent in owning up to this incredible admission. Probably most Calvinists would not go this far, and to that extent are seriously inconsistent. *Either the decree is all-encompassing or it is not!* For this reason we find the curious historical anomaly that when the Westminster Confession crossed the Atlantic, American Calvinists changed the wording from the singular "decree" to "decrees," undoubtedly to resolve this problem.[1] This was so that they could speak about *a decree to permit sin*, in contrast with one absolute decree. A single overarching decree does not allow this.

However, this still does not resolve the problem of their interpretation of Ephesians 1:11. If it is all-inclusive, then *all sin* must be included. If it is not all-inclusive, then it cannot be used of a *partially* exhaustive concept of sovereignty (excluding sin) and must be explained in its context, as was done in Chapter 2. Moderate Calvinists cannot exclude sin from its scope, and yet have it include everything else. There must be an exegetical basis for excluding sin from its purview, lest they are drawn in with the most extreme writers in making God the author of sin. A mediate view does not face this insuperable problem.

It is not just sin as an abstract concept with which Augustinians must deal but especially the worst outbreaks of human sin and depravity as well. What about the wicked violence of the pre-deluge society? Did God decree that? It is inconceivable that God had decreed such a sordid history of human depravity. Moses tells us that **the LORD was sorry that He had made man on the earth, and He was grieved in His heart** (Gen. 6:6). Although this may be understood as anthropomorphism, yet there must still be a core truth in this statement, which is irreconcilable with such a concept of God and His supposed decrees. In Chapters 1-3 we traced through the Old Testament and saw God's dealings with Israel in their sin and God's judgments as well and found the same tension. Any definition of sovereignty must by all means take this historical record fully into account.

To say that God had exhaustively decreed the sin and rebellion of mankind is to contradict everything in Scripture; it is solely based upon a philosophic concept of God. Can you imagine the Council of the Trinity in eternity past saying, "Let Us decree the slaughter of 20 million in World War I and 45 million in World War II, and let's make sure that Hitler gets six million Jews in the holocaust (along with Christians and Poles), Mao his over 20 million, and Stalin his 12 million white Russians. Let Us decree that the Sudanese Muslim government slaughters and enslaves thousands of south Sudanese Christians. And while the Muslims are at it We should have them rampage, rape, burn, slaughter, and terrorize Christians in Nigeria, Pakistan, Indonesia, and wherever. Don't leave out the World Trade Center! And while We are at it, before We create the human race, let Us decree to consign the vast majority of them to Hell without any possibility of them believing."[A] Calvin admitted the problem of the "horrible decree,"[B] but it is a problem of Augustine's own making. Apart from any attempt to give a philosophic solution to the problem of evil, it can be said assuredly that the Augustinian scenario has no basis inductively but is purely deductive, rationalistic, and absurd!

Norman Geisler has personalized the issue:

> A well-known conference speaker was explaining how he was unable to come to grips with the tragic death of his son. Leaning on his strong Calvinistic background, he gradually came to the conclusion: "*God* killed my son!" He triumphantly informed us that "then, and only then, did I get peace about the matter." A sovereign God killed his son, and therein he found ground for a great spiritual victory, he assured us I thought to myself, "I wonder what he would say if his daughter had been raped?" Would he not be able to come to grips with the matter until he concluded victoriously that "God raped my daughter!" God forbid! Some views do not need to be refuted; they simply need to be stated.[2]

Such decrees require paradox to explain free will.

For four centuries the church fathers never questioned man's free will. Indeed, they coined the term in response to the fatalism of some Greek

---

A   Just after I arrived back in Pakistan in 1997, 30 thousand Muslims rampaged through the Christian village of Shanti Nagar ("place of peace"), raping the girls, torching houses, a hospital, dispensaries, schools, and farm equipment. This, the worst anti-Christian incident in Pakistan's 50-year history, left a terrible psychological scar on all Pakistani Christians. I talked with the traumatized people The economic impact was devastating. That was only the beginning, as seen in more recent events Did God really do this? Although God *may* have been using the Muslims to judge America on 9/11, He did not do it! This is the reality of life in this sin-cursed world and makes Calvinistic theology incoherent

B   To be fair *horibilis* can be translated 'astonishing,' but the usual rendering 'horrible' is not inappropriate!

philosophies and religions, such as Manicheanism.[3] It wasn't until Augustine, relapsing back into his Manichean and neo-Platonist past by developing a deterministic concept of God (417-430), that free will was questioned. Today, it is a 'dirty word' in the minds of many Calvinists.[c]

But the question of determinism and free moral agency remains very real and serious for all Calvinists. The more extreme see God as the novelist, writing the whole script and us humans as mere players in the drama. God is the puppet master, and we are the puppets. Moderate Calvinists recognize that we have free moral agency and seek to harmonize it with God's sovereignty, by recourse to words such as paradox, antinomy, or mystery. They resort to Deuteronomy 29:29 to get them out of an insuperable bind, but it does not really resolve a very real contradiction.

Another response of Calvinists is to speak philosophically of "compatibilism, or soft determinism," whatever that means. There may be a few valid biblical examples, but it is irresponsible to extrapolate a few anecdotal cases into universal compatibilism. Geisler rightly refers to such abstruse terminology as "word magic," and Daane calls it "word games."

Certainly the biblical narrative portrays Adam and Eve as free moral agents, whom God held accountable for their actions. Even though in the fall man became a slave of sin, the continuing narrative portrays mankind as acting freely and still totally responsible for their actions, since God pronounces judgment upon disobedience to His commands and will. Resort to secondary causes, such as environment and heredity, is inadequate since mankind, created in God's image, distinct from the animals, is uniquely responsible to God. It is striking how many of the church fathers refer to the image of God in man in connection with free will, namely, Tertullian, Novatian, Cyril of Jerusalem, Gregory of Nyssa, etc.[4]

Norman Geisler points out that logically there are only three possible views: "self-determinism (self-caused actions), determinism (acts caused by another), and indeterminism (acts with no cause whatsoever)." He shows that philosophically the only defensible view is self-determinism, but more importantly, it is the only view which is biblically defensible.[5]

Such a God could never respond to mankind conditionally.

One hardly needs to adduce specific Scripture references to show that God responds to mankind conditionally, as seen in the many conditional statements of His laws, His will, His judgments, His salvation, and the Christian life. Calvinists and Arminians have been discussing the nature of that conditionality for centuries, but of the abundance of such conditional statements in Scripture there is no room for discussion. Does God actually

---

C. I was strongly criticized in a Calvinistic church for saying that the violence before the deluge and the apostasy of Israel in the book of Judges are examples of "free will gone amok." Although the pastor claims to be a compatibilist, who holds God's sovereignty as compatible with free will, his rebuke of my words indicates that he does not really believe in free will at all.

respond to man's response to His conditional warnings and promises? Does He really answer prayer? Are some of His blessings conditioned upon obedience? Does He really spare people from temporal judgments when they repent? Is salvation really conditioned on faith? The extreme Calvinist must see all of this as predetermined and not an actual response to human contingency. If this were true, then mankind could never have a relationship with a personal God who responds to us in any real sense.

If a spouse in marriage does not interact with his/her spouse in any responsive way, no real marriage is possible. A newspaper column reported a woman whose husband never had any serious conversation with her, they never went out for dinner or the like, over twelve years of marriage. It is not surprising that the marriage ended up in divorce. It was not a personal relationship since there was no interaction. In what sense can we call God a personal God if He does not really interact with us? He is Aristotle's God!

Such decrees must include reprobation.

James Daane suggested that the problem faced in the preaching of traditional Reformed theology is that *"reprobation is always there."*[6] Even though the Synod of Dort tried heroically to separate election and reprobation by denying that they operate "in the same manner," seventeenth and eighteenth-century scholastic Reformed theology gave them equal footing. "God was increasingly seen as determining alike the destiny of an amoral sparrow, the unbelief of the reprobate, and the faith of the elect." This led to the single decree of the Westminster Confession.[7] But decretal theology with its wall-to-wall decree cannot avoid making election and reprobation coordinate, thus making it unpreachable, unscriptural, and irrational.

Such decrees parallel the gross errors of Islam.

It is not surprising that some of the opponents of decretal theology see a parallel with the fatalism of Islam, but it is amazing that even some of its advocates have made this connection. Having lived in a Muslim country for seven years and having continued involvement in Muslim evangelism until the present, this tangency is of great personal concern. When people ask, "Why do Muslim extremists do the things they do, such as terrorism?" my response is that the root is their defective view of the character of God. Indeed, foundational to our ethics is our concept of the character of God. How could the inquisitors in Spain torture people in the name of Christ? Augustine's coercive God justified his persecution of the Donatists, which became the basis for the inquisition (cf. Ch. 24).

In a parallel way, Allah of the Muslims is a coercive God and a Muslim convert to Christ is to be starved and beaten to return to Islam, and failing that, should be murdered by his closest relatives. Most Calvinists seek to distance themselves from the fatalism of Islam, although unsuccessfully.[8]

Brother Andrew (of Open Doors' fame) tells of overhearing two Christian women discussing a hostage situation and lamenting that there was nothing that we can do about these things. He thought to suggest to them that they ought to become Muslims because they would find such thinking more conducive to Islamic theology, where fatalism reigns. His point is that prayer can and does make a vast difference. He went on to tell how in 1983 his Open Doors ministry issued a call to pray for the Soviet Union and the demise of the Iron Curtain. Within a year, Gorbachev emerged, and within six, the Berlin wall came tumbling down. The rest is history![9]

The fatalism of Islam is illustrated by the narrative of the film, *Lawrence of Arabia*. While Lawrence and the army of Sheikh Ali were crossing the desert to capture the Turk garrison at Aqaba, one of the men, Ghasim, fell off his camel unnoticed and was left behind in the worst part of the desert called, 'The Sun's Anvil.' When Lawrence proposed going back to rescue him, Sheik Ali said, "Ghasim's time has come, it is written." Lawrence responded, "Nothing is written." This provoked Sheikh Ali to react angrily, "Aqaba, what of Aqaba? You will not be at Aqaba, English! Go back, blasphemer, but you will not be at Aqaba!" Lawrence responded, "I shall be at Aqaba! It is written (pointing to his head) in here," upon which he turned back alone and rescued Ghasim. After the rescue, Sheikh Ali stated, "Truly for some men nothing is written unless they write it." Later, as they invest Lawrence with the robes of a Sharif, someone says, "People for whom nothing is written may write themselves a plan." As history records, they conquered the Turks at Aqaba and changed the course of the Middle East. This is a fascinating vignette into Lawrence's struggle with the fatalism of his Arab Muslim colleagues, which pervades the Islamic mindset.

Norman Geisler supports this understanding of Islamic thinking from the Qur'an itself: "If We [Allah] had so willed, We could certainly have brought Every soul its true guidance; But the Word from Me Will come true. 'I will Fill Hell with jinn and men all together'" (Surah 32:13). The Persian Muslim poet, Omar Khayyam graphically reinforced this:

> Tis all a chequer-board of night and days
> Where destiny with men for pieces plays;
> Hither and thither moves and mates and slays,
> And one by one back in the closet lays.[10]

This same fatalism about evangelism and world missions has been an albatross on the back of the church since the Reformation (cf. Ch. 25). Samuel M. Zwemer, great pioneer missionary to the Muslims, who was committed to Reformed doctrine, bluntly made the comparison:

> .. what might be called ultra-Calvinism has carried the day. The terminology of their teaching is Calvinistic, but its practical effect is pure fatalism. Most Moslem sects 'deny all free-agency in man and say that man is necessarily constrained by the force of God's eternal and immutable decree to act as he does.' God wills both good and evil; there is no escaping from the caprice of His decree. Religion is Islam, i.e., resignation. Fatalism has paralyzed progress; hope perishes under the weight of this iron bondage.[11]

Such decrees unduly limit God's love.

Donald Carson tries to resolve *The Difficult Doctrine of the Love of God*, a problems of Calvinism's own making. He suggests that one of the different ways in which God's love is spoken of in the Bible is: *"God's particular, effective, selecting love toward his elect."* In discussing another, *"God's salvific stance toward his fallen world"*, he admits that "God's love for the world cannot be collapsed into his love for the elect"[12] (as extreme Calvinists do). Jerom Zanchi, one of the originators of limited atonement, in his discussion of the attributes of God, *leaves out His love.* Undoubtedly, Carson's problem is exacerbated by his Calvinism. If God does not desire the salvation of the "non-elect" (not a biblical category), then it can hardly be said that He loves them (cf. Ch. 17).

God's Sovereignty in Salvation

It should be noted that it is not necessary for Augustinians to prove their concept of exhaustive sovereignty in order to establish their view of sovereignty in reference to salvation, that is, unconditional election and irresistible grace. They only need to prove that God's decrees in reference to *salvation* are all-inclusive. But instead of seeking to prove the more limited propositions relating to salvation, Augustinians always focus on God's decrees as being all-inclusive in reference to all events in the universe. Why do they do this? This is a type of *a fortiori* argument. That is, if the broader concept of God's decrees is true, then the narrower concept regarding matters of salvation-truth automatically follows; it does not need to be specifically argued. Since in Chapter 2 we have seen the incredible lack of evidence for the exhaustive exercise of sovereignty, sovereignty in relation to salvation truth must now be specifically investigated.

Arguments for the Augustinian view of God's sovereignty in salvation truth are usually dependent upon concepts of "predestination," unconditional election, foreknowledge, and irresistible grace. These arguments are supposedly based upon word studies of the relevant terms and exegesis of Romans 9:6-29 and Ephesians 1:4-13. Careful word studies of foreknowledge, election, and foreordination were given in Chapters 20 and 21, and the circular reasoning in the Augustinian construct was noted. Calvinistic treatments of foreknowledge, election, and predestination have as an unstated premise the Augustinian view of exhaustive sovereignty. Without that premise the inductive data is not at all supportive of their view of foreknowledge, election, and predestination upon which their view of God's sovereignty in salvation is built. This is why we refer to their approach as an *a fortiori* approach. That is, universal sovereignty is so strongly held that the other parts of the system fall into place almost automatically. This is why "sovereign grace" is really a catch phrase in Calvinistic circles. In any case, they always depend heavily on their understanding of Romans 9.

Romans Chapters 9 – 11

Romans 9 is a major focus of the discussion between Calvinists and others, since it is a lynchpin in their case for God's sovereignty manifest in the unconditional election of individuals. In examining this passage in the light of its context and the many Old Testament passages which Paul quotes in their contexts, there is absolutely no case for the unconditional election of individuals. The flow of Paul's thought in the broader context of Romans reveals that the subject is totally other than what Calvinists make it out to be. Careful examination of these contexts is absolutely essential for an honest dealing with the argument of the text.[13]

Context. First, the broader context of Romans must be considered. There was a Jew/Gentile issue in the church in Rome which keeps surfacing all through the epistle. This is so pervasive that liberal scholar F. C. Bauer claimed that the epistle was written to Hebrew Christians. His view has never been accepted because it is clearly wrong, but he had a point. Probably the original core of the church consisted of many Jews and prose-lytes converted on the day of Pentecost, augmented by converts from Paul's first two missionary journeys who migrated to Rome. However, when Claudius Caesar expelled the Jews from Rome (Acts 18:2), *the church naturally became totally Gentile.* When the Jews drifted back into Rome under Nero, including Priscilla and Aquila (Rom. 16:3), the Hebrew Christians were no longer running the church and probably felt marginalized as second-class members. They felt denigrated in the dispensational transition from Israel to the New Testament church—after all weren't they God's chosen ('choice') people? And now they heard that Paul was calling himself an "Apostle to the Gentiles," of all things! "Paul, you've abandoned your own people Israel," they must have been complaining. What about two millenniums of promises made to Israel—has the word of God been negated? Has God also abandoned Israel? Thus, we see Paul addressing these issues in Romans. Study the relevance of the following passages: 1:2, 3, 5, 16; 2:11, 17, 24, 25-29; 3:1, 9, 19-20, 21, 29, 31, 4:1, 6, 9, 12, 13-25; 6:14; 7:1-6, 7-25; 8:3-7; ch. 9-11; 14:1-23; 15:8-12, 16-18, 25-27, 31; 16:25-26.[14]

So in approaching Romans 9, not only the broader context of Chapters 9 through 11, but also this issue of the transition from Israel as God's choice people to its replacement by the body Church of both Jew and Gentile *permeates the whole book.* Most commentators recognize that the issue in this section is the vindication of God's righteousness in setting Israel aside in favor of the Church. First, 9:1-29 deals with God's sovereign justice in His dealings with Israel as a nation. Then, in 9:30 – 10:15 Paul focuses upon the proclamation of righteousness by faith to all mankind. In 10:16 – 11:32 Paul shows how God foreknew and used Israel's fall for world salvation.

The first 29 verses are the heart of the issue. *It is imperative that the reader open the biblical text at this point* in order to grasp this discussion, otherwise, stop reading! The major theological issue which must be decided in this passage is whether Paul is discussing the unconditional election of individuals or God's dealings with Israel corporately.

God's dealings with corporate Israel: Romans 9:1-29

In surveying God's just dealings with Israel, Paul shares his burden for the salvation of a people who had been greatly advantaged (9:1-5). Probably some of the Jewish Christians felt that Paul had abandoned them, so he uses very strong language to assure them of his great concern for the salvation of Jews. He expands the issue of Israel's advantage begun in 3:1-3 with an impressive list including the giving of the divine Messiah to the Jews.

Then in 9:6-13 he shows how in God's separating out the nation Israel, physical descent did not guarantee being retained in the chosen lineage. Paul makes this point explicitly in 9:6: "**For they are not all Israel who are descended from Israel.**" There are many who can trace their lineage back to Abraham, Isaac, and Jacob, who are not true Jews; they are not "**children of the promise**" (9:7, 8). Then he gives two examples of this. The lineage would be through Isaac, the miracle child procreated in harmony with God's order for the family. He says nothing about Ishmael's salvation or lack thereof. God blessed Ishmael, and the impression is given that he was a believer: "**God was with the lad ...**" (Gen. 16:10-12; 21:17-20). The focus is upon the lineage of the nation, not the salvation of individuals.

Then Paul pointed out the choice of Jacob over Esau for the promised lineage of the nation, quoting a part of God's word to Rebekah before their birth (but the whole is important here): "<u>Two nations</u> are in your womb; and <u>two peoples</u> shall be separated from your body; and <u>one people</u> shall be stronger than the other; and the older shall serve the younger" (Gen. 25:23). Is it not obvious that Paul's focus in using this quotation is not on the individuals, but upon the separation of national Israel from the Edomites? Esau as an individual never served Jacob; indeed, the opposite is true in that Jacob served Esau a red lentil stew to induce him to give up his birthright! Later we see Jacob's obeisance to Esau when they met on his return from Padan Aram. However, the subjugation of the Edomites to the Israelites began under David, was complete under Solomon, and continued on and off until the Babylonian captivity.

Paul then confirmed this by quoting from Malachi 1:2-4, *which was written about fifteen centuries later*, about God's judgment upon the Edomites and His continuing love for Israel (expanded in Obadiah): "**Jacob I loved, but Esau I hated, and I have made his mountains a desolation ... Though <u>Edom</u> says,...**" Is it not obvious that Jacob and Esau are euphemisms for the nations in the brief portion which Paul quoted? Malachi has personalized the nations by using the names of their progenitors. Certainly the Apostle Paul did not intend to wrench these sentences out of their prophetic contexts to make them teach a doctrine of unconditional individual election. Unfortunately, their close juxtaposition in 9:12-13 has allowed careless interpreters to read such a doctrine into them unjustifiably. But this is reading doctrine into the text, not careful contextual exegesis!

Four examples. In Romans 9:14-29 Paul gives four examples of God's sovereign justice in His dealings with the nation Israel, explicitly raising the issue of charges of God's injustice in v. 14. The first example is Moses' struggle with Israel when they sinned in worshiping a golden calf. At first, when God said He would destroy Israel and make a new nation from Moses, he interceded for Israel, and God heard him (Ex. 32:10-14). Then he pled again for God to forgive Israel, suggesting that God blot out his own name from His book (Ex. 32:32). When God expressed a reluctance to continue His presence in the midst of Israel, Moses interceded again and pled for God to show him His ways (33:1-16). God then favored Moses to see His presence in a special way, and the passage which Paul quoted is connected with this: "**I myself will make all My goodness pass before you, and I will proclaim the name of the Lord before you; and I will be gracious to whom I will be gracious, and will show compassion on whom I will show compassion**" (Ex. 33:19). The issue here is *the continuance of God's gracious and compassionate favor upon the nation Israel* in specially favoring their leader, Moses. It is in this regard that Paul argues in v. 16 that "**God's purpose ... does not depend on the man who wills and the man who runs, but on God who has mercy**" (Rom. 9:11, 16). The passage in Exodus has *nothing to do with individual, unconditional election to salvation, and therefore, neither could the passage in Romans*.

If that were the point which Paul was making, it would be a serious abuse of the Exodus narrative.[D] But thus far there is nothing in the Romans passage to support such an inference. Dave Hunt points out how Calvinists' treatments of this and other passages put a negative spin on them, emphasizing reprobation.[15] Note that neither in the Exodus passage, or in Paul's use of it, is there anything about reprobation—it is all about mercy and compassion upon Moses and Israel as a nation. Certainly Moses' salvation is not at issue, since he was the recipient of a unique blessing!

Paul's second example is God's dealings with Pharaoh, the god-king of a grossly idolatrous nation, in hardening him for judgment (9:17-18). It is commonly understood that each of the ten judgments related to the idolatrous religion of Egypt. Judgment came upon the gods of Egypt and their human regent, who himself was worshiped as god. This is a classic example of the principle which Paul had stated in Romans 1:24, 26, 28, that God judgmentally gave the most hardened heathen over to a depraved mind. First of all, God stated His sovereign intention to Moses: "**But I will harden Pharaoh's heart that I may multiply My signs and My wonders in the land of Egypt**" (Ex. 7:3). Then there are seven clear references to Pharaoh's heart being

---

D. It should be noted that Ex. 33.12, 17 is one of five passages in which Calvinists claim that *yada'* has an elective pregnant force However, God is simply expressing His close personal relationship with Moses, which has been greatly strengthened by his intercession for Israel. See App. F in *BCAA*.

characteristically hard (Ex. 7:13-14, 22; 8:19; 9:7) and even to Pharaoh hardening his own heart (8:15, 32), all *before* God then hardened his heart even further judgmentally (Ex. 9:12; 10:1, 20; 11:10; 14:8).

It was in this connection that the words of God to Pharaoh were spoken (Ex. 9:16), which Paul quoted: **"For this very purpose I raised you up, to demonstrate my power in you, and that my name might be proclaimed throughout the whole earth"** (Rom. 9:17). It helps to see the rest of God's words to Pharaoh: **"Still you exalt yourself against my people by not letting them go"** (Ex. 9:17). The issue here clearly was God's sovereign purpose to bring Israel out of Egypt and to make a signal demonstration of His judgment upon corrupt idolatrous religion in the process. Pharaoh and his nation were ripe for judgment (cf. Gen. 15:13-16). God was making an example of Pharaoh, his false prophets, and priests, who were forerunners of subsequent false prophets, singled out for denunciation by the Lord Jesus (Mt. 7:15-23), by Paul (Rom. 1:18-32; 2 Tim. 3:1-9, note reference to Jannes and Jambres), by Peter (2 Pet. 2), and by Jude (4-19). It must be emphasized that this has absolutely nothing to do with God's sovereignty in unconditional election of anybody to salvation or to reprobation. When Paul wrote that **"He hardens whom He desires"** (9:18b), he was not referring to an arbitrary reprobation in eternity past of people yet unborn, but of giving Satan's key representatives over judgmentally to a depraved mind (Rom. 1:24, 26, 28; 2:5). This passage has nothing to do with reprobation of the "non-elect" in eternity past, neither does Paul imply or state that.

Paul drew the third example from Jeremiah's observation of the potter's wheel (Jer. 18:1-11), although he did not quote him directly (Rom. 9:19-24). He responded to a fatalistic person who objects to what he has written thus far: **"You will say to me then, 'Why does He still find fault? For who resists His will?'"** (9:19). Note well that these are not Paul's words but those of an objector. In essence the objector argues, "If God has already decided to set Israel aside in favor of the Church, how can Israel be blamed, and how can Jews resist the will of a sovereign God in this regard?" Here instead of *boulē*, we find *boulēma*, which with the result ending *ma* indicates a more crystallized plan or counsel.[16] Perhaps it comes closest to the idea of a 'decree,' which seems to be the way it is used in First Clement (esp. 33:3). Note that the only use of *boulēma* in the whole New Testament is from the lips of a fatalistic objector, not as an expression of God's truth!

Paul's answer to this fatalistic objector comes from the potter's wheel. Let us note that Jeremiah saw the vessel being formed on the wheel being marred, but then remade by the potter, since the clay was still soft. Its form had not yet been fixed by firing in the kiln. The point that God explains to Jeremiah is that the nation Israel is clay in His hands, and the nation's future is contingent upon their response to His word:

> ... if <u>that nation</u> against which I have spoken turns from its evil, I will relent concerning the calamity I planned to bring on it... So now then, speak to the

men of Judah and against the inhabitants of Jerusalem saying, 'Thus says the LORD, "Behold, I am fashioning calamity against you and devising a plan against you. Oh turn back, each of you from his evil way, and reform your ways and your deeds"' (Jer. 18:8, 11).

Calvinists ignore the fact that the issues Paul is dealing with and the message of God through Jeremiah both relate to the nation Israel *corporately.* Indeed, *the conditional nature* of God's dealings with Israel are explicit in the Jeremiah passage. Paul later addresses the cause of Israel's being set aside as their unbelief (Rom. 9:30-33; 10:16-21). Here he speaks of God's patience with Israel over the years of His entreaty to them through Christ and His Apostles (9:22). The key word here is *katērtismena* (*"prepare, make, create"*). The question is whether this is middle or passive. The BAG lexicon suggests it may be a middle voice: *"having prepared themselves for destruction* Rom. 9:22."[17] This would harmonize with Jeremiah's context by putting the onus upon Israel.

The point which Paul is making here is that God has the sovereign right as a potter to use Israel for two millennia and then set them aside in favor of the Church. Additionally, in Romans 11 he shows the justice of this decision in the fact that a remnant of Jews are still being saved (11:1-10), and that He will ultimately restore Israel to the place of blessing corporately (11:11-32). Romans 9:23-24 is a segue into his later discussion of the Church's becoming vessels of mercy, by a plan prepared beforehand (*proetoimazein*) for glory. God was patient with Israel's unbelief so that He might reveal the glorious riches of the cross to and through the Church, which is being called from both Jews and Gentiles. The context gives no basis for individualizing this statement. Thus, this passage also says nothing about unconditional, individual election to salvation.

The fourth proof of God's sovereign justice in His dealings with national Israel is seen in the four prophetic passages Paul quoted in Romans 9:25-29 (Hosea 2:23; 1:10; Isa. 10:23; 1:9). Although the context of Hosea is about the end-time restoration of national Israel (3:4-5), Paul is drawing out the principle that those who were not God's people can become the people of God, in support of 9:23-24. The Isaiah quotations clearly refer to the preservation of a remnant of believing Jews, which point Paul reinforced in 11:1-10. In any case, there is nothing said here either about individual, unconditional election to salvation.

A universal gospel: Romans 9:30–10:15

The chapter divisions here and between Chapters 10 and 11 are poorly placed, since Paul moved into a new subject *before* the chapter division. He was vindicating the righteousness of God by discussing the proclamation of God's righteousness by faith to all mankind (9:30–10:15), and coming back to Israel's unbelief and failure (10:16–11:32). His emphasis upon the universality of the gospel message in the first section is totally contradictory to any notion of individual, unconditional election in Romans 9:[E]

> 'Whoever believes in Him will not be disappointed.' For there is no distinc-
> tion between Jew and Greek; for the same *Lord* is Lord of all, abounding in
> riches for all who call upon Him; for 'Whoever will call upon the name of the
> Lord will be saved' How then shall they call upon Him in whom they have not
> believed? And how shall they believe in Him whom they have not heard?
> And how shall they hear without a preacher? And how shall they preach
> unless they are sent? (Rom. 10:11-15a).

How much more clearly could Paul say that the salvation of the lost is
contingent upon human instrumentality?

In the segue to the next section, Paul's very simple principle must be
foundational to a theology of salvation: **"So faith comes from hearing, and hearing
by the word of Christ"** (10:17). Human instrumentality is paramount in preparing the lost for faith, but the new birth itself is totally a work of the Holy Spirit.

Since the Old Testament passages which Paul quotes in Romans 9 do
not in the least support the Calvinistic interpretation, they have a serious dilemma. Either Paul is grossly dishonest in his use of these passages, and the
integrity of Scripture comes into question, or else, Paul is fairly using these
passages and has been grossly misunderstood by Western, individualistic
Christians, who do not think corporately. The latter option is far more
preferable. Paul's first readers had no problem understanding his references
to God's corporate dealings with Israel because of their corporate-cultural
way of thinking and since Paul's discussion of Jew/Gentile issues directly
answered their concerns. Any issues related to individual, unconditional
election would have been farthest from their concerns or Paul's mind (cf.
App. B in *BCAA* for a critique of John Piper's *The Justification of God*). Do
we not believe in the sovereignty of God? Absolutely, but not in the sense in
which Augustinians believe it.

Conclusions

Delineating God's sovereignty

The following propositions about sovereignty can be fully justified from
the inductive data of Scripture unmixed with *a priori* considerations:

1. God as Creator has the right to rule His universe in any way He sees fit
   consistent with His own attributes. Since He chose to delegate spheres
   of autonomy to His creatures, this in no way limits His sovereignty.

2. Like human sovereigns, God exercises His sovereignty by punishing
   disobedience to His will at what times and ways suit His eternal plan.

3. God has continued to delegate authority to humans as He pleases:

E. Paul actually comes back to Israel's unbelief and failure in 10:16-21, which is the important context
for his reference to God's foreknowledge of Israel's failure in 11:2. This confirms that *proginoskein* has
its normative meaning of foreknowledge, as discussed in Chapter 20.

capital punishment and human government (Gen. 9:6); to priests, judges, and kings in Israel, elders in the church, and husbands in the family. This delegated authority intrinsically implies a limited autonomy.

4. By His omniscient foreknowledge of both eventualities and non-eventual possibilities God orchestrates and arranges those events He chooses without coercing the wills of the moral agents involved. God's foreknowledge cannot be contingent upon His will.

5. Since God completed creation and rested on the seventh day, much of His involvement is accomplished mediately, or indirectly, through His agents, and through orchestrating natural and human events.

6. Whenever it pleases Him, God intervenes in the world by supernatural acts, such as miracles, the new birth and other ministries of the Holy Spirit. This is implemented in harmony with His eternal plan.

7. There is no biblical basis for the notion that God has exhaustively decreed every last event which transpires in His universe.

8. By the nature of promises, covenants, and prophecies, God limits Himself voluntarily.

9. Romans 9 says nothing about unconditional election of individuals to salvation or reprobation of others to hell.

---

1 James Daane, *The Freedom of God*, pp. 41-42; the original Westminster Confession has "decree" in the singular

2 Norman L Geisler, *Chosen But Free*, p.133.

3 Geisler, pp 145-154

4 Ibid, pp 147-149

5 Ibid, pp. 175-180. Although I don't agree with all of his reasoning, I think his essential arguments are sound.

6. Daane, p 35 Daane was very concerned that election cannot be preached because it is unpreachable!

7 Ibid, pp 38-43

8. Gary North, *Dominion and Common Grace*, p 231; Talbot and Crampton, p 4, Coppes, p. 23,cited by Vance, p 703.

9. Brother Andrew, *And God Changed His Mind* . *Because His people dared to ask*, pp 11-25

10 Geisler, pp 133-34

11 Samuel M. Zwemer, *Religions of Mission Fields*, pp 244-5, as quoted by Fisk, *Calvinistic Paths*, p. 225

12 D. A Carson, *The Difficult Doctrine of the Love of God* (Wheaton. Crossway, 2000), pp 17-19

13 Cf Forster and Marston, Klein, *The New Chosen People*, commentaries by Blomberg and Leon Morris

14 D A. Carson, Douglas Moo, and Leon Morris, *An Introduction to the New Testament*, pp 244-45

15 Dave Hunt, *What Love Is This?*, pp 311-2.

16 William Douglas Chamberlain, *An Exegetical Grammar of the Greek New Testament*, pp 9-12.

17 Arndt and Gingrich, p 419; Wallace, *Grammar*, p 418 references 1 Cor 1·10 & 2 Cor 13 11 as examples

The Irresistible and the Indisputable are two weapons which the very nature of His [God's] scheme forbids Him to use. Merely to override a human will ... would be for Him useless. He cannot ravish. He can only woo....

There are only two kinds of people in the end: those who say to God, "Thy will be done," and those to whom God says, in the end, "Thy will be done." All that are in Hell, choose it. Without that self choice there could be no Hell.

-C. S. Lewis

IS GOD'S CALLING IRRESISTIBLE?

The biblical idea of 'calling' is a broad term to describe the process of how sinners come to repentant faith in Christ. God invites, yes, summons a lost human race to receive salvation in Christ and to appointment to service for Him. All are obligated to respond to that summons, but most do not. Why do some respond to the proclamation of the gospel, while others do not? Augustine answered that ultimately only the elect respond because they are the only ones whom God draws to Himself with irresistible grace. Since he was the first to advocate this notion, the majority Western church wrestled with it for a century until the Synod of Orange (AD 529), which omitted irresistible grace from the twenty-five canons of their concluding resolution. Calvin revived this doctrine as part of his tightly knit theology of salvation, and all Calvinists affirm irresistible grace, one of its five points. The standard Calvinistic works on this subject reveal a widespread lapse into proof-texting and an absence of exegesis* in discussing irresistible grace. Our agenda: a word study of the Greek words for calling, examination of the presuppositions, and exegesis of all relevant Scripture in context.

A Word Study of Calling
A survey of the usages of the words for calling (*kalein, klēsis, klētos*) indicates that in the Gospels they are used frequently in three of Christ's parables in the sense of an invitation to a feast (Mt. 22:1-14; Lk. 14:7-14, 15-24). Two of the parables are the basis for the idea of a general 'call' or invitation to all mankind to salvation. When the Lord Jesus capped the

parable of the king's wedding feast with the aphorism, **"For many are called, but few are chosen"** (Mt. 22:14), many recognize the meaning 'invited,' as in the margin of the NAS translation and in the text of the NIV. One other statement of the Lord Jesus, found in all three synoptic Gospels, is a reference to that general invitation: **"I have not come to call the righteous but sinners to repentance"** (Lk.5:32=Mt. 9:13=Mk. 2:17). It is obvious that the invitation to all sinners precedes the repentance.

Over fifty times in the epistles, mostly in Paul's letters, these words are used in a more technical sense, referred to as an 'effectual calling,' of the completed process in the life of believers by which they came to Christ. How that calling became effectual is the point of dispute between Calvinists and others. Is it an irresistible calling, or is it described as having been already effectuated because it is indeed a *fait accompli*, an accomplished fact? It seems that the Apostles used it in a narrower technical sense, especially of those who have responded to the general call or gospel invitation and are thus referred to as 'the called' by hindsight. To use the analogy of the parables of the Lord Jesus, it is as if the king at the banquet refers to those in the banquet hall as the 'invitees,' even though many others were invited but refused to come. It was an effectual calling (invitation) since those present responded to the invitation and are referred to as the invited ones in a narrower, technical sense. Those who refused to attend, although invited, are now irrelevant to the purpose of the invitation and thus not designated as invitees, the 'called.' This is all brought out so clearly in Christ's parable of the king's wedding feast in Matthew 22, already examined in detail in Chapter 21 (pp. 277-8). This parable is totally at odds with irresistible grace. However, there are other shades of meaning in this group of words which must be examined.

From the use of these words in secular Greek and the Septuagint, a prominent idea of 'commissioning' emerges. It is frequently used in Isaiah 42 to 55 of God calling and commissioning to service and dedication, in regard to Israel, King Cyrus, and the Messiah.[1] This meaning carries over to the usage of *kalein* in the New Testament, which is confirmed by Paul's usage: **"called as an apostle"** (Rom. 1:1; 1 Cor. 1:1; also Gal. 1:15). This is an aspect of the calling of all believers, that we are appointed or commissioned to His service. Paul affirms this in Ephesians 4:1: **"Therefore I, the prisoner of the Lord, implore you to walk in a manner worthy of the calling with which you have been called ..."** From Luther's exposition onward the idea of 'vocation' has been connected with this. All believers were privileged to be appointed as God's servants at the point of conversion. There is also a unique usage in 1 Corinthians 7:20 which supports the idea of *klēsis* as calling or vocation in a more secular sense: **"Let each man remain in that condition in which he was called."** Based upon parallel secular Greek usage the BAGD lexicon lists as a second meaning, "2. *Station* in life, *position, vocation*"[2] Thus, the Christian life itself is seen as a calling or vocation.

Further observations on the connotation of 'to summon' are in order.

This meaning is clear in the Gospels and Acts (Mt. 2:7; 20:8; 25:14; Lk. 19:13; Acts 4:18; 24:2).[3] In Chapter 3 (pp. 34-5) God's consistent confrontation of humanity in their sin was surveyed, with the concomitant implication of man's ability to respond. In the Septuagint and the Gospels the verb also has the sense of 'to name,' which is confirmed by Paul in Romans 1:7 and 1 Corinthians 1:2: "**called saints**," or possibly, "named saints."

Seeing the many aspects of this group of words, Schmidt, in *TDNT*, is undoubtedly correct in saying that "in the NT *kalein* is a technical term for the process of salvation."[4] Upon examining the many occurrences used in an effectual sense, the following definition emerges: *Calling is God's action in bringing the sinner to salvation, thus commissioning the believer to an exalted position with a new name for service to God.* It is used of the process and circumstances of our coming to faith viewed from the divine side, as contrasted with conversion, which is the human side. It is frequently used by Paul of the circumstances and process by which the sinner comes to faith (esp. 1 Cor. 7:15, 17-24), which implies a response to the general invitation, and thus, by hindsight is considered to be effectual.

Additional observations on key passages

2 Thessalonians 2:14 is an early significant usage: "**And it was for this He called you through our gospel, that you may gain the glory of our Lord Jesus Christ.**" First, a simple observation—that the calling was accomplished by means of the preaching of the gospel by Paul. Thus, calling is accomplished mediately, not directly (which might imply irresistible grace). As Paul's thought is unpacked, note that in the preceding verse (as discussed in Ch. 21) their salvation came "**through sanctification by the Spirit and faith in the truth.**" Allusion to a conditional element (faith in the truth) eliminates a direct work of irresistible grace. Of course, interpretation is strongly colored by one's pre-understanding of the relation of repentant faith to the new birth, already discussed in Chapter 17.

Another significant observation from 1 Corinthians 1:26ff should be noted. Paul stated that not many wise, mighty, or noble are called to salvation. Does God sovereignly discriminate against such people, or are there human factors involved in the sparseness of their response to the general calling of the gospel? It is common to human experience that pride is a major human factor which hinders the intelligencia, the nobility, and the powerful from putting faith in Christ. Although Paul's usage of these words emphasizes God's initiative in salvation, this is a counter indication to reading into the biblical concept of calling an irresistible, direct 'zapping' of the sinner by the Spirit. Indeed, the parable of the king's wedding feast, which Schmidt called the *crux interpretum*, indicates that those in the feast are the ones who responded to the general invitation.[5]

Later, we have Paul's most theological reference to calling:

But we know that for those who love Him, for those <u>called</u> in agreement

with His purpose, God makes all things work together for good. Because those whom He knew beforehand He appointed beforehand to share the likeness of His Son, so that He might be the First-born among many brothers (Rom. 8:28-29, NBV).

Note Paul's emphasis upon believers as **"those who love Him,"** which comes first in the emphatic position in the Greek sentence (as retained in the NBV). Then, in apposition to this, believers are designated as **"those called in agreement with His purpose."** As discussed in Chapter 2, there are three usages of *prothesis* in reference to God's plan of salvation, as confirmed by the BAGD listing: "plan, purpose, resolve, will,... design." Paul stressed the purpose of the calling to be that believers should **"share the likeness of His Son."** In other passages he expanded that purpose to include: called to freedom (Gal. 5:13), to hope (Eph. 1:18; 4:4), to peace in one body (Col. 3:15), not to impurity but in sanctification (1 Thess. 4:7), to suffering (1 Pet. 2:21), and to be a blessing (1 Pet. 3:9). Thus, God has many purposes in commissioning and calling saints. The means of implementing that plan are explained in Romans 8:29-30, as discussed in detail on pp. 263-7 in reference to foreknowledge and preappointment. That discussion also makes it clear that there is no basis here for an irresistible force in God's calling us to salvation.

Although Paul's use of calling in Romans 11:28-29 is not a reference to our individual salvation, but rather to God's ultimate plan for the nation Israel, nevertheless there is an applicable principle here: "... **for the gifts and the calling of God are irrevocable."** There is no hint in this context that the calling of Israel, in regard to their ultimate restoration back to the place of blessing, is irresistible. However, not only is God's plan for Israel irrevocable, but, based upon this principle, the true Christian's salvation is also irrevocable. This is the glorious truth of eternal security. *Thus, the calling to salvation is irrevocable, but not irresistible!*

One other theologically significant context from Peter's pen (2 Pet. 1:10) has already been discussed in Chapter 21 in its connection with election, where it was concluded that Peter is referring to the subjective assurance of salvation. This says little about the irresistibility of the calling, pro or con. Nor does it undermine the irrevocability of the calling, as Arminians might claim.

Presuppositions of Irresistible Grace

In reviewing the major Calvinistic works one is struck with the major part that presuppositions play in their discussion. Some of the discussions seem almost irrelevant to the subject at hand apart from some unstated presuppositions. It is only when the non-Calvinistic reader is reminded of their presuppositions, that one can even see the relevance of the discussion.[6] This is because this doctrine is very deductive.[7] These presuppositions have already been examined in detail in previous chapters:

❏   **Effectual calling necessarily implies irresistible grace.**

❏   **Irresistible grace presupposes unconditional election.[8]**

❏   **Irresistible grace presupposes an eternal decree.[9]**

❏   **Total inability necessitates irresistible grace.**

❏   **Regeneration is irresistible and precedes repentant faith.[10]**

❏   **Irresistible grace is effectuated by a direct gift of faith.[11]**

❏   **Monergism requires irresistible grace.**

Calvinists' Proof-texts Examined

As one examines the treatments of irresistible grace by Calvinists, the lack of serious exegetical discussion by most is a source of amazement, especially the failure to see each passage in its context. Many do not even bother to quote the passages, let alone focus on the important context.

Ezekiel 37:1-14. Gordon Clark claimed that the prophecy of dry bones in the valley is a proof of irresistible grace, as well as of all other points of the TULIP.[12] Clearly in making that claim, he has departed far from any literal interpretation of the passage and has ignored the Spirit-given interpretation in vv. 11-14: "**Son of man, these bones are the whole house of Israel ... I will bring you into the land of Israel.**" This comes in the context of many prophecies of the end-time restoration of Israel to the promised land and cannot be so spiritualized. It has nothing to do with irresistible grace!

Psalm 65:4. Clark also sees irresistible grace here:[13] "**To You all men come.... How blessed is the one whom You choose and bring near *to You* to dwell in Your courts. We will be satisfied with the goodness of Your house, Your holy temple.... You who are the trust of all the ends of the earth and of the farthest sea.**" (Ps. 65:2-5). Vance rightly faults Clark for not quoting the whole verse, thus omitting *the purpose of the choosing and bringing near, that is, to dwell in God's temple in Jerusalem.*[14] The main point is that Israel was chosen and favored above Gentiles to be able to worship in the temple. *The issue here is God's special favor to the nation Israel.* This privilege did not automatically save any Jew.

Luke 14:15-24. What was Augustine's basis for innovating irresistible grace from the parable of the great dinner invitation? Since those invited made irrational excuses, the host had his slaves not only bring in the handicapped, but also recruit others from the public thoroughfares. Augustine put the strongest spin on the word *anagkazein* by interpreting it in the sense of physical compulsion or coercion.[15] Although he misused Luke 14:23 in connection with coercing people (the Donatists) into the Catholic Church, its connection to coercion in irresistible grace is obvious.[16] The BAGD lexicon lists two meanings: "**1.** *compel, force*, of inner and outer compulsion.... **2.** weakened *invite (urgently), urge (strongly)...*"[17] It is most significant that of the other eight usages of this verb in the New Testament, only one refers to any sort of physical force (Acts 26:11). All the rest have to do with some personal (Mt. 14:22=Mk. 6:45), socio-religious (Gal. 2:3, 14; 6:12), or circumstantial (Acts 28:19; 2 Cor. 12:11) pressure to act. So Augustine's interpretation is extremely improbable.

In the parable, the slaves could not have used physical force since the host in the parable is not identified as a king. So the second meaning of an urgent invitation is really required. Otherwise, Augustine's misuse of the parable for physical coercion to faith might also be supported.

John 6:37, 44, 65

Calvinists see in Christ's statement that, **"All that the Father gives Me shall come to Me,"** a reference to the elect, who will irresistibly be drawn to Christ. They hold that this is confirmed by the converse in v. 44, **"No one can come to Me, unless the Father who sent Me draws him."** They do not consider any alternate interpretation suggested by the context.

Context. In the Bread of Life Discourse the Lord has been having a rather animated dialogue with a skeptical inquiring multitude (vv. 24ff). He had just stated that although they had seen Him, they still had not believed (6:36). Then in contrast he refers to the truly believing disciples in the crowd as **"all that the Father gives Me,"** who are inevitably coming to Him. The key issue all the way through the dialogue is faith or its lack (6:29, 35, 40, 47, 64), and He symbolizes faith as appropriating, that is, by eating and drinking Himself (6:35, 51, 53-58). A little later, He emphasized the human response factor: **"If anyone is willing to do His will, he will know of the teaching, whether it is of God or whether I speak from Myself"** (Jn. 7:17).

Identification. The first step is to identify who these people are whom Christ described as, **"all that the Father gives Me."** Since He used this phrase four other times, those contexts must also be examined. **"This is the will of Him who sent Me, that of all that He has given Me I lose nothing, but raise it up on the last day"** (Jn. 6:39). **"... that the Son may glorify You, even as You gave Him authority over all flesh, that to all whom You have given Him, He may give eternal life"** (Jn. 17:1-2) **"I manifested Your name to the men whom You gave Me out of the world. They were Yours and You gave them to Me, and they have kept Your word"** (17:6). **"I ask on their behalf; I do not ask on behalf of the world, but of those whom You hast given Me; for they are Yours"** (17:9). From this context of the Lord's high priestly prayer, it becomes clear that He is referring to the living disciples, whom the Father had given Him, especially the Apostles.

This could not be a reference to an abstract concept of the elect of all ages for a number of reasons. In 17:6 the Lord Jesus says that He had shown the Father to them personally. This could not be true of the elect of past ages, and the past tense He used (aorist) could not include the elect of future ages. The clause, **"they have kept Your word"** also eliminates believers of other ages, since it is obvious that this could not be said about future generations. Additionally, He later clarifies that those who in turn believe through their word are distinct from those whom the Father had given him: "**I do not ask on behalf of these alone, but for those also who believe in Me through their word ...**" (17:20). So the idea is clear in both John 6 and 17, that the Father is turning the godly Jewish remnant over to the Son during His earthly ministry. These are the already believing ones who inevitably come to Him, since *they were already regenerate*. Thus this passage has nothing to do with irresistible grace upon unbelievers, since these were already sincere believers. This is confirmed by the Lord's earlier statement, when He praised the Father for revealing His mysteries to these little children: "**All things have been handed over to me by my Father,...**" (Lk. 10:22a, ESV).

In previous ages, Old Testament saints had put their trust in the Father. Now that the Son has begun His ministry, that believing remnant is being given to the Son by the Father. This included many converts of John the Baptizer, as the Apostle John had described in John 1, including himself, James, Peter, Andrew, Nathaniel, and others. Previously they had "**heard and learned from the Father**" (John 6:45). Now they are transferring their faith to the Son, that is, they are coming to Him. Christ's quotation from Isaiah 54:13 in John 6:45 is strong confirmation of this: "**It is written in the prophets, 'And they shall all be taught of GOD.' Everyone who has heard and learned from the Father comes to Me**" (6:45). It becomes clear that these contemporary disciples, who were under His ministry and were open to the Father's teaching from the Old Testament, were the ones who came to Him in faith. A clear example is His comment at Caesarea Philippi after Peter's confession of His deity: "**Blessed are you, Simon Barjona, because flesh and blood did not reveal *this* to you, but My Father who is in heaven** " (Mt. 16:17).

Drawing. The 'drawing' of John 6:44 requires further consideration: "**No one can come to Me, unless the Father who sent Me draws him; and I will raise him up on the last day.**" Augustinians see this as an irresistible drawing. This is improbable, since the BAGD lexicon lists a second meaning for *helkuein*, "to draw a person in the direction of values for inner life, *draw, attract, an extended figurative use of meaning.*" A dozen references from the secular Greek and the Septuagint are given in support of this. None of these indicate any supposed irresistibility: "**I have loved you with an everlasting love; therefore I have drawn you with lovingkindness**" (Jer. 31.3). "**Therefore the maidens love you. Draw me after you and let us run together**" (Songs 1:3-4).[18] *Note that the primary literal meaning of the verb 'to draw, to drag' has reference to physical objects, whereas the figurative usage in reference to the inner life of a person is appropriately not coercive.*

The Lord Jesus used the same word, *helkuein*, again in John 12:32: "'**And I, if I be lifted up from the earth, will draw all men to Myself**'." Here it is the cross, not irresistible grace which draws sinners. Do some believe that God drags us kicking and screaming to salvation? Is our God really a coercive God? So, how are people drawn to Christ? The context of John 6:44 makes clear that they were drawn by the testimony of Abraham, Moses, and the prophets of the Old Testament Scriptures, as contemporary Jews checked out the supernatural credentials of Jesus of Nazareth and concluded with Nathaniel, "**Rabbi, You are the Son of God; You are the King of Israel**" (Jn. 1:49). Now since Pentecost, God has used the apostolic message and ministry, working mediately through Christian witnesses. It is as simple as that. Dean Henry Alford, that master exegete of a past century, confirmed this:

> That this 'drawing' is not irresistible grace, is confessed even by Augustine himself, the great upholder of the doctrines of grace.... The Greek expositors take the view which I have adopted above.... This *drawing* now is being exerted on all the world—in accordance with the Lord's prophecy (12:32) and His command (Matthew 28:19-20).[19]

John 6:65. "**And He was saying, 'For this reason I have said to you, that no one can come to Me, unless it has been granted him from the Father'.**" Although this is part of the same context of the contrast of believers with unbelievers, there are some additional contextual considerations here. Many of his professed disciples had just been grumbling at His words (6:61), and the immediately preceding verse is crucial, "**... 'But there are some of you who do not believe.' For Jesus knew from the beginning who they were who did not believe, and who it was that would betray Him**.... **As a result of this many of His disciples withdrew, and were not walking with Him anymore**.... '**Did I Myself not choose you, the twelve, and yet one of you is a devil?**'" (6:64, 66, 70). Obviously this choice was to apostleship, not to salvation!

Rejecting great light. Thus, in John 6:65 Christ refers to professed disciples, who had walked with Him for an extensive period of time, had sat under His teaching, and had seen His miracles, especially to Judas Iscariot. They were rejecting the greatest light that anybody could ever reject. They had professed to believe but, like Judas, were counterfeits. These are the ones to whom God was not granting the privilege to come to Him. What is the principle here? Is it the hidden counsel of God to which the Calvinists are so wont to flee? Or is it God's judgment upon the rejection of great light? The answer is given by Paul, who had resisted the convicting work of the Holy Spirit, kicking against the oxgoads (Acts 26:14). And yet God saved him! He tells us why in 1 Timothy 1:12-13. "**I thank Christ Jesus our Lord,... even though I was formerly a blasphemer and a persecutor and a violent aggressor. And yet I was shown mercy, because I acted ignorantly in unbelief.**" He had not closed his heart against great light. But Judas and the other counterfeit disciples sinned against the greatest light possible, and thus came under the judgmental blindness so frequently mentioned in Scripture.

Judgment. Not long afterward in a discussion with some Pharisees the Lord said, "'**For judgment I came into this world, that those who do not see may see; and that those who see may become blind.' Those of the Pharisees who were with Him heard these things and said to Him, 'We are not blind too, are we?' Jesus said to them, 'If you were blind, you would have no sin; but since you say, "We see," your sin** remains'" (John 9:39-41). So John 6:65 must be understood in a judgmental sense and not as having anything to do with election or reprobation in eternity past. Another passage also speaks of judgmental blindness upon those who closed their hearts to such great light: **"But though He had performed so many signs before them, yet they were not believing in Him;... He who rejects Me, and does not receive My sayings, has one who judges him; the word I spoke is what will judge him at the last day"** (Jn. 12:37, 48).

John 10:16

Calvinists assume that the "other sheep, which are not of this fold," is a reference to as yet unsaved elect who must be saved and brought into Christ's flock.[20] What other fold could He be referring to? All His disciples were Jews, and the day was coming in which that great missionary purpose of God would be fulfilled when He would bring Samaritans, proselytes, and Gentiles into the one flock with one shepherd.

Acts 9:1-19; 22:1-21; 26:1-20

Many Calvinists use the conversion of Saul of Tarsus as an example of irresistible grace.[21] However, there is nothing in the narrative or Paul's letters to support that idea. Certainly Saul went through a long spiritual struggle from the time he witnessed the martyrdom of Stephen, reinforced by hearing the repeated testimonies of the Christians he persecuted (Acts 26:10-11; 1 Tim. 1:12-16), until the very moment that he heard the words of the risen Lord, **"I am Jesus whom you are persecuting."** Instantaneously he realized that he had been tragically and absolutely wrong. He had thought sincerely that he was serving the true God of Israel, when in reality he was persecuting God's Messiah and His true people. It is very possible that as he heard the truth from the lips of Christians, he struggled with doubts about his own position. Certainly the Holy Spirit had been convicting him through their words, since that is the obvious meaning of the oxgoad the Lord referred to (Acts 26:14). At that point he had a choice to deny the truth or to face the new reality with which he was confronted. Granted the facts that he now faced were overwhelming, still God did not force his will. His own analysis in 1 Timothy 1:12-16, just referenced, was that he had acted **"ignorantly in unbelief."** His personal narrative is totally comprehensible without irresistible grace.

Acts 13:48

Another favorite Calvinistic proof-text is Luke's comment on the turning of the Apostles to Gentiles at Antioch of Pisidia after strong Jewish opposition: **"And when the Gentiles heard this, they began rejoicing and glorifying the word of the Lord; and as many as had been appointed [*tetagmenoi*] to eternal life believed."** A survey of translations shows agreement with the NAS version quoted above and seems supportive of the Calvinistic viewpoint. Since translators tend to follow the rut of tradition, this passage demands very careful study. Rotherham (**"as many as had become disposed for..."**), Alexander Campbell, R. J. Knowling in *EGT*, A. T. Robertson, and Alfred Marshall's Interlinear (**"having been disposed"**) are among the few to have broken out of the rut.[22] Most translators have overlooked important data.

Three issues. There are three issues which must be addressed in Acts 13:48: the context, the meaning of *tetagmenoi*, and whether this is a middle or passive verb. The BAGD lexicon gives as a primary meaning of *tassein*:

> 1. to bring about an order of things by arranging, *arrange, put in place* ...
> b of a pers. put into a specific position, used with a prep . . *tassein tina eis - assign someone to a (certain) classification* ... [middle or] pass. *belong to, be classed among those possessing - hosoi ēsan tetagmenoi eis zōēn aiōnion* **Ac 13:48.**— *tassein heauton eis diakonian - devote oneself to a service* [2 secular Greek examples] 1 Cor 16:15.[23]

Although it has been ignored that *tetagmenoi*, being a perfect participle in form, can be either middle or passive voice, this is of great significance in interpretation.[24] This is a periphrastic* pluperfect construction, which shows action antecedent to the main verb, *episteusan* (they believed).[25] The use of a neuter plural subject with a plural verb tends to emphasize the individuality of each subject.[26] The middle voice, being reflexive, could be rendered, "as many as had devoted themselves to eternal life believed" or "as many as had arranged (positioned) themselves toward eternal life believed." The first rendering is suggested by the usage in 1 Cor. 16:15: **"The household of Stephanas ... have devoted themselves for the ministry to the saints."** The second rendering is suggested by the first meaning listed in BAGD and the strong military use of the word in secular Greek, according to the LSJ lexicon: "—*draw up in order of battle, form, array, marshal,...* Med., *fall in, form in order of battle* ... 2. *post, station* ... III. c. acc. rei, *place in a certain order or relative position.*"[27] Delling, in *TDNT*, concurs with this general understanding in reference to Acts 13:48: "The idea that God's will to save is accomplished in Christians with their conversion is obviously not connected with the thought of predestination (IV, 192, 1ff.), but rather with that of conferring status (–>31, 20ff.); cf. *ouk axious* Ac 13:46."[28] Delling here is pointing to a contextual argument, so now the context must be carefully examined.

Context. First, examine the narrower context. When the Jews began to contradict and blaspheme, the Apostles said, **"It was necessary that the word of God should be spoken to you first; since you repudiate it, and judge yourselves unworthy of eternal life, behold, we are turning to the Gentiles"** (Acts 13:46). The contrast Luke makes between these words of the Apostles and his own statement in 13:48 is clear. Since the Jews had *put themselves* in a position hostile to eternal life, the Apostles very explicitly used the reflexive pronoun ('yourselves') to attribute the cause of their rejection to their attitude. Then Luke, in explaining the opposite response of the Gentiles, most probably intended a reflexive middle voice, rather than passive. Thus, he attributed the cause of the Gentile's faith to their attitude, which in 13:42 was evidenced in their pleading with the Apostles to come back on a second Sabbath to give the word of God. The contrasting parallel is striking.

Two other incidents immediately following have already been examined, when Luke attributes the faith of the converts to human factors (Acts 14:1; 17:11-12). Since Luke's theological perspective, presumably derived from Paul, allowed this, this is the most likely option in Antioch of Pisidia as well. The semantics, grammar, and syntax as explained above cogently lead to that conclusion. This exegesis is not new or novel, having been proposed by Dean Henry Alford a century and a half ago:

> The Jews had *judged themselves unworthy of eternal life:* the Gentiles, as many as were disposed to eternal life, believed.... but to find *in this text* pre-ordination to life asserted, is to force both the word and the context to a meaning which they do not contain.... Wordsworth well observes that it would be interesting to enquire what influence such renderings as this of *praeordinati* in the Vulgate version had on the minds of men like St. Augustine and his followers in the Western Church in treating the great questions of free will, election, reprobation, and final perseverance . . The tendency of the Eastern Fathers, who read the original Greek, was, he remarks, in a different direction from that of the Western School.[29]

Acts 16:14. "**A woman named Lydia,... a worshiper of God, was listening; and the Lord opened her heart to respond to the things spoken by Paul.**" Augustinians assume that Luke's statement that the Lord opened Lydia's heart to respond to the things spoken by the Apostles is a proof of irresistible grace. The Holy Spirit's initiative in opening the sinner's heart to the gospel message is not questioned, but it is by the conviction of the Holy Spirit (Jn. 16:8-11), which is neither irresistible nor immediate.   See Chapter 7 for the examples of conviction, which came through human instrumentality. The same is true with Lydia since Luke emphasizes that she was listening to the things spoken by Paul. There is also an important antecedent factor mentioned by Luke, that she was already "**a worshiper of God.**" Whether she was Jewish, a devout Gentile, or a proselyte, is not stated, but clearly she had been exposed to the Old Testament in her association with the Jewish women who had gathered for prayer on the Sabbath (16:13). *To foist the notion of irresistible grace upon this passage is theological extrapolation, not contextual exegesis.*

Then in Acts 26:17-18 Paul told how God charged him to minister to the Gentiles, "**to whom I am sending you, to open their eyes so that they may turn from darkness to light and from the dominion of Satan to God, that they may receive forgiveness of sins and an inheritance among those who have been sanctified by faith in Me.**" Paul was to be God's instrument to open the eyes of the Gentiles.

Romans 8:28-30. Augustinians seem to resort to this passage most consistently to prove irresistible grace. Please refer back to the discussion in Chapter 20 to see that there is no irresistible grace here.

Miscellaneous proof-texts. There are a number of proof-texts referred to by Calvinists, usually in a list without any exegetical support. Vance complains: "No exegesis is ever attempted, and little comment is made beside the standard Calvinistic cliches."[30] Vance's survey of Calvinistic works is most extensive, and his observation is undoubtedly correct. Some of the passages which seem irrelevant to the issue if taken literally are Psalm 110:3, John 5:21, and Philippians 2:12-13. James 1:18 is relevant and was discussed previously (cf. p. 59).

Passages Which Refute Irresistible Grace

There are a number of passages which stand in direct contradiction to the doctrine of irresistible grace, which are ignored by determinists, but must be examined in their contexts.

Matthew 13:1-43=Mark 4:1-20=Luke 8:4-15. When an explanation is sought as to why some people get saved and why others who hear the word of God remain unsaved, in the parable of the soils the Lord attributed the differing response to factors related to the soils themselves. This parable has already been explained in several places (pp. 165-6, 221) to which the reader is referred. Some raise the issue of Christ's quotation of Isaiah 6 in verses 10-15, especially, **"but to them it has not been granted"** (Mt. 13:11). However, it should be understood that all of these parables are judgmental in nature, occasioned in Matthew's sequence of events by the strong rejections of the Messiah in Matthew 12.[31] This is not the outworking of a decree of reprobation, but rather a response to Israel's rejection of Him.

Matthew 23:37. After three years of ministering to "this nation (genea)" of Israel and rebuking their unbelief, Christ cries out, **"O Jerusalem, Jerusalem, who kills the prophets and stones those who are sent to her! How often I wanted to gather your children together, the way a hen gathers her chicks under her wings, and you were unwilling."** A good case can be made for Israel's rejection of the Messiah as being part of God's eternal plan, yet the Lord attributes it to Israel's unwillingness. The cause of Israel's unbelief was not some lack of irresistible grace arising from a decree of reprobation which passed them by. No, Christ attributed it to Israel's willfulness.

Luke 7:30. Christ singled out the religious leaders of Israel as those who were resisting God's purpose: **"But the Pharisees and the lawyers rejected God's purpose for themselves, not having been baptized by John."** This statement is by itself simple and straightforward– that men can reject and thwart God's purpose for themselves. It is only a deterministic interpretation of 'irresistible grace' which would deny this fact. The fact that men are unsaved and going to Hell is attributed to their own self will, not to some mysterious elective purpose of God worked out by irresistible grace.

Acts 7:51. Stephen's accusation against the Jews who were about to kill him is most significant. **"You men who are stiff-necked and uncircumcised in heart and ears are always resisting the Holy Spirit; you are doing just as your fathers did."** From this statement it is difficult to avoid the conclusion that the Holy Spirit can be resisted. The implication is that the Holy Spirit had been seeking to convict them through Stephen's message, but they were resisting that convicting work. This is in harmony with Christ's reference in John 16:8 that the Spirit was to convict the world (*kosmos*) of unregenerate sinners. Acts 7:54 records their negative reaction to that convicting work: **"Now when they heard this, they were cut to the quick, and they began gnashing their teeth at him."** So conviction is not limited to the elect, nor is it irresistible.

1 Corinthians 4:15 and Philemon 10. In both of these passages, Paul speaks metaphorically of his having begotten Christians into Christian faith. It almost sounds as if he is taking credit for their new birth, but this certainly could not be the case! The new birth itself is one hundred percent the work of the Holy Spirit. Although Paul did not literally cause their actual new birth, per se, he used this figurative language to emphasize the point that he did have a lot to do with the circumstances which led them up to faith in Christ. There would have been no Corinthian church if he hadn't obeyed the Greatest Commission. But in any case Calvinists have failed to distinguish the human element in the ministry and circumstances of bringing people to faith, from the new birth itself, which is a distinct issue.

Problems of Coherence

The insincerity of the general call. George Bryson has described the bottom line of the message of extreme Calvinism very bluntly: "You will be saved or damned *for* all eternity because you were saved or damned *from* all eternity."[32] This statement makes many Calvinists angry, but it certainly represents the view of R. C. Sproul, among many others: "What predestination means, in its most elementary form, is that our final destination, heaven or hell, is decided by God not only before we get there, but before we are even born."[33] Those who believe in unconditional election and irresistible grace cannot escape from the force of this characterization. *This leaves the sincerity of the general call to salvation in a totally incoherent position.*

If all mankind is totally unable to respond to the general call, and only those unconditionally elected by God will be the recipients of irresistible grace, then there is no way that the sincerity of that general invitation of the gospel can be maintained. Some Calvinists say that people can reject Christ of their own free will, but they cannot accept Him of their own free will. John Wesley bluntly stated that the doctrine of predestination "represents our Lord as a hypocrite, a deceiver of the people, a man void of common sincerity, as mocking his helpless creatures by offering what he never intends to give, by saying one thing and meaning another."[34] Wesley's coherence argument is valid. The Calvinistic gospel mocks the 'non-elect' and is not "good news."

The God of the Bible is not coercive. As already observed, some Calvinists are willing to use words like 'coerce,' 'compel,' or 'constraint' to describe what is involved in irresistible grace. This raises the question already discussed in Chapter 2, "What kind of a God do we have?" Is He a coercive God? There is no evidence either in the biblical narrative or in the didactic books that God works coercively. Indeed, the age-long problem of the silence of God is a far greater mystery, that is, why does God seem so reticent to intervene in human affairs, especially when godless forces seem to be winning the day? Even today we struggle with this question. Why did God not intervene in the World Trade Center terrorism? The answer is that although God retains His ultimate sovereign power, He has chosen not to use it directly in most situations.

Why restrict irresistible grace to the elect?. Sproul recognizes the seriousness of this problem: "The nasty problem for the Calvinist is seen in the [question]. If God can and does choose to insure the salvation of some, why then does he not insure the salvation of all?"[35] While claiming that this is not a problem for Calvinists only, he seems unaware that the Calvinistic presuppositions cause the problem. Since non-Calvinists do not accept the premise that God saves by irresistible power, we do not have the problem. God has the power to insure the salvation of everyone, but since He hasn't chosen to implement the plan of salvation by irresistible power, He refrains from exercising it. Sproul thinks the non-Calvinist is concerned about God violating man's freedom, which may be the tenor of some Arminian arguments. However, those of us in the middle are more impressed with the way in which from Eden onward God has delegated responsibility to mankind, as spelled out in considerable detail in Chapters 2 and 3.

Conclusions

It is concluded that the doctrine of irresistible grace has been derived by Augustinians through a deductive process from the other points of the TULIP, rather than through a careful inductive,* exegetical* study of all relevant Scripture. When the historical context of the favorite proof-texts is given adequate consideration, the presuppositions brought out into the open, and careful word study of the usage of the term 'calling' is done, there is no basis left for irresistible grace.

---

1. Francis Brown, *The New Brown-Driver-Briggs-Gesenius Hebrew and English Lexicon*, pp. 895-6.

2. Arndt and Gingrich, *LexiconI*, p, 437

3. K L. Schmidt in Kittel, *Theological Dictionary of the New Testament*, III, p 490.

4. Ibid, p 489.

5 Schmidt, in *TDNT*, III, p 494

6 For example, Charles Hodge, *Systematic Theology* (GR Eerdmans, 1968), II, pp 687-714

7 R C Sproul, *Grace Unknown the Heart of Reformed Theology*, pp 179-96 The kind of irresistible grace he advocates is indeed unknown in the Scriptures, judging by the total lack of direct Scriptural evidence in his chapter

8. Bruce A. Ware, "The Place of Effectual Calling and Grace in a Calvinistic Soteriology," in Thomas R Schreiner and Bruce A. Ware, eds , *The Grace of God, The Bondage of the Will*, II 345 Edwin H Palmer, *The Five Points of Calvinism. a Study Guide*, pp 56-67. He references John 6 37, 44 and Acts 16 14, but doesn't even quote them

9 Duane Edward Spencer, *TULIP. The Five Points of Calvinism in the Light of Scripture*, p. 48

10 Loraine Boettner, *Predestination*, 5th ed., pp 162-181 Berkhof shows the close identification of effectual calling and regeneration in 17th century Reformed theology, and although he distinguished the two made no reference to faith in reference to regeneration; L Berkhof, *Systematic Theology*, rev ed., pp 469-476.

11   C Samuel Storms, *Chosen for Life* (GR· Baker, 1987), p. 46, as quoted by Vance, p 513

12   Gordon H Clark, *Predestination*, pp. 198-200.

13 Ibid, p 174.

14 Vance, *The Other Side of Calvinism* (rev. ed), p. 502.

15 Aurelius Augustine, "Letter to Vincentius," 2, 5. Also "Vincentius," 5 (AD 408); *Corr. Don.*, 21, 23; "Letter to Donatus," 3 (AD 416), as quoted and referenced by Forster and Marston, pp. 284, 292. Augustines's advocacy of the use of the physical force of the Roman government to coerce the Donatists back into the Catholic Church was the basis of the inquisition and consistent persecution of other Christian groups by the Roman church over the centuries. How much did it influence those Augustinians, Luther and Calvin, in their persecution and execution of Anabaptists and Servetus is an open question See Forster and Marston, pp 257-95.

16 Walter Grundmann in *TDNT*, I· 344-7 He doesn't use the adjective 'circumstantial' of "constraint," but all the references adduced in the LXX and Josephus lead to that conclusion. See Ps 107:13 (Gk. 106 13) for an example

17 Arndt and Gingrich, p 51

18 Bagster- Arndt-Gingrich-Danker, *A Greek-English Lexicon of the New Testament*, p.318

19 Henry Alford, *The New Testament for English Readers: John*, p 521.

20 Edwin H. Palmer, *The Five Points of Calvinism* (GR Guardian Press 1972) p.62

21 Custance, p 66. (The best texts do not have the goad in Acts 9·5, but rather 26·14.)

22 A. T Robertson, *Word Pictures*, II:200, R. J. Knowling,, in *Expositors' Greek Text*, II 300, references Rendall, Blass, Wendt, and Page, who so understands Chrysostom's interpretation, & Alexander Campbell, *Living Oracles*

23 Bagster-Arndt-Gingrich-Danker Lexicon, p. 991

24 Bagster's *Analytical Greek Lexicon*, p xx

25 Wallace, *Grammar Beyond Basics*, pp. 649, 626.

26 Ibid, p. 400f

27 Liddell-Scott-Jones, *Lexicon*, pp. 1759-60.

28 Gerhard Delling in *TDNT*, VIII, pp 28-9.

29. Henry Alford, *The Greek Testament*, II, 153-4.

30 Vance, p 503.

31 Alva J McClain, *The Greatness of the Kingdom* (Chicago: Moody, 1959), pp 322-3

32 George L Bryson, *The Five Points of Calvinism "Weighed and Found Wanting,"* p 121 Reformed professor, Douglas Wilson, says, "George Bryson is a very unusual non-Calvinist He is able to describe the doctrinal position of Calvinism without putting any extra eggs in the pudding His descriptions are fair and accurate, and he clearly knows his subject" (Quoted on the cover)

33 Sproul, *Chosen*, p. 22

34 John Wesley, "Sermon on Free Grace" in *Sermons*, I 482ff, as quoted by Philip Schaff, *History*, 8 566

35 Sproul, p 35.

History, I think, is probably a bit like a
pebbly beach, a complicated mass,
secretively three-dimensional. It is very
hard to chart what lies up against what, and
why and how deep. What does tend to get
charted is what looks manageable, most
recognisable (and usually linear) like the
wriggly flow of flotsam and jetsam, and
stubborn tar deposits.

-Richard Wentworth

A MIDDLE WAY IN CHRISTIAN HISTORY

In beginning historical research for this book, I discovered a significant reaction to extreme Calvinism in the seventeenth-century Amyraldian movement of the Reformed* churches of France. As my historical study broadened, a substantial trail of over a dozen historical movements emerged, many of which were supportive of a "middle way."

Ultimately this chapter does not determine the truth or falsity of the position advocated here, since there is only one standard of truth—the Bible as the inerrant* word of God. Christian history can only confirm the results of biblical exegesis;* it should not be preliminary to, or even a parallel study to the biblical investigation. That is, if there are no antecedents in the history of Christian thought, then the biblical data must be re-examined to see where the doctrinal study might have gone wrong. *But far too much theological study starts with historical material, which by its very nature is far more subjective than biblical data.*

There are a number of reasons why historical study must be so limited. The first is the imperfection of the historical record. Many documents upon which study should be based have long since perished, whether by barbarian or Muslim incursions, persecution by anti-Christian forces, or of smaller Christian groups by the political majority church (Catholic or Protestant), or by the ravages of time and bacterial action. Since the loss has not been impartial, the available data is skewed from the start.

We all have biases and theological presuppositions. We come to this historical study with a bias since we concluded, based on biblical studies, that an intermediate theology of salvation is true to God's word. Now we turn to Christian history to see whether others before us have come to a similar viewpoint. *This research does confirm substantial antecedents for a middle way; indeed, it raises serious problems for deterministic views.*

Augustine, the First Predestinarian
The great hiatus
My early research uncovered a startling statement by Reformed writer Paul K. Jewett: "As has often been observed, the first true predestinarian was Augustine."[1] This may not have given pause to Professor Jewett, but the question immediately arises about four centuries of church history without any predestinarian teaching or emphasis, as other historians confirm. How could this be, if it is a basic biblical doctrine? How could the disciples of the Apostles and their succeeding disciples for almost four hundred years have not discussed the subject? These early church fathers said much about free will, indeed, they coined the term, but nothing about predestination.[2]

The Augustine/Pelagius controversy
Pelagius (c.350-409) was a British monk who objected to Augustine's doctrine of original sin, since he denied that the sin of Adam constituted all mankind as sinners. Although they missed meeting personally, Augustine (353-430) wrote extensively against Pelagius' views after the conflict began in 406 and hardened his views of predestination and irresistible grace, which crystallized after 416. Pelagianism* was rejected at the Synod of Carthage in 412 and 418, and that rejection was confirmed at the Third Ecumenical Council at Ephesus (431). Neve affirms, "But the rejection of Pelagianism did not mean the acceptance of everything in the Augustinian system. It was Augustine's doctrine of predestination which gave offense, to those even who otherwise favored him in his controversy with Pelagius."[3]

The three categories sometimes used to classify the church fathers are a gross oversimplification: Pelagian, Semi-Pelagian*, and Augustinian. Pelagius was probably a heretic in emphasizing human ability, but attaching his name to mediating church fathers is to use a prejudicial term ('semi-Pelagian') of those who were not heretics. *They should be more accurately designated as semi-Augustinians.* * Both Philip Schaff and J. L. Neve use that terminology and make this distinction (which R. C. Sproul does not do).[4]

While all semi-Augustinians held to Augustine's view of original sin and emphasis upon God's grace in salvation, they did not follow him in his view of predestination and irresistible grace. Many emphasized God's initiative in salvation by some reference to prevenient (preceding) grace, but others, while stressing grace, thought that man had to take a first step by responding to the message of grace. Another confusing factor is that Augustine saw regeneration as a process, not as an instantaneous work of God.[5] Probably most of the early fathers should be considered semi-Augustinian. In any case, it is clear that all believed in general redemption and in 'free will.'

The triumph of semi-Augustinianism
There is no question that Augustine not only started a major battle with Pelagianism,* which he won, but for a century afterward a major contro-

322   GETTING THE GOSPEL RIGHT IN HISTORY

versy continued among those who accepted his essential view of original sin and his emphasis upon grace in salvation. But other than his disciple and defender, Prosper of Aquitaine (d. 463), virtually no one accepted his views on predestination and irresistible grace.[6] Confirming the novelty of his views, his contemporaries such as Jerome (347-415) and Ambrose (350-397) argued that very objection— *these views were absolutely new and not held by any in the church before Augustine.*

Augustine's view on election and irresistible grace spawned a strong reaction from many church fathers. Synods at Arles (472) and Lyon (475) sought to resolve the question and ultimately it was brought to the Synod of Orange (529), where the semi-Augustinians* won the day against Pelagianism, but without affirming predestination or irresistible grace. While the Synod of Orange affirmed much of Augustine's doctrine of grace, it departed from his views in the following particulars, as summarized by Neve: 1. The only statement about predestination was a rejection of predestination to perdition. 2. There was no affirmation of irresistible grace. 3. God foreknows all things, good and evil, but His prescience as such is not causative. 4. Prevenient grace is affirmed. 5. The grace of God and the merits of Christ are for all; God earnestly desires and wills the salvation of all men (1 Tim. 2:4). 6. Through the grace of God all may, by the cooperation of God, perform what is necessary for their soul's salvation.[7]

Jewett is clearly wrong when he claims that a "milder predestinarianism became the official teaching of the Latin church" after the Synod of Orange.[8] Schaff agrees with Neve's appraisal:

> At the synod of Orange (Arausio) in the year 529, at which Caesarius of Arles was leader, the Semi-Pelagian system, *yet without mention of its adherents,* was condemned in twenty-five chapters or canons, and the Augustinian doctrine of sin and grace was approved, without the doctrine of absolute or particularistic predestination. (italics his, underline mine)[9]

Thus, a semi-Augustinian view distinct from semi-Pelagianism won out.

Augustine's doctrinal limitations and problems

Since Augustine was such a towering figure in the history of Christian thought by permeating both Roman Catholic and Reformation theology, it is important to evaluate his impact. It was a mixed bag; he did move Christian theology back toward the doctrine of grace in a significant way. There were also some serious negative elements in his background, linguistic and exegetical skills, perspective, and hence, in his theology, which developed into absolute evils among both Catholics and Protestants.

His view of salvation. Augustine's theology of salvation was little developed. It certainly did not include the teaching of justification by faith, let alone the *sola fide* of the Reformers. The reason was his sacramental view of salvation through baptism, the eucharist, and membership in the majority, politically approved Roman church. Beyond that there was no need for salvation truth. Indeed, it was his strong emphasis upon baptism beginning *a process* of regeneration and an external organizational unity of the church allied with the state which set the pattern for the dead state-churchism of much of European Christendom over the centuries.[10] This is *the major heresy* in Christendom today, through which hundreds of millions are "damned through the church." One of the most offensive views to his contemporaries was that unbaptized infants are damned. Augustine had an incredible impact upon the medieval Latin-Catholic church, which clearly lapsed into scholasticism.* Schaff states: "He ruled the entire theology of the middle ages, and became the father of scholasticism in virtue of his dialectic mind, and the father of mysticism in virtue of his devout heart, without being responsible for the excesses of either system."

Coercive persecution of non-conformists. It was out of his controversy with the Donatist movement in North Africa that Augustine, not only put loyalty to the majority church above loyalty to the word of God, but actually began to advocate coercion in order to force the Donatist 'sectarians' back into the Roman church. He grossly misinterpreted the parable of the great wedding feast in Luke 14:15-24, by taking 'compel' (*anagkazein*) as implying physical force and using it as a basis for persecuting the Donatists, who were closer to the truth than he was. Subsequently, Augustine's misinterpretation became the basis for the infamous medieval inquisition and for the Reformers' persecution of the Anabaptists.* That centuries of persecution of true and godly believers can be traced back to Augustine's careless exegesis is outrageous! Connected with this is his view of the organizational nature of the universal (Catholic) church, in contrast with the biblical view of its mystical, organic nature. He saw apostolic succession and tradition as more important than conformity to Scripture. Schaff concludes that in Augustine "the state church found not only the first Christian leader of importance to advocate the use of persecution against non-conformists, but *they found the only Christian theologian of significance whose theological system could justify such persecution.*"[11] The reference here is to the relation of irresistible grace to coercion to faith.

Manichean influence. Some of Augustine's views can be traced back to his nine years in Manicheanism* before his conversion. A. H. Newman traces asceticism, the exaltation of virginity, viewing all sex as sinful, pompous ceremonials in the church, sacerdotalism, and indulgences as coming into the churches through the influence of Manicheanism.[12] There are Manichean roots to Augustine's deterministic theology as well. The pervasive influence of Manichean thought, although resisted by the other church fathers, gained entrance into the church through Augustine. He was the Trojan horse for Manichean determinism. In fact the Catholic church continued to reject determinism for another eleven centuries after the Synod of Orange, but an Augustinian monk named Martin Luther capitulated to it under the guise of grace and set the Protestant Reformation on this erroneous path. One other serious consequence of Augustine's determinism was his denial of assurance. He taught that the elect can only be known by perseverance to the end of life. Thus he robbed believers of the most precious salvation reality short of eternal life itself (cf. Ch. 9).

The root of Roman Catholic accretions. It is widely acknowledged that many of the errors of Roman Catholicism have their roots in Augustine. Sir Robert Anderson wrote, "Nearly all the errors prevalent in Romanism can be traced back to Augustine." Benjamin B. Warfield conceded that Augustine was "in a true sense the founder of Roman Catholicism." Zanchius referred to him as one of the four legs supporting the papal chair.[13]

Medieval determinism

The Greek Eastern church ignored Augustine and never showed any inclination toward absolute predestination. John of Damascus held to absolute foreknowledge but rejected absolute election since God cannot foreordain sin and does not force virtue upon the reluctant will. Schaff's summary of the Latin Western church is quite pointed:

> The Latin church retained a traditional reverence for Augustine, as her greatest divine, but never committed herself to his scheme of predestination.... *But the prevailing sentiment cautiously steered midway between Augustinianism and Semi-Pelagianism,* giving chief weight to the preceding and enabling grace of God, yet claiming some merit for man's consenting and co-operating will. *This compromise may be called Semi-Augustinianism, as distinct from Semi-Pelagianism. It was adopted by the Synod of Orange (Arausio) in 529* (emphasis mine).[14]

The subject was not significantly raised again until after the Reformation, but it is clear that the Roman church, on the popular level, drifted increasingly into semi-Pelagianism* in the centuries before the Reformation.

The Reformers and Their Successors
The German and Swiss Reformations

Undoubtedly the Protestant Reformation took place in a time of great ferment, intellectually, religiously, politically, and theologically. Mankind frequently tends to overreact in such times, and many examples of overreaction could be cited. Although in many areas we might criticize Martin Luther (1483-1546) for not going far enough, in reference to predestination he overreacted to the semi-Pelagianism* of the Catholic church. Clearly in the succeeding centuries there were over a dozen significant movements which sought to bring things back into better balance.

Luther never totally broke free from either his Augustinian background or a scholastic* way of thinking. His rationalizations about the faith of infants, the ubiquity of the body of Christ, consubstantiation, etc., reflect a scholastic* mode of thinking. He was, after all, an Augustinian monk and after his conversion he found Augustine's emphasis upon grace most conducive to his newly recovered understanding of justification by faith alone. Furthermore, he did not totally divest himself of Augustine's views of regeneration through baptism beginning a process either. Although Augustine knew nothing of justification by faith alone, his emphasis on grace seemed like a good fit to Luther. Undoubtedly, both Zwingli and Calvin were greatly influenced by Luther's determinism,* derived from Augustine.

The Anabaptist modifications.* Within a few years, some of Luther's and Zwingli's colleagues had second thoughts. By about 1521 Ulrich Zwingli (1484-1531) had drawn to himself a number of gifted young intellectuals, who were converted and joined with him in the Zurich Reformation. Within a few years some, such as Conrad Grebel and Simon Stumpf, were pressing Zwingli for a more thoroughgoing reformation. Dr. Balthasar Hubmaier joined them in their attack against the mass and other Catholic accretions. By 1524 a group of seven radical reformers broke with Zwingli over his failure to eliminate the mass, and the next year crystallized their opposition to infant baptism by immersing each other. Thus began the Swiss Anabaptist movement, which had many distinct strands.[15] Newman explains:

> They were almost without exception opposed to the Augustinian system of doctrine, especially in its Lutheran and Calvinistic forms, insisting upon the freedom of the will and the necessity of good works as the fruit of faith, and regarding faith as a great transforming process whereby we are brought not simply to participate in Christ's merits, but to enter into the completest union with him in a life of utter self-abnegation.[16]

Although determinism* was not the basic cause of the split with the Reformers, the Anabaptist* leaders, many of whom were well versed in the original languages and the church fathers, felt that the Scriptures militated against the Augustinian component of Reformation theology. Moreover, their unusually consistent Christian life and testimony could not be impugned by the Protestants and Catholics, who slaughtered them by the thousands. As they moved on to early martyrdom, they must have felt doubly convinced that Augustine's contribution to the Reformation was negative, especially in regard to his teaching of coercion to faith. Unfortunately, few of the leaders survived long enough to write any theological analysis of the issues, although men like Dr. Balthaser Hubmaier were fully competent to do so.[17] Hans Denck was a Bavarian Anabaptist leader who "was exceedingly trained in the word of the Scriptures and educated in the three main languages." Like many other Anabaptists, he was misrepresented as a universalist, but he actually held that Christ's death was sufficient for all humankind, but efficacious only to the believer.[18]

Bullinger's modification of Zwingli. It is clear that Henry Bullinger (1504-1575), Zwingli's successor in Zurich, did not go as far as Zwingli and Calvin on predestination. He was quoted by English Bishop John Davenant as holding to general redemption. Schaff says that he came closer to Calvin's view later in his ministry[19] and also alludes to Theodor Bibliander, Bullinger's colleague, as the father of biblical exegesis in Switzerland and a forerunner of Arminianism in opposing Calvin's rigid view.

Melanchthon's modification. Philip Melanchthon (1497-1560), began to moderate Luther's extreme views early on. Since Luther depended upon Philip to draft most of the important doctrinal standards of the Lutheran churches, these increasingly began to show evidence of his modifications. The Augsburg Confession, drawn up by Philip in 1530, does not state that faith is involuntary or that prevenient grace is necessary to faith. In 1532 he revised his earlier comments on Romans reflecting Luther's views, now to state, "And it is manifest that to resist belongs to the human will, because God is not the cause of sin." He ascribes conversion to three causes: the Word, the Holy Spirit, and the human will. He sought to avoid conflict with Luther in his lifetime, but by 1550 he was accused of 'synergism'*[20]

Calvin's actual views. The controversy over Calvin's views is surprising in the light of the massive amount of material in his *Institutes*, commentaries, and many other writings. Remember the number of times in previous chapters contemporary Calvinists were seen as dogmatically at odds with Calvin. The major issue is limited atonement. Much recent research proves that Calvin's successor, Theodore Beza (1519-1605) and his associates carried Calvin's doctrines to their extreme by introducing the notion of limited atonement, which Calvin did not affirm.[21] There is also evidence that Calvin softened his views in his later commentaries, as he was immersed in expounding Scripture itself, rather than developing a theological system. No doubt Beza and others developed Calvinism into a more scholastic type of rigid predestinarianism (cf. Ch. 18 & App. E of *BCAA*).

The spread and modification of the Reformation

Beginnings in Great Britain. Early in the British Reformation Bishop Hugh Latimer (c. 1485-1555), Miles Coverdale, the Bible translator, (1488-1569), and Thomas Cranmer, the Archbishop of Canterbury (1489-1556), can all be identified as holding to general redemption. Since they were contemporaries of the early Calvin, they probably did not get into the other issues of determinism. The 1553 version of the Articles of the Anglican Church clearly hold to general redemption.* Some writers have referred to the "free-willers" in the Anglican church during this time, while Calvinism was making increasing inroads. In the 1590s there was considerable controversy at Cambridge, and Peter Baro (1534-1599) was forced out for resisting Calvinism. In 1596 Nicholas Hemingius asked, "Do the elect believe or are the believers elect?" Richard Bancroft was a non-predestinarian bishop of London. However, William Perkins' 1598 book, *The Mode and Order of Predestination* was extreme Calvinism. Arminius wrote a refutation but never published it because of Perkins' death.[22] Toward the end of the sixteenth century there was a movement in England and Scotland to moderate the rigidity of the Calvinism coming from Geneva.[23]

Arminius and the Remonstrants. James Arminius (1560-1609) had all the right Calvinist credentials to become the theology professor at the Reformed University of Leyden. He had studied for three years under Theodore Beza in Geneva. Before becoming pastor of one of the principal Reformed churches in Amsterdam, he had traveled in Italy and heard the lectures of some of the great Catholic professors. Newman states:

> By this time he was recognized as among the ablest and most learned men of his time. His expository sermons were so lucid, eloquent, and well delivered as to attract large audiences. He was called upon from time to time to write against the opponents of Calvinism, which he did in a moderate and satisfactory way.... Before this time [1602] his intimate friends had become aware of the fact that he was no longer in full sympathy with the extreme predestinarianism of Beza, and he had written an exposition of Romans 9 in an anti-Calvinistic spirit. This, however, was not published till after his death.[24]

Unfortunately after Arminius joined the University faculty in 1603 and studiously avoided any anti-Calvinistic utterances, his colleague Gomarus instigated the authorities to require him to deliver a series of public lectures on predestination. "He defended the doctrine in a way that would have been acceptable to moderate Calvinists; but Gomar thought it necessary to supplement these lectures with a course of his own." This precipitated a hostile controversy on campus, which soon exploded into a national debate, involving the government of the Netherlands. Although the Supreme Court declined to hear the issue, in 1609 Arminius and Gomarus were required to engage in an extended discussion (debate?) on the issue. Arminius took sick and died two months later. The following year his many followers set forth the five points of the Remonstrance, which were responded to by the Calvinists with their five points (the TULIP).

This controversy ultimately precipitated the infamous Synod of Dort (1618-9), attended by delegates from Reformed churches in several other countries. Since the Arminians were excluded, the result was a foregone conclusion—the Arminians were excommunicated. John Barneveld, a leading statesman and advocate of freedom of conscience, was accused of treason and executed five days after the end of the Synod. Episcopius, the leader of the banished Arminians, published extensively against the Synod and the intolerance of the government and reiterated the charge of Calvinism being "Manichean* fatalism." This resulted in toleration being granted in 1625, and the establishment of an Arminian seminary in Amsterdam subsequently.[25] In England John Goodwin (1593-1665) wrote a defense of general redemption in 1640.[26] A century later the Wesleys developed a more evangelical form of Arminianism, which retained much of the Augustinian view of sin.

Modification at the Saumur seminary. Amyraldian theology can be traced back to John Cameron (1580-1625), who had studied in Glasgow under Andrew Melville, the "Scots Melanchthon." Cameron so excelled in his studies that upon graduation he was appointed as regent in Greek. Logic was taught there from Ramus, who espoused a more inductive* methodology, rather than Aristotle's more deductive* approach. By 1600 after only one year, he migrated to France, where he studied, taught, and pastored in many cities before beginning his teaching at the theological Academy at Saumur in 1618. In just three years his views on general redemption* were accepted with alacrity by his students and successors on the faculty, especially Moyse Amyraut (1596-1664). The Reformed* churches of France were grateful to Cameron for "his great services in the controversies against Arminians and Roman Catholics"[27]

After Cameron's untimely death, Amyraut proved to be such an effective exponent of Cameron's theology, that Amyraut's name became attached to it. After studying law, he had studied at Saumur under Cameron, and was called to minister at Saumur in 1626, sharing ministry with Louis Cappel, both at the church and Academy, where he served as principal from 1641 until his death. Life for the Protestants in France at that time was under the Edict of Nantes, which gave them some civil liberties. In 1631 Amyraut won an outstanding victory in the exercise of those liberties and was also partly responsible for attempts to improve relationships with the Lutherans. Amyraut was well known for developing good personal relationships with Roman Catholics while pursuing a strong apologetic for the Protestant faith.

It was in this connection that in 1634 he innocently started a controversy which was to become a central feature of his life for many years. He published *A Brief Treatise on Predestination*, which was occasioned by a dialog with a Roman Catholic nobleman while at dinner with the Bishop of Chartres. This nobleman was "filled with horror by the doctrine of predestination as taught in our churches," and regarded it as "contrary to the nature of God and His gospel to say that He created the greatest part of mankind with the express purpose of damning them." Amyraut's treatise stirred up a "civil war" among the Reformed churches. He responded to the opposition by publishing a defense that his doctrine was really that of Calvin. The attacks from the scholastic Calvinists eventuated in charges of heresy being leveled at Amyraut and Paul Testard in the national synod of Alençon in 1637. The charges focused on the universality and sufficiency of grace. "It is certain that Amyraut barely escaped being deposed and having his writings condemned." Although they were honorably acquitted from the synod, there were a few minor stipulations.[28] The synod decision did not end the controversy, however, but it is clear that the Amyraldian view was growing in acceptability within France.

After Amyraut's death, revocation of the Edict of Nantes (1685) forced many Protestants to flee France, many to the low countries and England, some to America. Apparently the Academy of Saumur did not survive to perpetuate the Amyraldian theology, which lost its geographical base as its adherents were scattered. Yet its impact can be traced right up to the present, even though its identity as a distinct theological school of thought has been seriously obscured. Even in Geneva some significant men were influenced by Saumur and came out in open sympathy with this theology.[A]

Seventeenth-century England. Archbishop James Ussher (1581-1656) clearly held to general redemption and told Richard Baxter (1615-1691) that he brought Bishop John Davenant (1572-1641) and Dr. John Preston (1578-1628) to this view. Ussher said that there must be a "middle way," but it was not yet clear to him. Baxter is considered a pre-eminent evangelist and refused to be called either a Calvinist or an Arminian (cf. p. 343).

Cocceius and Covenant Theology. Johannes Cocceius (1603-1669) was not the originator of Covenant Theology, but was certainly a major factor in its early development. Newman explains:

> He... became easily the most accomplished biblical scholar of his time. ... He was pre-eminently a scriptural theologian.... he may properly be regarded as the father of the federal theology. His great work, "Summary of the Doctrine Concerning the Covenant and Testament of God," was first published in 1648 and may be regarded as the first serious attempt at the working out of a biblical theology.... It is noticeable that the doctrine of predestination does not figure in this system and the entire doctrine of divine decrees is kept in the background. The aim of Cocceius was evidently to show that man was so endowed and conditioned that he need not have fallen, that he was responsible for his fall, and that after the fall God placed salvation within the reach of all by covenant and actually provided redemption in Christ for all who would believe.[29]

Charles Ryrie confirms Newman's opinion that it was Cocceius, having been influenced by Melanchthon, who saw in the covenant theme a "way to blunt the sharp and highly debated views on predestination current in his day." Herman Witsius (1636-1708) undermined Cocceius's intention by developing the idea of a Covenant of Redemption in eternity past, which in effect reverted Covenant Theology back to a deterministic mode of thought.[30] Although his effort was hijacked by extreme Calvinists, Cocceius represents another of the early reactions against the determinism of the Reformers.

The Pietistic* movement. Philip Spener (1635-1705) and August Francke (1663-1727) were the two key men in the beginnings of Pietism in

---

A   French refugees flooded into the Netherlands with their theology. In Germany, there already were similar views in Bremen. In England, Isaac Watts (1674-1748), Philip Doddridge (1702-51), John Newton (1725-1807), and Charles Simeon (1759-1836) all moved toward the middle. In Scotland James Fraser, Thomas Mair, the New Light Reformed Presbytery, James Morison's group, Thomas Chalmers (founder of the Free Church of Scotland), and Ralph Wardlaw were Amyraldian. In America, Amyraldian views influenced the neo-Edwardsian New Divinity movement, New School Presbyterianism (J. Richards), and among the Baptists, E. Dodge, Alva Hovey, and more recently A. H. Strong (Nicole, pp. 192-3).

the Lutheran state churches of Germany and Scandinavia. Spener sought to cultivate the spiritual life by small-group Bible study and prayer meetings and was grieved by the arid and bitter theological disputation and low moral state of the Lutheran state church. Francke helped found the University of Halle in 1694, out of which came the first Protestant missionaries and the Danish-Halle Mission in 1705. Although the pietistic movement did not stress theology, it definitely did not hold to the determinism of Luther (cf. p. 344).

The Moravian movement. Some persecuted followers of John Hus banded together with some Waldensians and Moravians to form the *Unitas Fratrum* (United Brethren) in 1467. Badly persecuted by the Catholics, a remnant under the leadership of Christian David (1690-1751) fled to the estate of the pietist Count Nicholas von Zinzendorf (1700-1760) in Saxony in 1722. Out of this Christian community, a most remarkable missionary movement developed. Between 1732 and 1760 this small movement sent out 226 missionaries to ten foreign countries, far outstripping all other Protestants combined. The Moravians stressed God's love for a lost world and resisted the determinism of the Reformers (cf. p. 344).

Thomas Boston and the Marrow men. The Marrow controversy of the Presbyterian Church of Scotland in the 1720s might be characterized as conflict between the 'legalists' and the 'evangelicals.' Edward Fisher's earlier book published in England in 1645, *The Marrow of Modern Divinity*, was a source of the view of the 'evangelicals,' that all men may apply to Christ for salvation, if they will, and that "a gospel warrant existed for offering Christ to the whole world." Thomas Boston (1677-1732) and his associates rejected the "covenant of redemption" in eternity past. A century later it led to the general redemption view of John McLeod Campbell (b. 1800), for which he was dismissed from ministry in 1831. He saw the Calvinism of his church as legalistic in denying that "all sinners are summoned to come to God with assurance of his love for them."[31]

The Wesleyan movement. No one can deny that the Wesleyan movement was the major spiritual force in eighteenth-century Great Britain and saved the nation from utter moral collapse. John (1703-91) and Charles Wesley were Anglican priests very devoted to a legalistic and mystical approach to the faith. As missionaries in Georgia, onboard their return ship, and back in London, they were very impressed with the simple faith of the Moravians with whom they had contact. In 1738 John's heart was "strangely warmed" in a Moravian meeting they attended. Afterward, Wesley visited Zinzendorf in Saxony. When he and his friend, George Whitefield (1714-70) began to preach forthright evangelistic sermons, pulpits in their Anglican churches began to close to them. Whitefield mentored Wesley in open-air preaching, which began to bear great fruit as the common people heard the gospel. Whitefield shifted a major focus of his ministry to the American colonies and became a major force in the first Great Awakening there.

Wesley developed a more evangelical form of Arminianism by coming back to a more Augustinian view of depravity than the Remonstrants, but added a new dimension with his view of entire sanctification in the Christian life. Whitefield was a Calvinist, and although they remained friends, they had a lifelong discussion about the issue. Wesleyan leader, Thomas Coke, initiated foreign missions in 1786 and the British Baptist mission of William Carey six years later was significantly stimulated by the Wesleyan revivals.

The New Divinity movement. The neo-Edwardsian New Divinity movement was the source of the Second Great Awakening in New England and the American foreign missions movement. Although they called themselves "consistent Calvinists," they were really neither. Although holding to an extreme view of sovereignty, they not only held to general redemption, but also to a governmental view of the cross, more harmonious with Arminianism. They were successors of Jonathan Edwards, Sr., whose immediate protégés, Samuel Hopkins became the theologian and Joseph Bellamy, the pastoral mentor. The junior Edwards moved even farther from his father's Calvinism, with grandson Timothy Dwight and his protégé Nathaniel Taylor representing a distinct strain called the New Haven theology, which stressed human free will, the "power to the contrary." Clearly both the Second Great Awakening in New England and the American foreign missions movement came out of the New Divinity movement. *Most historians have overlooked the fact that the unifying factor of the movement was their view of general redemption*[32] (cf. pp. 347-49).

The Restorationist movements. Barton W. Stone (1772-1844) and Alexander Campbell (1788-1866) were American Presbyterian ministers who early found "that Presbyterianism was not adequate for their revivalistic experience or for their theological views." In 1804 in Kentucky, Stone began "to organize groups that would answer to no name but 'Christians'." Similarly in 1811 in the Ohio valley Campbell started a movement rejecting traditional church forms and emphasizing New Testament doctrine and polity. "In 1832 the followers of Stone and Alexander Campbell came into a loose alliance known as the 'Christian' or 'Disciples' movement."[33] Early in the last century the movements separated again, but both have emphasized water baptism as necessary for salvation and have been decidedly Arminian.

Modern advocates

Samuel Fisk has done yeoman's work in amassing the quotations of hundreds of scholars, commentators, Bible teachers, church leaders, and theologians in recent centuries who have been generally supportive of a mediate view of salvation truth. Charles H. Spurgeon (1834-92) considered himself a Calvinist but spoke out strongly against determinism.* The following list includes only those who clearly held to eternal security and conditional election:[34] Baptists E. H. Johnson and Henry G. Weston's *An Outline* *of Systematic Theology* (1895); the great French commentator, Frederick L. Godet; Bishop Christopher Wordsworth's *The New Testament in the Original Greek* (1877); C. I. Scofield's original *Reference Bible* (1909); William Evans' *The Great Doctrines of the Bible* (1912); Nathan E. Wood, of Andover-Newton Seminary, *The Person and Work of Jesus Christ* (1908); W. H. Griffith-Thomas, a founder of Dallas Seminary; H. A. (Harry) Ironside of Moody Memorial Church and special Bible lecturer at Dallas Seminary; great expositor, G. Campbell Morgan; F. B. Meyer; Southern Baptists: Edgar Y. Mullins and Hershel H. Hobbs; W. E. Vine; E. Schuyler English; J. Sidlow Baxter; and Lehman Strauss, among many others.

Conclusions

There are a number of very significant conclusions which can be drawn from our historical investigation:

1. Determinists have a very serious problem with the silence of the church fathers regarding predestination and irresistible grace and their emphasis on free will before the latter years of Augustine (after 416).
2. Augustine's determinism and other errors, can be traced back to his years in Manicheanism* and neo-Platonism, not to careful biblical exegesis. His contemporaries considered his views as radically new.
3. Augustine's teaching and example on coercion to faith come from irresistible grace and have poisoned Christendom, resulting in persecution of myriads of true Christians. He was the source of many of the major errors of Roman Catholicism and of state-church Protestantism.
4. The ongoing controversy of the Augustine/Pelagius conflict was essentially settled for the church for a thousand years by the Synod of Orange (529), which took a semi-Augustinian position. The majority of the church fathers were semi-Augustinian, not semi-Pelagian..
5. Although the major Reformers represent a resurgence of Augustinian determinism, within a few years their associates and successors modified and blunted their rigid determinism. Almost to a man, these men were better versed in the original languages than the Reformers.
6. Theodore Beza reverted Calvinism to a more scholastic mode with his doctrine of limited atonement, first crystallized in the Canons of Dort.
7. There have been over a dozen significant reactions to the determinism of the Reformers, the outcome of which has continued to be a major force in evangelical Christianity. Much of the evangelism, church growth, and missions thrust has been spawned by these movements.
8. There have been hundreds of commentators and biblical writers in the last two centuries who held a mediating view of salvation truth.

---

1   Paul K Jewett, *Election and Predestination* (GR: Eerdmans, 1985), p 5; Boettner, p. 365

2   Forster and Marston give extensive quotations from the fathers before the council of Ephesus (431) who held to free will· *God's Strategy in Human History*, p 243-277, Geisler, *Chosen But Free*, Appendix 1.

3   Neve, I, 148

4   R. C Sproul, *Willing to Believe· The Controversy over Free Will* (GR· Baker Books, 1997), pp 69-86.

5   David R Anderson, "Regeneration: A *Crux Interpretum*" in *Journal of the Grace Evangelical Society*, 2000, ii

6   Douty, p. 138, extensive quotes of Prosper on general redemption.

7   Schaff, III, p 869; Neve, I, 151

8.   Jewett, p 7

9.   Schaff, III, 866, Neve, I, 1151. We must note the balance the Synod sought to attain

10   Anderson, "Regeneration, ii

11   Schaff, III, p 1018; p 283.

12   Albert Henry Newman, *A Manual of Church History*, 2 vols. (Phila American Baptist Publ., 1899), I, 197

13   Sir Robert Anderson, *The Gospel and its Ministry*, p. 95, B. B Warfield, *Calvin and Augustine*, ed. Samuel Craig, p 313; Jerom Zanchius, *The Doctrine of Absolute Predestination*, pp 168-9, as quoted by Laurence M Vance, *The Other Side of Calvinism* , pp. 18-19

14   Schaff, IV, 523-4

15   William R Estep, *The Anabaptist Story: An Introduction to Sixteenth-Century Anabaptism* , pp 11-21

16   Newman, II, 154-5

17   Estep, p 97.

18   Jan J. Kiwiet, "The Life of Hans Denck," *The Mennonite Quarterly Review* 31 (Oct 1957) 24 2, cited by Estep, p 110-1. Meic Pearse, *The Great Restoration: The Religious Radicals of the 16ᵗʰ and 17ᵗʰ Centuries*

19   John Davenant, *The Death of Christ*, ed Allport , II, 319, cited by Douty, p. 140, Schaff, VIII, 210-1, 618.

20   Newman, II, 322.

21   R T Kendall, *Calvin and English Calvinism to 1649*, 2ⁿᵈ ed , Clifford, Alan C , *Atonement and Justification*

22   Carl O. Bangs, *Arminius* ; O T Hargrave, "Free-willers in the English Reformation," *Church History*, XXXVII (1968), 271-280

23   A major source of these quotations is in Douty, pp. 143-149: Moule, *Outlines of Christian Doctrine*, p 43, Francis Goode, *The Better Covenant* (1848), pp. 334f ; Morris Fuller, T*he Life, Letters, and Writings of John Davenant* (London, 1897), p. 521, Davenant, *op. cit , p 386*; Joseph Hall, *Works*, X, 474.

24   Newman, II, 340

25   Ibid, II, 339-349

26   John Goodwin, *Redemption Redeemed: A Puritan Defense of Unlimited Atonement* (exp ed., 2004)

27   Roger Nicole, "Amyraldianism" in *Encyclopedia of Christianity* (1964), I: 187 Most of this section is derived from Nicole's article and from Brian G Armstrong, *Calvinism and the Amyraut Heresy*, pp. 42-119

28   Amyraut, *Preface to Six Sermons*, i-ii, as quoted by Armstrong, p. 81, 96 In a telephone conversation (December, 1981) Roger Nicole told me that Amyraut held to conditional election This is contradicted in dissertations by Armstrong and L Proctor (Univ. of Leeds, 1952), and in a conversation with Dr. Nicole in 2001 he agreed that they may be right

29   Newman, II, 575-6

30   Charles C Ryrie, *Dispensationalism*, rev. ed (Chicago Moody, 1995), pp 185-187

31   M Charles Bell, *Calvin and Scottish Theology*, pp. 153-161, 181-192.

32   The key evidence is in Edwards A. Park, *The Atonement Discourse and Treatises by*   (Boston, 1859) See also Conforti, *Samuel Hopkins and the New Divinity Movement*

33   John D Woodbridge, Mark A Noll, and Nathan O Hatch, *The Gospel in America* (Zondervan, 1979), pp 192-3

34   Samuel Fisk, *Divine Sovereignty and Human Freedom* (Loizeaux, 1973, rev. ed Wipf & Stock, 2002), *Calvinistic Paths Retraced* (Biblical Evangelism Press, 1985)

THE THEOLOGICAL LINEAGE CONNECTING

THE CONTINENT

Moyse Amyraut (1596-1664)
General redemption advocate ⇒⇒⇒⇒⇒⇒⇒⇒⇒⇒⇒⇒⇒
French Huguenot Seminary
Writings influenced Baxter

Philip Spener (1635-1705)
Started Pietistic Movement
Pia Desideria - 1675
⇓

August Francke (1663-1727)
German Pietistic leader
Danish-Halle Mission - 1705
University of Halle - 1694
⇓

Barth. Ziegenbalg (1682-1719)
Pietistic pioneer to India - 1705
Tamil Bible translation
⇓

Nicholas Zinzendorf (1700-60)
Moravian Church founder ⇒⇒
Sent 226 missionaries to 10
    countries - 1732-1760
Influenced by pietist Francke
⇓

Georg Schmidt (1709-85)
Moravian pioneer, S. Africa -1737
Successful mission to pygmies
Expelled by Calvinistic Boers
⇓

Christian Schwartz (1726-98)
Outstanding pietistic missionary
    to India - 1750-98
Telegu & Hindustani translations
Won incredible respect from
    Hindu & Muslim alike

GREAT BRITAIN

Robert Millar
History of the Propagation
    of Christianity - 1723
Prayer for heathen conversion
Free offer of the gospel to all

John Wesley (1703-91) ⇐⇐
Indefatigable evangelist
Evangelical Arminian theology
"The world is my parish"
Key to Great Awakening
Methodist founder

⇓
⇓
⇓
⇓
⇓

Thomas Coke (1747-1814)
1st Methodist Bishop in Amer.
Mission to W. Indies - 1786
Crossed Atlantic 19 times
Died en route to Ceylon

William Wilberforce (1759-1833)
Founded Anglican CMS -1799
Member of Parliament
Ended slave trade
Saved thru Doddridge's book

Henry Martyn (1781-1812)
East India Co. Anglican Chaplain - 1805
Pioneer to Muslims
Translated NT into Urdu, Persian, & Arabic
Challenged by Brainerd's *Diary*

Richard Baxter (1615-1691)
Call to the Unconverted - 1658
Mediate theology influenced many
Pioneer missiologist, mentored Eliot
Greatest evangelist of 17th century
⇓
⇓
⇓
⇓

Thomas Boston (1677-1732)
Man's Fourfold State -1720
    used in Judson's conversion

⇓
⇓
⇓

Philip Doddridge (1702-51)
Rise & Progress of Religion
General redemption theology
Proposed missions - 1741
Influenced Wesley & Griffin
Whitefield saved thru his book
⇓

George Whitefield (1714-70)
Powerful evangelist of 1st Great
    Awakening in England & Amer.
Partnered with Wesley & Edwards
Innovated extemp. open-air preaching
⇓

Andrew Fuller (1754-1815)
Gospel Worthy of All Acceptation
Carey's friend & theol. mentor
Home Director, Baptist Mission
⇓

William Carey (1761-1834)
Enquiry... Use of Means - 1792
Baptist Mission Soc. -1792
Pioneer to India -1793-1834
Major promoter of missions
Incredible Bible translations

KEY MISSIONS PERSONALITIES

AMERICA

John Eliot (1604-1690) ⟸⟸⟸
Pioneer miss. to Indians - 1644
Trans. Bible into Algonquin-1663
1000s converted & discipled
Trans. *Call to the Unconverted*
⇓
Cotton Mather (1663-1728)
Promoter of missions & literature for Indians and Negroes
Wrote biography of John Eliot, which impacted Carey
Promoted Francke's Halle mission

Roger Williams (1606-1683)
Founded Rhode Island
First American Baptist
Evangelized Indians
Promoted freedom of worship
Indian language handbook - 1643

Thomas Mayhew, Jr. (1620-55)
Evangelized island Indians
1643-1655
5 generations of Mayhews
carried on the work.

▶Theodore Frelinghuysen ⇒⇒
(1691-1747)
Pietistic evangelistic pastor
1st Great Awakening in NJ -1720
Connected with Tennants
and Whitefield

Jonathan Edwards (1703-58)
1st Gt. Awakening in Mass. -1733
Call to Prayer for Revival - 1748
Published Brainerd's Diary - 1749
Father of neoEdwardsian theology: urged sinners to seek God
Mentored Hopkins & Bellamy & impacted Fuller & Carey
⇓   ⇓

THE NEO-EDWARDSIAN "NEW DIVINITY" THEOLOGY

David Brainerd (1718-1747)
Miss. to Indians - 1743-46
Protégé of Edwards
Impactful *Diary* & Biography
Influenced by Whitefield

Samuel Hopkins (1721-1803)
Freed-slave mission - 1771
aborted by Amer. revolution
Miss. Soc. of R.I. - 1801
System of Doctrine - 1793
Neo-Edwardsian theologian
⇓

Joseph Bellamy (1719-1790)
True Religion Delineated
2nd Awakening pastor
General-redemption theology
Book impacted Fuller
Mentor of extemp. preachers
⇓

Dr. Jonathan Edwards, Jr. (1745-1801)
Indian mission with father: spoke Mohican
Mentored by Hopkins & Bellamy
Mediate theology; mentored Griffin   Timothy Dwight (1752-1817)
⇓   Yale revival -1802

Edward D. Griffin (1770-1837)   New Haven theology
2nd Awakening evangelist in Ct. & NJ   ⇓
Missions sermon - Phila. Gen. Assem. 1805   ⇓
Extent of Atonement - general red. -1819   ⇓
Andover Seminary faculty; Williams College Pres.   ⇓
Mentor of Mills, Judson & many missionaries   ⇓
⇓   ⇓

Adoniram Judson (1788-1850)
Saved & committed to missions
thru Andover faculty -1808-09
Amer. Board of Comm. - 1810
Pioneer to Burma - 1812-50
Amer. Baptist Mission -1814

Samuel Mills, Jr. (1783-1818)
Haystack prayer mtg - 1806
Soc. of Brethren at Williams
American Bible Soc. - 1814
United Foreign Miss. - 1816
both founded with Griffin

Nathaniel Taylor (1786-1858)
New Haven theology
Man able to repent & believe
Influenced 2nd Awakening
evangelist Charles G. Finney
(1792-1875)

To Sardis: I know your deeds, that you have a name that you are alive, but you are dead. Wake up, and strengthen the things which remain, which were about to die; for I have not found your deeds completed in the sight of My God.

To Philadelphia: I know your deeds. Behold, I have set before you an open door which no one can shut, because you have a little power, and have kept My word, and have not denied My name.

-The Lord Jesus Christ to His churches

THE DOCTRINAL BASIS OF GLOBAL EVANGELISM

There are three significant tests of any theological system. The historical and philosophic tests are given undue priority in many theological works. However, the test of global evangelism has been ignored. Since evangelism and missions are axiomatic, a theology's harmony with them must be investigated. Paul was both the greatest missionary and theologian of the early church. All his epistles were written in connection with his missionary ministry. How strange that much theology has developed since the Reformation without any reference to God's global missionary program. Indeed, a significant segment of theology has not been conducive to world evangelization, but even hostile to it. In actuality, theology ought to be the handmaiden of worldwide missions implementation.

For half a century missions and theology have been my focus. Since a major benefit is cross-pollenization between disciplines, the connections will be investigated. It is difficult to harmonize deterministic theology with global evangelism; in fact, it has had a negative historical impact. The great scandal of Protestantism is the "Great Protestant Omission," the two centuries in which Protestants did virtually nothing about world evangelization, with another century of inaction in the English-speaking world. *We must face the theological roots of that paralysis.* In order to do this, a biblical axiom comes to the fore, which strongly confirms a mediate theology.

Evangelism and Missions Are Axiomatic

It should not be necessary to be reminded of the clear priority, imperative, and urgency of global evangelism in the New Testament. Unfortu-

336

nately, theological static has obscured the reception of this clear message. Evangelism and missions are biblically axiomatic and therefore foundational to any sound theology, but not in the minds of many evangelical Christians, including many pastors, scholars, and theologians.

The evangelistic foundation. John the Baptizer was a very confrontational and effective evangelist. Certainly the Lord Jesus was a confrontational evangelist, a personal soul-winner, and at times, a cross-cultural missionary. When Christ recruited His early disciples to follow Him full-time, He invited them to **"follow Me, and I will make you fishers of men"** (Mt. 4:19). He did not call them to be identifiers of the elect. Every disciple of Christ is to be a fisher of men. If fish are to be caught, the fishermen must go to where the fish are and actively and diligently use the best skills possible. Fish do not usually jump into the boat, even by irresistible grace.

The greatest decree of the Sovereign. The Lord's ministry was not exclusively to His own people Israel, but included a number of Gentiles. He also alluded to the ultimate gospel outreach to Gentiles (Jn. 10:16; 12:20-24). During the forty days after His resurrection in which He appeared to the disciples, He charged them in five different ways to evangelize the whole world, comprising half of all His recorded words during this period. It has been misnamed "the Great Commission," but it is really the Greatest Decree of the King of the Universe.[A] Barna's surveys of Christians have revealed a gross ignorance of the Great Commission so the references are given here: Matthew 28:18-20; Mark 16:15; Luke 24:45-49; John 20:21; and Acts 1:8. His last words must not be ignored, soft-pedaled, rationalized, or obfuscated. They are unambiguous: our job is to go and make disciples of **"all the ethnic peoples"** **"in all the world"** **"all the days"** before He returns, because He has **"all authority"** in the universe. This is what we, feeble humans, are responsible to do. Just before His ascension He made it clear that the Holy Spirit will work in and through His witnesses to accomplish world evangelization (Acts 1:8).

Cross-cultural extension. The reticence of many Christians to obey this Greatest Commission belies some deep down questions about its genuineness, significance, uniqueness, priority and extent. (These issues are addressed in detail in my *What in the World Is God Doing?*) Although most of Christ's ministry and the witness of the church focused upon the Jewish nation for over a decade, the Commission clearly extends across cultures. Pentecost was anticipatory of the conversion of the Gentile Cornelius, the missionary ministry of Paul and his missionary teams, and the work of global missions until the end of the age. The giving of the Holy Spirit to the new-born Church on that day was adequate empowerment for what seemed to the Apostles a "mission impossible," and even today seems

---

A   For four centuries many theologians have argued about some presumed decrees in past eternity, when in reality the most important decree was explicitly and fully stated by the LORD of the universe during the most dramatic and central days of human history, the forty days after the resurrection.

overwhelming to most Christians. Accordingly, the Spirit-filled early disciples gave a bold, confrontational witness to the leaders of their nation, which resulted in persecution and martyrdom. The procrastination of these Jewish Apostles in following up the conversion of Cornelius may have prompted the calling of that intrepid Apostle to the Gentiles by a unique confrontation on the Damascus road. God formed Saul's bi-cultural, choleric personality into the premier missionary and theologian of the apostolic church. This not only teaches us that antecedent human factors are significant in God's molding of the clay to make the vessel He needs, but also that theology and world evangelism are intended to go hand in hand.[B] Romans is undoubtedly Paul's greatest theological treatise, but global evangelism pulses from beginning (1:14-17) to end (15:18-21), including a whole chapter (10):

> **I am under obligation both to Greeks and to barbarians, both to the wise and to the foolish. So, for my part I am eager to preach the gospel to you also who are in Rome. For I am not ashamed of the gospel, for it is the power of God for salvation to everyone who believes, to the Jew first and also to the Greek** (Rom. 1:14-17).

All his epistles were written in the course of his missionary ministry of three extensive tours and as a prisoner in connection with that cross-cultural ministry to the multicultural churches which he had planted on those tours. Indeed, the only history of the apostolic church came from a Gentile convert and companion of his. Somehow the missionary dimension of all of this had faded from the minds of the Reformation church, which claimed to be proclaiming its theology. *But a sound theology cannot be developed apart from this evangelistic and missionary foundation.*

The confrontational paradigm

The dilemma faced by all determinists is the place of persuasion in ministry and witness. There were many of Reformed* tradition in past generations who were opposed to any use of means in proclaiming the gospel message. Of course, that would make preaching itself an oxymoron since preaching is a human means. What some Calvinists mean is that any appeal, invitation, or persuasion of sinners to repent and believe the gospel would somehow deprive God of the glory of their conversion. The real issue is not the *use* of means, but *which* means are biblically valid. However, the answer is seen in examining the model, paradigm, and example of the Lord Jesus and His Apostles. What is the place of persuasion?

The contemporary debate in missions centers around three 'p's: *presence evangelism, proclamation evangelism, or persuasion evangelism.* Liberal writers are satisfied with mere 'presence evangelism,' as seen in the

---

B   How tragic it is that this great missionary's epistles have been distorted to contradict the missionary burden at the core of his ministry All his epistles were *missionary epistles,* and yet his last missionary epistles to individual missionaries have been misdesignated as "pastoral epistles" in most of the literature of the past century or more

mission institutions of the 'old-line' churches. Most evangelicals affirm 'proclamation evangelism.' Those of a more Calvinistic bent are reluctant to follow the biblical model of 'persuasion evangelism.'

Christ's example. What is the New Testament evidence for persuasion evangelism? Certainly Christ and His herald provoked many confrontations with the people and their leaders (Jn. 5:16-47; 6:26-66; 7:14-52; 8:12-59; 9:39-41; 10:22-42; 12:44-50; Mt. 21:12-13, 23-46; 22:1-46; 23:1-39). These chapters are filled with very effective argumentation of a very polemic and apologetic nature (Jn. 8:30; 10:42; 12:42, etc.). Christ was certainly a controversialist, and the words 'persuasion' and 'confrontation' are too weak a description. If we are to follow His example (WWJD?), Christ would not be satisfied with anything less than 'persuasion evangelism.'

The Apostles' model. The ministry of Peter and the other Apostles on the day of Pentecost was certainly argumentative, apologetic, confrontational, and controversial. It is clear that Peter must have given some sort of an overt "invitation" to the crowd since the Apostles separated out three thousand who were to be baptized. Luke doesn't tell us how they did it, but it had to have been something quite overt and directive. Succeeding days only intensified these aspects of their ministry, provoking arrest, intimidation, threats, imprisonment, etc. and resulting in incredible fruit of thousands converted. As the good news began to go out to the Gentiles through the ministry of Paul, Barnabas, and then Silas, Timothy, and many others whom Paul co-opted, the confrontational and persuasive element hardly diminished. Luke describes how immediately after Paul's conversion, in Damascus he *proclaimed* Christ by *confounding* the Jews in *proving* that Jesus was the Messiah (Acts 9:20-22). Back in Jerusalem he was "**speaking out boldly in the name of the Lord**" by "**talking and arguing with the Hellenistic Jews**" (9:28-29). This is just the beginning of the whole pattern of New Testament ministry (Acts 17:2-3; 18:4; 19:8-9).

The terms used. David Hesselgrave gives an excellent analysis of the words used in witness[c] and suggests that many writers are guilty of reductionism, since there are a score of words to be studied and most are overlooked. It is clear that superficial treatments do not do justice to the full range of these aspects of apostolic ministry and therefore lead to a truncated theology of how sinners come to faith in Christ. J. I. Packer concludes that these various verbs having to do with evangelism can be best summed up in the word 'teach'."[1] Hesselgrave suggests that terms like 'dispute,' 'reason,' 'persuade,' 'reprove,' 'rebuke,' or 'exhort' can hardly be subsumed under the

---

C   *Euangelizein* occurs 54 times and *euangelion*, 76 times, *kērussein* (herald, proclaim), its nouns *kērugma* and *kērux* over 60 times more, and *marturein* (bear witness) and its derived nouns well over one hundred times more We also find *sungchein* (confound), *sumbibazein* (prove), *diegeomai* (declare), *suzetein* (dispute), *lalein* (speak), *dialegomai* (reason with), *peithein* (persuade), *nouthetein* (admonish, warn), *katechein* (inform, instruct), *deomai*, (beg, beseech), *elengchein* (reprove), *epitimaein* (rebuke), and *parakalein* (exhort, urge) as well.

activity of 'teaching.' Knowing Packer's Calvinism, his agenda in soft-pedalling the confrontational dimension of evangelism is exposed. This is just one example of a mindset which could be exemplified a thousand fold.

Obstacles to Global Evangelism

Most moderate Calvinists would agree that the determinism of 'extreme Calvinism' hinders global evangelism. But the truth leads a step farther to state that Calvinism in general tends to be a hindrance to the kind of global evangelism stipulated in the New Testament and surveyed above, that is, persuasion evangelism and missions. There is both a historical connection and a logical, theological one as well.

The "Great Protestant Omission"

In my missions text a chapter is devoted to a survey of the paucity of missionary effort for two centuries after the Protestant Reformation until the beginning of the Danish-Halle mission in 1705 (three centuries in the English-speaking world). The Roman Catholics were sending out Jesuit, Dominican, Franciscan, and Augustinian missionaries all over the world, who are said to have gained more converts than were lost to Protestantism. But Protestants during this period were hostile to missions! In these two centuries there are less than a dozen incidents recorded in which any issue of missions arose, and most of these were strong reactions from the Protestant establishment to any such outrageous notion as world evangelism.[D] The few cases where there was positive action came from the fringes of Protestantism, not from the Lutheran or Reformed core. Gustav Warneck's comment on Protestant rationalizations is apt: "*Where there are Christians, missions are superfluous; and where there are no Christians, they are hopeless.*"[2]

Explanations and Rationalizations

How can this shocking fact– this great omission– be explained? Those who think the Reformation was a full-fledged restoration of apostolic

---

D Verceslaus Budovetz went on his own to Istanbul in 1577 and won one Muslim in five years In 1590 Hadrian Saravia wrote a chapter on missions in a book, which was disputed by Beza, who insisted that the Great Commission was binding only on the Apostles. By 1595 the Dutch Reformed were sending chaplains out with the colonialists to the East Indies and Ceylon (before 5-point Calvinism surfaced) They translated the Bible into Malay and baptized many converts, a substantial Reformed community in Indonesia resulting. In 1651 a Lutheran nobleman, Count Truchsess, challenged the theological faculty of Wittenberg as to why Lutherans were not sending out missionaries in obedience to the Great Commission. By echoing Beza's errors, they gave a sad testimony. If the heathen are lost, it is their own fault since they rejected God's word from Noah on down to the Apostles, who evangelized the whole human race In 1661 George Fox, the non-conformist founder of the Society of Friends (Quakers), sent three missionaries to China, but tragically they were never heard of again. In 1664 an Austrian Lutheran nobleman, Justinian Von Welz, began to advocate foreign missions. When Von Welz's sharp admonitions to Lutheran authorities fell on deaf ears, he "proceeded to Holland, where he abandoned his baronial title. Following ordination as an 'apostle to the Gentiles,' he sailed for Dutch Guiana (Surinam), where he died an early death before he could reap a harvest " An official refutation of Von Welz's views were given by Ursinus, citing the difficulty of the missionary task and of recruiting missionaries, the deep depravity of the heathen, making conversion next to impossible, the great need at home, and the responsibility of Christians already living in heathen lands to make the gospel known

Christianity cannot explain the facts. But since the Reformation was a complex movement involving political, social, cultural, and spiritual factors, it then becomes more comprehensible, though no less reprehensible. For the most part, the Reformation did not go far enough in the recovery of God's truth, resulting in a number of obstacles remaining to the restoration among Protestants of God's program of worldwide evangelism.

The difficult circumstances of the Protestants. Although the Protestant movement grew rapidly in northern Europe, it was in the minority. The Roman Church organized a religious and political Counter Reformation. Europe was wracked with religious wars, in which Protestants struggled for survival. To make matters worse, Lutherans and Calvinists hurled anathemas against each other, but worse yet, they persecuted the Anabaptists* and Mennonites, who rightly believed in the need for a more radical reformation of the church. Even after Protestants established colonies abroad, they still did little to evangelize non-Christians there. Indeed, their trading companies hindered the spread of the gospel in most cases.

Common rationalizations. The same rationalizations among Christians today were in vogue at that time. Lutheran theologian, Johann Ursinus, argued that Jews and heathen at home should be reached before going to pagans in far-off lands. However, since we can never totally reach our own homeland, the time will *never come* when missionaries would be sent out. Ursinus thought the heathen too depraved to respond to the gospel, but clearly his view of depravity and the power of the Holy Spirit were seriously deficient. Centuries of successful missions have put the lie to his pessimism.

The theology of the Reformers. It is generally acknowledged that the second generation Reformers rationalized away Christian responsibility, but what about Luther and Calvin? Although some try to defend the harmony of their viewpoint with missions,[3] not only are the arguments unconvincing, but the fact remains: for two centuries Protestant leaders did nothing to advance the cause of world evangelization. The best that can be said is that there was a concern for home missions within Europe. Although these rationalizations cannot be attributed directly to Luther or Calvin, Coates admits that:

> It cannot be gainsaid, however, that Luther's expositions of great missionary passages as Matt. 28:19-20 and Mark 16:15 are usually devoid of any missionary emphasis. Moreover, there is a good deal of validity to the contention that Luther's concept of "mission" dealt primarily with the correction of unchristian conditions prevailing within Christendom at his time [4]

Another weakness of the Reformers' theology was in their state-church concept of a *Landeskirche*, a territorial church. They rationalized that it was the responsibility of the government to send out missionaries, but governments can't be expected to do the work of the church.

The Reformers also had a distorted understanding of the implications of God's sovereignty. Luther, for example, did have a concern for Jews and Turks: "I do hope that our Gospel, now shining forth with a light so great, will before Judgment Day make an attack also on that abominable prophet Mohammed. May our Lord Jesus Christ do this soon."[5] Note that Luther left the responsibility with God to bring about the conversion of Muslims; the responsibility to fulfill the Great Commission is ours, not God's. Harry Boer faults all of the Reformers but Martin Bucer in this regard.[6] Certainly Beza's development of limited atonement did not help. Although many defend the Calvinistic view of sovereignty as compatible with missions, many Christians like William Carey's senior associate, John Ryland (cf. p. 347), have either misused the doctrine of God's sovereignty or else have a distorted view of it.

The Reformers also did not develop a biblical concept of missions. Luther's view that missions involved the church merely growing at its boundaries with heathen lands, using the illustration of ever-broadening ripples caused by a stone tossed into water, does not square with Scripture.[7]

The spiritual weakness of the Reformation. Although many reasons for the Great Omission are given, *ultimately there was only one, a spiritual one*. The Reformation did not have deep enough spiritual roots. It was not a great revival in which tens of millions of people were born again. Probably there were only a minority of Protestants who really came to the saving knowledge of Christ. The rest were swept along with the tide. Under the state church system, it was not hard to be a Protestant without being born again. There was much confusion about the nature of the new birth. Much reliance was placed upon baptism and communion, which were seen as 'sacraments'. Luther himself saw part of the problem:

> If one considers rightly how the people now act who wish to be Protestant (by profession), and who know how to talk much about Christ, there is nothing behind it. Thus the more part deceive themselves. Tenfold more were they who made a beginning with us, and who had serious pleasure in our teaching, but now not a tenth part of them remain steadfast.[8]

Christ's words to the Sardis church seem to apply to the spiritual state of the Reformation churches, "**I know your deeds; you have a reputation of being alive, but you are dead**" (Rev. 3:1). Before there could be world evangelism, there had to be spiritual renewal. That was two centuries in coming.

The Doctrinal Basis of Modern Missions

It is imperative to examine the movements, personalities, and theologies out of which the modern missions movement arose. Not only should the key players in that restoration be identified, but also a more precise study must be made of the theological roots which influenced them. In researching this book God providentially helped me discover virtually unknown key people, and after the unabridged edition many other significant discoveries are included here for the first time.[9] These discoveries have serious doctrinal implications, since there has been a pronounced 'spin' that

Calvinists have been at the forefront of the modern missions movement, which is far from the truth!

John Eliot. The significance of John Eliot's (1604-90) ministry to the Algonquins in Roxbury, Massachusetts has not been adequately recognized in recent works (including the first four editions of my own missions text). A century ago the Godbeys called him the "morning star of modern missions," but in a real sense he should be seen as *the father of the modern missionary movement.*[10] He did the whole thing in Roxbury: cross-cultural evangelism, Bible translation, training native-American pastors, getting a mission agency organized. He also translated Richard Baxter's *A Call to the Unconverted.* His was the beginning of centuries of missions to native Americans, *which provided the paradigm for foreign missions* a century and a half later. The significance of Roger Williams should also be recognized, since he was the first colonist to learn the Algonquin language. In 1643 he published an Algonquin phrase book, with observations about Indian culture. Williams provoked the other colonists to learn the language since their charters stated that their purpose was to evangelize the Indians, but they didn't even know the language. Apparently this impacted Eliot. Although Williams was a staunch friend of the Indians, it doesn't seem that he succeeded in planting indigenous churches among them.

Richard Baxter. Sidney Rooy's research indicates that Richard Baxter (1615-91) was virtually the first Protestant missiologist and the mentor of John Eliot by extended correspondence across the Atlantic. When Baxter was silenced by the king in 1660, he wrote extensively about the hindrances to world evangelization, focusing on kings, Catholic prelates, Muslims, and the indifference of Christians.[11] He had just published his classic, *A Call to the Unconverted*, which is a great example of confrontational evangelism. In his correspondence with Eliot he argued that we need "general, unfixed ministers" who are not pastors of churches, to do the work of evangelism and missions. This was out-of-the-box thinking for Protestants, but Eliot did not resign from his church to focus on the Algonquin ministry.[12] Baxter, influenced by Moyse Amyraut (cf. pp. 228-9), refused to be called either a Calvinist or an Arminian and advocated a "middle way" in theology. Apparently Eliot agreed with him, since he gave priority to translation of Baxter's book and also wrote to him of the spontaneity and freedom of the will seen in the "**likeness of God**" in Genesis 1:26-7. *The conviction of Baxter and Eliot that Christ died for all is the foundation of their missionary concern.*

Native American evangelism. For the next half a century, the only missionaries to native Americans continued to be settled pastors, who did double duty. The first ordination of three missionaries especially to Indian work was in 1733 by the Scottish S.P.C.K. The ordination sermon by Joseph Sewall, pastor of Old South Church in Boston, reflects a similar theology of salvation to that of Baxter and Eliot. In his exposition of Acts 26:16-19, he emphasized human responsibility and obedience to God in fulfilling the Great Commission and in going "**to open their eyes.**" He said, "And though the work itself is truly Divine ... yet is our glorious Lord pleased to put honour upon his Ministers in using them as instruments in his Hand, in this wonderful Work."[13] There was a continuing succession of missionaries to the native Americans, which laid *the foundation for foreign missions* in America. Cotton Mather's biography of Eliot was most significant, since William Carey referred to Eliot at least four times in his *Enquiry,* and gave Eliot's success in winning native Americans as refutation of the notion that the heathen were too depraved to be saved. *The theology of many of these New England pilgrims was developing in a moderate way, which was conducive to cross-cultural evangelism and missions.*

Pietists and Moravians. The initiative of the continental Pietists* and the Moravians in the restoration of missions is well known (cf. pp. 329-30). The Danish-Halle mission of the Lutheran Pietists in 1705 was the first significant Protestant mission and the logical outcome of their non-deterministic theology. Bartholomew Ziegenbalg (1682-1719) and his associates' initiative to India was a major turning point, but it was accomplished despite serious opposition and obstruction by mainstream Protestants.

Although the Pietists got Protestant missions started, the Moravian movement dominated the field for the rest of the eighteenth century. Count Nicholas von Zinzendorf (1700-60) was raised in a warm evangelical Pietism. By 1722 persecuted Christian refugees from Moravia and central Europe began to arrive at his estate in Saxony, and for the next five years he developed and nurtured a Christian community there. Influenced by seeing the fruit of pietistic missions, a revival among them led this Moravian community to begin sending out their own missionaries. By 1732 they sent out the first two to the West Indies, "and in the two decades that followed, the Moravians sent out more missionaries than all Protestants (and Anglicans) had sent out in the previous two centuries." This small group of persecuted Christians sent out 226 missionaries to ten foreign countries by 1760.[14]

The story of Georg Schmidt's African initiative has been buried for a century. When Ziegenbalg and Plutschau stopped off in South Africa on their way to India, they found out that the Calvinist Boers did not allow their African slaves to be baptized. It took years for that report to get to the Moravian center, where upon hearing it, Schmidt immediately set out for South Africa. After obstructionist delays from Calvinists in Holland, he arrived in Capetown in 1737 and was treated with contempt by the colonists. He was forced by their opposition to begin his witness beyond their frontiers. When after three years he baptized his first converts, the Boers were astonished to find them able to read and give a good account of their faith. Nevertheless, they expelled Schmidt! After fifty years when other Moravian missionaries regained entrance they found abiding fruit from his ministry. *The ultimate consequence of the unbiblical mindset of the Calvinist Boers was the scandalous policy of apartheid, which had theological roots.*

Jonathan Edwards. The missionary significance of Jonathan Edwards (1703-58) to both the British and American movements is only partly understood today. The publishing of Brainerd's diary and Edwards' own missionary service among the Mohicans are well known. Not only did Carey and Henry Martyn read the diary, but it influenced Philip Doddridge (1702-51) in 1741 to propose to the Congregational ministers in the English midlands the formation of a foreign mission society. However, they were not ready to move ahead. Doddridge had been influenced by Baxter's theology and had written *The Rise and Progress of Religion in the Soul*, which God greatly used in the conversion of George Whitefield and William Wilberforce, and later in the lives of John Wesley and Edward Griffin.[15]

Jonathan Edwards had been pastor of a church in New York City briefly in 1723 and was impacted by the beginnings of the First Great Awakening in New Jersey under Theodore Frelinghuysen, who had been influenced by pietism.* Frelinghuysen began to preach very confrontationally in his four Dutch Reformed churches in Raritan. Nominal Christians were saved and believers were revived. He connected with the Tennant family and George Whitefield, who were also practicing confrontational evangelism. Whitefield continued his barnstorming evangelistic tour through New England, which was the heart of the First Great Awakening. When Edwards assumed the pulpit of his grandfather Stoddard's church in Northampton in 1727, he began to preach forthright confrontational evangelistic sermons, and hundreds came to assurance of salvation.[E] His grandfather has previously seen five times of spiritual harvest there. Since Edwards was defending the revival, Whitefield briefly visited him. By 1784 John Erskine republished Edwards' *Call to Prayer for a Revival*, which impacted the principals of the British foreign mission movement and later contributed to the Second Awakening in New England, out of which the American missions movement arose.[16]

Rooy's discussion of Edwards' theology and sermons shows that his view of inability was not total.[17] John Gerstner's study of his manuscript sermons states: "Directions for seeking salvation are found in almost every sermon Edwards ever preached. No theme was so much on his heart and lips as this. This was the point of contact between sinners and the gospel, and he was constantly urging it on them."[18] Rooy backs this up from the published revival sermons: "In these sermons Edwards stacks promise upon promise to those who earnestly seek God.... But it is the last sermon, 'The Excellency of Christ,' that page after page gathers the invitations of Scripture to encourage the broken sinner in his 'choosing Christ'"[19]

Rooy then cites a number of writers who seriously qualify Edwards'

E His series on justification by faith prepared his congregation for the first revival, sermons of which impacted Andrew Fuller in England half a century later A series on the "History of Redemption" stimulated a second time of revival, which sermons were "put in treatise form by John Erskine and first published in 1774 in Edinburgh."

Calvinism.[F] Rooy, as a Calvinist, concludes that "Edwards held these two aspects [predestination and evangelism] in a healthy Biblical tension,"[20] but this really was an unhealthy contradiction. But it was good in that it moved New England Puritanism* away from extreme Calvinism and opened a door for aggressive evangelism and missions, which door his successors in the "New Divinity" movement clearly moved through. Joseph Conforti has shown that the Second Great Awakening and the American foreign missions movement both arose out of the neo-Edwardsian, New-Divinity movement and the New-Haven theology as well. The evangelist, Charles G. Finney (1792-1875) was influenced by New-Haven theology and moved even farther from Calvinism. Since Rooy was trying to show that foreign missions arose out of Calvinism, the data he provides undermines his own agenda.

One overlooked consequence of Edwards' own missionary ministry was that his son was only five years old when they came to Stockbridge, and like many missionary children, became very fluent in Mohican and later wrote a book about Indian dialects. The junior Edwards, a teenager when his father died, was taught theology by his father's two protégés, Hopkins and Bellamy, *who had both begun to teach general redemption.*

In 1771 Hopkins, as a pastor in Newport, R.I., proposed sending freed Negro slaves back to Africa as missionaries. He raised money to free two members of his congregation, but the Revolutionary War interrupted their plans. One prospective missionary was killed in the war, but Hopkins doggedly recruited two more. However, he lost support for this missionary venture by tying it to recolonization of Negroes to Africa and never saw his plan implemented before he died. He became the first president of the Missionary Society of Rhode Island in 1801.[21] Dr. Jonathan Edwards, Jr. (1745-1801) in turn discipled Edward Griffin in New Haven with New-Divinity theology and probably infected him with missionary insights as well. Before continuing, our narrative must go to England to put the story in sequence.

The Wesleyan initiative. The Wesleyan awakening was an important part of the root of British missions. George Whitefield (1714-70) had mentored John Wesley in confrontational open-air preaching. After the American revolution, Wesley sent Thomas Coke (1747-1814) to America to ordain Francis Asbury as the leader of the Methodists. By 1786 Coke brought five missionaries to the West Indies, who saw a great spiritual harvest among the Negroes, Carib Indians and whites.[22] This was six years before Carey's own Baptist mission, though little noted because Coke did not found a mission society but carried on his missionary projects under Wesley's personal oversight. On the first of his nineteen Atlantic crossings he read Brainerd's

---

F. "A. A van Schleven leaves the impression that Edwards' classification as a Calvinist is more formal than essential." He quotes Visser't Hooft as one who believes that "Edwards' views compromised the basic doctrine of God's sovereignty," and maintains that through Edwards Puritanism became Pietism. He cites H E Runner as judging Edwards to have compromised Calvinism and sees New England Puritanism as different from Genevan Calvinism "Ridderbos finds Edwards' preaching Methodistic."

dairy. Over the years he sent forty-three missionaries to America and the East and West Indies. Years later, he decided to become a missionary himself and died leading a team of missionaries out to Ceylon. *So actually the first British initiative came from the Arminian Methodists.*[23]

The British Baptist initiative. The major obstacle to missionary initiative by the British Particular Baptists was their antinomian,* extreme Calvinism. Andrew Fuller (1754-1815) was moved from extreme Calvinism by the writings of Abraham Taylor, President Edwards, and the neo-Edwardsians. His 1784 book, *The Gospel Worthy of All Acceptation*, caused a firestorm among his Particular Baptist colleagues. As a friend and mentor of Carey, he preached at his ordination. Carey himself had already been influenced to abandon extreme Calvinism by Robert Hall's *Help for Zion's Travelers.*[24] Fuller's book was probably the most important book of the century, because it opened up the minds of Carey and his associates to the theological basis for global evangelism.

Although by 1782 the writings of Edwards and Brainerd had caused the Baptist ministers to pray monthly for the conversion of unevangelized heathen, apparently many still didn't grasp that someone actually had to go out as missionaries to win them. Thus in 1791 when Carey published *An Enquiry into the Obligation of Christians to Use Means for the Conversion of the Heathens* and proposed the formation of a mission society to implement this, the Calvinistic reaction of the senior John Ryland was typical: "Sit down young man! You are a miserable enthusiast [fanatic]. When God chooses to convert the heathens, He will not consult you or me." Apparently he had not grasped the significance of Matthew 9:38 to pray for laborers for the harvest, since it didn't fit his Calvinistic theology.[25] Carey's title indicates the bias against *any use of means* in evangelism, which he had to counter.

Fuller was a founding member of the Baptist Missionary Society and became its first home director. Extensive preaching tours all over the British Isles, not only funded the mission, but put him in the middle of many theological debates of the day, which stimulated his prolific polemic and theological writing, all the while continuing in pastoral ministry.[26]

Although the anti-missions bias of the Particular Baptists was bad before Fuller and Carey, that of the Presbyterian church of Scotland was even worse. In 1796 the General Assembly passed this motion: "To spread abroad to barbarians and heathen natives the knowledge of the Gospel seems to be highly preposterous, in so far as it anticipates, nay even reverses, the order of Nature."[27] Now our narrative must cross the ocean again.

The neo-Edwardsian movement. The Second Great Awakening in New England was spawned by the New-Divinity movement of Edwards' successors. The American foreign missions movement was also a direct outcome of those revivals and its root theology. By 1799 Samuel Hopkins wrote John Ryland, Jr. in England of one hundred towns in New England and eastern New York State which were experiencing awakening, "mostly if not wholly under preachers of [neo-]Edwardian divinity." The result was that most of the candidates for the ministry were New-Divinity adherents, and the number of such pastors expanded rapidly: by 1792 there were 58 in Connecticut and by 1808, 170 in Massachusetts.[28] When Timothy Dwight became president of Yale in 1795 he faced widespread skepticism in the student body influenced by French deism, and he confronted it head on. He turned the tide on campus, and by 1802 "a student revival at Yale witnessed the conversion of one-third of the student body (75 out of 225 students). It touched off a series of awakenings which revived eastern colleges periodically during the next fifty years."[29] Conforti's claim about the impact of this movement is supported despite his overlooking the central part played by Edward D. Griffin (1770-1837), an unheralded key figure.

Edward Griffin, missionary mentor. Early in his fruitful evangelistic ministry in western Connecticut, Griffin led Samuel Mills, Jr. to the Lord. After 1800 he saw many hundreds come to Christ in his ministry in northern New Jersey and at First Presbyterian Church in Newark. He was invited to speak at the General Assembly in Philadelphia in 1805 and gave an unheard of missionary message, "The Kingdom of Christ."[30] Mills, by then a student at Williams College (in NW Mass.), came to hear his mentor and was so affected that he distributed copies of the sermon on campus. This is the untold background of the monumental Haystack Prayer Meeting at Williams College in August of 1806, as the Holy Spirit convinced Mills and his fellow students that they could become the first American foreign missionaries.

Although Adoniram Judson, Jr.'s was a pastor's son, he had been influenced to skepticism and deism at Boston College by a classmate, Jacob Eames. After graduation he went west to see the world, and one night stopped off in an inn. As he listened to the groans of a man dying in the next room, he wondered what skeptical Eames would say about death. In the morning he was shocked to find out that the dead man was indeed Jacob Eames. When he came back to his father's Plymouth parsonage in soul agony over the conflicting claims between the Bible and skepticism, in God's providence, Edward Griffin was there with Prof. Moses Stuart of the new Andover seminary. It was probably Griffin who gave Judson a copy of Thomas Boston's *Man's Fourfold State*, which convinced him to go to Andover as an incidental student to check out the claims of Christ. In three months he came to assurance of salvation. That summer Griffin arrived on campus as professor of "pulpit eloquence," and by September someone (probably Griffin) gave Judson a copy of Buchanan's missionary sermon, "The Star of the East," which started him on his way. Later when Samuel Mills and the other Williams graduates came on campus and connected with Judson, they consulted with Dr. Griffin about the next step. The founding of the American Board of Commissioners for Foreign Missions in 1810 is history. Griffin gave the invocation at the ordination of the first missionaries.

Mills became a home missionary to the frontier and connected with Griffin again in Newark, complaining about the lack of Bibles on the frontier. He got Griffin to promote the formation of the American Bible Society (1814) and the United Missionary Society (1816). By 1821 Griffin became the President of Williams College, where he recruited another generation of foreign missionaries until his retirement.[31]

The neo-Edwardsian theology. The New Divinity is poorly understood today. They called themselves "Consistent Calvinists," but they were neither consistent, nor really Calvinists. *They all held to general redemption,* as evidenced by the essays on the subject collected by Edwards A. Park in 1859. In his introductory essay Park argued that there were elements in the theology of the senior Edwards which paved the way for the New Divinity, which has rightly been called neo-Edwardsian theology. These elements were clearly manifest in Edwards' preaching, as noted above. Many of the neo-Edwardsians were effective, confrontational evangelistic preachers. Keith J. Hardman's analysis of the great awakenings in America indicates that they arose from confrontational evangelism, not the reverse.[32] In order to hold to general redemption, a number of these men denied substitution in the cross and held to free will. The New Haven theology of grandson, Timothy Dwight and his protégé, Nathaniel Taylor, moved farther from Calvinism. Apparently, most did continue to hold to unconditional election, which caused some internal tension. *Most significant, however, is that the New-Divinity movement spawned the Second Great Awakening and the American foreign missions movement.*

Conclusion. The lessons of history indicate that there is a fourfold sequence. First, an evangelism-friendly theology led to confrontational evangelism, which, in turn, led to both Great Awakenings, which, in turn, led to the development of the modern missions movement. Glover called this a step-by-step spiritual lineage of "true apostolic succession of spiritual grace and power and world-wide ministry."[33] The sequence thus is

Evangelism-friendly theology ⇒ Evangelism ⇒ Revival ⇒ Missions

Determinism Inconsistent with Evangelism

Since global persuasion evangelism should be axiomatic for biblical Christians, and since we have seen some serious historical tensions with deterministic theology, let us focus on the theological and logical tensions.

Determinism undermines motivation for evangelism. If the issue of who will be saved or lost was settled in eternity past, then there is nothing which any human being can do to change it. Moderate Calvinists insist that God has decreed the means as well as the end result, but if we refuse to witness for Christ, it follows that this also had been decreed by God, and nothing we can do could change it. We can rationalize *ad infinitum* that

God did not decree for us to be witnesses for Christ and assume no blame for inaction. There are already enough rationalizations to keep most Christians from a significant witness for Christ without another specious one! In this connection that great evangelistic pastor, Spurgeon remarked:

> But mark this, from the day when Fuller, Carey, Sutcliffe, and others, met together to send out missionaries to India, the sun began to dawn of a gracious revival which is not over yet.... The system of theology with which many identify his [Dr. John Gill's] name has chilled many churches to their very soul, for it has led them to omit the free invitations of the gospel, and to deny that it is the duty of sinners to believe in Jesus.[34]

Total inability promotes pessimism about salvation. The notion of total inability (cf. Ch. 3) has spread a pall of pessimism regarding the possibility of salvation, both among the unregenerate under Calvinistic teaching and the Christians who should be confronting them and explaining the simple plan of salvation to them. The logic of it is inexorable. If mankind is totally unable to respond to the gospel and must wait for God's irresistible grace based upon an eternal decree, why bother to try to get saved or to win a sinner to Christ? It is all set in concrete. *Even worse, it is a 'stacked deck.'*

Determinism leads to lack of persistence in evangelism. Few Christians are saved the first time they hear the gospel. This is true of those from nominally Christian cultures, but even more obviously of people from Muslim or Hindu backgrounds. In my lifelong involvement with missionaries to Muslims and Hindus, it has become clear that we must focus upon *the process of conversion*, that is, the process by which people come to repentant faith in Christ. The new birth is instantaneous, but the soul-struggle to come to faith may take years. However, the notion of irresistible grace leaves little room for such a protracted process. Thus, a Calvinist would not be inclined to see the necessity for dogged persistence in witness.

Determinism complicates the simple gospel message. If unconditional election and irresistible grace are true, then the simple gospel message of Christ and the Apostles was oversimplified and misleading. Repentant faith is not some mysterious, mystical intangible, which God arbitrarily gives to some hell-bound sinners and withholds from others. It is the human response to God's ultimatum of the gospel, which men are commanded to do in simply receiving God's Son. How many millions of anxious sinners have been lost because nobody explained to them how simple and available the promises of the gospel really are?

Determinism is counterproductive to church growth. Evangelist Robert Sumner has made an observation which can be substantiated over and over again today and through the centuries: "Many, many more souls are being 'elected' into the family of God where a strong program of New Testament evangelism is in operation than in the *non*-evangelistic–and sometimes even *anti*-evangelistic–atmosphere of the 'tulip' churches."[35]

Looking at the contemporary scene, Pentecostals and some other Arminian churches are far outstripping Calvinistic churches. When one checks the television schedule it is obvious that Pentecostals are way ahead in the use of modern media. The listings of evangelical Bible colleges over recent decades shows disproportionate Arminian growth. They have a more aggressive program of evangelism and missions and are seeing the fruit of it. However, if unconditional election were true, should not God be electing at least as many, if not more people in Calvinistic churches than in Arminian? Some say, "Gordon, you are a pragmatist!" Not at all! But theology must be tested by its fruit, or lack thereof.

Determinism raises serious missiological problems. In this connection two serious questions were previously raised on page 229: why are some kind of peoples, such as Muslims, harder to reach than others if irresistible grace is true? Is is it fair of God to save more Americans than Mongolians, Muslims, caste Hindus, etc., if unconditional election is true?

Conclusions

In short, there is not just inconsistency or paradoxical tension between deterministic theology and global evangelism, but *there is a serious logical, pragmatic, and historical disconnect and contradiction.* This does not disprove Calvinism. But it should cause determinists to go back and check their theology to see if perchance they might have gotten it wrong.

Before closing this chapter, the question must be raised as to how many millions are eternally condemned because of the failure of Protestant churches to pursue global persuasion evangelism from the Reformation until now? How many in the pagan world were condemned because deterministic theology restrained missions and persuasion evangelism? Indeed, how many European and American Protestants who desired to be saved were not because the simple offer of the gospel was not thought theologically appropriate? Some will respond that this was the sovereign will and decree of God. No, the responsibility is upon us Christians, who have complicated the message beyond belief! **"The Lord is not slow about His promise, as some count slowness, but is patient toward you [Christians], not wishing for any to perish but for all to come to repentance"** (2 Pet. 3:9).

1   David J Hesselgrave, Communicating Christ Cross-Culturally, p 55, He cites J I Packer, *Evangelism and the Sovereignty of God*, pp. 48-49, 413-23, & A. Duane Litfin, "The Perils of Persuasive Preaching, " *Christianity Today*, 21 (4 Feb , 1977).484-7.

2   Gustav Warneck, *Outline of a History of Protestant Missions*, trans George Robson, p 38.

3   Thomas Coates, "Were the Reformers Mission-Minded?" *Concordia Theological Monthly*, 40 9, 600-11, Charles Chaney, "The Missionary Dynamic in the Theology of John Calvin," *The Reformed Review*, 17 64, 24-38, Samuel M Zwemer, p 206-16, Harry R Boer, *Pentecost and Missions* (1961), p 18 Boer faults all the Reformers but Bucer in this regard.

4   Coates, "Reformers," p 604

5   Martin Luther, *Sammtliche Schriften*, 2d ed , ed Joh Georg Walch , vol. 14, p 305

6. Harry R. Boer, *Pentecost and Missions* (GR. Eerdmans, 1961), p 18.

7. Coates, "Reformers," p. 601

8   Martin Luther, cited by Johannes Warns, *Baptism* , trans G H. Lang (Paternoster, 1957), p 248, 252

9   It started with the discovery of a book of essays on general redemption by New-Divinity theologians collected by Edwards A. Park (1859), especially Edward Griffin, leading to the roots of missions at Williams College in 1806 Samuel Fisk highlighted the significance of Andrew Fuller in the British Baptist mission Sidney H. Rooy's published dissertation, *The Theology of Missions in the Puritan Tradition* (Eerdmans, 1965), to support a Calvinistic spin, actually backfired in that he did not understand the theology of some of the key players Other research discovered the significant role of Thomas Coke, Philip Doddridge, Samuel Hopkins, and others.

10 J E & A H Godbey, *Light in Darkness Missions and Missionary Heroes* (St Louis, Imperial, 1892), p 24

11 Baxter saw Muslims as the "devil's second army." and also wrote a commentary on some verses of the Qur'an He also expounded the "holy war" going on in which Satan uses heresies and persecution to obstruct world evangelization (Rooy, pp 135-44)

12 Rooy, pp 125-137

13 R Pierce Beaver, *Pioneers in Missions* (Eerdmans, 1966), p. 49

14 Kane, *Concise History* , pp 76-79

15 Rooy, pp 70, 292-3

16 Ibid, pp 286-294, C C Goen, *The Great Awakening*, "The Works of Jonathan Edwards," 4:155-6

17 Ibid, p. 299; Goen, 2: 392-3.

18 John Gerstner, *Steps to Salvation*, p. 78

19 Rooy, p 303, footnote 6.

20. Rooy, p. 302, 304.

21 Joseph A Conforti, *Samuel Hopkins and the New Divinity Movement* (Eerdmans, 1981), pp 142-158

22 This is alluded to by Carey in his *Enquiry.*

23 This is not referred to in any history of missions except Carey's own reference in his *Enquiry.*

24. Terry G. Carter, "The Calvinism of William Carey and its Effect on His Mission Work " A paper presented at ETS annual meeting at Colorado Springs, November, 2001. Carter was disappointed to find no reference to the doctrine of election in all of Carey's extensive correspondence.

25 Although the authenticity of this incident was challenged by Dr. John Ryland, Jr., the others present affirmed it, and Carey mentioned it to his colleague, Marshman. S Pierce Carey, *William Carey, D D* p. 50, Joseph Belcher, *William Carey· A Biography*, p. 52

26 Andrew Gunton Fuller, *The Complete Works of Andrew Fuller*, 2 vols. (Boston, 1833), I.20-65 Fuller was widely read on both sides of the Atlantic, since there are two British and two American editions of his complete works! Fuller's writings also impacted the Second Great Awakening in New England. He was one of the most widely read theologians on both sides of the Atlantic in the first half of the 19th century. Timothy Dwight had Yale College grant him an honorary doctorate after he refused a proffered doctorate from the College of New Jersey (Princeton)

27 Cited by Richard Fletcher, *The Barbarian Conversion: From Paganism to Christianity*, p. 1

28 Conforti, pp. 177-90.

29 Woodbridge, Noll, and Hatch, *The Gospel in America* (Zondervan, 1979), pp 107-8, 144.

30 The junior Edwards is Griffin's most likely source from which he got his missionary insights

31 John H Hewitt, *Williams College and Foreign Missions* (Boston· Pilgrim Press, 1914), additional documentation in my *What in the World Is God Doing? The Essentials of Global Missions*, 5th ed (2003)

32 Keith J Hardman, *Seasons of Refreshing Evangelism and Revivals in America* (Baker 1994), pp 15-19

33 Robert Hall Glover, *The Progress of World-Wide Missions* Rev. & enlarged by J Herbert Kane, p 88

34 Charles H. Spurgeon, cited by Iain Murray, *Spurgeon v Hyper-Calvinism* , pp. 112, 120, 127.

35 Robert L. Sumner, *An Examination of TULIP* (Murfreesboro, TN Biblical Evangelism Press, 1972), p. 22.

Christ sent His disciples into all the world, and He instructed them to preach the gospel to every creature. If, then, election means that all those whom God has arbitrarily chosen will certainly get to Heaven, and that all those whom He has not chosen will certainly not get there, no matter how faithfully and frequently the gospel may be preached to them, then why be greatly agitated about it? True, we have the command to take the gospel into all the world; but if only some are thus elected, why be greatly disturbed about it?

-Henry C. Thiessen

DOES IT *REALLY* MATTER?

Is this book a tempest in a teapot? Many naive or not doctrinally oriented Christians might think so. We have shown that both Calvinism and Arminianism, *as systems*, are seriously flawed. Each has some scriptural features and some unscriptural ones. As theological systems they fail in far too many points. But what difference does it make, after all?

Since doctrine is the only foundation for a sound Christian life, it makes a vast difference in our walk and service of God. It has a major impact upon our witness to the lost and the discipling of believers. All Christians should have a concern for truth and for the way Scripture is interpreted and preached in our pulpits. If our theological systems have deflected us from grasping and fulfilling the core of God's plan, this is indeed a serious problem. If we have majored on the minor and minored on the major from God's perspective, we are accountable at the judgment seat of Christ.

These days the secular media are filled with distorted images of evangelical Christianity, more than ever before. Deterministic* theology has given Christians bad press for centuries. We have a serious apologetic* problem, whether in academia, the media, within Christendom, with Jews, Muslims, Hindus, or cultists. We are viewed as gay-bashers, abortionist killers, haters of Muslims, a threat to Jews, and the list goes on. We don't need to add to that the thought that our God is an angry, arbitrary despot, who has already destined the mass of humanity to hell quite irrespective of anything anybody can do. *We must not add offense to that of the cross.*

The Impact on the Christian Life

Let us start where we all live, the Christian life. The track record of both determinists and Arminians in living a balanced Christian life is not great.

353

Assurance. The assurance of salvation is most significant as a basis for a stable Christian life. Both Arminians and extreme Calvinists deny that any Christian can be sure of ultimate salvation. Legions of Calvinists have agonized until their dying day over whether or not they were among the elect. This is not a defect in God's plan of salvation but of defective doctrine.

Prayer. The efficacy of prayer is another serious problem with which determinists struggle. Although they think that God does not really respond to the prayers of His people, the Bible is very clear that He does answer prayer.

Conditional love. The limitations on God's love make a tremendous difference in the Christian life for both Calvinists and Arminians. Conditional security means conditional love for Arminians, and the restriction of His love in limited atonement is just as serious a limitation. How can we have a good relationship with a God whose love in conditional, limited, and arbitrary?

Legalism. All serious Christians must fight legalism, but the evidence is clear that both extreme Calvinists and Arminians are prone to it. One serious form of legalism is writing off problem Christians as counterfeits because they don't measure up to our legalistic standard. Calvin was a legalist,[1] and extreme Calvinism falls into legalistic introspection very easily. It is rife among Arminians also. How many Arminians developed not only a lifestyle legalism, but also a legalistic understanding of the terms of salvation? The Lord Jesus said, **"For my yoke is easy and my burden is light."** He was the enemy of pharisaic legalism, which is not conducive to a balanced Christian life.

Self-righteous pride. Pride was the original sin of Lucifer, which made him Satan. Pride was a major factor in the mindset of the Pharisees of Christ's day. When we focus upon ourselves as God's 'elect,' there is a serious danger of denigrating both the 'non-elect' and those who do not agree with us. R. C. Sproul's calling those who believe in the priority of faith "barely Christian" is outrageous, and he is not alone. Ironically, this is usually portrayed as a view which magnifies God's grace. Evangelist John R. Rice put it bluntly: "The heresy of extreme Calvinism is particularly appealing to people.... to the scholarly intellect, the self-sufficient and proud mind. So brilliant, philosophical, scholarly preachers are apt to be misled on this matter more than the humble-hearted Bible believer."[2]

On the other hand, sinless perfectionism also is a great wellspring of pride. "I haven't sinned in ten years!" "I have received the second blessing and am now living on a higher plane of Christian experience." "I have been baptized in the Holy Ghost and speak in tongues." All of this is very intimidating to other Christians and is far from humble. Harry Ironside had an enlightening experience as a struggling young Salvation Army officer sent to a rest home. He found that those inmates who professed the least of "entire sanctification" were the most godly, and those who claimed the most showed the least evidences of the fruit of the Spirit.[3]

Irresponsible, unmotivated personal lives. Norman Geisler spelled it out: "Extreme Calvinism leads logically (if not practically) to personal irresponsibility: if our actions are good actions, they are such only because God has programmed us to do good; if evil, then we cannot help it because we are sinners by nature and God has not given us the desire to do good."[4] I have heard Calvinists rationalize sin as part of the will of God. On the other hand, my early Christian experience of my Arminian pastor calling sin "a mistake" in order to maintain his perfectionist theology is a similar rationalization. Drop the bar low so that you can jump over it!

It is difficult enough to motivate most Christians to actively seek and do the will of God without introducing contrary notions into their minds. Even some who are motivated, have an unbiblical motivation. Arminians are often motivated by fear of losing salvation, but then again Calvinists are often working hard to prove that they are among the elect. The true motivation should be our gratitude for what He has already done for us and is ready to do for "whosoever will" (2 Cor. 5:10). "**For the grace of God has appeared, bringing salvation to all men, instructing us to deny ungodliness and worldly desires and to live sensibly, righteously and godly in the present age ...**" (Titus 2:11-12).

Blaming God. Non-Christians quite regularly blame God for every calamity which comes into their lives. Isn't it a travesty then that deterministic Christians also attribute everything that happens directly to God? God gets enough blame from non-Christians without misguided determinists joining their ranks in blaming God.

The Impact on God's Truth
In our day of relativism most people do not believe in absolute truth. Most Christians really don't care much about doctrine and are very subjective in their Christian lives and faith. "Whatever turns you on," "whatever floats your boat,"--these are the mottoes of the day, even among Christians. Whatever seems to meet our material, emotional, and/or physical needs is acceptable, even if it is absolute heresy. *But truth does matter!* The Lord Jesus claimed to be absolute truth (Jn. 14:6) and He claimed that God's word is absolute truth (Mt. 5:18; Jn. 10:35). The Greek word for truth (*alētheia*) has as a key idea 'reality,' or 'actuality.'[5] So if we are prey to doctrinal error, we are living in a realm of unreality, believing things which are not actual or true! Our focus has been upon the theology of salvation, but actually all the categories of theology are affected by polarized error. As one might gather from Chapter 2, the biblical view of God is vastly impacted, and from Chapter 3, our understanding of man and sin. These systems impact our view of the Bible and the work of Christ. Thus, it bleeds through our whole view of God, Christ, man, sin, salvation, and even of the church.

Views of God. As Dave Hunt emphasizes, Calvinism misrepresents God as a loveless God. The notion of a passionless God connects with this. Arminianism fails to portray his justice adequately. In Christian ethics we learn that the whole of biblical ethics flows from the person and work of God.[6] God's character should be reflected in us. In Chapter 2 we saw that there is no biblical basis for an exaggerated concept of the sovereignty of God, which would make Him an arbitrary despot, like Allah of the Muslims.

Views of humanity. In Chapter 3 we saw that the extrapolation of human depravity into total inability is without biblical warrant. This had its devastating impact upon global missions for centuries, since the 'heathen' were represented as so depraved that it was useless to try to evangelize them. Even among nominal Christians the notion of total inability was made the basis for opposition to any confrontation of sinners with the gospel of Christ. The general impact of all of this upon the Christian community was a pessimism about the possibility of salvation, both on the part of the sinner and on the part of the preacher. What a thrill it was to discover that the myriads who were converted to Christ in the Second Great Awakening in New England were saved through New Divinity pastors *who preached that Christ died for all without exception.* For the first time in Calvinistic New England the common people were finding out that depravity did not mean inability to exercise repentant faith. That extrapolation of depravity into virtual denial of the image of God dehumanizes man and makes him out to be less than God's word shows him to be. On the other hand, Arminians tend to emphasize human ability too much.

Views of the Bible. It seems that many Arminians have a problem with the inerrancy of Scripture.* Many contemporary Arminians finds the Scripture to be self-contradictory. When the interpretation of diverse passages comes out with contradictory conclusions, trust in inerrancy is undermined. Many Arminian denominations do not even have a position on inerrancy.

On the other hand, determinists also have a problem they have not confronted. If the outworking of God's sovereignty and decrees is all encompassing, then how can it be that certain aspects of Scripture show human involvement, that is, the imperfect preservation of the text and of translations. Believing that God works mediately in many of His works in the world, we should have no problem with that. But if God has decreed "all that comes to pass" why did He not perfectly preserve the text? Even worse is the problem of translation. Why did God sovereignly allow that corrupt Vulgate version to dominate Christendom for over a millennium? But God overrules, and the Spirit uses our translations even though less than perfect.

Views of Christ. There have been many distorted pictures of Christ in past theology. When Catholic theology portrayed both Father and Son in a stern and wrathful way with Mary as the loving intercessor, Lutherans sought to correct that by portraying Christ as the loving intercessor with a God of wrath. Both Lutheran and Calvinistic theology has tended to portray Christ as propitiating and reconciling a wrathful God. Nineteenth-century pietists* in Scandinavia began to question that picture with the question, "Where is it written?" *The whole Tri-unity of God is united in their love for mankind.*

Views of salvation. The history of theology is one of human over-reaction. Doctrinal error in one direction was overcompensated for in the opposite direction. Pelagius' man-centered distortion of salvation was countered by Augustine's inconsistent overreaction of a deterministic concept of God's grace. Although a semi-Augustinian resolution was arrived at in the synod of Orange (529), the medieval Catholic church drifted increasingly to semi-Pelagianism.* The Reformers reacted by repackaging Augustine's determinism and restored justification by grace, but they retained much of his church-centered concept of salvation. Then, the Reformed* movement was hijacked by Beza and associates. A score of movements were identified which then sought to correct this over-reaction and to move away from determinism. Among them Arminius' correction itself got hijacked by the Remonstrants.[7] The Wesleyan movement brought theology back to a more evangelical position, although developing other unbiblical strains. Over the centuries there were constant universalist reactions against the narrow determinism of the Reformers and their successors. Those with a liberalizing mindset took the biblical truth of Christ's death for all, and failing to distinguish the objective ransom from the subjective liberation, sought to universalize salvation. This was clearly a reaction to the gross narrowness of determinism. Calvinists have no answer to universalism except to deny God's universal love. No wonder universalism has flourished in heavily Calvinistic areas. We could fairly say that *universalism is the unpaid debt of Calvinism!*

The Calvinistic gospel is not good news for all sinners. There is just a message of resignation to the inexorable will of God. This is more like the Islam I heard in Pakistan. Islam is a religion of submission to the inexorable will of a sovereign Allah. On the other hand, Arminian denial of eternal security does leave us with a temporary salvation, more akin to probation than the full acquittal of justification by faith alone. Such an insecure view of salvation held by both Arminians and extreme Calvinists is not a solid base for building a stable Christian life of assurance and blessing.

The Impact upon Preaching

Reformed homiletician and editor, James Daane, wrote his significant critique of decretal theology* because of his conviction that it is unpreachable.[8] Obviously Arminians are not preaching election, but he observed that the Reformed* are not preaching their Calvinism either, because it is unpreachable. This caused him to reexamine the biblical basis of what he termed 'decretal theology.' Daane suggested that the problem of preaching decretal theology is reprobation: "Simply stated, reprobation gets in the way of every attempt to take election seriously because in the traditional Reformed theology *reprobation is always there.*" Although I have not been a part of the Reformed tradition, I have sat under the ministry of at least three five-point Calvinists for an extensive period, one of whom even wrote a book on election. I cannot recall any one of the three giving any exposition of Calvinistic doctrine from the pulpit although all three inconsistently believed in evangelism and missions. Those Calvinists who believe in global evangelism are faced with an insuperable dilemma. Preaching their Calvinism along with the necessity of exercising repentant faith will prove counterproductive. Certainly Calvinism is not the gospel, and preaching them together will not only seem contradictory, but also will be offensive and a hindrance to unsaved hearers. Another urgent question is whether a preacher should believe something he cannot preach. It smacks of insincerity to have a Calvinistic hidden agenda, which cannot be preached to the unsaved.

The Impact upon Apologetics*

Much harm has been done by the oft-quoted statement of Charles Spurgeon that since the Bible is like a lion, you don't have to defend it, you just let it go. We know that the word of God is like a hammer, a mirror, and a sword, but there is no reference to the Bible being like a lion (2 Pet. 5:8). Today, lions are an endangered species! So we must question Spurgeon's simile and its negative impact for over a century. Most of us see Spurgeon as a hero of the faith in carrying to the next generation Andrew Fuller's emphasis on confronting sinners with the gospel. However, one wonders if his commitment to essential Calvinism did not distort his perspective on the value of apologetics. The root of Spurgeon's reticence toward apologetics may go back to Calvin. Dave Hunt demonstrates by extensive quotes from Calvin that he had "little use for evidence and proof." In emphasizing the internal testimony of the Spirit, Calvin denigrated external evidences for the inspiration of Scripture. Hunt points out that Muslims, Mormons, and others give their own subjective testimonies for the truth of their holy books since they lack any external objective support.[9] It is true that in the last century many Calvinists have been at the forefront of the use of apologetics.[A] However, it really is inconsistent with their view of man and salvation. If man is dead in total inability, apologetic argument is not going to have any impact. In Chapter 25 we saw the biblical paradigm for persuasion evangelism, of which apologetics is a vital part.

A starting point in apologetics is the arguments for the existence of God from creation. Starting with the premise of total inability it is obvious that if the word of God cannot impact the 'non-elect,' certainly the naturalistic

---

A. With the devastating inroads of liberalism in their denominations, Calvinists, such as Machen, Warfield, and Wilson, were forced to use apologetic tools to defend the faith, and Sproul, James Kennedy, and others have picked up the mantle, although not really compatible with their theology.

arguments would be even more useless. Extreme Calvinists face the same problem with making God the author of evil. They also have a problem of God being the ultimate discriminator of persons, since He supposedly gives the gift of faith to so few in many nations and to so many Americans.

Resorting to Philosophical Sophistries

There is a real concern about the harmful influence of philosophic systems upon theology, especially the evidence of philosophical sophistries in Calvinistic theology. The heavy dependence upon words like antinomy, paradox, and mystery are highly troubling. Expressions like "soft determinism" and compatibilism as explanations for the contradictions of the system are a smoke-screen, not a logical explanation. Daane charges that commitment to decretal theology* only produces "word games." Geisler calls it "word magic."[10]

We faulted the widespread failure to make a simple distinction between God's *certainty* of the whole future and God's *determining* of the whole future, as a fundamental error of logic and language. We also noted the theological recklessness of the *many extrapolations* of language and thought common among determinists. These involve such persistent subtle semantic shifts that we have no hesitation in calling them sophistries. They do not clarify God's truth; they only obfuscate and confuse the issues.

Usurping the True Meaning of Scripture

The main body of this book has been devoted to the interpretation of crucial Scripture passages, by carefully examining the contexts; the usage of key words in the literature; the grammar and syntax of each sentence; and the analogy of Scripture, without resort to parallelomania. We tried to consistently use an inductive, exegetical approach. Unless philosophical presuppositions and biases are eliminated as we handle the word of the living God, we are in danger of heresy. To fail to do so is to allow a theological or philosophical system to usurp the true meaning of God's word. In the parable of the soils the Lord Jesus spoke about the fourth kind of people, **"who have heard the word in an honest and good heart, hold it fast, and bear fruit with perseverance"** (Lk. 8:15). This must be the goal of every Christian. The content of the good news we bear is of highest importance in producing genuine fruit for God, fruit which will persist and survive the fires of God's judgments. It is not only foundational to bearing fruit for God, but also essential in honoring His inerrant word. *We bring discredit to God, His church, His word, and His gospel when we indulge in deductive, theological interpretation, which is Scripture twisting.*

Missing the Heart of God's Great Plan

God's great plan of the ages is the redemption and restoration of a lost human race. The full historical record is clear that deterministic theology, rather than helping world evangelism, has been a serious obstacle. In researching the modern missions movement, one wonders whether there has been a cover up of the negative impact of Calvinism by biased historians. The very least my discoveries show is that for over a century a very Calvinistic spin has been put on this history. This is most disturbing!

To the extent our theology of salvation is harmonious with that plan, to that extent it is the **"whole counsel of God"** (Acts 20:27); but to what extent it obscures or hinders that plan, to that extent it will be burned up in the fires of God's judgments. May every Christian be found searching the Scriptures with an **"honest and good heart"** to verify, understand, believe, obey, and proclaim accurately God's great eternal plan for the salvation of people of **"every nation and *all* tribes and peoples and tongues"** (Rev. 7:9).

Conclusions

Therefore, I appeal to Calvinistic readers to go beyond Calvin and Beza, back to the word of God. I appeal to Arminians to go beyond Arminius and Wesley, back to the Bible. I appeal to Lutherans to go beyond Luther and Melanchthon to a fresh exegesis of Scripture.

Let us break free from the destructive and divisive polarization of doctrine by going back to the full inspiration, sufficiency, and priority of the Scriptures in developing our theology. Let us make sure that we have a balanced theology, not majoring in the minor or perhaps even missing the major themes completely. Let us focus on the heart of God's plan of the ages—the redemption of lost humanity through the all-sufficient blood of Christ's cross by confronting the lost with the imperative of response to his bona fide offer of grace by repentant faith. Let us make sure that we are "telling it like it is," not binding on earth what God has not bound in heaven, and not loosing on earth what God has not loosed in heaven. *Only this will give the full glory to the Living God.*

1. Dave Hunt, *What Love Is This? Calvinism's Misrepresentation of God* (Sisters, OR. Loyal, 2002), pp 59-74.

2 John R Rice, *Predestined for Hell? No!* (Murfreesboro, TN: Sword of the Lord, 1958), p. 6, cited by Fisk, p. 198.

3 H A Ironside, *Holiness the False and the True* (Neptune, NJ. Loizeaux)

4. Geisler, *Chosen but Free*, p 132.

5 Abbott-Smith, *Lexicon*, p. 20

6 Carl F H Henry, *Christian Personal Ethics* (Eerdmans, 1957), pp 145-71 (not just limited to these pages)

7 Stephen M Ashby, "A Reformed Arminian View," in J Matthew Pinson, ed , *Four Views on Eternal Security* (Zondervan, 2002), pp 138, 150 See also the various writings of Carl Bangs.

8 James Daane, *The Freedom of God· A Study of Election and the Pulpit* (GR. Eerdmans, 1973).

9 Hunt, pp 394-6, cites Calvin's *Institutes*, III: pp. 71-73

10 Daane, p. 73.

GLOSSARY OF TERMS

Amillennialism: The view that the kingdom is now, inaugurated at the first coming of Christ, which denies a future literal reign of Christ on earth and equates Israel, the Church, and the kingdom.

Anabaptist: The group of radical reformation movements which broke from the mainline Reformation and insisted upon personal conversion and believers baptism by immersion.

Analogy of Scripture: A method of interpreting a passage by looking for parallel Scripture testimony for clarification. Also referred to as analogy of faith.

Anthropomorphism: A figure of speech describing God in human terms.

Antinomian: Literally, against law. Extreme Calvinists and others in emphasizing grace, have denied that any law is binding on them.

Aorist tense: A unique Greek verb tense, usually described as point action in past time, but perhaps more accurately, as giving the broader picture of the whole action of the verb.

Augustinian: The doctrine of Bishop Augustine of N. Africa (353-430) emphasizing predestination and irresistible grace. Used as synonymous with Calvinist and determinist.

Church fathers: Early Christian leaders and writers after the Apostles.

Compatibilism: A philosophical explanation of how a deterministic view of God's sovereignty can be compatible with human free will.

Contextualization: The process of communicating the message from one culture to another. Since the Bible was written in different cultures, the message must first be understood in its own cultural context before it can be communicated in diverse world cultures.

Crux Interpretum: A crucial passage or consideration in interpreting Scripture.

Decretal theology: Descriptive of a theological system based upon God's eternal decrees as determining all events, synonymous with Augustinian or Calvinistic theology.

Deductive reasoning: Deduction is "reasoning from a known principle to an unknown, from the general to the specific, or from a premise to a logical conclusion;" and "from the general to the particular, or from the universal to the individual."

Determinism: The view that all events in the universe have been determined in eternity by God.

Dispensational: An approach to Scripture which recognizes differing ages or dispensations in the outworking of God's plan, especially distinguishing the nation Israel, with its Mosaic rule of life, from the Church, with grace as its rule of life.

Etymology: Understanding word meaning by tracing a word to its root. Word usage is a preferred method.

Exegesis: The science of drawing out of Scripture its original meaning, emphasizing grammar, syntax, word meaning, and the immediate, broader, and cultural contexts of a passage. The analogy of Scripture must be carefully used by avoiding parallelomania.

Extrapolation: Going beyond the data to speculatively estimate results.

Hermeneutics: The science of the principles of interpretation of Scripture.

Inductive method: "the process of reasoning from particular instances to general conclusions." In logic, it is "reasoning from particular facts or individual cases to a general conclusion." In science it is parallel to the empirical or scientific method.

362

Inerrancy of Scripture: The Bible claims for itself verbal, plenary inspiration, which is confirmed by the phenomena of its internal consistency.

Isogesis: The opposite of exegesis, that is, reading back into Scripture another, usually theological, traditional, spiritualized, or desired meaning.

Lexicon: Usually a dictionary of words in a foreign language.

Manicheanism: An ancient Eastern religion formed from Persian Zoroastrianism and Christianity.

Middle voice: Describes the action of the subject of a verb back upon itself (reflexive), distinct from active and passive voice.

Neo-Puritans: Contemporary extreme Calvinists who show great reverence for the old Puritan writers.

Open theism: A recent theology, called extreme Arminianism, which holds that God does not know the whole future, only what He has determined.

Patristics: Study of church fathers.

Pelagian: The view of the British monk, Pelagius (350-409), who purportedly denied original sin and emphasized man's ability to please God.

Periphrastic, periphrasis: In grammar, an alternate, less direct way of structuring a sentence, usually for emphasis or to bring out an unusual idea.

Premillennialism: The view that Christ will return to earth to reign and rule in righteousness for the millennial kingdom before the final consummation.

Preparationism: The steps suggested by some Calvinists for sinners to prepare themselves while waiting for God's sovereign gift of the new birth and of faith to the elect.

Proof-texting: The false practice of merely listing or quoting a verse of the Bible apart from its context and careful exegesis, especially used by cults.

Providence: The biblical view that God is involved in the affairs of life and orchestrates circumstances, good and bad, for the ultimate good of believers.

Puritan: A term, which at first referred to those who wanted to purify the Anglican Church, but later came to refer to those of a more Calvinistic doctrine.

Reformed: A general term, which at first described a branch of the Reformation, but came to be more narrowly a reference to extreme Calvinism.

Scholasticism: A rationalistic philosophical approach to theology, developed by mediaeval scholars (schoolmen), grounded on the deductive methodology of Aristotle. It tends to put reason above Scripture by giving priority to deductive theological discussion before any attempt to exegete Scripture.

Semi-Augustinian: Those church fathers who accepted Augustine's emphasis on original sin and grace in salvation, while rejecting absolute predestination and irresistible grace.

Semi-Pelagian: The view that man is only partially depraved and therefore able to contribute to his soul's salvation, which means by faith plus works.

Septuagint (LXX): The ancient Greek translation of the Old Testament probably done by Jewish scholars in Alexandria, Egypt about 250 BC.

Sufficiency of Scripture: With the help of the Holy Spirit, Christians can accurately perceive salvation truth without recourse to traditions and rationalistic philosophies of men.

Synergism: Salvation by man working with God. Extreme Calvinists frequently accuse others of being synergists. Melanchthon was accused of being a synergist by extreme Lutherans.

Syntax: In grammar, sentence structure; the "arrangement of word forms to show their mutual relations in the sentence."

SCRIPTURE INDEX

363

NOTE:
Bold page numbers indicate reference is quoted in part or in whole.

SUBJECT INDEX

A

Abraham – **43-46**
All. Christ's death for– 67-8, **202-15**
Amyraldian Calvinism– 320, **328-9**
Amyraut, Moyse– **328**, 334
Anabaptists– 2, **325**
Analogy of Scripture –57, 128-30
Anticipations of the gospel – 41
Apologetics, impact on– 358-9
Apostates, apostasy– 183-7
Apostolic preacfhing – **76-81**, 219
Aramaic question in Mt. 16.18 – 126, 128
Arminianism– 2, **3**, 107, 109, 118, **151-5**
Arminius, James– 2, 32,151, **327**
Assurance of salvation– **109-122**, 247
Atonement, Old Testament– 56-7
Augustine, Aurelius– 2, 259-60, **321-24**, 332
Autonomy, man's– **17-18**, 25, **32**

B

Babel – **43**
Baptism, Water– 82, **231-242**
Baptismal regeneration– **231-242**
Baptism of the Spirit– **162**, 233
Backsliding Christians– 116
Baxter, Richard – 334, **343**
Beza, Theodor– **336**, 332
Binding and loosing – **133-135**
Blaming God – 355
Boston, Thomas -- **330**, 334, 348

C

Cain – 27
Calamities, impact on assurance – **116-7**
Calling, not irresistible – **305-319**
Calling, word study –**305-307**
Calvin, John–2, 216, 326
Calvinism, summary – **2, 3**, 109, 120-1, **151-4**
Carey, William– 334, **347**
Carnal Christians– **149**
Christ, the Rock–**126-31**
Christ, view of – **52-54, 245-6**
Chamberlain's Greek principle – 65, 127
Charismatic movement– 108
Cheap grace – 139
Church growth hindered – 350-1
Claims of Christ – 245
Cocceius, Johannes– 329
Coke, Thomas – 334, **346-7**
Compatiblism– 359
Confrontational paradigm– 33, **338-40**
Context in interpretation – 6, 21, 188-9
Conversion– **74-5, 105-6**
Conviction of the Spirit– **83-94**

Extent of – **93**
Historical actualization– **89-93**
Human instrumentality, by– **92-3**
Nature of– **93-4**
Reactions against– **92**
Cornelius – 38
Corporate passages individualized – 187
Corporate solidarity– **287-9**
Cost of Discipleship –142-3
Counsel, God's– **19-22**
Counterfeit Christians – 164, **169-70, 174-5, 183-87**
Covenants, biblical – 30, 44-5
Covenant theology– **329**
Creation -- **13-17**
Cross of Christ – 75, 113
Cultural overhang– 130

D

Death, spiritual– 26, **28-9**, 249
Decrees of God– **13**, 19, 23-4, **291-7**
Decretal theology– 357-8
Deductive methodology– **4-5**, 8, 216
Deity of Christ – 112-3, **118-9**, 245-6, 254
Demonstrative use of article– 21-22
Depravity, man's– 11, 26, **31-5**
Disciple– 139
Discipleship teachings-- 82, 180-1, **138-43**, 148-50
Discouragements, impact on assurance – **116-7**
Doctrine -- 4
Donatists – 323
Dwight, Timothy– 331, 335, 349

E.

Earnest of the Spirit – 160
Eastern Orthodoxy - 2
Edwards, Jonathan, Sr – 112, 335, **345-6**
Edwards, Jonathan, Jr – 335, 346
Election--
  Apostles, of– 279
  Christ, of –277
  Church, of– **279-85**
  Conditional– **259-61**
  Criteria of, revealed – **285-7**
  Ensuring – 181
  In Christ–**282-4**
  Israel, of –299-302
  Messiah, of– 275
  Mystery of– **284-7**
  Patriarchs, of– 274
  Relation to foreordination– 283-4
  Word study of– **276-82**
Elegchein, elegchos (conviction)– 85-6
Eliot, John – 335, 343
Empirical method – 4-5, 8

367

SELECTED BIBLIOGRAPHY

Alexander, Archibald *Thoughts on Religious Experience*. Carlisle, PA Banner of Truth, 1967 repr.

Alexander, W Lindsay *A System of Biblical Theology* 1888.

Allen, Ronald B *The Majesty of Man· The Dignity of Being Human* rev ed GR Kregel, 2000

Anderson, Sir Robert *Redemption Truths* GR: Kregel, 1980 (reprint).

Andrew, Brother. *And God Changed His Mind . . . Because His people dared to ask* Tarrytown. Revell, 1990.

Arminius, James *The Works of James Arminius*, trans James & William Nichols, 3 vols. GR Baker, 1986.

Armstrong, Brian G. *Calvinism and the Amyraut Heresy*. Madison Univ. of Wisconsin Press, 1969.

Bakker, Jim *I Was Wrong* Nashville: Thomas Nelson, 1996.

Bangs, Carl O *Arminius . A Study in the Dutch Reformation*, 2nd ed. GR Zondervan, 1985.

Barnes, Albert. *The Atonement* Minneapolis Bethany Fellowship, reprint of 1860.

Basinger, David & Randall, eds. *Predestination and Free Will Four Views* Downers Grove, IL· InterVarsity, 1986

Baxter, Richard. *The Practical Works of Richard Baxter· Selected Treatises* GR: Baker Book House, 1981 (1863)

Beaver, R Pierce *Pioneers in Mission* GR Eerdmans, 1966

_____. *To Advance the Gospel*. GR Eerdmans, 1967.

Beilby, James K and Eddy, Paul R. eds *Divine Foreknowledge. Four Views*. Downers Grove. InterVarsity, 2001.

Bell, M Charles. *Calvin and Scottish Theology:Theology of Assurance*. Edinburgh: Handsel Press, 1985.

Berkhof, L. *Systematic Theology*. GR. Eerdmanns, 1953.

Best, W E. *Justification before God (Not by Faith)* Houston. W E. Best Book Missionary Trust, n d

Bierma, Lyle D *German Calvinism in the Confessional Age*. GR, Baker Book, 1997.

Boer, Harry R *Pentecost and Missions* GR· Eerdmans, 1961.

Boettner, Loraine *The Reformed Faith* Phillipsburg· Presbyterian & Reformed, 1983

_____ *The Reformed Doctrine of Predestination*, 5th ed GR Eerdmans, 1941

Boice, James Montgomery *Awakening to God* Downers Grove, IL InterVarsity Press, 1979.

Brown, Colin ed *The New International Dictionary of New Testament Theology*, 3 vols GR· Zondervan,1967

Bryson, George L *The Five Points of Calvinism*. Costa Mesa, CA The Word for Today, 1996.

Buswell, Jr., James Oliver *A Systematic Theology of the Christian Religion* Grand Rapids. Zondervan, 1962

Cairns, Earle E *Christianity Through the Centuries A History of the Christian Church* GR Zondervan, 1996

Calvin, John *Institutes of the Christian Religion*, trans. By Henry Beveridge. GR Eerdmans, 1964

_____. *Commentaries*, trans William Pringle, 22 vols GR· Baker, 1979 reprint

Caragounis, Chrys C. *Peter and the Rock*. Berlin: DeGruyter, 1990.

Carson, D. A. *Exegetical Fallacies* Grand Rapids: Baker, 1984

_____ *The Difficult Doctrine of the Love of God*. Wheaton Crossway, 2000.

_____. *Divine Sovereignty and Human Responsibility. Biblical Perspectives in Tension*. GR. Baker, 1994

Carson, D. A., Moo, Douglas, and Morris, Leon. *An Introduction to the New Testament*. GR. Zondervan, 1992.

Carson, D. A. and Woodbridge, John D eds., *Hermeneutics, Authority and Canon* GR·Academie, 1986

Chafer, Lewis Sperry. *Systematic Theology*, 8 vols Dallas: Dallas Seminary Press, 1947.

Chantry, Walter. *Today's Gospel Authentic or Synthetic?* London: Banner of Truth, 1970

Clark, Gordon H *The Atonement*, 2nd ed Jefferson: The Trinity Foundation, 1987

_____ *Predestination*. Phillipsburg, NJ. Presbyterian and Reformed, 1987.

Clifford, Alan C. *Atonement and Justification. English Evangelical Theology (1640-1790)*, Oxford 1990.

Cocoris, G Michael *Lordship Salvation—Is It Biblical?* Dallas Redencion Viva, 1983

Conforti, Joseph A *Samuel Hopkins and the New Divinity Movement* GR· Eerdmans, 1981.

Craig, William Lane. *The Only Wise God· The Compatibility of Divine Foreknowledge and Human Freedom* Baker, 1987

Crampton, W Gary *What Calvin Says*. Jefferson, MD Trinity Foundation, 1992

Custance, Arthur C. *The Sovereignty of Grace* GR Baker, 1979

Daane, James *The Freedom of God: A Study of Election and Pulpit* GR Eerdmans, 1973

Davenant, John *The Death of Christ*, ed Allport London, 1832

Davis, Walter Bruce *William Carey Father of Modern Missions* Chicago Moody,1963

Demarest, Bruce *The Cross and Salvation The Doctrine of Salvation* Wheaton· Crossway, 1997

Dillow, Joseph C *The Reign of the Servant Kings* Miami Springs, FL: Schoettle Pub., 1992

Douty, Norman F. *The Death of Christ* Irving, TX Williams & Watrous Publishing, 1978.

Duty, Guy *If Ye Continue. A Study of the Conditional Aspects of Salvation* Minneapolis Bethany House, 1966

Eaton, Michael *No Condemnation: A New Theology of Assurance* Downers Grove, IL· InterVarsity Press, 1995

Elwell, Walter A ed. *Evangelical Dictionary of Theology.* GR Baker, 1984

Enns, Paul *The Moody Handbook of Theology* Chicago Moody Press, 1972

Erickson, Millard J *Christian Theology,* 3 vols. GR Baker, 1983

Estep, William R *The Anabaptist Story· An Introduction to Sixteenth-Century Anabaptism.* GR Eerdmans, 1996

Feinberg, John S *No One Like Him: The Doctrine of God* Wheaton Crossway, 2001.

Fisk, Samuel *Divine Sovereignty and Human Freedom.* rev ed Eugene, OR, Wipf and Stock, 2002

_____ *Calvinistic Paths Retraced,* Murfreesboro, TN Biblical Evangelism Press, 1985.

Fletcher, Richard. *The Barbarian Conversion from Paganism to Christianity.* NY. Henry Holt, 1997

Forlines, LeRoy. *The Quest for Truth: Answering Life's Inescapable Questions* Nashville Randall House, 2001

Forster, Roger T and Marston, V. Paul *God's Strategy in Human History* Minneapolis Bethany House, 1973

Fuller, Andrew Gunton ed *The Complete Wordks of Andrew Fuller,* 2 vols Boston Lincoln, Edmands, 1833

Geisler, Norman L *Chosen But Free.* Minneapolis: Bethany House, 1999.

George, Timothy *The Theology of the Reformers.* Nashville. Broadman, 1988

Grudem, Wayne *Systematic Theology· An Introduction to Biblical Doctrine* GR: Zondervan, 1994

Hardman, Keith J. *Seasons of Refreshing Evangelism and Awakenings in America,* GR· Baker Books, 1994.

Harrison, Everett F. *Baker's Dictionary of Theology.* GR Baker, 1960.

Heard, J B *The Tripartite Nature of Man Spirit, Soul, and Body* Edinburg: T. & T. Clark, 1866.

Heick, O W. and Neve, J. L. *A History of Christian Thought,* 2 vols Phila.: Muhlenberg, 1946

Hesselgrave, David J. *Communicating Christ Cross-Culturally.* GR· Zondervan, 1978.

Hewitt, John H. *Williams College and Foreign Missions.* Boston Pilgrim Press, 1914.

Hodge, Archibald A *The Atonement,* GR Baker, 1974 reprint (1867).

Hodge, Charles *Systematic Theology,* 3 vols. GR Eerdmanns, 1968 reprint.

Hodges, Zane C. *Absolutely Free* GR· Zondervan, 1989.

_____ *Harmony With God* Dallas Redencion Viva, 2001

_____. *The Gospel Under Siege A Study on Faith and Works* Dallas Redencion Viva, 1981

Hoekema, Anthony A. *Saved by Grace* GR· Eerdmans, 1989

Hoitenga, Dewey J., Jr *John Calvin and the Will* GR. Baker, 1997

Hopkins, Mark. *A Discourse occasioned by the death of Rev. Edward Dorr Griffin* Tuttle, Belcher, Burton, 1837.

Hull, J. Mervin *Judson the Pioneer* Phila.: American Baptist Publications, 1913.

Hunt, Dave. *What Love Is This? Calvinism's Misrepresentation of God.* Sisters, OR: Loyal, 2002

Ironside,H A. *Holiness the False and the True* Neptune, NJ. Loizeaux Bros.

Jewett, Paul K *Election and Predestination* GR: Eerdmans, 1985

Johnson, E. H , and Weston, Henry G. *An Outline of Systematic Theology.* Phila · American Baptist Publ.,1895

Judson, Edward *The Life of Adoniram Judson.* New York: Randolph, 1883

Kaiser, Jr , Walter C *Toward an Old Testament Theology* GR: Zondervan, 1978

_____. *Toward an Exegetical Theology.* GR Baker, 1981

Kane, Herbert J *A Concise History of the Christian World Mission* GR: Baker, 1978.

_____ *Understanding Christian Missions* GR: Baker, 1974, 1982

Kendall, R T *Calvin and English Calvinism to 1649,* 2nd ed. Carlisle, Cumbria, UK: Paternoster Press, 1997.

_____. *Once Saved, Always Saved.* Chicago: Moody, 1985

Klein, William W. *The New Chosen People.* GR· Zondervan, 1990.

Kling, David W *A Field of Divine Wonders: New Divinity and Revivals in W CT (1792-1822),* Penn State, 1993

Kuiper, R B. *For Whom Did Christ Die? A Study of the Divine Design of the Atonement.* GR Baker, 1959

Ladd, George Eldon *A Theology of the New Testament.* Eerdmans, 1974

Lane, A. N S , ed. Introduction to John Calvin's *The Bondage and Liberation of the Will* Baker, 1996

Latourette, Kenneth Scott, *A History of Christianity* NY. Harper & Row, 1953

Lewis, Gordon R and Demarest, Bruce A *Integrative Theology* Grand Rapids Zondervan, 1990

Lightner, Robert P *The Death Christ Died* Des Plaines, IL Regular Baptist Press, 1967

_____ *Sin, the Savior, and Salvation The Theology of Everlasting Life* Nashville Nelson, 1991.

Lovelace, Richard F *The American Pietism of Cotton Mather* Christian University Press, 1979

Luther, Martin *Sammtliche Schriften,* 2d ed , ed Joh Georg Walch St Louis Concordia, 1880-1910

_____ *The Bondage of the Will, trans* J I Packer & O R. Johnston Old Tappan, NJ· Revell, 1957

_____. *Martin Luther's Basic Theological Writings,* ed. Timothy F. Lull Minneapolis Fortress, 1989.

MacArthur, John F , Jr. *The Gospel According to Jesus.* GR Zondervan, 1988

_____. *Faith Works: The Gospel According to the Apostles* Dallas: Word, 1993.

Macleod, John *Scottish Theology*. Edinburgh Banner of Truth Trust, 1946.

McClain, Alva J The Greatness of the Kingdom Chicago: Moody, 1 959.

McDonald, H. D *The Christian View of Man* Wheaton Crossway, 1981

_____ *The Atonement of the Death of Christ: In Faith, Revelation, and History*. GR Baker, 1985

McGrath, Alister *History of the Doctrine of Justification* English Evangelical Theology *(1640-1790)*, Oxford, 1987

McKee, Elsie Anne and Armstrong, Brian G , eds. *Probing the Reformed Tradition*. Louisville John Knox, 1989

McNeil, John T. *The History and Character of Calvinism* NY: Oxford, 1967

Marshall, I. Howard. *Kept by the Power of God*, 3rd ed. Carlisle, UK Paternoster, 1995

Mell, Patrick H. *A Southern Baptist Looks at Predestination*. Cape Coral Christian Gospel Foundation, n d.

Moody, Dale, *The Word of Truth*. GR Eerdmans, 1981.

Morris, Leon *The Apostolic Preaching of the Cross*, 3rd ed GR: Eerdmans, 1965

Murray, Iain *The Puritan Hope. Revival and the Interpretation of Prophecy* London: Banner of Truth, 1975.

_____ *Spurgeon v Hyper-Calvinism: The Battle for Gospel Preaching* Carlisle: Banner of Truth,1995.

Murray John *Redemption Accomplished and Applied*. GR: Eerdmans, 1955.

Nash, Ansel. *Memoir of Edward Dorr Griffin*. New York, Benedict, 1842.

Neuser, Wilhelm H ed. *Calvinus Sacrae Scripturae Professor* Eerdmans, 1994.

Newman, Albert Henry *A Manual of Church History*, 2 vols. Phila American Baptist, 1899

Nettleton, David *Chosen to Salvation*. Schaumburg, IL: Regular Baptist Press, 1983

Noll, Mark A. *The Old Religion in a New World The History of North American Christianity* Eerdmans, 2002

Nichols, James *Calvinism and Arminianism*, 2 vols. London: Longmans, et al, 1824.

Olsen, Viggo B *Daktar Diplomat in Bangladesh* Chicago: Moody Press, 1973.

Olson, C Gordon *What in the World Is God Doing? The Essentials of Global Missions* , 5th ed , 2003

Olson, Roger E *The Story of Christian Theology: Twenty Centuries of Tradition & Reform* InterVarsity, 1999

Orr, James, ed *The International Standard Bible Encyclopedia*, 5 vols GR Eerdmans, 1955

Owen, John *The Death of Death in the Death of Christ* Carlisle Banner of Truth, 1959 reprint (1852)

Packer, J I *Evangelism and the Sovereignty of God* Chicago: IVP, 1961

Packer, J. I. & Johnston, O. R "Introduction ," in Luther's *Bondage of the Will*. Revell, 1957

Paine, Gustavus S *The Men Behind the King James Version*. GR Baker, 1977.

Palmer, Edwin H. *The Five Points of Calvinism in the Light of Scripture* GR. Guardian Press, 1972.

Park, Edwards A , ed. *The Atonement, Discourses and Treatises by Jonathan Edwards, John Smalley, Jonathan Maxcy, Nathanael Emmons, Edward D Griffin, Caleb Burge, and William R Weeks* Boston 1859

Pearse, Meic *The Great Restoration: The Religious Radicals of the 16th and 17th Centuries*. Paternoster, 1998

Peters, George W *A Biblical Theology of Missions* Chicago Moody Press, 1972

Pink, Arthur W *The Satisfaction of Christ* GR: Zondervan, 1955.

_____ *The Sovereignty of God* rev. ed Carlisle, PA: Banner of Truth, 1961

_____ . *Eternal Security*. GR Baker, 1974.

_____ . *Gleanings from the Scriptures: Man's Total Depravity* Chicago: Moody Press, 1969.

Pinnock, Clark H., ed *The Grace of God, The Will of Man: A Case for Arminianism*. GR Zondervan, 1989

_____ . ed *Grace Unlimited*. Minneapolis: Bethany, 1975.

Pinson, J Matthew, ed *Four Views on Eternal Security*. GR: Zondervan, 2002.

Piper, John *The Justification of God*, 2nd ed. GR Baker, 1993.

Radmacher, Earl D *What the Church Is All About: A Biblical and Historical Study* Chicago Moody Press, 1978

_____ *Salvation* Nashville: Word, 2000

Rice, John R *Predestined for Hell? No!* Murfreesboro, TN. Sword of the Lord, 1958.

Richards, James. *Lectures on Mental Philosophy and Theology* (1846)

Rooy, Sydney H *The Puritan Theology of Missions*, Eerdmans, 196?

Ryrie, Charles C *Basic Theology* Wheaton. Victor, 1986

_____ *Dispensationalism Today*, rev. ed Chicago Moody, 1995.

_____ *So Great Salvation. What It Means to Believe In Jesus Christ* Wheaton: Victor, 1989

Sauer, Erich *The Dawn of World Redemption: A Survey of Historical Revelation in the Old Testament* , 1951

_____ . *The Triumph of the Crucified* GR: Eerdmans, 1951.

Seaton, W J. *The Five Points of Calvinism* Edinburgh. Banner of Trusth, 1970

Schaff, Philip *History of the Christian Church*, 8 vols GR: Eerdmans, 1985 [1910]

Schaff-Herzog Encyclopedia

Schreiner, Thomas R & Ware, Bruce, eds *The Grace of God/ The Bondage of the Will*, 2vols GR: Baker, 1995

Shank, Robert *Life in the Son*. Springfield, MO: Westcott, 1960.

_____ . *Elect in the Son* Springfield, MO Westcott, 1970.

Shedd, W G T. *Dogmatic Theology* Nashville Thomas Nelson, 1980 reprint
Shelley, Bruce L *Evangelicalism in America* Eerdmans, 1967
Shelton, Dan O *Heroes of the Cross in America.* NY Young People's Missionary Movement, 1904
Spencer, Duane Edward *TULIP The Five Points of Calvinism in the Light of Scripture.* GR Baker, 1979.
Sproul, R C *Willing to Believe: The Controversy over Free Will* Grand Rapids· Baker, 1997
_____ *Grace Unknown the Heart of Reformed Theology.* GR Baker, 1997.
_____ *Faith Alone: The Evangelical Doctrine of Justification.* GR Baker, 1995.
_____ *Chosen by God* Wheaton· Tyndale, 1986.
_____. *Getting the Gospel Right.* GR: Baker Books, 1999.
Stanley, Charles *Eternal Security. Can You Be Sure?* Nashville. Nelson, 1990
Steele, David N & Thomas, Curtis C. *The Five Points of Calvinism*   Presby. & Reformed,1963
Stein, Robert H. *Difficult Passages in the New Testament.* Grand Rapids· Baker, 1990.
Storms, C Samuel *Chosen for Life* GR: Baker, 1987
Strobel, Lee. *The Case for Faith* GR: Zondervan, 2000
Strombeck, John F *Shall Never Perish* Moline, IL Strombeck Agency, 1936
Strong, Augustus Hopkins *Systematic Theology*, 2nd ed Philadelphia. Judson Press, 1906
Sumner, Robert L *An Examination of TULIP.* Murfreesboro, TN: Biblical Evangelism Press, 1972
Sweet, William Warren, *The Story of Religion in America.* NY· Harper, 1930
Tenney, Merrill C ed. *The Zondervan Pictorial Encyclopedia of the Bible.* 5 vols GR: Zondervan, 1975.
Thiessen, Henry C *Lectures in Systematic Theology* GR· Eerdmans, 1949.
Tiessen, Terrance *Providence and Prayer· How Does God Work in the World?* Downers InterVarsity, 2000
Tidball, Derek *The Message of the Cross* Downers Grove. InterVarsity, 2001
Tuttle, Robert G., Jr *John Wesley: His Life and Theology* GR Zondervan, 1978
Underwood, A C *A History of the English Baptists* London Baptist Union, 1970
Vance, Laurence M. *The Other Side of Calvinism* , 2nd ed , Pensacola Vance Publications,, 1991
Vos, Geerhardus *Biblical Theology· Old and New Testaments* GR· Eerdmans,
Vos, Howard F *Religions in A Changing World* Chicago Moody, 1959
Walvoord, John F *Jesus Christ, Our Lord* Chicago Moody, 1969
_____. *The Holy Spirit* Wheaton: Van Kampen Press, 1954.
Warfield, B. B *The Plan of Salvation* Eerdmans, 1935.
_____. *Calvin and Augustine*, ed Samuel Craig. Phila Presbyterian & Reformed, 1956
Warneck, Gustav. *Outline of a History of Protestant Missions.* trans by George Robson NY: Revell, 1901
Warns, Johannes *Baptism Studies in the Original Christian Baptism*, trans G. H Lang. Paternoster,1957
Wayland, Francis *Memoir of Judson* Boston Philips and Sampson, 1853.
White, James R *The Potter's Freedom* Amityville, NY Calvary Press, 2000
Wiley, H Orton *Christian Theology.* Kansas City, MO Beacon Hill, 1952
Wilkin, Robert N *Confident in Christ· Living by Faith Really Works.* Irving, TX. Grace Evangelical Soc , 1999.
Wills, Garry *Saint Augustine.* NY Viking Penguin, 1999
Woodbridge, John D ed. *Great Leaders of the Christian Church* Chicago. Moody, 1988
Woodbridge,John D , Noll, Mark A , and Hatch, Nathan O *The Gospel in America* Zondervan, 1979.
Woodbridge, John D and McComiskey, Thomas E , eds *Doing Theology in Today's World* Zondervan, 1991.
Wright, R K McGregor *No Place for Sovereignty What's Wrong with Freewill Theism* InterVarsity, 1996.
Zanchius, Jerom *The Doctrine of Absolute Predestination* GR· Baker Books, 1977

COMMENTARIES:
Alford, Henry *The Greek Testament* orig 4 vols Chicago· Moody, 1958 [1849]
Gundry, Robert H. *Matthew: A Commentary on his Literary and Theological Art* GR. Eerdmans, 1982
Henrichsen, Walter A *After the Sacrifice* Zondervan, 1979
Howley, G D C. ed. *A New Testament Commentary.* GR Zondervan, 1969.
Nichol, W Robertson ed , *The Expositor's Greek Testament.* GR Eerdmans, 1961.
Strauss, Lehman. *The Book of the Revelation* Neptune, NJ. Loizeaux Bos , 1964
Walvoord, John F and Zuck, Roy B , eds *The Bible Knowledge Commentary* Wheaton: Victor, 1983

LINGUISTIC TOOLS:
Abbott-Smith, G. *A Manual Greek Lexicon of the New Testament*, 3d ed Edinburgh T & T. Clark, 1937
Arndt, William F. and Gingrich, F Wilbur *A Greek-English Lexicon of the New Testament and Other Early Christian Literature* Zondervan, 1957.

Blass, F and DeBrunner, E A Greek Grammar of the New Testament and Other Literature, trans , Robert W
    Funk Chicago: Univ. of Chicago Press, 1961
Brown, Francis The New Brown-Driver-Briggs-Gesenius Hebrew and English Lexicon Hendrickson reprint, 1979
Burton, Ernest DeWitt. Syntax of the Moods and Tenses in New Testament Greek. Edinburgh T & T Clark,1898
Chamberlain, William Douglas An Exegetical Grammar of the Greek New Testament. NY: Macmillan, 1952
Cremer, Hermann. Biblico-Theological Lexicon of the New Testament Greek J & J Clark 1883
Dana, H. E. and Mantey, Julius R A Manual Grammar of the Greek New Testament NY Macmillan, 1927.
Davidson, A B Hebrew Syntax, 3rd ed. Edinburgh· T & T Clark, 1901.
Demosthenes, 31,4, Against Onetor   ·
Harris, R Laird, Archer, Gleason L., Jr. & Waltke, Bruce K , eds Theological Wordbook of the Old Testament
    Chicago Moody, 1980
Jastrow, Marcus Dictionary of Targumim, Talmud Babli, Yerushalmi and Midrashic Lit., NY: Judaica Press, 1982
Kittel, Gerhard, ed Theological Dictionary of the New Testament 10 vols.,Grand Rapids· Eerdmans, 1964.
Lampe, G. W. H. A Patristic Greek Lexicon Oxford, 1961.
Liddell, Henry George, Scott, Robert, and Jones. A Greek-English Lexicon, 9th ed. NY: Oxford Univ., 1996
Moulton James Hope, and Milligan, George The Vocabulary of the Greek Testament . London: 1914-1929.
Parkhurst, John A Greek and English Lexicon of the New Testament, ed. by Hugh James Rose London 1829
Robertson, A T and Davis, W Hersey. A New Short Grammar of the Greek Testament 10th ed Harper, 1958
Robertson, A T Word Pictures in the New Testament , 6 vols Nashville Broadman, 1930.
_____. A Grammar of the Greek New Testament in the Light of Historical Research
Rogers, Cleon L Jr and Cleon L. III. Linguistic and Exegetical Key to the New Testament. Zondervan, 1998
Ross, Allen P Introducing Biblical Hebrew GR Baker, 2001.
Thayer, John Henry A Greek-English Lexicon of the New Testament NY. American Book, 1886
Tregelles, Samuel P. Gesenius' Hebrew and Chaldee Lexicon of the Old Testament Scriptures
Turner, Nigel in Moulton, James Hope. Syntax, vol. III
Wallace. Daniel. Greek Grammar Beyond the Basics. Exegetical Syntax of the New Testament. Zondervan,1996
Watts, J Wash. A Survey of Syntax in the Hebrew Old Testament. Nashville Broadman, 1951.
Young, Robert. Analytical Concordance to the Bible GR. Eerdmans, 1936

ARTICLES:
Aldrich, Roy L "The Gift of God," Bibliotheca Sacra 122:487
Berg. J. Vanden. "Calvin and Missions," in Hoogstra, ed. John Calvin· Contemporary Prophet. GR: Baker, 1959
Berkouwer, G C. "Election and Doctrinal Reaction," Christianity Today 5:586
Chaney, Charles "The Missionary Dynamic in the Theology of John Calvin," Reformed Review, 17 64, 24-38
Coates, Thomas "Were the Reformers Mission-Minded?" Concordia Theological Monthly, 40.9, 600-611.
Constable,Thomas L. "The Gospel Message" in Campbell, Donald K ed, Walvoord: A Tribute Moody, 1982
Gerstner, John H. & Jonathan N "Edwardsean Preparation for Salvation," Westminster Theol. Jour , 42:5-50
Godfrey, W. Robert. "Reformed Thought on the Extent of the Atonement to 1618," WTJ, 37: 133-171
Gundry, Robert H. "The Language Milieu of First-Century Palestine " Jour Biblical Literature 83 (1964) 404-408
Hall, Basil. "Calvin Against the Calvinists," John Calvin: Courtenay Studies in Reformation Theology 1966
Hargrave, O T. "Free-willers in the English Reformation," Church History, XXXVII (1968), 271-280
Hoehner, Harold "Chronological Aspects of the Life of Christ Part V," Bibliotheca Sacra 524 (Oct '74) pp 340-8
James, Edgar C "Foreknowledge and Foreordination," Bibliotheca Sacra (July 1965)
Klooster, Fred H "Missions–The Heidelberg Catechism and Calvin," Calvin Theological Jour., 7:181-208 (1972)
McCoy, Charles S. "Johannes Cocceius Federal Theologian," Scottish Journal of Theology, 16.365.
Nicole, Roger. "Amyraldianism" in Encyclopedia of Christianity. (1964)
Olson, Roger. "Don't Hate Me Because I'm an Arminian," Christianity Today 43 (Sept 6, 1999) pp 87-90, 92-4
Sapaugh, Gregory "Is Faith a Gift? A study of Ephesians 2 8, " JOTGES, 7, no. 12 (Spring 1994), pp 39-40
Steffens, Nicholas M. "The Principle of Reformed Protestantism and Foreign Missions."P. & R. Review, 5 241-53
Ware, Bruce. "An Evangelical Reformulation of the Doctrine of the Immutability of God," JETS, 29.4, pp 431-449
Zwemer Samuel M "Calvinism and the Missionary Enterprise," Theology Today 7:206-216 (July 1950)

THEOLOGICAL PAPERS:
Carter, Terry G. "The Calvinism of William Carey and its Effect on his Mission Work," a paper delivered at ETS
    2001 at Colorado Springs, Nov 2001
Edgar, Thomas R "The Meaning of PROORIZO," a paper given at ETS Eastern Sect , March 30, 2001 at PBU.
Shahadeh, Imad. "Panel Discussion" at ETS 2000, Nashville, TN, November 2000.